Peterson's

Master the
GMAT
2014

PETERSON'S

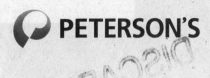

About Peterson's Publishing

To succeed on your lifelong educational journey, you will need accurate, dependable, and practical tools and resources. That is why Peterson's is everywhere education happens. Because whenever and however you need education content delivered, you can rely on Peterson's to provide the information, know-how, and guidance to help you reach your goals. Tools to match the right students with the right school. It's here. Personalized resources and expert guidance. It's here. Comprehensive and dependable education content—delivered whenever and however you need it. It's all here.

Credits
  "The American Renaissance," by James S. Turner, *Humanities*, Vol.13, No. 2 (March/April 1992). Published by The National Endowment for the Humanities.
  "Arnold's Double-Sided Culture," by John P. Farrell, *Humanities*, Vol. 12, No. 3 (May/June1991), pp. 26–30. Published by The National Endowment for the Humanities.
  "The Artful Encounter," by Richard Wendorf, *Humanities*, Vol. 14, No. 4 (July/August 1993), pp. 9–12. Published by The National Endowment for the Humanities.
  "The Debate Over Mozart's Music," by Neal Zaslaw, *Humanities*, Vol. 14, No. 5 (September/October 1993), pp. 26–27. Published by The National Endowment for the Humanities.
  "'I Am Christina Rossetti,'" by Antony H. Harrison, *Humanities*, Vol. 14, No. 4 (July/August 1993), pp. 33–37. Published by The National Endowment for the Humanities.
  "Images of Dorothea Lange," by Therese Thau Heyman, *Humanities*, Vol. 14, No. 5 (September/October 1993), pp. 6, 8–10. Published by The National Endowment for the Humanities.
  "Large Format Expands *Little Buddha*," by Bob Fisher, *American Cinematographer*, Vol. 75, No. 5 (May 1994), p. 41. Reprinted by permission of *American Cinematographer*.

For more information, contact Peterson's, 3 Columbia Circle, Suite 205, Albany, NY 12203; 800-338-3282 Ext. 54229; or find us online at www.petersonsbooks.com.

Bernadette Webster, Managing Editor; Ray Golaszewski, Publishing Operations Manager

ISBN-13: 978-0-7689-3759-6

Printed in the United States of America

10 9 8 7 6 5 4 3 2 1   15 14 13

Twentieth Edition

By printing this book on recycled paper (40% post-consumer waste) 142 trees were saved.

Petersonspublishing.com/publishingupdates

Check out our Web site at www.petersonspublishing.com/publishingupdates to see if there is any new information regarding the test and any revisions or corrections to the content of this book. We've made sure the information in this book is accurate and up-to-date; however, the test format or content may have changed since the time of publication.

Contents

PART III: GMAT ANALYTICAL WRITING ASSESSMENT

PART IV: GMAT INTEGRATED REASONING SECTION

PART V: GMAT QUANTITATIVE SECTION

PART VI: GMAT VERBAL SECTION

PART VII: FIVE PRACTICE TESTS

APPENDIXES

SPECIAL ADVERTISING SECTION

Before You Begin

HOW THIS BOOK IS ORGANIZED

Taking the GMAT is a skill. It shares some aspects with other endeavors, such as competing in athletics. It requires discipline and practice to succeed.

These are skills that can be improved through coaching, but ultimately, improvement also requires practice. This book gives you both.

- **Top 10 Strategies to Raise Your Score** lists the ten most important test-taking tips to help you score high on the GMAT.

- **Part I** provides essential information on the GMAT, including where to take it and how it's scored. You'll also learn what subjects are covered and what traps to watch out for. This part of the book also shows you each test section and each basic type of question up close; we've provided examples of each type of question (along with explanations), so you can get a good initial feel for the overall test.

- **Part II** is a complete Diagnostic Test that includes all four sections: Analytical Writing, Integrated Reasoning, Quantitative, and Verbal Sections. This will give you your first chance to work with samples of GMAT question types. Use the results of this test to determine where you need to focus your GMAT preparation.

- **Parts III through VI** make up the coaching program. This part of the book analyzes each section of the GMAT—Analytical Writing, Integrated Reasoning, Quantitative Questions, and Verbal Questions—and provides powerful test-taking strategies, both basic and advanced, for successfully attacking every question type you'll encounter in the actual exam.

- **Part VII** consists of five full-length practice tests with detailed answer explanations for each question. Each test contains the same number and mix of question types you will encounter on the actual GMAT. The answer explanations are invaluable for helping you learn from your mistakes. To accurately measure your performance, be sure to adhere strictly to the stated time limits for each section.

- **The Appendixes** provide resources for GMAT preparation, help you calculate your GMAT score, offer articles on graduate business degrees, and provide a handy vocabulary list to help you prepare for the Verbal Section of the GMAT.

Because the actual GMAT is computerized, you'll be entering answers on the actual exam by typing on a keyboard or using a mouse. Some parts of the exam, such as the Analytical Writing section, require you to type sentences and paragraphs. The other three sections require that you fill in the answer by typing a whole number in a box, checking off boxes in a grid using the computer mouse, or filling in blanks in a sentence with your mouse by "dragging and dropping" your chosen answer choices to the blanks. Obviously, answering in this fashion isn't possible in a book. To remain consistent with the actual exam, however, we've retained references to "clicking," "typing," or "dragging and dropping" the answers.

SPECIAL STUDY FEATURES

Peterson's Master the GMAT is designed to be as user-friendly as it is complete. To this end, it includes several features to make your preparation more efficient.

Overview

Each chapter begins with a bulleted overview listing the topics covered in the chapter. This will allow you to quickly target the areas in which you are most interested.

Summing It Up

Each chapter ends with a point-by-point summary that reviews the most important items in the chapter. The summaries offer a convenient way to review key points.

Bonus Information

As you work your way through the book, look for bonus information and advice in the margins of the pages. Information is in the following forms:

Note

Notes highlight need-to-know information about the GMAT, whether it's details about registration and scoring or the structure of a question type.

Tip

Tips provide valuable strategies and insider information to help you score your best on the GMAT.

Alert

Alerts do just what they say—alert you to common pitfalls and misconceptions you might face or hear regarding the GMAT.

YOU ARE WELL ON YOUR WAY TO SUCCESS

You've made the decision to apply to graduate school. *Peterson's Master the GMAT* will help prepare you for the steps you'll need to take to achieve your goal—from scoring high on the exam to being admitted to the graduate program of your choice. Good luck!

GIVE US YOUR FEEDBACK

Peterson's publishes a full line of resources to help guide you through the graduate school admission process. Peterson's publications can be found at college and university libraries and career centers and your local bookstore or library. Peterson's publications are also available as eBooks. Check our Web site, www.petersonsbooks.com, for more information about our eBook program.

We welcome any comments or suggestions you may have about this publication. Your feedback will help us make your education and career goals possible for you—and others like you.

TOP 10 STRATEGIES TO RAISE YOUR SCORE

Later in the book we'll review strategies and tips for specific test sections and question types. Right now, however, here's a list of general strategies for the GMAT. Even if you've read about these strategies elsewhere, or if they seem like common sense to you, it's a good idea to reinforce them in your mind.

1. **Know your optimal pace and stay on it.** Time is definitely a factor on every section of the GMAT. On the multiple-choice sections, expect to work at a quicker pace than is comfortable for you. Similarly, the 30-minute time limit for each Analytical Writing Assessment (AWA) response requires a lively writing pace, allowing little time for editing, revising, and fine-tuning.

   During the multiple-choice sections, check your pace after every 10 questions or so (three times during a section) and adjust it accordingly so that you have time to at least consider every question in the section. During each essay section, be sure to leave yourself enough time to cover all your main points and to wrap up your essay with a brief concluding paragraph. The best way to avoid the time squeeze is to practice under timed conditions so that you get a sense of your optimal pace.

2. **If you're not sure what the correct answer is, don't dwell on it—move on.** This tip is closely related to the previous one. You might find yourself reluctant to leave a question until you're sure your answer is correct. The design of the computer-adaptive test (CAT) contributes to this mindset, because your reward for correct responses to difficult questions is greater than your reward for easier questions. But a stubborn attitude will only defeat you, because it reduces the number of questions you may attempt, which in turn can lower your score. Remember: You can miss quite a few questions and still score high. Develop a sense of your optimal pace—one that results in the greatest number of correct responses.

3. **Take your time with the first few quantitative and verbal questions.**
   The CAT uses your responses to the first few questions to move you either up or down the ladder of difficulty. Of course, you want to move up the ladder. So take great care with the initial questions—perhaps move at a somewhat slower pace. Otherwise, you'll have to answer several questions just to reverse the trend by proving to the CAT that you're smarter than it thinks you are.

4. **Avoid random guessing.** If you must guess, always try to eliminate obvious wrong-answer choices first, then go with your hunch. Eliminating even one choice improves your odds. If you're out of time on a section, there's no advantage to guessing randomly on the remaining

questions. Why? You might luck out and guess correctly, but if you don't, incorrect responses move you down the ladder of difficulty, and correct responses to easier questions aren't worth as much as correct responses to more difficult questions. So on balance, there's no net advantage to guessing randomly.

5. **Read each question in its entirety, and read every answer choice.** You'll discover GMAT test designers sometimes "bait" test-takers with tempting wrong-answer choices. This applies to every type of multiple-choice question on the exam. So unless you're quickly running out of time, never confirm an answer until you've read all the choices. This mistake is among the leading causes of incorrect responses on the GMAT.

6. **Maintain an active mind set.** During the GMAT, it's remarkably easy to fall into a passive mode in which you let your eyes simply pass over the words while you hope that the correct response jumps out at you as you scan the answer choices. Fight this tendency. Try "interacting" with the test as you read it. Keep in mind that each question on the GMAT is designed to measure a specific ability or skill. Adopting an active, investigative approach to each question will help. Ask yourself:

   - What skill is the question measuring?

   - What is the most direct thought process to determine the correct response?

   - How might a careless test-taker be tripped up on this type of question? Answering these three questions is, in large part, what the rest of this book is all about.

7. **Use your pencil and scratch paper.** Using pencil and paper helps keep your mind in an active mode. Making brief notes and drawing diagrams and flow charts will help keep your thought process clear.

8. **Move the keyboard aside for the multiple-choice sections.** You won't use the keyboard at all for these sections, so put your scratch paper right in front of you and get the keyboard out of the way.

9. **Know the test directions inside and out**—before **you take the test.** Just before the first question of each type (e.g., Data Sufficiency or Reading Comprehension), the CAT will display the directions for that question type. The clock will be running while you're reading these directions. You can save valuable time by dismissing the directions as quickly as possible (by clicking on the DISMISS DIRECTIONS button)—presuming you've already made yourself familiar with the directions before exam time.

10. **Use the 10-minute breaks, but keep an eye on the time.** Remember: The GMAT CAT clock is always running, even during the two scheduled 10-minute breaks. By all means, take advantage of these breaks to leave the room, perhaps grab a quick snack from your locker, and do some stretching or relaxing. But don't get too relaxed: Ten minutes goes by very quickly and the test will begin after that time has elapsed—with or without you.

ACCESS THREE GMAT TESTS ONLINE

Peterson's is providing you with access to three additional GMAT practice tests. The testing content on these three practice tests was created by the test-prep experts at Peterson's. The Peterson's online testing experience resembles the testing experience you will find on the actual GMAT exam. You can access these three practice tests at http://www.petersonspublishing.com/gmat.

PART I
GMAT BASICS

All About the GMAT

chapter 1

OVERVIEW

- The GMAT at a glance
- An overview of the GMAT sections
- How the computer-adaptive GMAT works
- The GMAT CAT interface
- The GMAT CAT test-taking experience
- Your GMAT scores
- Score reporting
- How business schools evaluate GMAT scores
- Top 10 tips for GMAT prep
- Accommodations for test-takers with disabilities
- Commonly asked questions about the GMAT
- Summing it up

THE GMAT AT A GLANCE

The GMAT (Graduate Management Admission Test) is a standardized test of the Graduate Management Admission Council (GMAC), which develops guidelines, policies, and procedures for the graduate business school admission process and provides information about the admission process to the schools and to prospective applicants. The test provides graduate business schools, vocational counselors, and prospective applicants with predictors of academic performance in MBA programs. Approximately 1900 graduate business schools worldwide use GMAT scores as a part of their admissions process.

The GMAT is administered only by computer and given in a computer-adaptive (CAT) format for two of its four sections. This means that the Quantitative and Verbal sections of the test start with a question of moderate difficulty. If you answer the moderately difficult question correctly, it will be followed with a more difficult question. If you answer incorrectly, the question that follows will be easier. In terms of scoring, you want more difficult questions. Note that the Integrated Reasoning section introduced in 2012 is not computer-adaptive.

The GMAT contains four parts: an Analytical Writing Assessment (AWA) section, an Integrated Reasoning section, a Quantitative section, and a Verbal section. The total testing time (excluding breaks) is 3 hours and 30 minutes. With two 8-minute breaks, the testing time is 4 hours. Here's the basic structure of the test.

Analytical Writing Assessment (Section 1)

- Analysis of an Argument (one writing task, 30-minute time limit)
- Optional break (8-minute time limit)

Integrated Reasoning (Section 2)

- 12 questions, 30-minute time limit
- Table Analysis (2 questions)
- Two-Part Analysis (4 questions)
- Multi-Source Reasoning (3 questions)
- Graphics Interpretation (3 questions)

Quantitative Ability (Section 3)

- 37 multiple-choice questions, 75-minute time limit
- Problem Solving (22–23 questions)
- Data Sufficiency (14–15 questions)
- Optional break (8-minute time limit)

Verbal Ability (Section 4)

- 41 multiple-choice questions, 75-minute time limit
- Critical Reasoning (14–15 questions)
- Sentence Correction (14–15 questions)
- Reading Comprehension (12–13 questions, divided among four sets)

NOTE

The number of questions and question types for the Integrated Reasoning section may change over time.

Sequence of Exam Sections

The essay section always appears first. Section 2 is always Integrated Reasoning, coming before the two timed multiple-choice sections. Section 3 is always Quantitative Ability, and section 4 is always Verbal Ability.

Sequence of Questions in Integrated Reasoning, Quantitative, and Verbal Sections

In the Integrated Reasoning, Quantitative, and Verbal sections, the question types are interspersed. The following are typical sequences for each section (on any given GMAT, the sequences may be different):

Integrated Reasoning (A Typical Sequence of Question Types)

Question 1	Two-Part Analysis
Question 2	Table Analysis
Questions 3–5	Two-Part Analysis
Question 6	Table Analysis
Questions 7–9	Multi-Source Reasoning
Questions 10–12	Graphics Interpretation

Quantitative Ability (Typical Sequence of Questions)

Questions 1–2	Problem Solving
Questions 3–7	Data Sufficiency
Questions 8–13	Problem Solving
Question 14	Data Sufficiency
Question 15	Problem Solving
Question 16	Data Sufficiency
Questions 17–21	Problem Solving
Questions 22–27	Data Sufficiency
Questions 28–34	Problem Solving
Question 35	Data Sufficiency
Questions 36–37	Problem Solving

Verbal Ability (Typical Sequence of Questions)

Questions 1–3	Sentence Correction
Questions 4–5	Critical Reasoning
Questions 6–8	Reading Comprehension
Question 9	Sentence Correction
Questions 10–11	Critical Reasoning
Questions 12–14	Sentence Correction
Questions 15–17	Reading Comprehension
Questions 18–21	Critical Reasoning
Questions 22–24	Sentence Correction
Questions 25–26	Critical Reasoning
Question 27	Sentence Correction
Questions 28–30	Reading Comprehension
Questions 31–33	Critical Reasoning
Questions 34–35	Sentence Correction
Question 36	Critical Reasoning
Questions 37–39	Reading Comprehension
Question 40	Critical Reasoning
Question 41	Sentence Correction

NOTE

The order of sections may be different in the actual test.

Ground Rules

Here are some basic procedural rules for the GMAT (we cover test-taking procedures in greater detail later in this chapter):

- Once the timed test begins, you cannot stop the testing clock.

- If you finish any section before the time limit expires, you have the option of proceeding immediately to the next section.

- For the Integrated Reasoning section, you may review questions and answers if you have time. This is the only section that has a Review button because it is not computer-adaptive.

- Once you exit a section, you cannot return to it.

- Markers and noteboards are provided for all exam sections.

- You select a multiple-choice answer by clicking on an oval next to the choice. (Multiple-choice questions in the Quantitative and Verbal sections have five answer choices, but the number of answer choices vary in the Integrated Reasoning section.)

- Graphics Interpretation questions in the Integrated Reasoning section have drop-down windows to display answer choices.

- The Integrated Reasoning section has an on-screen calculator. There is no calculator for the Quantitative section.

- You compose your essay using the word processor built into the GMAT testing system. (Handwritten essays are not permitted.)

NOTE

The Next Generation GMAT has only one essay because, according to GMAC, research has shown that most test-takers score similarly on both the Issue and Argument essays, so having only one essay will still provide valid data for predicting performance in business school. Having one essay also enables the test-maker to keep the test to 3 hours and 30 minutes exclusive of breaks.

AN OVERVIEW OF THE GMAT SECTIONS

Here's a quick look at what each of the four timed test sections covers.

Analysis of an Argument (1 Essay, 30 Minutes)

This 30-minute section is designed to test your critical reasoning and analytical writing skills. Your task is to compose an essay in which you critique a paragraph-length argument based on the strength of the evidence presented in support of it and on the argument's logic (line of reasoning). You can also indicate what additional evidence would help you evaluate the argument and how the argument could be improved. Your Argument Analysis essay will be evaluated based on content, organization, writing style, and mechanics.

Integrated Reasoning (12 Questions, 30 Minutes)

This 30-minute section consists of 12 questions using multiple-choice formats to measure your "ability to evaluate information presented in new formats and from multiple sources." According to GMAC, the questions are tailored to measure the following skills:

- To assimilate and integrate information from different sources to solve challenging problems.

- To accurately interpret data presented visually in graphs to determine or estimate probabilities and statistics.

- To recognize and evaluate tradeoffs and the likelihood of outcomes.

- To convert quantitative data between graphical and verbal formats.

Each Integrated Reasoning question appears in one of four formats:

❶ Graphics Interpretation prompts ask test-takers to interpret a graphic such as a bar graph or scatterplot and then choose an answer from a drop-down menu. Rather than answer a question, the information completes a statement accurately.

❷ Table Analysis prompts present information and a table, which is sortable and similar to a spreadsheet. Test-takers can sort the table by any given column of information and then must analyze the data to determine which answer statement or statements are accurate.

❸ Multi-Source Reasoning prompts present data from two or three sources, which are given on tabbed pages. Test-takers click on each tab to read and analyze the information, which may be in the form of text, charts, tables, or a combination of types. The questions may be statements that the test-taker must determine the accuracy of, or they may require the test-taker to infer an answer from the data.

❹ Two-Part Analysis questions have, obviously, two parts. The question may be something like the following:

Indicate two different statements as follows: one statement identifies an assumption required by the argument, and the other identifies a possible fact that, if true, would provide significant logical support for the required assumption.

The answers are in a two-column table format. Each question has its own column and the answers are to the right.

Quantitative Ability (37 Questions, 75 Minutes)

This 75-minute section consists of 37 multiple-choice questions designed to measure your basic mathematical skills; understanding of basic mathematical concepts; and ability to reason quantitatively, solve quantitative problems, and interpret graphical data. The Quantitative Ability section covers the following topics:

- Arithmetical operations

- Integers, factors, and multiples

- The number line and ordering

- Decimals, percentages, ratios, and proportion

- Exponents and square roots

- Descriptive statistics (mean, median, mode, range, standard deviation)

- Basic probability, permutations, and combinations

- Operations with variables

- Algebraic equations and inequalities

- Functions

- Geometry, including coordinate geometry

> **NOTE**
> Often, in finding the answer for one column, you've also found the answer for the other one.

Algebraic concepts on the GMAT are those normally covered in a first-year high school algebra course. The GMAT does not cover more advanced areas such as trigonometry and calculus.

Each Quantitative question appears in one of two formats (any of the previously listed topics is fair game for either format):

1. **Problem Solving** questions require you to solve a mathematical problem and then select the correct answer from among five answer choices. Some of these questions will be "story" problems—cast in a real-world setting.

2. **Data Sufficiency** problems each consist of a question followed by two statements labeled (1) and (2). Your task is to analyze each of the two statements to determine whether it provides sufficient data to answer the question and, if neither suffices alone, whether both statements together suffice. Every Data Sufficiency question has the same five answer choices. As with certain Problem Solving questions, some of these questions will be so-called "story" problems, cast in a real-world setting.

Verbal Ability (41 Questions, 75 Minutes)

This 75-minute section consists of 41 multiple-choice questions. Each question will be one of the following three types (each type covers a distinct set of verbal and verbal reasoning skills):

1. **Critical Reasoning** questions measure your ability to understand, criticize, and draw reasonable conclusions from arguments. Each argument consists of a brief one-paragraph passage.

2. **Sentence Correction** questions measure your command of the English language and of the conventions of Standard Written English. Areas tested include grammar, diction, usage, and effective expression (but not punctuation). In each question, part (or all) of a sentence is underlined. Your task is to determine which is correct—the original underlined part or one of four alternatives.

3. **Reading Comprehension** questions measure your ability to read carefully and accurately, to determine the relationships among the various parts of the passage, and to draw reasonable inferences from the material in the passage. You'll encounter four sets of questions; all questions in a set pertain to the same passage. The passages are drawn from a variety of subjects, including the humanities, the social sciences, the physical sciences, ethics, philosophy, and law.

HOW THE COMPUTER-ADAPTIVE GMAT WORKS

The "computer-adaptive" feature of the GMAT CAT for the Quantitative and Verbal sections makes it an entirely different animal from conventional paper-based tests. The following are five key features that set the CAT apart.

1. **During the Quantitative and Verbal sections, the GMAT CAT will continuously adapt to your ability level.**

   The "A" in CAT stands for "Adaptive," which means that during the two multiple-choice sections, the testing system tailors its difficulty level to your level of ability. How? The initial few questions of each type are average in difficulty level. As you respond correctly

NOTE

Early in an exam section, the CAT can shift from the easiest level to a very challenging level (or vice versa) in as few as 3 or 4 successive questions. Later in the section, when your ability level is established, the difficulty level will not vary as widely.

to questions, the CAT system steps you up to more difficult questions. Conversely, as you respond incorrectly to questions, the CAT steps you down to easier ones. Thus, the CAT builds a customized test for you, drawing on its very large pool of multiple-choice questions.

❷ The GMAT CAT does not let you skip questions.

Given the adaptive nature of the test, this makes sense. The computer-adaptive algorithm cannot determine the appropriate difficulty level for the next question without a response (correct or incorrect) to each question presented in sequence.

❸ The GMAT CAT does not let you return to any question already presented (and answered).

Why not? The computer-adaptive algorithm that determines the difficulty of subsequent questions depends on the correctness of previous responses. For example, suppose you answer Question 5 incorrectly. The CAT responds by posing slightly easier questions. Were the CAT to let you return to Question 5 and change your response to the correct one, the questions following Question 5 would be easier than they should have been, given your amended response. In other words, the process by which the CAT builds your GMAT and determines your score would be undermined.

❹ The GMAT CAT does not require you to answer all available questions.

The CAT gives you the opportunity to respond to a total of 37 Quantitative and 41 Verbal questions. But the CAT does not require you to finish either section. The CAT will tabulate a score regardless of the number of available questions you've answered, except if you fail to respond to at least one question during a section, in which case an "NS" (no score) will appear on your score report for *that section only*.

❺ During each section, the GMAT CAT automatically warns you when time is running out.

When 5 minutes remain during each timed section, the on-screen clock (in the upper left corner of the screen) will blink silently several times to warn you. This 5-minute warning will be your only reminder.

NOTE

If you fail to type at least one character, you'll automatically receive a score of 0 (on a scale of 0 to 6) for that section. This score will appear on your report.

THE GMAT CAT INTERFACE

The five simulated screen shots that follow show the GMAT CAT interface for the AWA section, the Integrated Reasoning section, the Quantitative section, and the Verbal section. Let's first examine the features of the interface that are common to all exam sections.

The CAT Title Bar

A dark title bar will appear across the top of the computer screen at all times during all test sections. (You cannot hide this bar.) The CAT title bar displays three items:

❶ Left corner: The time elapsed for the current section (hours and minutes)

❷ Middle: The name of the test (GMAT) and current section number

❸ Right corner: The current question number and total number of questions in the current section

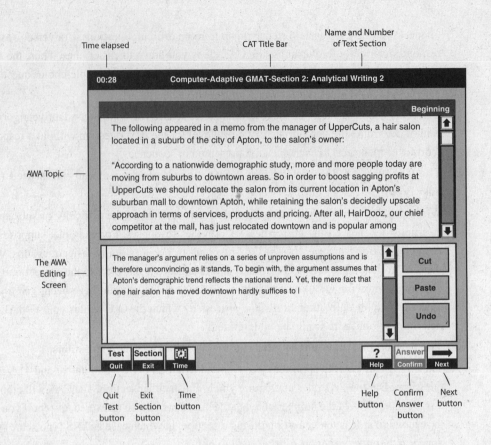

The CAT Toolbar

A series of six buttons appears in a toolbar across the bottom of the computer screen at all times during all test sections. (You cannot hide the toolbar.) Here's a description of each button's function:

1 **Test / Quit** Click on this button to stop the test and cancel your scores for the entire test. (Partial score cancelation is not allowed in any event.) If you click here, a dialog box will appear on the screen, asking you to confirm this operation. Stay away from this button unless you're absolutely sure that you want to erase your GMAT score for the day and you're willing to throw away your GMAT registration fee.

2 **Section / Exit** Click on this button if you finish the section before the allotted time expires and wish to proceed immediately to the next section. A dialog box will appear on the screen asking you to confirm this operation. Stay away from this button unless you've already answered every question in the current section and you don't feel as though you need a breather before starting the next one.

3 **Time** Click on this button to display the time remaining to the nearest second. By default, the time elapsed is displayed (in the upper left corner) in hours and minutes, but not to the nearest second.

4 **? Help** Click on this button to access the directions for the current question type (for example, Data Sufficiency or Sentence Correction), general test directions, and instructions for using the toolbar items.

5 **Answer Confirm** Until you confirm, you can change your answer as often as you wish (by clicking on a different oval). But once you confirm, the question disappears forever and the next one appears in its place. Whenever the NEXT button is enabled (appearing dark gray), the CONFIRM ANSWER button is disabled (appearing light gray), and vice versa.

6 **→ Next** Click on the NEXT button when you're finished with the current question. When you click on NEXT, the current question will remain on the screen until you click on CONFIRM ANSWER.

The AWA Screen

As illustrated in the previous screen shot, the AWA prompt appears at the top of your screen, and your essay response appears below it as you type your response. (The screen in the figure includes the first several lines of a response.) Notice that you have to scroll down to read the entire topic and question. You compose your essays using the CAT word processor. (Later in this chapter, we'll review its features and limitations.)

The Integrated Reasoning Screens

The screens for Integrated Reasoning differ depending on the format, but for the most part, the answers require test-takers to click on ovals next to the correct answer. The two-part analysis questions provide the ovals in two columns in a table format with the answers listed to the right. The two columns represent the two types of answer choices, which may be fact/assumption or strengthen/weaken. Typically, the prompt and question are presented above the answer table.

NOTE

In the sample questions throughout this book, the answer choices are lettered for easy reference to corresponding explanations.

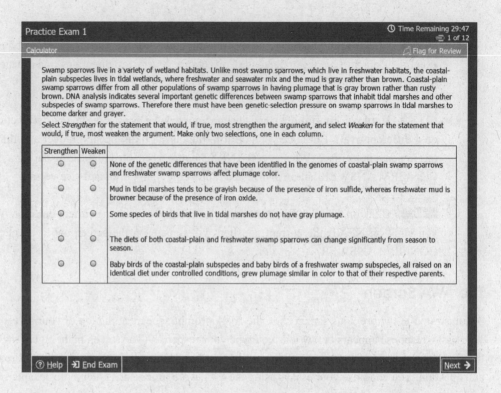

Table analysis questions list the information above the table across the entire screen the same way the two-part analysis questions do. Then the table is presented on the left and the question/directions and answers on the right. The answers are set up in two columns, similar to the arrangement for the two-part analysis questions. The table analysis question type includes a function by which you can re-sort the data in the table in a variety of ways, dependent on the subject of each column. At the top of the table is a "Select" box. Click on it and the list of potential ways you can sort the table drops down. You can choose all of them one at a time if you want. To choose your answer, you click on the oval next to the correct answer in the question-and-answer field on the right of the screen.

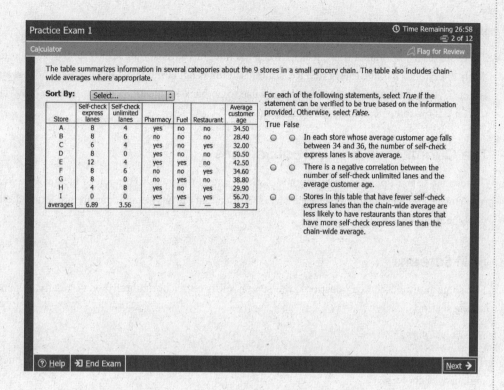

Split screens are used for the multi-source reasoning questions. The left screen presents the data on tabbed pages that you click on to open and read. The answers may be set up similarly to the table analysis question-and-answer column format, or the question and its answers may be in the more traditional multiple-choice format—question followed by a list of answers and you answer by clicking on the oval next to the correct answer. Whichever format for answers is used, the question and answers are on the screen to the right.

The graphics interpretation questions are answered by choosing the correct answer from a drop-down menu. The format of these questions and answers appears closer to the traditional multiple-choice test format—a question and list of answers—except that the answers are chosen from a drop-down menu. The data may be on the left of the screen and the question and answers to the right or the data may be across the screen at the top and the question and answers below it. It seems to depend on the size and type of data.

NOTE

With the on-screen calculator, you can add, subtract, multiple, divide, and do square roots. The calculator also has memory capability for memory add and memory recall.

Important Differences for the Integrated Reasoning Section

There are three important differences between the Integrated Reasoning section and the Quantitative Ability section. First, the Integrated Reasoning section is not computer-adaptive. Second, because it is not CAT, there is a review button you can use to go back to questions in this section only. Third, there is an on-screen calculator for this section only.

The Quantitative and Verbal Screens

To respond to multiple-choice questions, click on one of the ovals to the left of the answer choices. You can't use the keyboard to select answers. Notice that the answer choices are not lettered; you'll click on blank ovals.

Split Screens

For some multiple-choice questions, the screen splits either horizontally or vertically, depending on the section.

Reading Comprehension

The screen splits vertically. The left side displays the passage; the right side displays the question and answer choices.

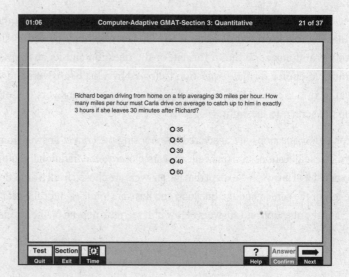

Quantitative Questions Including Figures

The screen splits horizontally. The figures appear at the top; the question and answer choices appear at the bottom.

Vertical Scrolling

For some multiple-choice questions, you'll have to scroll up and down (using the vertical scroll bar) to view all the material that pertains to the current question.

Reading Comprehension

Passages are too long for you to see on the screen in their entirety, so you'll need to scroll as you review them.

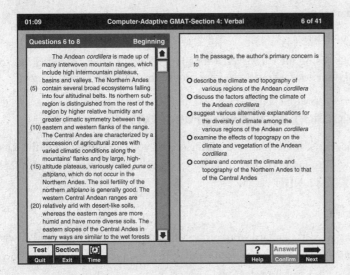

Quantitative Questions Including Figures

Some figures—especially charts and graphs—won't fit on the screen in their entirety; you might need to scroll.

The CAT's Word Processor

In writing your essay, you'll use the simple word processor built into the CAT system. While the word processor includes some features that are standard in programs like Word® and WordPerfect®, it also lacks many of these programs' features.

Keyboard Commands for Navigation and Editing

Here are the navigational and editing keys available in the CAT word processor:

- Backspace removes the character to the left of the cursor
- Delete removes the character to the right of the cursor
- Home moves the cursor to the beginning of the line
- End moves the cursor to the end of the line
- Arrow keys move the cursor up, down, left, or right
- Enter inserts a paragraph break (starts a new line)
- Page Up moves the cursor up one page (screen)
- Page Down moves the cursor down one page (screen)

NOTE

Don't worry about words that you might otherwise italicize or underline (such as titles or non-English words). The exam readers understand the limitations of the CAT word processor.

Certain often-used features of standard word processing programs are not available in the CAT word processor. For example, no keyboard commands are available for:

- TAB—disabled
- Beginning/end of paragraph
- Beginning/end of document
- No key combinations (using the CTRL, ALT, or SHIFT key) or other so-called macros are available for editing functions. (You'll use your mouse for cutting and pasting text.)

Mouse-Driven Navigation and Editing Functions

Just as with other word processors, to navigate the editing screen you can simply point the cursor to the position at which you wish to begin typing, then click. The CAT word processor also includes mouse-driven CUT, PASTE, and UNDO.

Selecting Text You Wish to Cut

You select text the same way as with standard word processing programs: either (1) hold down your mouse button while sweeping the I-beam on the screen over the desired text, or (2) hold down the SHIFT key and use the navigation keys to select text.

The CUT Button

If you wish to delete text but want to save it to a temporary clipboard for pasting elsewhere, select that text, and then click on the CUT button. Cutting text is not the same as deleting it.

When you delete text (using the DELETE key), you cannot paste it elsewhere in your document (but see UNDO below). The drag-and-drop cut-and-paste function of most computers is not available on the GMAT computer. To copy, you must first cut the text and then paste it in the desired spot.

The PASTE Button

If you wish to move text from one position to another, select and cut the text, and then reposition your cursor where you want the text to go and click on the PASTE button.

The UNDO Button

Click on this button to undo the most recent delete, cut, or paste that you performed. There is no multiple undo function on the GMAT computer. The CAT word processor stores only your most recent delete, cut or paste, or keyboard entry.

The Vertical Scroll Bar

Once you key in ten lines or so, you'll have to scroll to view your entire response. A vertical scroll bar also appears to the right of the AWA prompt. Be sure to scroll all the way down to make sure you've read the entire prompt.

Spell-Checking, Grammar-Checking, Fonts, Attributes, Hyphenation

The CAT word processor does not include a spell-checker or grammar-checker, nor does it allow you to choose typeface or point size. Neither manual nor automatic hyphenation is available. Attributes such as bold, italics, and underlining are not available.

THE GMAT CAT TEST-TAKING EXPERIENCE

When you take a test as important as the GMAT, it's a good idea to minimize test anxiety by knowing exactly what to expect on exam day—aside from the timed test itself. Let's walk you through the various pre-test and post-test procedures and describe the physical testing environment.

When You Arrive at the Test Center

Here's what you can expect when you arrive at the test center:

- The test administrator will request that you present valid photo identification and will ask you to agree to the GMAT Examination Testing Rules & Agreement.

- The administrator will digitally take your fingerprint, signature, and/or palm vein pattern and will photograph you. Audio and video are recorded in the testing room at all centers during the exam. If you refuse to participate in any part of the check-in process or if you do not agree to allow audio/video recording, you will not be permitted to take the GMAT, and you will forfeit your entire test fee.

- Before you begin taking the exam at a test center workstation, you'll be asked to agree electronically to the "GMAT Nondisclosure Agreement and General Terms of Use" statement. This is required for you to be permitted to take the exam. If you don't agree to the statement, you cannot take the GMAT, and you will forfeit your test fee.

- Testing aids are not allowed during the test session or during breaks between sessions. These include beepers, pagers, calculators, books, pamphlets, notes, blank paper, rulers or any other measuring devices, iPods, MP3 players, radios, cell phones, stopwatches, watch alarms, dictionaries, translators, thesauri, and PDAs.

- Testing begins promptly once you're seated at your workstation. Expect to be there for about 4 hours.

- Two optional 8-minute breaks are scheduled during the test administration. If you exceed the time allowed for these breaks, that amount of time will automatically be deducted from the time you have to complete the next section of the test. The computer clock starts ticking on the next section of the exam whether or not you're back from your break.

- The test administrator will replace wet erase pens if they dry out during the test.

Testing Procedures and Rules

- If you want to exit the testing room for any reason, you must raise your hand and wait for the administrator to come in and escort you from the room. (You won't be able to pause the testing clock for any reason.)

- No guests are allowed in the waiting room during your test.

- No food, drink, or tobacco is allowed in the testing room, although you may be able to store such items in a locker and take them outside during breaks.

- No hats are allowed.

- Your palm vein pattern will be recorded when you arrive at the testing center, and your pattern will be matched whenever you exit and return to the testing room after a break.

ALERT!

In 2009, the digital fingerprinting used at many GMAT testing centers was replaced with a sensor that records the unique pattern formed by a person's palm veins. The new technology ensures that each test-taker has a single GMAT record, and prevents people from taking the test for others.

ALERT!

First-time GMAT test-takers will have both palms digitally scanned. If you are retaking the test and have a fingerprint on file, you will be asked to provide a matching print as well as palm scans. You will also be required to sign a digital signature pad.

- You'll receive a booklet of five "noteboards" before the exam. If you need more during the exam, raise your hand and request it from the administrator. You cannot remove any noteboards from the testing room during or after the exam.

- The administrator will replace your dull pencils with fresh, sharp ones upon your request anytime during the exam (just raise your hand).

What You Should Know About the CAT Testing Environment

- Individual testing stations are like library carrels; they're separated by half-walls.

- The height of your chair's seat will be adjustable, and the chair will swivel. Chairs at most testing centers have arms.

- Computer monitors generally measure 15 inches. You can adjust contrast. If you notice any flickering, ask the administrator to move you to another station. (You won't be able to tell if your monitor has color capability, though; the GMAT is strictly black and white.)

- If your mouse has two buttons, you can use either button to click your way through the exam (both buttons serve the same function). Don't expect a mouse with a scrolling wheel. Trackballs are available, but only if you request one before you begin the test.

- Testing rooms are not soundproof. During your test, you might hear talking and other noise from outside the room.

- Expect the administrator to escort other test-takers in and out of the room during your test. Do your best to ignore this potential distraction.

- If the testing room is full, expect to hear lots of mouse-clicking during your test.

- Earplugs are available upon request.

- Room temperatures may vary, so it's a good idea to dress in layers.

- You'll be under continuous audio and video surveillance. To guard against cheating, and to record any irregularities or problems in the testing room as they occur, the room is continuously audiotaped and videotaped.

Before You Begin the Test—The Computer Tutorial

The administrator has just escorted you into the exam room and to your workstation and has wished you luck. Before you begin the exam, the CAT System will lead you through a tutorial that explains:

1 How to use the mouse

2 How to select and change an answer

3 How to scroll the screen display up and down

4 How to use the toolbars. Here you'll learn how to:

- Quit the test.

- Exit the current section.

- Access the directions.

- Confirm your response and move to the next question.

5 How to use the special features in the AWA word processor and calculator for the Integrated Reasoning section

ALERT!

You can't change the size of the font on the GMAT computer screen unless you specifically request before the exam begins that a special ZOOMTEXT function be made available to you.

Here's what you need to know about the tutorial:

- You won't be able to skip any section or any screen during the tutorial.

- As you progress, the system requires that you demonstrate competency in using the mouse, selecting and confirming answer choices, and accessing the directions. You can't begin taking the actual test unless you've shown that you know how to use the system.

- At the end of each tutorial section (series of screens), you can repeat that section if you'd like—but you will have to step through the entire sequence of screens in that section again. You can't return to a section once you've left it.

- The AWA section of the tutorial allows you to practice using the word processor.

- If you carefully read all the information presented to you, expect to spend about 20 minutes on the tutorial.

Post-Test GMAT CAT Procedures

It's been four hours since you first entered the testing center, and you've just completed all the sections. You may think you've finished the test, but you haven't—not quite, anyway. You need to do four more things before you're done.

1 **Respond to a brief questionnaire.** The CAT will expect you to complete a brief questionnaire about your demographics, background, plans for graduate school, and whether you'd like to participate in surveys or receive information from GMAC, graduate business schools, organizations that grant scholarships, and/or strategic partners of GMAC. The answers may be prepopulated with responses you previously provided if you're retaking the GMAT.

2 **Cancel your test, at your option.** The most important question you'll answer while seated at your testing station is this one. The CAT will ask you to choose whether to cancel your scores (no scores are recorded; partial cancelation is not provided for) or see your scores immediately.

Once you elect to see your scores, you can no longer cancel them—ever! So be sure to take a few minutes and think it over. The CAT gives you 5 minutes to decide; if you haven't decided within 5 minutes, the CAT will automatically show you your scores, and you forfeit your option to cancel.

The scores that you receive immediately do not include scores for the AWA or the Integrated Reasoning sections.

3 **View and record your scores.** If you elect to see your scores, write them down on your noteboard. Although you can't take your noteboard outside the exam room, the supervisor will allow you to transcribe your scores onto another sheet of paper that you can take home with you.

4 **Direct your scores to the schools of your choice.** Once you've elected to see your scores, the CAT will ask you to select the schools you wish to receive your score report (the CAT provides a complete list of schools).

TIP

Read the prior review of the CAT tutorial, and you can step more quickly through it on test day. The less time you spend on the tutorial, the less fatigued you'll be during the actual exam.

ALERT!

If you click on the CANCEL SCORES button, the CAT will then give you another 5 minutes to think over your decision. So you really have 10 minutes altogether to make up your mind.

Before You Leave the Testing Center

When you exit the testing room for the final time, the following three things will happen:

1. The administrator will collect your marker and noteboard.
2. The administrator will remind you to collect your belongings from your locker (if you used one) and turn in your locker key.
3. The administrator will provide you with a pamphlet that explains how to interpret your test scores. (You can take this home with you.)

YOUR GMAT SCORES

You'll receive five scores for the GMAT:

1. A scaled Quantitative score on a 0–60 scale
2. A scaled Verbal score on a 0–60 scale
3. A Total score, on a 200–800 scale, based on both your Quantitative and Verbal scores
4. An AWA score on a 0–6 scale for your Argument Analysis essay
5. An Integrated Reasoning score on a 0–8 scale

Like the AWA, the Integrated Reasoning score will not count toward the total score. For each score, you'll also receive a percentile rank (0–99%). A percentile rank of 60%, for example, indicates that you scored higher than 59% (and lower than 40%) of all other test-takers. Percentile ranks reflect your performance relative to the entire GMAT test-taking population during the most recent three-year period.

How the Quantitative and Verbal Sections Are Scored

The scoring system for the Quantitative and Verbal sections is a bit tricky. Your score for each of these two sections is based on three factors:

1. The number of questions you answer correctly
2. The difficulty level of the questions you answer correctly
3. The range of question types and topics among the questions you answer correctly

So even if you don't respond to all 37 Quantitative or all 41 Verbal questions, you can still attain a good score for that section if a high percentage of your responses are correct—especially if you respond correctly to a wide variety of question types. The CAT system's scoring algorithms are well-guarded secrets; however, knowing exactly how the system works wouldn't affect your exam preparation or test-taking strategy anyway.

How the GMAT Essays Are Scored

The evaluation and scoring system for the GMAT essay is also a bit tricky. Initially, one person will read and evaluate your Argument essay and award a single score on a scale of 0–6 in intervals of 0.5 points with 6 being the highest.

Readers apply a holistic scoring approach, meaning that a reader will base his or her evaluation on the overall quality of your writing. In other words, instead of awarding separate sub-scores for content, organization, writing style, and mechanics, the reader will consider how effective your essay is as a whole—accounting for all of these factors.

Scoring Criteria for the Argument Essay

All readers are trained to apply the same scoring criteria. Here are the essential requirements for a top-scoring (6) Argument Analysis essay:

- You identify the key features of the argument and analyze each one in a thoughtful manner.
- You support each point of critique with insightful reasons and examples.
- You develop ideas in a clear, organized manner, with appropriate transitions to help connect ideas.
- You demonstrate proficiency, fluency, and maturity in the use of sentence structure, vocabulary, and idiom.
- You demonstrate an excellent command of the elements of Standard Written English, including grammar, word usage, spelling, and punctuation—even if the essay contains minor flaws in these areas.

The criteria for lower scores are the same as those listed above; the only difference is that the standard for quality decreases for successively lower scores.

Computerized Rating of Your Essay

Although a human reader evaluates your GMAT essay, a computer program called E-Rater® will also evaluate your essay in terms of grammar, syntax (sentence structure), repetitiveness (overuse of the same phrases), sentence length, and spelling. Like a human reader, E-Rater awards a score of 0–6 for each essay.

In many respects, E-Rater is similar to the grammar- and spell-checkers built into popular word processing programs such as Word and WordPerfect. However, E-Rater is custom-designed to weigh certain criteria more heavily than others. For instance, very little weight is given to minor mechanical errors (e.g., in punctuation and spelling). Also, E-Rater overlooks so-called gray areas of grammar (for example, use of the passive voice), and flags certain problems (such as repetitiveness) that off-the-shelf checkers might not. Of course, E-Rater is only useful to a point. It cannot evaluate your ideas or how persuasively you have presented and supported those ideas. That's what the human readers are for.

Computing Your AWA Score

Here are the four specific steps involved in calculating your AWA score:

1 As mentioned above, one reader will read and score your Argument Analysis essay. He or she will award a single score on a scale of 0–6 in half-point intervals (6 is the highest).

2 E-Rater will also evaluate and award a score of 0–6 for the essay.

3 The human reader's score differs from E-Rater's score by more than one point, a second human reader will read and score the essay (and E-Rater's score will be disregarded).

4 Your final score is the average of the scores awarded by the human reader and the E-Rater; AWA scores are rounded up to the nearest half-point.

NOTE

All GMAT readers are college or university faculty; most teach in the field of English or communications. Each reader evaluates your writing independently of other readers, and no reader is informed of other readers' scores.

NOTE

The scoring criteria for all six score levels are published in the official GMAT Information Bulletin and on the official GMAT Web site.

NOTE

According to the testing service, the human readers' and E-Rater's combined evaluation takes into account more than fifty structural and linguistic criteria.

NOTE

GMAT absences and cancelations also appear on your official report, but they will not adversely affect your chances of admission.

SCORE REPORTING

Once the essay has been read and scored and the Integrated Reasoning section has been scored, Pearson VUE mails out an official score report for all four sections and the total score for the Quantitative and Verbal sections. Expect your score report in twenty days after you take the exam. Pearson VUE had been sending out scores in fewer than twenty days, but because the Integrated Reasoning section is still new and the test-maker wants "to ensure that all Integrated Reasoning scores are equivalent," GMAC has been cautioning candidates to expect twenty days for their official reports.

At the same time, Pearson VUE will transmit a score report to each business school you've designated to receive your score report. You can direct that reports be sent to as many as five schools without charge.

HOW BUSINESS SCHOOLS EVALUATE GMAT SCORES

Each business school develops and implements its own policies for evaluating GMAT scores. Some place equal weight on GMAT scores and grade-point averages (GPAs), others weigh GMAT scores more heavily, and still others weigh GPA more heavily. Pearson VUE reports your three most recent GMAT scores to each business school receiving your scores and transcripts. Most schools simply average reported scores. (Quantitative, Verbal, Total, Integrated Reasoning, and AWA scores are each averaged separately for this purpose.)

A minority of schools have refined this approach by disregarding a score that is sufficiently lower than another score for the same ability—on the basis that the low score unfairly distorts the test-taker's ability in this area. Other schools disregard all but your highest score of each type in any event. (This approach is increasingly uncommon, since it discriminates in favor of test-takers who can afford to take the GMAT repeatedly.)

TOP 10 TIPS FOR GMAT PREP

Regardless of what books, software, or other GMAT-prep resources you're using, certain time-tested strategies for GMAT preparation never go out of style. To attain your best possible GMAT score, and to maximize your chances of getting into your first-choice business school, follow these ten tips:

 Don't Neglect Your Weaknesses.

In preparing for the GMAT, many test-takers mistakenly focus on their areas of strength and neglect areas where they have weaknesses. They may tell themselves: "I can't handle this tough material right now; I'll either review it later or skip it and hope to make some lucky guesses on the exam."

The fact is, you can't hide any of your individual GMAT scores from business school admissions officers, so don't waste time by spending energy on an area of the GMAT that you already know. You'll use your time more efficiently by devoting it to improving on your weaknesses.

2 **Don't Neglect the GMAT Essay Sections.**

GMAT "prep neglect" is especially common with the GMAT essay—and ironically, business schools are focusing more and more on the GMAT essay to help them make tough decisions among applicants, many of whom appear equally qualified otherwise. So your AWA score might very well make the difference between being accepted or rejected, especially for a business school that considers you a borderline candidate.

3 **Practice Under Exam Conditions.**

When it comes to GMAT prep, there's simply no substitute for "putting yourself to the test" by taking practice questions under simulated testing conditions. Here are some suggestions:

- Adhere to the time limits imposed by each exam section.

- If possible, use a word processor for composing your practice essays; try to use only the features available on the CAT word processor.

- If possible, take at least one computer-based practice test.

- Don't underestimate the role that endurance plays in taking the GMAT. Half the battle is just making it through the 4-hour ordeal with your wits intact. Condition yourself by taking at least one full-length practice test straight through, with only a few short breaks.

4 **Take the Real GMAT Once—Just for Practice.**

If you have time and can afford it, register for and take the real GMAT once as a "dress rehearsal," just to get comfortable with the testing environment. You'll rid yourself of a lot of anxiety and nervousness and, if you're like most test-takers, you'll be far more relaxed and focused the second time around. In fact, GMAT statistics show that among repeaters, more than 90 percent improve their score the second time around.

5 **Keep Practice Scores in Perspective.**

If you're like most GMAT test-takers, you've set your sights on two or three particular colleges or universities as your top choices, and you have a good idea what GMAT scores you'll need for getting into those schools. If that's the case, you've probably also set a goal for yourself with GMAT scores. That's understandable, but don't psyche yourself out by obsessing over your practice-test scores—you'll be sabotaging yourself. The bottom line: Try to concern yourself not with test scores themselves, but with what you can constructively do between now and exam day to improve these scores.

6 **Maintain a Positive Attitude.**

It's important to maintain a positive attitude about the GMAT—but it's also important to keep your self-confidence from turning into complacency and overconfidence. Think you can just "wing it" on the GMAT and still crush the competition? Think again. Even if you were a curve-raiser in college, thousands of other test-takers like you are taking the GMAT very seriously, and they can easily bump you down on the GMAT-scoring curve.

7 **Have Realistic Expectations.**

You'd love perfect GMAT scores, wouldn't you? In theory, of course, you can attain them. But in reality, you probably won't score as high as you'd like to. Accept your limitations. With regular study and practice, you'll perform as well as you can reasonably expect to. Also be realistic about the benefits you expect from this or any other GMAT-preparation book. There's only so much that you can do in a few weeks or months to boost your GMAT score.

8 Take Steps to Minimize GMAT Anxiety.

Test anxiety, whether before or during a test, can hinder your performance. Although it's a good idea to try and minimize it, don't expect to eliminate it entirely. If you're starting to feel the heat, try the following anxiety-busting techniques:

- Practice testing under exam conditions is the best method of reducing test anxiety. As you become more comfortable in a simulated testing environment, your nerves will begin to settle down, and the real test will seem more like "just another day at the office."

- Join (or form) a GMAT study group. Openly discuss your insecurities about the GMAT and you'll notice that they begin to dissipate.

- Before taking practice tests, try simple relaxation techniques such as stretching, quieting your thoughts, deep breathing, or whatever else works for you. Some people find a quick burst of vigorous exercise to be highly effective.

- You'll be anxious about the GMAT only if you're actually thinking about it. So during the weeks that you're gearing up for the test, keep yourself preoccupied with your everyday activities. Try not to discuss the GMAT with others except during planned study sessions or classes.

9 Know When You've Peaked.

Preparing for the GMAT is a bit like training for an athletic event. You need to familiarize yourself with the event, learn to be comfortable with it, and build up your skill and endurance. At some point—hopefully around exam day—your motivation, interest, and performance will peak. Sure, it takes some time and effort to get comfortable with the exam, to correct poor test-taking habits, to bone up on whatever math and grammar you might have forgotten, to develop an instinct for recognizing wrong answer choices, and to find your optimal pace. But there's a point beyond which additional study and practice confer little or no additional benefit. Don't drag out the process by starting several months in advance or by postponing the GMAT to give yourself more time than you really need for preparation.

10 Take the GMAT Early to Allow Yourself the Option of Retaking It.

Most graduate business schools admit new students for the fall term only. Although application deadlines vary widely among schools, if you take the GMAT no later than the November prior to matriculation, you'll meet almost any application deadline. Ideally, you should take the GMAT early enough so that you can take the exam a second time if necessary and still meet application deadlines. In any event, schedule the GMAT so that you're sure you will have adequate time to prepare.

ALERT!

Fast, accurate typists have a clear advantage in the GMAT essay sections. If you're a poor typist, work on improving your speed and skill before exam day.

ACCOMMODATIONS FOR TEST-TAKERS WITH DISABILITIES

The Graduate Management Admission Council® (GMAC®) offers reasonable accommodations to GMAT test-takers with disabilities in accordance with applicable law. Testing accommodations are available for those individuals who meet certain eligibility criteria and properly document their request.

Accommodations may include the following for those qualifying test-takers with documented disabilities:

- Additional testing time (all tests are timed)
- Additional or extended rest breaks
- Allowance of a medical device in the testing rooms
- A trackball mouse
- A reader who can read the test items to the test-taker and record test-taker responses
- A recorder to record test-taker responses
- Enlarged font on the PC monitor
- A sign language interpreter

To request test accommodations, you need to take the following five steps:

1 Download the *GMAT Information Bulletin*, and read it carefully. To receive a copy of the *GMAT Information Bulletin* in the mail, order a copy of the Bulletin on www.mba.com or contact GMAT Customer Service online at www.pearsonvue.com/contact/gmat.

2 Download the *Supplement for Test Takers with Disabilities*, and review it carefully. To receive a copy of the *Supplement for Test Takers with Disabilities* in the mail, contact GMAT Customer Service.

3 Complete the GMAT Test Accommodations Request Form found in the *Supplement for Test Takers with Disabilities*.

4 Obtain supporting documentation describing the need for accommodation. To ensure that the documentation is complete, review the "Guidelines for Documentation" in the *Supplement for Test Takers with Disabilities*.

5 Send completed GMAT Test Accommodations Request Form and all supporting documentation, along with the test fee (US $250), to Pearson VUE at one of the following addresses:

Standard Mail:
Pearson VUE
Attention: GMAT Disability Services
P.O. Box 581907
Minneapolis, MN 55458-1907
USA

Express Mail or Courier Service:
Pearson VUE
Attention: GMAT Disability Services
5601 Green Valley Drive, Suite 220
Bloomington, MN 55437
USA

The following comfort aids DO NOT require a GMAT Test Accommodations Request Form:

- Eyeglasses and hearing aids
- Pillow for supporting neck, back, or injured limb
- Neck braces or collars
- Insulin pump, if attached to your body (Medical equipment not attached to your body requires an accommodation request.)

If you are planning to request test accommodations, you must submit all of the required forms and information well in advance of your testing date. It may take up to six to eight weeks for a decision regarding an accommodation request, as the forms and supporting documentation must be reviewed to determine whether the request is adequately supported and to identify appropriate accommodations, consistent with the Americans with Disabilities Act (ADA) or applicable law.

COMMONLY ASKED QUESTIONS ABOUT THE GMAT

Question: What ID do I need to bring to the test center?

Answer: The ID must be government-issued, valid (not expired), original (no photocopies), and legible. It should include:

- A recent, recognizable photo
- Your name in the Roman alphabet, spelled exactly as you provided when you registered
- Your signature
- Your date of birth as you provided at registration

Acceptable IDs include a driver's license, government-issued ID, military ID, permanent resident/green card, or passport. Visit www.mba.com for more information.

Question: What do I do if I'm a citizen of one country and am taking the test in a different country?

Answer: You must present a valid, current (not expired) passport. If you do not have proper identification, you should contact the GMAT Customer Service in your region before your test date.

Question: What if my name has changed between the time I registered and the test appointment?

Answer: You should contact the GMAT Customer Service in your region to request a name change.

Question: What if I need my cellular (mobile) phone at the test center?

Answer: You may not take your cell phone into the testing room, and you may not check or use your phone during breaks. You may store your phone in a locker during your test, but remember that the test administrator is not responsible for lost or stolen items. If there is an emergency, you may ask the test administrator to use the center's phone during a break.

Question: May I access anything from the storage locker during one of my breaks?

Answer: You are permitted to access snacks and necessary items, such as medication that has to be taken at a specified time. You may not access cell phones, study aids, or any electronic devices during the breaks.

Question: What if I need more break time than I am given?

Answer: Breaks are timed, and any additional time you take during the break will be deducted from the time you are given to complete the next section of the exam.

Question: What if I need an unscheduled break?

Answer: If there is an emergency, raise your hand to get the administrator's attention. The administrator will set your workstation to break mode, and you may leave the testing room. Be aware that the exam timer will NOT stop during your unscheduled break.

Question: What if I need to reschedule my exam?

Answer: To reschedule your exam, go online to www.mba.com or call GMAT Customer Service. If you reschedule at least seven days before your original test date, you will be charged a service fee, but you won't lose the entire test payment. Your new appointment must be within six months of your original appointment.

Question: When will I get my scores?

Answer: Immediately after you complete the test you will receive an unofficial score report with Verbal, Quantitative, and Total scores. Official Score Reports are available online within twenty days to you as well as the programs you requested to receive them. The Official Report includes your AWA and Integrated Reasoning scores, which are not available immediately after you finish taking the test.

Question: If I've taken the GMAT exam more than once, will the score report contain all of my scores?

Answer: Official Score Reports include all GMAT exams you've taken within the past five years. If you have taken the exam and canceled your scores, your report will note that the scores are unreportable, but it will not include what the scores were.

Question: How do I order additional score reports, and how long do they take to arrive?

Answer: As part of your test fee, your scores can be sent to up to five school programs that you must select at the time of the test. You can order additional score reports for a fee by credit card at www.mba.com or by faxing a request. You can download the form on www.mba.com or call GMAT Customer Service in your region to request a form, which can then be mailed with a check or money order.

Question: What if I want a score report for a GMAT exam taken more than five years ago?

Answer: Score reports from tests taken from five to ten years ago are available, but they are sent to schools with the stipulation that they should be interpreted with caution. You should check with the school before requesting an old score report, because many do not accept them. Scores that are more than a decade old are not available. Only scores from within the last five years are reported.

SUMMING IT UP

- The GMAT contains four sections: Analytical Writing, Integrated Reasoning, Quantitative, and Verbal. The total testing time (excluding breaks) is 3 hours, 30 minutes.

- You receive five scores for the GMAT exam: a scaled Quantitative score on a 0–60 scale, a scaled Verbal score on a 0–60 scale, a Total score on a 200–800 scale (based on your Quantitative and Verbal scores), an AWA score on a 0–6 scale in half-point intervals, and an Integrated Reasoning score on a 0–8 scale. Percentile rankings are also included.

- Every business school has its own policies for evaluating GMAT scores. Pearson VUE reports your three most recent GMAT scores to each business school receiving your scores and transcripts.

- The Quantitative and Verbal sections of the GMAT are computer-adaptive, meaning that the testing system tailors its difficulty level to your level of ability. When you respond correctly to questions, it steps up to more difficult questions; if you respond incorrectly, it steps down to less difficult ones.

- The Integrated Reasoning section of the GMAT is not CAT. You may review questions and answers on this section of the test.

- You cannot skip questions or return to already answered questions on the GMAT CAT.

- For the essay section, you must use the simple word processor built into the CAT system, which includes some (but not all) standard features included in programs like Word and WordPerfect.

- A good way to minimize test anxiety is to know what to expect on exam day. Review the description of a typical testing environment in this chapter to become familiar with your physical surroundings on exam day.

- The Integrated Reasoning section has an on-screen calculator, whereas the Quantitative Section does not allow the use of a calculator.

- The Graduate Management Admission Council (GMAC) offers reasonable accommodations to GMAT test-takers with disabilities in accordance with applicable law. If you are planning to request test accommodations, you must submit all of the required forms and information well in advance (six to eight weeks) of your testing date.

GMAT Questions:
A First Look

OVERVIEW

- **Analytical Writing Assessment (AWA)**
- **The Integrated Reasoning section**
- **The Quantitative section**
- **The Verbal section**
- **Summing it up**

The GMAT consists of four parts, and test questions come in ten formats:

Test Section	Question Format
Analytical Writing Assessment (Section 1)	Analysis of an Argument
Integrated Reasoning section (Section 2)	Table Analysis
	Graphics Interpretation
	Multi-Source Reasoning
	Two-Part Analysis
Quantitative section (Section 3)	Problem Solving
	Data Sufficiency
Verbal section (Section 4)	Critical Reasoning
	Sentence Correction
	Reading Comprehension

Here you'll examine each format in detail. Specifically, you'll:

- Learn what abilities and content areas the format covers
- Examine the test directions
- Look at one or two example questions
- Review the question formats' key features

ANALYTICAL WRITING ASSESSMENT (AWA)

The GMAT Analytical Writing Assessment (AWA) consists of a single essay prompt that requires you to analyze an argument. In this section:

chapter 2

- You compose an essay response using the test's built-in word processor.
- Your time limit is 30 minutes.
- Your essay topic, or "prompt," is drawn randomly from a large pool.
- Your essay will be evaluated based on four broad areas: content, organization, writing style, and mechanics (grammar, syntax, word usage, etc.).

Analysis of an Argument
(1 Essay, 30 Minutes)

During the Argument Analysis section, your task is to compose an essay in which you critique a paragraph-length argument based on the strength of the evidence presented in support of it and on the argument's logic (line of reasoning). You can also indicate what additional evidence would help you evaluate the argument and how the argument could be improved. The Argument Analysis section is designed to test your critical reasoning and analytical writing skills. In scoring your Argument essay, the reader will consider how effectively you do the following:

- Identify and analyze the key elements of the argument
- Organize, develop, and express your critique
- Support your ideas (with reasons and examples)
- Control the elements of Standard Written English

Test Directions

During the pre-test tutorial, as well as at the start of your timed Argument Analysis section, the GMAT will present two screens of directions and guidelines specific to the Argument Analysis writing task. The first screen will describe the task generally and indicate the four general scoring criteria. Here's essentially what you'll see on the first screen:

This writing task is designed to test your critical-reasoning skills as well as your writing skills. Your task is to critique the stated argument in terms of its logical soundness and in terms of the strength of the evidence offered in support of the argument. In scoring your Argument essay, the reader will consider how effectively you:

- Identify and analyze the key elements of the argument
- Organize, develop, and express your critique
- Support your ideas (with reasons and examples)
- Control the elements of Standard Written English

The screen will then indicate additional rules and guidelines. Here's essentially what you'll see farther down the screen:

- Your time limit is 30 minutes.
- You must critique the logical soundness of the argument presented.
- A critique of any other argument is unacceptable.
- You should take a few minutes to plan your response before you begin typing.

- You should develop your ideas fully and organize them in a coherent manner.
- You should leave time to reread your response and make any revisions you think are needed.

The second screen will indicate specific guidelines for critiquing the Argument. Here's essentially what you'll see on the second screen:

- You are not being asked to agree or disagree with any of the statements in the argument.
- You should analyze the argument's line of reasoning.
- You should consider questionable assumptions underlying the argument.
- You should consider the extent to which the evidence presented supports the argument's conclusion.
- You may discuss what additional evidence would help strengthen or refute the argument.
- You may discuss what additional information, if any, would help you to evaluate the argument's conclusion.

NOTE
You can access the two screens of directions and guidelines any time during the Argument Analysis section by clicking on the HELP button.

What Argument Analysis Questions Look Like

The Argument on your exam will be drawn randomly from a large pool. Each Argument in the official pool consists of a paragraph-length passage, which presents the *argument* itself, followed by a *directive* (statement of your task). The directive is the same for every Argument in the official pool.

The Argument will appear as a quotation from a specified fictitious source. Here's an example similar to the ones in the official pool—although you won't see this one on your exam (the directive follows the Argument):

Directions: Using a word processor, compose an essay for the following argument and directive. Do not use any spell-checking or grammar-checking functions.

The following recommendation appeared in a memo from the Hillsville City Council to the city's mayor:

> "The private firm Trashco provides refuse pickup and disposal as well as recycling services for the town of Plattsburg. Trashco's total fees for these services are about two thirds of what Hillsville pays Ridco for the same services. In order to save enough money to construct a refuse transfer station within our city limits, Hillsville should discontinue using Ridco's services and use Trashco's services instead."

Discuss how well reasoned you find this argument. In your discussion, be sure to analyze the line of reasoning and the use of evidence in the argument. For example, you may need to consider what questionable assumptions underlie the thinking and what alternative explanations or counterexamples might weaken the conclusion. You can also discuss what sort of evidence would strengthen or refute the argument, what changes in the argument would make it more logically sound, and what, if anything, would help you to better evaluate its conclusion.

Key Facts About GMAT Argument Analysis

Here are some key facts about the Argument Analysis section (most are review):

- **The CAT will randomly select your Argument Analysis prompt from a large pool.** You won't be able to choose among topics.

- **All Arguments in the official pool contain the same directive.** Learn the directive that follows the quoted Argument before the exam, and you won't need to read it during the exam.

- **There is a right answer—or at least, a right way to go about answering the prompt.** Unlike essays that ask for your opinion, the argument that you are asked to critique will contain at least three major problems in the use of evidence, reasoning, and logic. To score high on this Argument Analysis essay, you must identify and discuss each major problem.

- **You don't need technical knowledge or special training in logic to score high.** GMAT Arguments are designed so that you can analyze them by applying general reasoning skills and common sense.

- **GMAT readers appreciate your time constraint and focus less on minutia than on the big picture.** The readers will focus primarily on substance and organization. You writing "style" and your mechanics (grammar, syntax, word usage, etc.) are secondary factors, and you won't be penalized for errors in spelling and punctuation unless these errors are frequent and egregious.

THE INTEGRATED REASONING SECTION
(12 Questions, 30 Minutes)

The Integrated Reasoning Section contains questions in four distinct formats:

1. Two-Part Analysis (approximately 4 questions)
2. Table Analysis (approximately 2 questions)
3. Multi-Sources Reasoning (approximately 3 questions)
4. Graphics Interpretation (approximately 3 questions)

The test-maker indicates that the number of questions per type may change over time. Each type not only has a different format for the prompt, but also a different number of and setup for answer choices. However, the purpose of the four types of questions are similar. They are meant to assess how well test-takers are able to evaluate information presented in different ways. As you read in Chapter 1, the GMAC has identified through research four key skills that business school faculty consider important for students to possess. They are looking for the ability to:

- Assimilate and integrate information from different sources to solve challenging problems.

- Accurately interpret data presented visually in graphs to determine or estimate probabilities and statistics.

- Recognize and evaluate tradeoffs and the likelihood of outcomes.

- Convert quantitative data between graphical and verbal formats.

While some questions require the ability to solve math problems, all the questions require good reading comprehension and critical thinking skills. There is no special list of content to study to prepare for the Integrated Reasoning section of the GMAT. If you review the math topics in this book and take the practice tests, you'll also be reviewing for any math questions in the Integrated Reasoning section. The same is true if you study the review sections for the Verbal part of the GMAT and take the practice tests.

Two-Part Analysis (Approximately 4 Questions)

Two-Part Analysis questions ask two questions, but in one set of directions. You won't find two separate questions and two sets of answer choices. The information to be analyzed is presented in the form of a prompt followed by a set of directions, which serves as the questions. The directions give you two tasks to perform—that is, answer choices to find—such as determining which of the statements listed as answer choices supports an argument and which statement weakens it. In other words, you're being asked to identify a set of contradictions. Or, the tasks may require solutions to math problems.

Test Directions

The general directions at the beginning of the Integrated Reasoning section of the GMAT say simply that Two-Part Analysis questions present a two-component task with answer options in a two-column table format. Actual directions vary based on the task. Some examples are the following:

Identify a speed, in miles per hour, for Truck A and a speed, in miles per hour, for Truck B that together are consistent with the given information. Make only one selection in each column.

Select the number that equals the ratio, *r*, of the sequence, and the number that equals the number, *n*, of the terms. Make only one selection in each column.

Select *Strengthen* for the statement that, if true, would most strengthen the analyst's argument, and select *Weaken* for the statement that, if true, would most weaken the analyst's argument. Make only two selections, one in each column.

Indicate two different statements as follows: one statement identifies an *assumption required* by the company's decision, and the other identifies a *possible fact* that, if true, would provide significant logical support for the required assumption. Make only two selections, one in each column.

The one constant in each set of directions is the need to find two answers.

What Two-Part Analysis Questions Look Like

The following is similar to the type of Two-Part Analysis question you will find on the actual test. Some questions will require calculations. If so, click on the Calculator button to use the onscreen calculator, or use the noteboard for simple calculations. A number of the Two-Part questions will require critical thinking rather than calculation to figure out the correct answers.

1. Two cars, Car A and Car B, are driving toward each other along the same road at constant speeds. They start 210 miles apart, and in 3 hours they will meet.

   In the table, identify a speed, in miles per hour, for Car A and a speed, in miles per hour, for Car B that together are consistent with the given information. Make only one selection in each column.

NOTE
To view the explanations of the question types while taking the test, click on HELP.

	1.1		1.2	

Car A	Car B	
(A)	(A)	20
(B)	(B)	30
(C)	(C)	35
(D)	(D)	45
(E)	(E)	55
(F)	(F)	60

Answer letters will not appear above the columns on the actual test. They have been placed here as a convenience in helping you relate the answer explanations to the questions.

1.1. **The correct answer is (C).** Two-Part Analysis questions may be quantitative or verbal; and the correct answers in the two columns may be independent of or dependent on each other. In this case, you have a quantitative question with answers that are dependent on each other.

Let r_A be Car A's speed and r_B be Car B's speed, and let d_A be the distance that Car A will have traveled when the two cars meet, and d_B be the distance that Car B will have traveled when they meet. The two distances will add up to 210 miles when the two cars meet:

$$d_A + d_B = 210 \Rightarrow d_B = 210 - d_A$$

You also know that distance equals speed times time, and since time in this case is 3 hours (the time it will take for the two cars to meet), you have:

$$d_A = 3r_A$$

and

$$d_B = 3r_B$$
$$210 - d_A = 3r_B$$
$$210 - 3r_A = 3r_B$$
$$3r_B + 3r_A = 210$$
$$r_B + r_A = 70$$

So, you have arrived at an expression that relates the speeds of the two cars. You cannot go further than this and calculate what the speeds are—but you also don't have to do that. You simply have to pick two answer choices that, together, satisfy this expression. In other words, you are looking for two answer choices whose sum equals 70. Here's a further tricky point: These two answer choices may be different from each other, but they don't have to be. In this case, the only way two of the answer choices can add up to 70 is if they are both 35. Thus, choice (C) is the correct answer for the speed of both cars.

1.2. **The correct answer is (C).** See the above explanation.

Key Facts About GMAT Two-Part Analysis

Keep in mind the following important features of Two-Part Analysis questions:

- **There are two answers to find—or tasks to perform—but only one set of directions.** The one set of directions lists both tasks, or answers, you must find. Be sure that you read the directions carefully and understand what you are to find. Often, the answers are contradictions such as weaken/strengthen and assumption/fact.

- **Not all Two-Part Analysis questions require math calculations.** Some questions require you to think through an argument and determine an assumption underlying it and a fact supporting the argument or whether particular information strengthens or weakens the argument.

- **Be sure you click on the correct oval for the question part you are answering.** Sometimes, you may reach the answer to the second part of the task before you determine the answer to the first part. Be sure to click on the answer oval in the correct column.

- **The number of answer choices may be more than or fewer than five.** The multiple-choice sections of the GMAT, the Quantitative and Verbal, have five multiple-choice answers per question. The Two-Part Analysis questions may have more than or less than five answer choices. The answer choices are the same for both tasks.

- **To receive credit, you must answer both parts of the question correctly.** Answering only one of the two tasks won't get you any credit. You must answer both correctly to receive credit.

Table Analysis (Approximately 2 Questions)

The Table Analysis questions provide data in the form of a table. But the difference between this question type and table questions found in traditional standardized tests is that the data in the GMAT is presented in a table that test-takers may re-sort. The data is presented in a format similar to a spreadsheet. Based on what the question is asking, you may sort the table in as many ways as the table has columns. Say the table has four columns, you may re-sort it in the three ways not shown. However, you need to read the question and statements carefully and note what you are to do and what the statement says. You may not need to re-sort in all the ways possible to work out your answer.

The question is again in the form of directions that ask you to determine something about a set of three statements. You must choose an answer for each of the three statements. You may need to do some computation to determine answers, but for the most part the calculations will not be complex.

Test Directions

The general directions state that the table is to be analyzed and the task will require the test-taker to determine if certain statements are accurate. The following are questions similar to what you might find on the GMAT for Table Analysis questions:

For each of the following statements, select *Inferable* if the statement is reasonably inferable from the given information. Otherwise, select *Not inferable*.

For each of the following statements, select *Yes* if the statement is true based on the information in the table. Otherwise, select *No*.

Note the word *each* in the directions. Answer only one and you won't receive credit.

NOTE

If you fail to type at least one character, you'll automatically receive a score of 0 (on a scale of 0 to 6) for that section. This score will appear on your report.

What Table Analysis Questions Look Like

The actual test question will appear on the screen as a prompt, a table, and three statements. It will be up to you to determine how much re-sorting of the data on the table you will need to do in order to determine the accuracy of each of the three statements. By accuracy, test-makers mean whether something is true or false based on the data or inferable or not inferable based on the data.

2. The table gives information about the area and population size of 18 U.S. states, as well as U.S. rankings of these states in terms of area and population. Each of these states is among the top 30 U.S. states for both area and population.

Sort By: | Select ▼ |

| State | Area | | Population | |
	Size (thousand square miles)	U.S. Rank	Size (millions)	U.S. Rank
Alabama	52.4	30	4.8	23
Arizona	147	6	6.5	16
California	163.7	3	37.7	1
Colorado	104.1	8	5.1	22
Florida	65.8	22	19.1	4
Georgia	59.4	24	9.8	9
Illinois	57.9	25	12.9	5
Iowa	56.3	26	3	30
Michigan	96.7	11	9.9	8
Minnesota	86.9	12	5.3	21
Missouri	69.7	21	6	18
New York	54.6	27	19.5	3
North Carolina	53.8	28	9.7	10
Oklahoma	69.9	20	3.8	28
Oregon	98.4	9	3.9	27
Texas	268.6	2	25.7	2
Washington	71.3	18	6.8	13
Wisconsin	65.5	23	5.7	20

For each of the following statements, select *Yes* if the statement is true based on the information in the table. Otherwise, select *No*.

	(A) Yes	(B) No	
2.1	○	○	New York State has 0.357 people per square mile.
2.2	○	○	The median population among the listed states is 6.5 million.
2.3	○	○	More than half of the states listed have areas of less than 70,000 square miles.

You will not have answer numbers and letters on the actual test, but for your convenience in relating answer explanations to statements, we have inserted numbers before each statement line and letters above the columns.

On the computer test, this will be the end of the question prompt and statements. To demonstrate how to answer such questions, the various other ways you may re-sort the data are given.

Sort By: | Area: Size ▼ |

State	Area		Population	
	Size (thousand square miles)	U.S. Rank	Size (millions)	U.S. Rank
Alabama	52.4	30	4.8	23
North Carolina	53.8	28	9.7	10
New York	54.6	27	19.5	3
Iowa	56.3	26	3	30
Illinois	57.9	25	12.9	5
Georgia	59.4	24	9.8	9
Wisconsin	65.5	23	5.7	20
Florida	65.8	22	19.1	4
Missouri	69.7	21	6	18
Oklahoma	69.9	20	3.8	28
Washington	71.3	18	6.8	13
Minnesota	86.9	12	5.3	21
Michigan	96.7	11	9.9	8
Oregon	98.4	9	3.9	27
Colorado	104.1	8	5.1	22
Arizona	147	6	6.5	16
California	163.7	3	37.7	1
Texas	268.6	2	25.7	2

Sort By: | Area: U.S. Rank ▼ |

State	Area		Population	
	Size (thousand square miles)	U.S. Rank	Size (millions)	U.S. Rank
Texas	268.6	2	25.7	2
California	163.7	3	37.7	1
Arizona	147	6	6.5	16
Colorado	104.1	8	5.1	22
Oregon	98.4	9	3.9	27
Michigan	96.7	11	9.9	8
Minnesota	86.9	12	5.3	21
Washington	71.3	18	6.8	13

Oklahoma	69.9	20	3.8	28
Missouri	69.7	21	6	18
Florida	65.8	22	19.1	4
Wisconsin	65.5	23	5.7	20
Georgia	59.4	24	9.8	9
Illinois	57.9	25	12.9	5
Iowa	56.3	26	3	30
New York	54.6	27	19.5	3
North Carolina	53.8	28	9.7	10
Alabama	52.4	30	4.8	23

Sort By: | Population: Size   ▼ |

| State | Area | | Population | |
	Size (thousand square miles)	U.S. Rank	Size (millions)	U.S. Rank
Iowa	56.3	26	3	30
Oklahoma	69.9	20	3.8	28
Oregon	98.4	9	3.9	27
Alabama	52.4	30	4.8	23
Colorado	104.1	8	5.1	22
Minnesota	86.9	12	5.3	21
Wisconsin	65.5	23	5.7	20
Missouri	69.7	21	6	18
Arizona	147	6	6.5	16
Washington	71.3	18	6.8	13
North Carolina	53.8	28	9.7	10
Georgia	59.4	24	9.8	9
Michigan	96.7	11	9.9	8
Illinois	57.9	25	12.9	5
Florida	65.8	22	19.1	4
New York	54.6	27	19.5	3
Texas	268.6	2	25.7	2
California	163.7	3	37.7	1

Sort By: Population: U.S. Rank ▼

State	Area		Population	
	Size (thousand square miles)	U.S. Rank	Size (millions)	U.S. Rank
California	163.7	3	37.7	1
Texas	268.6	2	25.7	2
New York	54.6	27	19.5	3
Florida	65.8	22	19.1	4
Illinois	57.9	25	12.9	5
Michigan	96.7	11	9.9	8
Georgia	59.4	24	9.8	9
North Carolina	53.8	28	9.7	10
Washington	71.3	18	6.8	13
Arizona	147	6	6.5	16
Missouri	69.7	21	6	18
Wisconsin	65.5	23	5.7	20
Minnesota	86.9	12	5.3	21
Colorado	104.1	8	5.1	22
Alabama	52.4	30	4.8	23
Oregon	98.4	9	3.9	27
Oklahoma	69.9	20	3.8	28
Iowa	56.3	26	3	30

2.1. **The correct answer is (B).** Using common sense, you would guess that this statement is incorrect—surely New York is more densely populated than that—but you should not evaluate it that way. Rather, evaluate it using mathematics. The key here is that the population figures are given in *millions* of people, while the area figures are given in *thousands* of square miles. Thus, in order to find a state's exact population, you should multiply the given figure by 1,000,000, and in order to find its area, you should multiply the given figure by 1000. So, New York's population per square mile is:

$$\frac{19.5 \times 1,000,000}{54.6 \times 1000} = 0.357 \times 1000 = 357$$

2.2. **The correct answer is (B).** You did not have to re-sort the table for Question 2.1, but you should re-sort it by "Population: Rank" for Question 2.2. There are 18 listed states in total, so the median population among them will be the average of the populations of the two states that are 9th and 10th among the listed states (not ranked 9th and 10th among all U.S. states). These are Washington and Arizona, which have populations of 6.8 million and 6.5 million, respectively. Thus, the median population among the listed states is 6.65 million, not 6.5 million. (Note that, if all 30 states with the highest population were given, then the median population would have been the average of the populations of the 15th and 16th states. Since some states are missing, however, don't worry about what the population of the 15th-most populous state may be, but rather just work with what you are given.)

2.3. **The correct answer is (A).** Re-sort the table by "Area: U.S. Rank." Oklahoma, which is the 20th-largest state in the country, is the largest of the listed states whose area is less than 70,000 square miles. You might think, then, that since only from the 20th state down does size get smaller than 70,000 square miles, that fewer than half of the top 30 states are smaller than 70,000 square miles in size. Once again, however, that's not what the question is asking! You're only interested in the states that appear in the table, and among them 10 have an area less than 70,000 square miles, while only 8 have an area greater than 70,000 square miles. Thus, the statement is correct.

Note the importance of reading the data and the statements carefully. Had you re-sorted by all four categories, you would have wasted some time. You needed to re-sort only by Population: Rank and Area: U.S. Rank.

Key Facts About GMAT Table Analysis

- **Table Analysis directions are the questions.** Like Two-Part Analysis questions, the directions for each Table Analysis test item are really the questions.

- **Table Analysis questions have three parts.** Each Table Analysis test item requires that you determine something about each of three statements. It may look like a single question, but each row is a separate "question" and two answer choices.

- **Though you can re-sort the table, you may not need to re-sort every column.** Read the directions and statements carefully and you may find that you don't need to re-sort every column on the table to determine the answers.

- **You may need to do some computation to determine the answers.** For the most part, any calculations for this question type will be fairly simple.

- **Click on the correct oval for the answer. This can't be said too often.** With the time pressure of the test situation and the newness of the question formats, you might click the oval in the wrong line or the wrong column. Be alert when you click on your answer.

- **To receive credit, you must answer all three parts of the question correctly.** Answering only one or two of the statements won't get you any credit. You must click on the right answer for each of the three statements to receive credit for the question.

Multi-Source Reasoning (Approximately 3 Questions)

Multi-Source Reasoning questions provide several pieces of information, often in different forms, that test-takers must analyze, interpret, and synthesize in order to answer questions. The form for the data may be text such as e-mail messages, sections of reports, or someone's analysis and opinion as well as tables, and charts. The questions themselves may be in a standard multiple-choice format, that is, one question and several answer choices. Or, the questions may be presented as statements and you must determine their accuracy; the format is similar to the two-column setup for some Two-Part Analysis and Table Analysis questions. Not all Multi-Source Reasoning items require math calculations.

Test Directions

The general directions at the beginning of the Integrated Reasoning section tell test-takers to click on all the tabs to analyze the information presented in order to determine the answers. On the actual test, you may find directions similar to the following when the setup for the test item is the two-column yes/no and inferable/not inferable format of Table Analysis questions:

> For each of the following statements, select *Inferable* if the statement is reasonably inferable from the information provided. Otherwise, select *Not inferable*.

Or, you may find specific questions such as the following when the question-and-answer setup follows the traditional multiple-choice format:

> Based on the given information, which of the following can be most reasonably inferred to be a view held by the producer?

> The poetry of which of the following is more likely to have been performed with musical accompaniment?

What Multi-Source Reasoning Questions Look Like

Managing Director	Theaters

Message from the Managing Director of a theater company to the Artistic Director

I have information about six theaters that could be suitable for our upcoming production. Their capacities range from 142 seats to 199 seats, and their rental rates range from $6000 per week to $12,000 per week. Location ac-counts for much of the difference in prices: Theaters in Center City are pricier than the others. On the other hand, we are likely to sell more tickets in a centrally located theater than in one of the others. Judging by our recent productions, I think that we should be able to achieve 50% of our weekly box office potential (that is, 50% of what we would earn in a week if we sold all tickets to all performances at the maximum price) in Center City. Otherwise, 40% is a more reasonable expectation.

Take a look at the attached table for more details.

Managing Director	Theaters					

This table has further details about location, capacity, and rental price of each theater.

				Box Office Potential		
Theater	Seats	Weekly Rental	Center City?	30%	40%	50%
The Lark	150	$6500	No	$14,175	$18,900	$23,625
The Jewel Box	142	$6000	No	$13,419	$17,892	$22,365
Williams Center	199	$9000	No	$18,806	$25,074	$31,343
The Tulip	150	$11,000	Yes	$14,175	$18,900	$23,625
The Stage	175	$12,000	Yes	$16,538	$22,050	$27,563
The Attic	150	$10,000	Yes	$14,175	$18,900	$23,625

For each of the following theaters, select *Yes* if the managing director believes it is reasonable that each week the theater company will be able to earn more than $13,000 above the weekly rental price at that theater. Otherwise, select *No*.

	(A)	(B)	
	Yes	No	
3.1	o	o	The Lark
3.2	o	o	The Tulip
3.3	o	o	The Attic

You will not have answer numbers and letters on the actual test, but for your convenience in relating answer explanations to statements, we have inserted numbers before each statement line and letters above the columns.

Note the similarity in answer setup to some of the test items for the Two-Part Analysis and Table Analysis questions. Note also that there are only two tabs for this question and that each presents data in different ways. The first tab has text in the form of an e-mail and the second tab presents quantitative data.

3.1. **The correct answer is (B).** The question is an inference question that involves numbers. The managing director believes it is reasonable that the company will achieve 50% of its weekly box office potential in theaters located in Center City, and 40% of box office potential in theaters located outside of Center City. The Lark is not in Center City, while the Tulip and the Attic are. Thus, for the Lark, calculate the difference between the 40% Box Office Potential value and its rental price:

$18,900 – $6500 = $12,400

So, for this theater, the managing director does not believe it is reasonable that the theater company will be able to earn more than $13,000 over the weekly rental price.

3.2. **The correct answer is (B).** Subtracting the Tulip's weekly rental price from the value of 50% of Box Office Potential gives $12,625. Thus, the managing director does not believe it is reasonable that the theater company will be able to earn more than $13,000 over the weekly rental price at this theater, either.

3.3. **The correct answer is (A).** Performing the same calculation here as in Question 3.2, but for the Attic figures yields $13,625. Thus, the managing director believes it is reasonable that the theater company will be able to earn more than $13,000 over the weekly rental price at the Attic.

Key Facts About GMAT Multi-Source Reasoning

- **Multi-Source Reasoning items will have two or three tabs.** Read the questions quickly to see what they are about and then read the tabs. Determine what is relevant information in each tab based on the questions.

- **Questions for the Multi-Source Reasoning part vary in format.** Some questions may be presented as three statements and you have to determine the accuracy of each, or the questions may be set up as traditional multiple-choice items and you have to choose the one correct answer. The latter tend to be quantitative questions.

- **To receive credit, you must answer all parts of the question correctly.** If the question is a traditional multiple-choice item, then you have to answer only one part. But if the question is a multi-part statement question, then you must analyze all statements correctly to receive credit.

Graphics Interpretation (Approximately 3 Questions)

According to the general directions at the beginning of the Integrated Reasoning section, the task with Graphics Interpretation questions is to interpret the image and "select the option from a drop-down menu list to accurately complete response statements." The graphical image presenting the data may be a line graph, bar graph, scatterplot, bubble graph, or pie chart. The graphics are similar to ones you've seen and worked with on other tests; it's the format for answering the questions—the drop-down menu—that's different.

However, once you click to open the menu, the setup for the answer choices is similar to a traditional multiple-choice test. The drop-down menu will list three or more answers, and you click on the answer that you believe is correct.

Test Directions

Unlike the other formats for Integrated Reasoning, the directions for Graphics Interpretation questions are basically the same from item to item. Like traditional multiple-choice test items, which this part of the Integrated Reasoning section most closely resembles, it's the questions that vary—except they are statements, not questions as such. All the test items for Graphics Interpretation are statements that you will have to complete. Think fill-in-the-blanks. The basic directions for this type of question will be similar to the following:

On the basis of the information provided, select from the drop-down menus the options that completes the statement the most accurately.

Use the drop-down menus to fill in the following statements with the most accurate answers.

Based on the information on the graph, use the drop-down menus to fill in the blanks to make the most accurate statements.

ALERT!

Figures in the Integrated Reasoning section are drawn to scale. This is not true in the Quantitative section.

What Graphics Interpretation Questions Look Like

The graphics used as the basis for the questions vary in format, but each test item has two statements that you must complete accurately.

4. The graph shows a company's unit sales during the course of a year.

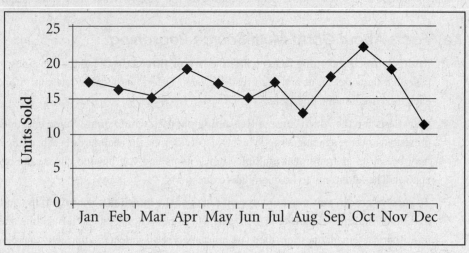

Based on the given information, use the drop-down menus to fill in the blanks to make the most accurate statements based on the graph.

4.1. The percent increase in unit sales in May compared to March was

    (A) 13.3

    (B) 26.7

    (C) 88.2

    (D) 113.3

4.2. The company sold as many units in October as it did in August.

    (A) 0.62

    (B) 1.17

    (C) 1.24

    (D) 1.62

On the actual GMAT, you will not see the answer choices listed like they are here, but rather as items in a drop-down menu, which is placed in line with the statements. Your task will be to select the menu item that best completes each statement. For the purposes of this book, however, the answers are shown in a lettered list, for ease of presentation.

4.1. **The correct answer is (A).** The graph gives you absolute values, and the question asks for a percentage. In March, the company sold 15 units, while in May it sold 17 units. In other words, the original value was 15 and the change was 2, so the percent increase was:

$$\frac{2}{15}100 = 13.3$$

4.2. **The correct answer is (D).** In October the company sold 21 units; in August it sold 13. If October sales were x times as many as August sales, then:

$$21 = 13x$$
$$x = \frac{21}{13}$$
$$x = 1.62$$

Key Facts About GMAT Graphics Interpretation

- **The graphical images are similar to ones you've seen on other tests**. You've worked with all the types of images used for Graphics Interpretation questions—bar graphs, line graphs, pie charts, scatterplots, and bubble graphs.

- **The format of the questions and answers is different for Graphics Interpretation test items, but not really.** You have to click on a drop-down menu to open the answer window, but the answers are arranged in a list like traditional multiple-choice answers. You select an answer and click on it to fill in a blank and complete a statement.

- **To receive credit, you must answer both parts of the question correctly.** Graphics Interpretation questions have two separate questions and sets of answer choices. You must answer both questions correctly to receive credit.

THE QUANTITATIVE SECTION
(37 Questions, 75 Minutes)

Before examining the two question formats—Problem Solving and Data Sufficiency—that the test-makers use for Quantitative Section questions, let's first cover what's common to both formats.

Both types of questions—Problem Solving and Data Sufficiency—are designed to measure the following general skills:

- Your proficiency in arithmetical operations
- Your proficiency at solving algebraic equations
- Your ability to convert verbal information to mathematical terms
- Your ability to visualize geometric shapes and numerical relationships
- Your ability to devise intuitive and unconventional solutions to conventional mathematical problems

Here's a breakdown of the specific areas covered on the Quantitative section, along with their frequency of appearance:

Properties of Numbers and Arithmetical Operations (13–17 Questions)

- Linear ordering (positive and negative numbers, absolute value)
- Properties of integers (factors, multiples, prime numbers)
- Arithmetical operations
- Laws of arithmetic
- Fractions, decimals, and percentages
- Ratio and proportion
- Exponents (powers) and roots
- Average (arithmetic mean), mode, and median
- Basic probability

Algebraic Equations and Inequalities (11–15 Questions)

- Simplifying linear and quadratic algebraic expressions
- Solving equations with one variable (unknown)
- Solving equations with two variables (unknowns)
- Solving factorable quadratic equations
- Inequalities
- Functions

Geometry, Including Coordinate Geometry (5–8 Questions)

- Intersecting lines and angles
- Perpendicular and parallel lines
- Triangles
- Quadrilaterals (four-sided polygons)
- Circles
- Rectangular solids (three-dimensional figures)
- Cylinders
- Pyramids
- Coordinate geometry

Interpreting Statistical Charts, Graphs, and Tables (2–4 Questions)

- Pie charts
- Tables
- Bar graphs
- Line charts

Algebraic concepts on the GMAT are those normally covered in a first-year high school algebra course. The Quantitative section does NOT cover the following skills and math areas:

- Complex calculations involving large and/or unwieldy numbers
- Advanced algebra concepts
- Formal geometry proofs
- Trigonometry
- Calculus
- Statistics (except for simple probability, arithmetic mean, and median)

The following assumptions apply to all Quantitative questions:

- All numbers used are real numbers.
- All figures lie on a plane unless otherwise indicated.
- All lines shown as straight are straight. Lines that appear "jagged" can be assumed to be straight (lines can look somewhat jagged on the computer screen).

NOTE

Additional assumptions about figures (diagrams and graphics) are different for Problem Solving questions than for Data Sufficiency questions.

Problem Solving (22–23 questions)

Problem Solving questions require you to work to a solution (a numerical value or other expression) and then find that solution among the five answer choices. Any of the Quantitative areas listed is fair game for a Problem Solving question.

Test Directions

The directions that follow are essentially what you'll see during the pre-test tutorial and just prior to your first Problem Solving questions (you can access these directions at any time by clicking on the HELP button).

Directions for Problem Solving Questions: Solve this problem and indicate the best of the answer choices given.

Numbers: All numbers used are real numbers.

Figures: A figure accompanying a Problem Solving question is intended to provide information useful in solving the problem. Figures are drawn as accurately as possible EXCEPT when it is stated in a specific problem that its figure is not drawn to scale. Straight lines may sometimes appear jagged. All figures lie on a plane unless otherwise indicated.

To review these directions for subsequent questions of this type, click on HELP.

What Problem Solving Questions Look Like

Let's look at two Problem Solving questions that are similar to what you might see on the GMAT. (Answer choices are lettered (A) through (E) here. Remember, though, that on the actual GMAT, you'll select among choices by clicking on one of five blank ovals, not letters.) This first problem is easy to understand, and no formulas or tricky math are needed to solve it. Among GMAT test-takers, about 80 percent would answer this question correctly.

1. Village A's population, which is currently 6800, is decreasing at a rate of 120 each year. Village B's population, which is currently 4200, is increasing at a rate of 80 each year. At these rates, in how many years will the population of the two villages be equal?

   (A) 9

   (B) 11

   (C) 13

   (D) 14

   (E) 16

The correct answer is (C). One way to solve this problem is to subtract 120 from A's population while adding 80 to B's population—again and again until the two are equal—keeping track of the number of times you perform these simultaneous operations. (You'll find that number to be 13.) But there's a faster way to solve the problem that also helps you avoid computation errors. The difference between the two populations is currently 2600 (6800 − 4200). Each year, that gap closes by 200 (120 + 80). So you can simply divide 2600 by 200 to determine the number of years it will take for the gap to close completely. That's easy math: 2600 ÷ 200 = 13.

2. If $-27 = \left(-\dfrac{1}{3}\right)^k$, what is the value of k?

   (A) −9

   (B) −3

   (C) $-\dfrac{1}{3}$

   (D) $\dfrac{1}{3}$

   (E) 3

NOTE

Remember that on the actual GMAT screen, you'll select your choice by clicking on one of five blank ovals instead of choosing among lettered answer choices.

The correct answer is (B). This question is asking you to determine the power that $-\dfrac{1}{3}$ must be raised to in order to obtain −27. First, look at the numbers in the question. Note that $-27 = (-3)^3$. That's a good clue that the answer to the question must involve the number −3. If the number we were raising to the power of k were − 3, then the value of k would be 3. But the number we're raising to the power of k is $-\dfrac{1}{3}$, which is the *reciprocal* of −3. (By definition, the product of a number and its reciprocal is 1.) So, you need to apply the rule that a negative exponent reciprocates its base. In other words, raising a base number to a negative power is the same as raising the base number's reciprocal to the power's absolute value. Therefore:

$$\left(-\dfrac{1}{3}\right)^{-3} = (-3)^3$$

As you can see, the value of k is −3.

Key Facts About GMAT Problem Solving

Important features of the Problem Solving format to keep in mind (some of these points are review):

- **Numerical answer choices are listed in order—from smallest in value to greatest in value.** Notice in our first sample question that the numerical values in the answer choices got *larger* as you read down from (A) to (E). That's the way it is with every Problem Solving question whose answer choices are all numbers. There is one exception to this pattern. If a question asks you which answer choice is greatest (or smallest) in value, the answer choices will not necessarily be listed in ascending order of value—for obvious reasons.

- **Some Problem Solving questions will include figures (geometry figures, graphs, and charts).** Most of the 5–8 geometry questions will be accompanied by some type of figure. Also, each data interpretation question will be accompanied by a chart or graph.

- **Figures are drawn accurately unless the problem indicates otherwise.** Accompanying figures are intended to provide information useful in solving the problems. They're intended to help you, not to mislead or trick you by their visual appearance. If a figure is not drawn to scale, you'll see this warning near the figure: "Note: Figure not drawn to scale."

Data Sufficiency (14–15 Questions)

The Data Sufficiency format is unique to the GMAT; you won't find it on any other standardized test. Each Data Sufficiency problem consists of a question followed by two statements—labeled (1) and (2). Your task is to analyze each of the two statements to determine whether it provides sufficient data to answer the question and, if neither suffices alone, whether both statements together suffice.

Data Sufficiency problems cover the same mix of arithmetic, algebra, and geometry as Problem Solving questions. (Any of the listed Quantitative areas is fair game for a Data Sufficiency question.)

Test Directions

The following directions are essentially what you'll see during the pre-test tutorial and just prior to your first Data Sufficiency question. (You can access these directions at any time by clicking on the HELP button.) Notice that some of the directions are new. In other words, they don't apply to Problem Solving questions.

Directions for Data Sufficiency Questions: This Data Sufficiency problem consists of a question and two statements, labeled (1) and (2), in which certain data are given. You have to decide whether the data given in the statements are <u>sufficient</u> for answering the question. Using the data given in the statements <u>plus</u> your knowledge of mathematics and everyday facts (such as the number of days in July or the meaning of *counterclockwise*), you must indicate whether:

- **(A)** Statement (1) ALONE is sufficient, but Statement (2) alone is not sufficient to answer the question asked;
- **(B)** Statement (2) ALONE is sufficient, but Statement (1) alone is not sufficient to answer the question asked;
- **(C)** BOTH Statements (1) and (2) TOGETHER are sufficient to answer the question asked, but NEITHER statement ALONE is sufficient;
- **(D)** EACH statement ALONE is sufficient to answer the question asked;
- **(E)** Statements (1) and (2) TOGETHER are NOT sufficient to answer the question asked, and additional data specific to the problem are needed.

ALERT!

In Data Sufficiency questions, figures are not necessarily drawn to scale. Figures in the Integrated Reasoning section are drawn to scale.

Numbers: All numbers used are real numbers.

Figures: A figure accompanying a Data Sufficiency problem will conform to the information given in the question, but will not necessarily conform to the additional information in Statements (1) and (2).

Lines shown as straight can be assumed to be straight and lines that appear jagged can also be assumed to be straight.

You may assume that positions of points, angles, regions, etc., exist in the order shown and that angle measures are greater than zero.

All figures lie in a plane unless otherwise indicated.

Note: In Data Sufficiency problems that ask you for the value of a quantity, the data given in the statements are sufficient only when it is possible to determine exactly one numerical value for the quantity.

To review these directions for subsequent questions of this type, click on HELP.

What Data Sufficiency Questions Look Like

As already noted, each Data Sufficiency problem consists of a question followed by two statements labeled (1) and (2). Let's look at two examples, similar to what you'll encounter on the GMAT. (Answer choices are lettered (A) through (E) here. Remember, though, that on the actual GMAT, you'll select among choices by clicking on one of five blank ovals, not letters.) This first question is a bit easier than average. Of all GMAT test-takers, about 85 percent would respond correctly to it.

3. How many quarts of oil will a car burn during a 3600-mile trip?

    (1) The car burns half a quart of oil every 1000 miles.

    (2) At a price of $1.50 per quart, the car uses $2.70 worth of oil during the trip.

    (A) Statement (1) ALONE is sufficient, but Statement (2) alone is not sufficient to answer the question asked;

    (B) Statement (2) ALONE is sufficient, but Statement (1) alone is not sufficient to answer the question asked;

    (C) BOTH Statements (1) and (2) TOGETHER are sufficient to answer the question asked, but NEITHER statement ALONE is sufficient;

    (D) EACH statement ALONE is sufficient to answer the question asked;

    (E) Statements (1) and (2) TOGETHER are NOT sufficient to answer the question asked, and additional data specific to the problem are needed.

The correct answer is (D). To answer the question, you need to know the rate (the number of miles per quart) at which the car burns oil. Statement (1) provides the information you need. A half quart of oil is burned per 1000 miles; therefore, the car will burn 3.6 that amount over 3600 miles. Although you don't need to do the math, the answer to the question is (3.6)(0.5) = 1.8. You've narrowed the answer choices to (A) and (D). But can you see that Statement (2) alone also provides the information you need to determine the rate? The amount of oil used = $2.70 ÷1.50. Again, although you don't need to do the math, the quotient (and the answer to the question) is 1.8. Since either statement alone suffices to answer the question, the correct answer is choice (D).

This next Data Sufficiency question is a bit more difficult than average. Only about 55 percent of all GMAT test-takers would respond correctly to it.

4. What is the absolute value of the sum of two numbers?

   (1) The product of the two numbers is 6.

   (2) One number is 5 less than the other number.

   (A) Statement (1) ALONE is sufficient, but Statement (2) alone is not sufficient to answer the question asked;

   (B) Statement (2) ALONE is sufficient, but Statement (1) alone is not sufficient to answer the question asked;

   (C) BOTH Statements (1) and (2) TOGETHER are sufficient to answer the question asked, but NEITHER statement ALONE is sufficient;

   (D) EACH statement ALONE is sufficient to answer the question asked;

   (E) Statements (1) and (2) TOGETHER are NOT sufficient to answer the question asked, and additional data specific to the problem are needed.

The correct answer is (C). Calling one number x and the other number y, Statement (1) alone tells us only that $xy = 6$, but gives no information about their sum. This narrows the answer choice options to (B), (C), and (E). Statement (2) alone tells us that the relationship between the two numbers can be written as $y = x - 5$, but gives no information about their sum. The correct answer choice must be either (C) or (E). By considering Statements (1) and (2) together, you can substitute $x - 5$ for y in the equation $xy = 6$:

$$x(x-5) = 6$$
$$x^2 - 5x = 6$$
$$x^2 - 5x - 6 = 0$$

You can factor the quadratic expression into two binomial factors, then find the roots of the equation—that is, the possible values of x:

$$x - 6 = 0 \quad \text{or} \quad x + 1 = 0$$
$$x = 6 \quad \text{or} \quad x = -1$$

Hence, either $x = 6$ and $y = 1$, with sum 7, or $x = -1$ and $y = -6$, with sum -7. In either case, the absolute value of their sum is the same: 7. Since both statements together provide one and only one answer to the question, the correct answer choice is (C).

You can also analyze this problem less formally. Based on statement (1) alone, try to think of some possibilities for the values of the two numbers that satisfy statement (1). Just using integers, the following four pairs should occur to you: 1 and 6, 2 and 3, –1 and –6, or –2 and –3. Since there's more than one possibility, you can rule out answer choices (A) and (D). Statement (2) alone presents an infinite number of possibilities, doesn't it? So you can also rule out choice (B). Together, Statements (1) and (2) seem to rule out all integer pairs except (1, 6) and (–1, –6). In either case, the absolute value of their sum is 7. But what about non-integers? Answering this question is where a bit of intuition or trial-and-error is required. You may try a few non-integer number pairs to satisfy yourself that none works.

TIP

In Data Sufficiency
questions, just as
in Problem Solving
questions, rely on
the information in
the question and
statements, not on a
figure's appearance.

Key Facts About GMAT Data Sufficiency

Keep in mind the following important features of the Data Sufficiency format (some of these points are review):

- **The answer choices are exactly the same for all Data Sufficiency questions.** This is one feature that makes Data Sufficiency questions unique among other types of GMAT questions.

- **Data Sufficiency questions can vary widely in difficulty level.** Assuming you're familiar with their unique format, these questions are neither inherently easier nor more difficult than Problem Solving questions. The level of difficulty and complexity can vary widely (depending on the correctness of your responses to earlier questions).

- **A Data Sufficiency question that asks for a specific numerical value is answerable only if *one and only one value* results.** Some, but not all, Data Sufficiency questions will ask for a particular numerical value. For example:

  - What is the area of the circle?

  - What is the value of *x*?

  - What is the area of triangle *ABC*?

  - How much did Sam pay for his book?

- **The two statements (1 and 2) will not conflict with each other.** Perhaps you're wondering which response you should choose—(D) or (E)—if you can answer the question with either statement alone, but get two conflicting answers. Don't worry; this won't happen. If you can answer the question using either statement alone, the answer will be the same in both cases. In other words, Statements (1) and (2) will never conflict with one another. Why? The test-makers design Data Sufficiency questions to avoid the "(D) vs. (E)" conundrum.

- **Figures are not necessarily drawn to scale, unless noted otherwise.** Any figure accompanying a Data Sufficiency question will conform to the information in the question itself but will not necessarily conform to either Statement (1) or (2). So although the figures are not designed to mislead you, they are not necessarily drawn to scale.

- **Calculating is not what Data Sufficiency is primarily about.** Expect to do far less number crunching and equation solving for Data Sufficiency questions than for Problem Solving questions. What's being tested here is your ability to recognize and understand principles, not to work step-by-step toward a solution. (That's what Problem Solving is about.)

THE VERBAL SECTION
(41 Questions, 75 Minutes)

The Verbal Section contains questions in three distinct formats:

1. Critical Reasoning (14–15 questions)
2. Sentence Correction (14–15 questions)
3. Reading Comprehension (12–13 questions)

Regardless of the format, each and every question in the Verbal Section offers five answer choices. Otherwise, each of the three formats is quite distinct. In the pages ahead, you can examine each one up close.

Critical Reasoning (14–15 Questions)

Critical Reasoning questions are designed to measure your ability to understand, criticize, and draw reasonable conclusions from arguments. GMAT Critical Reasoning questions cover various aspects of reasoning and evaluating arguments. Here are the three basic aspects on which most of the exam's 14–15 Critical Reasoning questions are based:

- Identifying assumptions underlying an argument
- Understanding the effect of additional evidence on an argument
- Drawing strong inferences from stated premises

Some GMAT Critical Reasoning questions will involve specific forms of reasoning or argument evaluation. Look for any of the following forms on your exam:

- Recognizing a hypothesis that provides a good explanation for a set of observations
- Recognizing an effective strategy, based on a set of premises and a stated objective
- Making valid deductions from stated premises or recognizing an additional premise needed to validate a stated conclusion
- Recognizing similarities in reasoning between different arguments

Test Directions

There are no special instructions for GMAT Critical Reasoning questions. The following simple directions are essentially what you'll see during the pre-test tutorial and just prior to your first Critical Reasoning question (you can access these directions at any time by clicking on the HELP button):

Directions for Critical Reasoning Questions: For this question, select the best of the answer choices given.

What Critical Reasoning Questions Look Like

Each Critical Reasoning question consists of a paragraph-length passage, followed by a question about the passage and five answer choices. Let's look at two Critical Reasoning questions that are similar to what you might see on the GMAT. (Answer choices are lettered (A) through (E) here. Remember, though, that on the actual GMAT you'll select among choices by clicking on one of five blank ovals, not letters.)

This first question is a bit easier than average; among GMAT test-takers, about 80 percent would answer it correctly.

5. Ten years ago, Brand 1 was the most popular beer among consumers. Today, however, consumers buy twice as much Brand 2 beer as Brand 1, even though Brand 2 is nearly twice as expensive as Brand 1.

   Which of the following, if true, would best explain the apparent discrepancy described above?

   (A) Consumers of beer as a group consider a beer's taste more important than its price.

   (B) Brand 2 beer has decreased in price over the last ten years.

   (C) Over the last ten years, wine has become a more popular beverage among consumers than beer.

   (D) Brand 2 beer is more readily available to consumers today than Brand 1 beer.

   (E) The minimum age at which a person can legally drink beer is lower today than ten years ago.

The correct answer is (D). The best answer choice must explain why Brand 2 beer is more popular than Brand 1 beer despite its higher price. Only choice (D) provides an adequate explanation. If Brand 1 beer is not available, while Brand 2 is, then obviously a consumer will purchase Brand 2 and not Brand 1. Choice (A) might explain the discrepancy if consumers prefer the taste of Brand 2 beer over that of Brand 1 beer; however, we don't know whether this is the case. Choice (B) might explain an increase in sales of Brand 2 beer; however, it fails to explain why Brand 2 is more popular today than Brand 1. Choice (C) might explain declining beer consumption generally; however, the popularity of wine is irrelevant to the popularity of one brand of beer compared to another brand of beer. Choice (E) might explain an increase in beer sales generally, but it does not explain why consumers buy more Brand 2 beer than Brand 1 beer.

This next Critical Reasoning question is a bit more difficult than average. Only about 50 percent of all GMAT test-takers would respond correctly to it.

6. *Company Spokesperson:* Charges that our corporation has discriminated against women in its hiring and promotion practices are demonstrably untrue. In fact, statistics show that greater than 60 percent of our corporation's employees are women.

   The answer to which of the following questions would be most relevant in evaluating the argument above?

   (A) What is the average tenure, or length of employment, among the company's women employees?

   (B) What percentage of the company's employees in higher-level management positions are women?

   (C) What percentage of employees in competing companies are women?

   (D) How has the percentage of women employees at the company changed over time?

   (E) Is the chief executive officer of the company a man or a woman?

The correct answer is (B). What makes this question difficult is that some of the incorrect answer choices are somewhat relevant to the argument, but their relevance is neither as clear nor as direct as choice (B). Let's start with the correct answer. Although a large percentage of the company's employees are women, it is entirely possible that these women generally occupy low-level positions while male employees generally hold higher-level jobs. One possible explanation for such a discrepancy would be that, when deciding whom to promote, the company discriminates against women. Hence, the answer to the question in choice (B) is highly relevant to evaluating the spokesperson's denial that the company engages in this type of discrimination. The issue raised in choice (A) would be relevant to whether the company's employee-termination practices are discriminatory, especially if the average tenure for women turned out to be significantly briefer than for men. However, the issue of tenure is not directly relevant to the company's hiring or promotion practices. Nor is the issue raised in choice (C) directly relevant to the argument. For example, assume that the percentage of the company's employees that are women is typical among firms in its industry. So what? Perhaps all of the firms discriminate against women or perhaps none does. As for choice (D), the company's practices in the past are not directly relevant to its current practices. Choice (E) focuses on only one high-level employee, hardly a sufficient statistical sampling to prove a pattern of discrimination. Also, even with a female CEO, a company could very well engage in hiring and promotion practices that are unfair to women.

Key Facts About GMAT Critical Reasoning

Keep in mind the following important features of Critical Reasoning questions:

- **Your knowledge of the topic at hand is not important in answering Critical Reasoning questions.** The test-makers design Critical Reasoning questions so that you can analyze and answer them without regard to what is factual (or not) in the real world. Also, whatever your personal opinions or viewpoints about the issue that an argument raises, they are irrelevant to analyzing the argument and answering the question.

- **Distinctions in quality between answer choices can be subtle.** GMAT Critical Reasoning is not a "black-and-white" affair in which one answer is perfect while each of the others is completely wrong. A typical Critical Reasoning question stem contains a word such as "best" or "most." That's because more than one answer choice usually has merit—it's just that the correct answer choice is the strongest among the bunch. (To master GMAT Critical Reasoning, you'll need to become comfortable with these shades of gray.)

- **Each piece of information in the paragraph is usually important in answering the question.** Occasionally, a Critical Reasoning paragraph will include superfluous information, which does not come into play at all in analyzing the argument and answering the question. But this is the exceptional case.

Sentence Correction (14–15 Questions)

Sentence Correction questions are designed to measure your command of the English language and of the conventions of Standard Written English. GMAT Sentence Correction covers two areas of English language proficiency:

1. Correct expression, measured by your ability to recognize errors in grammar, diction, and word usage

2. Effective expression, measured by your ability to improve sentences that are poorly worded or structured

GMAT Sentence Correction does NOT cover three other areas of English language proficiency:

1. Punctuation (except that comma placement can come into play if it affects the meaning of a sentence)

2. Vocabulary (you won't have to memorize long lists of obscure words just for GMAT Sentence Correction)

③ Slang and colloquialisms (informal expressions don't appear at all in Sentence Correction questions)

Test Directions

The following directions are essentially what you'll see during the pre-test tutorial and just prior to your first Sentence Correction question (you can access these directions at any time by clicking on the HELP button):

Directions for Sentence Correction Questions: This question presents a sentence, all or part of which is underlined. Beneath the sentence you will find five ways of phrasing the underlined part. The first of these repeats the original; the other four are different. If you think the original is best, choose the first answer; otherwise, choose one of the other answers.

This question tests correctness and effectiveness of expression. In choosing your answer, follow the requirements of Standard Written English; that is, pay attention to grammar, choice of words, and sentence construction. Choose the answer that produces the most effective sentence; this answer should be clear and exact, without awkwardness, ambiguity, redundancy, or grammatical error.

What Sentence Correction Questions Look Like

In each Sentence Correction question, part of a sentence (or the whole sentence) will be underlined. The first answer choice will simply restate the underlined part "as is." The other four choices present alternatives to the original underlined phrase.

Let's look at two questions that are similar to what you might see on the GMAT. (Answer choices are lettered (A) through (E) here. Remember, though, that on the actual GMAT you'll select among choices by clicking on one of five blank ovals, not letters.) This first question is a bit easier than average; among GMAT test-takers, about 80 percent would answer this question correctly.

7. A thesaurus can be a useful tool for <u>writers, providing he knows how to use it</u> correctly.

   (A) writers, providing he knows how to use it

   (B) writers, providing he knows how to use such a book

   (C) a writer, providing he knows how to use them

   (D) writers, providing she knows how to use it

   (E) writers, providing they know how to use it

The correct answer is (E). A pronoun and the noun to which it refers (called the *antecedent*) should be consistent; both should be either singular or plural. In the original sentence, however, the singular pronoun he is inconsistent with its plural antecedent *writers*. Among the four alternatives, only choices (C) and (E) fix this problem. In choice (C), both are singular, while in choice (E) both are plural; either is acceptable. Choice (C), however, creates another pronoun-antecedent error. Notice that it replaces the singular pronoun *it* with the plural *them*. Since the intended antecedent is *thesaurus*, which is singular, the plural pronoun *them* is incorrect, and you can eliminate choice (C). Choice (E) is the best version of the underlined part; it fixes the problem with the original version without creating any new errors.

Here's a Sentence Correction question that's a bit more difficult than average. Of all GMAT test-takers, only about 55 percent would respond correctly to it.

8. Frank Lloyd Wright was a preeminent architect of the twentieth century, and <u>there have been many less talented people who, both in the past and today, have</u> imitated his style.

   (A) there have been many less talented people who, both in the past and today, have

   (B) a great number of less talented people of today, as well as in the past, have

   (C) many less talented people, both in the past and today, have

   (D) there are many less talented people, today as well as in the past, who

   (E) many people less talented than Wright who, today as well as in the past, have

The correct answer is (C). The original version contains no grammatical errors. However, the phrase *there have been many less talented people who* is wordy. Choice (C) provides a more concise and graceful version, without introducing any new errors. In choice (B), *a great number of* is wordy; also, the two phrases of *today* and *in the past* lack grammatical parallelism. Choice (D) provides a less wordy version than the original, but is still not as effective as choice (C). As for choice (E), it too is unnecessarily wordy; what's more, within the construction of choice (E), the word *who* creates an incomplete sentence and should be omitted.

Key Facts About GMAT Sentence Corrections

Keep in mind the following important features of Sentence Correction questions (some of these points are review):

- **Any part of the sentence might be underlined.** The underlined part may appear at the beginning, middle, or end of the sentence. Also, in some cases, the entire sentence will be underlined. Expect all of these variations on your exam.

- **The first answer choice simply repeats the underlined part.** The other four choices present alternatives to the original underlined phrase.

- **The best answer choice isn't always perfect.** The best choice among the five will not contain any grammatical errors. However, it may make for a less-than-ideal sentence, at least in your opinion. But remember: You're looking for the best version of the five, not the perfect version.

- **More than one answer choice may be grammatically correct.** These questions cover not just grammar but also effective expression. So don't select an answer choice just because it results in a grammatically correct sentence. Another answer choice may be clearer, more concise, or less awkward—and therefore better.

- **A single Sentence Correction item can cover a lot of ground.** Don't expect each Sentence Correction item to isolate and test you on one, and only one, rule of grammar or aspect of written expression. Typically, by the time you've read all five choices, you've seen a variety of grammatical errors and other problems—at least among the four incorrect choices.

- **Punctuation doesn't matter.** You won't find errors in punctuation in these sentences (except as part of larger errors involving sentence structure).

- **You won't need any knowledge of the topic at hand in order to handle a question.** You're at no disadvantage if you know little or nothing about the topic of any particular sentence.

For instance, in handling the second question above, experts on Frank Lloyd Wright would not have any advantage over other test-takers, would they?

Reading Comprehension (12–13 Questions)

GMAT Reading Comprehension questions are designed to measure your ability to read carefully and accurately, to determine the relationships among the various parts of the passage, and to draw reasonable inferences from the material in the passage. On the GMAT, you'll encounter four sets of Reading Comprehension questions; all questions in a set pertain to the same passage and are presented in sequence. GMAT Reading Comprehension tests the following reading skills (you can think of these skills as question types):

- Recognizing the main point or primary purpose of the passage
- Recalling information explicitly stated in the passage
- Making inferences from specific information stated in the passage
- Recognizing the purpose of specific passage information
- Applying and extrapolating from the ideas presented in the passage

Test Directions

The following directions are essentially what you'll see during the pre-test tutorial and just prior to your first group of Reading Comprehension questions (you can access these directions at any time by clicking on the HELP button):

Directions for Reading Comprehension Questions: The questions in this group are based on the content of a passage. After reading the passage, choose the best answer to each question. Answer all questions on the basis of what is stated or implied in the passage.

What Reading Comprehension Sets Look Like

Each Reading Comprehension set consists of a reading passage along with a series of 3–4 questions about the passage. Here's a typical passage. Go ahead and read it now.

Line   Urodeles, a class of vertebrates that includes small, lizard-like creatures such as newts and salamanders, have an enviable ability to regenerate arms, legs, tails, heart muscle, jaws, spinal cords, and other organs that are injured or destroyed by accidents or those who prey on them. Planaria, which are a type of simple worm, have their own form of regenerative power. A

(5) single worm can be sliced and diced into hundreds of pieces, each piece giving rise to a completely new animal. However, while both urodeles and planaria have the capacity to regenerate, they use different means to accomplish this feat.

    In effect, urodeles turn back the biological clock. First, the animal heals the wound at the site of the missing limb. Then, various specialized cells at the site, such as bone, skin, and

(10) blood cells, lose their identity and revert to cells as unspecialized as those in the embryonic limb bud. This process is called dedifferentiation, and the resulting blastema, a mass of unspecialized cells, proliferates rapidly to form a limb bud. Ultimately, when the new limb takes shape, the cells take on the specialized roles they had previously cast off.

    In contrast, planaria regenerate using cells called neoblasts. Scattered within the planarian

(15) body, these neoblasts remain in an unspecialized, stem-cell state, which enables them at need to differentiate into any cell type. Whenever planaria are cut, the neoblasts migrate to the site

and form a blastema by themselves. It is interesting to note that this mechanism is similar to that following reproductive fission in these animals, and that species incapable of this form of asexual reproduction have poorly developed regenerative capacities.

Now, look at two questions based on the preceding passage. (Answer choices are lettered (A) through (E) here. Remember, though, that on the actual GMAT you'll select among choices by clicking on one of five blank ovals, not letters.) This first question is a bit easier than average; among GMAT test-takers, about 80 percent would answer this question correctly.

9. The author's primary purpose in the passage is to

   (A) describe the roles of blastema in regenerating urodeles and planaria.

   (B) describe how urodeles use the process of dedifferentiation to regenerate.

   (C) contrast the mechanisms by which urodeles and planaria accomplish regeneration.

   (D) show how methods of cellular regeneration have evolved in different animal species.

   (E) explain the link between reproductive fission and regeneration in simple worms.

The correct answer is (C). The last sentence of the first paragraph sets forth this central theme: that urodeles and planaria differ in the means they use to regenerate. The paragraphs that follow provide the details that reveal those differences. The second paragraph discusses how urodeles regenerate, while the third paragraph discusses how planaria regenerate. (Notice the phrase "In contrast," which begins the third paragraph.) Each of the incorrect choices distorts the author's central focus in the passage.

Here's a question that's a bit more difficult than average. Of all GMAT test-takers, only about 50 percent would respond correctly to it.

10. In the final sentence of the passage, the author implies that

   (A) reproductive fission and regeneration in certain planaria differ solely in the quantity of new planaria produced.

   (B) planaria that reproduce sexually use the process of dedifferentiation to regenerate entirely new animals.

   (C) asexual reproduction is related to regeneration in planaria but not in urodeles.

   (D) the genetic makeup of planaria created through regeneration would be the same as in those created through reproductive fission.

   (E) those planaria that reproduce by splitting themselves in two are more likely to regenerate using the same mechanism.

The correct answer is (E). The idea in the final sentence of this passage is difficult to grasp, making this question difficult to answer. The sentence says essentially that those species of planaria that do not engage in reproductive fission (i.e., splitting) are less likely to regenerate themselves in this way. Choice (E) expresses the same essential idea conversely: species of planaria that reproduce asexually (by fission or splitting) are the ones that are more likely to be able to regenerate in the same way.

Key Facts About GMAT Reading Comprehension

Keep in mind the following important features of GMAT Reading Comprehension (some of these points are review):

- **Passages appear on the left side of the computer screen, and questions appear (one at a time) on the right side.** You'll have to scroll vertically to read each entire passage, even the short ones.

- **Reading Comprehension questions are designed to test a lot more than just your short-term memory and your knack for finding information quickly.** Although your ability to recall what you've read is part of what's being tested, all but the easiest questions also gauge your ability to assimilate, interpret, and apply the ideas presented.

- **Some questions require that you focus on an isolated sentence or two; others require that you assimilate information from various parts of the passage.** Understandably, questions that cover disparate parts of a passage tend to be tougher than ones that you can answer just by reading a particular sentence or two.

- **Questions about information appearing early in the passage tend to come before other questions.** However, this isn't a hard-and-fast rule; don't assume you can simply scroll down the passage to answer each question in turn.

- **Tougher questions include not only a "best" response but also a tempting second-best response.** Recognizing the difference in quality between the two most viable responses is the key to answering the questions correctly.

- **Reading Comprehension questions are not designed to test your vocabulary.** Sure, you'll find the occasional advanced, technical, or obscure word. But the test-makers don't intentionally load the passages with tough vocabulary. Also, if a reading passage introduces a technical term, don't worry—the passage will supply all you need to know about the term to respond to the questions.

- **Reading Comprehension passages are condensed from larger works in the humanities, social sciences, and physical sciences.** Specific sources include professional journals, dissertations, and periodicals of intellectual interest. The test-makers edit the source material in order to pack it with test-worthy material.

- **All reading passages are not created equal—that is, equally difficult.** Comparatively tough passages are typically written in a dryer, more "academic" style than easier ones. Syntax is more complex and vocabulary more advanced. The passage's topic might deal with ideas and concepts that are more difficult to grasp, or it might be written, organized, or edited in a way that makes it more difficult to assimilate.

- **Prior knowledge of a passage's subject matter is not important. All questions are answerable** based solely on information in the passage. The exam includes passages from a variety of disciplines, so it is unlikely that any particular test-taker knows enough about two or more of the areas included on the test to hold a significant advantage over other test-takers.

SUMMING IT UP

- The Analytical Writing Assessment (AWA) requires you to compose an essay using the GMAT's built-in word processor. You have 30 minutes for the essay; your topic is randomly selected from a large pool.

- In your AWA essay, you critique a paragraph-length argument based on the strength of the evidence presented in support of it and on the argument's logic.

- Your essay will be graded for content, organization, writing style, and mechanics.

- The Integrated Reasoning questions have four formats: Two-Part Analysis, Table Analysis, Multi-Source Reasoning, and Graphics Interpretation. Each has a different setup and number of answer choices. For Graphics Interpretation questions, rather than clicking on an oval to choose an answer as you'll do with the other three formats, you'll have to select an answer from a drop-down menu.

- The Table Analysis questions have a sorting function, so you can re-sort the data to help you find the accurate solution.

- The Integrated Reasoning section has an on-screen calculator, but the Quantitative section does not.

- Problem Solving and Data Sufficiency questions in the Quantitative section of the GMAT measure your proficiency in arithmetical operations and solving algebraic equations, your ability to convert verbal information into mathematical terms, to visualize geometric shapes and numerical relationships, and to devise solutions to mathematical problems.

- The Verbal section of the GMAT consists of three parts: Critical Reasoning, Sentence Correction, and Reading Comprehension.

- Critical Reasoning measures your ability to understand, criticize, and draw reasonable conclusions from arguments.

- Sentence Correction measures your command of the English language and the conventions of Standard Written English.

- Reading Comprehension tests your ability to read carefully and accurately, determine the relationships among the various parts of the passage, and draw reasonable inferences from the material in the passage.

PART II
DIAGNOSING STRENGTHS AND WEAKNESSES

ANSWER SHEET PRACTICE TEST 1: DIAGNOSTIC

ANALYTICAL WRITING ASSESSMENT

_____

_____

_____

_____

_____

_____

_____

_____

_____

_____

_____

_____

_____

_____

_____

_____

_____

_____

_____

_____

_____

_____

_____

_____

_____

_____

_____

answer sheet

answer sheet

INTEGRATED REASONING

1.1 (A)(B)(C)(D)(E)(F)   4.1 (A)(B)(C)(D)(E)(F)   7.1 (A)(B)   10.1 (A)(B)(C)(D)
1.2 (A)(B)(C)(D)(E)(F)   4.2 (A)(B)(C)(D)(E)(F)   7.2 (A)(B)   10.2 (A)(B)(C)
2.1 (A)(B)   5.1 (A)(B)(C)(D)(E)(F)   7.3 (A)(B)   11.1 (A)(B)(C)(D)
2.2 (A)(B)   5.2 (A)(B)(C)(D)(E)(F)   8. (A)(B)(C)(D)(E) 11.2 (A)(B)(C)(D)
2.3 (A)(B)   6.1 (A)(B)   9.1 (A)(B)   12.1 (A)(B)(C)(D)
3.1 (A)(B)(C)(D)(E)(F)   6.2 (A)(B)   9.2 (A)(B)   12.2 (A)(B)(C)(D)
3.2 (A)(B)(C)(D)(E)(F)   6.3 (A)(B)   9.3 (A)(B)

QUANTITATIVE SECTION

1. (A)(B)(C)(D)(E)   9. (A)(B)(C)(D)(E)   17. (A)(B)(C)(D)(E)   25. (A)(B)(C)(D)(E)   33. (A)(B)(C)(D)(E)
2. (A)(B)(C)(D)(E)   10. (A)(B)(C)(D)(E)   18. (A)(B)(C)(D)(E)   26. (A)(B)(C)(D)(E)   34. (A)(B)(C)(D)(E)
3. (A)(B)(C)(D)(E)   11. (A)(B)(C)(D)(E)   19. (A)(B)(C)(D)(E)   27. (A)(B)(C)(D)(E)   35. (A)(B)(C)(D)(E)
4. (A)(B)(C)(D)(E)   12. (A)(B)(C)(D)(E)   20. (A)(B)(C)(D)(E)   28. (A)(B)(C)(D)(E)   36. (A)(B)(C)(D)(E)
5. (A)(B)(C)(D)(E)   13. (A)(B)(C)(D)(E)   21. (A)(B)(C)(D)(E)   29. (A)(B)(C)(D)(E)   37. (A)(B)(C)(D)(E)
6. (A)(B)(C)(D)(E)   14. (A)(B)(C)(D)(E)   22. (A)(B)(C)(D)(E)   30. (A)(B)(C)(D)(E)
7. (A)(B)(C)(D)(E)   15. (A)(B)(C)(D)(E)   23. (A)(B)(C)(D)(E)   31. (A)(B)(C)(D)(E)
8. (A)(B)(C)(D)(E)   16. (A)(B)(C)(D)(E)   24. (A)(B)(C)(D)(E)   32. (A)(B)(C)(D)(E)

VERBAL SECTION

1. (A)(B)(C)(D)(E)   9. (A)(B)(C)(D)(E)   17. (A)(B)(C)(D)(E)   25. (A)(B)(C)(D)(E)   33. (A)(B)(C)(D)(E)
2. (A)(B)(C)(D)(E)   10. (A)(B)(C)(D)(E)   18. (A)(B)(C)(D)(E)   26. (A)(B)(C)(D)(E)   34. (A)(B)(C)(D)(E)
3. (A)(B)(C)(D)(E)   11. (A)(B)(C)(D)(E)   19. (A)(B)(C)(D)(E)   27. (A)(B)(C)(D)(E)   35. (A)(B)(C)(D)(E)
4. (A)(B)(C)(D)(E)   12. (A)(B)(C)(D)(E)   20. (A)(B)(C)(D)(E)   28. (A)(B)(C)(D)(E)   36. (A)(B)(C)(D)(E)
5. (A)(B)(C)(D)(E)   13. (A)(B)(C)(D)(E)   21. (A)(B)(C)(D)(E)   29. (A)(B)(C)(D)(E)   37. (A)(B)(C)(D)(E)
6. (A)(B)(C)(D)(E)   14. (A)(B)(C)(D)(E)   22. (A)(B)(C)(D)(E)   30. (A)(B)(C)(D)(E)   38. (A)(B)(C)(D)(E)
7. (A)(B)(C)(D)(E)   15. (A)(B)(C)(D)(E)   23. (A)(B)(C)(D)(E)   31. (A)(B)(C)(D)(E)   39. (A)(B)(C)(D)(E)
8. (A)(B)(C)(D)(E)   16. (A)(B)(C)(D)(E)   24. (A)(B)(C)(D)(E)   32. (A)(B)(C)(D)(E)   40. (A)(B)(C)(D)(E)
                                                                                          41. (A)(B)(C)(D)(E)

answer sheet

Practice Test 1: Diagnostic

ANALYTICAL WRITING ASSIGNMENT
Analysis of an Argument
1 Question • 30 Minutes

Directions: Using a word processor, compose an essay for the following argument and directive. Do not use any spell-checking or grammar-checking functions.

The following appeared as part of an article in a national business publication:

> "Workforce Systems, a consulting firm specializing in workplace productivity and efficiency, reports that nearly 70 percent of Maxtech's employees who enrolled in Workforce Systems' one-week seminar last year claim to be more content with their current jobs than prior to enrolling in the seminar. By requiring managers at all large corporations to enroll in the kinds of seminars that Workforce System offers, productivity in our economy's private sector is certain to improve."

Discuss how well reasoned you find this argument. In your discussion, be sure to analyze the line of reasoning and the use of evidence in the argument. For example, you may need to consider what questionable assumptions underlie the thinking and what alternative explanations or counterexamples might weaken the conclusion. You can also discuss what sort of evidence would strengthen or refute the argument, what changes in the argument would make it more logically sound, and what, if anything, would help you better evaluate its conclusion.

INTEGRATED REASONING

12 Questions • 30 Minutes

1. Truck A is 40 miles ahead of Truck B on a highway. Both trucks are moving in the same direction at constant but different speeds, such that in 4 hours Truck B will reach Truck A.

   In the following table, identify a speed, in miles per hour, for Truck A and a speed, in miles per hour, for Truck B that together are consistent with the given information. Make only one selection in each column.

1.1	Truck A	1.2	Truck B	
(A)	○	(A)	○	45
(B)	○	(B)	○	48
(C)	○	(C)	○	52
(D)	○	(D)	○	56
(E)	○	(E)	○	58
(F)	○	(F)	○	61

2. The table gives information about the vehicle types and models that an automaker produces. The "Fuel-Efficient Models" column shows the number of models of each type that average more than 30 miles per gallon on the highway. The safety rating of each model is given in increments of 0.5 stars, from 0 to 5. For each type of vehicle, the "Starting Price" column shows the price of the vehicle with the lowest starting price and the price of the vehicle with the highest starting price.

Sort By: | Select ▼ |

Vehicle Type	Number of Models	Fuel-Efficient Models	Average Safety Rating	Starting Price
Compact	4	4	4.25	$17,000–$25,000
Sedan	4	4	4.5	$19,500–$28,000
Sport	2	0	3.75	$28,000–$33,000
SUV	3	1	3.67	$24,000–$30,500
Truck	2	0	4	$24,000–$28,000

For each of the following statements, select *Inferable* if the statement is reasonably inferable from the given information. Otherwise, select *Not inferable*.

	(A) Inferable	**(B)** Not Inferable	
2.1	○	○	The average highway fuel consumption of all the automaker's sedans is greater than 30 miles per gallon.
2.2	○	○	The average highway fuel consumption of all the automaker's models is greater than 18 miles per gallon.
2.3	○	○	The average starting price of all compact cars is lower than the average starting price of all sedans.

(On the computer test, this will be the end of the question prompt and statements. For this paper test and your convenience, we are providing the various other ways you may sort the data for ease in determining the answers.)

Sort By: | Number of Models ▼ |

Vehicle Type	Number of Models	Fuel-Efficient Models	Average Safety Rating	Starting Price
Sport	2	0	3.75	$28,000–$33,000
Truck	2	0	4	$24,000–$28,000
SUV	3	1	3.67	$24,000–$30,500
Compact	4	4	4.25	$17,000–$25,000
Sedan	4	4	4.5	$19,500–$28,000

Sort By: | Fuel-Efficient Models ▼ |

Vehicle Type	Number of Models	Fuel-Efficient Models	Average Safety Rating	Starting Price
Sport	2	0	3.75	$28,000–$33,000
Truck	2	0	4	$24,000–$28,000
SUV	3	1	3.67	$24,000–$30,500
Compact	4	4	4.25	$17,000–$25,000
Sedan	4	4	4.5	$19,500–$28,000

Sort By: [Average Safety Rating ▼]

Vehicle Type	Number of Models	Fuel-Efficient Models	Average Safety Rating	Starting Price
SUV	3	1	3.67	$24,000–$30,500
Sport	2	0	3.75	$28,000–$33,000
Truck	2	0	4	$24,000–$28,000
Compact	4	4	4.25	$17,000–$25,000
Sedan	4	4	4.5	$19,500–$28,000

Sort By: [Starting Price ▼]

Vehicle Type	Number of Models	Fuel-Efficient Models	Average Safety Rating	Starting Price
Compact	4	4	4.25	$17,000–$25,000
Sedan	4	4	4.5	$19,500–$28,000
Truck	2	0	4	$24,000–$28,000
SUV	3	1	3.67	$24,000–$30,500
Sport	2	0	3.75	$28,000–$33,000

3. *Economist:* When a country is in a recession, fiscal austerity measures, such as cuts to public services and pensions, especially when coupled with higher taxes, exacerbate a country's recession instead of helping the country move out of the recession. It is exactly when an economy is hurting that government should pursue expansionary policies, such as increasing government spending or lowering interest rates, even at the risk of higher inflation.

If County X is in a recession, then the economist suggests that a certain type of *prediction* about the country can be made based on a certain action by the country's government. In the table, indicate the possible *action* and *prediction* that most strongly conform to the economist's suggestion. Make only two selections, one in each column.

	3.1 Action	3.2 Prediction	
(A)	○	○	Country X's government keeps its interest rates low.
(B)	○	○	Country X's government cuts the salaries of public sector employees and increases real estate taxes.
(C)	○	○	Country X's government increases spending on infrastructure and raises interest rates.
(D)	○	○	Country X's recession will be alleviated.
(E)	○	○	Country X's inflation will increase.
(F)	○	○	Country X's recession will worsen.

4. A certain number of men and women have entered a trivia contest. All the contestants have the same likelihood of winning the contest, and the probability that a man wins is seven-eighths of the probability that a woman wins.

In the table below, identify a number of male contestants and a number of female contestants that together are consistent with the given information. Make only one selection in each column.

4.1	Male	4.2	Female	
(A)	○	(A)	○	21
(B)	○	(B)	○	28
(C)	○	(C)	○	30
(D)	○	(D)	○	32
(E)	○	(E)	○	40
(F)	○	(F)	○	42

5. A dentist is scheduling ten appointments, five on each of two consecutive days. These appointments may be for cleanings, fillings, or root canals, according to the following rules:

• No more than two root canals can be scheduled on the same day.

• Root canals must be scheduled before noon.

• In total, at least three fillings must be scheduled between the two days.

All but four of the appointments have been scheduled already, as shown in the table below. Masha, Melissa, Sanjay, and Xavier will take the remaining four time slots, one time slot each. Xavier needs a root canal and Sanjay is not available after 11 a.m. on Day 2.

	Day 1	Day 2
9 a.m.		
10 a.m.	Root Canal	Cleaning
11 a.m.	Root Canal	Cleaning
Noon	Cleaning	
1 p.m.		Cleaning

In the table below, select *Must occur* for the appointment that is certain to occur as described in the statement, and select *Cannot occur* for the appointment that is certain not to occur as described in the statement. Make only one selection in each column.

	5.1 Must occur	5.2 Cannot occur	
(A)	○	○	Sanjay's appointment is on Day 1.
(B)	○	○	Sanjay's appointment is at 9 a.m.
(C)	○	○	Masha's appointment is on Day 1.
(D)	○	○	Melissa's appointment is at noon.
(E)	○	○	Melissa's appointment is on Day 2.
(F)	○	○	The 1 p.m. appointment on Day 1 is for a cleaning.

6. The table gives the results for the top 25 finishers in a 10K street race. Finish times are given in hours:minutes:seconds. Most runners competed for one of several athletics clubs, while a few runners did not compete for any club.

Sort By: [Select ▼]

Name	Gender	Age	Club	Finish Place	Time (Net)	Time (Age-Adjusted)
Bikila	M	24	WRRC	1	0:30:44	0:30:44
Tanui	M	27	No club	2	0:30:51	0:30:51
Gerima	M	22	KLR	3	0:30:56	0:30:56
Ramos	M	25	WRRC	4	0:31:07	0:31:07
Korir	M	29	MVAC	5	0:31:22	0:31:22
Fiorelli	M	35	SCPN	6	0:31:48	0:31:08
Schulz	M	28	SCPN	7	0:32:16	0:32:16
Manesh	M	23	KLR	8	0:32:18	0:32:18
Elliott	M	30	MVAC	9	0:32:30	0:32:25
Zatopek	M	41	No club	10	0:32:35	0:30:34
Martinez	M	28	SCPN	11	0:32:41	0:32:41
Hester	M	32	MVAC	12	0:32:49	0:32:34
Dominguez	M	29	WRRC	13	0:33:00	0:33:00
Bryzgylova	F	21	No club	14	0:33:06	0:33:06
Yakatomi	F	25	KLR	15	0:33:09	0:33:09
Nurmi	M	42	SCPN	16	0:33:11	0:30:54
Bronkovic	M	34	SCPN	17	0:33:16	0:32:44
Selim	M	31	SCPN	18	0:33:34	0:33:25

Name	Gender	Age	Club	Finish Place	Time (Net)	Time (Age-Adjusted)
Lipmanson	F	23	MVAC	19	0:33:38	0:33:38
Litvinova	F	37	No club	20	0:33:55	0:33:17
Bogomilov	M	32	KLR	21	0:34:02	0:33:46
Lewis	M	31	KLR	22	0:34:29	0:34:19
Linares	F	38	MVAC	23	0:35:00	0:34:11
Marchand	M	43	WRRC	24	0:35:16	0:32:36
Ostrowski	M	26	WRRC	25	0:35:22	0:35:22

For each of the following statements, select *Yes* if the statement can be shown to be true based on the information in the table. Otherwise, select *No*.

	(A) Yes	(B) No	
6.1	o	o	The range of net finish times for members of the KLR club was greater than the range of net finish times for members of the WRRC club.
6.2	o	o	The fastest age-adjusted time among female runners was the same as the median age-adjusted time among all runners who did not compete for a particular club.
6.3	o	o	If the course record is 29:37, then exactly 9 runners achieved net times that are no more than 10% slower than the record

(On the computer test, this will be the end of the question prompt and statements. For this paper test and your convenience, we are providing you the various other ways you may sort the data.)

Sort By: Gender ▼

Name	Gender	Age	Club	Finish Place	Time (Net)	Time (Age-Adjusted)
Bryzgylova	F	21	No club	14	0:33:06	0:33:06
Yakatomi	F	25	KLR	15	0:33:09	0:33:09
Lipmanson	F	23	MVAC	19	0:33:38	0:33:38
Litvinova	F	37	No club	20	0:33:55	0:33:17
Linares	F	38	MVAC	23	0:35:00	0:34:11
Bikila	M	24	WRRC	1	0:30:44	0:30:44
Tanui	M	27	No club	2	0:30:51	0:30:51
Gerima	M	22	KLR	3	0:30:56	0:30:56
Ramos	M	25	WRRC	4	0:31:07	0:31:07
Korir	M	29	MVAC	5	0:31:22	0:31:22
Fiorelli	M	35	SCPN	6	0:31:48	0:31:08
Schulz	M	28	SCPN	7	0:32:16	0:32:16
Manesh	M	23	KLR	8	0:32:18	0:32:18
Elliott	M	30	MVAC	9	0:32:30	0:32:25
Zatopek	M	41	No club	10	0:32:35	0:30:34
Martinez	M	28	SCPN	11	0:32:41	0:32:41
Hester	M	32	MVAC	12	0:32:49	0:32:34
Dominguez	M	29	WRRC	13	0:33:00	0:33:00
Nurmi	M	42	SCPN	16	0:33:11	0:30:54
Bronkovic	M	34	SCPN	17	0:33:16	0:32:44
Selim	M	31	SCPN	18	0:33:34	0:33:25
Bogomilov	M	32	KLR	21	0:34:02	0:33:46
Lewis	M	31	KLR	22	0:34:29	0:34:19
Marchand	M	43	WRRC	24	0:35:16	0:32:36
Ostrowski	M	26	WRRC	25	0:35:22	0:35:22

Sort By: Age ▼

Name	Gender	Age	Club	Finish Place	Time (Net)	Time (Age-Adjusted)
Bryzgylova	F	21	No club	14	0:33:06	0:33:06
Gerima	M	22	KLR	3	0:30:56	0:30:56
Manesh	M	23	KLR	8	0:32:18	0:32:18
Lipmanson	F	23	MVAC	19	0:33:38	0:33:38
Bikila	M	24	WRRC	1	0:30:44	0:30:44
Ramos	M	25	WRRC	4	0:31:07	0:31:07
Yakatomi	F	25	KLR	15	0:33:09	0:33:09
Ostrowski	M	26	WRRC	25	0:35:22	0:35:22
Tanui	M	27	No club	2	0:30:51	0:30:51
Schulz	M	28	SCPN	7	0:32:16	0:32:16
Martinez	M	28	SCPN	11	0:32:41	0:32:41
Korir	M	29	MVAC	5	0:31:22	0:31:22
Dominguez	M	29	WRRC	13	0:33:00	0:33:00
Elliott	M	30	MVAC	9	0:32:30	0:32:25
Selim	M	31	SCPN	18	0:33:34	0:33:25
Lewis	M	31	KLR	22	0:34:29	0:34:19
Hester	M	32	MVAC	12	0:32:49	0:32:34
Bogomilov	M	32	KLR	21	0:34:02	0:33:46
Bronkovic	M	34	SCPN	17	0:33:16	0:32:44
Fiorelli	M	35	SCPN	6	0:31:48	0:31:08
Litvinova	F	37	No club	20	0:33:55	0:33:17
Linares	F	38	MVAC	23	0:35:00	0:34:11
Zatopek	M	41	No club	10	0:32:35	0:30:34
Nurmi	M	42	SCPN	16	0:33:11	0:30:54
Marchand	M	43	WRRC	24	0:35:16	0:32:36

Sort By: | Club ▼ |

Name	Gender	Age	Club	Finish Place	Time (Net)	Time (Age-Adjusted)
Gerima	M	22	KLR	3	0:30:56	0:30:56
Manesh	M	23	KLR	8	0:32:18	0:32:18
Yakatomi	F	25	KLR	15	0:33:09	0:33:09
Bogomilov	M	32	KLR	21	0:34:02	0:33:46
Lewis	M	31	KLR	22	0:34:29	0:34:19
Korir	M	29	MVAC	5	0:31:22	0:31:22
Elliott	M	30	MVAC	9	0:32:30	0:32:25
Hester	M	32	MVAC	12	0:32:49	0:32:34
Lipmanson	F	23	MVAC	19	0:33:38	0:33:38
Linares	F	38	MVAC	23	0:35:00	0:34:11
Tanui	M	27	No club	2	0:30:51	0:30:51
Zatopek	M	41	No club	10	0:32:35	0:30:34
Bryzgylova	F	21	No club	14	0:33:06	0:33:06
Litvinova	F	37	No club	20	0:33:55	0:33:17
Fiorelli	M	35	SCPN	6	0:31:48	0:31:08
Schulz	M	28	SCPN	7	0:32:16	0:32:16
Martinez	M	28	SCPN	11	0:32:41	0:32:41
Nurmi	M	42	SCPN	16	0:33:11	0:30:54
Bronkovic	M	34	SCPN	17	0:33:16	0:32:44
Selim	M	31	SCPN	18	0:33:34	0:33:25
Bikila	M	24	WRRC	1	0:30:44	0:30:44
Ramos	M	25	WRRC	4	0:31:07	0:31:07
Dominguez	M	29	WRRC	13	0:33:00	0:33:00
Marchand	M	43	WRRC	24	0:35:16	0:32:36
Ostrowski	M	26	WRRC	25	0:35:22	0:35:22

Sort By: [Time (Age-Adjusted)   ▼]

Name	Gender	Age	Club	Finish Place	Time (Net)	Time (Age-Adjusted)
Zatopek	M	41	No club	10	0:32:35	0:30:34
Bikila	M	24	WRRC	1	0:30:44	0:30:44
Tanui	M	27	No club	2	0:30:51	0:30:51
Nurmi	M	42	SCPN	16	0:33:11	0:30:54
Gerima	M	22	KLR	3	0:30:56	0:30:56
Ramos	M	25	WRRC	4	0:31:07	0:31:07
Fiorelli	M	35	SCPN	6	0:31:48	0:31:08
Korir	M	29	MVAC	5	0:31:22	0:31:22
Schulz	M	28	SCPN	7	0:32:16	0:32:16
Manesh	M	23	KLR	8	0:32:18	0:32:18
Elliott	M	30	MVAC	9	0:32:30	0:32:25
Hester	M	32	MVAC	12	0:32:49	0:32:34
Marchand	M	43	WRRC	24	0:35:16	0:32:36
Martinez	M	28	SCPN	11	0:32:41	0:32:41
Bronkovic	M	34	SCPN	17	0:33:16	0:32:44
Dominguez	M	29	WRRC	13	0:33:00	0:33:00
Bryzgylova	F	21	No club	14	0:33:06	0:33:06
Yakatomi	F	25	KLR	15	0:33:09	0:33:09
Litvinova	F	37	No club	20	0:33:55	0:33:17
Selim	M	31	SCPN	18	0:33:34	0:33:25
Lipmanson	F	23	MVAC	19	0:33:38	0:33:38
Bogomilov	M	32	KLR	21	0:34:02	0:33:46
Linares	F	38	MVAC	23	0:35:00	0:34:11
Lewis	M	31	KLR	22	0:34:29	0:34:19
Ostrowski	M	26	WRRC	25	0:35:22	0:35:22

7.

Producer	Critic	

Statement by theater producer:

Producers do not expect blind adoration by critics, but a little loyalty and support for the artists are not too much to ask for.

A production that reaches a Broadway stage represents thousands of hours spent by countless individuals with track records of excellence in their fields. Surely such a production is of some worth—and yet, from reading recent reviews, one would be excused to think that all new productions are worthless.

Meanwhile, rising real estate and labor costs mean that producers are taking ever-increasing risks to bring major productions to the stage. Inevitably, these increasing costs are shared with audiences in the form of higher ticket prices. Yet why would a consumer who is choosing between a play and a considerably less expensive movie pick the play if that has been proclaimed "soporific" by the press?

It is unconscionable that critics should treat so carelessly the art they are supposed to love.

Producer	Critic	

Statement by theater critic:

It is precisely because the theater critic loves the theater that he must be ruthless in his assessment of it. Every time a critic reviews a stage production, he may be responding to that production, but he is responsible for all theater. Rather than individuals, he must serve the art form. If he upgrades a mediocre production to winning, or lauds a decent one as great, he harms all productions. The Smiths may not pay a king's ransom for tickets to a show they've been warned is bad, but if they do pay a king's ransom for tickets to a show that has received good notices in the press, but is in fact mediocre, then they may never pay for theater tickets again. Surely producers are not asking that critics should harm the stellar shows of tomorrow by lying to audiences about the lamentable shows of today.

For each of the following statements, select *Inferable* if the statement is reasonably inferable from the information provided. Otherwise, select *Not inferable*.

	(A) Yes	(B) No	
7.1	○	○	The higher cost of theatrical labor is one of the factors that have led to higher ticket prices for theatrical productions.
7.2	○	○	The critic would prefer to risk harming a bad production via a negative review in the interest of helping good productions in the future.
7.3	○	○	The critic laments that at present theatrical productions are of poor quality, but expects them to be of good quality in the future.

8.

Producer	Critic

Statement by theater producer:

Producers do not expect blind adoration by critics, but a little loyalty and support for the artists are not too much to ask for.

A production that reaches a Broadway stage represents thousands of hours spent by countless individuals with track records of excellence in their fields. Surely such a production is of some worth—and yet, from reading recent reviews, one would be excused to think that all new productions are worthless.

Meanwhile, rising real estate and labor costs mean that producers are taking ever-increasing risks to bring major productions to the stage. Inevitably, these increasing costs are shared with audiences in the form of higher ticket prices. Yet why would a consumer who is choosing between a play and a considerably less expensive movie pick the play if that has been proclaimed "soporific" by the press?

It is unconscionable that critics should treat so carelessly the art they are supposed to love.

Producer	Critic

Statement by theater critic:

It is precisely because the theater critic loves the theater that he must be ruthless in his assessment of it. Every time a critic reviews a stage production, he may be responding to that production, but he is responsible for all theater. Rather than individuals, he must serve the art form. If he upgrades a mediocre production to winning, or lauds a decent one as great, he harms all productions. The Smiths may not pay a king's ransom for tickets to a show they've been warned is bad, but if they do pay a king's ransom for tickets to a show that has received good notices in the press, but is in fact mediocre, then they may never pay for theater tickets again. Surely producers are not asking that critics should harm the stellar shows of tomorrow by lying to audiences about the lamentable shows of today.

Based on the given information, which one of the following can most reasonably be inferred to be a view held by the producer?

(A) Consumers prefer going to the movies to going to the theater.

(B) A good review will make consumers choose the theater over the movies.

(C) A theatrical production is likely to be of some worth if it is put together by individuals with track records of excellence in their fields.

(D) Critics should laud decent productions as great.

(E) Critics do not have a responsibility toward the theatrical art form.

9.

Producer	Critic

Statement by theater producer:

Producers do not expect blind adoration by critics, but a little loyalty and support for the artists are not too much to ask for.

A production that reaches a Broadway stage represents thousands of hours spent by countless individuals with track records of excellence in their fields. Surely such a production is of some worth—and yet, from reading recent reviews, one would be excused to think that all new productions are worthless.

Meanwhile, rising real estate and labor costs mean that producers are taking ever-increasing risks to bring major productions to the stage. Inevitably, these increasing costs are shared with audiences in the form of higher ticket prices. Yet why would a consumer who is choosing between a play and a considerably less expensive movie pick the play if that has been proclaimed "soporific" by the press?

It is unconscionable that critics should treat so carelessly the art they are supposed to love.

Producer	Critic

Statement by theater critic:

It is precisely because the theater critic loves the theater that he must be ruthless in his assessment of it. Every time a critic reviews a stage production, he may be responding to that production, but he is responsible for all theater. Rather than individuals, he must serve the art form. If he upgrades a mediocre production to winning, or lauds a decent one as great, he harms all productions. The Smiths may not pay a king's ransom for tickets to a show they've been warned is bad, but if they do pay a king's ransom for tickets to a show that has received good notices in the press, but is in fact mediocre, then they may never pay for theater tickets again. Surely producers are not asking that critics should harm the stellar shows of tomorrow by lying to audiences about the lamentable shows of today.

For each of the following topics, select *Disagree* if, based on the producer's and the critic's statements, it can be inferred that the producer and the critic would hold opposing views on the topic. Otherwise, select *Cannot infer disagreement*.

	(A) Disagree	(B) Cannot infer disagreement	
9.1	○	○	The degree to which critics love the theater.
9.2	○	○	Where the theater critic's loyalty lies.
9.3	○	○	The quality of new productions.

10. The graph shows the number of student-athletes who participated during the 2010−11 school year in four team sports at certain schools in a six-school league. Each student participated in no more than one of these sports. The combined number of student-athletes who participated in these four sports at all six schools in 2010−11 was 425.

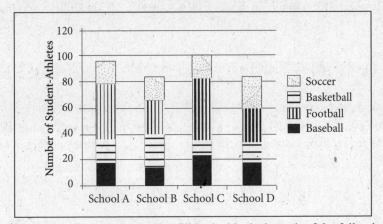

Based on the given information, fill in the blanks in each of the following statements.

10.1. Among the four schools shown in the graph, the one with the most students who participated in the sports shown in the graph, not counting football, is _____.

   (A) School A
   (B) School B
   (C) School C
   (D) School D

10.2. The two schools with the most student-athletes accounted for _____ of the student-athletes in the league.

   (A) between 30% and 40%
   (B) between 40% and 50%
   (C) over 50%

11. The graph shows the distribution of a family's expenses in January of a given year.

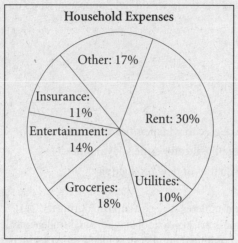

Based on the given information, fill in the blanks in each of the following statements.

11.1. If the family spent $1200 in rent in January, then it spent _____ in Utilities and Insurance that month.

(A) $400

(B) $440

(C) $800

(D) $840

11.2. If the family's total January expenses were $4000, and if 20% of the family's "Other" expenses went toward buying baby clothes, then the family spent _____ for baby clothes in January.

(A) $136

(B) $163

(C) $680

(D) $800

12. The graph plots seven countries in terms of the size of their Merchant Navy, Military Navy, and total population, with the area of each country's bubble corresponding to that country's total population.

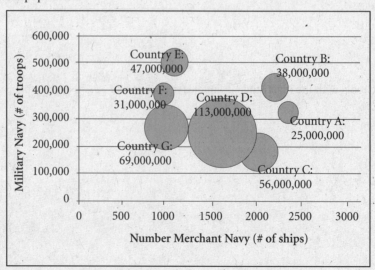

Based on the given information, fill in the blanks in each of the following statements.

12.1. The country that has the most ships in its Merchant Navy relative to the country's population is _____.

(A) Country A

(B) Country B

(C) Country D

(D) Country G

12.2. The probability that a country is in the top four in terms of the both number of ships in its Merchant Navy and number of troops in its Military Navy is _____.

(A) 0.14

(B) 0.29

(C) 0.5

(D) 0.71

QUANTITATIVE SECTION

37 Questions • 75 Minutes

Directions for Problem Solving Questions: *(These directions will appear on your screen before your first Problem Solving question.)*

Solve this problem and indicate the best of the answer choices given.

Numbers: All numbers used are real numbers.

Figures: A figure accompanying a Problem Solving question is intended to provide information useful in solving the problem. Figures are drawn as accurately as possible EXCEPT when it is stated in a specific problem that its figure is not drawn to scale. Straight lines may sometimes appear jagged. All figures lie on a plane unless otherwise indicated.

To review these directions for subsequent questions of this type, click on HELP.

Directions for Data Sufficiency Questions: *(These directions will appear on your screen before your first Data Sufficiency question.)*

This Data Sufficiency problem consists of a question and two statements, labeled (1) and (2), in which certain data are given. You have to decide whether the data given in the statements are *sufficient* for answering the question. Using the data given in the statements *plus* your knowledge of mathematics and everyday facts (such as the number of days in July or the meaning of *counterclockwise*), you must indicate whether:

(A) Statement (1) ALONE is sufficient, but Statement (2) alone is not sufficient to answer the question asked;

(B) Statement (2) ALONE is sufficient, but Statement (1) alone is not sufficient to answer the question asked;

(C) BOTH Statements (1) and (2) TOGETHER are sufficient to answer the question asked, but NEITHER statement ALONE is sufficient;

(D) EACH statement ALONE is sufficient to answer the question asked;

(E) Statements (1) and (2) TOGETHER are NOT sufficient to answer the question asked, and additional data specific to the problem are needed.

Numbers: All numbers used are real numbers.

Figures: A figure accompanying a Data Sufficiency problem will conform to the information given in the question, but will not necessarily conform to the additional information in statements (1) and (2).

Lines shown as straight can be assumed to be straight and lines that appear jagged can also be assumed to be straight.

You may assume that positions of points, angles, regions, etc., exist in the order shown and that angle measures are greater than zero.

All figures lie in a plane unless otherwise indicated.

Note: In Data Sufficiency problems that ask you for the value of a quantity, the data given in the statements are sufficient only when it is possible to determine exactly one numerical value for the quantity.

To review these directions for subsequent questions of this type, click on HELP.

1. $4\dfrac{1}{2}+3\dfrac{3}{4}-2\dfrac{2}{5}=$

   (A) $\dfrac{29}{5}$

   (B) $\dfrac{23}{4}$

   (C) $\dfrac{117}{20}$

   (D) $\dfrac{231}{40}$

   (E) $\dfrac{57}{10}$

2. Lyle's current age is 23 years, and Melanie's current age is 15 years. How many years ago was Lyle's age twice Melanie's age?

   (A) 5
   (B) 7
   (C) 8
   (D) 9
   (E) 16

3. If x and y are integers, is $x + y - 1$ divisible by 3?

   (1) When x is divided by 3, the remainder is 2.

   (2) When y is divided by 6, the remainder is 5.

4. Four knots—A, B, C, and D—appear in that order along a straight length of rope. Is the distance between B and D the same as the distance between A and B?

   (1) The distance between A and C is less than the distance between B and D.

   (2) Half the distance between A and D is the same as the distance between C and D.

5. Is $x > y$?

   (1) x is the arithmetic mean of all two-digit prime numbers less than 23.

   (2) y is the sum of all factors of 60 that are greater than −1 but less than 6.

6. In a boat race between David and Jeff, when Jeff had covered half the 30-mile race distance, David was 2 miles ahead of Jeff. How long did it take David to travel the entire 30-mile distance?

   (1) David traveled the last 15 miles of the race's distance in 40 minutes.

   (2) Jeff traveled the first 15 miles of the race's distance in 45 minutes.

7.

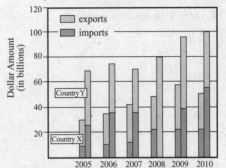

IMPORTS AND EXPORTS FOR COUNTRY X AND COUNTRY Y, 2005–2010

   According to the chart shown above, during the year that Country X's exports exceeded its own imports by the greatest dollar amount, Country Y's imports exceeded Country X's imports by approximately

   (A) $23 billion.
   (B) $75 billion.
   (C) $90 billion.
   (D) $110 billion.
   (E) $160 billion.

8. If $a - b = 2d$ and $2c - 4a = d$, what is $2b - c$?

   (A) $-\dfrac{7}{2}d$

   (B) $-\dfrac{9}{2}d$

   (C) $-2a - 3d$

   (D) $4a - \dfrac{7}{2}d$

   (E) $4a - \dfrac{9}{2}d$

9. If n is the first of two consecutive odd integers, and if the difference of their squares is 120, which of the following equations can be used to find their values?

   (A) $(n+1)^2 - n^2 = 120$

   (B) $n^2 - (n+2)^2 = 120$

   (C) $[(n+2)-n]^2 = 120$

   (D) $n^2 - (n+1)^2 = 120$

   (E) $(n+2)^2 - n^2 = 120$

10. M is P % of what number?

   (A) $\dfrac{MP}{100}$

   (B) $\dfrac{100P}{M}$

   (C) $\dfrac{M}{100P}$

   (D) $\dfrac{P}{100M}$

   (E) $\dfrac{100M}{P}$

11.

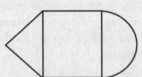

   Three carpet pieces—in the shapes of a square, a triangle, and a semi-circle—are attached to one another, as shown in the figure above, to cover the floor of a room. If the area of the square is 144 feet and the perimeter of the triangle is 28 feet, what is the perimeter of the room's floor, in feet?

   (A) $32 + 12\pi$

   (B) $40 + 6\pi$

   (C) $34 + 12\pi$

   (D) $52 + 6\pi$

   (E) $52 + 12\pi$

12. If $(b \square a \square c) = ab - c$, then

   $(4 \square 3 \square 5) + (6 \square 5 \square 7) =$

   (A) 6

   (B) 11

   (C) 15

   (D) 30

   (E) 40

13. Two competitors battle each other in each match of a tournament with nine participants. What is the minimum number of matches that must occur for every competitor to battle every other competitor?

   (A) 27

   (B) 36

   (C) 45

   (D) 64

   (E) 81

14. What is the value of x?

   (1) $4x^2 - 4x = -1$

   (2) $2x^2 + 9x = 5$

15. If $\dfrac{1}{1-x} = \dfrac{3}{4x}$, then $x =$

   (A) $-\dfrac{3}{7}$

   (B) $\dfrac{3}{7}$

   (C) $\dfrac{3}{5}$

   (D) $\dfrac{7}{3}$

   (E) 3

16. A 30-ounce pitcher is currently filled to exactly half its capacity with a lemonade mixture consisting of equal amounts of two lemonade brands—A and B. If the pitcher is then filled to capacity to conform to a certain recipe, how many ounces of each lemonade brand must be added to fill the pitcher?

   (1) The recipe calls for a mixture that includes 60 percent brand A.

   (2) When filled to capacity, the pitcher contains 12 ounces of brand B.

17. Lisa has 45 coins, which are worth a total of $3.50. If the coins are all nickels and dimes, what is the difference between the number of dimes and the number of nickels?

   (A) 5

   (B) 10

   (C) 15

   (D) 20

   (E) 25

18. A university's Natural Sciences division employs 140 professors, 70% of whom are men. If the university wishes to increase the percentage of its female natural sciences professors to at least 40%, and if no existing professors quit and it hires no new male professors, at least how many female natural sciences professors must the division hire?

    (A) 10
    (B) 14
    (C) 23
    (D) 24
    (E) 105

19. Barbara invests $2400 in the National Bank at 5%. How much additional money must she invest at 8% so that the total annual income will be equal to 6% of her entire investment?

    (A) $1200
    (B) $3000
    (C) $1000
    (D) $3600
    (E) $2400

20. ABC Company pays an average of $140 per vehicle each month in outdoor parking fees for three of its eight vehicles. The company pays garage parking fees for the remaining five vehicles. If ABC pays an average of $240 per vehicle overall each month for parking, how much does ABC pay per month in garage parking fees for its vehicles?

    (A) $300
    (B) $420
    (C) $912
    (D) $1420
    (E) $1500

21. If $m = n$ and $p < q$, which of the following must be true?

    (A) $m - p > n - q$
    (B) $p - m > q - n$
    (C) $m - p < n - q$
    (D) $mp > nq$
    (E) $m + q < n + p$

22. If $ab \neq 0$, is ?

    (1) $c \neq 0$
    (2) $a > b$

23. If the price of a candy bar is doubled, by what percent will sales of the candy bar decrease?

    (1) For every 10 cent increase in price, the sales will decrease by 5 percent.
    (2) Each candy bar now costs 60 cents.

24. What is the numerical value of the second term in the following sequence: $x, x + 1, x + 3, x + 6, x + 10, x + 15, \ldots$?

    (1) The sum of the first and second terms is one-half the sum of the third and fourth terms.
    (2) The sum of the sixth and seventh terms is 43.

25. On the xy-plane, what is the area of a right triangle, one side of which is defined by the two points having the (xy) coordinates (2,3) and (−4,0)?

    (1) The triangle crosses the y-axis at exactly two points.
    (2) The y-coordinate of two of the triangle's three vertices is 0 (zero).

26.

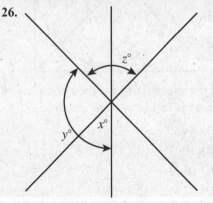

In the figure above, what is the value of x?

    (1) $y = 130$
    (2) $z = 100$

27. If $xy < 0$, and if x and y are both integers, what is the difference in value between x and y?

    (1) $x + y = 2$
    (2) $-3 < x < y$

28. A photographic negative measures $1\frac{7}{8}$ inches by $2\frac{1}{2}$ inches. If the longer side of the printed picture is to be 4 inches, what will be the length of the shorter side of the printed picture?

(A) $2\frac{3}{8}$ inches

(B) $2\frac{1}{2}$ inches

(C) $2\frac{3}{4}$ inches

(D) 3 inches

(E) $3\frac{1}{8}$ inches

29.

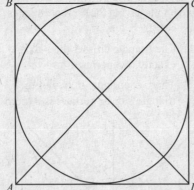

If the circumference of the circle pictured above is 16π, what is the length of $\overline{AC}$?

(A) $4\sqrt{2}$

(B) 16

(C) $16\sqrt{2}$

(D) 32

(E) 16π

QUESTIONS 30 AND 31 REFER TO THE FOLLOWING FIGURE.

AVERAGE YEAR-ROUND TEMPERATURES, CITY X AND CITY Y

Month of the year (January - December)

Note: Drawn to Scale

30. With respect to the two-month period over which the average daily temperature in City X increased by the greatest percentage, City Y's average daily temperature was approximately

(A) 38°

(B) 42°

(C) 52°

(D) 64°

(E) 68°

31. During the time periods in which City Y's average daily temperature was increasing while City X's was decreasing, the average daily temperature in City Y exceeded that in City X by approximately

(A) 0°

(B) 4°

(C) 10°

(D) 15°

(E) 19°

32.

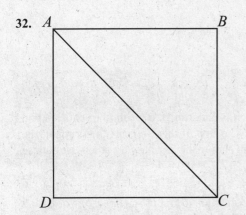

In the figure above, $ABCD$ is a square. If $\overline{AC}$ is 8 units long, what is the perimeter of the square?

(A) 16

(B) $12\sqrt{2}$

(C) 24

(D) $16\sqrt{2}$

(E) 30

33. Dan drove home from college at an average rate of 60 miles per hour. On his trip back to college, his rate was 10 miles per hour slower and the trip took him one hour longer than the drive home. How far is Dan's home from the college?

(A) 65 miles

(B) 100 miles

(C) 200 miles

(D) 280 miles

(E) 300 miles

34.
$$\sqrt{\frac{y^2}{2} - \frac{y^2}{18}} =$$

(A) 0

(B) $\dfrac{2|y|}{3}$

(C) $\dfrac{19y}{3}$

(D) $\dfrac{y\sqrt{3}}{6}$

(E) $\dfrac{y\sqrt{5}}{3}$

35. A certain cylindrical tank set on its circular base is 7.5 feet in height. If the tank is filled with water, and if the water is then poured out of the tank into smaller cube-shaped tanks, how many cube-shaped tanks are required to hold all the water?

(1) The length of a cube-shaped tank's side is equal to the radius of the cylindrical tank's circular base.

(2) If three cube-shaped tanks are stacked on top of one another, the top of the third cube stacked is the same distance above the ground as the top of the cylindrical tank.

36. Marisa took six tests in her physics class, and averaged a score of 79 over the six tests. If the average of her five best scores was 82, what was Marisa's worst score?

(A) 61

(B) 64

(C) 68

(D) 76

(E) 85

37. A solution of 60 ounces of sugar and water is 20% sugar. How much water must be added to make a solution that is 5% sugar?

(A) 20 ounces

(B) 80 ounces

(C) 100 ounces

(D) 120 ounces

(E) 180 ounces

VERBAL SECTION
41 Questions • 75 Minutes

Directions for Sentence Correction Questions: *(These directions will appear on your screen before your first Sentence Correction question.)*

This question presents a sentence, all or part of which is underlined. Beneath the sentence you will find five ways of phrasing the underlined part. The first of these repeats the original; the other four are different. If you think the original is best, choose the first answer; otherwise choose one of the others.

This question tests correctness and effectiveness of expression. In choosing your answer, follow the requirements of Standard Written English; that is, pay attention to grammar, choice of words, and sentence construction. Choose the answer that produces the most effective sentence; this answer should be clear and exact, without awkwardness, ambiguity, redundancy, or grammatical error.

Directions for Critical Reasoning Questions: *(These directions will appear on your screen before your first Critical Reasoning question.)*
For this question, select the best of the answer choices given.

Directions for Reading Comprehension Questions: *(These directions will appear on your screen before your first group of Reading Comprehension questions.)*
The questions in this group are based on the content of a passage. After reading the passage, choose the best answer to each question. Answer all the questions following the passage on the basis of what is stated or implied in the passage.

1. The mangrove forests of the Sundarbans, which is a region of both Bangladesh and India, provides vital protection from coastal storms which threaten the region.

    (A) provides vital protection from coastal storms which threaten
    (B) provides vital protection from coastal storms, which threaten
    (C) provide vital protection from coastal storms which threaten
    (D) provide vital protection from coastal storms that threaten
    (E) provides vital protection from coastal storms that threaten

2. After being injected, one participant from each of the three groups was taken to an observation room where, they believed, they encountered someone that had had the same injection.

    (A) they believed, they encountered someone that had had
    (B) as they believed, they encountered someone who had had

    (C) they believed that they encountered someone having had
    (D) the participant believed they encountered someone who had
    (E) the participant believed, he or she encountered someone who had had

3. While many doctors are loathe to discredit folk remedies entirely, they sometimes privately react to cures for the common cold that range from teas from various herbs, cooked foods such as rice porridge and chicken soup, and placing a hot stone on the site of congestion with reactions ranging from polite laughter to disdain.

    (A) teas from various herbs, cooked foods such as rice porridge and chicken soup, and placing a hot stone on the site of congestion
    (B) teas made from various herbs, foods such as rice porridge and chicken soup, and placing a hot stone on the site of congestion

(C) drinking teas from various herbs, eating foods such as rice porridge and chicken soup, and placing a hot stone on the site of congestion

(D) teas from various herbs, eating foods such as rice porridge and chicken soup, and the placement of a hot stone on the site of congestion

(E) herbal teas, rice porridge and chicken soup, and placing a hot stone on the site of congestion

4. In a recent survey, 9 out of 10 people using Slim-Ease for two weeks as directed reported that they lost weight during this period. This fact surely proves that Slim-Ease is effective for anyone wanting to shed some unwanted pounds.

The claim made above depends on which of the following assumptions?

(A) The survey participants were not using Slim-Ease immediately prior to the two-week period.

(B) The survey participants did not exercise during the two-week period.

(C) The survey participants were overweight prior to the two-week period.

(D) The survey participants' dietary habits were otherwise similar during the two-week period and prior to that period.

(E) No other product is more effective than Slim-Ease to help lose weight.

5. Compared to older houses, new houses are sure to have newer, more efficient heating and cooling units, more modern kitchen appliances, and more contemporary-style bathroom fixtures. They also generally conform to current building-code regulations, whereas many older houses do not. Accordingly, it is always advantageous to purchase a new home rather than an old home.

Which of the following, if true, is the best criticism of the advice given in the argument above?

(A) Some people prefer more traditional styles of bathroom fixtures over contemporary styles.

(B) Whether a house has new equipment and fixtures and conforms to current code requirements are not the only factors home buyers consider important when choosing a house.

(C) New houses are generally more expensive than older houses of comparable size.

(D) When an older house is sold, correcting any code violations is the responsibility of the seller.

(E) In general, older houses have more of the kinds of details that lend charm to a home than do new houses.

QUESTIONS 6–8 ARE BASED ON THE FOLLOWING PASSAGE.

Line   In the 1970s, the idea of building so-called "New Towns" to absorb growth was considered a potential cure-all for urban problems in the United States. It was (5) erroneously assumed that by diverting residents from existing centers, current urban problems would at least get no worse. It was also wrongly assumed that, since European New Towns had been financially (10) and socially successful, the same could be expected in the United States.

However, the ill-considered projects not only failed to relieve pressures on existing cities, but also weakened those (15) cities further by drawing away high-income citizens. This increased the concentration of low-income groups—who were unable to provide the necessary tax base to support the cities. Taxpayers who (20) remained were left to carry a greater burden, while industry and commerce sought to escape.

As it turned out, the promoters of New Towns were the developers, builders, and (25) financial institutions, all whose main interest was financial gain. Not surprisingly, development occurred in areas where land was cheap and construction profitable

Line rather than where New Towns were genu-
(30) inely needed. Moreover, poor planning
and legislation produced not the sort of
successful New Towns seen in Britain but
rather nothing more than sprawling
suburbs. Federal regulations designed to
(35) promote the New Town concept failed to
consider social needs as the European plans
did. In fact, the regulations specified virtually all of the ingredients of the typical
suburban community.

6. The author's primary concern in the passage
is to

(A) describe the characteristics of
American New Towns that made
them unsuccessful.

(B) trace the development of the New
Town concept in the United States.

(C) list the differences between New
Towns in the United States and those
in Europe.

(D) explain why New Towns in the
United States failed to meet general
expectations.

(E) analyze the impact of New Towns on
urban centers in the United States.

7. Based only on the information in the passage,
with which of the following statements about
New Towns in the United States would the
author most likely agree?

(A) They helped dissuade businesses in
urban centers from relocating to other
areas.

(B) They provided a thriving social
center away from the problems of the
older city.

(C) They helped reduce air pollution by
relocating workplaces to suburbs,
where most workers lived.

(D) They thwarted economic
redevelopment plans for decaying
urban centers.

(E) They provided affluent urban
residents an escape from the city.

8. Which of the following phenomena is most
closely analogous to the New Towns established in the United States?

(A) A business that fails as a result of
insufficient demand for its products
or services

(B) A new game that fails to attain
widespread popularity because its
rules are unfair

(C) New utility software that solves one
computer problem but creates another

(D) A new drug whose side effects are
severe enough to discourage people
from using it

(E) A scientific theory that lacks
supporting empirical evidence

9. Because hearing loss is cumulative, <u>it often
comes to pass that the person whose losing
her hearing</u> is not aware of what is happening until the loss is quite severe.

(A) it often comes to pass that the person
whose losing her hearing

(B) the person who is losing her hearing
often

(C) it often comes to pass that the person
whose hearing is being lost

(D) it often comes to pass that the person
who's experiencing hearing loss

(E) the person whose hearing is being
lost often

10. *Company X spokesperson:* Although several
of our key managerial employees have left
our company since we merged with our leading competitor two months ago, we have no
reason to believe that a significant number of
our other employees will follow suit. Virtually all of Company X's current employees
are the same people who we employed prior
to the merger, and our employee-relations
department is making every effort to ensure
that these employees are content here.

Which of the following, if true, would tend to
support most effectively the spokesperson's
prediction in the argument above?

(A) The employees who left Company X since the merger did so because they received more attractive employment offers from other firms.

(B) Worsening economic conditions may force Company X to reduce the size of its workforce in the near future.

(C) Company X has just hired a highly respected consultant who specializes in employee relations.

(D) None of the employees who worked for the company that has merged with Company X have left voluntarily.

(E) Most companies lose some workers to other firms as a result of a merger, but the number of workers lost is usually insignificant.

11. *Gwen:* As we both know, the most popular restaurants among college students here in Collegetown are the ones that provide delivery service. So, local economic conditions, which rely on the student population, would improve if expensive Collegetown restaurants were replaced by less expensive ones that also provide delivery service.

Jose: I disagree. After all, many expensive Collegetown restaurants also provide delivery service.

Which of the following best expresses the point of disagreement between Gwen and Jose?

(A) Whether inexpensive restaurants are more popular among Collegetown students than expensive restaurants

(B) Whether Collegetown should reduce the number of restaurants providing delivery service

(C) Whether inexpensive restaurants in Collegetown should provide delivery service

(D) Whether Collegetown students prefer delivery meal service over sit-down meal service

(E) Whether inexpensive restaurants are popular among Collegetown students

12. What both puzzles and intrigues many investigators is the differing tendencies of the cloned lines of PBA in causing cerebral changes.

(A) What both puzzles and intrigues many investigators is

(B) What both puzzle and intrigue many investigators are

(C) What both puzzles and intrigues many investigators are

(D) What both puzzle and intrigue many investigators is

(E) What are both puzzles and intrigues for many investigators are

13. Of the 1000 chemicals in coffee, less than thirty have been tested, most of which produce cancer in laboratory rats.

(A) less than thirty have been tested, most of which produce cancer in laboratory rats.

(B) most of which produce cancer in laboratory rats, fewer than thirty have been tested.

(C) most of the less than thirty tested produced cancer in laboratory rats.

(D) less than thirty of which have been tested, most of them produce cancer in laboratory rats.

(E) fewer than thirty have been tested, and most of these produce cancer in laboratory rats.

14. If the corporate bureaucracy persists in its discriminatory hiring and job advancement practices, its chief executives will expose themselves to class-action litigation by the groups prejudiced thereby.

(A) its chief executives will expose themselves

(B) its chief executives would expose themselves

(C) their chief executives will expose themselves

(D) its chief executives themselves would become exposed

(E) the chief executives will, by themselves, be exposed

QUESTIONS 15–17 ARE BASED ON THE FOLLOWING PASSAGE.

Line   When Ralph Waldo Emerson pronounced America's declaration of cultural independence from Europe in his "American Scholar" address, he was
(5) actually articulating the transcendental assumptions of Jefferson's political independence. In the ideal new world envisioned by Emerson, America's becoming a perfect democracy of free and
(10) self-reliant individuals was within reach. Bringing Emerson's metaphysics down to earth, Henry David Thoreau's *Walden* (1854) asserted that one can live without encumbrances. Emerson wanted to
(15) visualize Thoreau as the ideal scholar in action that he had called for in the "American Scholar." In the end, however, Emerson regretted Thoreau's too-private individualism, which failed to signal the
(20) vibrant revolution in national consciousness that Emerson had prophesied. For Emerson, what Thoreau lacked, Walt Whitman embodied in full. On reading *Leaves of Grass* (1855), Emerson saw in
(25) Whitman the "prophet of democracy" whom he had sought. Other American Renaissance writers were less optimistic than Emerson and Whitman about the fulfillment of the democratic ideal. In The
(30) Scarlet Letter (1850), Nathaniel Hawthorne concluded that antinomianism such as the "heroics" displayed by Hester Prynne leads to moral anarchy; and Herman Melville, who saw in his story of *Pierre* (1852) a
(35) metaphor for the misguided assumptions of democratic idealism, declared the transcendentalist dream unrealizable. Ironically, the literary vigor with which both Hawthorne and Melville explored the
(40) ideal showed their deep sympathy with it even as they dramatized its delusions.

15. The author of the passage seeks primarily to

   (A) explore the impact of the American Renaissance writers on the literature of the late eighteenth century.

   (B) illustrate how American literature of the mid-eighteenth century differed in form from European literature of the same time period.

   (C) identify two schools of thought among American Renaissance writers regarding the democratic ideal.

   (D) point out how Emerson's democratic idealism was mirrored by the works of the American Renaissance writers.

   (E) explain why the writers of the American Renaissance believed that an ideal world was forming in America.

16. Based on the passage's information, it can be inferred that Emerson might be characterized as any of the following EXCEPT:

   (A) a transcendentalist.

   (B) an American Renaissance writer.

   (C) a public speaker.

   (D) a would-be prophet.

   (E) a political pragmatist.

17. With which of the following statements about Melville and Hawthorne would the author most likely agree?

   (A) Both men were disillusioned transcendentalists.

   (B) Hawthorne sympathized with the transcendental dream more so than Melville.

   (C) They agreed as to what the transcendentalist dream would ultimately lead to.

   (D) Both men believed the idealists to be misguided.

   (E) Hawthorne politicized the transcendental ideal, whereas Melville personalized it.

18. Last year, two drownings occurred at Lake Serene, so this year the lake's owner added one more lifeguard to the lakefront staff. No drownings have occurred at the lake this year. However, the new lifeguard has been home with the flu for nearly half the summer, so it appears that the new lifeguard was not needed after all.

    Which of the following, if true, would be most damaging to the argument above?

    (A) This year, the lake's owner posted a warning about swimming without a lifeguard present.

    (B) Drowning is not the lake owner's only safety concern.

    (C) The lake has been equally crowded with swimmers this year as last year.

    (D) Lake activities are safer in the presence of lifeguards.

    (E) The new lifeguard has never saved a person from drowning.

19. Analyst Q predicts that the share price of MetaCorp stock will remain at its current level or higher as long as most stock analysts continue to recommend that investors buy the company's stock, and that stock analysts will continue to recommend MetaCorp stock to investors as long as the company continues to show a profit. Analyst T predicts that the share price of MetaCorp stock will at least remain at its current level, even if economic conditions worsen for MetaCorp's industry as a whole, as long as MetaCorp continues to show a profit.

    If the predictions of Analyst Q and Analyst T are all accurate, which of the following is logically inferable from them?

    (A) Stock analysts would be more likely to recommend MetaCorp stock to investors if economic conditions for MetaCorp's industry are good than if they are poor.

    (B) If MetaCorp stops showing a profit, stock analysts will be less inclined to recommend the company's stock to investors.

    (C) If stock analysts stop recommending MetaCorp stock to investors, then the price of MetaCorp stock is less likely to at least remain at its current level than if stock analysts continue to recommend it.

    (D) If economic conditions worsen for MetaCorp's industry as a whole, stock analysts will be less inclined to recommend MetaCorp stock.

    (E) If MetaCorp continues to show a profit, then the price of MetaCorp stock will either remain at its current level or increase.

20. A national performing arts association conducted a survey that appears to confirm the public's interest in high culture. More than 90 percent of those surveyed said that they were either "somewhat interested" or "very interested" in attending performances of opera, ballet, or classical music.

    Which of the following, if true, would most seriously weaken the argument above?

    (A) Not all performances of opera, ballet, and classical music should be considered "high culture."

    (B) Not all those who are interested in attending performances of opera, ballet, or classical music are willing to support an arts association.

    (C) Most of those surveyed reported being "somewhat interested" rather than "very interested."

    (D) Other statistics show that more people attend sporting events than performances of opera, ballet, or classical music.

    (E) The association conducting the survey receives most of its funding from sources other than the general public.

21. The high level of violence in television programming today has often been cited as an explanation for the increasing level of violence in our society. And, in fact, some recent studies show that the level of violence in television programming has increased considerably over the past twenty years. However, other recent studies indicate that the level, while high, is only slightly greater than it was twenty years ago.

Which of the following, if true, would provide the best explanation for the discrepancy among the recent studies cited in the argument above?

(A) Numerous studies of television violence have been conducted since the advent of television, and their results have not always been in agreement.

(B) All of those involved in conducting the cited studies shared the same perception of what constitutes "violence" in television programming.

(C) Television programming designed specifically for children accounts for a greater portion of television programming today than it did twenty years ago.

(D) Many factors other than violence in television programming have a significant impact on the level of violence in society.

(E) Over the last twenty years, the level of violence in television programming has increased more than in society as a whole.

22. All modern computer languages derive from a more basic "assembly" language that originated many decades ago.

(A) All modern computer languages derive from

(B) Derived from all modern computer languages is

(C) Resulting in all modern computer languages was

(D) Modern computer languages, which all resulted from

(E) All modern computer languages are derived from

23. Despite his admiration of the great jazz musicians that preceded him, Blakey opposed them trivializing the popular genre.

(A) them trivializing the popular genre.

(B) their trivializing of the popular genre.

(C) them when trivializing the popular genre.

(D) the popular genre being trivialized by them.

(E) their trivializing the popular genre.

24. Inventors have yet to learn that something that does two things does one of them better.

(A) Inventors have yet to learn

(B) Having not yet learned, inventors need to learn

(C) Inventors have not as of yet learned

(D) Inventors as yet have to learn

(E) Not having yet learned, inventors have to learn

25. In general, obesity is caused not by the ingestion of foods that are high in fat content but rather by eating foods that contain too much sugar. For proof, consider that over the past ten years, even as sales of low-fat meals, snacks, and desserts have increased sharply throughout the world's developed countries, the incidence of obesity in those countries, as a percentage of overall population, has reached a new high.

Which of the following, if true, would most support the claim made in the argument above?

(A) Ninety percent of the low-fat foods sold in developed countries are purchased by just 10 percent of the population.

(B) Sales of foods with a high sugar content have increased significantly over the past ten years.

(C) Government-approved standards of obesity have changed several times during the past ten years.

(D) Some foods labeled "low-fat" actually contain relatively high levels of fat.

(E) Most physicians consider regular exercise to be an important component of any effective program to prevent or reverse obesity.

26. The increasing scarcity of available rental housing, particularly apartments with two or more bedrooms, is attributable to two recent trends: the increasing number of new office buildings as compared to new apartment buildings and the increasing number of apartments being sold as condominiums rather than rented.

The passage above best supports which of the following conclusions?

(A) The rate at which new apartment buildings are being built is decreasing.

(B) The current demand for reasonably priced rental housing is greater than the current supply.

(C) Most apartments being sold as condominiums have at least two bedrooms.

(D) More new office buildings than rental apartment buildings are currently being built.

(E) The current demand for offices is greater than the current demand for rental apartments.

27. Scientist and artist Leonardo Da Vinci <u>was, and always will be considered by many,</u> as a singular figure among those whose scientific, artistic, and other cultural contributions defined the Renaissance period of European history.

(A) was, and always will be considered by many, as

(B) was and always will be considered by many as being

(C) was, and always will be by many, considered

(D) was, and always will be considered by many as,

(E) was considered by many and always will be by many

QUESTIONS 28–30 ARE BASED ON THE FOLLOWING PASSAGE.

Line   During the process of embryonic development, cells become progressively restricted in their developmental potential and finally acquire the biochemical and
(5) morphological specialization necessary for their respective functions in an adult. Since enzymatic and structural proteins are required for the appearance and maintenance of this specialization, the differ-
(10) entiated state results from the synthesis and activity of cell-specific proteins during development.

Since all cells of an organism contain the same genotype as the fertilized egg,
(15) cellular differentiation is the result of variable gene activity rather than selective gene loss. Thus, cellular specialization and cell-specific protein synthesis result from the expression of appropriately selected
(20) groups of genes in each cell type. As development proceeds, the progressive differentiation of cells is correlated with changes in the population of protein species within the embryo, which in turn reflect
(25) the accurate programming of the time and sequence of the biosynthesis of different proteins by the genome. In the absence of opportunities for genetic analysis, determining the mechanisms involved in the
(30) regulation of protein synthesis is key to understanding genome control during development.

The majority of studies on gene activity in embryogenesis have been done on the
(35) sea urchin system, where large numbers of embryos undergoing relatively synchronous development can be easily obtained. Also, sea urchins' permeability to radioactive isotopes and to inhibitors of
(40) RNA and protein synthesis provides a distinct advantage for study over amphibian material. Especially well documented are the maternal programming of early development and the genomic control of later
(45) differentiation in the urchin. Maternal products, stored in the egg cytoplasm from oogenesis, can support development from fertilization through the hatching blastula stage; however, development from the
(50) mesenchyme blastula stage is dependent

upon gene products synthesized under the direction of the embryonic genome.

28. With which of the following statements would the author of the passage most likely disagree?

   (A) Morphological specialization requires the synthesis of cell-specific proteins.

   (B) Embryonic development involves differentiation in cell genotype.

   (C) The population of protein species with the embryo is dependent upon the timing of protein biosynthesis.

   (D) Enzymatic proteins are required for an organism's full development.

   (E) Selective gene loss is not a factor in cellular differentiation during embryonic development.

29. Which of the following statements about embryonic development in sea urchins is best supported by the passage?

   (A) Genomic control over early embryonic development is especially well documented.

   (B) Permeability to RNA inhibitors is comparable to that in amphibian embryos.

   (C) Development during the hatching blastula stage requires gene products synthesized under the direction of the embryonic genome.

   (D) Maternal products can support embryonic development following the mesenchyme blastula stage.

   (E) Genomic control of later cell differentiation has been studied extensively.

30. The last paragraph of the passage:

   (A) illustrates a biological process by way of an example.

   (B) describes a methodology for studying a biological phenomenon.

   (C) compares two stages of biological development.

   (D) defines and explains an important term mentioned earlier.

   (E) provides an example which disproves a scientific theory.

31. Equipment used by private biotechnology research firms becomes obsolete more quickly than any other business equipment, simply because biotechnology advances so rapidly. A proposed tax law would provide significant tax incentives for businesses in every industry to replace their old equipment with new equipment. Obviously, political lobbyists for the biotechnology industry were the instigators of this tax proposal.

Which of the following most supports the claim that biotechnology industry lobbyists are responsible for the tax proposal?

   (A) Equipment used in the biotechnology industry loses its value more quickly than equipment used in any other industry.

   (B) Biotechnology firms expect biotechnology advances to outpace those in other industries for the foreseeable future.

   (C) The legislator introducing the proposed law used to work in the biotechnology industry.

   (D) Other industries have not lobbied for the proposed law.

   (E) Unless a biotechnology firm replaces its obsolete equipment, it will be driven out of business by competing firms.

32. Due to sharply escalating tuition at four-year colleges, debt on student loans has increased to the point that many new graduates are forced either to pursue graduate-level degrees, thereby postponing repayment of their student loans, or to pursue only the highest-paying jobs. An unfortunate result of this trend is that fewer and fewer new graduates are entering important, but lower-paying, professions that require only a four-year degree.

Which of the following strategies would be most effective in reversing the decline in the number of college graduates entering lower-paying professions that require only a four-year degree?

(A) Encourage college students to enroll in classes year-round in order to graduate early.

(B) Expand opportunities for graduate-level students to obtain paying jobs while still in school.

(C) Expand course offerings that prepare college students for these lower-paying professions.

(D) Establish higher admission standards for graduate-level programs.

(E) Increase the number of academic units required to obtain a four-year college degree.

33. International environmental regulations do not protect hybrid species, but they are protected by way of domestic laws.

(A) but they are protected by way of domestic laws.

(B) although domestic laws do.

(C) and so domestic laws only protect hybrid species.

(D) yet the laws of domestic protection will so protect.

(E) which require legal protection domestically.

34. Even for high school freshmen and sopho-mores, theories concerning the psychology of death and dying among the elderly can hold considerable significance and interest for many students.

(A) Even for high school freshmen and sophomores, theories concerning the psychology of death and dying among the elderly can hold considerable significance and interest for many students.

(B) Even for high school freshmen and sophomores with considerable interest in theories concerning the psychology of death and dying among the elderly, these theories can hold considerable significance.

(C) Theories concerning the psychology of death and dying among the elderly, for many students, even high school freshmen and sophomores, can hold considerable significance and interest.

(D) Theories concerning the psychology of death and dying among the elderly can hold considerable significance and interest even for high school freshmen and sophomores.

(E) Considerable significance and interest for even high school freshmen and sophomores is held in theories concerning the psychology of death and dying among the elderly.

35. In order for a new third-world democratic country to achieve and maintain political stability, its government must afford its citizens the power to elect and remove the country's leaders. After all, Country X is among the most stable countries in the world, and its government affords its citizens this power.

The argument above is flawed in that it ignores the possibility that

(A) many third-world countries already grant their citizens the power to elect and remove their leaders.

(B) a large percentage of third-world countries have already achieved, and are maintaining, political stability.

(C) Country X's leaders are more popular among Country X's citizens than are the leaders of most third-world countries among their citizens.

(D) specific procedures for electing a country's leaders vary significantly from one country to another.

(E) Country X was already politically stable when its citizens were first afforded the power to elect and remove their leaders.

QUESTIONS 36–39 ARE BASED ON THE FOLLOWING PASSAGE.

Line   For investors looking for a stellar investment, Planetary Resources, with its goal of mining asteroids, may just be the launch pad. Although company officials
(5) admit that the real payoff is probably decades away, Planetary Resources is planning, eventually, to bring precious metals and minerals from space to Earth. It also aims to tap the water resources of
(10) asteroids in order to supply others in space such as NASA, other explorers, and, conceivably, other commercial ventures. (To gauge the value of becoming space's water tap, think space prices not Earth prices:
(15) The current cost of sending a liter of water to the International Space Station is about $20,000.)

    "Sky's the limit" is not too farfetched an idiom to describe possible profits from
(20) the venture. Eric Anderson, Planetary Resource's co-founder, recently estimated the worth of each asteroid at $12 trillion. A company promotional video states that a single asteroid could supply more
(25) platinum than all of the platinum that has already been mined on Earth. Right now, there are 9000 known near-Earth asteroids deemed large enough to mine. More important, NASA has recently brought the
(30) idea's plausibility down to Earth by releasing plans for how the mining of near-Earth asteroids might be accomplished.

    Should Planetary Resources succeed in
(35) its attempts to robotically extract platinum group metals and more, a monopoly on space mining will exist until the competition catches up—if it ever does. If the barrier to future entry in the space-mining
(40) market remains the technological hegemony of Planetary Resources (not to mention its funding, which comes in part from the deep pockets of two billionaires from the darling of all alleged monopolies,
(45) Google), public ire might not be aroused. At some point, investors believe, Planetary Resources could establish a formidable economy of scale and fulfill its projected goal of adding billions of dollars annually
(50) to the nation's GDP.

36. The author implies that public response to a monopoly on space mining

    (A) would be about the same as the response to the accusations that Google is a monopoly.

    (B) could be particularly angry if the competition suffered a barrier to entry based on economy of scale.

    (C) might be accepting if Planetary Resources' technological supremacy limited other market entry.

    (D) might be so intense as to make Planetary Resources a target for antitrust legislation.

    (E) would be focused on the issues of relevant markets and structural competitiveness.

37. The fact in the passage that gives the greatest credence to the feasibility of the project is the

    (A) participation of investors from Google.

    (B) potential benefits to future space exploration.

    (C) existence of NASA plans for asteroid mining.

    (D) likely development of an economy of scale.

    (E) technological preeminence of Planetary Resources.

38. The author's attitude toward the venture can best be described as

    (A) objective and reportorial.

    (B) guardedly optimistic.

    (C) amused and slightly sarcastic.

    (D) pointedly and bitterly negative.

    (E) vacillating from paragraph to paragraph.

39. The passage mentions all of the following as possible venture outcomes EXCEPT:

    (A) the eventual supply of water from space to space exploration teams.

    (B) the use of robots to extract precious metals, particularly platinum-group metals.

(C) enormous potential profits and a profoundly positive effect on the nation's GDP.

(D) the collaboration of NASA with Planetary Resources in a public/private venture.

(E) the likely inability of other private space-mining ventures to catch up and compete.

40. Veterinarians have developed a new cat food that contains medication to prevent hair balls from accumulating in a cat's stomach and digestive tract. Hair balls are generally not harmful to cats, but they do cause discomfort. Although the medicated food is effective, many cats develop an allergic reaction to it that, left untreated, can result in a harmful infection. Accordingly, those concerned about the health of their cats should not feed this food to them.

The answer to which of the following questions would be most useful to cat owners considering whether to feed the medicated food to their cats?

(A) How much of the medicated food must a cat eat in order to develop an allergic reaction?

(B) How noticeable to humans are the allergic reactions associated with ingesting the medicated food?

(C) Are there effective methods of preventing hairballs other than feeding a cat the medicated food?

(D) Do cats typically develop similar allergic reactions to other types of food as well?

(E) What percentage of all cat owners feed the medicated food to their pet cats?

41. <u>On this issue, this state's elected officials ignored the wishes of their electorate, which</u> cannot reasonably be disputed in light of the legislative record.

(A) On this issue, this state's elected officials ignored the wishes of their electorate, which

(B) This state's elected officials, ignoring on this issue the wishes of their electorate,

(C) That this state's elected officials ignored the wishes of their electorate

(D) On this issue, the wishes of the electorate were ignored by this state's elected officials, and

(E) That the wishes of the electorate on this issue were ignored by this state's elected officials

ANSWER KEY AND EXPLANATIONS

See Appendix B for score conversion tables to determine your score. Be sure to keep a tally of correct and incorrect answers for each test section.

Analysis of an Argument—Evaluation and Scoring

Evaluate your Argument Analysis essay on a scale of 1 to 6 (6 being the highest score) according to the following five criteria:

1. Does your essay identify the key features of the argument and analyze each one in a thoughtful manner?

2. Does your essay support each point of its critique with insightful reasons and examples?

3. Does your essay develop its ideas in a clear, organized manner, with appropriate transitions to help connect ideas?

4. Does your essay demonstrate proficiency, fluency, and maturity in its use of sentence structure, vocabulary, and idiom?

5. Does your essay demonstrate command of the elements of Standard Written English, including grammar, word usage, spelling, and punctuation?

The following series of questions, which serve to identify the Argument's five distinct problems, will help you evaluate your essay in terms of Criteria 1 and 2. To earn a score of 4 or higher, your essay should identify at least three of these problems and, for each one, provide at least one example or counterexample that supports your critique. (Your examples need not be the same as the ones below.) Identifying and discussing at least four of the problems would help earn you an even higher score.

- Do Maxtech employees, at least those whose claim Workforce cites, constitute a sufficiently *representative statistical sample* of the entire private-sector workforce? (Perhaps these Maxtech employees were more receptive or responsive to Workforce's particular methods than the average private-sector worker.)

- Is the report from Workforce Systems *credible*? (Perhaps the company overstates the benefits of its seminars in order to attract clients.)

- Was the seminar the *actual cause* of the improved level of contentment among the participants from Maxtech? (The answer might depend on how much time has passed since the seminar, whether Maxtech's participants have the same jobs as before, and whether the seminar is designed to help workers become more content to begin with.)

- Are the claims by Maxtech's employees *credible*? (Perhaps they felt pressure to exaggerate the benefits of the seminar, or falsely report improvement in order to take time off from work to enroll again in the seminar.)

- Might the argument assume that *all other conditions remain unchanged*? (Overall productivity of the economy's private sector depends also on many extrinsic factors having nothing to do with the benefits of these types of seminars.)

INTEGRATED REASONING SECTION

1. B, E	4. B, D	7.1 A	9.2 A	11.1 D
2.1 A	5. A, F	7.2 A	9.3 B	11.2 A
2.2 A	6.1 B	7.3 B	10.1 D	12.1 A
2.3 B	6.2 B	8. C	10.2 B	12.2 B
3. B, F	6.3 A	9.1 B		

1. **The correct answers are (B) (*Truck A*) and (E) (*Truck B*).** Let r_A be Truck A's speed and r_B be Truck B's speed. You should look for an expression that relates r_A and r_B. Distance equals speed multiplied by time, and in this case time is the same for both trucks: 4 hours. So, you have:

$$D_A = 4r_A$$
$$D_B = 4r_B$$

You also know that Truck B will have traveled 40 more miles than Truck A when the two trucks meet. Therefore, $D_B = D_A + 40$. Substitute this in the expression for Truck B above and you get $D_A + 40 = 4r_B$. Next, substitute the expression for D_A from the Truck A expression above, in order to get a new expression with only two unknowns: r_A and $4r_B$:

$$D_A + 40 = 4r_B$$
$$4r_A + 40 = 4r_B$$
$$r_A + 10 = r_B$$
$$r_B - r_A = 10$$

So you are looking for two answer choices that differ by 10. The only two choices are 48 and 58, so these are the speeds of Truck A and B, respectively.

2.1. **The correct answer is (A).** Because all four of the automaker's sedans are fuel-efficient—that is, they average more than 30 mpg on the highway—it is true that the average highway fuel consumption of all the automaker's sedans is greater than 30 mpg.

2.2. **The correct answer is (A).** The lowest possible value of the average highway fuel consumption of all the automaker's models will occur if each model gets the lowest possible highway fuel consumption. Assume that the nine fuel-efficient models get exactly 30 miles per gallon on the highway, and that the remaining six models get 0 miles per gallon on the highway. Then the sum of the fuel consumption of all fifteen models is 270 miles per gallon, and the average of all fifteen models is 18 miles per gallon. Since the fuel-efficient models get more than 30 miles per gallon, it is inferable that the average highway fuel consumption of all the automaker's models is greater than 18 miles per gallon.

2.3. **The correct answer is (B).** It is true that the lowest and highest starting prices in the sedan category are higher than the corresponding prices in the compact category, but this does not prove that the average starting price of all sedans is higher than the average starting price of all compacts. You can be certain that the lowest and highest starting prices in each row give the starting prices for two of the four cars of each type, but you cannot infer anything about the starting prices of the other two cars of each type. If the starting prices of the four cars in each category are evenly distributed within the range of starting prices for that category, then the average starting price of all compact cars is, indeed, lower than the average starting price of all sedans. On the other hand, it is possible that three of the four compacts all have the highest starting price of $25,000, and one has the lowest starting price of $17,000, in which case their average starting price is $23,000, while three of the four sedans all have the lowest starting price of $19,500, and one has the highest starting price of $28,000, in which case their average starting price is $21,625. In this scenario, the average starting price of all compact cars is greater than the average starting price of all sedans. (Incidentally, the questions in this Table Analysis set were actually answerable without any re-sorting of the table.)

3.1. and **3.2. The correct answers are (B) (*Action*) and (F) (*Prediction*).** The economist says that cuts in government spending and increased taxes will make a recession worse. These are the action and prediction combinations that appear in Statements B and F. Note that the economist does not guarantee that low interest rates will lead to higher inflation, so Statement A will not necessarily lead to Statement E. Finally, Statement C lists government actions that pull in different directions, according to the economist: increasing spending on infrastructure is an expansionary policy, but raising interest rates is not. Thus, no clear prediction can be made based on this action.

4.1. and **4.2. The correct answers are (B) (*Male*) and (D) (*Female*).** Let M be the number of male contestants, F be the number of female contestants, and T be the number of total contestants. Then, $T = M + F \Rightarrow F = T - M$. Next, the probabilities that a male or a female contestant will win are:

$$P(\text{Male}) = \frac{\text{Male contestants}}{\text{Total contestants}} = \frac{M}{T}$$

$$P(\text{Female}) = \frac{\text{Female contestants}}{\text{Total contestants}} = \frac{T - M}{T}$$

You also know that $P(\text{Male}) = \frac{7}{8} P(\text{Female})$, so:

$$\frac{M}{T} = \frac{7}{8}\left(\frac{T - M}{T}\right)$$

$$M = \frac{7}{8}(T - M)$$

$$8M = 7T - 7M$$

$$15M = 7T$$

$$M = \frac{7}{15}T$$

Correspondingly, $F = \frac{8}{15}T$. This means that out of every 15 contestants, 7 are male and 8 are female, so if the number of total contestants is the nth multiple of 15, then the number of male contestants is the nth multiple of 7, and the number of female contestants is the nth multiple of 8 (for instance, there could be 15 contestants in total, 7 male and 8 female, or 30 contestants in total, 14 male and 16 female, and so on). So, among the answer choices, you are looking for two numbers that are the 7th and 8th multiple of the same positive integer. The only two choices that work are B and D: 28 is the 7th multiple of 4, and 32 is the 8th multiple of 4, so the number of men is 28 and the number of women is 32.

5.1. and **5.2. The correct answers are (A) (*Must occur*) and (F) (*Cannot occur*).** The best way to go about this is to make as many deductions as possible based on the rules before you examine the answer choices. Note that rules are not only the three that are highlighted in the bulleted points. Two more rules are masquerading in the text: Xavier needs a root canal, and Sanjay is not available after 11 a.m. on Day 2. Since no more than two root canals can be scheduled on each day, Xavier's root canal has to be on Day 2. Furthermore, it has to be at 9 a.m. on Day 2, because root canals must be scheduled before noon. Next, note that you have three time slots left and no fillings scheduled. However, at least three fillings must be scheduled in total, so all three of the remaining time slots must be for fillings. Finally, Sanjay's limitation (that he's not available after 11 a.m. on Day 2) combined with the fact that the 9 a.m. slot on Day 2 is now taken by Xavier means that Sanjay's appointment must be on Day 1.

Now you can move on to the answer choices. Right away you notice that your last deduction appears in the first answer choice: Sanjay's appointment has to be on Day 1, so choice (A) is the correct answer in the "must occur" column. Scanning through the rest of the choices, you should note that choice (F) is impossible: since all of the non-Xavier appointments must be for fillings, the 1 p.m. appointment on Day 1 must be for a filling, not a cleaning. Thus, choice (F) is the correct answer in the "cannot occur" column. All other choices describe appointments that may occur, but do not have to.

6.1. The correct answer is (B). Sort the table by "Club." For KLR, the fastest time was 30:56 and the slowest time was 34:29. For WRRC, the fastest time was 30:44 and the slowest time was 35:22. In other words, the fastest WRRC time was faster than the fastest KLR time, and the slowest WRRC time was slower than the slowest KLR time. This means that the range of times was greater for WRRC than for KLR, so the statement is incorrect.

6.2. The correct answer is (B). Sort the table first by "Gender" and then by "Club." The fastest age-adjusted time among female runners was Bryzgylova's 33:06. Now, four runners did not compete for a club, so the median of their age-adjusted times is the average of the two middle times when the times are arranged in ascending or descending order. These two middle times are Zatopek's 30:34 and Bryzgylova's 33:06. Therefore, the median age-adjusted time among the runners who did not compete for a particular club is less than 33:06, so the statement is incorrect.

6.3. The correct answer is (A). Return the table to its original sorting, by "Time (Net)." When you considered the other two statements, you did not need to perform any calculations. Here, however, you have to. First, convert the course record to seconds: 29 minutes and 37 seconds is equal to 1777 seconds. Ten percent more than that is 1954.7 seconds. Rather than converting this back to minutes and seconds, use the statement to help you save some time. The statement says that exactly 9 runners achieved net times that are no more than 10% slower than the record. Go to the ninth-best finisher (Elliott) and convert his net time to seconds: 32 minutes and 30 seconds equals 1950 seconds. It's true, then, that the top 9 finishers recorded times no more than 10% slower than the record. Next, check the tenth-best finisher. Zatopek finished at 32:35, which equals 1955 seconds, so he missed the 10% cut-off by 0.3sec. Thus, exactly 9 runners achieved net times that are no more than 10% slower than the record.

7.1. The correct answer is (A). This statement is inferable: The producer says that "rising . . . labor costs . . . are shared with audiences in the form of higher ticket prices."

7.2. The correct answer is (A). This statement is inferable as well. The critic implies that if he gives a false good review for a bad production, he's harming future good productions. His ending statement that "surely producers are not asking that" he do that implies that he would rather not—he would rather not harm future good productions. From his statement that his responsibility to the theatrical art form means he must be ruthless in his reviews, you can infer that he would prefer to risk harming a bad production via a negative review in the interest of helping good productions in the future.

7.3. The correct answer is (B). This statement is not inferable. The critic does not state that current productions are bad or that future ones will be good. He merely says that those current ones that are bad should be called out as such for the benefit of those future ones that are good.

8. **The correct answer is (C).** The producer says that "a production that reaches a Broadway stage represents thousands of hours spent by countless individuals with track records of excellence in their fields. Surely such a production is of some worth." In other words, she uses the "track records of excellence" of the participants in the production as evidence that the production is of some worth. This is precisely what choice (C) says, so it is the correct answer. Choice (A) is too broad: The producer does not claim that consumers prefer the movies to the theater under all circumstances. Choice (B) does not follow logically from the given information. The producer claims that a bad review is likely to make a consumer pick the movies over theater, but this does not mean that a good review will change the consumer's choice from movie to theater. It may, or it may not. Choice (D) is not fully supported by the producer's statement: She does not appreciate negative reviews, but it is too much of a leap to conclude that she feels critics should laud decent productions as great. Finally, choice (E) is counter, if anything, to the producer's statement "It is unconscionable that critics should treat so carelessly the art they are supposed to love." This implies that the producer sees some responsibility by critics toward the art form, even if she interprets this responsibility differently from how the critic does.

9.1. **The correct answer is (B).** The critic states that critics love the theater. The producer states that it is unconscionable that critics should treat carelessly the art they "are supposed to love." This does not necessarily mean that she doubts critics' love of the theater. It could also mean that she is astounded that critics who, indeed, love the theater should treat it, in her words, carelessly. Thus, you cannot infer disagreement on this score.

9.2. **The correct answer is (A).** Producer and critic do disagree here. The producer claims that the individuals involved in a particular production deserve loyalty from the critic. The critic, on the other hand, retorts that his responsibility is to the theatrical art form over any individual practitioners—in other words, that his main loyalty is with the theater, not with individuals.

9.3. **The correct answer is (B).** The critic does not say that new productions are bad; he merely says that, if they are bad, then the critic has a responsibility to say so. It is the producer who implies that recent reviews make new productions seem bad, but that is not necessarily the opinion of the critic. All in all, you cannot infer exactly how the critic feels about the quality of new productions, and so you cannot infer agreement or disagreement between the critic and the producer.

10.1. **The correct answer is (D).** For each school, the second area from the top (the one with the vertical stripes) represents that school's football players. School A had a total of approximately 95 student-athletes, approximately 42 of whom played football. So, approximately 53 students played one of the other three sports in School A. For the other schools these numbers are: 50 non-football players in School B (82 total athletes minus 32 football players), 54 non-football players in School C (100 total athletes minus 46 football players), and 60 non-football players in School D (82 total athletes minus 22 football players). These figures are not exact, but it appears clear that School D had the most non-football players.

10.2. **The correct answer is (B).** The four schools in the graph had 95, 82, 100, and 82 student-athletes, for a total of 359 student-athletes. The remaining two schools had 425 minus 359, or 66 athletes. Therefore, the two schools with the most student-athletes are Schools A and C, which, together, had 195 student-athletes. Now you need to find what percent of 425 the total is for Schools A and C:

$$195 = \frac{x}{100}(425)$$
$$x \approx 45.88$$

So, Schools A and C had approximately 45.88% of the league's student-athletes.

11.1. **The correct answer is (D).** If the $1200 that the family spent on rent represents 30% of January's total expenses, and if x stands for these total expenses, then you have:

$$\$1200 = 30\%(x)$$
$$x = \frac{\$1200}{30}(100)$$
$$x = \$4000$$

So, the family's total expenses in January were $4000. Combined, Utilities and Insurance represented 21% of that amount:

$$y = 21\%(\$4000)$$
$$y = \frac{21 \times \$4000}{100}$$
$$y = \$840$$

Therefore, the family spent $840 for utilities and insurance in January.

11.2. **The correct answer is (A).** First, find out how much the family's "Other" expenses were. Seventeen percent of $4000 is:

$$17\%(\$4000) = \frac{17 \times \$4000}{100} = \$680$$

Next, find what 20% of $680 is:

$$20\%(\$680) = \frac{20 \times \$680}{100} = \$136$$

12.1. **The correct answer is (A).** The smaller the bubble, the smaller the country's population. The farther to the right the bubble is, the more ships the country has in its Merchant Navy. Thus, you are looking for the smallest possible bubble that is as far to the right as possible. Luckily, Country A's bubble is both the smallest one and the one that's farthest to the right. Thus, of all the countries plotted in the graph, Country A has the most ships in its Merchant Navy relative to its population.

12.2. **The correct answer is (B).** The four countries that have the most ships in their Merchant Navy are A, B, D, and C. The four countries that have the most troops in their Military Navy are G, B, F, and A. Countries A and B are in both of those list, so they are the only two that rank in the top four in both categories. Thus, the probability you are looking for is 2 out of 7, or 0.29.

QUANTITATIVE SECTION

1. C	9. E	17. A	25. E	33. E
2. B	10. E	18. D	26. C	34. B
3. C	11. B	19. A	27. E	35. C
4. D	12. D	20. E	28. D	36. B
5. C	13. B	21. A	29. C	37. E
6. E	14. A	22. E	30. D	
7. A	15. B	23. C	31. C	
8. B	16. D	24. D	32. D	

1. **The correct answer is (C).** Your first step is to rewrite mixed numbers as fractions:

$$\frac{9}{2} + \frac{15}{4} - \frac{12}{5}$$

The least common denominator is 20. You can eliminate answer choice (D). Rewrite each fraction, then combine:

$$\frac{9}{2} + \frac{15}{4} - \frac{12}{5} = \frac{90 + 75 - 48}{20} = \frac{117}{20}$$

2. **The correct answer is (B).** You can solve the problem algebraically as follows:

$$23 - x = 2(15 - x)$$
$$23 - x = 30 - 2x$$
$$x = 7$$

An alternative method is to subtract the number given in each answer choice, in turn, from both Lyle's age and Melanie's age.

3. **The correct answer is (C).** Neither Statement (1) nor (2) alone provides any information about the second variable or, in turn, about the value of $x + y - 1$. Thus choices (A), (B), and (D) can easily be eliminated. Next, consider Statements (1) and (2) together. Given a remainder of 2 when x is divided by 3, the value of x must be greater than a multiple of 3 by exactly 2: $x = \{5,8,11,14,\ldots\}$. Given a remainder of 5 when y is divided by 6, the value of y must be greater than a multiple of 6 by exactly 5: $y = \{11,17,23,29,\ldots\}$. Adding together any x-value and any y-value will always result in a sum that exceeds a multiple of 3 by exactly 7 (or by exactly 1). Accordingly, subtracting 1 from that sum will always result in a multiple of 3. Thus, given Statements (1) and (2), $x + y - 1$ is divisible by 3.

4. **The correct answer is (D).** Statement (1) alone suffices to answer the question. Given $AC < BD$, AB (which is less than AC) must be less than BD. $BD > AB$, and the answer to the question is *no*. Statement (2) also suffices alone to answer the question. Given $\frac{AD}{2} = CD$, C bisects AD, and $AC = CD$. Thus, AB (which is smaller than AC) must be smaller than CD. Because CD is less than BD, $AB < BD$, and the answer to the question is *no*.

5. **The correct answer is (C).** Neither Statement (1) nor (2) alone suffices to determine the values of both x and y. Thus, you can easily eliminate choices (A), (B), and (D). Next, consider both

statements together. The two-digit prime numbers less than 23 include 11, 13, 17, and 19. Their sum is 60, and the average of the four numbers is 15 ($x = 15$). Considering Statement (2), the positive factors of 60 that are less than 6 include 1, 2, 3, 4, and 5. Their sum is 15 ($y = 15$). $x = y$, and the answer to the question, based on Statements (1) and (2) together, is *no*.

6. **The correct answer is (E).** Statement (1) alone provides no information about how long it took David to travel the first 15 miles, and it is therefore insufficient by itself to answer the question. Statement (2) alone provides even less information about how long it took David to travel the entire distance. Although you can determine from Statement (2) that David traveled the first 17 miles in 45 minutes, you cannot determine how long it took David to travel the remaining 13 miles. Statements (1) and (2) together establish that David traveled 32 miles (17 + 15) in 85 minutes (45 + 40). However, 2 of the 32 miles are accounted for twice. Without knowing either the time that it took David to travel the 16th and 17th miles of the race, or his average speed over those two miles, you cannot determine David's total time for the 30-mile race. Thus, Statements (1) and (2) together are insufficient to answer the question.

7. **The correct answer is (A).** This question involves two steps. First, visually compare the difference in height between Country X's solid bar and shaded bar for each year. (Be careful to look at County X's bar, *not* Country Y's.) You don't need to determine amounts at this point. A quick inspection reveals that 2007 was the year that Country X's exports exceeded its own imports by the greatest amount. Now go to the second step. During 2007, Country Y's imports were approximately $35 billion and Country X's imports were approximately $13 billion. The difference is $22 billion. Choice (A) is the only one that approximates this dollar figure.

8. **The correct answer is (B).** Solve the first equation for $2b$:

    $$a - b = 2d$$
    $$b = a - 2d$$
    $$2b = 2a - 4d$$

    Next, solve the second equation for c: $2c - 4a = d$
    $$2c = 4a + d$$
    $$c = 2a + \frac{d}{2}$$

    Now, combine the two results: $2b - c = 2a - 4d - \left(2a + \frac{d}{2}\right)$
    $$= -\frac{9}{2}d$$

9. **The correct answer is (E).** The other integer is $n + 2$. The difference between n and $n + 2$ must be positive, so the term $(n + 2)$ must appear first in the equation.

10. **The correct answer is (E).** Convert the question into an algebraic equation, and solve for x:

    $$M = \frac{P}{100}(x)$$
    $$100M = Px$$
    $$\frac{100M}{P} = x$$

11. **The correct answer is (B).** The length of each side of the square is 12 feet. The length of the remaining two sides of the triangle totals 16 feet. The perimeter of the semicircle $= \frac{1}{2}\pi d = \frac{1}{2}\pi(12) = 6\pi$. The length of the two sides of the square included in the overall perimeter totals 24. The total perimeter of the floor $= 16 + 6\pi + 24 = 40 + 6\pi$.

12. **The correct answer is (D).** Apply the defined operation to each of the two expressions as follows:

$$(4 \times 3 - 5) = 12 - 5 = 7$$
$$(6 \times 5 - 7) = 30 - 7 = 23$$

Then add the two results: $7 + 23 = 30$

13. **The correct answer is (B).** Competitor 1 must engage in eight matches. Competitor 2 must engage in seven matches not already accounted for. (The match between Competitors 1 and 2 has already been tabulated.) Similarly, Competitor 3 must engage in six matches other than those accounted for, and so on. The minimum number of total matches: $8 + 7 + 6 + 5 + 4 + 3 + 2 + 1 = 36$.

14. **The correct answer is (A).** Both equations are quadratic. For each one, you can determine the number of possible values of x by setting the quadratic expression equal to 0 (zero) and factoring that expression. Perform these tasks for the equation in Statement (1):

$$4x^2 - 4x = -1$$
$$4x^2 - 4x + 1 = 0$$
$$(2x - 1)(2x - 1) = 0$$

The equation's two roots are the same—that is, there's only one possible value for x. Thus, Statement (1) alone suffices to answer the question. Now perform the same tasks for the equation in Statement (2):

$$2x^2 + 9x = 5$$
$$2x^2 + 9x - 5 = 0$$
$$(x + 5)(2x - 1) = 0$$

As you can see, based on the equation given in Statement (2), there are two different roots—that is, two possible values of x. Thus, Statement (2) alone is insufficient to answer the question.

15. **The correct answer is (B).** Cross-multiply and solve:

$$\frac{1}{1 - x} = \frac{3}{4x}$$
$$4x = 3(1 - x)$$
$$4x = 3 - 3x$$
$$7x = 3$$
$$x = \frac{3}{7}$$

16. **The correct answer is (D).** The question itself provides that the pitcher currently contains $7\frac{1}{2}$ ounces of each brand. Given Statement (1), 60% of the 30-ounce mixture, or 18 ounces, must be Brand A. Subtract $7\frac{1}{2}$ from 18 to find the remaining amount of Brand A needed ($10\frac{1}{2}$ ounces). Then subtract 18 from 30 to find the amount of Brand B (12). Finally, subtract $7\frac{1}{2}$ from 12 to find the remaining amount of Brand B needed ($4\frac{1}{2}$ ounces). We've answered the question with Statement (1) alone. Statement 2 would lead to the same answer.

17. **The correct answer is (A).** Let x equal the number of nickels:

$$45 - x = \text{the number of dimes}$$
$$5x = \text{the value of all nickels (in cents)}$$
$$450 - 10x = \text{the value of all dimes (in cents)}$$

Given a total value of 350 cents:

$$5x + 450 - 10x = 350$$
$$-5x = -100$$
$$x = 20$$

Lisa has 20 nickels and 25 dimes; thus she has five more dimes than nickels.

18. **The correct answer is (D).** The number of female professors currently is 30% of 140, which equals 42. Let x be the number of female professors the university hires. Then, the number of female professors will be $42 + x$ and the total number of professors will be $140 + x$. If the number of female professors is to be at least 40% of the total number of professors, then $42 + x$ must be at least 40% of $140 + x$:

$$42 + x \geq 40\% \left(140 + x\right)$$
$$42 + x \geq \frac{2}{5}\left(140 + x\right)$$
$$42 + x \geq \frac{2}{5} \times 140 + \frac{2}{5}x$$
$$42 + x \geq 56 + \frac{2}{5}x$$
$$\frac{3}{5}x \geq 14$$
$$x \geq 23.\overline{3}$$

Because 35% of 40% of the voters (female) voted for Lange, 14% (0.40 × 0.35) of all voters Therefore, the university must hire at least 24 female professors to achieve its goal.

19. **The correct answer is (A).** If Barbara invests x additional dollars at 8%, her total investment will amount to $(2400 + x)$ dollars.

$$0.050\left(2400\right) + 0.08x = 0.06\left(2400 + x\right)$$
$$5\left(2400\right) + 8x = 6\left(2400 + x\right)$$
$$12{,}000 + 8x = 14{,}400 + 6x$$
$$2x = 2400$$
$$x = 1200$$

20. **The correct answer is (E).** The total parking fee that ABC pays each month is $1920 ($240 × 8). Of that amount, $420 is paid for outdoor parking for three cars. The difference ($1920 – $420 = $1500) is the total garage parking fee that the company pays for the other five cars.

21. **The correct answer is (A).** In choice (A), unequal quantities are subtracted from equal quantities. The differences are unequal, but the inequality is reversed because unequal numbers are being subtracted from, rather than added to, the equal numbers.

22. **The correct answer is (E).** Statement (1) alone is insufficient to answer the question, since it provides no information about a or b. Many test-takers would conclude incorrectly that Statement (2) alone is sufficient to answer the question. (About half of these test-takers would assert that the

answer to the question is *no*, while the other half would claim that the answer to the question is *yes*.) Both groups would be wrong, of course. If you're the least bit unsure about this, it's a good idea to plug in a few simple numbers. For example, let $a = 2$ and $b = 1$. If $c = 1$ (a positive value), then $\frac{c}{a} < \frac{c}{b}$ because $\frac{1}{2} < \frac{1}{1}$. But if $c = -1$ (a negative number), then $\frac{c}{a} > \frac{c}{b}$ because $-\frac{1}{2} > -\frac{1}{1}$.

23. **The correct answer is (C).** Statement (1) alone is insufficient to answer the question because it fails to indicate what percent a 10-cent increase amounts to. Statement (2) alone is insufficient because it fails to provide any information as to the change in sales resulting from an increased price. Together, however, Statements (1) and (2) provide the information needed. You do not need to calculate the percent decrease in sales; you know that the correct answer is (C). Here's how you would perform the calculation, however: A 60-cent increase is 6 increases of 10 cents, so the decrease in sales is 30% (6 × 5).

24. **The correct answer is (D).** Statement (1) establishes a linear equation with one variable:

$$x + (x + 1) = \frac{1}{2}[(x + 3) + (x + 6)]$$

You can determine the second term by solving for x, and Statement (1) suffices to answer the question. [The second term is 4.5 ($x = 3.5$); however, you need not determine these values.] Statement (2) also establishes a linear equation in one variable: $(x + 15) + (x + 21) = 43$. The seventh term must be $(x + 21)$ because each successive term in the sequence is greater than the previous by an increasing consecutive integer. Statement (2) alone suffices to answer the question. (Again, $x = 3.5$ and the second term is 4.5, although you need not determine either value.)

25. **The correct answer is (E).** Statement (1) alone allows for more than one possible area, as illustrated below (A and B):

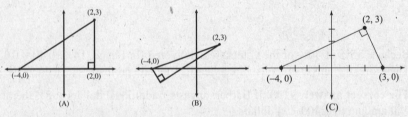

Statement (2) also allows for more than one possible area (A and C), as illustrated above.

26. **The correct answer is (C).** It's obvious that neither Statement (1) nor Statement (2) alone provides sufficient information to determine the degree measure of $\angle x$. Thus, you can easily eliminate choices (A), (B), and (D). Next, consider Statements (1) and (2) together. Notice that $\angle y$ and $\angle z$ together form an angle whose degree measure exceeds 180 (a straight line) by x. Thus, $y + z - x = 180$. Statements (1) and (2) provide the values of y and z and thus suffice to answer the question ($x = 50$).

27. **The correct answer is (E).** Given $xy < 0$, either x or y (but not both) must be negative. Despite this restriction, Statement (1) alone is insufficient to answer the question because it specifies one equation in two variables. Statement (2) alone is also insufficient. Although x must equal either -2 or -1 (x must be a negative integer), y could be any positive integer. Now, consider Statements (1) and (2) together. Since there are two possible values of x (-2 and -1) in the equation $x + y = 2$, the difference between x and y could be either -4 or -6. Thus, Statements (1) and (2) together are insufficient to answer the question.

28. **The correct answer is (D).** Equate the proportions of the negative with those of the printed picture:

$$\frac{2\frac{1}{2}}{4} = \frac{1\frac{7}{8}}{x}$$

$$\frac{\frac{5}{2}}{4} = \frac{\frac{15}{8}}{x}$$

$$\frac{5}{2}x = \frac{15}{2}$$

$$5x = 15$$

$$x = 3$$

29. **The correct answer is (C).** $\overline{AC}$ is a diagonal of the square $ABCD$. To find the length of any square's diagonal, multiply the length of any side by $\sqrt{2}$. So first you need to find the length of a side. Half the length of a side equals the circle's radius, and the perimeter of any circle equals $2\pi r$, where r is the radius. Thus, the radius here is 8, and the length of each of the square's sides is 16. Therefore, the length of diagonal $\overline{AC} = 16\sqrt{2}$.

30. **The correct answer is (D).** The two greatest two-month percent increases for City X were from 1/1 to 3/1 and from 5/1 to 7/1. Although the temperature increased by a greater amount during the latter of these two periods, the percent increase was greater from 1/1 to 3/1:

    January–February: from 30° to 50°, a 66% increase

    May–June: from 60° to 90°, a 50% increase

During the period from 1/1 to 3/1, City Y's average daily temperature was midway between its highest and lowest temperatures (between 66° and 62°), or about 64°.

31. **The correct answer is (C).** The only two-month periods in which City Y's temperature was increasing while City X's was decreasing were September–October and November–December. Compare the two midpoints of the line segments for each period:

    September–October: City X's average was 50 and City Y's was 46.

    November–December: City X's average was 36 and City Y's average was 60.

For each city, find the average of the two midpoints:

City X's average: $\frac{50 + 36}{2} = 43$

City Y's average: $\frac{46 + 60}{2} = 53$

City Y's average overall temperature was about 10 degrees greater than City X's during these four months.

32. **The correct answer is (D).** The diagonal of a square is the hypotenuse of a $1:1:\sqrt{2}$ right triangle where the two legs are sides of the square. Given a hypotenuse of 8, the length of each side of the square is $\frac{8}{\sqrt{2}}$, or $4\sqrt{2}$. Accordingly, the square's perimeter $= 4 \times 4\sqrt{2} = 16\sqrt{2}$.

33. **The correct answer is (E).** You can express the distance both in terms of Dan's driving time going home and going back to college. Letting x equal the time (in hours) it took Dan to drive home, you can express the distance between his home and college both as $60x$ and as $50(x + 1)$. Equate the two distances (because distance is constant) and solve for x as follows:

$$60x = 50(x+1)$$
$$60x = 50x + 50$$
$$x = 5$$

It took Dan 5 hours at 60 miles per hour to drive from college to home, so the distance is 300 miles.

34. **The correct answer is (B).** Combine the terms under the radical into one fraction:

$$\sqrt{\frac{y^2}{2} - \frac{y^2}{18}} = \sqrt{\frac{9y^2 - y^2}{18}} = \sqrt{\frac{8y^2}{18}} = \sqrt{\frac{4y^2}{9}}$$

Then factor out "perfect squares" from both numerator and denominator: $\sqrt{\frac{4y^2}{9}} = \frac{2|y|}{3}$

35. **The correct answer is (C).** To answer the question, you need to compare the volume of the cylindrical tank with the volume of a cube-shaped tank. Statement (1) fails to provide sufficient information to determine these volumes. The volume of the cylindrical tank is $7.5\pi r^2$ and, given Statement (1), you can express the cube's volume as r^3. The ratio of the two volumes, then, is $7.5\pi r^2 : r^3$, or $7.5\pi : r$. Accordingly, the comparative volumes of the containers vary, depending on the value of r. Statement (2) is also insufficient to answer the question. Given Statement (2), the length of a cube's side is 2.5 feet, and you can determine its volume (s^3). However, you cannot determine the cylindrical tank's volume because the size of its circular base remains unknown. Statement (1) provides this missing information. Thus, Statements (1) and (2) together suffice to answer the question. Given Statements (1) and (2), the ratio of V [cylinder] to V [cube] is $3\pi : 1$, so 10 cube-shaped tanks are required.

36. **The correct answer is (B).** If Marisa's six tests averaged a score of 79, then these six tests added up to a total score of 79×6, which equals 474. Similarly, her five highest scoring tests added up to a total score of 82×5, which equals 410. Marisa's worst score was 474 minus 410, which equals 64.

37. **The correct answer is (E).** You can solve this problem by working backward from the answer choices—trying out each one in turn. Or, you can solve the problem algebraically. You can express the amount of sugar after you add water as $0.05(60 + x)$, where $60 + x$ represents the total amount of solution after you add the additional water. This amount of sugar is the same as (equal to) the original amount of sugar (20% of 60). Set up an equation, multiply both sides by 100 to remove the decimal point, and solve for x:

$$5(60 + x) = 1200$$
$$300 + 5x = 1200$$
$$5x = 900$$
$$x = 180$$

VERBAL SECTION

1. D	10. E	18. C	26. C	34. D
2. E	11. A	19. E	27. D	35. E
3. C	12. A	20. A	28. B	36. C
4. D	13. E	21. A	29. E	37. C
5. B	14. A	22. E	30. A	38. B
6. D	15. C	23. E	31. B	39. D
7. E	16. E	24. A	32. D	40. C
8. C	17. D	25. B	33. B	41. C
9. B				

1. **The correct answer is (D).** The original answer is faulty because the subject, *forests*, does not agree with the verb *provides*; also *which* is incorrectly used to introduce a restrictive clause. Choice (D) creates correct subject-verb agreement and replaces *which* with *that* to correctly introduce the relative clause.

2. **The correct answer is (E).** The original answer is faulty in two ways: the pronoun *they*, which is plural, does not agree with the singular antecedent *participant*, which is singular, and the pronoun *that* is used where the pronoun *who* belongs. Choice (E) remedies both problems by replacing the pronoun *they* with the singular *he or she* to agree with the antecedent and by replacing *that* with *who*.

3. **The correct answer is (C).** The original sentence is not parallel; the items in the series should all be the same in grammatical structure. Choice (D) corrects these problems by creating a series of three gerund phrases that serve as compound and parallel objects of the preposition *from*.

4. **The correct answer is (D).** The claim (in the second sentence) relies on the assumption that all other factors in weight loss—such as exercise and dietary habits—remained unchanged from prior to the two-week period through the two-week period.

5. **The correct answer is (B).** The passage draws the general conclusion that home buyers should "always" buy a new house based on a few specific advantages that new houses offer. Choice (B) is the best criticism of the argument because it suggests that these factors are not necessarily the only factors, or the most important ones, in the home-buying decision.

6. **The correct answer is (D).** In the first paragraph, the author cites certain erroneous assumptions upon which the U.S. New Town concept was based. Then, in the next two paragraphs, the author describes how and why New Towns in the United States failed to solve urban problems and to provide the sort of social environment hoped for. Choice (D) provides a good recapitulation of this entire discussion.

7. **The correct answer is (E).** In the second paragraph, the author states that one of the effects of New Towns was to draw high-income citizens away from the cities—essentially what choice (E) indicates.

8. **The correct answer is (C).** According to the first sentence of the passage, New Towns were originally conceptualized as a way to absorb growth. Based on other information in the passage, it appears that U.S. New Towns achieved this objective—at least to some extent—since city residents who could afford to move away from urban centers did so. At the same time, however,

the cities were left with new problems, such as an insufficient tax base to support themselves and to retain businesses. Thus, like the phenomenon that choice (C) describes, New Towns were an innovation that served to solve one problem but created another along the way.

9. **The correct answer is (B).** The original sentence contains two problems: the phrase "it often comes to pass that" is both wordy and superfluous; and the relative pronoun *whose*, which shows possession, is used instead of the subject pronoun *who* and the verb *is*. Choice (B) corrects these problems by eliminating excess words and by replacing *whose* with *who is*.

10. **The correct answer is (E).** If the statement in choice (E) is true, it suggests that Company X's experience is comparable to that of other merging companies, and therefore it is unlikely that many more Company X workers will leave as a result of the merger.

11. **The correct answer is (A).** Gwen's argument relies on the assumption that expensive restaurants are not so popular among the college students as inexpensive restaurants. Jose provides one reason why expensive restaurants are not necessarily less popular among the college students, suggesting that the disagreement is about whether expensive restaurants are in fact less popular among the college students than inexpensive ones.

12. **The correct answer is (A).** The original sentence correctly begins with a noun clause; when the subject of a sentence is a noun clause, a singular verb is required.

13. **The correct answer is (E).** The original sentence improperly uses *less* instead of *fewer* in reference to a numerical quantity (the number of chemicals tested). Also, the modifier *most of which* is separated from its antecedent (*thirty*), resulting in confusion as to whether *most of which* refers to the thirty chemicals tested or the tests themselves. Choice (E) remedies both problems in the original sentence.

14. **The correct answer is (A).** The original sentence correctly uses the singular pronoun *its* in referring to the singular *bureaucracy*. Also, choice (A) is consistent in its use of the future tense.

15. **The correct answer is (C).** The passage describes an imaginary debate over the American democratic ideal among the writers of the American Renaissance, in which Emerson, Thoreau, and Whitman are grouped together in one school of thought, while Hawthorne and Melville are paired in another. Choice (C) nicely matches this recap.

16. **The correct answer is (E).** The passage is clear throughout that Emerson is an idealist, which is just the opposite of a pragmatist.

17. **The correct answer is (D).** According to the passage, Melville, through his story *Pierre*, conveyed the notion that democratic idealism was based on "misguided assumptions." Although the author is not so explicit that Hawthorne also believed idealists to be misguided, Hawthorne's conclusion that transcendental freedom leads to moral anarchy can reasonably be interpreted this way.

18. **The correct answer is (C).** The argument's conclusion is that the new lifeguard was not a factor in the declining number of deaths from last year to this year. Choice (C) rules out one other possible explanation for the decline in the number of drownings, in turn rendering it more likely that the additional lifeguard *did* contribute to the decline.

19. **The correct answer is (E).** The conclusion in choice (E) is logically inferable from two premises given in the passage: (1) If MetaCorp continues to show a profit, then analysts will continue to recommend it (in symbolic form: *If A, then B*), and (2) if analysts recommend MetaCorp stock, then the stock's price will at least remain at its current level—in other words, either remain the same or increase (in symbolic form: *If B, then C*). From these two premises, choice (E) is logically inferable (in symbolic form: *If A, then C*).

20. **The correct answer is (A).** The argument that the public is interested in high culture relies on the assumption that opera, ballet, and classical music are considered "high culture." Choice (A) provides some evidence that this necessary assumption is a questionable one.

21. **The correct answer is (A).** The discrepancy among the cited studies involves the increase in the level of violence in television programming over the last twenty years. One possible explanation for the discrepancy is that the recent studies relied on different previous studies, which disagreed as to what the level was twenty years ago.

22. **The correct answer is (E).** The original version improperly uses *derive* instead of the proper idiom *are derived from*. Choice (E) corrects this diction error.

23. **The correct answer is (E).** The original sentence is faulty in its use of the pronoun *them* instead of the possessive *their* where the object of a verb (*opposed*) is a gerund (*trivializing*). Choice (E) corrects the improper use of *them*, replacing it with the possessive *their*, which properly precedes the gerund *trivializing*.

24. **The correct answer is (A).** The original sentence is correct in its use of the idiomatic phrase *have yet to*.

25. **The correct answer is (B).** The factual information cited in the passage suggests that eating high-fat foods does not cause obesity. However, that information is no help in determining the real cause. By showing that the rise in obesity has coincided with an increase in the sales of high-sugar foods, choice (B) suggests that excessive sugar consumption might be the cause. Although this correlation in itself does not irrefutably prove that sugar is the culprit, it nevertheless helps strengthen the case.

26. **The correct answer is (C).** The argument's first sentence suggests that the supply-demand ratio for rental apartments with two or more bedrooms is decreasing at a faster rate than the supply-demand ratio of rental apartments with one or fewer bedrooms. One possible explanation for the difference is the one that choice (C) provides.

27. **The correct answer is (D).** The original version is faulty in two respects. First, the placement of the commas sets up a flawed parallel structure between the progressive verbs *was considered* and *will be considered*. Second, the phrase *considered as* is idiomatically questionable here. A person is *considered* or *considered to be*, not *considered as*, at least in the broader context of this sentence. Choice (D) remedies both problems with the original sentence.

28. **The correct answer is (B).** According to the passage, all cells of an organism contain the same genotype as the fertilized egg (lines 13–15). Thus, choice (B) contradicts the information in the passage.

29. **The correct answer is (E).** According to the passage, the maternal programming of early development and the genomic control of later differentiation are "especially well documented" (lines 43–44).

30. **The correct answer is (A).** In the first two paragraphs, the author discusses the process of cell differentiation in embryonic development. While the author is particularly concerned with examining the mechanisms involved, no specific type of organism (animal) is discussed as an illustration until the final paragraph (which focuses on the sea urchin). Accordingly, choice (A) properly reflects the flow of the author's discussion.

31. **The correct answer is (B).** The passage allows you to confidently conclude that biotechnology firms will in fact continue to replace equipment more frequently than other businesses and therefore will stand to benefit from the proposed law more than other businesses. It would make sense, then, that the biotechnology lobbyists might be behind the proposal.

32. **The correct answer is (D).** Higher admission standards would reduce the number of options available to new college graduates, thereby increasing the likelihood that a new college graduate would enter one of the lower-paying professions that requires only a four-year degree.

33. **The correct answer is (B).** The original sentence awkwardly mixes the active voice (first clause) and the passive voice (second clause). It also includes the unnecessarily wordy *by way of*. Choice (B) corrects both problems with a concise second clause in the active voice.

34. **The correct answer is (D).** The original sentence misplaces the phrase *Even for high school freshmen and sophomores.* This phrase is intended to modify *many students;* therefore, the author should reconstruct the sentence so that the two phrases appear nearer to each other. Choice (D) moves the initial phrase to the end of the sentence, clarifying the sentence's meaning.

35. **The correct answer is (E).** The argument suggests that the key to a third-world country's political stability is to afford its citizens certain powers. However, the argument relies entirely on one observed case (Country X) in which both characteristics are present. To be convincing, the argument must at least show that these powers actually contributed to Country X's political stability. Choice (E) provides one plausible scenario in which these powers could have nothing to do with the country's political stability.

36. **The correct answer is (C).** Choice (C) is the correct answer because the author notes in the last paragraph that public ire might not be aroused if the entry barrier (to competition) is technological ascendancy. Choice (A) must be ruled out because, while the author does attempt to link Google and Planetary Resources as alleged or probable monopolies, the author does not equate criticism against them. After all, Planetary Resources is yet to become a monopoly—if it ever does. Choice (B) must be ruled out because the author, while suggesting public ire, discounts the idea that it would exist and does not link it to this cause. Choice (D) is incorrect because the author does not allude to negative public response or antitrust legislation. Choice (E) should be eliminated because, while such arguments are germane to the discussion of monopolies, they are not mentioned in this passage.

37. **The correct answer is (C).** Choice (C) gives the only fact in the passage that points to scientific research that could validate such a venture. Choice (A) is tempting; nevertheless, the participation of Google investors probably lends more credence to financial viability and the assumption of high start-up costs than to the feasibility of successfully and profitably mining asteroids over the long term. Choice (B) must be ruled out because it names a possible effect of the endeavor, rather than something that makes it feasible. Choice (D) is incorrect because an economy of scale will develop only if the project is feasible to begin with. Choice (E) should be eliminated because no mention is made of this as a fact; moreover, would-be investors should wonder just exactly what the company's current capabilities are.

38. **The correct answer is (B).** The tone and connotations must be considered carefully to arrive at this choice, and readers must distinguish between puns related to stars, a launch pad, the sky being "the limit," the plan being "down to Earth," and sarcasm, which has a more critical bite. The author's attitude may also be gauged, in general, by a general lack of criticism, as well as by the first sentence, which guardedly anoints the investment. Choice (A) is incorrect because the author does actually suggest in the first sentence that the venture might be a good investment. Choice (C) is tempting; the punning does suggest amusement. Nevertheless, there is no sarcasm present. Furthermore, there are a large number of facts and no amusement whatsoever in the reporting of possible economic implications. Choice (D) is incorrect because the author actually puts a more positive spin on the endeavor than the level of scientific fact in the passage might warrant. Choice (E) should be eliminated because, while the puns cease after the second paragraph, the view throughout is fairly consistent: If this unlikely and farfetched plan does succeed, there are billions, if not trillions, of dollars to be made.

39. **The correct answer is (D).** Even though NASA research may be the basis of some part of the endeavor, there is no mention of any past, current, or future collaboration. Choice (A) must be ruled out because it is specifically mentioned in Paragraph 1. Choice (B) must be ruled out because the first sentence of the third paragraph mentions "attempts to robotically extract platinum group metals." Choice (C) is incorrect because the author mentions both: the first in the second-paragraph context of the estimated worth of a single asteroid and the second in the final sentence. Choice (E) should be eliminated because the author treats this as a distinct possibility in Paragraph 3.

40. **The correct answer is (C).** If there are other ways to prevent one's cat from accumulating hairballs, then there is no reason to risk the cat's developing an allergic reaction (and in turn a harmful infection) by feeding it the medicated food.

41. **The correct answer is (C).** The original sentence contains a misplaced modifying phrase (following the comma). The sentence's construction suggests that it is the electorate that cannot reasonably be disputed, although this makes little sense in the context of the sentence as a whole. Choice (C) remedies the underlined phrase's faulty construction by rephrasing it as a noun clause.

PART III

GMAT ANALYTICAL WRITING ASSESSMENT

Argument Analysis

OVERVIEW

- **The 7-step plan**
- **Common reasoning flaws and how to handle them**
- **Adding optional elements to your essay**
- **Keys to writing a successful GMAT Argument Analysis essay**
- **Summing it up**

In this part of the book, you'll learn the basics and some advanced techniques for writing an effective GMAT Argument Analysis essay that will earn you a better-than-average score of at least 4 on the 0–6 scale. Specifically, you'll learn the following:

- A step-by-step approach to planning and organizing, composing, and proofreading your essay, all comfortably within the 30-minute time limit for the task

- Success keys to scoring higher with your essays than most GMAT test-takers

- Useful tips for writing mechanics and for developing a writing style appropriate for the GMAT

THE 7-STEP PLAN

For a high-scoring Argument essay, you need to accomplish these four basic tasks:

1 Identify and analyze the Argument's key elements

2 Organize, develop, and express your critique in a coherent and logically convincing manner

3 Support your ideas with sound reasons and supporting examples

4 Demonstrate adequate control of the elements of Standard Written English (grammar, syntax, and usage)

The 30 minutes that you're allowed to write your essay isn't much time, so you will need to use the time wisely. This does *not* mean using every one of your 30 minutes to peck away at the keyboard like mad. You should spend some time up front thinking about what you will write and how you will organize your ideas. You'll also want to save some time at the end of this section of the exam to proofread and fine-tune your essay. Here's a 7-step game plan to help you budget your time so you can accomplish all four tasks listed above within your 30-minute time limit (suggested times are in parentheses):

chapter 4

NOTE

The time limits for these steps are guidelines. As you practice composing your Argument essay under timed conditions, you'll be able to adjust to a pace that works best for you.

1 Read the Argument and identify its conclusion(s) (1 min.)

2 Examine the evidence for its support of the conclusion(s) (3 min.)

3 Organize and prioritize your points of critique (1 min.)

4 Compose a brief introductory paragraph (2 min.)

5 Compose the body of your response (16 min.)

6 Compose a concluding paragraph (2 min.)

7 Proofread for significant mechanical problems (5 min.)

Notice that by following the suggested time limits for each step, you'll spend about 5 minutes planning your essay, 20 minutes writing it, and 5 minutes proofreading it.

In the following pages, you'll walk through each step in turn, using the following Argument statement, which is similar to some of the statements in the official pool:

Argument 1 (and directive)

The following appeared in a memo from the manager of UpperCuts hair salon:

"According to a nationwide demographic study, more and more people today are moving from suburbs to downtown areas. In order to boost sagging profits at UpperCuts, we should take advantage of this trend by relocating the salon from its current location in Apton's suburban mall to downtown Apton, while retaining the salon's decidedly upscale ambiance. Besides, HairDooz, our chief competitor at the mall, has just relocated downtown and is thriving at its new location, and the most prosperous hair salon in nearby Brainard is located in that city's downtown area. By emulating the locations of these two successful salons, UpperCuts is certain to attract more customers."

Discuss how well reasoned you find this argument. In your discussion be sure to analyze the line of reasoning and the use of evidence in the argument. For example, you may need to consider what questionable assumptions underlie the thinking and what alternative explanations or counterexamples might weaken the conclusion. You can also discuss what sort of evidence would strengthen or refute the argument, what changes in the argument would make it more logically sound, and what, if anything, would help you better evaluate its conclusion.

Step One: Read the Argument and Identify Its Conclusion(s) (1 min.)

Every GMAT Argument consists of the following basic elements:

- *Evidence* (stated premises that the Argument does not dispute)
- *Assumptions* (unstated premises needed to justify a conclusion)
- *Conclusions* (inferences drawn from evidence and assumptions)

As you read an Argument for the first time, identify its *final* conclusion as well as its *intermediate* conclusion (if any). Why is this first step so important? Unless you are clear about the Argument's conclusions, it's impossible to evaluate the author's reasoning or the strength of the evidence offered in support of it—and that's what this section of the GMAT is all about.

You'll probably find the *final* conclusion in the Argument's first or last sentence. The Argument might refer to it as a "claim," a "recommendation," or a "prediction." An intermediate conclusion, upon which the final conclusion depends, might appear anywhere in the Argument. Not every Argument contains an intermediate conclusion.

Did you identify and distinguish between the intermediate and final conclusions in the Argument involving UpperCuts? Here they are:

Intermediate conclusion:

"By emulating the locations of these two successful salons, UpperCuts is certain to attract more customers."

Final conclusion:

"In order to boost sagging profits at UpperCuts, we should... relocat[e] the salon from its current location in Apton's suburban mall to downtown Apton, while retaining the salon's decidedly upscale ambiance."

Notice that the Argument's final conclusion relies on its intermediate conclusion. Here's the essential line of reasoning:

UC will gain customers if it moves downtown. (*Intermediate conclusion*)

Therefore, UC will boost its profits simply by moving downtown. (*Final conclusion*)

Always jot down an Argument's intermediate conclusion (if any) and its final conclusion—in shorthand like we've provided above. You'll need to refer to them time and again as you develop your points of critique and compose your essay.

Step Two: Examine the Evidence for Its Support of the Conclusion(s) (3 min.)

Most Arguments contain at least two or three items of information, or evidence, that are used in support of its conclusion(s). Identify them, label them, and jot them down in shorthand on your scratch paper. Argument 1 contains three distinct items of evidence:

Evidence (Item 1):

"According to a nationwide demographic study, more and more people today are moving from suburbs to downtown areas."

Evidence (Item 2):

"HairDooz, our chief competitor at the mall, has just relocated downtown and is thriving at its new location."

Evidence (Item 3):

". . . the most prosperous hair salon in nearby Brainard is located in that city's downtown area."

Next, analyze each item as to how much support it lends to the Argument's intermediate and final conclusions. For the most part, what you should look for are any unsubstantiated or unreasonable

TIP

Use your notebook to help you keep track of information as you develop your argument.

assumptions upon which the Argument's conclusions depend. For example, an Argument might rely on one of these assumptions, yet fail to provide evidence to support it.

An event that occurs after another was caused by the other (a false-cause problem)

Two things that are similar in one way are similar in other ways (a false-analogy problem)

A statistical sample of a group is representative of the group as a whole

Also check for problems with the Argument's *internal logic* (for example, self-contradictions or circular reasoning). These types of problems don't occur commonly in GMAT Arguments, but you should be on the lookout for them anyway.

Don't filter your ideas during this crucial brainstorming step. Get them all down onto your scratch paper. (You'll sort them out in Step 3.)

Below is an example of what a test-taker's notes for Argument 1 might look like after a few minutes of brainstorming:

inter. concl. UC   will gain customers downtown
final concl. UC   will improve profits downtown
• demog. study is   Apton typical? <   no trend
                                        reverse
                                        trend
• success of HD is   location key? <   marketing
                                         key stylist
• success of B salon downtown   location key?
                    is   Apton like Brainard?
                    (demog.)
• other problems
    relocation   expenses offset revenues
    UC   must establish new clientele
    competition   from HD
        (suff. demand for both salons?)
    demand   for upscale   salon downtown?

Step Three: Organize and Prioritize Your Points of Critique (1 min.)

Using your notes from Step 2 as a guide, arrange your ideas into paragraphs (probably three or four, depending on the number of problems built into the Argument). Take a minute to consider whether any of the flaws you identified overlap and whether any can be separated into two distinct problems. In many cases, the best sequence in which to organize your points of critique is the same order in which reasoning problems arise in the Argument.

Try to use your notes as an outline, numbering points according to their logical sequence. Below is an example of what the test-taker's notes for Argument 1 look like after organizing them (arrows indicate where he intends to discuss a point; [FC] refers to final conclusion):

Step Four: Compose a Brief Introductory Paragraph (2 min.)

You've spent about 5 minutes planning your essay; now it's time to compose it. Don't waste time repeating the quoted Argument; the reader, whom you can assume is already familiar with the Argument, is interested in your critique—not in your transcription skills. Here are three tasks you should try to accomplish in your initial paragraph:

1. *Identify* the Argument's final conclusion.
2. *Describe* briefly the Argument's line of reasoning and evidence in support of its conclusion.
3. *Allude* generally to the problems with the Argument's line of reasoning and use of evidence.

You can probably accomplish all three tasks in two or three sentences. Here's a concise introductory paragraph of a response to Argument 1:

Citing a general demographic trend and certain evidence about two other hair salons, the manager of UpperCuts (UC) concludes here that UC should relocate from suburban to downtown Apton in order to attract more customers and, in turn, improve its profitability. However, the manager's argument relies on a series of unproven assumptions and is therefore unconvincing as it stands.

Although you want to stick to your outline, remember to stay flexible. Start with the points that strike you as the most important and easiest to articulate. You can always rearrange them later.

Your introductory paragraph is the least important component of your essay, so you might consider waiting until you've completed your critique of the Argument before composing your introduction. If you're running out of time for your introduction, begin your essay with a sentence like one of the following two, and then delve right into your first point of critique—without a paragraph break:

This argument suffers from numerous flaws which, considered together, render untenable the conclusion that UpperCuts should relocate to downtown Apton. One such flaw involves...

I find the argument for moving UpperCuts salon downtown specious at best, because it relies on a series of unproven and doubtful assumptions. One such assumption is that...

Step Five: Compose the Body of Your Response (16 min.)

- Try to devote a separate paragraph to each major point of your critique—but be flexible. Sometimes it makes more sense to discuss related points in the same paragraph.

- Be sure the first sentence of each paragraph conveys to the reader the essence of the problem you're dealing with in that paragraph.

- For each of the Argument's assumptions, try to provide at least one example or counterexample (a hypothetical scenario) that, if true, would undermine the assumption.

- Try to devote no more than three or four sentences to any one point in your outline. Otherwise, you risk running out of time without discussing all of the Argument's major problems.

- Arrange your paragraphs so that your essay flows logically from one point of critique to the next.

- Don't worry if you don't have time to discuss each and every point of critique or example that you noted during Step 2. The readers understand your time constraint.

Here's the body of a test-taker's response to Argument 1. As you read these four paragraphs, notice that each paragraph addresses a distinct, critical assumption—a certain condition that must be true to justify one of the Argument's conclusions. Also notice that each paragraph describes at least one scenario that, if true, would serve to undermine an assumption.

One such assumption is that Apton reflects the cited demographic trend. The mere fact that one hair salon has moved downtown hardly suffices to show that the national trend applies to Apton specifically. For all we know, in Apton there is no such trend, or perhaps the trend is in the opposite direction, in which event the manager's recommendation would amount to especially poor advice.

Even assuming that downtown Apton is attracting more residents, relocating downtown might not result in more customers for UC, especially if downtown residents are not interested in UC's upscale style and prices. Besides, HairDooz might draw potential customers away from UC, just as it might have at the mall. Without ruling out these and other reasons why UC might not benefit from the trend, the manager can't convince me that UC would attract more customers by moving downtown.

Even if there was a high demand for UC's service in downtown Apton, an increase in the number of patrons would not necessarily improve UC's profitability. UC's expenses might be higher downtown, in which case it might be no more, or perhaps even less, profitable downtown than at the mall.

As for the Brainard salon, its success might be due to particular factors that don't apply to UC. For example, perhaps the Brainard salon thrives only because it is long-established in downtown Brainard. Or perhaps hair salons generally fare better in downtown Brainard than downtown Apton, due to demographic differences between the two areas. In short, the manager simply cannot justify his proposal on the basis of the Brainard salon's success.

Step Six: Compose a Concluding Paragraph (2 min.)

Unless your essay has a clear ending, the reader might think you didn't finish on time. Be sure to make time for a final paragraph that clearly "wraps up" your essay. Your final paragraph is *not* the place to introduce any new points of critique. Instead, *recapitulate* the Argument's problems—e.g., a series of unproven assumptions—in two or three sentences. Here's a final paragraph in response to Argument 1:

> In sum, the argument relies on what might amount to two poor analogies between UC and two other salons, as well as a sweeping generalization about demographic trends, which may or may not apply to Apton. Thus, even though the manager has provided some scant evidence to support the recommendation, on balance I find the argument unconvincing at best.

Notice that this paragraph does not introduce any new points of critique. It's just a brief recap of the argument's major problems, along with a reiteration of why the Argument is weak.

Another tack you could take with your concluding paragraph is to recap how the argument could be strengthened and/or how additional information might be needed to evaluate it. Although these two elements are optional, incorporating one or both into your essay can boost your score.

From beginning to end (including the introductory, body, and concluding paragraphs), the preceding sample essay runs just under 400 words in length—brief enough to plan and write in 30 minutes. It's well organized; it articulates the Argument's major problems; it supports each point of critique with relevant examples; and it's crisp, clear, and convincing. In short, it contains all the elements of a high-scoring GMAT Argument essay.

Step Seven: Proofread for Significant Mechanical Problems (5 min.)

Be sure to reserve time to check the flow of your essay, paying particular attention to the first sentence of each paragraph. Check to see if you should rearrange paragraphs so that they appear in a more logical sequence. To score high, you don't need to compose a flawless work of art. The readers won't reduce your score for the occasional awkward sentence and minor error in punctuation, spelling, grammar, or diction (word choice and usage). Don't get hung up on whether each sentence is something your English composition professor would be proud of. Instead, use whatever time remains to read your essay from start to finish and fix the most glaring mechanical problems. Here are some suggestions for what you should and, just as important, should *not* try to accomplish during this final step:

- Find and rework awkward sentences, especially ones where the point you're trying to make is not clear.

- Find and correct accidental omission of words, garbled phrases, grammatical errors, and typographical errors. It doesn't take much time to fix these kinds of errors, and the time spent will go a long way toward making a positive impression on the reader.

- Correct spelling errors *only* when they might prevent the reader from understanding the point at hand.

- Don't spend *any* of your valuable time correcting punctuation or removing extra character spaces between words.

- Don't get drawn into drastic rewriting. Accept that your essay is what it is and that you don't have time to reshape it substantially.

COMMON REASONING FLAWS AND HOW TO HANDLE THEM

GMAT test designers intentionally incorporate numerous reasoning flaws into Arguments that render them vulnerable to criticism. In a typical Argument Analysis section, you can find three or four distinct areas for critique. The following are the most common types of problems with GMAT Arguments. If you have time, try to memorize this list to help you brainstorm and ferret out flaws in any GMAT Argument.

- Confusing cause-and-effect with mere correlation or time sequence
- Drawing a weak analogy between two things
- Relying on a potentially unrepresentative statistical sample
- Relying on a potentially unreliable survey or poll
- Assuming that a certain condition is necessary and/or sufficient for a certain outcome
- Assuming that characteristics of a group apply to each group member (or vice versa)
- Assuming that all things remain unchanged over time
- Assuming that two courses of action are mutually exclusive
- Relying on undefined, vague, or ambiguous terms

In the following pages, you'll learn more about each type of flaw and how to address each one in your Argument Analysis essay.

Confusing Cause-and-Effect with Mere Correlation or Time Sequence

Many GMAT Arguments rely on the claim that certain events cause certain other events. A cause-and-effect claim might be based on these two circumstances:

1 A significant *correlation* between the occurrences of two phenomena (both phenomena generally occur together)

2 A *temporal relationship* between the two (one event occurred after another)

A significant correlation or a temporal relationship between two phenomena is one indication of a cause-and-effect relationship between them. However, neither in itself proves such a relationship. Unless the Argument also considers and eliminates all other plausible causes of the presumed "result," the Argument is vulnerable to criticism. To show the reader you understand this sort of false-cause problem, you need to accomplish all three of the following tasks:

❶ *Identify* the false-cause problem (e.g., as one of the Argument's crucial assumptions).

❷ *Elucidate* by providing at least one or two examples of other possible causes.

❸ *Explain* how the false-cause problem undermines the Argument.

Here's an Argument that confuses causation with mere *temporal sequence,* followed by a succinct and effective critique.

Argument:

The following appeared in the editorial section of a newspaper:

"Two years ago, State X enacted a law prohibiting environmental emissions of certain nitrocarbon by-products, on the basis that these by-products have been shown to cause Urkin's disease in humans. Last year, fewer State X residents reported symptoms of Urkin's disease than in any prior year. Since the law is clearly effective in preventing the disease, in the interest of public health, this state should adopt a similar law."

Response:

The editorial infers that State X's new law is responsible for the apparent decline in the incidence of Urkin's disease (UD) symptoms. However, the editorial's author ignores other possible causes of the decline—for example, a new UD cure or new treatment for UD symptoms. Without eliminating alternative explanations such as these, the author cannot justify either the inference or the additional assertion that a similar law would be similarly effective in the author's state.

Drawing a Weak Analogy Between Two Things

A GMAT Argument might draw a conclusion about one thing (perhaps a city, school, or company) on the basis of an observation about a similar thing. However, this line of thinking assumes that because the two things are similar in certain respects, they are similar in all respects, at least as far as the Argument is concerned. Unless the Argument provides sufficient evidence to substantiate this assumption, the Argument is vulnerable to criticism. The Argument cannot rely on these claims to support its recommendation.

To show the reader you understand the weak-analogy problem, you need to accomplish all three of the following tasks:

❶ *Identify* the analogy (e.g., as one of the Argument's crucial assumptions).

❷ *Elucidate* by providing at least one or two significant ways in which the two things might differ.

❸ *Explain* how those differences, which render the analogy weak, undermine the Argument's conclusion.

Here's an Argument that contains a questionable analogy, followed by an effective 3-sentence analysis.

Argument:

The following was part of a speech made by the principal of Valley High School:

"Every year, Dunston High School wins the school district's student Math SuperBowl competition. The average salary of teachers at Dunston is greater than at any other school in the district. Hence in order for Valley High students to improve their scores on the state's standardized achievement exams, Valley should begin awarding bonuses to Valley teachers whenever Valley defeats Dunston in the Math SuperBowl."

Response:

The principal's recommendation relies on what might be a poor analogy between Dunston and Valley. Valley teachers might be less responsive than Dunston teachers when it comes to monetary incentives, or Valley students might be less gifted than Dunston students when it comes to math. In short, what might have helped Dunston perform well at the Math SuperBowl would not necessarily help Valley perform better either at the SuperBowl or on the state exams.

Relying on a Potentially Unrepresentative Statistical Sample

A GMAT Argument might cite statistical evidence from a study, survey, or poll involving a "sample" group, then draw a conclusion about a larger group or population that the sample supposedly represents. But in order for a statistical sample to accurately reflect a larger population, the sample must meet two requirements:

❶ The sample must be *significant in size* (number) as a portion of the overall population.

❷ The sample must be *representative* of the overall population in terms of relevant characteristics.

Arguments that cite statistics from studies, surveys, and polls often fail to establish either of these two requirements. Of course this failure is by design of the test-maker, who is inviting you to call into question the reliability of the evidence. To show the reader you understand this statistical problem, you need to accomplish all three of the following tasks:

❶ *Identify* the problem (e.g., as one of the Argument's crucial assumptions).

❷ *Elucidate* by providing at least one or two respects in which key characteristics of a sample group might differ from those of the larger population.

❸ *Explain* how those differences would undermine the Argument's conclusion.

Here's an Argument that relies on two potentially unrepresentative sample groups: (1) new graduates from a certain state's undergraduate programs and (2) new graduates from the state's graduate-level programs. The response that follows it provides a brief but effective critique.

Argument:

The following was part of an article appearing in a national magazine:

"Our nation's new college graduates will have better success obtaining jobs if they do not pursue advanced degrees after graduation. After all, more than 90 percent of State X's undergraduate students are employed full-time within one year after they graduate, while less than half of State X's graduate-level students find employment within one year after receiving their graduate degrees."

Response:

The argument fails to consider that State X's new graduates might not be representative of the nation's as a whole, especially if the former group constitutes only a small percentage of the latter group. If it turns out, for example, that State X's undergraduate students are less motivated than the nation's average college student to pursue graduate-level study, then the argument's recommendation for all undergraduate students would be unwarranted.

Relying on a Potentially Unreliable Survey or Poll

As you just learned, a GMAT Argument might draw some conclusion involving a group based on statistical data about an *insufficient* or *unrepresentative* sample. However, this is not the only potential problem with statistical data. The process of collecting the data (i.e., the methodology) might be flawed in a way that calls into question the *quality* of the data. This will render the data "tainted" and therefore unreliable for drawing any conclusions. In order for survey or poll results to be reliable in quality:

- The survey or poll responses must be *credible* (truthful and accurate). If respondents have reason to provide incomplete or false responses, the results are tainted (and therefore unreliable).

- The method of collecting the data must be *unbiased*. If responses are not mandatory or if the survey's form predisposes subjects to respond in certain ways, then the results are tainted (and therefore unreliable).

To show the reader that you recognize and understand this statistical problem, you need to accomplish all three of the following tasks:

1. *Identify* the problem (e.g., as one of the Argument's crucial assumptions).
2. *Elucidate* by providing at least one or two reasons, based on the Argument's information, why the statistical data might be tainted (and therefore unreliable).
3. *Explain* how the potentially tainted data might undermine the Argument's conclusion.

The following Argument relies on a survey that poses a potential *bias* as well as a *credibility* problem. The response contains all three elements required to address each problem, in a single paragraph.

Argument:

The following appeared in a memo from the director of human resources at Webco:

"Among Webco employees participating in our department's most recent survey, about half indicated that they are happy with our current four-day work week. These survey results show that the most effective way to improve overall productivity at Webco is to allow each employee to choose for himself or herself either a four-day or five-day work week."

Response:

The survey methodology might be problematic in two respects. First, we are not informed whether the survey required that respondents choose their work week preference between alternatives. If it did, then the results might distort the preferences of the respondents, who might very well prefer a work schedule choice not provided for in the survey. Secondly, we are not informed whether survey responses were anonymous or even confidential. If they were not, then respondents might have provided responses that they believed their superiors would approve of, regardless of whether the responses were truthful. In either event, the survey results would be unreliable for the purpose of drawing any conclusions about Webco employee preferences, let alone about how to improve overall productivity at Webco.

Assuming That a Condition Is Necessary and/or Sufficient for a Certain Outcome

A GMAT Argument might recommend a certain course of action, based on one or both of the following claims:

- The course of action is *necessary* to achieve a desired result.
- The course of action is *sufficient* to achieve the desired result.

With respect to Claim 1, the Argument must provide evidence that no other means of achieving the same result are available. For Claim 2, the Argument must provide strong evidence that the proposed course of action by itself would be sufficient to bring about the desired result. Lacking this sort of evidence, the Argument cannot rely on these claims to support its recommendation.

To show the reader you understand necessary-condition and sufficient-condition problems, you need to accomplish all three of the following tasks:

  1 *Identify* the problem (e.g., as one of the Argument's crucial assumptions).

  2 *Elucidate* by providing at least one or two examples. For a necessary-condition problem, suggest other possible means of achieving the stated objective. For a sufficient-condition problem, suggest other conditions that might also be sufficient for the outcome.

  3 *Explain* how the problem undermines the Argument's conclusion.

Here's an Argument that assumes that a certain condition is *necessary* for a certain outcome. The response provides a brief but incisive analysis of the problem.

Argument:

The following appeared in a memo from a vice president at Toyco, which operates a large chain of toy stores:

"Last year was the first year in which Playtime Stores, our main competitor, sold more toys than Toyco. Playtime's compensation for its retail sales force is based entirely on their sales. If Toyco is to recapture its leadership position in the toy-sales market, we must reestablish our former policy of requiring all our retail associates to meet strict sales quotas in order to retain their jobs."

Response:

The argument assumes that the proposed compensation policy is the only way that Toyco can once again sell more toys than Playtime. However, the vice president fails to consider and rule out possible alternative means of achieving this end—for example, opening new stores or adding new types of toys to the ones its stores already carry. Until the president does so, I will remain unconvinced that the proposed policy is a necessary means for Toyco to recapture market leadership.

Assuming That Characteristics of a Group Apply to Each Group Member (or Vice Versa)

A GMAT Argument might point out some fact about a general group—such as students, employees, or cities—to support a claim about one particular member of that group. Or conversely, the Argument might point out some fact about a particular group member to support a claim about the entire group. In either scenario, unless the Argument supplies clear evidence that the member is representative of the group as a whole (by the way, it won't), the Argument is vulnerable to criticism.

To show the reader you understand a group-member problem, you need to accomplish all three of the following tasks:

1. *Identify* the problem (e.g., as one of the Argument's crucial assumptions).
2. *Elucidate* by providing at least one or two significant ways in which the member might differ from the general group.
3. *Explain* how those key differences, which serve to refute the assumption, would undermine the Argument's conclusion.

Here's an Argument that assumes that characteristics of a group member apply to the group as a whole. Following the Argument is a response that shows how to handle the problem in one very succinct paragraph.

Argument:

The following is part of an article that appeared several years ago in the entertainment section of a local newspaper:

"At the local Viewer Choice video store, the number of available movies in DVD format remains about the same as three years ago, even though the number of available movies on Blu-ray has increased tenfold over the past three years. People who predict the impending obsolescence of the DVD format are mistaken, since demand for DVD movie rentals today clearly remains just as strong as ever."

Response:

This argument assumes that Viewer Choice (VC) is typical of all video stores as a group. However, this isn't necessarily the case; VC might carry far more DVDs, as a percentage of its total inventory, than the average store. If so, then the argument has failed to discredit the prediction for the industry as a whole.

Assuming That All Things Remain Unchanged Over Time

A GMAT Argument might rely on evidence collected in the past to formulate some conclusion or recommendation concerning the present or the future. Similarly, an Argument might rely on evidence about present conditions to make a prediction or recommendation for the future. But unless the Argument provides clear evidence that key circumstances have remained, or will remain, unchanged over the relevant time period, the Argument is vulnerable to criticism.

To address this problem, you should accomplish each of the following three tasks:

1. *Identify* the problem (i.e., the poor assumption that all key circumstances remain fixed over time).
2. *Elucidate* by providing examples of conditions that might change from one time frame to the other.
3. *Evaluate* the argument in light of the problem.

Here's an Argument that provides evidence about the past to draw a conclusion about the present as well as the future, followed by a 3-sentence paragraph that addresses the problem.

Argument:

The following appeared in a political campaign advertisement:

"Residents of this state should vote to elect Kravitz as state governor in the upcoming election. During Kravitz's final term as a state senator, she was a member of a special legislative committee that explored ways the state can reduce its escalating rate of violent crime. Elect Kravitz for governor, and our cities' streets will be safer than ever."

Response:

Assuming that at one time Kravitz was genuinely committed to fighting violent crime, the ad unfairly infers a similar commitment on Kravitz's part today and in the future while Kravitz serves as governor. Kravitz might hold entirely different views today, especially if her participation as a member of the committee occurred some time ago. Lacking better evidence that as governor Kravitz would continue to make crime fighting a high priority, the ad cannot persuade me to vote for Kravitz based on her committee membership.

Assuming That Two Courses of Action Are Mutually Exclusive

An Argument might recommend one course of action over another to achieve the stated objective, without considering that it is possible to pursue both courses (that is, they are not mutually exclusive alternatives), thereby increasing the likelihood of achieving the objective. Here's a good example, along with a response that handles the flaw.

Argument:

Rivertown's historic Hill district used to be one of the city's main tourist attractions. Recently, however, the district's quaint older shops and restaurants have had difficulty attracting patrons. In order to reverse the decline in tourism to the district, Rivertown's City Council intends to approve the construction of a new shopping center called Hill Hub on one of the district's few remaining vacant parcels. However, the city's interests in attracting revenue from tourism would be better served were it to focus instead on restoring Hill district's older buildings and waging a publicity campaign touting the historically authentic character of the district.

Response:

The argument seems to assume that the city must either approve the Hill Hub project or engage in the restoration and publicity efforts that the argument suggests but that the city cannot do both. However, the argument provides absolutely no evidence that the city must choose between the two courses of action. Lacking any such evidence, it is entirely possible that implementing both plans would attract more dollars from tourists to the district than implementing either one alone.

Relying on Undefined, Vague, or Ambiguous Terms

An Argument might contain a statement (or word or phrase) that carries more than one possible meaning or is simply too vague to reasonably rely upon when it comes to drawing conclusions. Look for references to "some," "many," and "several" in lieu of providing precise percentages or numbers. Also look for references to a particular class, category, or group, without a clear explanation of what it includes or excludes. Here's an example, followed by an effective response:

Argument:

A reliable recent study attests to the value of physical activity in increasing attention span among young children. Accordingly, in order to improve the overall learning levels among elementary-school children in our state, the state's board of education should mandate a daily exercise regimen for students at all our state's elementary schools.

Response:

The Argument neglects to indicate what types of "physical activity" the study observed. For all I know, those activities amounted to play, as opposed to the recommended exercise "regimen," which might be more like work for children. Nor does the Argument indicate the age range of the "young children" observed in the study. Perhaps the children were preschoolers, whose attention spans might respond differently than school-age children to certain types of physical activity. In short, before I can determine the extent to which the study supports the recommendation, I need specific definitions of these important terms.

ADDING OPTIONAL ELEMENTS TO YOUR ESSAY

The directive for every GMAT Argument indicates that you *may* include either or both of the following in your essay:

1 Suggestions about how the Argument can be strengthened

2 Additional information needed to evaluate the Argument

These two elements are optional, and you can score high on your Argument essay without using them, so don't take time to add them unless you're certain that you've adequately addressed all of the Argument's major problems. Otherwise, you risk running out of time to accomplish that essential task.

But keep in mind: You're more likely to attain a top score of 6 if you add these additional elements, all else being equal. So as you brainstorm your Argument essay, by all means jot down your ideas about how the Argument can be strengthened and/or what additional information is needed to evaluate the Argument. Then, after you've finished your critique of the Argument and proofread your critique, check the clock. If you still have at least a few minutes, go ahead and add one or both elements.

You have two realistic choices as to where to include them in your essay:

1 List the suggestions (and/or additional information needed) in your *final*, concluding paragraph.

2 Incorporate the suggestions (and/or additional information needed) into your *body paragraphs*.

Here's how you might incorporate both elements into a final paragraph of an essay on Argument 1 about UpperCuts hair salon (we've underlined words and phrases that you could use in the final paragraph of nearly any Argument essay):

Optional elements added to an essay's final, concluding paragraph:

In sum, the argument is a dubious one that relies on a series of unproven assumptions—about Apton's and Brainard's demographics, the reasons for the success of the two other salons, and UC's future expenses. To strengthen the argument, the manager should provide better evidence of a demographic shift in Apton toward the downtown area, and clear evidence that those demographics portend success there for an upscale hair salon. Even with this additional evidence, in order to properly evaluate the argument I would need to know why HairDooz relocated, what factors have contributed to the Brainard salon's success, what factors other than location might have contributed to UC's sagging profits at the mall, and what additional, offsetting expenses UC might incur at the new location.

Now here's how you might incorporate the same two elements into the body of an essay on the same Argument. (The optional elements are in italics—just to help you locate them.) Again, we've underlined words and phrases that you could use in nearly any Argument essay:

Optional elements incorporated into an essay's body paragraphs:

To begin with, the argument assumes that Apton's demographic trend reflects the national trend. Yet, the mere fact that one hair salon has moved downtown hardly suffices to infer any such trend in Apton; HairDooz might owe its success at its new location to factors unrelated to Apton's demographics. In fact, for all we know, the trend in Apton might be in the opposite direction. *Thus, I would need to know whether more people are in fact moving to downtown Apton before I could either accept or reject the manager's proposal.*

Even if Apton's demographics do reflect the national trend, it is unfair to assume that UC will attract more customers simply by relocating downtown. It is entirely possible that the types of people who prefer living in downtown areas tend not to patronize upscale salons. It is also possible that HairDooz will continue to impede upon UC's business, just as it might have at the mall. *Before I can accept that UC would attract more customers downtown, the manager would need to supply clear proof of a sufficient demand downtown for UC's service.*

Nor can the manager justify the recommended course of action on the basis of the Brainard salon's success. Perhaps hair salons generally fare better in downtown Brainard than downtown Apton, due to demographic differences between the two areas. Or perhaps the salon thrives only because it is long-established in downtown Brainard—an advantage that UC clearly would not have in its new location. *Accordingly, in order to determine whether the success of the Brainard salon portends success for UC in downtown Apton, I would need to know why the Brainard salon is successful in the first place.*

Finally, even assuming that the proposed relocation would attract more customers, an increase in the number of patrons would not necessarily result in improved profits. After all, profit is a function of expenses as well as revenue. Thus an increase in UC's expenses—due perhaps to higher rents downtown than at the mall—might very well offset increasing revenues, thereby frustrating UC's efforts to improve its profitability. *Before I could agree with the proposal, I would need to examine a comparative cost-benefit analysis for the two locations.*

KEYS TO WRITING A SUCCESSFUL GMAT ARGUMENT ANALYSIS ESSAY

In the following pages, we've distilled our very best advice for GMAT Argument Analysis into easily "digestible" nuggets of information. Many of them reiterate suggestions we've already made, but they're well worth underscoring. Others are new here. Apply these points of advice to the Practice Tests in PART VII, then review them again just before exam day. You'll be glad you did.

Ferreting Out the Flaws Is Half the Battle

Built into each and every GMAT Argument are at least three or four distinct reasoning problems. That's how the test-makers design them. To earn a high score, your essay must first and foremost identify these problems. If you haven't isolated at least three major flaws after brainstorming and making notes, then you can be sure that you've missed at least one. Read the Argument again more carefully. Even a few overlooked words can be key.

Ration your time to be sure the reader knows you've recognized each and every problem listed in your notes. Don't worry if 30 minutes isn't enough time for you to discuss each problem in detail. When it comes to analyzing GMAT Arguments, remember that breadth is better than depth.

Keep in mind: GMAT Arguments are not all created equal. Some are flawed in more ways than others. The greater the number of distinct flaws, the more forgiving the reader will be. So if an Argument contains as many as five or six distinct problems and you overlook one or two of them, you can still attain a high score—perhaps even a top score of 6—assuming your essay is outstanding in all other respects.

Viewpoints and Opinions Don't Matter

Your Argument essay is not the place to present viewpoints or opinions about an issue that the Argument might touch on. Your analysis must focus strictly on the Argument's logical features and on how strongly its evidence supports its conclusions.

For instance, consider an Argument for electing a certain political candidate because she has a record of being tough on crime. Presenting various viewpoints on this social issue and weighing alternative approaches to reducing crime are inappropriate topics for an Argument Analysis essay. These viewpoints are irrelevant.

Don't Leave Any Point of Critique Without Support

Don't neglect to support each point of your critique with at least one example or counterexample that helps the reader understand the particular flaw you're pointing out. Keep your examples and counterexamples hypothetical ("What if . . .," "Suppose that . . .," "It's possible that . . .," or "Perhaps . . ."). You don't need to go into great detail; one or two for each point of critique will suffice. Unless you provide some support for each point of critique, your score might suffer.

What if you think you won't have enough time to provide supporting detail for each point of critique in your notes? Don't despair. Look for two or three points that are related to the same item of evidence (for example, points that all involve the same statistical survey). Then, plan to touch briefly on each one *in the same paragraph*. Grouping them together this way will make sense to the reader, who might not notice what's missing as much as the fact that you're very organized!

Don't Look for the "Fatal Flaw"

Avoid dwelling on one particular flaw that you think is the most serious or on one realistic example or counterexample that you think, if true, would spell certain death for the entire Argument. You risk running out of time to identify all the problems you've listed in your notes.

In addition, don't try to rank any flaw as "more serious" or "less serious" than another. True, one particular flaw might be more damaging to an Argument than others. But by identifying it as "the most serious problem with the Argument," you're committing yourself to defend this claim by weighing that problem against all the others. Do you really have time for this kind of analysis? No! Nor do the GMAT readers expect or want this from you. In short, you're better off applying equal treatment to each of the Argument's problems.

Don't Use Technical Terminology

Scholars in the academic fields of Critical Reasoning and Logic rely on all sorts of formal terminology, much of which comes from Latin, for the kinds of reasoning flaws that you'll find in GMAT Arguments. For example, post hoc reasoning refers to faulty "After this, therefore because of this" reasoning. But you won't score any points with GMAT readers by tossing around such terminology in your Argument essay. Besides, if you use a technical term, you'll need to define it for the reader, which will only consume your precious time.

Go with the Logical Flow

Try to organize your points of critique to reflect the Argument's line of reasoning, from its evidence and assumptions to its intermediate conclusion (if any), then to its final conclusion. Fortunately, most GMAT Arguments are already organized this way, so that your points of critique can simply follow the quoted Argument from beginning to end.

Don't assume, though, that this sequence will be the most logical one. Regardless of the sequence of ideas in the quoted Argument, try to group together all your points of critique that involve the same item of evidence (for example, a statistical survey or study). Also, it makes logical sense to address problems involving the Argument's intermediate conclusion before those involving its final conclusion.

Look Organized and in Control of the Task

Use every tool at your disposal to show the reader that you can write well under pressure. Use logical paragraph breaks—one after your introduction, one between each of your main points, and one before your concluding paragraph. Be sure to present your main points in a logical, easy-to-follow sequence. (If you don't get it right the first time, you can use the word processor's cut-and-paste feature to rearrange your ideas.) Your essay's "bookends"—the introductory and concluding paragraph—are especially key to looking organized and in control. First of all, make sure they're there. Then, make sure they're consistent with each other and that they reveal your viewpoint and recap the reasons for your viewpoint.

Quality Counts, Not Quantity

The only limitation on your essay's length is the practical one that the 30-minute time limit imposes. A lengthy essay that's articulate and that includes many insightful ideas that are well supported by examples will score higher than a brief essay that lacks substance. On the other hand, an essay that's concise and to the point can be more effective than one that is long-winded and rambling.

Don't worry about the word length of your essay. GMAT readers don't count words. As long as you incorporate into your essay all the suggested elements you learned about in this lesson, you don't need to worry about length. Just keep in mind that it's quality, not quantity, that counts.

Don't Lose Sight of Your Primary Objectives

The official scoring criteria for the Argument Analysis essay boil down to four broad objectives. Never lose sight of them during your 30-minute Argument section. After brainstorming and making notes but before you start typing, ask yourself these three questions:

1. Have I clearly identified each of the Argument's major problems?
2. Can I support each point of my critique with at least one relevant example or counterexample?
3. Do I have in mind a clear, logical structure for presenting my points of critique?

Once you can confidently answer "Yes" to each question, start composing your essay. When you've finished your draft, ask yourself the same questions as well as this fourth one:

4. Have I demonstrated good grammar, diction (word choice and usage), and syntax (sentence structure)?

Once you can answer "Yes" to all four questions, rest assured that you've produced a solid, high-scoring Argument essay.

SUMMING IT UP

- Follow the 7-step plan in this chapter for a high-scoring Argument Analysis essay: read the argument and identify its conclusions; examine the Argument's evidence to determine how strongly it supports the conclusion; organize and prioritize your points of critique; compose an introduction; compose the body of your response; compose a concluding paragraph; and proofread your essay for significant mechanical problems.

- Identifying and analyzing the Argument's main elements is key to composing a successful essay.

- Be sure to reinforce your ideas with sound reasons and supporting examples.

- It's important that you show adequate command of the elements of Standard Written English, such as grammar, syntax, and usage.

Writing Style and Mechanics

OVERVIEW

- The basics
- Advanced techniques
- Summing it up

THE BASICS

The testing service instructs GMAT readers to place less weight on writing style and mechanics than on content and organization. But this doesn't mean that these two factors won't influence the reader or affect your Analytical Writing Assessment (AWA) score. Indeed, they might. If the way you write interferes with the reader's understanding of your ideas, be prepared for a disappointing score. In any event, poor writing will predispose the reader to award a lower score, regardless of your ideas or how you organize them. To ensure yourself a high AWA score, strive for writing that is:

- Appropriate in tone and "voice" for graduate-level academic writing

- Varied in sentence length and structure (to add interest and variety and to demonstrate a mature and sophisticated writing style)

- Clear and concise (easy to follow and direct, not wordy or verbose)

- Correct in grammar, mechanics, and usage (conforming to the requirements of Standard Written English)

- Stylistically persuasive (using rhetorical devices effectively)

All of this is easier said than done, of course. Don't worry if you're not a natural when it comes to writing effective prose. You can improve your writing for your exam, even if your time is short. Start by reading the suggestions and guidelines in this book. Keep in mind, however, that improvement in writing comes mainly with practice, so you'll also need to apply what you learn here to the Practice Tests in Part VII of this book.

Overall Tone and Voice

In general, try to maintain a somewhat formal tone throughout your essays. An essay that comes across as conversational is probably a bit too informal for the GMAT. Here are some additional guidelines:

chapter 5

- The overall tone should be critical but not inflammatory or emotional. Don't overstate your position with extreme or harsh language. Don't attempt to elicit a visceral or emotional response from the reader. Appeal instead to the reader's intellect.

- When it comes to your main points, a very direct, even forceful voice is perfectly acceptable. But don't overdo it; when it comes to the details, use a more dispassionate approach.

- Avoid making your point with "cutesy" or humorous remarks. Avoid puns, double meanings, plays on words, and other forms of humor. It isn't that GMAT readers don't have a sense of humor; it's just that this is not the appropriate venue for it.

- Sarcasm is entirely inappropriate for your GMAT essay. You run the risk that the reader might not realize that you're being sarcastic—and in that case, your remark will only confuse the reader and muddle your essay.

Sentence Length and Variety

To ensure a high AWA score, strive to write sentences that are varied in length and structured to help convey their intended meaning, rather than obscuring or distorting it. Here are some specific warnings and suggestions:

- Sentences that vary in length make for a more interesting and persuasive essay. For rhetorical emphasis, try using an abrupt short sentence for a crucial point, either before or after longer sentences that elucidate that point. For additional variety, use a semicolon to transform two sentences involving the same train of thought into one.

- Sentences that use the same essential structure can help convey your line of reasoning to the reader. Try using the same structure for a list of reasons or examples.

- Sentences that essentially repeat throughout your essay suggest an immature, unsophisticated writing style. Try to avoid using so-called "template" sentences over and over—especially for the first (or last) sentence of each body paragraph.

TIP

The rules of grammar reviewed in the Sentence Correction lessons in this book should help you compose and proofread your essay as well.

Clear and Concise Writing

You're more likely to score high on your GMAT essay with clear and concise writing. Frequently occurring awkward, wordy, or redundant phrases can lower your AWA score by a notch, especially if they interfere with the reader's understanding of your essay. And though punctuation is the least important aspect of your GMAT essay, habitually overusing, underusing, or misusing commas can also contribute to lowering your score.

Wordy and Awkward Phrases

With enough words, anyone can make the point, but it requires skill and effort to make your point with concise phrases. As you proofread your essay, if you detect a sentence that's clumsy or too long, check for a wordy, awkward phrase that you can replace with a clearer, more concise one. Here are two examples (replace italicized phrases with the ones in parentheses):

Discipline is crucial to *the attainment of* one's objectives. (attain)

To indicate the fact that they are in opposition to a bill, legislators sometimes engage in filibusters. (To show their)

Look for the opportunity to change prepositional phrases into one-word modifiers:

The employee *with ambition* . . .

The *ambitious* employee . . .

You can often rework clauses with relative pronouns (that, who, which, etc.), omitting the pronoun:

The system, *which* is most efficient and accurate . . .

The most efficient and accurate system . . .

In your Argument essay, you can replace wordy phrases that signal a premise with a single word:

Wordier: the reason for, for the reason that, due to the fact that, in light of the fact that, on the grounds that

More concise: because, since, considering that

Redundant Words and Phrases

As you proofread your essays, check for words and phrases that express the same essential idea twice.

Both unemployment levels *as well as* interest rates can affect stock prices. (Replace *as well as* with *and* or omit *both*.)

The reason science is being blamed for threats to the natural environment *is because* scientists fail to see that technology is only as useful, or as harmful, as those who decide how to use it. (Replace *because* with *that*, or omit *the reason* and *is*.)

Using Too Few (or Too Many) Commas

Although punctuation is the least important aspect of your GMAT essay, misplacement, overuse, or underuse of commas might interfere with the reader's understanding of a sentence. Too few commas might confuse the reader; too many can unduly interrupt the sentence's flow. Here's the guideline: Use the minimum number of commas needed to ensure that the reader will understand your point.

Your Facility with the English Language

To ensure a top score on your essay, strive to convince the reader that you possess a strong command of the English language—in other words, that you can use the language correctly, clearly, and persuasively in writing. To show the reader the requisite linguistic prowess, try to do these three things:

1. Demonstrate a solid vocabulary.
2. Use proper idioms (especially prepositional phrases).
3. Use proper diction (word usage and choice).

NOTE

The GMAT word processor does not allow you to italicize or mark accents on foreign words. It's okay to leave them as is, but make sure they're commonly understood words.

Demonstrating a Solid Vocabulary

By all means, show the reader that you possess the vocabulary of a broadly educated individual and that you know how to use it. But keep the following five caveats in mind:

1. Don't overuse SAT-style words just to make an impression. Doing so will only serve to warn the reader that you're trying to mask poor content with window dressing.

2. Avoid obscure or archaic words that few readers are likely to know. The reader will not take time to consult an unabridged dictionary.

3. Avoid technical terminology that only specialists and scholars in a specific field understand. GMAT readers are typically English-language generalists from the academic fields of English and communications, not economic-policy analysts.

4. Use Latin and other non-English terms *very* sparingly. After all, one of the primary skills being tested through the GMAT essays is your facility with the *English* language. However, the occasional use of Latin terms and acronyms—for example, *per se, de facto, ad hoc,* and especially *i.e.* and *e.g.*—are perfectly acceptable. Non-English words used commonly in academic writing—such as *vis-à-vis, caveat,* and *laissez faire*—are acceptable as well. Again, just don't overdo it.

5. Avoid colloquialisms (slang and vernacular).

Your Diction and Use of Idioms

In evaluating essays, GMAT readers also take into account your diction and use of idioms—again, especially when problems in these areas interfere with the readers' understanding of the meaning. In this section, you'll learn tips for avoiding, or at least minimizing, diction and idiom errors in your essay.

Diction (Word Choice and Usage)

Diction refers to word choice and the manner in which you use the word. For instance, you might confuse one word with another because they look or sound similar, or you may choose a word that doesn't accurately convey your idea. Here's an example of each type of diction error:

Word choice error:

The best way to *impede* employees to improve their productivity is to allow them to determine for themselves the most efficient way of performing their individual job tasks.

(The word *impede* means "to hinder or hamper." In the context of this sentence, *impede* should be replaced with a word such as *impel*, which means "propel or drive." The test-taker might have confused these two words.)

Word usage error:

Unless the department can supply a comparative cost-benefit analysis for the two alternative courses of action, I would remain *diffident* about following the department's recommendation.

(The word *diffident* means "reluctant, unwilling, or shy." A more appropriate word here would be ambivalent, which means "undecided or indecisive." Or perhaps the test-taker meant to use the word *indifferent* (thereby committing the first type of diction error).

What appear to be diction errors might, in many instances, be mere clerical (typing) errors. Accordingly, problems with your word choice and usage will adversely affect your scores only if they are obvious and occur frequently.

Idiom

An *idiom* is a distinctive (idiosyncratic) phrase that is considered proper or improper based on whether it has become acceptable over time, through repeated and common use. Here are two sentences, each of which contains an idiomatic prepositional phrase and another idiom.

The speaker's contention *flies in the face* of the empirical evidence and, *in any event,* runs contrary to common sense.

For all we know, last year was the only year in which the company earned a profit, in which case the vice president's advice might turn out especially poor in retrospect.

Tips for Avoiding Diction and Idiom Errors

Idioms don't rely on any particular rules of grammar; they are learned over time by experience. As you might suspect, the English language contains more idiomatic expressions than you can imagine. Moreover, the number of possible diction errors isn't limited to the number of entries in a comprehensive unabridged English dictionary. Although it is impossible in these pages to provide an adequate diction or idiom review, we can provide some guidelines to these aspects of your writing:

- If you're the least bit unsure about the meaning of a word you intend to use in your essay, don't use it. Why risk committing a diction blunder just to impress the reader with an erudite vocabulary? (And if you're not sure what "erudite" means, either find out or don't use it in your essays!)

- If a phrase sounds wrong to your ear, change it until it sounds correct to you.

- The fewer words you use, the less likely you'll commit an error in diction or idiom. So when in doubt, go with a relatively brief phrase that you still think conveys your point.

- If English is your second language, take heart: In evaluating and scoring your essay, GMAT readers take into account diction or idiom problems only to the extent that those problems interfere with understanding your sentence's intended meaning. As long as your writing is understandable to your EFL (English-as-first-language) friends, you don't need to worry.

If you have ample time before your exam and you think your diction and use of idioms could stand improvement, check for errors in your practice essays by consulting a reputable guidebook to English usage. Or you might consult a trusted professor, colleague, or acquaintance who has a firm grasp of the conventions of Standard Written English.

ADVANCED TECHNIQUES

As you know by now, although GMAT readers place less weight on writing style and mechanics than on content and organization, the way you write can affect your AWA score, especially if you've written an otherwise borderline essay that has the reader "on the fence" between two scores.

Earlier in the chapter, you learned some basic tips for style and mechanics. Here, we'll move on to more advanced techniques. We'll review the following:

- A variety of rhetorical devices that, if used appropriately and prudently, add persuasiveness to essays
- How to connect your ideas together with words and phrases that will help the reader follow your reasoning as you proceed from one point to the next
- The parlance of Critical Reasoning and how to use it properly
- How to refer to yourself, to the statement or Argument, and to the author of the statement or Argument

Developing a Persuasive Writing Style

To further ensure a high AWA score, you should try to use particular words and phrases that can be rhetorically effective. However, you should also avoid words and phrases that amount to so-called empty rhetoric. You can also use punctuation for rhetorical emphasis.

Rhetorical Words and Phrases by Functional Category

Here's a reference list of rhetorical words and phrases categorized by function. Some list items you encountered as underlined words and phrases in the examples throughout this book; others are new.

Use phrases such as these to subordinate an idea:

> although it might appear that, at first glance it would seem/appear that, admittedly

Use phrases such as these to argue for a position, thesis, or viewpoint:

> promotes, facilitates, provides a strong impetus, serves to, directly, furthers, accomplishes, achieves, demonstrates, suggests, indicates

Use phrases such as these to argue for a solution or direction based on public policy or some other normative basis:

> ultimate goal/objective/purpose, overriding, primary concern, subordinate, subsumed

Use phrases such as these to refute, rebut, or counter a proposition, theory, or viewpoint:

> however, closer scrutiny reveals, upon closer inspection/examination, a more thorough analysis, in reality, actually, when viewed more closely, when viewed from another perspective, further observation shows

Use phrases such as these to point out problems with a proposition, theory, or viewpoint:

> however, nevertheless, yet, still, despite, of course, serious drawbacks, problematic, counter-vailing factors

Use phrases such as these to argue against a position or viewpoint:

works against, undermines, thwarts, defeats, runs contrary to, fails to achieve/ promote/accomplish, is inconsistent with, impedes

Use phrases such as these to argue that the merits of one position outweigh those of another:

on balance, on the whole, all things considered, in the final analysis

Avoid Empty Rhetoric

Many test-takers try to mask weak ideas by relying on strong rhetoric. Be careful in using words and phrases such as these for emphasis:

clearly, absolutely, definitely, without a doubt, nobody could dispute that, extremely, positively, emphatically, unquestionably, certainly, undeniably, without reservation

It's okay to use them, but keep in mind that by themselves, they add absolutely no substance to your ideas. You must be certain that you have convincing reasons and/or examples to back up your rhetoric.

Using Punctuation for Rhetorical Emphasis

You can also use punctuation for rhetorical emphasis. Here are four suggestions (try them out during the Practice Tests in Part VII):

1 Use em-dashes (two hyphens or one hyphen preceded and followed by a space) in the middle of a sentence—instead of commas or parentheses—to set off particularly important parenthetical material (as in this sentence). You can also use an em-dash instead of a comma before a concluding phrase to help set off and emphasize what follows. But don't overuse the dash or it will lose its punch.

2 Use exclamation points for emphasis very sparingly. As in this paragraph, one per essay is plenty!

3 Sentences that pose questions can be a useful rhetorical device. Like short, abrupt sentences, rhetorical questions can help persuade the reader or at least help to make your point. They also add interest and variety. Yet how many test-takers think to incorporate them into their essays? Not many. (By the way, we just posed a rhetorical question.) Just be sure to provide an answer to your question. And don't overdo it; one rhetorical question per essay is plenty.

4 Avoid using UPPERCASE letters, asterisks (*), or similar devices to flag words you would emphasize in rhetorical speech. To get your point across, rely instead on your choice of words and phrases and your sentence construction.

Connecting Your Ideas

Your essays will not earn top scores unless your ideas flow naturally from one to the next, allowing the reader to easily follow your train of thought. To connect your ideas, develop your own arsenal of transition devices—words and phrases that serve as bridges between ideas—to convey your line of reasoning to the reader.

Each transition device should help the reader make certain connections or assumptions about the two areas that you are connecting. For example, some devices lead your reader forward and imply the building of an idea or thought, while others prompt the reader to compare ideas or draw conclusions from the preceding thoughts.

Here's a reference list that includes many of those devices—by functional category.

To signal addition:

and, again, and then, equally important, finally, further, furthermore, nor, too, next, lastly, what's more, in addition

To connect ideas:

furthermore, in addition, also, [first, second . . .], moreover, most important/significantly, consequently, simultaneously, concurrently, next, finally

To signal comparison or contrast:

but, although, conversely, in contrast, on the other hand, whereas, except, by comparison, where, compared to, weighed against, vis-à-vis, while, meanwhile

To signal proof:

because, for, since, for the same reason, obviously, evidently, furthermore, moreover, indeed, in fact, in addition, in any case, that is

To signal exception:

yet, still, however, nevertheless, in spite of, despite, of course, occasionally, sometimes, in rare instances, infrequently

To signal sequence (chronological, logical, or rhetorical):

[first, second(ly), third(ly) . . .], next, then, now, at this point, after, in turn, subsequently, finally, consequently, previously, beforehand, simultaneously, concurrently

To signal examples:

for example, for instance, perhaps, consider, take the case of, to demonstrate, to illustrate, as an illustration, one possible scenario, in this case, in another case, on this occasion, in this situation

To signal your reasoning from premise to conclusion:

therefore, thus, hence, accordingly, as a result, it follows that, in turn

Use these phrases for your concluding or summary paragraph:

in sum, in the final analysis, in brief, summing up, in conclusion, to conclude, to recapitulate, in essence, in a nutshell

Using the Language of Critical Reasoning

You don't need to resort to the technical terminology of formal logic in your essays. However, you will need to use less technical words, such as "argument," "assumption," "conclusion," and possibly "premise" and "inference." Be sure you understand what these words mean and that you're using them correctly. Here are definitions and usage guidelines for these terms.

Argument: The process of reasoning from premises to conclusion

To describe a flawed argument, use adjectives such as *weak, poor, unsound, poorly reasoned, dubious, poorly supported,* and *problematic.*

To describe a good argument, use adjectives such as *strong, convincing, well reasoned,* and *well supported.*

You don't "prove an argument"; rather, you "prove an argument (to be) true." (However, the word "prove" implies deduction and should be used sparingly, if at all, in your Argument essay.)

Premise: A proposition helping to support an argument's conclusion

Use the words *premise* and *evidence* interchangeably to refer to stated information that is not in dispute.

Assumption: Something taken for granted to be true in the argument (Strictly speaking, assumptions are unstated, assumed premises.)

To describe an assumption, use adjectives such as unsupported, unsubstantiated, and unproven.

To describe a particularly bad assumption, use adjectives such as unlikely, poor, questionable, doubtful, dubious, and improbable.

To strengthen an argument, you substantiate an assumption (or show or demonstrate) that the assumption is true. (However, be careful in using the word "prove"; it is a strong word that implies deduction.)

Strictly speaking, an assumption is neither "true" nor "false," neither "correct" nor "incorrect." Also, you don't "prove an assumption."

Conclusion: A proposition derived by deduction or inference from the premises of an argument

To describe a poor conclusion, use adjectives such as indefensible, unjustified, unsupported, improbable, and weak.

To describe a good conclusion, use adjectives such as well-supported, proper, probable, well-justified, and strong.

Although you can "prove a conclusion" or "provide proof for a conclusion," again the word "proof" implies deduction. You're better off "supporting a conclusion" or "showing that the conclusion is probable."

Inference: The process of deriving from assumed premises (assumptions) either a strict conclusion or a conclusion that is to some degree probable

> You can describe an inference as poor, unjustified, improbable, or unlikely.

> You can also describe an inference as strong, justified, probable, or likely.

> You can "infer that . . .", but the phrase "infer a conclusion" is awkward.

Deduction: The process of reasoning in which the conclusion follows necessarily from the premises (Deduction is a specific kind of inference.)

References to Yourself and to the Argument

While writing your essays, you may occasionally need to refer to the Argument or its hypothetical source, whether a person or entity. You might also wish to refer to yourself from time to time. Here are some guidelines for handling these references.

Self-References

Self-references—singular and plural—are perfectly acceptable, though optional. Just be consistent.

> "I disagree with . . ."

> "In my view, . . ."

> "Without additional evidence, we cannot assume that . . ."

References to the Argument

In your Argument essay, try using "argument" to refer to the passage's line of reasoning as a whole or "recommendation" or "claim" to refer to specific conclusions.

References to the Source of the Argument

Be sure your references to an Argument's source are appropriate. The first time you refer to the source, be specific and correct—e.g., "this editorial," "the ad," "the vice president," or "ACME Shoes." If no specific source is provided, try using "author" or "argument."

ALERT!

GMAT Argument Analysis essays do not involve deduction, so avoid using any form of the word "deduction" in that essay.

Pronoun References to an Argument's Proponent

In your Argument essay, it's okay to save keystrokes by using an occasional pronoun. Just be sure that your pronouns are appropriate and consistent (he/she or neither):

"The speaker argues . . . *Her* line of reasoning is . . . but *she* overlooks."

"The manager cites . . . in support of *his* argument . . . *He* then recommends . . ."

"To strengthen *its* conclusion, the city council must . . . *It* must also . . ."

Also, be sure that your pronoun references are clear. Don't use a pronoun if it is separated from its antecedent (the noun that it describes) by one or more sentences.

Shorthand References to an Argument's Source and Evidence

It's perfectly acceptable to save keystrokes with shorthand names or acronyms in place of multiple-word proper nouns. If you use an acronym, be sure to identify it the first time you use it. For example:

In this Argument, the marketing director for Specialty Manufacturing (SM) recommends that SM discontinue its line of . . .

Quoting the Argument

Occasionally, it may be appropriate to quote key words or phrases from the Argument. For example, you may wish to point out to the reader a key phrase that is ambiguous or vague (e.g., "certain respondents") or a term that is overly inclusive or exclusive (e.g., "only" or "all"). Just keep the number of quoted words and phrases to a minimum. And remember: There's never any justification for quoting entire sentences.

> **NOTE**
>
> Readers don't care whether you use masculine, feminine, or gender-neutral terms in your essay, but be sure to keep it consistent. Alternating male and female examples and expressions might confuse the reader.

SUMMING IT UP

- The GMAT places less emphasis on writing style and mechanics than on content and organization—but these factors can influence the exam reader and affect your score if the way you write interferes with the reader's understanding of your ideas.

- Keep your overall tone and voice relatively formal, and try to vary sentence length.

- Work on writing as clearly and concisely as possible.

- If you feel as though you need to build your vocabulary to strengthen your essay writing, consult the Word List in Appendix C of this book.

- Watch your diction and use of idioms; make sure whatever you write is commonly understood.

- For stronger essays, use the tools of rhetoric, such as irony, punctuation, and effective key words and phrases; connect your ideas with transitional words or phrases; and apply the language of critical reasoning in your writing.

PART IV

GMAT INTEGRATED REASONING SECTION

CHAPTER 6   Integrated Reasoning

Integrated Reasoning

OVERVIEW

- The 3-step plan for graphics interpretation and table analysis questions
- The 3-step plan for multi-source reasoning questions
- The 4-step plan for two-part analysis questions
- Keys for answering integrated reasoning questions successfully
- Summing it up

You'll work with four different question formats in the GMAT's Integrated Reasoning section: table analysis, graphics interpretation, multi-source reasoning, and two-part analysis. In this chapter, you'll learn step-by-step approaches for handling all four types of questions and also strategies for applying the approaches.

In order to succeed in the Integrated Reasoning section, you will need to be familiar with these four question types. This book has many opportunities for practice so you can become fluent in recognizing and answering these new formats.

Next, you need to be confident about the content. Luckily, although the Integrated Reasoning section and some of the question formats may be new to you, the content itself is not. You may be surprised to see that the content references not only quantitative skills, but also the same skills you need to answer questions in the Reading Comprehension and Critical Reasoning sections of the test. Be sure to review statistics, percents, algebraic expressions, probability, inferences, assumptions, and the strengthening and weakening of arguments in the relevant chapters of this book.

Finally, you need to use an approach to answering these questions that has proven successful for test-takers on a variety of standardized tests. In this chapter, you'll review this approach, with which you're probably already familiar:

- Read the prompt and get the big picture—but ignore some of the details.
- Read the questions and hone in on those particular details that you need to answer the question.
- Answer the questions.

However, there are some fine differences from one question type to the next in the Integrated Reasoning section so it's important to break down each question type and look at its parts.

THE 3-STEP PLAN FOR GRAPHICS INTERPRETATION AND TABLE ANALYSIS QUESTIONS

The following 3-step plan will help you figure out answers to both the graphics interpretation and table analysis question formats.

Step One: Size Up the Prompt to Get the Big Picture

At this point, you're interested only in getting an overview of what the prompt and data are about.

- **Data:** In general terms, what data are presented in the table or graph? Read the title of the table or graph, read the column headings or axes labels, and glance at the body of the table or graph. What type of data (such as countries, companies, products, unit sales, and so on) is displayed?

- **Accompanying text:** Take note of any text above or below the table or graph. It's a good idea to read this text before you read the data on the table or graph because it will provide the context for the table or graph.

- **Numbers:** Are any numbers absolute values, percents, or ranks—or, what is likely, a mix of these?

- **Units:** Are they consistent from column to column or axis to axis, or not—for instance, does one column present information in meters, and another column present it in kilometers?

- **Details:** Ignore most of them! At this stage, you do not need to figure out exactly what information is in each cell or at each part of the graph. Much of the data will not be relevant to the questions, anyway—but of course, at this stage you do not know what is relevant and what is not. Only when you get to the questions should you scrutinize the appropriate parts of the table or graph in detail.

- **Extreme values:** That said, do take note of any values that are significantly different from the rest. For instance, does the graph spike or dip dramatically at some point? Is some value on the table much larger or smaller than the other values in its column? Make a quick mental note of any such extreme differences and move on.

Step Two: Size Up the Question

Consider the statements/questions one at a time, and determine the following:

- **Wording:** What exactly is the question asking? Be specific. For instance, do you have to determine whether a statement is true or false, or whether you can or cannot infer something?

- **Content:** What content is being tested? Are you looking for a probability, a percent change, a positive or negative correlation, an average or median, or something else such as the weakness or strength of an argument? What rules or formulas are likely to come into play?

- **Location on graph/table:** Where should you look in order to get to the answer? If the graph presents unit sales over a twelve-month period, which months are the relevant ones? If a table presents school rankings across different categories, on which schools or categories should you focus?

- **Sorting:** For tables, what is the best way to sort the data in order to get the answer in the safest and fastest way?

Step Three: Answer the Question

Now, it's time to put the information together and answer the question or questions related to the table or graph.

- **Noteboard or calculator:** Since a calculator is available to you, take advantage of it for any complicated calculations. However, do not always resort to the calculator: Certain calculations may be easy to simplify and solve quickly on your noteboard.

- **Shortcuts:** Are there any? Think of any shortcuts you picked up in your GMAT Quantitative practice, such as plugging in "100" as the starting value in a percent change question in order to simplify the calculations. Additionally, there may be an Integrated Reasoning–specific shortcut available. For instance, if a table lists certain entities by rank, and if all of the top 25 entities are listed, then you do not need to count them one by one to know there are twenty-five of them (in order to find, say, the median). Be careful, however: a GMAT table may give you only some of the top-ranked entries.

- **Estimation and Rounding:** Table Analysis questions give you precise data, and often ask for precise answers. In those cases, it's best to perform all calculations first and round in the end, if necessary. Since you are able to use a calculator, these calculations are not difficult to perform. On the other hand, on Graphics Interpretation questions you may or may not be able to discern specific values—that will depend, for instance, on how fine the scale of the x- and y-axis is. If a graph gives a general idea rather than specific values, you may be able to estimate and save time.

- **Double-check your result:** Check for any careless mistakes. Did you select the "Yes" column when you meant to choose "No"? Did you calculate the answer by looking at the wrong column of the table?

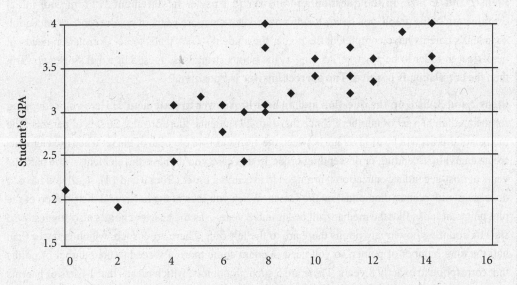

Number of Years of Parents' Post-Secondary Education

For each of 26 students in a high school class, the chart above shows the student's grade point average and the number of combined years of post-secondary education (college, graduate school, etc.) that this student's parents have completed.

NOTE

At this point on the GMAT, you will not see the answer choices in a bulleted list, but as items in a drop-down menu, which is placed to align with the statements. Your task will be to select the menu item that best completes each statement. For the purposes of this book, however, the bulleted list is used for ease of presentation.

Based on the given information, use the drop-down menus to fill in the blanks in each of the following statements:

1. The correlation between the GPA of the students in the study and the number of years of post-secondary education that the students' parents completed is

   o positive

   o negligible

   o negative

2. The median number of years of post-secondary education the students' parents completed is

   o less than 8

   o 8

   o more than 8

Apply the 3-Step Plan

Step 1: Size up the prompt/graph and the accompanying text: The text tells you that you are looking at the GPA of students in a high school class, as well as the number of years of post-secondary education their parents completed. The data is presented in a scatterplot. The students' GPA varies from just under 2 to 4, and the number of years of post-secondary education that the parents have completed ranges from 0 to 14. The data suggests a rather regular trend from the lower left corner to the upper right corner of the graph. That is, there is a positive correlation between the two variables. Finally, note that for a majority of the cases, the students' parents have completed more than 4 years of post-secondary education.

Steps 2 and 3: Size up the question and answer it: Answer to statement 1: From your initial examination of the graph, you have already noticed that the more years of post-secondary education a student's parents have completed, the higher the student's GPA tends to be. Correlation need not be perfect in order to be positive: As long as the points strongly suggest a line that slopes upward, then the correlation is positive. **The correct answer is "positive."**

Steps 2 and 3: Size up the question and answer it: Answer to statement 2: Here you're looking for the median of a set of numbers. Since there are 26 students, there are also 26 sets of parents. The median of this set will be the average between the 13th and 14th element of the set when the elements are arranged in ascending or descending order. In this case you do have the elements—the parents' years of post-secondary education—arranged in ascending order (from 0 and 14), so all you have to do is count plot points (diamonds) on the screen. When you look at the horizontal distribution of the plot points, it looks like the median will be around 8 years—as the answer choices also suggest—so start by counting how many points there are to the left of 8. There are 9 such, which is fewer than half the total number of points; so you need to count some more. Proceed to the number of points that correspond to exactly 8 years. There are 5 such plot points, which means that 14 sets of parents (9 plus 5) had 8 years of post-secondary education or fewer. Most importantly, the 13th and 14th element of the set are both 8, so the median of the set is 8. **The correct answer is "8."**

Examples of Graphs

Here are some of the various types of graphs you are likely to see on the GMAT:

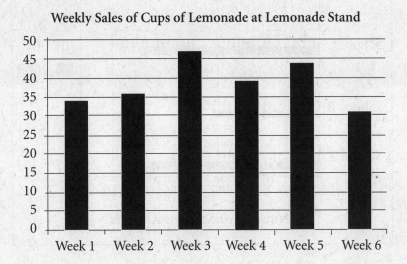

Bar Graph

- May be vertical (column) or horizontal (bar)
- The height of the column or length of the bar corresponds to the value of the entry (e.g., the number of cups of lemonade sold in a given week)

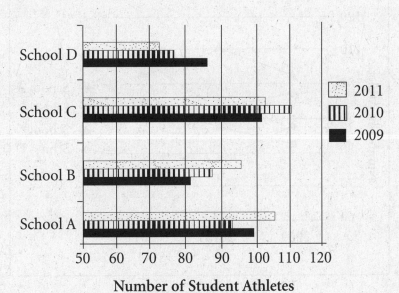

Stacked Bar Graph

- Displays multiple data points in a single column/bar
- Highlights the sum of each set of data points

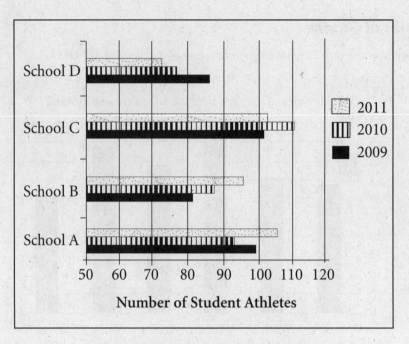

Clustered Column or Bar Graph

- Displays multiple data points in a single cluster
- Highlights comparisons within each cluster, as well as across clusters (e.g., the comparison of the number of athletes at the same school from one year to the next, as well as at different schools, whether in the same year or not)

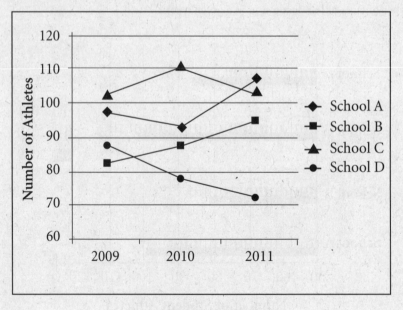

Line Graph

- Usually shows changes over time
- May include one or more lines to allow comparisons vertically (e.g., across schools on a given year) as well as horizontally (e.g., for the same school one year to the next

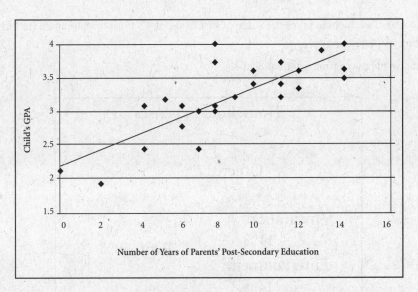

Scatterplot

- Each dot as a data point
- *x*- and *y*-coordinates for each data point
- May or may not include a trend (or "regression") line
- A trend line of positive slope means a positive correlation between the two variables (i.e., as one rises, the other rises, too)
- A trend line of negative slope means a negative correlation between the two variables (i.e., as one rises, the other falls)
- Sometimes no correlation between the variables

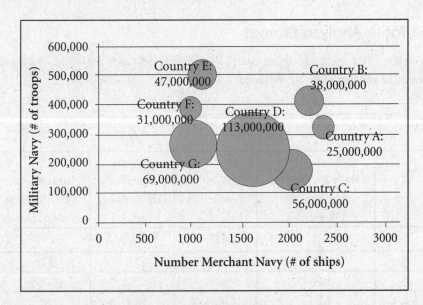

Bubble Graph

- Like a scatterplot, but includes a third measurement for each data point
- The center of each circle gives that data point's *x*- and *y*-coordinates

- The size of each circle gives the value of that data point's third measurement (in this case, the country's population)
- Data points may or may not have labels

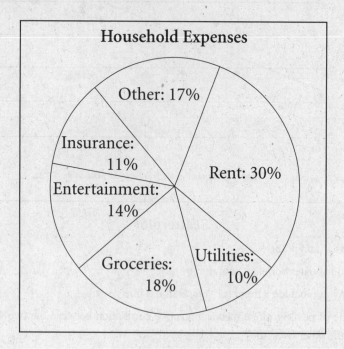

Pie Graph

- The full circle represents the whole (e.g., the entire household expenses, in this case)
- Each slice represents the size of each component part

Sample Table Analysis Prompt

The table displays data on the top fifteen crude oil-producing nations in the world. The data are from November, 2010, unless otherwise indicated

Sort By: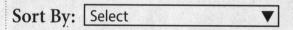

Country	Daily Production (millions of barrels)	Share of World Production as %	Proven Reserves (billions of barrels)	Daily exports to the U.S. (thousands of barrels)
Algeria	2.16	2.47%	12.2	262
Brazil	2.75	3.20%	12.8	271
Canada	3.70	4.30%	175.2	2,060
China	4.26	5.00%	20.4	8*
Iran	4.20	4.90%	137.6	0
Iraq	2.39	2.81%	115	336

Country	Daily Production (millions of barrels)	Share of World Production as %	Proven Reserves (billions of barrels)	Daily exports to the U.S. (thousands of barrels)
Kuwait	2.50	2.93%	101.5	125
Mexico	2.88	3.39%	10.4	1,220
Nigeria	2.51	2.95%	37.2	1,020
Norway	2.14	2.45%	6.7	35
Russia	9.91	11.60%	60	158
Saudi Arabia	10.30	12.10%	259.9	1,080
UAE	2.81	3.30%	97.8	10**
USA	8.85	10.40%	19.2	n/a
Venezuela	2.35	2.80%	99.4	825

* The data for China's Daily Exports to the U.S. are from December 2010

** The data for the UAE's Daily Exports to the U.S. are from September 2010

(Data are from the Energy Information Association)

For each of the following statements, select *Yes* if the statement can be shown to be true based on the information in the table. Otherwise, select *No*.

Yes	No	
○	○	The top six countries in terms of daily crude oil production accounted for more than half of the world's daily crude oil production.
○	○	No country exported to the United States more than half the crude oil that that country produced daily.
○	○	No country produced more crude oil daily relative to the amount of its own proven reserves than did the United States.

This is all the information you will see when you first land on this question. However, let's do one more thing before we examine the statements: For illustration purposes, let's see what the table looks like sorted by each of its other columns. (On the exam, of course, you should not sort and re-sort by each column head. You should use the sort function only as necessary in order to evaluate each statement.)

Sort By: Daily Production ▼

Country	Daily Production (millions of barrels)	Share of World Production as %	Proven Reserves (billions of barrels)	Daily exports to the U.S. (thousands of barrels)
Norway	2.14	2.45%	6.7	35
Algeria	2.16	2.47%	12.2	262
Venezuela	2.35	2.80%	99.4	825
Iraq	2.39	2.81%	115	336
Kuwait	2.50	2.93%	101.5	125
Nigeria	2.51	2.95%	37.2	1,020
Brazil	2.75	3.20%	12.8	271
UAE	2.81	3.30%	97.8	10**
Mexico	2.88	3.39%	10.4	1,220
Canada	3.70	4.30%	175.2	2,060
Iran	4.20	4.90%	137.6	0
China	4.26	5.00%	20.4	8*
USA	8.85	10.40%	19.2	n/a
Russia	9.91	11.60%	60	158
Saudi Arabia	10.30	12.10%	259.9	1,080

Sort By: [Shares of World Production ▼]

Country	Daily Production (millions of barrels)	Share of World Production as %	Proven Reserves (billions of barrels)	Daily exports to the U.S. (thousands of barrels)
Norway	2.14	2.45%	6.7	35
Algeria	2.16	2.47%	12.2	262
Venezuela	2.35	2.80%	99.4	825
Iraq	2.39	2.81%	115	336
Kuwait	2.50	2.93%	101.5	125
Nigeria	2.51	2.95%	37.2	1,020
Brazil	2.75	3.20%	12.8	271
UAE	2.81	3.30%	97.8	10**
Mexico	2.88	3.39%	10.4	1,220
Canada	3.70	4.30%	175.2	2,060
Iran	4.20	4.90%	137.6	0
China	4.26	5.00%	20.4	8*
USA	8.85	10.40%	19.2	n/a
Russia	9.91	11.60%	60	158
Saudi Arabia	10.30	12.10%	259.9	1,080

Sort By: | Proven Reserves   ▼ |

Country	Daily Production (millions of barrels)	Share of World Production as %	Proven Reserves (billions of barrels)	Daily exports to the U.S. (thousands of barrels)
Norway	2.14	2.45%	6.7	35
Algeria	2.16	2.47%	12.2	262
Venezuela	2.35	2.80%	99.4	825
Iraq	2.39	2.81%	115	336
Kuwait	2.50	2.93%	101.5	125
Nigeria	2.51	2.95%	37.2	1,020
Brazil	2.75	3.20%	12.8	271
UAE	2.81	3.30%	97.8	10**
Mexico	2.88	3.39%	10.4	1,220
Canada	3.70	4.30%	175.2	2,060
Iran	4.20	4.90%	137.6	0
China	4.26	5.00%	20.4	8*
USA	8.85	10.40%	19.2	n/a
Russia	9.91	11.60%	60	158
Saudi Arabia	10.30	12.10%	259.9	1,080

Sort By: | Daily Exports to the U.S. ▼ |

Country	Daily Production (millions of barrels)	Share of World Production as %	Proven Reserves (billions of barrels)	Daily exports to the U.S. (thousands of barrels)
Iran	4.20	4.90%	137.6	0
China	4.26	5.00%	20.4	8*
UAE	2.81	3.30%	97.8	10**
Norway	2.14	2.45%	6.7	35
Kuwait	2.50	2.93%	101.5	125
Russia	9.91	11.60%	60	158
Algeria	2.16	2.47%	12.2	262
Brazil	2.75	3.20%	12.8	271
Iraq	2.39	2.81%	115	336
Venezuela	2.35	2.80%	99.4	825
Nigeria	2.51	2.95%	37.2	1,020
Saudi Arabia	10.30	12.10%	259.9	1,080
Mexico	2.88	3.39%	10.4	1,220
Canada	3.70	4.30%	175.2	2,060
USA	8.85	10.40%	19.2	n/a

Apply the 3-Step Plan

Step 1: Size up the prompt/table and accompanying text: The table gives you data about the daily production, proven reserves, and exports to the United States of the top fifteen nations in terms of crude oil production. The default sorting of the data is alphabetical by country name—a sorting that will probably not be useful to you because it does not organize the figures in any meaningful way.

All columns feature absolute figures, except the "Share of World Production" column that lists the data by percents.

The units are not consistent among the columns: One column gives figures in thousands of barrels, another in millions, and a third in billions. These differences may come into play as you consider the statements.

Note also some extreme values. A few values in the "Exports" column are over 1,000, whereas most are in the low hundreds, or even lower, which means that a few countries, such as Canada and Mexico, export far more crude to the United States than do other countries. Also, in the "Daily Production" column, many entries are 2.xx range, whereas a few—such as Saudi Arabia's 10.30—are significantly larger. Once you have noted these easy-to-spot extreme values, don't waste more time poring over the numbers. Proceed to the statements.

Steps 2 and 3: Size up the question and answer it: Answer for statement 1: By default, the table is sorted alphabetically by "Country." Re-sort it by "Share of World Production in %" so you get the top six producers grouped together. Once you have done this, your job is simple: Add the percentages of these six countries (Saudi Arabia, Russia, USA, China, Iran, and Canada) to see whether the sum is greater than 50% or not:

$$12.10\% + 11.60\% + 10.40\% + 5.00\% + 4.90\% + 4.30\% = 48.30\%$$

The daily production of the top six crude oil producers falls short of 50% of the world's daily production. **The correct answer is "No."**

Steps 2 and 3: Size up the question and answer it: Answer for statement 2: You have to compare the "Daily Exports to the U.S." value for each country to the value of that country's "Daily Production," looking for any ratio of "Daily Exports" to "Daily Production" that is greater than $\frac{1}{2}$. For this task, you're not comparing values vertically along one column, but rather horizontally along the rows, so it's not imperative that you re-sort the data in one particular way. However, it is still helpful to keep the table sorted by the "Daily Production" column so you have one of the two sets of values involved in the comparison ordered neatly.

Because you're comparing, be sure to keep the units straight! The "Daily Production" and "Daily Exports to the U.S." figures are not given in the same units. The former are given in millions of barrels, whereas the latter are in thousands of barrels. Convert one of the two values into the other's units in order to compare correctly. For instance, in thousands of barrels, Norway's daily production is 2,140 thousand barrels, which is quite a bit more than twice the 35 thousand it exports to the United States. In fact, because all the countries on the list produce more than 2 million barrels daily, no country that exports to the United States fewer than 1 million barrels (that is, 1,000 thousand barrels) could possibly be one that exports to the United States more than half its daily production. You can easily eliminate all these countries, so you are left with only Nigeria, Mexico, Canada, and

Saudi Arabia. Canada's 2,060 thousand barrels exported daily to the United States are more than half of Canada's 3,700 thousand barrels produced daily, so there is at least one country that exports to the United States more than half its daily production. Thus, statement 2 is incorrect. **The correct answer is "No."**

Steps 2 and 3: Size up the question and answer it: Answer for statement 3: Here you have to compare the ratio of "Daily Production" to "Proven Reserves" for the United States to that ratio for each of the other countries. For the United States, this ratio is:

$$\frac{8.85 \text{ million}}{19.2 \text{ billion}} = \frac{8.85 \times 10^6}{19.2 \times 10^9} = 0.46 \times 10^{-3}$$

You do not need to actually calculate this ratio precisely for each of the other countries. While on many Integrated Reasoning questions you have to be precise and should not estimate, here is one case when it is safe to estimate. Why? Because the question does not ask you to provide an exact value, but rather to compare certain values to certain other values.

All countries produced barrels in the millions daily and had reserves in the billions. Thus, the ratio for all countries will look like the ratio for the United States: it will be in the form of $R \times 10^{-3}$. For the purposes of the comparison, you can ignore the 10^{-3} and estimate the various values of R. For the United States, R equals almost 0.5. A quick look at the table shows you that for most countries R is considerably smaller than 0.5 (e.g., for Saudi Arabia it is $\frac{10.3}{259.9}$, or approximately 0.04; and for Canada, it is $\frac{3.7}{175.2}$, or approximately 0.02). Scan through the table and look for a country whose

Daily Production (ignoring the unit—millions of barrels) is close to half its Proven Reserves (again ignoring the unit). The only country that comes close is Norway, and even then the ratio is closer to one-third rather than one-half ($\frac{2.14}{6.7}$). Thus, no country produces more crude oil daily relative to the amount of its own proven reserves than does the United States. **The correct answer is Yes.**

THE 3-STEP PLAN FOR MULTI-SOURCE REASONING QUESTIONS

As the name implies, these questions are based on more than one source of data or information. The prompt may be a table and a graph, two graphs, or like the example below, exposition. For multi-source reasoning questions, you will need your critical thinking skills, but you may also need certain quantitative and reading comprehension skills, because reading and quantitative content are often integrated in the same prompt.

Step One: Size Up the Prompt to Get the Big Picture

Content: What's under each tab? How does each tab relate to the other(s)? For instance, is this a point/counterpoint by two authors on a certain topic? An e-mail exchange? Perhaps a scientific analysis accompanied by a table or graph? Read "interactively," that is, identify the main idea of the passage or passages and keep track of the way information is organized. Look for structural clues, such as "furthermore," "in contrast," "therefore," "consequently," and so on. (Check out the Reading Comprehension chapter in this book for more about such clues.)

Data, numbers and units: Examine in general terms any tables or graphs in the prompt as you would in a table analysis or graphics interpretation prompt (see the 3-Step Plan earlier). Do not forget about any text above or below the table or graph.

Details: At this stage, don't try to retain in detail each example or table entry.

Step Two: Size Up the Question

Question format: Multi-source reasoning questions are of two types: either traditional multiple choice, with five answer choices only one of which is correct, or of the new format, in which you are given three statements and you must make a "yes or no" choice for each.

Wording: What exactly is the question asking? Be specific. For instance, do you have to determine whether a statement is true or false, whether you can or cannot infer something, or whether two different authors or organizations agree or disagree with certain statements?

Location: Which tab(s), paragraph(s), graph(s), or table(s) hold the relevant information? You may have to look in more than one place—that is, you may have to combine information from multiple tabs to determine the information. Incidentally, you won't be able to re-sort any tables included here—but you won't need to, either.

Content: What content areas are being tested? Are you strictly in Verbal-land, or are there also Quantitative topics involved? If so, what rules or formulas are likely to come into play?

Step Three: Answer the Question

Location: Go to the appropriate source(s)—graph(s), tab(s), or table(s)—and locate the necessary information.

Shortcuts: Are there any? On traditional multiple-choice questions, can you use the answer choices to your advantage—for instance, by working backwards? Can you plug in numbers to help you reach the right answer quickly?

Scratch pad and calculator: Use them if necessary. Do not try to set up any complicated equations or perform complex calculations in your head. But remember that sometimes, you don't need to actually calculate the answer. Estimating can be enough to get to the right answer.

Double-check your answer: Check for any careless mistakes. Did you select the "Yes" column when you meant to choose "No"? Did you calculate the answer by looking at the wrong column of the table? Make sure you did not fall for a "trap" answer in a traditional multiple-choice question.

Sample Multi-Source Reasoning Prompt

First Analyst	Second Analyst

The Widget world has grown from a niche interest of teenage and college boys to a multi-billion dollar industry attracting men and women of all ages. In particular, Next Widget Corporation has had great success, increasing its revenues almost threefold over the past decade, and boasting six of the ten most popular products in the market.

Yet investors have become jittery recently, fearing that widget sales will decline—as gizmo sales did last year—and knocked Next Widget's stock price down 33% from its peak of $113.17 in late 2011. These fears are misguided. Unlike the gizmo industry, the widget industry should continue to grow, as more consumers switch from higher-priced Gizmos to more affordable Widgets. Next Widget should also get a boost in revenues from its upcoming expansion into South America.

For now, Next Widget's stock remains a buy.

First Analyst	Second Analyst

Next Widget's stock has skyrocketed over the past decade, reaching its all-time high of $113.17 per share on December 19, 2011—a 415% increase over its initial public offering share price in 2002—as the company's revenues increased from $570 million in 2002 to $1.62 billion in 2011.

This run cannot continue. The revenue gains came mostly prior to 2009: The increases in the company's top line of $210 million and $193 million in 2010 and 2011, respectively, were the smallest of the past decade. This trend is likely to continue in 2012, at least in the domestic market, given increased competition from the up-and-coming Widgitainers, Inc.

Furthermore, Next Widget's planned expansion into South America may be trickier than expected. Even if successful in the long term, it will certainly contribute a loss in the near term, thus putting a strain on the company's operating margins.

Now is a good time to sell your Next Widget stock.

1. For each of the following statements, select *Inferable* if the statement is reasonably inferable from the information provided. Otherwise, select *Not inferable*.

Inferable	Not inferable	
○	○	The first analyst expects that Next Widget will make a profit in South America in the coming year.
○	○	The second analyst expects that Widgitainers' share price will increase in 2012.
○	○	The second analyst expects that Next Widget's profits will not increase by more than $193 million in 2012.

2. On the day of the first analyst's report, Next Widget's stock price was approximately what percent of its stock price at its initial public offering?
   (A) 245%
   (B) 278%
   (C) 345%
   (D) 382%
   (E) 482%

Apply the 3-Step Plan: Question 1

Step 1: Begin with the big picture. This prompt presents two sources of information, reports by two analysts about the company Next Widget. The first analyst believes the company's stock is worth buying, whereas the second one disagrees. The first analyst supports his opinion by saying that Next Widget is a very successful company, has many popular products, and should increase its revenues due to its expansion in South America. The analyst also expects that the widget industry in general stands to gain from softness in the gizmo industry. Note also the figures: the share price is down in 2012, having reached its high late in 2011. (Don't worry about the exact numbers at this stage; just take note that they're there, and you can come back to them if you need to when you look at the questions.)

The second analyst acknowledges that Next Widget has been very successful to date, but sees reason for concern. In support of her argument, she cites the declining rate of increase in the company's revenues in 2010 and 2011 and increased domestic competition from another company. She is also not enthusiastic about the South American expansion, forecasting a loss at first for the company. This analyst quotes more figures than the first one. In addition to the declining rate of revenue increase, she also mentions the percent increase in the share price since the IPO and quotes the same high price as the one the first analyst mentions. Make a mental note and move on to the first question.

Step 2: Size up the question. This is a yes/no question asking you to determine whether you can infer certain statements based on the two analyst reports. The statements appear to be self-contained to one tab per statement: that is, in this case you need to look only in the first tab for statements referring to the first analyst, and only in the second tab for statements referring to the second analyst.

NOTE

You are likely to see such a mix of question formats in multi-source reasoning prompts on the GMAT.

Step 3: Answer the question: Answer for Statement 1: Does the first analyst say anything about profits in South America? No, he expects a boost in revenues, but that's about it. Therefore, you cannot infer that he expects Next Widget to make a profit in South America in the coming year. **The correct answer is "Not inferable."**

Step 3: Answer the question: Answer for Statement 2: The second analyst mentions Widgitainers as an up-and-coming company that should give Next Widget increased competition in the future. However, the analyst makes no mention of Widgitainers' stock. **The correct answer is "Not inferable."**

Step 3: Answer the question: Answer for Statement 3: The second analyst says that Next Widget's revenue increases of $210 million in 2010 and $193 million in 2011 were the smallest of the past decade, and that this trend will likely continue in 2012. What trend is this? If these two figures were the smallest in a decade, then the revenue increase in 2009 must have been greater than (or possibly equal to) the revenue increase in 2010. Furthermore, the revenue increase in 2011 is smaller than that in 2010, so the trend the analyst mentions is that of a declining rate of revenue increase at least for the years 2009–2011. She expects this trend to continue, so she believes Next Widget will either not increase its revenues in 2012, or it will increase them by less than (or at least no more than) the 2011 figure: $193 million. **The correct answer is "Inferable."**

Apply the 3-Step Plan: Question 2

Steps 1 and 2: Size up the prompt/question: Whereas the first question was based on an analysis of written information, this question is quantitative and a traditional multiple-choice question, like all the problem-solving questions in the Quantitative section of the GMAT. Finally, you will need to consult both tabs in order to answer this question correctly.

Both analysts mention the $113.17 share price in late 2011 as the all-time high price the stock has reached. The second analyst says that this price is 415% higher than the initial public offering (IPO) price, while the first analyst says that the share price has dropped by 33% since reaching $113.17. You're in Percent Change-land here, and even though you're given an absolute value ($113.17), you should ignore it for the purpose of answering this question. It's true that based on the stock's all-time high price you can calculate its IPO price and its price at the time of the first analyst's report (let's call this the current price), and then find what percent of the IPO price is the current price—but that would be unnecessarily complicated. You're only looking for a percent change, not actual values.

Step 3: Answer the question: Let the IPO price be 100. Then, since the all-time high price is 415% higher than the IPO price, the all-time high price is $515. The current price is 33% lower than $515, so it is 67% of $515:

$$67\% \times 515 = \frac{67}{100} \times 515 = 345$$

So the current price of (approximately) 345 is (approximately) 345% of the IPO price of 100. **The correct answer is (C).**

THE 4-STEP PLAN FOR TWO-PART ANALYSIS QUESTIONS

Two-Part Analysis may test quantitative, critical thinking, and/or reading comprehension skills.

Step One: Preview the Task at Hand

Often, though not always, it helps to read the last sentence of the prompt—the one that describes the task you have to perform—and the answer choices—the statements in the table and the table's column headings—in order to orient yourself. For instance, if you see numbers or variables in the answer choices, you are looking at a quantitative question. If you see "Strengthen" and "Weaken" in the column headings, you are in the world of critical thinking. Sometimes, however, you may not be able to make much sense by reading just the last sentence and perusing the table with the answer choices. If so, don't worry! All will become clear once you've read the full prompt. In any event, be quick at this stage. Do not spend too much time looking at numbers or trying to understand fully the situation just by reading the last sentence of the prompt.

Step Two: Read the Prompt

Read the entire prompt to get a complete view of the situation. Use what you learned when you previewed the task to help you focus your examination of the prompt.

Step Three: Examine the Task in Details

Wording: In order to understand precisely what you have to do, reread carefully the task you have to perform as well as the answer choices and column headings.

Content: Confirm what content areas are being tested. If this is a quantitative prompt, what rules or formulas are likely to come into play? Are you looking for absolute values, percents, or expressions with variables? Do you have to set up any equations?

Dependent tasks: Recognize whether the tasks you have to perform are dependent on, or independent of, each other. On some two-part analysis prompts, the correct answer in each column will be dependent on the correct answer in the other column, while on other prompts the two correct answers will stand on their own, independent of each other.

Step Four: Answer the Question

Solve and verify: If the question is quantitative, solve and then look for your answer among the answer choices. If the tasks are independent of each other, work on them one at a time.

Read the answer choices for the best choice: If the question is verbal, select the best statements, one for each column, among the answer choices.

Scratch pad and calculator: Use them if necessary. Do not try to set up any complicated equations or perform complex calculations in your head. But remember that you don't always need to use the calculator. Sometimes an estimate will be enough to find the right answer.

Do not work backward: Though you may be tempted to work backward from the answer choices, do not. You will end up testing many different combinations of answer choices, thus wasting too much time.

Double-check your result: Make sure you did not fall for a "trap" answer or make any careless errors. Did you mistakenly select in the "Strengthen" column the choice that best weakens the argument? Did you make exactly two selections, one in each column? Remember: the same answer choice may be correct in both columns.

Sample Two-Part Analysis Prompt

LightTheStage, a stage lighting equipment rental company, charges $\$x$ for the first four weeks that a lighting instrument is rented, and $\$y$ per week for each week after that. The company 1564 Theatre Group has budgeted $2,000 to spend on the rental of lighting instruments from LightTheStage for its upcoming production.

In the table, indicate which expression corresponds to the maximum number of weeks per instrument for which 1564 Theatre Group can rent 10 instruments given its budget, as well as which expression corresponds to the maximum number of instruments 1564 Theatre Group can rent for a total of 10 weeks per instrument given its budget. Make only two selections, one in each column.

Number of weeks per instrument	Number of instruments per week	Expression
○	○	$\dfrac{1,000}{2x + 3y}$
○	○	$\dfrac{2,000}{x + 6y}$
○	○	$\dfrac{2,000}{x + 9y}$
○	○	$\dfrac{4(50 + y - x)}{y}$
○	○	$\dfrac{200 + 4y - x}{y}$
○	○	$\dfrac{2000 + 4y - x}{y}$

Apply the 4-Step Plan

Step 1: Preview the task. A quick glance at the answer table tells you that this is a quantitative question. Additionally, all answer choices are algebraic expressions in x and y, so you will have to set up some sort of equation and solve for an unknown quantity.

NOTE

All parts of multi-part questions need to be correct to earn you credit.

Step 2: Read the prompt. You have a vendor, a customer, the customer's budget, and the vendor's rental prices. Two absolute values are given (the theater's lighting rental budget and the 4 weeks of the initial rental rate) and two variables for the two rental rates.

Circle back to the tasks you have to perform. Note that they are similar but independent of each other. You will have to set up two algebraic expressions, one for each column, and solve the first one for the number of weeks per instrument, and the second one for the number of instruments per week.

Step 3: Proceed to solving, one column at a time.

Column 1: Let W be the maximum number of weeks that 1564 Theatre Group rents each of the 10 instruments. Then $W - 4$ is the maximum number of weeks per instrument during which 1564 Theatre Group pays $\$y$ per instrument (since for the first 4 weeks it pays $\$x$ per instrument—and remember, that's $\$x$ in total for each instrument for the first 4 weeks, not $\$x$ per week). The total cost per instrument, then, is $x + y(W - 4)$. The theater company is renting 10 instruments, so its total cost is $10[x + y(W - 4)]$. Equate this expression to \$2,000 and solve for W:

$$10[x + y(W - 4)] = 2,000$$
$$x + y(W - 4) = 200$$
$$x + yW - 4y = 200$$
$$yW = 200 + 4y - x$$
$$W = \frac{200 + 4y - x}{y}$$

The correct answer is $\frac{200 + 4y - x}{y}$.

Column 2: Follow the same process you did for column 1. If 1564 Theatre Group is renting each instrument for 10 weeks, then it is paying $\$x$ for the first four weeks and $\$y$ per week for the remaining 6 weeks. Thus, it is paying $x + 6y$ in total for each instrument. Let I be the maximum number of instruments the theater company rents. Then, its total cost is $I(x + 6y)$. Equate this expression to \$2,000 and solve for I:

$$I(x + 6y) = 2,000$$
$$I = \frac{2,000}{x + 6y}$$

The correct answer is $\frac{2,000}{x + 6y}$.

KEYS FOR ANSWERING INTEGRATED REASONING QUESTIONS SUCCESSFULLY

So far, you have read, learned, and worked through strategies specific to each of the four formats you'll find on the Integrated Reasoning section of the GMAT. The following seven strategies are ones that you can and should apply to all the formats—and to any of the quantitative multiple-choice questions.

Use Your Time Wisely: Ignore Most of the Details

Integrated Reasoning questions will usually come with a plethora of data, most of which you will not need. Do not waste time reading over every last detail in the prompt—particularly in tables and graphs. So, while you're thinking of that 2.5-minute-per-prompt-average for the entire section, you may find you need less time than that for graphics interpretation or table analysis questions. That's good, because you may need more time for multi-source reasoning or two-part analysis questions! Wherever possible, avoid wasting time perusing details unnecessarily.

Guess If You Have To

If you've wrestled with a question for a while, but are still not sure about it, make an educated guess and move on. There's no penalty for wrong answers, so give yourself the chance to answer the next question, which may be more familiar to you.

Keep Figures and Units Straight

Do not confuse absolute values with percents or meters with kilometers. Always read carefully what the question is asking, and what data the prompt provides. Pay attention to the scales of axes, the headings of columns, and the accompanying text: Relevant information about figures may be found in all of those places.

Know When to Estimate and When to Calculate Precisely

The calculator can be your friend in this section, but it is not always needed. In general, on a table analysis question that asks for a precise value, you should calculate an exact answer, and not merely a ballpark one. On the other hand, if the question asks for a comparison among values, you may be able to estimate. For instance, if you need to compare 1.4 to the ratio of 1,396 over 257, you do not need to waste time performing the division. You just need to realize that the ratio will be far greater than 1.4.

Read Every Answer Choice in Its Entirety

Frequently, answer choices use language taken directly from the prompt. This does not make them correct, however! If you're asked to judge whether a statement is true or not based on the given information, do not assume that a statement is true because it mentions, say, a vase-painting process that's discussed in the prompt. Read fully each statement and weigh it carefully against the prompt so that you do not make any careless mistakes.

Review Relevant Quantitative and Verbal Content

Remember that the Integrated Reasoning section tests content from the same general pool that's also tested in the other sections of the GMAT. In particular, statistics, percents, algebraic expressions, probability, inferences, strengthening/weakening arguments, and assumptions appear frequently in integrated reasoning questions. Sharpen your skills in those areas to give yourself the best chance at a strong integrated reasoning score.

Double-Check Your Answers

. . . unless you're running out of time!

SUMMING IT UP

- Make sure you are familiar with the new question formats so that you can move quickly from one prompt/question to the next on test day.

- Integrated Reasoning is just a new way to test content that has been tested on the GMAT for years. This new section often combines quantitative, critical reasoning, and reading comprehension concepts in the same question.

- In general terms, you should approach all Integrated Reasoning questions in a similar way:

  o Read the prompt first, focusing on the big picture and ignoring the details.

  o Read the questions next and look for particular details that are relevant to each question. Ignoring all irrelevant details is particularly important. You are likely to see many numbers in tables or quantities plotted in graphs, but you should not waste valuable time trying to learn what each of them is.

  o Answer the questions.

- A calculator is available in this section, but not in the Quantitative section. That's okay because you may need it here, but you will not need it for the Quantitative section. Even in the Integrated Reasoning section, you may find it easier for some questions to estimate rather than work out equations.

- You'll also have a noteboard and a wet-erase pen for scratch paper.

- Graphs and charts are drawn accurately in the Integrated Reasoning section.

PART V

GMAT QUANTITATIVE SECTION

Problem Solving

OVERVIEW

- **The 5-step plan for problem solving**
- **Some advanced techniques**
- **Use common-sense "guesstimates" to narrow the field**
- **When to plug in numbers for variables**
- **When—and when not—to work backward from numerical answer choices**
- **Find the easiest route to the answer**
- **Search geometry figures for clues**
- **Sketch a geometry figure to solve a problem**
- **Plug in numbers for "defined operation" questions**
- **Keys to successful GMAT problem solving**
- **Summing it up**

In this chapter, you'll learn:

- A step-by-step approach to handling any Problem Solving question
- Keys for successfully tackling Problem Solving questions

To handle GMAT Problem Solving questions, you'll need to be well versed in the fundamental rules of arithmetic, algebra, and geometry. Your knowledge of these basics is, to a large extent, what's being tested. (That's what the math reviews in Chapters 9–11 are all about.)

But the test-makers are just as interested, if not more interested, in gauging your mental agility, flexibility, creativity, and efficiency in solving quantitative problems. More specifically, they design Problem Solving questions to help determine the following:

- Can you manipulate numbers with a certain end result already in mind?
- Can you see the dynamic relationships between numbers as you apply operations to them?
- Can you visualize geometric shapes and relationships between shapes?
- Can you devise unconventional solutions to conventional quantitative problems?
- Can you solve problems efficiently, by recognizing the easiest, quickest, or most reliable route to a solution?

chapter 7

This chapter will help give you the skills you need to answer "yes" to these questions. What follows might strike you as merely a series of tips, shortcuts, or secrets for GMAT Problem Solving. However, the skills you'll learn here are intrinsic to the test and, along with your knowledge of substantive rules of math, they're precisely what Problem Solving questions are designed to measure.

THE 5-STEP PLAN FOR PROBLEM SOLVING

The first task in this chapter is to learn the five basic steps for handling any GMAT Problem Solving question:

1. Size up the question.
2. Size up the answer choices.
3. Look for a shortcut.
4. Set up the problem and solve it.
5. Verify your response before moving on.

We'll apply this approach to three sample Problem Solving questions.

Step One: Size Up the Question

Read the question and then pause for a moment to ask yourself:

- What specific subject area is being covered?
- What rules and formulas are likely to come into play?
- How complex is this question? (How many steps are involved in solving it? Does it require setting up equations, or does it require merely a few quick calculations?)
- Do I have a clue, off the top of my head, how I would begin solving this problem?

Determine how much time you're willing to spend on the problem, if any. Recognizing a tough question when you see it may save you valuable time; if you don't have a clue, take a guess and move on.

Step Two: Size Up the Answer Choices

Before you attempt to solve the problem at hand, examine the answer choices. They can provide helpful clues about how to proceed in solving the problem and about what sort of solution you should be aiming for. Pay particular attention to the following.

Form

Are the answer choices expressed as percentages, fractions, or decimals? Ounces or pounds? Minutes or hours? If the answer choices are expressed as equations, are all variables together on one side of the equation? As you work through the problem, rewrite numbers and expressions in the same form as the answer choices.

Value

Are the answer choices extremely small valued numbers? Numbers between 1 and 10? Greater numbers? Negative or positive numbers? Do the answer choices vary widely in value or are their values clustered closely around an average? If all answer choices are tightly clustered in value, you can probably disregard decimal points and extraneous zeros in performing calculations. At the same time, however, you should be more careful about rounding off your figures where answer choices do not vary widely. Wide variation in value suggests that you can easily eliminate answer choices that don't correspond to the general value of numbers suggested by the question.

Other Distinctive Properties and Characteristics

Are the answer choices integers? Do they all include a variable? Does one or more include radicals (roots)? Exponents? Is there a particular term, expression, or number that they have in common?

Step Three: Look for a Shortcut

Before plunging headlong into a problem, ask yourself if there's a quick, intuitive way to get to the correct answer. If the solution is a numerical value, perhaps only one answer choice is in the right ballpark. Also, some questions can be solved intuitively, without resorting to equations and calculations. (You'll see how when we apply this step to our sample questions.)

Step Four: Set Up the Problem and Solve It

If your intuition fails you, grab your pencil and do whatever computations, algebra, or other procedures you need to do to solve the problem. Simple problems may require just a few quick calculations; complex algebra and geometry questions may require setting up and solving a series of equations.

Step Five: Verify Your Response Before Moving On

After solving the problem, if your solution does *not* appear among the answer choices, check your work—you obviously made at least one mistake. If your solution *does* appear among the choices, don't celebrate quite yet. Although there's a good chance your answer is correct, it's possible your answer is wrong and that the test-maker anticipated your error by including a "sucker" answer choice. (We'll look at examples of this type of answer choice in a little while.) So check the question to verify that your response corresponds to what the question calls for in value, expression, units of measure, and so forth. If it does, and you're confident that your work was careful and accurate, don't spend any more time checking your work. Confirm your response and move on to the next question.

Sample Questions

Question 1 is a word problem involving *changes in percent*. (Word problems account for about half of the Quantitative questions.)

1. If Susan drinks 10% of the juice from a 16-ounce bottle immediately before lunch and 20% of the remaining amount with lunch, approximately how many ounces of juice are left to drink after lunch?

    (A) 4.8

    (B) 5.5

    (C) 11.2

    (D) 11.5

    (E) 13.0

Question 2 involves the concept of *arithmetic mean* (simple average).

2. The average of 6 numbers is 19. When one of those numbers is removed, the average of the remaining 5 numbers is 21. What number was taken away?

    (A) 2

    (B) 8

    (C) 9

    (D) 11

    (E) 20

Question 3 is a somewhat more difficult Problem Solving question involving the concept of *proportion*.

3. If p pencils cost $2q$ dollars, how many pencils can you buy for c cents? [Tip: 1 dollar = 100 cents]

    (A) $\dfrac{pc}{2q}$

    (B) $\dfrac{pc}{200q}$

    (C) $\dfrac{50pc}{q}$

    (D) $\dfrac{2pq}{c}$

    (E) $200\,pcq$

Notice that in question 3, instead of performing a numerical computation, your task is to express a *computational process* in terms of letters. Expressions such as these are known as *literal expressions*, and they can be perplexing. On the GMAT, you'll probably find two or three of them among the 25–26 Problem Solving questions.

Apply the 5-Step Plan

Let's review the three sample questions one at a time using the 5-step plan you just learned.

Question 1

Question 1 is a relatively easy question. Approximately 80% of test-takers respond correctly to questions like this one. Here it is again:

1. If Susan drinks 10% of the juice from a 16-ounce bottle immediately before lunch and 20% of the remaining amount with lunch, approximately how many ounces of juice are left to drink after lunch?

   (A) 4.8
   (B) 5.5
   (C) 11.2
   (D) 11.5
   (E) 13.0

Step 1: This problem involves the concept of *percent*—more specifically, *percentage decrease.* The question is asking you to perform two computations—in sequence. (The result of the first computation is used to perform the second one.) Percent questions tend to be relatively simple. All that is involved here is a two-step computation.

Step 2: The five answer choices in this question provide two useful clues:

❶ Notice that they range in value from 4.8 to 13.0. That's a broad spectrum, isn't it? But what general value should we be looking for in a correct answer to this question? Without crunching any numbers, it's clear that most of the juice will still remain in the bottle, even after lunch. So you're looking for a value much closer to 13 than to 4. Eliminate choices (A) and (B).

❷ Notice that each answer choice is carried to exactly one decimal place, and that the question asks for an *approximate* value. These two features are clues that you can probably round off your calculations to the nearest "tenth" as you go.

Step 3: You already eliminated choices (A) and (B) in Step 1. But if you're on your toes, you can eliminate all but the correct answer without resorting to precise calculations. Look at the question from a broader perspective. If you subtract 10% from a number, then 20% from the result, that adds up to a *bit less* than a 30% decrease from the original number. Thirty percent of 16 ounces is 4.8 ounces. So the solution must be a number that is a bit greater than 11.2 (16 − 4.8). Answer choice (D), 11.5, is the only choice that works.

Step 4: If your intuition fails you, work out the problem. First, determine 10% of 16, then subtract that number from 16:

$16 \times 0.1 = 1.6$

$16 - 1.6 = 14.4$

Susan now has 14.4 ounces of juice. Now perform the second step. Determine 20% of 14.4, then subtract that number from 14.4:

$$14.4 \times 0.2 = 2.88$$

Round off 2.88 to the nearest tenth: 2.9

$$14.4 - 2.9 = 11.5$$

Step 5: The decimal number 11.5 is indeed among the answer choices. Before moving on, however, ask yourself whether your solution makes sense—in this case, whether the value of our number (11.5) "fits" what the question asks for. If you performed Step 2, you should already realize that 11.5 is in the right ballpark. If you're confident that your calculations were careful and accurate, confirm choice (D), and move on to the next question. **The correct answer is (D).**

Question 2

Question 2 is average in difficulty. Approximately 60% of test-takers respond correctly to questions like it. Here's the question again:

2. The average of 6 numbers is 19. When one of those numbers is removed, the average of the remaining 5 numbers is 21. What number was taken away?

   (A) 2
   (B) 8
   (C) 9
   (D) 11
   (E) 20

Step 1: This problem involves the concept of *arithmetic mean* (simple average). To handle this question, you need to be familiar with the formula for calculating the average of a series of numbers. But notice that the question does not ask for the average, but rather for one of the numbers in the series. This curveball makes the question a bit tougher than most arithmetic mean problems.

Step 2: Take a quick look at the answer choices for clues. Notice that the middle three are clustered closely together in value. So take a closer look at the two aberrations: choices (A) and (E). Choice (A) would be the correct answer to the question: "What is the difference between 19 and 21?" But this question is asking something entirely different, so you can probably rule out (A) as a sucker bait answer choice. Choice (E) might also be a sucker choice, since 20 is simply 19 + 21 divided by 2. If this solution strikes you as too simple, you've got good instincts! The correct answer is probably either choice (B), (C), or (D). If you're pressed for time, guess one of these, and move on to the next question. Otherwise, go to Step 3.

Step 3: If you're on your toes, you might recognize a shortcut here. You can solve this problem quickly by simply comparing the two sums. Before the sixth number is taken away, the sum of the numbers is 114 (6 × 19). After removing the sixth number, the sum of the remaining numbers is 105 (5 × 21). The difference between the two sums is 9, which must be the value of the number removed.

Step 4: If you don't see a shortcut, here's how to solve this problem conventionally. The formula for arithmetic mean (simple average) can be expressed this way: $AM = \dfrac{\text{sum of terms in the set}}{\text{number of terms in the set}}$

In the question, you started with six terms. Let a through f equal those six terms:

$$19 = \frac{a+b+c+d+e+f}{6}$$

$$114 = a+b+c+d+e+f$$

$$f = 114 - (a+b+c+d+e)$$

Letting f = the number removed, here's the arithmetic mean formula, applied to the remaining five numbers:

$$21 = \frac{a+b+c+d+e}{5}$$

$$105 = a+b+c+d+e$$

Substitute 105 for $(a+b+c+d+e)$ in the first equation:

$$f = 114 - 105$$

$$f = 9$$

Step 5: If you have time, check to make sure you got the formula right, and check your calculations. Also make sure you didn't inadvertently switch the numbers 19 and 21 in your equations. (It's remarkably easy to commit this careless error under time pressure!) If you're satisfied that your analysis is accurate, confirm your answer and move on to the next question. **The correct answer is (C).**

Question 3

Question 3 is moderately difficult. Approximately 50% of test-takers respond correctly to questions like it. Here's the question again:.

3. If p pencils cost $2q$ dollars, how many pencils can you buy for c cents? [Tip: 1 dollar = 100 cents]

    (A) $\dfrac{pc}{2q}$

    (B) $\dfrac{pc}{200q}$

    (C) $\dfrac{50pc}{q}$

    (D) $\dfrac{2pq}{c}$

    (E) $200\,pcq$

Step 1: The first step is to recognize that this question involves a literal expression. Although it probably won't be too time-consuming, it may be a bit confusing. You should also recognize that

> **ALERT!**
>
> Careless errors, such as switching two numbers in a problem, is by far the leading cause of incorrect GMAT responses.

the key to this question is the concept of proportion. It might be appropriate to set up an equation to solve for *x*. Along the way, expect to convert dollars into cents.

Step 2: The five answer choices provide a couple of useful clues:

- Notice that each answer choice includes all three letters (*p*, *q*, and *c*). So the solution you're shooting for must also include all three letters.

- Notice that every answer choice but (E) is a fraction. So anticipate building a fraction to solve the problem algebraically.

Step 3: Is there any way to answer this question besides setting up an algebraic equation? Yes. In fact, there are two ways. One is to use easy numbers for the three variables—for example, $p = 2$, $q = 1$, and $c = 100$. These simple numbers make the question easy to work with: "If 2 pencils cost 2 dollars, how many pencils can you buy for 100 cents?" Obviously, the answer to this question is 1, so you can plug the numbers into each answer choice to see which choice provides an expression that equals 1. Only choice (B) fits the bill:

$$\frac{(2)(100)}{(200)(1)} = 1$$

Another way to shortcut the algebra is to apply some intuition to this question. If you strip away the pencils, *p*'s, *q*'s and *c*'s, in a very general sense the question is asking:

"If you can buy an item for a dollar, how many can you buy for one *cent*?"

Since one cent (a penny) is $\frac{1}{100}$ of a dollar, you can buy $\frac{1}{100}$ of one item for a cent. So you're probably looking for a fractional answer with a large number such as 100 in the denominator (as opposed to a number such as 2, 3, or 6). Answer choice (B) is the only choice that appears to be in the correct ballpark. Choice (B) is indeed the correct answer.

Step 4: You can also answer the question in a conventional manner using algebra. (This is easier said than done.) Here's how to approach it:

❶ Express 2*q* dollars as 200*q* cents (1 dollar = 100 cents).

❷ Let *x* equal the number of pencils you can buy for *c* cents.

❸ Think about the problem "verbally," then set up an equation and solve for *x:*

"*p* pencils is to 200*q* cents as *x* pencils is to *c* cents"

"The ratio of *p* to 200*q* is the same as the ratio of *x* to *c*" (in other words, the two ratios are proportionate)

Step 5: Our solution, $\frac{pc}{200q}$, is indeed among the answer choices. If you arrived at this solution using the conventional algebraic approach (Step 4), you can verify your solution by substituting simple numbers for the three variables (as we did in Step 3). Or if you arrived at your solution by plugging in numbers, you can check your work by plugging in a different set of numbers or by thinking about the problem conceptually (as in Step 3). Once you're confident you've chosen the correct expression among the five choices, confirm your choice, and then move on to the next question. **The correct answer is (B).**

SOME ADVANCED TECHNIQUES

Now let's take a look at some more advanced methods of Problem Solving. In this next section, you'll:

- Apply the success keys you learned earlier to more challenging Problem Solving questions.
- Learn additional success keys that apply to certain types of Problem Solving questions and apply these keys to example questions.

The first thing you'll want to do is scan the answer choices to see what all or most of them have in common, such as radical signs, exponents, factorable expressions, or fractions. Then try to formulate a solution that looks like the answer choices.

4. If $a \neq 0$ or 1, then $\dfrac{\frac{1}{a}}{2-\frac{2}{a}} =$

   (A) $\dfrac{1}{2a-2}$

   (B) $\dfrac{2}{a-2}$

   (C) $\dfrac{1}{a-2}$

   (D) $\dfrac{1}{a}$

   (E) $\dfrac{2}{2a-1}$

The correct answer is (A). Notice what all the answer choices have in common: Each one is a fraction in which the denominator contains the variable a, and no fractions appear in the numerator or denominator. That's a clue that your job is to manipulate the expression given in the question so that the result includes these features. First, place the denominator's two terms over the common denominator a. Then, divide a from the denominators of both the numerator fraction and the denominator fraction (this is a shortcut to multiplying the numerator fraction by the reciprocal of the denominator fraction):

$$\frac{\frac{1}{a}}{2-\frac{2}{a}} = \frac{\frac{1}{a}}{\frac{2a-2}{a}} = \frac{1}{2a-2}$$

USE COMMON-SENSE "GUESSTIMATES" TO NARROW THE FIELD

If the question asks for a numerical value, you can probably narrow the answer choices by estimating the value and type of number you're looking for. Use your common sense and real-world experience to formulate a rough estimate for word problems. However, don't expect to eliminate all answer choices except the correct one by using common sense alone.

5. A spinner containing seven equal regions numbered 1 through 7 is spun two times in a row. What is the probability that the first spin yields an odd number and the second spin yields an even number?

   (A) $\dfrac{2}{7}$

   (B) $\dfrac{12}{49}$

   (C) $\dfrac{5}{14}$

   (D) $\dfrac{1}{2}$

   (E) $\dfrac{4}{7}$

This problem involves the concept of probability. Common sense about basic probability should tell you that, with odds of close to 50% of spinning the desired type of number on each of the two spins, the odds of spinning such a number twice in a row should be less than 50%. So you can eliminate choices (D) and (E). Your odds of answering the question correctly are now 1 in 3. But notice that the remaining choices—(A), (B), and (C)—are closely grouped in value. Also notice that, in each of these remaining choices, the denominator contains the sort of number you could end up with when you apply a mathematical operation to the numbers given in the question.

Conclusion: You've probably reached the limits of applying common sense, and you'll need to solve the problem mathematically to find the correct choice. Here's how to do it. There are four odd numbers (1, 3, 5, and 7) and three even numbers (2, 4, and 6) on the spinner. So the chances of yielding an odd number with the first spin are 4 in 7, or $\dfrac{4}{7}$. The chances of yielding an even number with the second spin are 3 in 7, or $\dfrac{3}{7}$. To determine the probability of both events occurring, combine the two individual probabilities by multiplication:

$$\frac{4}{7} \times \frac{3}{7} = \frac{12}{49}$$

Notice the "sucker" answer choice in this question: Answer choice (D) provides the simple average of the two individual probabilities: $\dfrac{4}{7}$ and $\dfrac{3}{7}$. Aside from the fact that $\dfrac{1}{2}$, or 50%, is too high a probability from a common-sense viewpoint, choice (D) should strike you as too easy a solution to what appears to be a complex problem. **The correct answer is (B).**

WHEN TO PLUG IN NUMBERS FOR VARIABLES

If the answer choices contain variables (like x and y), the question might be a good candidate for the "plug-in" strategy. Pick simple numbers (so the math is easy) and substitute them for the variables. You'll definitely need your pencil for this strategy.

6. If a train travels $r + 2$ miles in h hours, which of the following represents the number of miles the train travels in 1 hour and 30 minutes?

(A) $\dfrac{3r+6}{2h}$

(B) $\dfrac{3r}{h+2}$

(C) $\dfrac{r+2}{h+3}$

(D) $\dfrac{r}{h+6}$

(E) $\dfrac{3}{2}(r+2)$

This is an algebraic word problem involving rate of motion (speed). You can solve this problem either conventionally or by using the plug-in strategy.

The conventional way: Notice that all of the answer choices contain fractions. This is a clue that you should try to create a fraction as you solve the problem. Here's how to do it. Given that the train travels $r + 2$ miles in h hours, you can express its rate in miles per hour as $\dfrac{r+2}{h}$. In $\dfrac{3}{2}$ hours, the train would travel this distance:

$$\left(\dfrac{3}{2}\right)\left(\dfrac{r+2}{h}\right) = \dfrac{3r+6}{2h}$$

The plug-in strategy: Let $r = 8$ and $h = 1$. Given these values, the train travels 10 miles $(8 + 2)$ in 1 hour. Obviously, in $1\dfrac{1}{2}$ hours the train will travel 15 miles. Start plugging these r and h values into the answer choices. You won't need to go any further than choice (A):

$$\dfrac{3r+6}{2h} = \dfrac{3(8)+6}{2(1)} = \dfrac{30}{2}, \text{ or } 15$$

Plugging the values into choice (E) also gives an answer of 15, but you should eliminate choice (E) because it omits h. Common sense should tell you that the correct answer must include both r and h. **The correct answer is (A).**

WHEN—AND WHEN NOT—TO WORK BACKWARD FROM NUMERICAL ANSWER CHOICES

If a Problem Solving question asks for a number value and if you draw a blank as far as how to set up and solve the problem, don't panic. You might be able to work backward by testing the answer choices, each one in turn.

7. A ball is dropped 192 inches above level ground, and after the third bounce, it rises to a height of 24 inches. If the height to which the ball rises after each bounce is always the same fraction of the height reached on its previous bounce, what is this fraction?

   (A) $\frac{1}{8}$

   (B) $\frac{1}{4}$

   (C) $\frac{1}{3}$

   (D) $\frac{1}{2}$

   (E) $\frac{2}{3}$

The fastest route to a solution is to plug in an answer. Try choice (C) and see what happens. If the ball bounces up $\frac{1}{3}$ as high as it started, then after the first bounce it will rise up $\frac{1}{3}$ as high as 192 inches, or 64 inches. After a second bounce, it will rise $\frac{1}{3}$ as high, or about 21 inches. But the problem states that the ball rises to 24 inches after the third bounce. Obviously, if the ball rises less than that after two bounces, it'll be way too low after three. So choice (C) cannot be the correct answer.

We can see that the ball must be bouncing higher than one third of the way; so the correct answer must be a greater fraction, either choice (D) or choice (E). You've already narrowed your odds to 50%. Try plugging in choice (D), and you'll see that it works: $\frac{1}{2}$ of 192 is 96; $\frac{1}{2}$ of 96 is 48; and $\frac{1}{2}$ of 48 is 24. **The correct answer is (D).**

Although it would be possible to develop a formula to answer the question, doing so would be senseless, considering how quickly and easily you can work backward from the answer choices.

Working backward from numerical answer choices works well when the numbers are easy and when few calculations are required, as in the preceding question. In other cases, however, applying algebra might be a better way.

8. How many pounds of nuts selling for 70 cents per pound must be mixed with 30 pounds of nuts selling at 90 cents per pound to make a mixture that sells for 85 cents per pound?

   (A) 10
   (B) 12
   (C) 15
   (D) 20
   (E) 24

Is the easiest route to the solution to test the answer choices? Let's see. First of all, calculate the total cost of 30 pounds of nuts at 90 cents per pound: $30 \times 0.90 = \$27$. Now, start with choice (C). Fifteen pounds of nuts at 70 cents per pound cost \$10.50. The total cost of this mixture is \$37.50, and the total weight is 45 pounds. Now you'll need to perform long division. The average weight of the mixture turns out to be between 83 and 84 cents—too small valued for the 85 cent average given in the question. At least you can eliminate choice (C).

You should realize by now that testing the answer choices might not be the most efficient way to tackle this question. Besides, there are ample opportunities for calculation errors. Instead, try solving this problem algebraically—by writing and solving an equation. Here's how to do it. The cost (in cents) of the nuts selling for 70 cents per pound can be expressed as $70x$, letting x equal the number that you're asked to determine. You then add this cost to the cost of the more expensive nuts ($30 \times 90 = 2700$) to obtain the total cost of the mixture, which you can express as $85(x + 30)$. You can state this algebraically and solve for x as follows:

$$70x + 2700 = 85(x + 30)$$
$$70x + 2700 = 85x + 2550$$
$$150 = 15x$$
$$10 = x$$

Ten pounds of 70-cents-per-pound nuts must be added in order to make a mixture that sells for 85 cents per pound. **The correct answer is (A).**

FIND THE EASIEST ROUTE TO THE ANSWER

If the question asks for an approximation, then you know that precise calculations won't be necessary and you can safely "round off the numbers" as you go. But even in other questions, you can sometimes eliminate all but the correct answer without resorting to precise calculations.

9. What is the difference between the sum of all positive odd integers less than 102 and the sum of all positive even integers less than 102?

   (A) 0
   (B) 1
   (C) 50
   (D) 51
   (E) 101

To see the pattern, compare the initial terms of each sequence:

   odd integers: $\{1,3,5, ..., 99,101\}$

   even integers: $\{2,4,6, ..., 100\}$

Notice that, for each successive term, the even integer is one more than the corresponding odd integer. There are a total of 50 corresponding integers, so the difference between the sums of all these corresponding integers is -50. But the odd-integer sequence includes one additional integer: 101. So the difference is $(-50 + 101)$, or 51. **The correct answer is (D).**

SEARCH GEOMETRY FIGURES FOR CLUES

Most geometry problems are accompanied by figures. The pieces of information a figure provides can lead you, step-by-step, to the answer.

10.

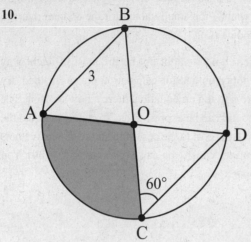

If O is the center of the circle in the figure above, what is the area of the shaded region, expressed in square units?

(A) $\dfrac{3}{2}$

(B) 2π

(C) $\dfrac{5}{2}$

(D) $\dfrac{8}{3}$

(E) 3π

This question asks for the area of a portion of the circle defined by a central angle. To answer the question, you'll need to determine the area of the entire circle as well as what percent (portion) of that area is shaded. This multi-step question is as complex as any you might encounter on the GMAT. But there's no need to panic; just start with what you know, then move step-by-step toward the answer. Mine the figure for a piece of information that might provide a starting point. $\triangle OCD$ is your first "stepping stone." Here are the steps to the answer:

Step 1: You know that $\overline{OC}$ and $\overline{OD}$ are congruent (equal in length) because each one is the circle's radius. In any triangle, angles opposite congruent sides are also congruent (the same size, or degree measure). Thus, $\angle OCD$ must measure 60°—just like $\angle OCD$.

Step 2: For any triangle, the sum of the measures of all three interior angles is 180°. Thus, $\angle COD$ measures 60°, just like the other two angles.

Step 3: Vertical angles created by two intersecting lines are congruent. Thus, $\angle AOB$ also measures 60°.

By the same reasoning as in Steps 1 and 2, each angle of $\triangle ABO$ measures 60°. Notice that the length of $\overline{AB}$ is given as 3. Accordingly, the length of each and every side of both triangles is 3.

Since this length (3) is also the circle's radius (the distance from its center to its circumference), you can determine the circle's area. The area of any circle is πr^2, where r is the circle's radius. Thus, the area of the circle is 9π.

Now determine what portion of the circle's area is shaded. The four angles formed at the circle's center (O) total 360°. You know that two of these angles account for 120°, or $\dfrac{1}{3}$ of those 360°. $\angle AOC$ is supplementary to $\angle DOC$; that is, the two angles combine to form a straight line, and so their measures total 180°. Therefore, $\angle AOC$ measures 120°. 120° is $\dfrac{1}{3}$ of 360°. Thus, the shaded portion accounts for $\dfrac{1}{3}$ the circle's area, or 3π.

If you look at the 60° angle in the figure, you might recognize right away that both triangles are equilateral and, extended out to their arcs, form two "pie slices," each one $\dfrac{1}{6}$ the size of the whole "pie" (the circle). What's left are two big slices, each of which is twice the size of a small slice. So the shaded area must account for $\dfrac{1}{3}$ of the circle's area. With this intuition, the problem is reduced to the simple mechanics of calculating the circle's area, then dividing it by 3. **The correct answer is (E).**

SKETCH A GEOMETRY FIGURE TO SOLVE A PROBLEM

A geometry problem that does not provide a diagram might cry out for one. That's your cue to take pencil to scratch paper and draw one yourself.

11. A rancher uses 64 feet of fencing to create a rectangular horse corral. If the ratio of the corral's length to width is 3:1, which of the following most closely approximates the minimum length of additional fencing needed to divide the rectangular corral into three triangular corrals, one of which is exactly twice the area of the other two?

   (A) 24 feet
   (B) 29 feet
   (C) 36 feet
   (D) 41 feet
   (E) 48 feet

Your first step is to determine the dimensions of the rectangular corral. Given a 3:1 length-to-width ratio, you can solve for the width (w) of the field using the perimeter formula:

$$2(3w) + 2(w) = 64$$
$$8w = 64$$
$$w = 8$$

Accordingly, the length of the rectangular corral is 24 feet. Next, determine how the rancher must configure the additional fencing to meet the stated criteria. This calls for a bit of sketching to help you visualize the dimensions. Only two possible configurations create three triangular corrals with the desired ratios:

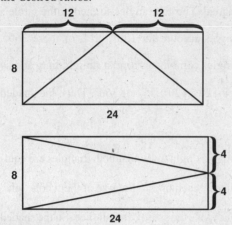

The top figure requires less fencing. You can determine this fact by calculating each length (using the Pythagorean theorem). Or you can use logic and visualization. Here's how. As a rectangle becomes flatter ("less square"), the shorter length approaches zero (0), at which point the minimum amount of fencing needed in the top configuration would decrease, approaching the length of the longer side. However, in the bottom design, the amount of fencing needed would increase, approaching twice the length of the longer side.

Your final step is to calculate the amount of fencing required by the top design, applying the theorem (let x = either length of cross-fencing):

$$8^2 + 12^2 = x^2$$
$$64 + 144 = x^2$$
$$208 = x^2$$
$$x = \sqrt{208} \approx 14.4$$

Thus, a minimum of approximately 28.8 feet of fencing is needed. Answer choice (B) approximates this solution.

Since the question asks for an approximation, it's a safe bet that estimating $\sqrt{208}$ to the nearest integer will suffice. If you learned your "times table," you know that $14 \times 14 = 196$, and $15 \times 15 = 225$. So $\sqrt{208}$ must be between 14 and 15. That's close enough to zero in on choice (B), which provides twice that estimate. **The correct answer is (B).**

PLUG IN NUMBERS FOR "DEFINED OPERATION" QUESTIONS

At least one of your 25–26 Problem Solving questions will probably be an example of what's called a "defined operation." These questions look weird and therefore might strike you as difficult. But they're really not. In fact, the math turns out to be ridiculously easy. What's being tested is your ability to understand what the problem requires and then to perform the simple arithmetical calculations—carefully!

12. Let ⟨a b c d⟩ be defined for all numbers a, b, c, and d by ⟨a b c d⟩ $= ac - bd$. If $x = $ ⟨5 4 2 1⟩,

what is the value of ⟨x 10 2 1⟩?

(A) 1
(B) 2
(C) 18
(D) 38
(E) 178

In defining the diamond-shaped figure as "$ac - bd$," the test-makers are saying that whenever you see four numbers in a diamond like this, you should plug them into the mathematical expression shown in the order given. The question itself then requires you to perform this simple task twice.

First, let's figure out the value of x. If x is the diamond labeled as x, then $a = 5$, $b = 4$, $c = 2$, and $d = 1$. Now, we plug those numbers into the equation given, and do the simple math:

$x = (5 \times 2) - (4 \times 1)$

$x = 10 - 4$

$x = 6$

Now, we tackle the second step. Having figured out the value of x, we can plug it into our second diamond, where $a = 6$, $b = 10$, $c = 2$, and $d = 1$. Again, plug in the numbers and do the math:

$(6 \times 2) - (10 \times 1) = 12 - 10 = 2$

The correct answer is (B).

As you can see, the math is very easy; the trick is understanding what the test-makers are doing, which is "defining" a new math operation and then carefully plugging in the numbers and working out the solution. With a little practice, you'll never get a "defined operation" question wrong.

KEYS TO SUCCESSFUL GMAT PROBLEM SOLVING

Here are some basic tips you should follow for any type of Problem Solving question. Apply these "keys" to the Practice Tests in Part VII, and then review them again just before exam day.

Narrow Down Answer Choices Up Front by Sizing Up the Question

If the question asks for a number value, you can probably narrow down the answer choices by estimating the value and type of number you're looking for. Use your common sense and real-world experience to formulate a "ballpark" estimate for word problems.

Question 1

You can narrow down answer choices by looking at the problem from a "common-sense" viewpoint. The five answer choices in this question provide some useful clues. Notice that they range in value from 4.8 to 13.0. That's a wide spectrum, isn't it? But what general value should you be looking for in a correct answer to this question? Without crunching any numbers, it's clear that most of the juice will still remain in the bottle, even after lunch. So you're looking for a value much closer to 13 than to 4. So you can safely eliminate (A) and (B).

Common Sense Can Sometimes Reveal the Right Answer

In many questions, you can eliminate all but the correct answer without resorting to precise calculations.

Question 1

Look at the question from a broader perspective. If you subtract 10% from a number, then 20% from the result, that adds up to a bit less than a 30% decrease from the original number. Thirty percent of 16 ounces is 4.8 ounces. So the solution must be a number that is a bit greater than 11.2 (16 − 4.8). Choice (D), 11.5, is the only choice that fits the bill!

Question 3

In Question 3, notice that we made c a much greater number than either p or q. Only a fraction with c in the numerator and a large number in the denominator (or vice versa) is likely to yield a quotient you're looking for. With this in mind, choice (B) jumps off the paper at you as the likely choice!

Scan the Answer Choices for Clues to Solving the Problem

Scan the answer choices to see what all or most of them have in common—such as radical signs, exponents, factorable expressions, or fractions. Then try to formulate a solution that looks like the answer choices.

Question 3

Notice that each answer choice includes all three letters (p, q, and c). So the solution you're aiming for must also include all three letters. Also, notice that every answer but choice (E) is a *fraction*. So anticipate building a fraction to solve the problem.

Don't Be Fooled by Too-Obvious Answer Choices

The test-makers will intentionally tempt or "bait" you with wrong-answer choices that result from making common errors in calculation and in setting up and solving equations. Don't assume that your response is correct just because your solution appears among the five answer choices! Rely instead on your sense of whether you understood what the question called for and performed the calculations and other steps carefully and accurately.

Question 1

In this question, each of the four incorrect choices is sucker bait:

(A)	4.8	You performed the wrong calculation: 30% of 16 ounces = 4.8 ounces
(B)	5.5	This is the number of ounces Susan drank. (The question asks for the amount remaining.)
(C)	11.2	You performed the wrong calculation: 30% of 16 ounce = 4.8 ounces 16 − 4.8 = 11.2
(D)	11.5	This is the correct answer.
(E)	13.0	You confused percentages with raw numbers, erroneously converting 30% (10% + 20%) into 3.0: 16 − 3.0 = 13.0

Question 2

This question contains two sucker answer choices:

| (A) | 2 | This would be the correct answer to the question: "What is the difference between 19 and 21?" But this question is asking something entirely different. |
| (B) | 20 | 20 is simply 19 + 21 divided by 2. If this solution strikes you as too simple, you've got good instincts. |

Don't Do More Work Than Needed to Get to the Answer

If the question asks for an approximation, that's a huge clue that precise calculations aren't necessary.

Question 1

Notice that each answer choice is carried to exactly one decimal place and that the question asks for an approximate value. These two features are clues that you can probably round off your calculations to the nearest tenth as you go.

Look for Shortcuts to Conventional Ways of Solving Problems

The adage "There's more than one way to skin a cat" applies to many GMAT Problem Solving questions.

Question 2

You can solve this problem quickly by simply comparing the two sums. Before the sixth number is removed, the sum of the numbers is 114 (6 × 19). After removing the sixth number, the sum of the remaining numbers is 105 (5 × 21). The difference between the two sums is 9, which must be the value of the number.

Know When to Plug In Numbers for Variables

If the answer choices contain variables (like x and y), the question might be a good candidate for the "plug-in" strategy. Pick simple numbers (so the math is easy), and substitute them for the variables. You'll definitely need your pencil for this strategy.

Question 3

This question was a perfect candidate for the plug-in strategy. Instead of trying to figure out how to set up and solve an algebraic equation, in Step 3 we used easy numbers for the three variables, then plugged those numbers into each answer choice to see which choice worked.

Know When to Work Backward from Numerical Answer Choices

If a Problem Solving question asks for a number value and if you draw a blank about how to set up and solve the problem, don't panic. You might be able to work backward by testing each answer choice. This might take a bit of time, but if you test the answer choices in random order, the statistical odds are that you'll only need to test three choices to find the correct one.

Question 2

You already learned that comparing the two sums is the quickest shortcut to the answer. But if this strategy didn't occur to you, working backward from the answer choices would be the next quickest method. After the sixth number is removed, the sum of the five remaining numbers is $21 \times 5 = 105$. So to test an answer choice, add this sum to the number provided in the choice, dividing the new sum by 6. If the result is 19, you've found the correct choice. Here's how to do the math for choice (C), which is the correct answer:

$$\frac{105+9}{6} = \frac{114}{6} = 19$$

Problem Solving questions always list numerical answer choices in ascending order of value. So if you use the strategy of working backward, start with the median value: choice (C). If choice (C) turns out too great, you know the correct answer must be either choice (A) or choice (B). Conversely, if choice (C) turns out too small, then either choice (D) or choice (E) must be correct. Of course, you might also be able to eliminate an answer choice right away by sizing up the questions (a previous strategy). Doing so would make your job even easier!

Always Check Your Work

Always check your work. Here are three suggestions for doing so:

❶ Do a reality check. Ask yourself whether your solution makes sense based upon what the question asks. (This check is especially appropriate for word problems.)

❷ For questions where you solve algebraic equations, plug your solution into the equation(s) to make sure it works.

Confirm your calculations (except for the simplest no-brainers) with your calculator. It's amazingly easy to accidentally push the wrong button.

Checking your calculations is especially crucial for questions asking for an approximation. Why? If your solution doesn't precisely match one of the five answer choices, you might conclude that you should just pick the choice that's closest to your solution—a big mistake if you miscalculated!

Question 1

A reality check on this question will tell you that answer choice (C), 11.5, seems about right, but that most of the other choices don't.

Read the Question One Last Time Before Moving On

Among GMAT test-takers, simple carelessness in reading a Problem Solving question is by far the most likely cause of an incorrect answer. So even if your solution is among the choices and you're confident your calculations are accurate, don't move on quite yet. Read the question again. Make sure you answered the precise question asked. For example, does the question ask for:

- Arithmetic mean or median?
- A circumference or an area?
- A sum or a difference?
- A perimeter or a length of one side only?
- An aggregate rate or a single rate?
- Total time or average time?

Also check to make sure you:

- Used the same numbers provided in the question
- Didn't inadvertently switch any numbers or other expressions
- Didn't use raw numbers where percentages were provided or vice versa

Question 1

The question asked for the amount of juice remaining, not the amount Susan drank. Also, a careless test-taker might subtract 10 ounces instead of 10%.

Question 2

A careless test-taker might inadvertently switch the numbers 19 and 21.

Question 3

The question asks for an answer in cents, not dollars.

SUMMING IT UP

- For success in the GMAT Problem Solving questions, follow the 5-step approach in this chapter: size up the question, appraise the answer choices, check for shortcuts to finding the answer, set up the problem and solve it, and verify your response before moving to the next question.

- Problem Solving questions are designed to "reward" you for recognizing easier or more intuitive ways of finding the correct answer, so be on the alert for possible shortcuts.

- Don't look for easy solutions to complex problems, however. Those that involve algebraic formulas generally aren't solved by adding or subtracting a few numbers.

- Always check your calculations. Careless mistakes are the leading cause of incorrect responses on the GMAT Quantitative section.

- Problem Solving questions list numerical choices in ascending order of value. So if you have to work backward, start from the middle choice (C). If it turns out to be too great, you know the correct answer must be choice (A) or choice (B); if it turns out to be too small, you can focus on choice (D) or choice (E) as the correct answer.

Data Sufficiency and Analysis

OVERVIEW

- **The 5-step plan for Data Sufficiency problems**
- **Data Sufficiency strategies**
- **Keys to successful GMAT Data Sufficiency**
- **The 5-step plan for Data Analysis problems**
- **Keys to successful GMAT Data Analysis**
- **Summing it up**

In this chapter, you'll learn:

- A step-by-step approach to handling all Data Sufficiency and Analysis questions
- Keys for successfully tackling Data Sufficiency and Analysis questions

The Data Sufficiency format is unique to the GMAT; you won't find it on any other standardized test. Each Data Sufficiency consists of a question followed by two statements—labeled (1) and (2). Your task is to analyze each of the two statements to determine whether it provides sufficient data to answer the question and, if neither suffices alone, whether both statements together suffice. These are your answer choices:

- **(A)** Statement (1) ALONE is sufficient, but Statement (2) alone is not sufficient to answer the question asked;
- **(B)** Statement (2) ALONE is sufficient, but Statement (1) alone is not sufficient to answer the question asked;
- **(C)** BOTH Statements (1) and (2) TOGETHER are sufficient to answer the question asked, but NEITHER statement ALONE is sufficient;
- **(D)** EACH statement ALONE is sufficient to answer the question asked;
- **(E)** Statements (1) and (2) TOGETHER are NOT sufficient to answer the question asked, and additional data specific to the problem are needed.

You'll also learn several more advanced techniques for achieving your highest possible score on the Quantitative section of the GMAT. These include:

- Applying the basic techniques to more challenging Data Sufficiency questions
- Learning additional ways to apply techniques to certain types of Data Sufficiency questions, with example questions for practice
- Learning a step-by-step approach to handling any Data Analysis question
- Learning how to tackle Data Analysis questions
- Further exploring some of the strategies listed above by applying them to GMAT-style questions that are more challenging

chapter 8

THE 5-STEP PLAN FOR DATA SUFFICIENCY PROBLEMS

The first task in this chapter is to learn the five basic steps for handling any GMAT Data Sufficiency problem:

1 Size up the question.

2 Size up the two statements and look for a shortcut.

3 Consider Statement (1) alone.

4 Consider Statement (2) alone.

5 If neither statement alone answers the question, consider both together.

Later in this chapter, we'll apply this 5-step approach to four sample Data Sufficiency questions.

Step One: Size Up the Question

As with Problem Solving questions, assess what specific mathematical area is being tested (e.g., what mathematical rules and formulas come into play). By determining what you're up against, you're well on your way to dealing with the question. Data Sufficiency questions, just like Problem Solving questions, vary widely in difficulty level. Try to get a feel for your limitations in handling complex questions. Determine how much time you're willing to spend on the question, if any.

Step Two: Size Up the Two Statements and Look for a Shortcut

- Do the statements provide essentially the same information? If so, the answer is probably either choice (D) ("Each statement ALONE is sufficient to answer the question asked") or choice (E) ("Statements 1 and 2 TOGETHER are NOT sufficient to answer the question asked, and additional data specific to the problem are needed").

- Does either statement establish a solvable system of equations (for example, two equations in two variables)?

- Does a statement seem to merely repeat (paraphrase) all or some of the information in the question? (If so, you can't answer the question with that statement alone.)

Asking yourself questions such as these may in some cases enable you to determine the correct answer choice without doing any more work. Otherwise, proceed to Step 3.

Step Three: Consider Statement (1) Alone

TIP

If you're pressed for time, take your best guess and move on after Step 3. Your odds of selecting the correct answer choice are fairly good at this point.

If the information provided in Statement (1) suffices to answer the question, eliminate choices (B), (C), and (E) as viable answer choices. On the other hand, if Statement (1) is insufficient alone, eliminate choices (A) and (D) as viable answer choices.

Step Four: Consider Statement (2) Alone

If the information provided in Statement (2) answers the question, eliminate choices (A), (C), and (E) as viable answer choices. On the other hand, if Statement (2) is insufficient alone, eliminate choices (B) and (D) as viable answer choices.

Step Five: If Neither Statement Alone Answers the Question, Consider Both Together

Now if you can answer the question, the correct answer choice is (C). If you still don't have enough information, the correct answer choice is (E).

Sample Questions

1. If a jewelry merchant bought a particular ring for $10,000 and sold the ring to Judith, how much did Judith pay for the ring?

    (1) The merchant's profit from the sale was 50%.

    (2) The amount that the merchant paid for the ring was two-thirds the amount that Judith paid for the ring.

    (A) Statement (1) ALONE is sufficient, but Statement (2) alone is NOT sufficient to answer the question asked;

    (B) Statement (2) ALONE is sufficient, but Statement (1) alone is NOT sufficient to answer the question asked;

    (C) BOTH Statements (1) and (2) TOGETHER are sufficient to answer the question asked, but NEITHER statement ALONE is sufficient;

    (D) Each statement ALONE is sufficient to answer the question asked;

    (E) Statements (1) and (2) TOGETHER are NOT sufficient to answer the question asked, and additional data specific to the problem are needed.

2. The symbol $\square$ represents the third digit in the 5-digit number 62,$\square$79. What number does $\square$ represent?

    (1) 62,$\square$79 is a multiple of 3.

    (2) The sum of the digits of 62,$\square$79 is divisible by 4.

    (A) Statement (1) ALONE is sufficient, but Statement (2) alone is NOT sufficient to answer the question asked;

    (B) Statement (2) ALONE is sufficient, but Statement (1) alone is NOT sufficient to answer the question asked;

    (C) BOTH Statements (1) and (2) TOGETHER are sufficient to answer the question asked, but NEITHER statement ALONE is sufficient;

    (D) Each statement ALONE is sufficient to answer the question asked;

    (E) Statements (1) and (2) TOGETHER are NOT sufficient to answer the question asked, and additional data specific to the problem are needed.

NOTE

On the actual GMAT CAT screen, you'll select your choice by clicking on one of five blank ovals (instead of lettered answer choices).

3. If $xy \neq 0$, is $x > y$?
    (1) $|x| > |y|$
    (2) $x = 2y$

(A) Statement (1) ALONE is sufficient, but Statement (2) alone is NOT sufficient to answer the question asked;

(B) Statement (2) ALONE is sufficient, but Statement (1) alone is NOT sufficient to answer the question asked;

(C) BOTH Statements (1) and (2) TOGETHER are sufficient to answer the question asked, but NEITHER statement ALONE is sufficient;

(D) Each statement ALONE is sufficient to answer the question asked;

(E) Statements (1) and (2) TOGETHER are NOT sufficient to answer the question asked, and additional data specific to the problem are needed.

4.

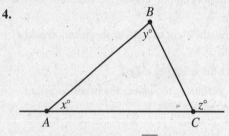

In the figure above, is $\overline{AB}$ equal in length to $\overline{AC}$?
    (1) $x + y = z$
    (2) $y = 180 - z$

(A) Statement (1) ALONE is sufficient, but Statement (2) alone is NOT sufficient to answer the question asked;

(B) Statement (2) ALONE is sufficient, but Statement (1) alone is NOT sufficient to answer the question asked;

(C) BOTH Statements (1) and (2) TOGETHER are sufficient to answer the question asked, but NEITHER statement ALONE is sufficient;

(D) Each statement ALONE is sufficient to answer the question asked;

(E) Statements (1) and (2) TOGETHER are NOT sufficient to answer the question asked, and additional data specific to the problem are needed.

> **NOTE**
>
> Most Data Sufficiency questions will not include diagrams (geometry figures, graphs, and charts).

Apply the 5-Step Plan

Let's review the four sample questions one at a time using the 5-step plan you just learned. By now, you're probably familiar with the five answer choices, so we won't bother including them with the questions from now on.

Question 1

Question 1 is a relatively easy question. Approximately 85% of test-takers respond correctly to questions like it. Here's the question again:

1. If a jewelry merchant bought a particular ring for $10,000 and sold the ring to Judith, how much did Judith pay for the ring?

    (1) The merchant's profit from the sale was 50%.

    (2) The amount that the merchant paid for the ring was two-thirds of the amount that Judith paid for the ring.

Step 1: The focus of this question is the concept of *percent increase*—in the context of a word problem involving *profit*. This type of question is usually fairly easy, so you can expect to determine the correct response within a minute—without resorting to an educated guess. It should be worth investing your time on this one.

Step 2: Notice that the two statements (1 and 2) provide the same information—only in different ways! This is a huge clue that the correct answer choice is either (D) or (E). You'll still have to consider one of the two statements alone, but that should suffice.

Step 3: Consider the premise, along with Statement (1) *alone*. (Disregard Statement (2) for now.) Given that the merchant paid $10,000 for the ring, if the merchant earned a 50% profit from the sale to Judith, determining Judith's ring price is a simple matter of adding 50% of $10,000 to $10,000:

$10,000 + 0.5($10,000) = Judith's ring price

At this point, it's clear that you can determine Judith's ring price by simple multiplication and addition. Don't waste time actually computing Judith's ring price. You know that Statement (1) alone suffices to answer the question and that's all you need to know! Eliminate choices (B), (C), and (E) from consideration. The correct choice must be either (A) or (D).

Step 4: If you're not convinced that both statements say essentially the same thing, go ahead and consider the premise along with Statement (2) *alone*. (Disregard Statement (1) for now.) If the merchant's cost was $\frac{2}{3}$ the amount Judith paid, then Judith paid $\frac{3}{2}$ of the merchant's cost. Determining Judith's ring price is a simple matter of multiplying $10,000 by $\frac{3}{2}$:

$10,000 \times \frac{3}{2}$ = Judith's ring price

At this point, it's clear that you can determine Judith's ring price by simple multiplication. As in Step 3, don't waste time actually computing that price. You know that Statement (2) alone suffices to answer the question, and that's all you need to know.

Step 5: This step is unnecessary here. There's no need to consider both statements together. You know that either Statement (1) or (2) alone suffices to answer the question, so you can eliminate choice (A). **The correct answer is (D).**

Question 2

Question 2 is average in difficulty level. Approximately 65% of test-takers respond correctly to questions like it. Here's the question again:

2. The symbol □ represents the third digit in the 5-digit number 62,□79. What number does □ represent?

    (1) 62,□79 is a multiple of 3.

    (2) The sum of the digits of 62,□79 is divisible by 4.

Step 1: This question is testing factors and divisibility. The peculiar use of a "placeholder" is a typical GMAT technique for testing your understanding of integers and digits. Questions such as these are usually straightforward once you know the basic rules, as well as a few shortcuts for divisibility.

Step 2: Both statements appear to add different information to the question. So there's no obvious shortcut here. (Go on to Step 3.)

Step 3: Consider Statement (1) alone. If the sum of the digits of a number is divisible by 3, the number is also divisible by 3. Excluding the digit represented by □, the sum of the digits in the number 62,□79 is 24. Accordingly, if the number is a multiple of (divisible by) 3, the missing digit must be 0, 3, 6, or 9. Since there's more than one possible value for □, Statement (1) alone is insufficient to answer the question. Eliminate answer choices (A) and (D).

Step 4: Consider Statement (2) alone. The number that □ represents can be 0, 4, or 8. Thus, Statement (2) alone is insufficient to answer the question. Eliminate answer choice (B).

Step 5: Consider Statements (1) and (2) together. The two statements together establish that the missing digit is 0, because 0 is the only common number in the two lists of possible values for □. Thus, Statements (1) and (2) together are sufficient to answer the question. **The correct answer is (C).**

Question 3

Question 3 is moderately difficult. Approximately 45% of test-takers respond correctly to questions like it. Here's the question again:

3. If $xy \neq 0$, is $x > y$?
    (1) $|x| > |y|$
    (2) $x = 2y$

Step 1: This is a typical *absolute value question*. Whenever you see inequalities and variables but no numbers, that's a clue that you'll need to consider different types of numbers—such as negative numbers, positive numbers, fractions, and perhaps the numbers 0 and 1—to determine the correct answer choice. Getting to the answer might entail performing some simple calculations, and perhaps a bit of trial and error (plugging in possible values).

Step 2: Both statements appear to add different information to the question. So there's no obvious shortcut here. But a good reasoned guess at this point would be that the correct answer choice is (E). Why? Because the question doesn't restrict the value of either *x* or *y* (except that neither can equal 0). So if you're pressed for time, guess choice (E) and move on to the next question. Otherwise, go on to Step 3.

Step 3: You must consider both positive and negative values for x and y. Given $|x| > |y|$, an x-value of either 4 or -4 and a y-value of 2, for example, satisfies the inequality but results in two different answers to the question. Thus, Statement (1) alone is insufficient to answer the question. Eliminate answer choices (A) and (D).

Step 4: Similarly, given $x = 2y$, if you use negative values for both x and y (for example, $x = -4$ and $y = -2$), the answer to the question is no; but if you use positive values (for example, $x = 4$ and $y = 2$), the answer to the question is yes. Thus, Statement (2) alone is insufficient. Eliminate answer choice (B).

Step 5: Statements (1) and (2) together are still insufficient. For example, if $x = -4$ and $y = -2$, both Statements (1) and (2) are satisfied, $x < y$, and the answer to the question is no. However, if $x = 4$ and $y = 2$, Statements (1) and (2) are both satisfied, but $x > y$, and the answer to the question is yes. Eliminate answer choice (C). **The correct answer is (E).**

Question 4

Question 4 is a relatively difficult question. Approximately 30% of test-takers respond correctly to questions like it. Here's the question again:

4.

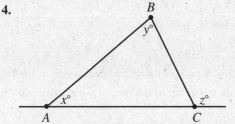

In the figure above, is $\overline{AB}$ equal in length to $\overline{AC}$?

(1) $x + y = z$

(2) $y = 180 - z$

Step 1: This question is a geometry problem involving the *isosceles triangle*. (You'll see anywhere from five to eight geometry questions on your GMAT.) This question involves three distinct rules of geometry. Two of these rules (A and C below) apply specifically to triangles:

Rule A: If two angles of a triangle are congruent, then the two sides opposite those angles are congruent.

Rule B: If angles formed from the same vertex form a straight line, their degree measures total 180 (and they are known as "supplementary" angles).

Rule C: In any triangle, the sum of the degree measures of the three interior angles is 180.

If you're unfamiliar with any of the three rules in Step 1, you won't get very far with this question! So if you're pressed for time and if you're particularly weak in this area of geometry, consider taking a guess and moving on.

Step 2: Intuition alone probably won't get you very far on this question. If you're really on your toes, you'll notice that Statement (1) merely restates Rule C (see Step 1) in a different form. Also because Statement (2) includes a number, this statement is probably more likely than Statement (1) to suffice in answering the question. (This amounts to little more than a guess, however.) So let's move on to Step 3.

Beware: Don't shortcut the analysis by simply measuring the lengths with your eye. Data Sufficiency figures are not necessarily drawn to scale, so analyze these problems using your knowledge of mathematics, not your eye.

Step 3: Consider Statement (1) alone. Given Rule A (see Step 1) to answer the question, you need to know whether angle y is congruent to the triangle's unidentified angle—the interior angle at point C. Let's call this angle a. If $a = y$, then the answer to the question is yes. Otherwise, the answer is no. In either case, we need to know whether $a = y$ in order to answer the question. Together, angles a and z form a straight line—the line passing through points A and C:

$$a + z = 180$$
$$a = 180 - z$$

The sum of x, y, and a is 180 (Rule C). You can substitute $(180 - z)$ for a in this equation, and manipulate the result so that it is identical to the equation in Statement (1):

$x + y + a = 180$	Rule C (sum of angle measures is 180°)
$x + y + (180 - z) = 180$	substituting $(180 - z)$ for a
$x + y - z = 0$	subtract 180 from each side
$x + y = z$	add z to each side

Notice that you could have "shortcut" this entire analysis had you already been aware of the rule that the measure of an exterior angle of a triangle is always equal to the sum of the measures of the two remote interior angles.

Step 4: Now consider Statement (2), disregarding Statement (1) for now. The expression $(180 - z)$ equals our third unidentified angle, which we called a in Step 3. Given that $(180 - z)$ also equals y, the two angles a and y are congruent (equal in degree measure). The two sides opposite a and y must also be congruent (see Rule A). Thus, Statement (2) alone suffices to answer the question.

Step 5: Because Statement (1) alone is insufficient to answer the question, while Statement (2) alone is sufficient, the answer must be choice (B). There's no need to consider the two statements together. Based on Statement (2), the answer to the question itself is yes, but you don't need to go this far. Had neither (1) nor (2) alone been sufficient to answer the question, you would have then considered both statements together to determine whether the correct answer choice was (C) or (E). **The correct answer is (B).**

DATA SUFFICIENCY STRATEGIES

In this section, you'll learn strategies for handling Data Sufficiency problems and see examples of each strategy.

Plug In "Easy" Numbers, but Don't Forget Negatives, Fractions, Zero, and One

If a Data Sufficiency question involves variables, you can easily confuse yourself by thinking about the problem purely abstractly. You should also experiment with different numerical values. Take pencil to paper and scratch out some scenarios. This technique will help you see what's behind the problem at hand. Just be sure to try all the different "types" of numbers that the problem allows (greater numbers, lesser numbers, positive and negative numbers, non-integers, as well as 0 and 1). If the answer to the question depends on what kind of values you plug in, then the correct answer choice must be (E).

5. If a, b, c, and d are all positive integers, is $\dfrac{a}{b}$ greater than $\dfrac{c}{d}$?

   (1) $a > c$
   (2) $b > d$

Neither statement alone allows you to compare the values of the two fractions. To see this, try plugging in some simple numbers. For example, let $a = 4$ and $c = 2$, in accordance with Statement (1). Since you can choose any values for b and d, the possible values of either fraction are infinite in number, and so you can see that Statement (1) alone is insufficient to answer the question. By the same reasoning, Statement (2) alone is also insufficient.

Now, consider the two statements together. Again, let $a = 6$ and $c = 2$, in accordance with Statement (1). Now, start plugging in some values for b and d that meet the condition in Statement (2), which is that $b > d$. Can you answer yes to the question? Easily; for example, $b = 2$ and $d = 1$. Can you answer no to the question? Easily; here's just one possible way: $b = 4$ and $d = 1$. Stop here! You've found two different answers to the question and so you know the correct answer must be choice (E). **The correct answer is (E).**

Look for Two Statements That Say Essentially the Same Thing

In most Data Sufficiency questions, one numbered statement will provide information that is different from the other statement. But this isn't always the case. One skill that the test-makers will test is your ability to recognize two statements that provide essentially the same information—just in a slightly different form. If they're the same, you know the correct answer choice must be either (D) or (E).

6.

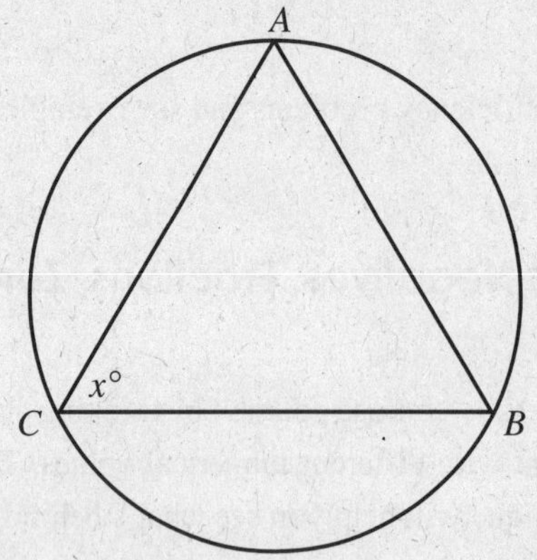

Is the triangle in the figure above equilateral?

(1) Minor arc AB has a degree measure of 120°.

(2) $x = 60$

The two statements tell us the same thing—that angle C measures 60°, as it would if the triangle were equilateral. But without further information, we can't tell that angles A and B are also 60° angles. It's possible, for instance, that angle A measures 59° while angle B measures 61°—in which case the triangle is *not* equilateral. Since we can't know for sure, the answer must be choice (E).

Take Note: The triangle inscribed in the circle certainly looks equilateral (which means that all three sides are equal in length). But the apparent dimensions of the triangle in the diagram are irrelevant to answering the question. Only the facts given in the question and in the two numbered statements are important. **The correct answer is (E).**

Focus on Quantitative Concepts, Not on Number Crunching

Data Sufficiency focuses more on mathematical concepts than on working toward a quantitative solution (which is what Problem Solving questions are primarily about). So be sure to size up the problem at hand. Ask yourself: "What rule, principle, or formula is the question covering?" Once you've figured this out, you should be able to handle the problem relatively easily.

7. What is the value of $p^2 - q^2$?

(1) $p + q = -4$

(2) $p - q = 4$

Many test-takers would jump headlong into trying various values for p and q in trial-and-error fashion. That's not the way to approach this problem or, for that matter, any Data Sufficiency problem. Before you evaluate either statement alone, look at the expressions given in the problem. Did you notice that $p^2 - q^2$ is the difference of two squares, and that the expressions given in the two statements provide its two binomial factors? In other words: $p^2 - q^2 = (p + q)(p - q)$. This is the concept that the question is designed to cover. Once you see this, handling the problem is a snap. Although neither statement alone suffices to answer the question (because you're dealing with a quadratic rather than a linear equation), Statements (1) and (2) together provide the two binomials, allowing you to answer the question. (To calculate the answer, you would simply multiply: $-4 \times 4 = -16$.) **The correct answer is (C).**

Don't Do More Work Than Necessary

Keep in mind that the Data Sufficiency format does not require you to answer the question. So once you've convinced yourself which statement(s), if any (1, 2, both, neither), suffices to answer the question, stop right there! You'd only be wasting your precious time by figuring out the answer itself.

8. What is the average weight of the 5 members of a football team?
   (1) The average weight of the 3 heaviest team members is 340 pounds.
   (2) The 2 lightest team members weigh 275 and 290 pounds.

To calculate the average of a group of numbers, you must have two pieces of information: The total of the numbers and the number of numbers. In this case, the only missing piece of information is the total weight of the team members. (You already know the number of numbers involved: 5.) Neither Statement (1) nor (2) alone gives you the players' total weight. But if you combine Statements (1) and (2), you can determine it. You'd multiply 340 by 3 (to get the combined weight of the heaviest team members) and add 275 and 290 (the weights of the two lightest members). *But there's no need to actually perform these steps.* All that matters is that you can tell that it would be theoretically possible to make these calculations and so determine the average. This is enough to get the correct answer. **The correct answer is (C).**

Don't Assume Any Information Not Stated in the Problem

One of the skills the test-makers are measuring is your ability to distinguish facts provided in a Data Sufficiency problem from unsupported assumptions made out of carelessness or inattention. There's a natural tendency to "invent" facts that aren't really there so that you can answer the question. No test-taker is immune to this tendency. You might be surprised how many "smart" GMAT test-takers slip up in this way, robbing themselves of precious Quantitative score points.

9. What percentage of the female students in a certain history class is majoring in economics?
   (1) 50 percent of the students in the class are male and 50 percent are female.
   (2) 50 percent of all students in the class are majoring in economics.

Many test-takers would carelessly *assume* that the percent of students majoring in economics is the same for the class's male students as for its female students. If this were the case, then you could easily answer the question. (The answer would be 50.) But the problem provides no information to support this assumption! Thus, the correct answer must be choice (E). **The correct answer is (E).**

Beware of Statements That Are Irrelevant or Provide Facts Already Supplied in the Question

Ask yourself what kind of information each statement provides. A statement is more likely to be sufficient to answer the question if:

- It provides specific numerical values not given in the premise.
- It adds something new to the premise.
- It provides information that strikes you as relevant to the question.

On the other hand, a statement is more likely to be *insufficient* to answer the question if:

- It does not provide any specific numerical values that the premise leaves unknown.
- It seems redundant—simply paraphrasing the premise (or some part of it).
- The information strikes you as irrelevant to the premise or question.

10. A certain granola recipe calls for a simple mixture of raisins costing $3.50 per pound with oats. At a cost of $2.00 per pound for the granola mixture, how many pounds of oats must be added to 10 pounds of raisins?

   (1) The granola mixture is packaged in one-pound bags.

   (2) Oats cost $1.00 per pound.

The question itself provides two of the three facts you need to answer it: the cost per pound of raisins and the cost per pound of the mixture. Statement (1) alone provides no useful information for answering the question. So without even looking at Statement (2), you've eliminated answer choices (A), (C), and (D)! Statement (2) provides the third needed fact: the cost per pound of oats. **The correct answer is (B).**

Although you don't need to do the math, here's how you would answer the question with the additional information provided by Statement (2). Think of the quantities as costs per pound, and multiply the cost by the weight. The total mixture will consist of 10 pounds of raisins at $3.50 per pound, or ($3.50)(10), plus "*x*" pound of oats at $1.00 per pound, or ($1.00)(*x*). The mixture costs $2.00 per pound, and it will be (10 + *x*) pounds:

$$(3.50)(10) + (1.00)(x) = (2.00)(10 + x)$$
$$35 + x = 20 + 2x$$
$$15 = x$$

Fifteen pounds of oats are needed.

Don't Assume That Diagrams Are Accurate

Although a diagram will conform to the information in the question, it won't necessarily conform to either Statement (1) or (2). So don't use a Data Sufficiency figure to estimate or measure values, shapes, lengths, or other sizes. For example, don't rely on a figure's appearance to determine:

- Whether one line segment is longer than another
- Whether one angle is larger (greater in degree measure) than another
- Whether two lines are parallel or perpendicular
- Whether two triangles are the same shape or size
- Whether one segment of a pie chart is larger than another segment

Rely instead on the numbers and the textual information provided in the question and in the two statements.

11.

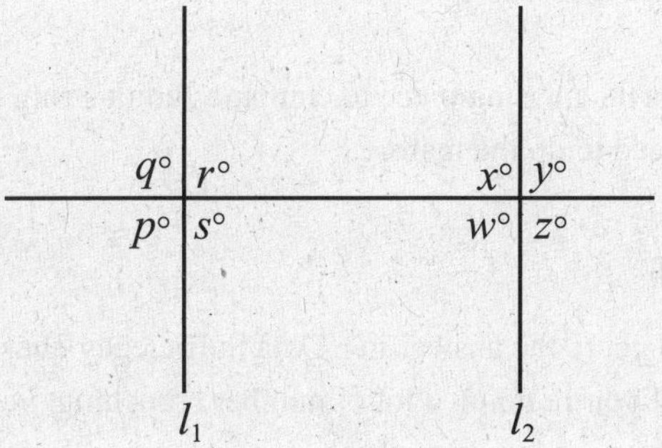

In the figure above, is l_1 parallel to l_2?

(1) $q + y = s + w$

(2) $p + x = 180$

If you were to rely on the appearance of the figure, you'd see that the two lines look parallel. But remember: When it comes to GMAT Data Sufficiency, never measure with your eye! Rely instead on the numbers and other information in the problem. Here's how to analyze this problem. Vertical angles (formed by intersecting lines) are always congruent. Thus, $q = s$ and $y = w$. Accordingly, $q + y$ must equal $s + w$ in any event, and Statement (1) alone does not suffice to answer the question. Given Statement (2) alone, since p and x are supplementary, p must equal w (because $w + x = 180$). Thus, corresponding angles are congruent, and the two lines are parallel. **The correct answer is (B).**

KEYS TO SUCCESSFUL GMAT DATA SUFFICIENCY

Here are some basic tips for solving Data Sufficiency problems. Apply these keys to the Practice Tests in Part VII, and then review them again just before exam day.

Memorize the Answer Choices

Don't just learn the directions—memorize the answer choices. (Remember: they are always the same.) This way you'll save time because you won't need to refer to them for every question.

Be Sure to Consider Each Statement Alone

After analyzing Statement (1), you'll be surprised how difficult it can be to purge the information in Statement (1) from your mind and start with a clean slate in considering Statement (2). Be alert at all times to this potential problem.

Don't Do More Work Than Necessary

Keep in mind that the Data Sufficiency format does not require you to answer the question. So once you've convinced yourself that a statement (1 or 2) suffices to answer the question, stop right there! You'd only be wasting your precious time by figuring out the answer itself.

Question 1

Once you recognized that each statement provides the missing piece to compute Judith's ring cost, you know the correct answer is (D). There's no need to do the math.

Don't Perform Endless Calculations

You shouldn't have to do involved calculations to get to the answer in a Data Sufficiency question. A few simple calculations may be required. But if you're doing a lot of number crunching, you've probably missed the mathematical principle the question is asking about.

Question 2

Had we not used an organized approach to the problem, we would have had no choice but to start plugging in digit after digit (0 through 9). The more number crunching, the greater the chance for error.

Look for a Quicker, More Intuitive Route to the Correct Answer

The GMAT is testing, among other skills, your ability to find ingenious, unconventional, and intuitive solutions to conventional problems. Always look for a shortcut to performing calculations. You'll save time, and you'll avoid common computational errors.

Question 2

As you tackle more questions like Question 2, you'll learn to recognize when an answer depends on which values are used and you won't have to bother plugging in "test" numbers.

Never Rely Solely on a Diagram or Figure

Although a figure will conform to the information in the question, it won't necessarily conform to either Statement (1) or (2). So don't use a Data Sufficiency figure to estimate or measure values, shapes, lengths, or other sizes. For example, don't rely on a figure's appearance to determine whether:

- One line segment is longer than another
- One angle is larger (greater in degree measure) than another
- Two lines are parallel or perpendicular
- Two triangles are the same shape or size
- One segment of a pie chart is larger than another segment

Rely instead on the numbers and textual information provided in the question and statements.

Question 4

In the figure, it appears that $\overline{AB}$ is equal in length to $\overline{AC}$. If you had relied on the figure, your response to the question would have been wrong!

Consider All the Possibilities for Unknowns

When analyzing a Data Sufficiency question involving unknowns (variables such as x and y), unless the question explicitly restricts their value, consider positive and negative values, as well as fractions and the numbers zero (0) and 1. If the answer to the question depends on what kind of value you plug in, then the correct answer must be (E).

Question 3

We needed to consider negative as well as positive numbers; otherwise, we would have gotten the answer wrong.

Look for Two Statements That Say Essentially the Same Thing

Check to see if the two statements provide essentially the same information—just in a slightly different form. If they're the same, you know the correct answer choice must be either (D) or (E).

Question 1

Notice that the two statements provided the same information—just in different forms.

Check Each Statement for Numbers Needed to Answer the Question

Use this approach for any Data Sufficiency problem involving formulas and calculations and when the question asks for a number. In a problem involving rate of motion (speed), for instance, if the question asks for a speed but does not provide the time (or does not provide the distance), rule out a statement that doesn't supply the missing piece of the formula.

Question 3

In analyzing this question, we recognized early that neither statement alone supplied the numbers we needed.

Don't Try to Do All the Work in Your Head

As with Problem Solving questions, don't try to do too much work in your head. Avoid careless errors by using your pencil and scratch paper for all but the simplest mathematical steps. (Remember: Scratch paper and pencils will be provided at the testing center.)

Question 3

How far would you get with Question 3 without doing some pencil work—at a minimum, scratching out the two statements in different forms? Not very far!

If Short on Time, Make a Reasoned Guess by Eliminating Answer Choices

Keep in mind that if Statement (1) alone is insufficient to answer the question, you can eliminate choices (A) and (D). On the other hand, once you've determined that one of the statements alone is sufficient, you can eliminate choices (C) and (E). At this point, your odds of guessing correctly are 1 in 3, which is a lot better than 1 in 5 for a completely random guess. So if you're having trouble analyzing one statement but are confident that the other statement is sufficient alone, make a guess and move on to the next question.

Questions 1–4

In any of the four example questions, we could have stopped part way through our analysis and taken a reasoned guess. Remember: If you can get as far as ruling out one answer choice, you can rule out two. At that point, your odds look pretty good.

THE 5-STEP PLAN FOR DATA ANALYSIS PROBLEMS

Now that we've reviewed the basic strategies for solving Data Sufficiency problems, let's try to tackle another special type of GMAT Quantitative problem, which the test-makers call Data Analysis. This type of question is designed to gauge your ability to read and analyze data presented in graphical form and to calculate figures such as percentages, ratios, fractions, and averages based on the numbers you glean from the data. They can appear in either of the two basic formats: Problem Solving and Data Sufficiency.

Expect to find two to four Data Analysis questions (typically in sets of two questions) interspersed with other questions in the GMAT Quantitative section. Each question in a set pertains to the same graphical data, and each involves either *one* or *two* distinct graphical displays. Four types appear most frequently:

1. Pie charts
2. Tables
3. Bar graphs
4. Line graphs

Here's a 5-step approach that will help you to handle any set of Data Analysis questions:

1. Look at the "big picture" first.
2. Read the entire question very carefully and look for a shortcut.
3. Perform the steps required to get the answer.
4. Check all answer choices for your own answer.
5. Check your calculations carefully.

We'll apply this approach to two sample Data Analysis questions later in this chapter.

Step One: Look at the "Big Picture" First

Before plunging into the question(s), read all the information above and below the figure(s). Look particularly for:

- Totals (dollar figures or other numbers)
- Whether the numbers are in thousands or millions
- How two or more figures are labeled
- Whether graphical data are expressed in numbers or percentages

Step Two: Read the Entire Question Very Carefully and Look for a Shortcut

As you read, divide the question into parts, each of which involves a distinct step in getting to the answer. Pay particular attention to whether the question asks for:

- An approximation
- A percentage or a raw number
- A comparison
- An increase or a decrease

In breaking the question down into tasks, look for a shortcut to save yourself work.

Step Three: Perform the Steps Required to Get the Answer

As you work, round numbers up or down (but not too far).

Step Four: Check All Answer Choices for Your Own Answer

If the question asks for a number, find the choice closest to your answer. Look for other answer choices that are "too close for comfort." If you see any, or if your solution is nowhere near any of the choices, go to Step 5.

Step Five: Check Your Calculations Carefully

Make sure that the value and form (number, percentage, total, etc.) of your solution conforms to what the question asks. Check your rounding technique. Did you round off in the wrong direction? Did you round off too far?

Sample Questions

Both of these questions are based on the same two pie charts.

INCOME AND EXPENSES–DIVISIONS A, B, C,
AND D OF XYZ COMPANY (YEAR X)

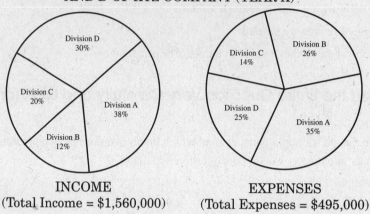

INCOME
(Total Income = $1,560,000)

EXPENSES
(Total Expenses = $495,000)

12. During year X, by approximately what amount did Division C's income exceed Division B's expenses?

(A) $125,000

(B) $127,000

(C) $140,000

(D) $180,000

(E) $312,000

13. With respect to the division whose percent of total income exceeded its percent of total expenses by the greatest amount among the four divisions, by approximately what amount did the division's income exceed its own expenses?

(A) $69,000

(B) $90,000

(C) $150,000

(D) $185,000

(E) $240,000

Before learning and applying the 5 steps, note the following key features of Data Analysis question sets:

- The questions tend to be long and wordy. Get used to it; that's the way the test-makers design them. You'll probably find that you have more trouble interpreting the questions than the figures.

- Bar graphs and line charts are drawn to scale. Pie charts are not necessarily drawn to scale (you'll see a note letting you know that it's not). Visual scale is irrelevant when it comes to analyzing tables.

- Important assumptions will be provided. Any additional information that you might need to know to interpret the figures will be indicated above and below the figures. (Be sure to read this information.)

- Nearly all questions ask for an approximation. You'll see some form of the word *approximate* in nearly all Data Analysis questions. This is because the test-makers are trying to gauge your ability to interpret graphical data, not your ability to crunch numbers to the "*n*th" decimal place.

- Many of the numbers used are *almost* round. This feature relates to the previous one. The GMAT rewards test-takers who recognize that rounding off numbers (to an appropriate extent) will suffice to get to the right answer. So they pack Data Analysis figures with numbers that are close to "easy" ones. (The numbers in our pie chart set serve as good examples. For example, $1,560,000 is close to $1,500,000 and $495,000 is close to $500,000.)

- Figures are not drawn to deceive you or to test your eyesight. In bar graphs and line charts, you won't be asked to split hairs to determine values. These figures are designed with a comfortable margin for error in visual acuity. Just don't round up or down too far.

Apply the 5-Step Plan

Now let's apply the steps you just learned to the above sample questions.

Step 1: Size up the two charts, and read the information above and below them. Notice that we're only dealing with one company during one year here. Notice also that dollar totals are provided but that the pie segments are expressed only as percentages. That's a clue that your main task in this set will be to calculate dollar amounts for various pie segments. Now read the first question.

Question 12

Question 12 is a moderately difficult question. Approximately 50% of test-takers respond correctly to questions like it. Here's the question again:

12. During year X, by approximately what amount did Division C's income exceed Division B's expenses?

   (A) $125,000
   (B) $127,000
   (C) $140,000
   (D) $180,000
   (E) $312,000

You already performed Step 1, so move ahead to Step 2.

Step 2: This question involves three tasks: (1) calculate Division C's income, (2) calculate Division B's expenses, and (3) compute their difference. There's no shortcut to these three tasks, so go on to Step 3.

Step 3: Division B's expenses accounted for 26% of XYZ's total expenses, given as $495,000. Rounding off these figures to 25% and $500,000, Division B's expenses totaled approximately $125,000. Income from Division C sales was 20% of total XYZ income, given as $1,560,000. Rounding this total down to $1,500,000, income from Division C sales was approximately $300,000. Income from Division C sales exceeded Division B's expenses by approximately $175,000.

Step 4: The correct answer is (D). If you have extra time, go to Step 5.

Step 5: Make sure you started with the right numbers. Did you compare C's income with B's expenses (and not some other combination)? If you're satisfied that the numbers you used were the right ones and that your calculations are okay, move on to the next question.

Question 13

Question 13 is a difficult question. Approximately 30% of test-takers respond correctly to questions like it. Here's the question again:

13. With respect to the division whose percent of total income exceeded its percent of total expenses by the greatest amount among the four divisions, by approximately what amount did the division's income exceed its own expenses?

    (A) $69,000

    (B) $90,000

    (C) $150,000

    (D) $185,000

    (E) $240,000

Step 1: Take another close look at the charts.

Step 2: This is a complex question. First, you need to compare profitability among the four divisions. You can rule out Division B, since its percent of total expenses exceeded its percent of total income. That leaves Divisions A, C, and D.

Step 3: For Divisions A, C, and D, compare percent of income and percent of expenses:

    Division A: 38% of total income and 35% of total expenses (3% difference)

    Division C: 20% of total income and 14% of total expenses (6% difference)

    Division D: 30% of total income and 25% of total expenses (5% difference)

For Division C, $(20\%)(\$1,560,000) - (14\%)(\$495,000) = \$242,700$.

Step 4: Answer choice (E), $240,000, is the only one close to our approximation. **The correct answer is (E).**

Step 5: If you have time, rethink Step 3. Make sure you're convinced that the difference in Division C's percentages was greater than either A's or D's. Also ask yourself if $240,000 is in the right ballpark. If you're confident in your analysis, move on to the next question.

KEYS TO SUCCESSFUL GMAT DATA ANALYSIS

Here are some basic tips you should follow for any type of Data Analysis question. Apply these keys to the Practice Tests in Part VII, then review them again just before exam day.

Scroll Vertically to See the Entire Display

Some vertical scrolling may be necessary to view the entire display, especially the information above and below the chart, graph, or table. Don't forget to scroll up and down as you analyze each question.

Don't Confuse Percentages with Raw Numbers

Most data analysis questions involve raw data as well as proportion—in terms of either percent, fraction, or ratio (usually percent). Always ask yourself: "Is the solution to this problem a raw number or a proportional number?" You can be sure that the testing service will "bait" you with appealing incorrect answer choices!

Go to the Appropriate Chart (or Part of a Chart) for Your Numbers

This point of advice may seem obvious; nevertheless, reading the wrong data is probably the leading cause of incorrect responses to Data Analysis questions! To ensure that you don't commit this careless error, point your finger to the proper line, column, or bar on the screen; put your finger right on it, and don't move it until you're sure you've got the correct data.

To Save Time, Round Off Numbers—but Don't Distort Values

Most Data Analysis questions ask for approximate values. So to save time, it's okay to round off numbers; rounding off to the nearest appropriate unit or half-unit usually suffices to get to the correct answer. But don't get too rough in your approximations. Also be sure to round off numerators and denominators of fractions in the same direction (either both up or both down), unless you're confident that a rougher approximation will suffice. Otherwise, you'll distort the value of the number.

Handle Lengthy, Confusing Questions One Part at a Time

Data Analysis questions can be wordy and confusing. Don't panic. Keep in mind that lengthy questions almost always call for two discrete tasks. For the first task, read only the first part of the question. When you're done, go back to the question and read the next part.

Don't Split Hairs Reading Line Charts and Bar Graphs

These are the two types of figures that are drawn to scale. If a certain point on a chart appears to be about 40% of the way from one hash mark to the next, don't hesitate to round up to the halfway point. (The number 5 is usually easier to work with than 4 or 6.)

Formulate a Clear Idea About the Overall Size of the Number Called For

The test-makers pack Data Analysis questions with "sucker bait" answer choices for test-takers who make common computational errors. The best way to keep yourself from falling into their trap is to ask yourself what sort of ballpark number you're looking for in a correct answer. You might ask yourself:

- Is it a double-digit number?
- Is it a percentage that is obviously greater than 50 percent?
- Is it a raw number in the thousands?

By keeping the big picture in mind, you'll catch the fact that you made an error in calculation.

SUMMING IT UP

- To successfully solve Data Sufficiency questions, size up the question first; size up the two statements, and look for a shortcut to the correct answer; consider Statement (1) alone; consider Statement (2) alone; and consider both statements together if neither one alone is enough to answer the question.

- Data Sufficiency questions focus on mathematical concepts rather than working toward a quantitative solution (as Problem Solving questions do)—so it's important to size up the problem before trying to work the actual numbers or equations.

- Watch for "red herring" statements that are irrelevant to the problem at hand. You're looking for a statement that is *sufficient* to answer the question correctly.

- Never assume that graphical figures are accurate.

- For success in more advanced Data Analysis problems, handle parts one at a time before tackling the question as a whole.

Math Review: Number Forms, Relationships, and Sets

chapter 9

OVERVIEW

- **Percents, fractions, and decimals**
- **Simplifying and combining fractions**
- **Decimal place values and operations**
- **Simple percent problems**
- **Percent increase and decrease**
- **Ratios and proportion**
- **Altering fractions and ratios**
- **Ratios with more than two quantities**
- **Proportion problems with variables**
- **Arithmetic mean, median, mode, and range**
- **Standard deviation**
- **Geometric sequences**
- **Arithmetic sequences**
- **Permutations**
- **Combinations**
- **Probability**
- **Summing it up**

In this chapter, you'll focus first on various forms of numbers and relationships between numbers. Specifically, you'll learn how to:

- Combine fractions using the four basic operations
- Combine decimal numbers by multiplication and division
- Compare numbers in percentage terms
- Compare percent changes with number changes
- Rewrite percents, fractions, and decimal numbers from one form to another
- Determine ratios between quantities and determine quantities from ratios
- Set up equivalent ratios (proportions)

Next, you'll explore the following topics, all of which involve sets (defined groups) of numbers or other objects:

- Simple average and median (two ways that a set of numbers can be described as a whole)
- Arithmetic sequences (the pattern from one number to the next in a linear list of numbers)
- Permutations (the possibilities for arranging a set of objects)
- Combinations (the possibilities for selecting groups of objects from a set)
- Probability (the statistical chances of a certain event, permutation, or combination occurring)

PERCENTS, FRACTIONS, AND DECIMALS

Any real number can be expressed as a fraction, a percent, or a decimal number. For instance, $\frac{2}{10}$, 20%, and 0.2 are all different forms of the same quantity or value. GMAT math questions often require you to rewrite one form as another as part of solving the problem at hand. You should know how to write any equivalent quickly and confidently.

To rewrite a percent as a decimal, move the decimal point two places to the *left* (and drop the percent sign). To rewrite a decimal as a percent, move the decimal point two places to the *right* (and add the percent sign).

$$95\% = 0.95$$

$$0.004 = 0.4\%$$

To rewrite a percent as a fraction, *divide* by 100 (and drop the percent sign). To rewrite a fraction as a percent, *multiply* by 100 (and add the percent sign). Percents greater than 100 are equivalent to numbers greater than 1.

$$810\% = \frac{810}{100} = \frac{81}{10} = 8\frac{1}{10}$$

$$\frac{3}{8} = \frac{300}{8}\% = \frac{75}{2}\% = 37\frac{1}{2}\%$$

Beware: Percents greater than 100 or less than 1 (such as 457% and 0.067%) can be confusing, because it's a bit harder to grasp their magnitude. To guard against errors when writing, keep in mind the general magnitude of the number you're dealing with. For example, think of 0.09% as just less than 0.1%, which is one-tenth of a percent, or a thousandth (a pretty small valued number). Think of $\frac{0.45}{5}$ as just less than $\frac{0.5}{5}$, which is obviously $\frac{1}{10}$, or 10%. Think of 668% as more than 6 times a complete 100%, or between 6 and 7.

To rewrite a fraction as a decimal, simply divide the numerator by the denominator, using long division. A fraction-to-decimal equivalent might result in a precise value, an approximation with a repeating pattern, or an approximation with no repeating pattern:

$\frac{5}{8} = 0.625$	The equivalent decimal number is precise after three decimal places.
$\frac{5}{9} \approx 0.555$	The equivalent decimal number can only be approximated (the digit 5 repeats indefinitely).
$\frac{5}{7} \approx 0.714$	The equivalent decimal number can safely be approximated.

Certain fraction-decimal-percent equivalents show up on the GMAT more often than others. The numbers in the following tables are the test-makers' favorites because they reward test-takers who recognize quick ways to deal with numbers. Memorize these conversions so that they're second nature to you on exam day.

Percent	Decimal	Fraction	Percent	Decimal	Fraction
50%	0.5	$\frac{1}{2}$	$16\frac{2}{3}\%$	$0.16\frac{2}{3}$	$\frac{1}{6}$
25%	0.25	$\frac{1}{4}$	$83\frac{1}{3}\%$	$0.83\frac{1}{3}$	$\frac{5}{6}$
75%	0.75	$\frac{3}{4}$	20%	0.2	$\frac{1}{5}$
10%	0.1	$\frac{1}{10}$	40%	0.4	$\frac{2}{5}$
30%	0.3	$\frac{3}{10}$	60%	0.6	$\frac{3}{5}$
70%	0.7	$\frac{7}{10}$	80%	0.8	$\frac{4}{5}$
90%	0.9	$\frac{9}{10}$	$12\frac{1}{2}\%$	0.125	$\frac{1}{8}$
$33\frac{1}{3}\%$	$0.33\frac{1}{3}$	$\frac{1}{3}$	$37\frac{1}{2}\%$	0.375	$\frac{3}{8}$
$66\frac{2}{3}\%$	$0.66\frac{2}{3}$	$\frac{2}{3}$	$62\frac{1}{2}\%$	0.625	$\frac{5}{8}$
			$87\frac{1}{2}\%$	0.875	$\frac{7}{8}$

SIMPLIFYING AND COMBINING FRACTIONS

GMAT question might ask you to combine fractions using one or more of the four basic operations (addition, subtraction, multiplication, and division). The rules for combining fractions by addition and subtraction are very different from the ones for multiplication and division.

Addition and Subtraction and the LCD

To combine fractions by addition or subtraction, the fractions must have a common denominator. If they already do, simply add (or subtract) numerators. If they don't, you'll need to find one. You can always multiply all of the denominators together to find a common denominator, but it might be a big number that's clumsy to work with. So instead, try to find the *least* (or *lowest*) *common denominator* (LCD) by working your way up in multiples of the largest of the denominators given. For denominators of 6, 3, and 5, for instance, try out successive multiples of 6 (12, 18, 24, . . .), and you'll hit the LCD when you get to 30.

1. $\dfrac{5}{3} - \dfrac{5}{6} + \dfrac{5}{2} =$

   (A) $\dfrac{15}{11}$

   (B) $\dfrac{5}{2}$

   (C) $\dfrac{15}{6}$

   (D) $\dfrac{10}{3}$

   (E) $\dfrac{15}{3}$

To find the LCD, try out successive multiples of 6 until you come across one that is also a multiple of both 3 and 2. The LCD is 6. Multiply each numerator by the same number by which you would multiply the fraction's denominator to give you the LCD of 6. Place the three products over this common denominator. Then, combine the numbers in the numerator. (Pay close attention to the subtraction sign!) Finally, simplify to lowest terms:

$$\frac{5}{3} - \frac{5}{6} + \frac{5}{2} = \frac{10}{6} - \frac{5}{6} + \frac{15}{6}$$

$$= \frac{20}{6}$$

$$= \frac{10}{3}$$

The correct answer is (D).

Multiplication and Division

To multiply fractions, multiply the numerators and multiply the denominators. The denominators need not be the same. To divide one fraction by another, multiply by the reciprocal of the divisor (the number after the division sign).

Multiplication: Division:

$$\dfrac{\dfrac{2}{5}}{\dfrac{3}{4}} = \dfrac{2}{5} \times \dfrac{4}{3} = \dfrac{(2)(4)}{(5)(3)} = \dfrac{8}{15} \qquad \dfrac{1}{2} \times \dfrac{5}{3} \times \dfrac{1}{7} = \dfrac{(1)(5)(1)}{(2)(3)(7)} = \dfrac{5}{42}$$

To simplify the multiplication or division, cancel factors common to a numerator and a denominator before combining fractions. It's okay to cancel across fractions. Take, for instance, the operation $\dfrac{3}{4} \times \dfrac{4}{9} \times \dfrac{3}{2}$. Looking just at the first two fractions, you can cancel out 4 and 3, so the operation simplifies to $\dfrac{1}{1} \times \dfrac{1}{3} \times \dfrac{3}{2}$. Now, looking just at the second and third fractions, you can cancel out 3 and the operation becomes even simpler: $\dfrac{1}{1} \times \dfrac{1}{1} \times \dfrac{1}{2} = \dfrac{1}{2}$.

Apply the same rules in the same way to variables (letters) as to numbers.

2. $\dfrac{2}{a} \times \dfrac{b}{4} \times \dfrac{a}{5} \times \dfrac{8}{c} = ?$

     (A) $\dfrac{ab}{4c}$

     (B) $\dfrac{10b}{9c}$

     (C) $\dfrac{8}{5}$

     (D) $\dfrac{16b}{5ac}$

     (E) $\dfrac{4b}{5c}$

Since you're dealing only with multiplication, look for factors and variables (letters) in any numerator that are the same as those in any denominator. Canceling common factors leaves:

$$\dfrac{2}{1} \times \dfrac{b}{1} \times \dfrac{1}{5} \times \dfrac{2}{c}$$

Multiply numerators and denominators and you get $\dfrac{4b}{5c}$. **The correct answer is (E).**

Mixed Numbers and Multiple Operations

A mixed number consists of a whole number along with a simple fraction—for example, the number $4\frac{2}{3}$. Before combining fractions, you might need to rewrite a mixed number as a fraction. To do so, follow these three steps:

❶ Multiply the denominator of the fraction by the whole number.

❷ Add the product to the numerator of the fraction.

❸ Place the sum over the denominator of the fraction.

For example, here's how to rewrite the mixed number $4\frac{2}{3}$ into a fraction:

$$4\frac{2}{3} = \frac{(3)(4)+2}{3} = \frac{14}{3}$$

To perform multiple operations, always perform multiplication and division before you perform addition and subtraction.

3. $\dfrac{4\frac{1}{2}}{1\frac{1}{8}} - 3\frac{2}{3} = ?$

(A) $\dfrac{1}{3}$

(B) $\dfrac{3}{8}$

(C) $\dfrac{11}{6}$

(D) $\dfrac{17}{6}$

(E) $\dfrac{11}{2}$

First, rewrite all mixed numbers as fractions. Then, eliminate the complex fraction by multiplying the numerator fraction by the reciprocal of the denominator fraction (cancel across fractions before multiplying):

$$\frac{\frac{9}{2}}{\frac{9}{8}} - \frac{11}{3} = \left(\frac{9}{2}\right)\left(\frac{8}{9}\right) - \frac{11}{3} = \left(\frac{1}{1}\right)\left(\frac{4}{1}\right) - \frac{11}{3} = \frac{4}{1} - \frac{11}{3}$$

Then, express each fraction using the common denominator 3, and then subtract:

$$\frac{4}{1} - \frac{11}{3} = \frac{12-11}{3} = \frac{1}{3}$$

The correct answer is (A).

DECIMAL PLACE VALUES AND OPERATIONS

Place value refers to the specific value of a digit in a decimal. For example, in the decimal 682.793:

- The digit 6 is in the "hundreds" place.
- The digit 8 is in the "tens" place.
- The digit 2 is in the "ones" place.
- The digit 7 is in the "tenths" place.
- The digit 9 is in the "hundredths" place.
- The digit 3 is in the "thousandths" place.

So you can express 682.793 as follows:

$$600 + 80 + 2 + \frac{7}{10} + \frac{9}{100} + \frac{3}{1000}$$

To approximate, or round off, a decimal, round any digit less than 5 down to 0, and round any digit 5 or greater up to 0 (adding one digit to the place value to the left).

- The value of 682.793 to the nearest hundredth is 682.79.
- The value of 682.793 to the nearest tenth is 682.8.
- The value of 682.793 to the nearest whole number is 683.
- The value of 682.793 to the nearest ten is 680.
- The value of 682.793 to the nearest hundred is 700.

Multiplying Decimals

The number of decimal places (digits to the right of the decimal point) in a product should be the same as the total number of decimal places in the numbers you multiply. So to multiply decimals quickly, follow these three steps:

1. Multiply, but ignore the decimal points.
2. Count the total number of decimal places among the numbers you multiplied.
3. Include that number of decimal places in your product. Here are two simple examples:

Example 1

$(23.6)(0.07)$	Three decimal places altogether
$(236)(7) = (1652)$	Decimals temporarily ignored
$(23.6)(0.07) = 1.652$	Decimal point inserted

Example 2

$(0.01)(0.02)(0.03)$	Six decimal places altogether
$(1)(2)(3) = 6$	Decimals temporarily ignored
$(0.01)(0.02)(0.03) = 0.000006$	Decimal point inserted

TIP

Eliminate decimal points from fractions, as well as from percents, to help you see more clearly the magnitude of the quantity you're dealing with.

Dividing Decimals

When you divide (or compute a fraction), you can move the decimal point in both numbers by the same number of places either to the left or the right without altering the quotient (value of the fraction). Here are three related examples:

$$11.4 \div 0.3 = \frac{11.4}{0.3} = \frac{114}{3} = 38$$

$$1.14 \div 3 = \frac{1.14}{3} = \frac{114}{300} = 0.38$$

$$114 \div 0.003 = \frac{114}{0.003} = \frac{114,000}{3} = 38,000$$

GMAT questions involving place value and decimals usually require a bit more from you than just identifying a place value or moving a decimal point around. Typically, they require you to combine decimals with fractions or percents.

4. Which of the following is nearest in value to $\frac{1}{3} \times 0.3 \times \frac{1}{30} \times 0.03$?

   (A) $\dfrac{1}{10,000}$

   (B) $\dfrac{33}{100,000}$

   (C) $\dfrac{99}{100,000}$

   (D) $\dfrac{33}{10,000}$

   (E) $\dfrac{99}{10,000}$

There are several ways to combine the four numbers provided in the question. One method is to combine the two fractions: $\frac{1}{3} \times \frac{1}{30} = \frac{1}{90}$. Then, combine the two decimals: $0.3 \times 0.03 = 0.009 = \frac{9}{1000}$. Finally, combine the two fractions:

$$\frac{1}{90} \times \frac{9}{1000} = \frac{9}{90,000} = \frac{1}{10,000}$$

The correct answer is (A).

SIMPLE PERCENT PROBLEMS

On the GMAT, a simple problem involving percent might ask you to perform any one of these four tasks:

1 Find a percent of a percent.

2 Find a percent of a number.

3 Find a number when a percent is given.

4 Find what percent one number is of another.

The following examples show you how to handle these four tasks (Task 4 is a bit trickier than the others):

Finding a percent of a percent	*What is 2% of 2%?* Rewrite 2% as 0.02, then multiply: $0.02 \times 0.02 = 0.0004$, or 0.04%
Finding a percent of a number	*What is 35% of 65?* Rewrite 35% as 0.35, then multiply: $0.35 \times 65 = 22.75$
Finding a number when a percent is given	*7 is 14% of what number?* Translate the question into an algebraic equation, writing the percent as either a fraction or decimal: $7 = 14\%$ of x $7 = 0.14x$ $x = \dfrac{7}{0.14} = \dfrac{1}{0.02} = \dfrac{100}{2} = 50$
Finding what percent one number is of another	*90 is what % of 1500?* Set up an equation to solve for the percent: $\dfrac{90}{1500} = \dfrac{x}{100}$ $1500x = 9000$ $15x = 90$ $x = \dfrac{90}{15}$, or 6

PERCENT INCREASE AND DECREASE

In example 4, you set up a proportion. (90 is to 1500 as x is to 100.) You'll need to set up a proportion for other types of GMAT questions as well, including questions about ratios, which you'll look at a bit later in this chapter.

The concept of percent change is one of the test-makers' favorites. Here's the key to answering questions involving this concept: Percent change always relates to the value *before* the change. Here are two simple illustrations:

10 increased by what percent is 12?	1. The amount of the increase is 2. 2. Compare the change (2) to the original number (10). 3. The change in percent is $\left(\dfrac{2}{10}\right)(100) = 20$, or 20%.
12 decreased by what percent is 10?	1. The amount of the decrease is 2. 2. Compare the change (2) to the original number (12). 3. The change is $\dfrac{1}{6}$, or $16\dfrac{2}{3}$% , or approximately 16.7%.

Notice that the percent increase from 10 to 12 (20%) is not the same as the percent decrease from 12 to 10 $\left(16\dfrac{2}{3}\%\right)$. That's because the original number (before the change) is different in the two questions.

A typical GMAT percent change problem will involve a story—about a type of quantity such as tax, profit or discount, or weight—in which you need to calculate successive changes in percent. For example:

- An increase, then a decrease (or vice versa)
- Multiple increases or decreases

Whatever the variation, just take the problem one step at a time and you'll have no trouble handling it.

5. A stereo system originally priced at $500 is discounted by 10%, then by another 10%. If a 20% tax is added to the purchase price, how much would a customer buying the system at its lowest price pay for it, including tax, to the nearest dollar?

   (A) $413
   (B) $480
   (C) $486
   (D) $500
   (E) $512

After the first 10% discount, the price was $450 ($500 minus 10% of $500). After the second discount, which is calculated based on the $450 price, the price of the stereo is $405 ($450 minus 10%

of \$450). A 20% tax on \$405 is \$81. Thus, the customer has paid \$405 + \$81 = \$486. **The correct answer is (C).**

A percent change problem might also involve an accompanying chart or graph, which provides the numbers needed for the calculation.

6.

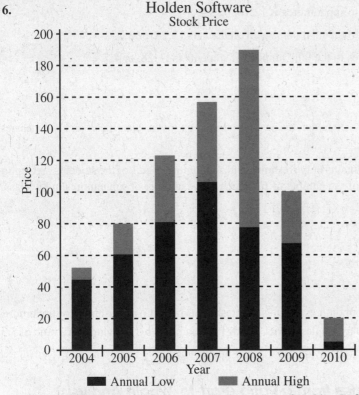

Holden Software
Stock Price

Based on the graph above, the average low price of Holden Software stock for the two-year period 2005–2006 was approximately what percent lower than its average high price for the two-year period 2008–2009?

(A) 25

(B) 37

(C) 45

(D) 52

(E) 75

Annual *low* prices (represented by black bars) for 2005 and 2006 were \$60 and \$80, respectively, which yield an average of \$70 for the two-year period. Annual *high* prices (represented by gray bars) for 2008 and 2009 were approximately \$190 and \$100, respectively, which yield an average of \$145. The percent decrease from \$145 to \$70 ≈ 52%. The only possible answer choice is (D). **The correct answer is (D).**

Something to keep in mind: If a question based on a bar graph, line graph, or pie chart asks for an approximation, the test-makers are telling you that it's okay to round off numbers you glean from the chart or graph. For example, in the preceding question, a rough estimate of \$190 for the high 2008 stock price was close enough to determine the correct answer choice.

RATIOS AND PROPORTION

A *ratio* expresses proportion or comparative size—the size of one quantity *relative* to the size of another. As with fractions, you can simplify ratios by dividing common factors. For example, given a class of 28 students—12 freshmen and 16 sophomores:

- The ratio of freshmen to sophomores is 12:16, or 3:4.
- The ratio of freshmen to the total number of students is 12:28, or 3:7.
- The ratio of sophomores to the total number of students is 16:28, or 4:7.

Finding a Ratio

A GMAT question might ask you to determine a ratio based on given quantities. This is the easiest type of GMAT ratio question.

7. A class of 56 students contains only freshmen and sophomores. If 21 of the students are sophomores, what is the ratio of the number of freshmen to the number of sophomores in the class?

   (A) 3:5
   (B) 5:7
   (C) 5:3
   (D) 7:4
   (E) 2:1

Since 21 of 56 students are sophomores, 35 must be freshmen. The ratio of freshmen to sophomores is 35:21. To simplify the ratio to simplest terms, divide both numbers by 7, giving you a ratio of 5:3. **The correct answer is (C).**

Determining Quantities from a Ratio (Part-to-Whole Analysis)

You can think of any ratio as parts adding up to a whole. For example, in the ratio 5:6, 5 parts + 6 parts = 11 parts (the whole). If the actual total quantity were 22, you'd multiply each element by 2: 10 parts + 12 parts = 22 parts (the whole). Notice that the ratios are the same: 5:6 is the same ratio as 10:12.

You might be able to solve a GMAT ratio question using this part-to-whole approach.

8. A class of students contains only freshmen and sophomores. If 18 of the students are sophomores, and if the ratio of the number of freshmen to the number of sophomores in the class is 5:3, how many students are in the class?

   (A) 30
   (B) 36
   (C) 40
   (D) 48
   (E) 56

Using a part-to-whole analysis, look first at the ratio and the sum of its parts: 5 (freshmen) + 3 (sophomores) = 8 (total students). These aren't the actual quantities, but they're proportionate to those quantities. Given 18 sophomores altogether, sophomores account for 3 parts—each part containing 6 students. Accordingly, the total number of students must be $6 \times 8 = 48$. **The correct answer is (D).**

Determining Quantities from a Ratio (Setting Up a Proportion)

Since you can express any ratio as a fraction, you can set two equivalent, or proportionate, ratios equal to each other, as fractions. So the ratio 16:28 is proportionate to the ratio 4:7 because $\frac{16}{28} = \frac{4}{7}$. If one of the four terms is missing from the equation (the proportion), you can solve for the missing term using algebra. So if the ratio 3:4 is proportionate to 4:x, you can solve for x in the equation $\frac{3}{4} = \frac{4}{x}$.

Using the cross-product method, equate products of numerator and denominator across the equation:

$$(3)(x) = (4)(4)$$
$$3x = 16$$
$$x = \frac{16}{3}, \text{ or } 5\frac{1}{3}$$

Or, since the numbers are simple, shortcut the algebra by asking yourself what number you multiply the first numerator (3) by for a result that equals the other numerator (4):

$$3 \times \frac{4}{3} = 4 \text{ (a no-brainer calculation)}.$$

So, you maintain proportion (equal ratios) by also multiplying the first denominator (4) by $\frac{4}{3}$:

$$4 \times \frac{4}{3} = \frac{16}{3} \text{ (another no-brainer calculation)}.$$

Even if the quantities in a question strike you as decidedly "unround," it's a good bet that doing the math will be easier than you might first think.

9. If 3 miles are equivalent to 4.83 kilometers, then 11.27 kilometers are equivalent to how many miles?

   (A) 1.76
   (B) 5.9
   (C) 7.0
   (D) 8.4
   (E) 16.1

The question essentially asks, "3 is to 4.83 as *what* is to 11.27?" Set up a proportion, then solve for x by the cross-product method:

$$\frac{3}{4.83} = \frac{x}{11.27}$$
$$(4.83)(x) = (3)(11.27)$$
$$x = \frac{(3)(11.27)}{4.83}$$
$$x = \frac{33.81}{4.83}, \text{ or } 7$$

The correct answer is (C).

Notice that, despite all the intimidating decimal numbers, the solution turns out to be a tidy number: 7. That's typical of the GMAT.

Now let's focus on more advanced applications of fractions, percents, decimals, ratios, and proportion. We'll place special emphasis on how the test-makers incorporate algebraic features into GMAT questions covering these concepts:

- Altering fractions and ratios
- Ratios involving more than two quantities
- Proportion problems with variables

We'll take a look at how test-makers design tougher-than-average GMAT questions involving:

- Arithmetic mean (simple average) and median (two ways that a set of numbers can be measured as a whole)
- Standard deviation (a quantitative expression of the dispersion of a set of measurements)
- Geometric sequences (the pattern from one number to the next in an exponential list of numbers)
- Permutations (the possibilities for arranging a set of objects)
- Combinations (the possibilities for selecting groups of objects from a set)
- Probability (the statistical chances of a certain event, permutation, or combination occurring)

ALTERING FRACTIONS AND RATIOS

TIP

Remember: When you add (or subtract) the same number from both the numerator and denominator of a fraction—or from each term in a ratio—you alter the fraction or ratio, unless the original ratio was 1:1 (in which case the ratio is unchanged).

An average test-taker might assume that *adding* the same *positive* quantity to a fraction's numerator (p) and to its denominator (q) leaves the fraction's value $\left(\dfrac{p}{q}\right)$ unchanged. But this is true *if and only*

if the original numerator and denominator were equal to each other. Otherwise, the fraction's value will change. Remember the following three rules, which apply to any positive numbers x, p, and q (the first one is the no-brainer you just read):

If $p = q$, then $\dfrac{p}{q} = \dfrac{p+x}{q+x}$. (The fraction's value remains unchanged and is always 1.)

If $p > q$, then $\dfrac{p}{q} > \dfrac{p+x}{q+x}$. (The fraction's value will *decrease*.)

, If $p < q$, then $\dfrac{p}{q} < \dfrac{p+x}{q+x}$. (The fraction's value will *increase*.)

A GMAT question might ask you to alter a ratio by adding or subtracting from one (or both) terms in the ratio. The rules for altering ratios are the same as for altering fractions. In either case, set up a proportion and solve algebraically for the unknown term.

10. A drawer contains exactly half as many white shirts as blue shirts. If four more shirts of each color were to be added to the drawer, the ratio of white to blue shirts would be 5:8. How many blue shirts does the drawer contain?

   (A) 14

   (B) 12

   (C) 11

   (D) 10

   (E) 9

Represent the original ratio of white to blue shirts by the fraction $\dfrac{x}{2x}$, where x is the number of white shirts, then add 4 to both the numerator and denominator. Set this fraction equal to $\dfrac{5}{8}$ (the ratio after adding shirts). Cross-multiply to solve for x:

$$\frac{x+4}{2x+4} = \frac{5}{8}$$
$$8x + 32 = 10x + 20$$
$$12 = 2x$$
$$x = 6$$

The original denominator is $2x$, or 12. **The correct answer is (B).**

RATIOS WITH MORE THAN TWO QUANTITIES

You approach ratio problems involving three or more quantities the same way as those involving only two quantities. The only difference is that there are more "parts" that make up the "whole."

11. Three lottery winners—X, Y, and Z—are sharing a lottery jackpot. X's share is $\dfrac{1}{5}$ of Y's share and $\dfrac{1}{7}$ of Z's share. If the total jackpot is \$195,000, what is the dollar amount of Z's share?

  (A) \$15,000
  (B) \$35,000
  (C) \$75,000
  (D) \$105,000
  (E) \$115,000

At first glance, this problem doesn't appear to involve ratios. (Where's the colon?) But it does. The ratio of X's share to Y's share is 1:5, and the ratio of X's share to Z's share is 1:7. So you can set up the following triple ratio:

  X:Y:Z = 1:5:7

X's winnings account for 1 of 13 equal parts (1 + 5 + 7) of the total jackpot. $\dfrac{1}{13}$ of \$195,000 is \$15,000. Accordingly, Y's share is 5 times that amount, or \$75,000, and Z's share is 7 times that amount, or \$105,000. **The correct answer is (D).**

In handling word problems involving ratios, think of a whole as the sum of its fractional parts, as in the method used to solve the preceding problem $\dfrac{1}{13}$ (X's share) $+ \dfrac{5}{13}$ (Y's share) $+ \dfrac{7}{13}$ (Z's share) = 1 (the whole jackpot).

PROPORTION PROBLEMS WITH VARIABLES

A GMAT proportion question might use *letters* instead of numbers—to focus on the process rather than the result. You can solve these problems algebraically or by using the plug-in strategy.

12. A candy store sells candy only in half-pound boxes. At *c* cents per box, which of the following is the cost of *a* ounces of candy? [1 pound = 16 ounces]

   (A) $\dfrac{c}{a}$

   (B) $\dfrac{a}{16c}$

   (C) ac

   (D) $\dfrac{ac}{8}$

   (E) $\dfrac{8c}{a}$

This question is asking: "*c* cents is to one box as *how many cents* are to *a* ounces?" Set up a proportion, letting *x* equal the cost of *a* ounces. Because the question asks for the cost of ounces, convert 1 box to 8 ounces (a half pound). Use the cross-product method to solve quickly:

$$\frac{c}{8} = \frac{x}{a}$$

$$8x = ac$$

$$x = \frac{ac}{8}$$

The correct answer is (D).

You can also use the plug-in strategy for this question, either instead of algebra or, better yet, to check the answer you chose using algebra. Pick easy numbers to work with, such as 100 for *c* and 16 for *a*. At 100 cents per 8-ounce box, 16 ounces of candy cost 200 cents. Plug your numbers for *a* and *c* into each answer choice. Only choice (D) gives you the number 200 you're looking for.

ARITHMETIC MEAN, MEDIAN, MODE, AND RANGE

Arithmetic mean (simple average), median, mode, and range are four different ways to describe a set of terms quantitatively. Here's the definition of each one:

- **Arithmetic mean (average):** In a set of *n* measurements, the sum of the measurements divided by *n*.

- **Median:** The middle measurement after the measurements are ordered by size (or the average of the two middle measurements if the number of measurements is even).

- **Mode:** The measurement that appears most frequently in a set.

- **Range:** The difference between the greatest measurement and the least measurement.

For example, given a set of six measurements, (8,–4,8,3,2,7):

mean = 4	$(8 - 4 + 8 + 3 + 2 + 7) \div 6 = 24 \div 6 = 4$
median = 5	The average of 3 and 7—the two middle measurement in the set ordered in this way: $\{-4,2,3,7,8,8\}$
mode = 8	8 appears twice (more frequently than any other measurement
range = 12	The difference between 8 and –4

For the same set of values, the mean (simple average) and the median can be, but are not necessarily, the same. For example: $\{3,4,5,6,7\}$ has both a mean and median of 5. However, the set $\{-2,0,5,8,9\}$ has a mean of 4 but a median of 5.

The GMAT covers arithmetic mean far more frequently than median, mode, or range, so let's focus on problems involving mean. First of all, in finding a simple average, be sure the numbers being added are all of the same form or in terms of the same units.

13. What is the average of $\frac{1}{5}$, 25%, and 0.09?

    (A) 0.18

    (B) 20%

    (C) $\frac{1}{4}$

    (D) 0.32

    (E) $\frac{1}{3}$

Since the answer choices are not all expressed in the same form, first rewrite numbers as whichever form you think would be easiest to work with when you add the numbers together. In this case, the easiest form to work with is probably the decimal form. So rewrite the first two numbers as decimals, and then find the sum of the three numbers: $0.20 + 0.25 + 0.09 = 0.54$. Finally, divide by 3 to find the average: $0.54 \div 3 = 0.18$. **The correct answer is (A).**

To find a missing number when the average of all the numbers in a set is given, plug into the arithmetic mean formula all the numbers you know—which include the average, the sum of the other numbers, and the number of terms. Then, use algebra to find the missing number. Or, you can try out each answer choice, in turn, as the missing number until you find one that results in the average given.

14. The average of five numbers is 26. Four of the numbers are –12, 90, –26, and 10. What is the fifth number?

    (A) 16

    (B) 42

    (C) 44

    (D) 68

    (E) 84

TIP

Numerical answer choices are listed in ascending order of value, so if you're working backward from the choices, start with (C), the median value. If (C) is either too great or too little, you've narrowed down the options either to (A) and (B) or to (D) and (E).

To solve the problem algebraically, let x = the missing number. Set up the arithmetic mean formula, then solve for x:

$$26 = \frac{(90+10-12-26)+x}{5}$$

$$26 = \frac{62+x}{5}$$

$$130 = 62+x$$

$$68 = x$$

The correct answer is (D).

Or, you can try out each answer choice in turn. Start with the middle value, 44, choice (C). The sum of 44 and the other four numbers is 106. Dividing this sum by 5 gives you 21.2—a number less than the average of 26 that you re aiming for. So you know the fifth number is greater than 44—and that leaves choices (D) and (E). Try out the number 68, choice (D), and you'll obtain the average of 26.

If the numbers are easy to work with, you might be able to determine a missing term, given the simple average of a set of numbers, without resorting to algebra. Simply apply a dose of logic.

15. If the average of six consecutive multiples of 4 is 22, what is the greatest of these integers?

    (A) 22
    (B) 24
    (C) 26
    (D) 28
    (E) 32

You can answer this question with common sense—no algebra required. Consecutive multiples of 4 are 4, 8, 12, 16, etc. Given that the average of six such numbers is 22, the two middle terms (the third and fourth terms) must be 20 and 24. (Their average is 22.) Accordingly, the fifth term is 28, and the sixth and greatest term is 32. **The correct answer is (E).**

On the GMAT, easier questions involving simple average might ask you to add numbers together and divide a sum. A tougher question might ask you to perform the following task (which involves algebra) such as:

Find the value of a number that changes an average from one number to another.

When an additional number is added to a set, and the average of the numbers in the set changes as a result, you can determine the value of the number that's added by applying the arithmetic-mean formula twice.

16. The average of three numbers is –4. If a fourth number is added, the arithmetic mean of all four numbers is –1. What is the fourth number?

    (A) –10
    (B) 2
    (C) 8
    (D) 10
    (E) 16

To solve the problem algebraically, first determine the sum of the three original numbers by the arithmetic-mean formula:

$$-4 = \frac{a+b+c}{3}$$

Then, apply the formula again accounting for the additional (fourth) number. The new average is -1, the sum of the other three numbers is -12, and the number of terms is 4. Solve for the missing number (x):

$$-1 = \frac{-12+x}{4}$$
$$-4 = -12+x$$
$$8 = x$$

The correct answer is (C).

You approach arithmetic mean problems that involve variables instead of (or in addition to) numbers in the same way as those involving only numbers. Just plug the information you're given into the arithmetic mean formula, and then solve the problem algebraically.

17. If A is the average of P, Q, and another number, which of the following represents the missing number?

   (A) $3A - P - Q$
   (B) $A + P + Q$
   (C) $A + P - Q$
   (D) $A - P + Q$
   (E) $3A - P + Q$

Let x = the missing number. Solve for x by the arithmetic-mean formula:

$$A = \frac{P+Q+x}{3}$$
$$3A = P+Q+x$$
$$3A - P - Q = x$$

The correct answer is (A).

ALERT!
Don't try the plug-in strategy to solve the problem on this page; it's too complex. Be flexible and use shortcuts wherever you can—but recognize their limitations.

STANDARD DEVIATION

Standard deviation is a measure of dispersion among members of a set. Computing standard deviation involves these five steps:

1. Compute the arithmetic mean (simple average) of all terms in the set.
2. Compute the difference between the mean and each term.
3. Square each difference you computed in Step 2.
4. Compute the mean of the squares you computed in Step 3.
5. Compute the non-negative square root of the mean you computed in Step 4.

For example, here's how you'd determine the standard deviation of Distribution A: $\{-1,2,3,4\}$:

$$\text{Arithmetic mean} = \frac{-1+2+3+4}{4} = \frac{8}{4} = 2$$

The difference between the mean (2) and each term: $2 - (-1) = 3$; $2 - 2 = 0$; $3 - 2 = 1$; $4 - 2 = 2$

The square of each difference: $\{3^2, 0^2, 1^2, 2^2\} = \{9, 0, 1, 4\}$

The mean of the squares: $\dfrac{9 + 0 + 1 + 4}{4} = \dfrac{14}{4} = \dfrac{7}{2}$

The standard deviation of Distribution A: $A = \sqrt{\dfrac{7}{2}}$

A GMAT question might ask you to calculate standard deviation (as in the preceding example). Or, a question might ask you to *compare* standard deviations. You might be able to make the comparison without precise calculations—by remembering to follow this general rule: *The greater the data are spread away from the mean, the greater the standard deviation.* For example, consider these two distributions:

Distribution A: {1,2.5,4,5.5,7}

Distribution B: {1,3,4,5,7}

In both sets, the mean and median is 4, and the range is 6. But the standard deviation of *A* is greater than that of *B*, because 2.5 and 5.5 are further away than 3 and 5 from the mean.

18. Which of the following distributions has the greatest standard deviation?
    (A) {−1,1,3}
    (B) {1,2,5}
    (C) {0,4,5}
    (D) {−3,−1,2}
    (E) {2,3,6}

Notice that in each of the choices (A), (B), and (E), the distribution's range is 4. But in choice (C) and choice (D), the range is 5. So the correct answer is probably either (C) or (D). Focusing on these two choices, notice that the middle term in choice (C), 4, is skewed further away from the mean than the middle term in choice (D). That's a good indication that (C) provides the distribution having the greatest standard deviation. **The correct answer is (C).**

GEOMETRIC SEQUENCES

In a geometric sequence of numbers, each term is a constant multiple of the preceding one; in other words, the ratio between any term and the next one is constant. The multiple (or ratio) might be obvious by examining the sequence—for example:

In the geometric sequence 2, 4, 8, 16, . . ., you can easily determine that the constant multiple is 2 (and the ratio of each term to the next is 1:2).

In the geometric sequence 1, −3, 9, −27, . . ., you can easily determine that the constant multiple is − 3 (and the ratio of each term to the next is 1:−3).

Once you know the multiple (or ratio), you can answer any question asking for an unknown term—or for either the sum or the average of certain terms.

19. In a geometric sequence, each term is a constant multiple of the preceding one. If the third and fourth numbers in the series are 8 and –16, respectively, what is the first term in the sequence?

(A) –32

(B) –4

(C) 2

(D) 4

(E) 64

The constant multiple is –2. But since you need to work backward from the third term (8), apply the reciprocal of that multiple twice. The second term is $(8)\left(-\frac{1}{2}\right) = -4$. The first term is $(-4)\left(-\frac{1}{2}\right) = 2$.

The correct answer is (C).

20. In a geometric sequence, each term is a constant multiple of the preceding one. What is the sum of the first four numbers in a geometric sequence whose second number is 4 and whose third number is 6?

(A) 16

(B) 19

(C) $22\frac{1}{2}$

(D) $21\frac{2}{3}$

(E) 20

The constant multiple is $\frac{3}{2}$. In other words, the ratio of each term to the next is 2:3. Since the second term is 4, the first term is $4 \times \frac{2}{3} = \frac{8}{3}$. Since the third term is 6, the fourth term is $6 \times \frac{3}{2} = \frac{18}{2}$, or 9.

The sum of the four terms $= \frac{8}{3} + 4 + 6 + 9 = 21\frac{2}{3}$. **The correct answer is (D).**

You can also solve geometric sequence problems by applying a special formula. But you'll need to memorize it because the test won't provide it. In the following formula, r = the constant multiple (or the ratio between each term and the preceding one), a = the first term in the sequence, n = the position number for any particular term in the series, and T = the particular term itself:

$ar^{(n-1)} = T$

You can solve for any of the formula's variables, as long as you know the values for the other three. Following are two examples:

If $a = 3$ and $r = 2$, then the third term $= (3)(2)^2 = 12$, and the sixth term $= (3)(2)^5 = (3)(32) = 96$.

If the sixth term is $-\frac{1}{16}$ and the constant ratio is $\frac{1}{2}$, then the first term $(a) = -2$:

ALERT!

You can't calculate the average of terms in a geometric series by averaging the first and last term in the series: The progression is geometric, not arithmetic. You need to add up the terms, then divide by the number of terms.

$$a\left(\frac{1}{2}\right)^5 = -\frac{1}{16}$$

$$a\left(\frac{1}{32}\right) = -\frac{1}{16}$$

$$a = \left(-\frac{1}{16}\right)(32) = -2$$

The algebra is simple enough—but you need to know the formula, of course.

21. In a geometric series, each term is a constant multiple of the preceding one. If the first three terms in a geometric series are –2, x, and –8, which of the following could be the sixth term in the series?

    (A) –32

    (B) –16

    (C) 16

    (D) 32

    (E) 64

Since all pairs of successive terms must have the same ratio, $\frac{-2}{x} = \frac{x}{-8}$. By the cross-product method, $x^2 = 16$, and hence $x = \pm 4$. For $x = 4$, the ratio is $\frac{4}{-2} = -2$. Applying the formula you just learned, the sixth term would be $(-2)(-2)5 = 64$. For $x = -4$, the ratio is $\frac{-4}{-2} = 2$. The sixth term would be $(-2)(2)^5 = -64$. **The correct answer is (E).**

ARITHMETIC SEQUENCES

In an arithmetic sequence of numbers, there is a constant (unchanging) difference between successive numbers in the sequence. In other words, all numbers in an arithmetic sequence are evenly spaced. All of the following are examples of an arithmetic sequence:

- Successive integers
- Successive even integers
- Successive odd integers
- Successive multiples of the same number
- Successive integers ending in the same digit

On the GMAT, questions involving an arithmetic sequence might ask for the average or the sum of a sequence. When the numbers to be averaged form an arithmetic (evenly spaced) sequence, the average is simply the median (the middle number or the average of the two middle numbers if the number of terms is even). In other words, the mean and median of the set of numbers are the same. Faced with calculating the average of a long sequence of evenly-spaced integers, you can shortcut the addition.

22. What is the average of the first 20 positive integers?

   (A) $7\frac{1}{2}$

   (B) 10

   (C) $10\frac{1}{2}$

   (D) 15

   (E) 20

Since the terms are evenly spaced, the average is halfway between the 10th and 11th terms—which happen to be the integers 10 and 11. So the average is $10\frac{1}{2}$. (This number is also the median.) If you take the average of the first term (1) and the last term (20), you get the same result:

$$\frac{1+20}{2} = \frac{21}{2}, \text{ or } 10\frac{1}{2}$$

The correct answer is (C).

Finding the sum (rather than the average) of an arithmetic (evenly spaced) sequence of numbers requires only one additional step: multiplying the average (which is also the median) by the number of terms in the sequence. The trickiest aspect of this type of question is determining the number of terms in the sequence.

23. What is the sum of all odd integers between 10 and 40?

   (A) 250

   (B) 325

   (C) 375

   (D) 400

   (E) 450

The average of the described numbers is 25—halfway between 10 and 40 (in other words, half the sum of 10 and 40). The number of terms in the sequence is 15. (The first term is 11, and the last term is 39.) The sum of the described series of integers $= 25 \times 15 = 375$. **The correct answer is (C).**

When calculating the average or sum of a sequence of evenly spaced numbers, be careful counting the number of terms in the series. For instance, the number of positive *odd* integers less than 50 is 25, but the number of positive *even* integers less than 50 is only 24.

PERMUTATIONS

A *permutation* is an arrangement of objects in which the order (sequence) is important. Each arrangement of the letters A, B, C, and D, for example, is a different permutation of the four letters. There are two different ways to determine the number of permutations for a group of distinct objects.

   ❶ List all the permutations, using a methodical process to make sure you don't overlook any. For the letters A, B, C, and D, start with A in the first position, then list all possibilities for the second position, along with all possibilities for the third and fourth positions (you'll discover six permutations):

A B C D	A C B D	A D B C
A B D C	A C D B	A D C B

Placing B in the first position would also result in 6 permutations. The same applies to either C or D in the first position. So the total number of permutations is $6 \times 4 = 24$.

❷ Use the following formula (let n = the number of objects) and limit the number of terms to the counting numbers, or positive integers:

Number of permutations $= n(n - 1)(n - 2)(n - 3) \ldots (1)$

The number of permutations can be expressed as $n!$ ("n" factorial). Using the factorial is much easier than compiling a list of permutations. For example, the number of arrangements (permutations) of the four letters A, B, C, and D:

$$4! = 4(4 - 1)(4 - 2)(4 - 3) = 4 \times 3 \times 2 \times 1 = 24$$

TIP

You can shortcut common factorial calculations by memorizing them: $3! = 6$, $4! = 24$, and $5! = 120$.

24. Five tokens—one red, one blue, one green, and two white—are arranged in a row, one next to another. If the two white tokens are next to each other, how many arrangements according to color are possible?

(A) 12

(B) 16

(C) 20

(D) 24

(E) 30

The two white tokens might be in positions 1 and 2, 2 and 3, 3 and 4, or 4 and 5. For each of these four possibilities, there are 6 possible color arrangements (3!) for the other three tokens (which all differ in color). Thus, the total number of possible arrangements is 4×6, or 24. **The correct answer is (D).**

COMBINATIONS

ALERT!

Notice that each parenthetical combination backtracks to an earlier letter. Be sure you don't repeat any combination, and make sure you don't backtrack to an earlier object.

A *combination* is a group of certain objects selected from a larger set. The order of objects in the group is not important. You can determine the total number of possible combinations by listing the possible groups in a methodical manner. For instance, to determine the number of possible three-letter groups among the letters A, B, C, D, and E, work methodically, starting with A as a group member paired with B, then C, then D, then E. Be sure not to repeat combinations (repetitions are indicated in parentheses here):

A, B, C	(A, C, B)	(A, D, B)	(A, E, B)
A, B, D	A, C, D	(A, D, C)	(A, E, C)
A, B, E	A, C, E	A, D, E	(A, E, D)

Perform the same task assuming B is in the group, then assuming C is in the group (all combinations not listed here repeat what's already listed):

B, C, D	C, D, E
B, C, E	
B, D, E	

The total number of combinations is 10.

25. How many two-digit numbers can be formed from the digits 1 through 9, if no digit appears twice in a number?

(A) 36

(B) 72

(C) 81

(D) 144

(E) 162

Each digit can be paired with any of the other 8 digits. To avoid double counting, account for the possible pairs as follows: 1 and 2–9 (8 pairs), 2 and 3–9 (7 pairs), 3 and 4–9 (6 pairs), and so forth. The total number of distinct pairs is $8 + 7 + 6 + 5 + 4 + 3 + 2 + 1 = 36$. Since the digits in each pair can appear in either order, the total number of possible two-digit numbers is 2×36, or 72. **The correct answer is (B).**

Here's something to consider: You can approach combination problems as *probability* problems as well. Think of the "probability" of any single combination as "1 divided by" the total number of combinations (a fraction between zero (0) and 1). Use whichever method is quickest for the question at hand. We'll review probability next.

PROBABILITY

Probability refers to the statistical chances of an event occurring (or not occurring). By definition, probability ranges from zero (0) to 1. (Probability is never negative, and it's never greater than 1.) Here's the basic formula for determining probability:

$$\text{Probability} = \frac{\text{number of ways the event can occur}}{\text{total number of possible occurrences}}$$

26. If you randomly select one candy from a jar containing two cherry candies, two licorice candies, and one peppermint candy, what is the probability of selecting a cherry candy?

(A) $\dfrac{1}{6}$

(B) $\dfrac{1}{5}$

(C) $\dfrac{1}{3}$

(D) $\dfrac{2}{5}$

(E) $\dfrac{3}{5}$

There are two ways among five possible occurrences that a cherry candy will be selected. Thus, the probability of selecting a cherry candy is $\frac{2}{5}$. **The correct answer is (D).**

To calculate the probability of an event *not* occurring, just subtract the probability of the event occurring from 1. So, referring to the preceding question, the probability of not selecting a cherry candy is $\frac{3}{5}$. (Subtract $\frac{2}{5}$ from 1.)

Here's another example of probability, but a bit tougher this time. A standard deck of 52 playing cards contains 12 face cards. The probability of selecting a face card from a standard deck is $\frac{12}{52}$, or $\frac{3}{13}$. On the GMAT, a tougher probability question will involve this basic formula, but it will also add a complication of some kind. It might require you to determine any of the following:

- Certain missing facts needed for a given probability
- Probabilities involving two (or more) *independent* events
- Probabilities involving an event that is *dependent* on another event

For the next three types of probability questions, don't try to "intuit" the answer. Probabilities involving complex scenarios such as these are often greater or less than you might expect.

Missing Facts Needed for a Given Probability

In this question type, instead of calculating probability, you determine what missing number is needed for a given probability. Don't panic; just plug what you know into the basic formula and solve for the missing number.

27. A piggy-bank contains a certain number of coins, of which 53 are dimes and 19 are nickels. The remainder of the coins in the bank are quarters. If the probability of selecting a quarter from this bank is $\frac{1}{4}$, how many quarters does the bank contain?

   (A) 30
   (B) 27
   (C) 24
   (D) 21
   (E) 16

On its face, this question looks complicated, but it's really not. Just plug what you know into the probability formula. Let x be the number of quarters in the bank (this is the numerator of the formula's fraction), and let $x + 72$ be the total number of coins (the fraction's denominator). Then solve for x (use the cross-product method to clear fractions):

$$\frac{1}{4} = \frac{x}{x + 72}$$
$$x + 72 = 4x$$
$$72 = 3x$$
$$24 = x$$

The correct answer is (C).

Probability Involving Two (or More) Independent Events

Two events are independent if neither event affects the probability that the other will occur. (You'll look at dependent events next.) On the GMAT, look for either of these two scenarios involving independent events:

❶ The random selection of one object from *each of two or more groups*

❷ The random selection of one object from a group, then *replacing* it and selecting again (as in a "second round" or "another turn" of a game)

In either scenario, the simplest calculation involves finding the probability of two events both occurring. All you need to do is multiply together their individual probabilities: (probability of event 1 occurring) × (probability of event 2 occurring) = (probability of both events occurring).

For example, assume that you randomly select one letter from each of two sets: {A,B} and {C,D,E}. The probability of selecting A and $C = \frac{1}{2} \times \frac{1}{3}$, or $\frac{1}{6}$.

To calculate the probability that two events will *not both* occur, *subtract from* 1 the probability of both events occurring. To determine the probability that *three* events will all occur, just multiply the third event's probability by the other two.

28. If one student is chosen randomly out of a group of seven students, then one student is again chosen randomly from the same group of seven, what is the probability that two different students will be chosen?

(A) $\frac{36}{49}$

(B) $\frac{6}{7}$

(C) $\frac{19}{21}$

(D) $\frac{13}{14}$

(E) $\frac{48}{49}$

You must first calculate the chances of picking a particular student twice by multiplying together the two individual probabilities for the student: $\frac{1}{7} \times \frac{1}{7} = \frac{1}{49}$. The probability of picking any one of the 7 students twice is then $7 \times \frac{1}{49} = \frac{7}{49}$. The probability of picking the same student twice, added to the probability of not picking the same student twice, equals 1. So to answer the question, subtract $\frac{7}{49}$ from 1, and you get $\frac{6}{7}$. **The correct answer is (B).**

Beware: In one selection, the probability of not selecting a certain student from the group of seven is $\frac{6}{7}$ (the probability of selecting the student, subtracted from 1). But does this mean that the probability of not selecting the same student twice $= \frac{6}{7} \times \frac{6}{7} = \frac{36}{49}$? No, it doesn't. Make sure you understand the difference.

Probability Involving a Dependent Event

Two distinct events might be related in that one event affects the probability of the other one occurring—for example, randomly selecting one object from a group, then selecting a second object from the same group *without replacing the first selection*. Removing one object from the group increases the odds of selecting any particular object from those that remain.

You handle this type of problem as you would any other probability problem: Calculate individual probabilities, then combine them.

29. In a random selection of two people from a group of five—A, B, C, D, and E—what is the probability of selecting A and B?

   (A) $\frac{2}{5}$

   (B) $\frac{1}{5}$

   (C) $\frac{1}{10}$

   (D) $\frac{1}{15}$

   (E) $\frac{1}{20}$

You need to consider each of the two selections separately. In the first selection, the probability of selecting either A or B is $\frac{2}{5}$. But the probability of selecting the second of the two is $\frac{1}{4}$, because after the first selection only 4 people remain from whom to select. Since the question asks for the probability of selecting both A and B (as opposed to either one), multiply the two individual probabilities: $\frac{2}{5} \times \frac{1}{4} = \frac{2}{20} = \frac{1}{10}$. **The correct answer is (C).**

You can also approach a question such as this one as a *combination* problem. For this question, here are all the possibilities:

   A and either B, C, D, or E (4 combinations)

   B and either C, D, or E (3 combinations)

   C and either D or E (2 combinations)

   D and E (1 combination)

There are 10 possible combinations, so the probability of selecting A and B is 1 in 10.

SUMMING IT UP

- Although the types of questions reviewed in this chapter are the most basic of the math problems you'll encounter on the GMAT Quantitative section, don't underestimate how useful they'll be as building blocks for solving more complex problems.

- Certain fraction-decimal-percent equivalents show up more frequently than others on the GMAT. If you have time, memorize the standard conversions to save yourself time on the actual exam.

- Percent change questions are typical on the GMAT Quantitative section, so be ready for them.

- As with fractions, you can simplify ratios by dividing common factors.

- Review the definitions of arithmetic mean, median, mode, and range, so you're better equipped to solve such problems on the exam.

- Many arithmetic sequence questions ask for the average or sum of a series. You may be able to "shortcut" the addition instead of calculating the average of a long series of evenly spaced integers.

- Memorizing common factorial combinations will save you time when you encounter permutation questions on the GMAT.

- Work methodically on combination questions to avoid backtracking to an earlier object.

- It's wise not to try "intuiting" the answers to probability questions. Many of these problems are too complex to arrive at an accurate answer this way.

Math Review: Number Theory and Algebra

chapter 10

OVERVIEW

- Basic properties of numbers
- Factors, multiples, and divisibility
- Prime numbers and prime factorization
- Exponents (powers)
- Exponents and the real number line
- Roots and radicals
- Roots and the real number line
- Linear equations with one variable
- Linear equations with two variables
- Linear equations that cannot be solved
- Factorable quadratic expressions with one variable
- The quadratic formula
- Nonlinear equations with two variables
- Solving algebraic inequalities
- Weighted-average problems
- Currency problems
- Mixture problems
- Investment problems
- Problems of rate of production or work
- Problems of rate of travel (speed)
- Problems involving overlapping sets
- Summing it up

In this chapter, you'll first broaden your arithmetical horizons by dealing with numbers in more abstract, theoretical settings. You'll examine the following topics:

- The concept of absolute value
- Number signs and integers—and what happens to them when you apply the four basic operations

263

- Factors, multiples, divisibility, prime numbers, and the "prime factorization" method
- The rules for combining exponential numbers (base numbers and "powers") using the four basic operations
- The rules for combining radicals using the four basic operations
- The rules for simplifying terms containing radical signs

Then you'll review the following basic algebra skills:

- Solving a linear equation with one variable
- Solving a system of two equations with two variables—by substitution and by addition-subtraction
- Recognizing unsolvable linear equations when you see them
- Handling algebraic inequalities

BASIC PROPERTIES OF NUMBERS

You'll begin this chapter by reviewing the basics about integers, number signs (positive and negative), and prime numbers. First, make sure you're up to speed on the following definitions, which you'll need to know for this chapter as well as for the test:

- **Absolute value (of a real number):** The number's distance from zero (the origin) on the real-number line. The absolute value of x is indicated as $|x|$. (The absolute value of a negative number can be less than, equal to, or greater than a positive number.)
- **Integer:** Any non-fraction number on the number line: $\{\ldots, -3, -2, -1, 0, 1, 2, 3, \ldots\}$. Except for the number zero (0), every integer is either positive or negative. Every integer is either even or odd.
- **Factor (of an integer n):** Any integer that you can multiply by another integer for a product of n.
- **Prime number:** Any positive integer that has exactly two positive factors: 1 and the number itself. In other words, a prime number is not divisible by (a multiple of) any positive integer other than itself and 1.

Number Signs and the Four Basic Operations

The four basic operations are addition, subtraction, multiplication, and division. Be sure you know the sign of a number that results from combining numbers using these operations. Here's a table that includes all the possibilities (a "?" indicates that the sign depends on which number has the greater absolute value):

Addition	Subtraction	Multiplication	Division
$(+) + (+) = +$	$(+) - (-) = (+)$	$(+) \times (+) = +$	$(+) \div (+) = +$
$(-) + (-) = -$	$(-) - (+) = (-)$	$(+) \times (-) = -$	$(+) \div (-) = -$
$(+) + (-) = ?$	$(+) - (+) = ?$	$(-) \times (+) = -$	$(-) \div (+) = -$
$(-) + (+) = ?$	$(-) - (-) = ?$	$(-) \times (-) = +$	$(-) \div (-) = +$

GMAT problems involving combining numbers by addition or subtraction usually incorporate the concept of absolute value, as well as the rule for subtracting negative numbers.

1. $|-1-2| - |5-6| - |-3+4| = ?$

   (A) -5

   (B) -3

   (C) 1

   (D) 3

   (E) 5

First, determine each of the three absolute values:

$$|-1-2| = |-3| = 3$$

$$|5-6| = |-1| = 1$$

$$|-3+4| = |1| = 1$$

Then combine the three results: $3 - 1 - 1 = 1$. **The correct answer is (C).**

Because multiplication (or division) involving two negative terms always results in a positive number:

- Multiplication or division involving any *even* number of negative terms gives you a positive number.

- Multiplication or division involving any *odd* number of negative terms gives you a negative number.

2. A number M is the product of seven negative numbers, and the number N is the product of six negative numbers and one positive number. Which of the following holds true for all possible values of M and N?

   I. $M \times N < 0$

   II. $M - N < 0$

   III. $N + M < 0$

   (A) I only

   (B) II only

   (C) I and II only

   (D) II and III only

   (E) I, II, and III

The product of seven negative numbers is always a negative number. (M is a negative number.) The product of six negative numbers is always a positive number, and the product of two positive numbers is always a positive number. (N is a positive number.) Thus, the product of M and N must be a negative number; I is always true. Subtracting a positive number N from a negative number M always results in a negative number less than M; II is always true. However, whether III is true depends on the values of M and N. If $|N| > |M|$, then $N + M > 0$, but if $|N| < |M|$, then $N + M < 0$. **The correct answer is (C).**

Integers and the Four Basic Operations

When you combine integers using a basic operation, whether the result is an odd integer, an even integer, or a non-integer depends on the numbers you combined. Here's a summary of all the possibilities:

Addition and Subtraction

- integer $\pm$ integer = integer
- even integer $\pm$ even integer = even integer
- even integer $\pm$ odd integer = odd integer
- odd integer $\pm$ odd integer = even integer

Multiplication and Division

- integer $\times$ integer = integer
- integer $\div$ non-zero integer = integer, but only if the numerator is divisible by the denominator (if the result is a quotient with no remainder)
- odd integer $\times$ odd integer = odd integer
- even integer $\times$ non-zero integer = even integer
- even integer $\div$ 2 = integer
- odd integer $\div$ 2 = non-integer

GMAT questions that test you on the preceding rules sometimes look like algebra problems, but they're really not. Just apply the appropriate rule, or if you're not sure of the rule, plug in simple numbers to zero in on the correct answer.

3. If P is an odd integer and if Q is an even integer, which of the following expressions CANNOT represent an even integer?

   (A) $3P - Q$
   (B) $3P \times Q$
   (C) $2Q \times P$
   (D) $3Q - 2P$
   (E) $32P - 2Q$

Since 3 and P are both odd integers, their product ($3P$) must also be an odd integer. Subtracting an even integer (Q) from an odd integer results in an odd integer in all cases. **The correct answer is (A).**

FACTORS, MULTIPLES, AND DIVISIBILITY

Figuring out whether one number (f) is a factor of another (n) is no big deal. Just divide n by f. If the quotient is an integer, then f is a factor of n (and n is divisible by f). If the quotient is not an integer, then f is not a factor of n, and you'll end up with a remainder after dividing. For example,

2 is a factor of 8 because $8 \div 2 = 4$, which is an integer. On the other hand, 3 is not a factor of 8 because $8 \div 3 = \frac{8}{3}$, or $2\frac{2}{3}$, which is a non-integer. (The remainder is 2.)

Remember these four basic rules about factors, which are based on the definition of the term "factor":

❶ Any integer is a factor of itself.

❷ 1 and –1 are factors of all integers.

❸ The integer zero has an infinite number of factors but is not a factor of any integer.

❹ A positive integer's greatest factor (other than itself) will never be greater than one half the value of the integer.

On the "flip side" of factors are multiples. If f is a factor of n, then n is a multiple of f. For example, 8 is a multiple of 2 for the same reason that 2 is a factor of 8—because $8 \div 2 = 4$, which is an integer.

As you can see, factors, multiples, and divisibility are simply different aspects of the same concept. So, a GMAT question about factoring is also about multiples and divisibility.

4. If $n > 6$, and if n is a multiple of 6, which of the following is always a factor of n?

(A) $n - 6$

(B) $n + 6$

(C) $\frac{n}{2}$

(D) $\frac{n}{2} + 3$

(E) $\frac{n}{2} + 6$

Since 3 is a factor of 6, 3 is also a factor of any positive-number multiple of 6. Thus, if you divide any multiple of 6 by 3, the quotient will be an integer. In other words, 3 will be a factor of that number (n). As for the incorrect choices, $n - 6$ (choice (A)) is a factor of n only if $n = 12$. $n + 6$ (choice (B)) can never be a factor of n because $n + 6$ is greater than n. You can eliminate choices (D) and (E) because the greatest factor of any positive number (other than the number itself) is half the number, which in this case is $\frac{n}{2}$. **The correct answer is (C).**

Although the plug-in strategy works for the preceding question, you should try out more than one sample value for n. If $n = 12$, choices (A), (C), and (E) are all viable. But try out the number 18, and choice (C) is the only factor of n. (To be on the safe side, you should try out at least one additional sample value as well, such as 24.)

PRIME NUMBERS AND PRIME FACTORIZATION

A *prime number* is a positive integer that is divisible by only two positive integers: itself and 1. Just for the record, here are all the prime numbers less than 50:

2 3 5 7 11 13 17 19 23 29 31 37 41 43 47

To find the prime factorization of a number (or composite number), divide the number by the primes in order and use each repeatedly until it is no longer a factor. For example:

$$110 = 2 \times 55$$

$$= 2 \times 5 \times 11$$

This is the prime factorization of 110.

Stop when all factors are prime. Then if a factor occurs more than once, use an exponent to indicate this (i.e., write it in exponential form).

5. Which of the following is a prime factorization of 144?

   (A) $2^4 \times 3^2$

   (B) 4×3^3

   (C) $2^3 \times 1^4$

   (D) $2^4 \times 3 \times 5$

   (E) $2 \times 32 \times 4$

Divide 144 by the smallest prime, which is 2. Continue to divide the result by 2, and you ultimately obtain a prime-number quotient:

$$144 = 2 \times 72$$

$$= 2 \times 2 \times 36$$

$$= 2 \times 2 \times 2 \times 18$$

$$= 2 \times 2 \times 2 \times 2 \times 9$$

$$= 2 \times 2 \times 2 \times 2 \times 3 \times 3$$

$$= 2^4 \times 3^2$$

The correct answer is (A).

EXPONENTS (POWERS)

An *exponent*, or *power*, refers to the number of times a number (referred to as the *base*) is used as a factor. In the number 2^3, the base is 2 and the exponent is 3. To calculate the value of 2^3, you use 2 as a factor three times: $2^3 = 2 \times 2 \times 2 = 8$.

On the GMAT, questions involving exponents usually require you to combine two or more terms that contain exponents. To do so, you need to know some basic rules. Can you combine base numbers—using addition, subtraction, multiplication, or division—before applying exponents to the numbers? The answer depends on which operation you're performing.

Combining Exponents by Addition or Subtraction

When you add or subtract terms, you cannot combine bases or exponents. It's as simple as that.

$$a^x + b^x \neq (a + b)^x$$

$$a^x - b^x \neq (a - b)^x$$

If you don't believe it, try plugging in a few easy numbers. Notice that you get a different result depending on which you do first: combine bases or apply each exponent to its base:

$$(3 + 4)^2 = 7^2 = 49$$

$$3^2 + 4^2 = 9 + 16 = 25$$

6. If $x = -2$, then $x^5 - x^2 - x = ?$

   (A) -70

   (B) -58

   (C) -34

   (D) 4

   (E) 26

You cannot combine exponents here, even though the base is the same in all three terms. Instead, you need to apply each exponent, in turn, to the base, then subtract:

$$x^5 - x^2 - x = (-2)^5 - (-2)^2 - (-2) = -32 - 4 + 2 = -34$$

The correct answer is (C).

Combining Exponents by Multiplication or Division

It's a whole different story for multiplication and division. First, remember these two simple rules:

1 You can combine bases first, but only if the exponents are the same:

$$a^x \times b^x = (ab)^x$$

2 You can combine exponents first, but only if the bases are the same. When multiplying these terms, add the exponents. When dividing them, subtract the denominator exponent from the numerator exponent:

$$a^x \times a^y = a^{(x+y)}$$

$$\frac{a^x}{a^y} = a^{(x-y)}$$

When the same base appears in both the numerator and denominator of a fraction, you can cancel the number of powers common to both.

7. Which of the following is a simplified version of $\dfrac{x^2 y^3}{x^3 y^2}$?

   (A) $\dfrac{y}{x}$

   (B) $\dfrac{x}{y}$

   (C) $\dfrac{1}{xy}$

   (D)   1

   (E) $x^5 y^5$

The simplest approach to this problem is to cancel x^2 and y^2 from the numerator and denominator. This leaves you with x^1 in the denominator and y^1 in the numerator. "Canceling" a base's powers in a fraction's numerator and denominator is actually a shortcut to applying the rule $\dfrac{a^x}{a^y} = a^{(x-y)}$ along with another rule, $a^{-x} = \dfrac{1}{a^x}$, that you'll review immediately ahead. **The correct answer is (A).**

Additional Rules for Exponents

To cover all your bases, also keep in mind these three additional rules for exponents:

1 When raising an exponential number to a power, multiply exponents:
$(a^x)^y = a^{xy}$

2 Any number other than zero (0) raised to the power of 0 equals 1:
$a^0 = 1 \; [a \neq 0]$

3 Raising a base other than zero to a negative exponent is equivalent to 1 divided by the base raised to the exponent's absolute value:

$a^{-x} = \dfrac{1}{a^x}$

The preceding three rules are all fair game for the GMAT. In fact, a GMAT question might require you to apply more than one of these rules.

8. $(2^3)^2 \times 4^{-3} =$

   (A) $\dfrac{1}{8}$

   (B) $\dfrac{1}{2}$

   (C) $\dfrac{2}{3}$

   (D)   1

   (E)   16

$$\left(2^4\right)^4 \times 4^{-3} = 2^{(2)(3)} \times \dfrac{1}{4^3} = \dfrac{2^6}{4^3} = \dfrac{2^6}{4^6} - 1$$

The correct answer is (D).

Exponents You Should Know

For the GMAT, memorize the exponential values in the following table. You'll be glad you did, since these are the ones you're most likely to see on the exam.

Power and Corresponding Value

Base	2	3	4	5	6	7	8
2	4	8	16	32	64	128	256
3	9	27	81	243			
4	16	64	256				
5	25	125	625				
6	36	216					

EXPONENTS AND THE REAL NUMBER LINE

Raising bases to powers can have surprising effects on the magnitude and/or sign—negative vs. positive—of the base. You need to consider four separate regions of the real-number line:

1. Values greater than 1 (to the right of 1 on the number line)
2. Values less than –1 (to the left of –1 on the number line)
3. Fractional values between 0 and 1
4. Fractional values between –1 and 0

The next table indicates the impact of positive-integer exponent (x) on base (n) for each region.

$n > 1$	n raised to any power: $n^x > 1$ (the greater the exponent, the greater the value of n^x)
$n < -1$	n raised to even power: $n^x > 1$ (the greater the exponent, the greater the value of n^x)
	n raised to odd power: $n^x < -1$ (the greater the exponent, the lesser the value of n^x)
$0 < n < 1$	n raised to any power: $0 < n^x < 1$ (the greater the exponent, the lesser the value of n^x)
$-1 < n < 0$	n raised to even power: $0 < n^x < 1$ (the greater the exponent, the lesser the value of n^x, approaching 0 on the number line)
	n raised to odd power: $-1 < n^x < 0$ (the greater the exponent, the greater the value of n^x, approaching 0 on the number line)

The preceding set of rules are simple enough to understand. But when you apply them to a GMAT question, it can be surprisingly easy to confuse yourself, especially if the question is designed to create confusion.

9. If $-1 < x < 0$, which of the following must be true?

   I. $x < x^2$

   II. $x^2 < x^3$

   III. $x < x^3$

   (A) I only

   (B) II only

   (C) I and II only

   (D) I and III only

   (E) I, II, and III

The key to analyzing each equation is that raising x to successively greater powers moves the value of x closer to zero (0) on the number line. I must be true. Since x is given as a negative number, x^2 must be positive and thus greater than x. II cannot be true. Since x is given as a negative number, x^2 must be positive, while x^3 must be negative. Thus, x^2 is greater than x^3. III must be true. Both x^3 and x are negative fractions between 0 and -1, but x^3 is closer to zero (0) on the number line—that is, greater than x. **The correct answer is (D).**

ROOTS AND RADICALS

On the flip side of exponents and powers are roots and radicals. The *square root* of a number n is a number that you "square" (multiply by itself, or raise to the power of 2) to obtain n.

$2 = \sqrt{4}$ (the square root of 4) because 2×2 (or 2^2) $= 4$

The cube root of a number n is a number that you raise to the power of 3 (multiply by itself twice) to obtain n. You determine greater roots (for example, the "fourth root") in the same way. Except for square roots, the radical sign will indicate the root to be taken.

$2 = \sqrt[3]{8}$ (the cube root of 8) because $2 \times 2 \times 2$ (or 2^3) $= 8$

$2 = \sqrt[4]{16}$ (the fourth root of 16) because $2 \times 2 \times 2 \times 2$ (or 2^4) $= 16$

For the GMAT, you should know the rules for simplifying and for combining radical expressions.

Simplifying Radicals

On the GMAT, always look for the possibility of simplifying radicals by moving what's under the radical sign to the outside of the sign. Check inside your square-root radicals for perfect squares: factors that are squares of nice tidy numbers or other terms. The same advice applies to perfect cubes, and so on.

$\sqrt{4a^2} = 2\lvert a \rvert$	4 and a^2 are both perfect squares; remove them from under the radical sign, and find each one's square root.
$\sqrt{8a^3} = \sqrt{(4)(2)a^3} = 2a\sqrt{2a}$	8 and a^3 are both perfect cubes, which contain perfect-square factors; remove the perfect squares from under the radical sign, and find each one's square root.

You can simplify radical expressions containing fractions in the same way. Just be sure that what's in the denominator under the radical sign stays in the denominator when you remove it from under the radical sign.

$$\sqrt{\frac{20x}{x^3}} = \sqrt{\frac{(4)(5)}{x^2}} = \frac{2\sqrt{5}}{x}$$

$$\sqrt[3]{\frac{3}{8}} = \sqrt[3]{\frac{3}{2^3}} = \frac{1}{2}\sqrt[3]{3}$$

10. $\sqrt{\dfrac{28a^6b^4}{36a^4b^6}} =$

   (A) $\dfrac{a}{b}\sqrt{\dfrac{a}{2b}}$

   (B) $\dfrac{a}{2b}\sqrt{\dfrac{a}{b}}$

   (C) $\dfrac{|a|}{3|b|}\sqrt{7}$

   (D) $\dfrac{a^2}{3b^2}\sqrt{2}$

   (E) $\dfrac{2a}{3b}$

TIP

Whenever you see a non-prime number under a square-root radical sign, factor it to see whether it contains perfect-square factors you can move outside the radical sign. More than likely, you need to do so to solve the problem at hand.

Divide a^4 and b^4 from the numerator and denominator of the fraction. Also, factor out 4 from 28 and 36. Then, remove perfect squares from under the radical sign:

$$\sqrt{\frac{28a^6b^4}{36a^4b^6}} = \sqrt{\frac{7a^2}{9b^2}} = \frac{|a|\sqrt{7}}{3|b|}, \text{ or } \frac{|a|}{3|b|}\sqrt{7}$$

The correct answer is (C).

In GMAT questions involving radical terms, you might want to remove a radical term from a fraction's denominator to match the correct answer. To accomplish this, multiply both numerator and denominator by the radical value. (This process is called "rationalizing the denominator.") Here's an example of how to do it:

$$\frac{3}{\sqrt{15}} = \frac{3\sqrt{15}}{\sqrt{15}\sqrt{15}} = \frac{3\sqrt{15}}{15} \text{ or } \frac{1}{5}\sqrt{15}$$

Combining Radical Terms

The rules for combining terms that include radicals are quite similar to those for exponents. Keep the following two rules in mind; one applies to addition and subtraction, while the other applies to multiplication and division.

Addition and subtraction: If a term under a radical is being added to or subtracted from a term under a different radical, you cannot combine the two terms under the same radical.

$$\sqrt{x} + \sqrt{y} \neq \sqrt{x + y}$$
$$\sqrt{x} - \sqrt{y} \neq \sqrt{x - y}$$
$$\sqrt{x} + \sqrt{x} = 2\sqrt{x}, \text{ not } \sqrt{2x}$$

On the GMAT, if you're asked to combine radical terms by adding or subtracting, chances are you'll also need to simplify radical expressions along the way.

11. $\sqrt{24} - \sqrt{16} - \sqrt{6} =$

    (A) $\sqrt{6} - 4$

    (B) $4 - 2\sqrt{2}$

    (C) 2

    (D) $\sqrt{6}$

    (E) $2\sqrt{2}$

Although the numbers under the three radicals combine to equal 2, you cannot combine terms this way. Instead, simplify the first two terms, then combine the first and third terms:

$$\sqrt{24} - \sqrt{16} - \sqrt{6} = 2\sqrt{6} - 4 - \sqrt{6} = \sqrt{6} - 4$$

The correct answer is (A).

Multiplication and Division: Terms under different radicals can be combined under a common radical if one term is multiplied or divided by the other, but only if the radical is the same.

$$\sqrt{x}\sqrt{x} = (\sqrt{x})^2, \text{ or } x$$
$$\sqrt{x}\sqrt{y} = \sqrt{xy}$$
$$\frac{\sqrt{x}}{\sqrt{y}} = \sqrt{\frac{x}{y}}$$
$$\sqrt[3]{x}\sqrt{x} = ?$$

You cannot easily combine $\sqrt[3]{x}\sqrt{x} = x^{\frac{1}{3}}x^{\frac{1}{2}} = x^{\frac{1}{3} + \frac{1}{2}} = x^{\frac{5}{6}}$.

12. $\left(2\sqrt{2a}\right)^2 =$

    (A) $4a$

    (B) $4a^2$

    (C) $8a$

    (D) $8a^2$

    (E) $6a$

Square each of the two terms, 2 and $\sqrt{2a}$, separately. Then combine their squares by multiplication: $(2\sqrt{2a})^2 = 2^2 \times (\sqrt{2a})^2 = 4 \times 2a = 8a$. **The correct answer is (C).**

Roots You Should Know

For the GMAT, memorize the roots in the following table. If you encounter one of these radical terms on the exam, chances are you'll need to know its equivalent integer to answer the question.

In the following table, notice that the cube root of a negative number is negative and the cube root of a positive number is positive.

Square roots of "perfect square" integers	Cube roots of "perfect cube" integers (positive and negative)
$\sqrt{121} = 11$	$\sqrt[3]{(-)8} = (-)2$
$\sqrt{144} = 12$	$\sqrt[3]{(-)27} = (-)3$
$\sqrt{169} = 13$	$\sqrt[3]{(-)64} = (-)4$
$\sqrt{196} = 14$	$\sqrt[3]{(-)125} = (-)5$
$\sqrt{225} = 15$	$\sqrt[3]{(-)216} = (-)6$
$\sqrt{625} = 25$	$\sqrt[3]{(-)343} = (-)7$
	$\sqrt[3]{(-)512} = (-)8$
	$\sqrt[3]{(-)729} = (-)9$
	$\sqrt[3]{(-)1000} = (-)10$

ROOTS AND THE REAL NUMBER LINE

As with exponents, the root of a number can bear a surprising relationship to the magnitude and/or sign (negative vs. positive) of the number (another of the test-makers' favorite areas). Here are three rules you should remember:

❶ If $n > 1$, then $1 < \sqrt[3]{n} < \sqrt{n} < n$ (the greater the root, the lesser the value). However, if n lies between 0 and 1, then $n < \sqrt{n} < \sqrt[3]{n} < 1$ (the greater the root, the greater the value).

$n = 64$ $1 < \sqrt[3]{64} < \sqrt{64} < 64$ $1 < 4 < 8 < 64$	$n = \dfrac{1}{64}$ $\dfrac{1}{64} < \sqrt{\dfrac{1}{64}} < \sqrt[3]{\dfrac{1}{64}} < 1$ $\dfrac{1}{64} < \dfrac{1}{8} < \dfrac{1}{4} < 1$

2 Every negative number has exactly one cube root, and that root is a negative number. The same holds true for all other odd-numbered roots of negative numbers.

$\sqrt[3]{-27} = -3$ $(-3)(-3)(-3) = -27$	$\sqrt[5]{-32} = -2$ $(-2)(-2)(-2)(-2)(-2) = -32$

3 Every positive number has only one cube root, and that root is always a positive number. The same holds true for all other odd-numbered roots of positive numbers.

13. Which of the following inequalities, if true, is sufficient alone to show that $\sqrt[3]{x} < \sqrt[5]{x}$?

  (A) $-1 < x < 0$

  (B) $x > 1$

  (C) $|x| < -1$

  (D) $|x| > 1$

  (E) $x < -1$

If $x < -1$, then applying a greater root yields a lesser negative value—farther to the left on the real number line. **The correct answer is (E).**

LINEAR EQUATIONS WITH ONE VARIABLE

Algebraic expressions are usually used to form equations, which set two expressions equal to each other. Most equations you'll see on the GMAT are linear equations, in which the variables don't come with exponents. To solve any linear equation containing one variable, your goal is always the same: Isolate the unknown (variable) on one side of the equation. To accomplish this, you may need to perform one or more of the following four operations on both sides, depending on the equation:

  1 Add or subtract the same term from both sides.

  2 Multiply or divide by the same term on both sides.

  3 Clear fractions by cross-multiplication.

  4 Clear radicals by raising both sides to the same power (exponent).

Performing any of these operations on both sides does not change the equality; it merely restates the equation in a different form.

Let's take a look at each of these four operations to see when and how to use each one.

  1 *Add or subtract the same term from both sides of the equation.*

  To solve for x, you may need to either add or subtract a term from both sides of an equation— or do both.

NOTE

The square root (or other even-number root) of any negative number is an imaginary number, not a real number. That's why the preceding rules don't cover these roots.

ALERT!

The operation you perform on one side of an equation must also be performed on the other side; otherwise, the two sides won't be equal.

14. If $2x - 6 = x - 9$, then $x =$

    (A) -9

    (B) -6

    (C) -3

    (D) 2

    (E) 6

First, put both x-terms on the left side of the equation by subtracting x from both sides; then combine x-terms:

$$2x - 6 - x = x - 9 - x$$
$$x - 6 = -9$$

Next, isolate x by adding 6 to both sides:

$$x - 6 + 6 = -9 + 6$$
$$x = -3$$

The correct answer is (C).

② *Multiply or divide both sides of the equation by the same non-zero term.*

To solve for x, you may need to either multiply or divide a term from both sides of an equation. Or, you may need to multiply and divide.

15. If $12 = \dfrac{11}{x} - \dfrac{3}{x}$, then $x =$

    (A) $\dfrac{3}{11}$

    (B) $\dfrac{1}{2}$

    (C) $\dfrac{2}{3}$

    (D) $\dfrac{11}{12}$

    (E) $\dfrac{11}{3}$

First, combine the x-terms:

$$12 = \frac{11 - 3}{x}$$

Next, clear the fraction by multiplying both sides by x:

$$12x = 11 - 3$$

$$12x = 8$$

Finally, isolate x by dividing both sides by 12:

$$x = \frac{8}{12}, \text{ or } \frac{2}{3}$$

The correct answer is (C).

③ *If each side of the equation is a fraction, your best bet is to cross-multiply.*
Where the original equation equates two fractions, use cross-multiplication to eliminate the fractions. Multiply the numerator from one side of the equation by the denominator from the other side. Set the product equal to the product of the other numerator and denominator. (In effect, cross-multiplication is a shortcut method of multiplying both sides of the equation by both denominators.)

16. If $\dfrac{7a}{8} = \dfrac{a+1}{3}$, then $a =$

   (A) $\dfrac{8}{13}$

   (B) $\dfrac{7}{8}$

   (C) 2

   (D) $\dfrac{7}{3}$

   (E) 15

First, cross-multiply as we've described:

   $(3)(7a) = (8)(a + 1)$

Next, combine terms (distribute 8 to both a and 1):

   $21a = 8a + 8$

Next, isolate a-terms on one side by subtracting $8a$ from both sides; then combine the a-terms:

   $21a - 8a = 8a + 8 - 8a$
   $13a = 8$

Finally, isolate a by dividing both sides by its coefficient 13:

   $\dfrac{13a}{13} = \dfrac{8}{13}$

   $a = \dfrac{8}{13}$

The correct answer is (A).

④ *Square both sides of the equation to eliminate radical signs.* Where the variable is under a square-root (radical) sign, remove the radical sign by squaring both sides of the equation. (Use a similar technique for cube roots and other roots.)

17. If $3\sqrt{2x} = 2$, then $x =$

   (A) $\dfrac{1}{18}$

   (B) $\dfrac{2}{9}$

   (C) $\dfrac{1}{3}$

   (D) $\dfrac{5}{4}$

   (E) 3

First, clear the radical sign by squaring all terms:

$$(3^2)(\sqrt{2x})^2 = 2^2$$
$$(9)(2x) = 4$$
$$18x = 4$$

Next, isolate x by dividing both sides by 18:

$$x = \frac{4}{18}, \text{ or } \frac{2}{9}$$

The correct answer is (B).

LINEAR EQUATIONS WITH TWO VARIABLES

What we've covered up to this point is pretty basic stuff. If you haven't quite caught on, you should probably stop here and consult a basic algebra workbook for more practice. On the other hand, if you're with us so far, let's forge ahead and add another variable. Here's a simple example:

$$x + 3 = y + 1$$

Quick . . . what's the value of x? It depends on the value of y, doesn't it? Similarly, the value of y depends on the value of x. Without more information about either x or y, you're stuck—but not completely. You can express x in terms of y, and you can express y in terms of x:

$$x = y - 2$$
$$y = x + 2$$

Let's look at one more:

$$4x - 9 = \frac{3}{2}y$$

Solve for x in terms of y:

$$4x = \frac{3}{2}y + 9$$
$$x = \frac{3}{8}y + \frac{9}{4}$$

Solve for y in terms of x:

$$\frac{4x - 9}{\frac{3}{2}} = y$$
$$\frac{2}{3}(4x - 9) = y$$
$$\frac{8}{3}x - 6 = y$$

To determine numerical values of x and y, you need a system of two linear equations with the same two variables. Given this system, there are two different methods for finding the values of the two variables:

① The substitution method

② The addition-subtraction method

Next, we'll apply each method to determine the values of two variables in a two-equation system.

The Substitution Method

To solve a system of two equations using the substitution method, follow these four steps (we'll use x and y here):

① In either equation, isolate one variable (x) on one side.

② Substitute the expression that equals x in place of x in the other equation.

③ Solve that equation for y.

④ Now that you know the value of y, plug it into either equation to find the value of x.

ALERT!

You can't solve an equation if it contains two unknowns (variables). You either need to know the value of one of the variables or you need a second equation.

18. If $\dfrac{2}{5}p + q = 3q - 10$, and if $q = 10 - p$, then $\dfrac{p}{q} =$

   (A) $\dfrac{5}{7}$

   (B) $\dfrac{3}{2}$

   (C) $\dfrac{5}{3}$

   (D) $\dfrac{25}{6}$

   (E) $\dfrac{36}{6}$

Don't let the fact that the question asks for $\dfrac{p}{q}$ (rather than simply p or q) throw you. Because you're given two linear equations with two unknowns, you know that you can first solve for p and q, then divide p by q. First things first: Combine the q-terms in the first equation:

$$\frac{2}{5}p = 2q - 10$$

Next, substitute $(10 - p)$ for q (from the second equation) in the first equation:

$$\frac{2}{5}p = 2(10 - p) - 10$$

$$\frac{2}{5}p = 20 - 2p - 10$$

$$\frac{2}{5}p = 10 - 2p$$

Move the p-terms to the same side, then isolate p:

$$\frac{2}{5}p + 2p = 10$$

$$\frac{12}{5}p = 10$$

$$p = \left(\frac{5}{12}\right)(10)$$

$$p = \frac{25}{6}$$

Substitute $\frac{25}{6}$ for p in either equation to find q (we'll use the second equation):

$$q = 10 - \frac{25}{6}$$

$$q = \frac{60}{6} - \frac{25}{6}$$

$$q = \frac{35}{6}$$

The question asks for $\frac{p}{q}$, so do the division:

$$\frac{p}{q} = \frac{\frac{25}{6}}{\frac{35}{6}} = \frac{25}{35}, \text{ or } \frac{5}{7}$$

The correct answer is (A).

The Addition-Subtraction Method

Another way to solve for two unknowns in a system of two equations is with the addition-subtraction method. Here are the five steps:

1. Make the coefficient of either variable the same in both equations (you can disregard the sign) by multiplying every term in one of the equations.
2. Make sure the equations list the same variables in the same order.
3. Place one equation above the other.
4. Add the two equations (work down to a sum for each term), or subtract one equation from the other, to eliminate one variable.
5. You can repeat Steps 1–3 to solve for the other variable.

19. If $3x + 4y = -8$, and if $x - 2y = \frac{1}{2}$, then $x =$

   (A) -12

   (B) $-\frac{7}{5}$

   (C) $\frac{1}{3}$

   (D) $\frac{14}{5}$

   (E) 9

To solve for x, you want to eliminate y. You can multiply each term in the second equation by 2, then add the equations:

$$3x + 4y = -8$$
$$\underline{2x - 4y = 1}$$
$$5x + 0y = -7$$

$$x = -\frac{7}{5}$$

The correct answer is (B).

NOTE

If a question requires you to find values of both unknowns, combine the two methods. For example, after using addition-subtraction to solve for x, substitute the value of x into either equation to find y.

Since the question asked only for the value of x, stop here. If the question had asked for both x and y (or for y only), you could have multiplied both sides of the second equation by 3, then subtracted the second equation from the first:

$$3x + 4y = -8$$
$$3x - 6y = \frac{3}{2}$$
$$\overline{0x + 10y = -9\frac{1}{2}}$$
$$10y = -\frac{19}{2}$$
$$y = -\frac{19}{20}$$

Which Method Should You Use?

Which method, substitution or addition-subtraction, you should use depends on what the equations look like to begin with. To see what we mean, look again at this system:

$$\frac{2}{5}p + q = 3q - 10$$
$$q = 10 - p$$

Notice that the second equation is already set up nicely for the substitution method. You could use addition-subtraction instead; however, you'd just have to rearrange the terms in both the equations first:

$$\frac{2}{5}p - 2q = -10$$
$$p + q = 10$$

Now, look again at the following system:

$$3x + 4y = -8$$
$$x - 2y = \frac{1}{2}$$

TIP

To solve a system of two linear equations with two variables, use addition-subtraction if you can quickly and easily eliminate one of the variables. Otherwise, use substitution.

Notice that the x-term and y-term already line up nicely here. Also, notice that it's easy to match the coefficients of either x or y: Multiply both sides of the second equation by either 3 or 2. This system is an ideal candidate for addition-subtraction. To appreciate this point, try using substitution instead. You'll discover that it takes far more number crunching.

LINEAR EQUATIONS THAT CANNOT BE SOLVED

Never assume that one linear equation with one variable is solvable. If you can reduce the equation to $0 = 0$, then you can't solve it. In other words, the value of the variable could be any real number. The test-makers generally use the Data Sufficiency format to cover this concept.

20. If $3x - 3 - 4x = x - 7 - 2x + 4$, then what is the value of x?

(1) $x > -1$

(2) $x < 1$

All terms on both sides subtract out:

$$3x - 3 - 4x = x - 7 - 2x + 4$$
$$-x - 3 = -x - 3$$
$$0 = 0$$

Thus, even considering both statements together, x could equal any real number between -1 and 1 (not just the integer 0). **The correct answer is (E).**

In some cases, what appears to be a system of two equations with two variables might actually be the same equation expressed in two different ways. In other words, what you're really dealing with are two equivalent equations that you cannot solve. The test-makers generally use the Data Sufficiency format to cover this concept.

21. Does $a = b$?

(1) $a + b = 30$

(2) $2b = 60 - 2a$

An unwary test-taker might assume that the values of both a and b can be determined with both equations together, because they appear at first glance to provide a system of two linear equations with two unknowns. Not so! You can easily manipulate the second equation so that it is identical to the first:

$$2b = 60 - 2a$$
$$2b = 2(30 - a)$$
$$b = 30 - a$$
$$a + b = 30$$

As you can see, the equation $2b = 60 - 2a$ is identical to the equation $a + b = 30$. Thus, a and b could each be any real number. You can't solve one equation in two unknowns, so the correct answer must be choice (E). **The correct answer is (E).**

Whenever you encounter a Data Sufficiency question that calls for solving one or more linear equations, stop in your tracks before taking pencil to paper. Size up the equation to see whether it's one of the two unsolvable kinds you learned about here. If so, unless you're given more information, the correct answer will be choice (E).

FACTORABLE QUADRATIC EXPRESSIONS WITH ONE VARIABLE

A *quadratic expression* includes a "squared" variable, such as x^2. An equation is quadratic if you can express it in this general form:

$ax^2 + bx + c = 0$,

where:

x is the variable

a, b, and c are constants (numbers)

$a \neq 0$

b can equal 0

c can equal 0

Here are four examples (notice that the b-term and c-term are not essential; in other words, either b or c, or both, can equal zero):

Quadratic Equation	Same Equation, but in the form: $ax^2 + bx + c = 0$
$2w^2 = 16$	$2w^2 - 16 = 0$ (no b-term)
$x^2 = 3x$	$x^2 - 3x = 0$ (no c-term)
$3y = 4 - y^2$	$y^2 + 3y - 4 = 0$
$7z = 2z^2 - 15$	$2z^2 - 7z - 15 = 0$

Every quadratic equation has exactly two solutions, called *roots*. (But the two roots might be the same.) On the GMAT, you can often find the two roots by *factoring*. To solve any factorable quadratic equation, follow these three steps:

❶ Put the equation into the standard form: $ax^2 + bx + c = 0$.

❷ Factor the terms on the left side of the equation into two linear expressions (with no exponents).

❸ Set each linear expression (root) equal to zero and solve for the variable in each one.

Factoring Simple Quadratic Expressions

Some quadratic expressions are easier to factor than others. If either of the two constants b or c is zero, factoring requires no sweat. In fact, in some cases, no factoring is needed at all:

A quadratic with no c-term	A quadratic with no b-term
$2x^2 = x$	$2x^2 - 4 = 0$
$2x^2 - x = 0$	$2(x^2 - 2) = 0$
$x(2x - 1) = 0$	$x^2 - 2 = 0$
$x = 0, \ 2x - 1 = 0$	$x^2 = 2$
$x = 0, \ \dfrac{1}{2}$	$x = \sqrt{2}, -\sqrt{2}$

NOTE

When dealing with a quadratic equation, your first step is usually to put it into the general form $ax^2 + bx + c = 0$. But keep in mind: The only essential term is ax^2.

Factoring Quadratic Trinomials

A trinomial is simply an algebraic expression that contains three terms. If a quadratic expression contains all three terms of the standard form $ax^2 + bx + c$, then factoring becomes a bit trickier. You need to apply the FOIL method, in which you add together these terms:

(F) the product of the *first* terms of the two binomials

(O) the product of the *outer* terms of the two binomials

(I) the product of the *inner* terms of the two binomials

(L) the product of the *last* (second) terms of the two binomials

Note the following relationships:

(F) is the first term (ax^2) of the quadratic expression

(O + I) is the second term (bx) of the quadratic expression

(L) is the third term (c) of the quadratic expression

You'll find that the two factors will be two binomials. The GMAT might ask you to recognize one or both of these binomial factors.

22. Which of the following is a factor of $x^2 - x - 6$?

    (A) $(x + 6)$

    (B) $(x - 3)$

    (C) $(x + 1)$

    (D) $(x - 2)$

    (E) $(x + 3)$

Notice that x^2 has no coefficient. This makes the process of factoring into two binomials easier. Set up two binomial shells: $(x\ )(x\ )$. The product of the two missing second terms (the "L" term under the FOIL method) is -6. The possible integral pairs that result in this product are $(1, -6)$, $(-1, 6)$, $(2, -3)$, and $(-2, 3)$. Notice that the second term in the trinomial is $-x$. This means that the sum of the two integers whose product is -6 must be -1. The pair $(2, -3)$ fits the bill. Thus, the trinomial is equivalent to the product of the two binomials $(x + 2)$ and $(x - 3)$. **The correct answer is (B).**

To check your work, multiply the two binomials using the FOIL method:

$$(x + 2)(x - 3) = x^2 - 3x + 2x - 6$$
$$= x^2 - x + 6$$

If the preceding question had asked you to determine the roots of the equation $x^2 - x - 6 = 0$, you'd simply set each of the binomial factors equal to zero (0), then solve for x in each one. The solution set (the two possible values of x) includes the roots -2 and 3.

23. How many different values of x does the solution set for the equation $4x^2 = 4x - 1$ contain?

    (A) None

    (B) One

    (C) Two

    (D) Four

    (E) Infinitely many

First, express the equation in standard form: $4x^2 - 4x + 1 = 0$. Notice that the c-term is 1. The only two integral pairs that result in this product are $(1,1)$ and $(-1,-1)$. Since the b-term $(-4x)$ is negative, try using $(-1,-1)$. Set up a binomial shell:

$$(? - 1)(? - 1)$$

Notice that the a-term contains the coefficient 4. The possible integral pairs that result in this product are $(1,4)$, $(2,2)$, $(-1,-4)$, and $(-2,-2)$. A bit of trial-and-error reveals that only the pair $(2,2)$ works. Thus, in factored form, the equation becomes $(2x - 1)(2x - 1) = 0$. To check your work, multiply the two binomials using the FOIL method:

$$(2x-1)(2x-1) = 4x^2 - 2x - 2x + 1$$
$$= 4x^2 - 4x + 1$$

Since the two binomial factors are the same, the two roots of the equation are the same. In other words, x has only one possible value. **The correct answer is (B).** (Although you don't need to find the value of x in order to answer the question, solve for x in the equation $2x - 1 = 0$; $x = \dfrac{1}{2}$. Note that the negative form of the binomial $2x - 1$, that is, $-2x + 1$, can be used and will yield the same result.)

Stealth Quadratic Equations

Some equations that appear linear (variables include no exponents) may actually be quadratic. Following, you will see the two GMAT situations you need to be on the lookout for.

❶ The same variable inside a radical also appears outside:

$$\sqrt{x} = 5x$$
$$\left(\sqrt{x}\right)^2 = (5x)^2$$
$$x = 25x^2$$
$$25x^2 - x = 0$$

❷ The same variable that appears in the denominator of a fraction also appears elsewhere in the equation:

$$\frac{2}{x} = 3 - x$$
$$2 = x(3 - x)$$
$$2 = 3x - x^2$$
$$x^2 - 3x + 2 = 0$$

In both scenarios, you're dealing with a quadratic (nonlinear) equation with one variable. So, in either equation, there are two roots. (Both equations are factorable, so go ahead and find their roots.) The test-makers often use the Data Sufficiency format to cover this concept.

24. What is the one, unique value of x?

   (1) $6x = \sqrt{3x}$

   (2) $x > 0$

An unwary test-taker might assume that the equation in Statement (1) is linear—because x is not squared. Not so! Clear the radical by squaring both sides of the equation, then isolate the x-terms on one side of the equation and you'll see that the equation is quite quadratic indeed:

$$36x^2 = 3x$$
$$36x^2 - 3x = 0$$

To ferret out the two roots, factor out $3x$, then solve for each root:

$$3x(12x - 1) = 0$$
$$3x = 0; \ 12x - 1 = 0$$
$$x = 0, \ \frac{1}{12}$$

Since there is more than one possible value for x, Statement (1) alone is insufficient to answer the question. Statement (2) alone is obviously insufficient. But the two together eliminate the root value 0, leaving $\frac{1}{12}$ as the only possible value of x. **The correct answer is (C).**

THE QUADRATIC FORMULA

For some quadratic equations, although rational roots exist, they're difficult to find. For example, $12x^2 + x - 6 = 0$ can be solved by factoring, but the factors are not easy to see:

$$12x^2 + x - 6 = (3x - 2)(4x + 3)$$

Faced with a quadratic equation that's difficult to factor, you can always use the quadratic formula, which states that for any equation of the form $ax^2 + bx + c = 0$:

$$x = \frac{-b \pm \sqrt{b^2 - 4ac}}{2a}$$

In the equation $12x^2 + x - 6 = 0$, for example, $a = 12$, $b = 1$, and $c = -6$. Plugging these values into the quadratic formula, you'll find that the two roots are $\frac{2}{3}$ and $-\frac{3}{4}$.

Some quadratic equations have no rational roots (solutions). Referring to the quadratic formula, if $\sqrt{b^2 - 4ac}$ turns out to be a negative number, then its square root will be imaginary, and hence so will the roots of the quadratic equation at hand. But the GMAT doesn't test you on imaginary numbers. In other words, you'll find only real-number roots in any GMAT quadratic equation.

NONLINEAR EQUATIONS WITH TWO VARIABLES

In the world of math, solving nonlinear equations with two or more variables can be very complicated, even for bona-fide mathematicians. But on the GMAT, all you need to remember are these three general forms:

❶ Sum of two variables, squared: $(x + y)^2 = x^2 + 2xy + y^2$

❷ Difference of two variables, squared: $(x - y)^2 = x^2 - 2xy + y^2$

❸ Difference of two squares: $x^2 - y^2 = (x + y)(x - y)$

You can verify these equations using the FOIL method:

$(x+y)^2$	$(x-y)^2$	$(x+y)(x-y)$
$=(x+y)(x+y)$	$=(x-y)(x-y)$	$=x^2+xy-xy-y^2$
$=x^2+xy+xy+y^2$	$=x^2-xy-xy+y^2$	$=x^2-y^2$
$=x^2+2xy+y^2$	$=x^2-2xy+y^2$	

For the GMAT, memorize the three equations listed here. When you see one form on the exam, it's a sure bet that your task is to rewrite it as the other form.

TIP

You usually can't solve quadratics using a shortcut. Always look for one of the three common quadratic forms. If you see it, rewrite it as its equivalent form to answer the question as quickly and easily as possible.

25. If $x^2 - y^2 = 100$, and if $x + y = 2$, then $x - y =$

    (A) –2
    (B) 10
    (C) 20
    (D) 50
    (E) 200

If you're on the lookout for the difference of two squares, you can handle this question with no sweat. Use the third equation you just learned, substituting 2 for $(x + y)$, then solving for $(x - y)$:

$$x^2 - y^2 = (x+y)(x-y)$$
$$100 = (x+y)(x-y)$$
$$100 = (2)(x-y)$$
$$50 = (x-y)$$

The correct answer is (D).

SOLVING ALGEBRAIC INEQUALITIES

You can solve algebraic inequalities in the same manner as equations. Isolate the variable on one side of the inequality symbol, factoring and eliminating terms wherever possible. However, one important rule distinguishes inequalities from equations: Whenever you multiply or divide both sides of an inequality by a negative number, you must reverse the inequality symbol. Simply put: If $a > b$, then $-a < -b$.

$12 - 4x < 8$	original inequality
$-4x < -4$	12 subtracted from each side; inequality unchanged
$x > 1$	both sides divided by –4; inequality reversed

Here are five general rules for dealing with algebraic inequalities. Study them until they're second nature to you because you'll put them to good use on the GMAT.

❶ Adding or subtracting unequal quantities to (or from) equal quantities:

   If $a > b$, then $c + a > c + b$

   If $a > b$, then $c - a < c - b$

❷ Adding unequal quantities to unequal quantities:

   If $a > b$, and if $c > d$, then $a + c > b + d$

③ Comparing three unequal quantities:

If $a > b$, and if $b > c$, then $a > c$

④ Combining the same positive quantity with unequal quantities by multiplication or division:

If $a > b$, and if $x > 0$, then $xa > xb$

⑤ Combining the same negative quantity with unequal quantities by multiplication or division:

If $a > b$, and if $x < 0$, then $xa < xb$

26. If $a > b$, and if $c > d$, then which of the following must be true?

   (A) $a - b > c - d$

   (B) $a - c > b - d$

   (C) $c + d < a - b$

   (D) $b + d < a + c$

   (E) $a - c < b + d$

Inequality questions can be a bit confusing, can't they? In this problem, you need to remember that if unequal quantities (c and d) are added to unequal quantities of the same order (a and b), the result is an inequality in the same order. This rule is essentially what answer choice (D) says. **The correct answer is (D).**

ALERT!

Be careful when handling inequality problems: The wrong answers might look right, depending on the values you use for the different variables.

WEIGHTED-AVERAGE PROBLEMS

You solve *weighted-average* problems using the arithmetic mean (simple average) formula, except you give the set's terms different weights. For example, if a final exam score of 90 receives *twice* the weight of each of two midterm exam scores 75 and 85, think of the final exam score as two scores of 90—and the total number of scores as 4 rather than 3:

$$WA = \frac{75 + 85 + (2)(90)}{4} = \frac{340}{4} = 85$$

Similarly, when some numbers among terms might appear more often than others, you must give them the appropriate "weight" before computing an average.

27. During an 8-hour trip, Brigitte drove 3 hours at 55 miles per hour and 5 hours at 65 miles per hour. What was her average rate, in miles per hour, for the entire trip?

   (A) 58.5

   (B) 60

   (C) 61.25

   (D) 62.5

   (E) 66.25

Determine the total miles driven: $(3)(55) + (5)(65) = 490$. To determine the average over the entire trip, divide this total by 8, which is the number of total hours: $490 \div 8 = 61.25$. **The correct answer is (C).**

A tougher weighted-average problem might provide the weighted average and ask for one of the terms, or require conversions from one unit of measurement to another—or both.

28. A certain olive orchard produces 315 gallons of oil annually, on average, during four consecutive years. How many gallons of oil must the orchard produce annually, on average, during the next six years, if oil production for the entire 10-year period is to meet a goal of 378 gallons per year?

   (A) 240
   (B) 285
   (C) 396
   (D) 420
   (E) 468

In the weighted-average formula, 315 annual gallons receives a weight of 4, while the average annual number of gallons for the next six years (x) receives a weight of 6:

$$378 = \frac{1260 + 6x}{10}$$
$$3780 = 1260 + 6x$$
$$3780 - 1260 = 6x$$
$$2520 = 6x$$
$$420 = x$$

This solution (420) is the average number of gallons needed per year, on average, during the next six years. **The correct answer is (D).**

To guard against calculation errors, check your answer by sizing up the question. Generally, how great a number are you looking for? Notice that the stated goal is a bit greater than the annual average production over the first four years. So you're looking for an answer that is greater than the goal—a number somewhat greater than 378 gallons per year. You can eliminate choices (A) and (B) out of hand. The number 420 fits the bill.

CURRENCY PROBLEMS

Currency problems are similar to weighted-average problems in that each item (bill or coin) is weighted according to its monetary value. Unlike weighted-average problems, however, the "average" value of all the bills or coins is not at issue. In solving currency problems, remember the following:

- You must formulate algebraic expressions involving both *number* of items (bills or coins) and *value* of items.
- You should convert the value of all monies to a common currency unit before formulating an equation. If converting to cents, for example, you must multiply the number of nickels by 5, dimes by 10, and so forth.

29. Jim has $2.05 in dimes and quarters. If he has four fewer dimes than quarters, how much money does he have in dimes?

   (A) 20 cents
   (B) 30 cents
   (C) 40 cents
   (D) 50 cents
   (E) 60 cents

Letting x equal the number of dimes, $x + 4$ represents the number of quarters. The total value of the dimes (in cents) is $10x$, and the total value of the quarters (in cents) is $25(x + 4)$ or $25x + 100$. Given that Jim has \$2.05, the following equation emerges:

$$10x + 25x + 100 = 205$$
$$35x = 105$$
$$x = 3$$

Jim has three dimes, so he has 30 cents in dimes. **The correct answer is (B).**

You could also solve this problem without formal algebra, by plugging in each answer choice in turn. Let's try this strategy for choices (A) and (B):

(A) 20 cents is 2 dimes, so Jim has 6 quarters. 20 cents plus \$1.50 adds up to \$1.70. Wrong answer!

(B) 30 cents is 3 dimes, so Jim has 7 quarters. 30 cents plus \$1.75 adds up to \$2.05. Correct answer!

TIP

You can solve most GMAT currency problems by working backward from the answer choices.

MIXTURE PROBLEMS

In GMAT mixture problems, you combine substances with different characteristics, resulting in a particular mixture or proportion, usually expressed as percentages. Substances are measured and mixed by either volume or weight—rather than by number (quantity).

30. How many quarts of pure alcohol must you add to 15 quarts of a solution that is 40% alcohol to strengthen it to a solution that is 50% alcohol?

(A) 4.0

(B) 3.5

(C) 3.25

(D) 3.0

(E) 2.5

You can solve this problem by working backward from the answer choices—trying out each one in turn. Or, you can solve the problem algebraically. The original amount of alcohol is 40% of 15. Letting x equal the number of quarts of alcohol that you must add to achieve a 50% alcohol solution, $0.4(15) + x$ equals the amount of alcohol in the solution after adding more alcohol. You can express this amount as 50% of $(15 + x)$. Thus, you can express the mixture algebraically as follows:

$$(0.4)(15) + x = (0.5)(15 + x)$$
$$6 + x = 7.5 + 0.5x$$
$$0.5x = 1.5$$
$$x = 3$$

You must add 3 quarts of alcohol to obtain a 50% alcohol solution. **The correct answer is (D).**

INVESTMENT PROBLEMS

GMAT investment problems involve interest earned (at a certain percentage rate) on money over a certain time period (usually a year). To calculate interest earned, multiply the original amount of money by the interest rate:

amount of money × interest rate = amount of interest on money

For example, if you deposit $1000 in a savings account that earns 5% interest annually, the total amount in the account after one year will be $1000 + 0.05($1000) = $1000 + $50 = $1050.

GMAT investment questions usually involve more than simply calculating interest earned on a given principal amount at a given rate. They usually call for you to set up and solve an algebraic equation. When handling these problems, it's best to eliminate percent signs.

31. Dr. Kramer plans to invest $20,000 in an account paying 6% interest annually. How much more must she invest at the same time at 3% so that her total annual income during the first year is 4% of her entire investment?

    (A) $32,000
    (B) $36,000
    (C) $40,000
    (D) $47,000
    (E) $49,000

Letting x equal the amount invested at 3%, you can express Dr. Kramer's total investment as 20,000 + x. The interest on $20,000 plus the interest on the additional investment equals the total interest from both investments. You can state this algebraically as follows:

$$0.06(20,000) + 0.03x = 0.04(20,000 + x)$$

Multiply all terms by 100 to eliminate decimals, then solve for x:

$$6(20,000) + 3x = 4(20,000 + x)$$
$$120,000 + 3x = 80,000 + 4x$$
$$40,000 = x$$

She must invest $40,000 at 3% for her total annual income to be 4% of her total investment ($60,000). **The correct answer is (C).**

Beware: In solving GMAT investment problems, by all means size up the question to make sure your calculated answer is in the ballpark. But don't rely on your intuition to derive a precise solution. Interest problems can be misleading. For instance, you might have guessed that Dr. Kramer would need to invest more than *twice* as much at 3% than at 6% to lower the overall interest rate to 4%, which is not true.

PROBLEMS OF RATE OF PRODUCTION OR WORK

A *rate* is a fraction that expresses a quantity per unit of time. For example, the rate at which a machine produces a certain product is expressed this way:

$$\text{rate of production} = \frac{\text{number of units produced}}{\text{time}}$$

A simple GMAT rate question might provide two of the three terms and then ask you for the value of the third term. To complicate matters, the question might also require you to convert a number from one unit of measurement to another.

32. If a printer can print pages at a rate of 15 pages per minute, how many pages can it print in $2\frac{1}{2}$ hours?

   (A) 1375
   (B) 1500
   (C) 1750
   (D) 2250
   (E) 2500

Apply the following formula:

$$\text{rate} = \frac{\text{no. of pages}}{\text{time}}$$

The rate is given as 15 minutes, so convert the time ($2\frac{1}{2}$ hours) to 150 minutes. Determine the number of pages by applying the formula to these numbers: no. of pages

$$15 = \frac{\text{no. of pages}}{150}$$
$$(15)(150) = \text{no. of pages}$$
$$2250 = \text{no. of pages}$$

The correct answer is (D).

A more challenging type of rate-of-production (work) problem involves two or more workers (people or machines) working together to accomplish a task or job. In these scenarios, there's an inverse relationship between the number of workers and the time that it takes to complete the job; in other words, the more workers, the quicker the job gets done.

A GMAT work problem might specify the rates at which certain workers work alone and ask you to determine the rate at which they work together, or vice versa. Here's the basic formula for solving a work problem:

$$\frac{A}{x} + \frac{A}{y} = 1$$

In this formula:

- x and y represent the time needed for each of two workers, x and y, to complete the job alone.

- A represents the time it takes for both x and y to complete the job working in the *aggregate* (together).

NOTE

In the real world, a team may be more efficient than the individuals working alone. But for GMAT questions, assume that no additional efficiency is gained this way.

So each fraction represents the portion of the job completed by a worker. The sum of the two fractions must be 1 if the job is completed.

33. One printing press can print a daily newspaper in 12 hours, while another press can print it in 18 hours. How long will the job take if both presses work simultaneously?

   (A) 7 hours, 12 minutes
   (B) 9 hours, 30 minutes
   (C) 10 hours, 45 minutes
   (D) 15 hours
   (E) 30 hours

Just plug the two numbers 12 and 18 into our work formula, then solve for A:

$$\frac{A}{12} + \frac{A}{18} = 1$$

$$\frac{3A}{36} + \frac{2A}{36} = 1$$

$$\frac{5A}{36} = 1$$

$$5A = 36$$

$$A = \frac{36}{5}, \text{ or } 7\frac{1}{5}$$

Both presses working simultaneously can do the job in $7\frac{1}{5}$ hours—or 7 hours, 12 minutes. **The correct answer is (A).**

PROBLEMS OF RATE OF TRAVEL (SPEED)

GMAT rate problems often involve rate of travel (speed). You can express a rate of travel this way:

$$\text{rate of travel} = \frac{\text{distance}}{\text{time}}$$

An easier speed problem will involve a single distance, rate, and time. A tougher speed problem might involve different rates, such as:

- Two different times over the same distance
- Two different distances covered in the same time

In either type, apply the basic rate-of-travel formula to each of the two events. Then solve for the missing information by algebraic substitution. Use essentially the same approach for any of the following scenarios:

- One object making two separate "legs" of a trip—either in the same direction or as a round trip
- Two objects moving in the same direction
- Two objects moving in opposite directions

TIP

In work problems, use your common sense to narrow down answer choices.

TIP

Regardless of the type of speed problem, start by setting up two distinct equations patterned after the simple rate-of-travel formula: ($r \times t = d$).

34. Janice left her home at 11 a.m., traveling along Route 1 at 30 mph. At 1 p.m., her brother Richard left home and started after her on the same road at 45 mph. At what time did Richard catch up to Janice?

    (A) 2:45 p.m.

    (B) 3:00 p.m.

    (C) 3:30 p.m.

    (D) 4:15 p.m.

    (E) 5:00 p.m.

Notice that the distance Janice covered is equal to that of Richard—that is, distance is constant. Letting x equal Janice's time, you can express Richard's time as $x - 2$. Substitute these values for time and the values for rate given in the problem into the speed formula for Richard and Janice:

Formula: rate × time = distance

Janice: $(30)(x) = 30x$

Richard: $(45)(x - 2) = 45x - 90$

Because the distance is constant, you can equate Janice's distance to Richard's, then solve for x:

$$30x = 45x - 90$$
$$15x = 90$$
$$x = 6$$

Janice had traveled 6 hours when Richard caught up with her. Because Janice left at 11:00 a.m., Richard caught up with her at 5:00 p.m. **The correct answer is (E).**

35. How far in kilometers can Scott drive into the country if he drives out at 40 kilometers per hour (kph), returns over the same road at 30 kph, and spends 8 hours away from home, including a 1-hour stop for lunch?

    (A) 105

    (B) 120

    (C) 145

    (D) 180

    (E) 210

Scott's actual driving time is 7 hours, which you must divide into two parts: his time spent driving into the country and his time spent returning. Letting the first part equal x, the return time is what remains of the 7 hours, or $7 - x$. Substitute these expressions into the motion formula for each of the two parts of Scott's journey:

Formula: rate × time = distance

Going: $(40)(x) = 40x$

Returning: $(30)(7 - x) = 210 - 30x$

Because the journey is round trip, the distance going equals the distance returning. Simply equate the two algebraic expressions, then solve for x:

$$40x = 210 - 30x$$
$$70x = 210$$
$$x = 3$$

Scott traveled 40 kph for 3 hours, so he traveled 120 kilometers. **The correct answer is (B).**

PROBLEMS INVOLVING OVERLAPPING SETS

Overlapping set problems involve distinct sets that share some number of members. GMAT overlapping set problems come in one of two varieties:

1 Single overlap (easier)

2 Double overlap (tougher)

36. Each of the 24 people auditioning for a community-theater production is an actor, a musician, or both. If 10 of the people auditioning are actors and 19 of the people auditioning are musicians, how many of the people auditioning are musicians but not actors?

   (A) 10

   (B) 14

   (C) 19

   (D) 21

   (E) 24

You can approach this relatively simple problem without formal algebra: The number of actors plus the number of musicians equals 29 (10 + 19 = 29). However, only 24 people are auditioning. Thus, 5 of the 24 are actor-musicians, so 14 of the 19 musicians must not be actors.

You can also solve this problem algebraically. The question describes three mutually exclusive sets: (1) actors who are not musicians, (2) musicians who are not actors, and (3) actors who are also musicians. The total number of people among these three sets is 24. You can represent this scenario with the following algebraic equation (n = number of actors/musicians), solving for $19 - n$ to answer the question:

$$(10 - n) + n + (19 - n) = 24$$
$$29 - n = 24$$
$$n = 5$$
$$19 - 5 = 14$$

The correct answer is (B).

37. Adrian owns 60 neckties, each of which is either 100% silk or 100% polyester. Forty percent of each type of tie is striped, and 25 of the ties are silk. How many of the ties are polyester but not striped?

   (A) 18

   (B) 21

   (C) 24

   (D) 35

   (E) 40

This double-overlap problem involves four distinct sets: striped silk ties, striped polyester ties, non-striped silk ties, and non-striped polyester ties. Set up a table representing the four sets, filling in the information given in the problem, as shown in the next figure:

	silk	polyester	
striped		.	40%
non-striped		?	60%
	25	35	

Given that 25 ties are silk (see the left column), 35 ties must be polyester (see the right column). Also, given that 40% of the ties are striped (see the top row), 60% must be non-striped (see the bottom row). Thus, 60% of 35 ties, or 21 ties, are polyester and non-striped. **The correct answer is (B).**

SUMMING IT UP

- Make sure you're up to speed on the definitions of absolute numbers, integers, factors, and prime numbers to better prepare yourself for the number theory and algebra questions on the GMAT Quantitative section.

- Use prime factorization to factor composite integers.

- GMAT questions involving exponents usually require that you combine two or more terms that contain exponents, so review the basic rules for adding, subtracting, multiplying, and dividing them.

- On the GMAT, always look for a way to simplify radicals by moving what's under the radical sign to the outside of the sign.

- Most algebraic equations you'll see on the GMAT exam are linear. Remember the operations for isolating the unknown on one side of the equation. Solving algebraic inequalities is similar to solving equations: Isolate the variable on one side of the inequality symbol first.

- Weighted-average problems and currency problems can be solved in a similar manner by using the arithmetic mean formula.

- Mixture and investment problems on the GMAT can be solved using what you've learned about solving proportion and percentage questions. Rate of production and travel questions can be solved using the strategies you've learned about fraction problems.

Math Review: Geometry

chapter 11

OVERVIEW

- Lines and angles
- Triangles
- Isosceles and equilateral triangles
- Rectangles, squares, and parallelograms
- Circles
- Advanced circle problems
- Polygons
- Cubes and other rectangular solids
- Cylinders
- Coordinate signs and the four quadrants
- Defining a line on the coordinate plane
- Graphing a line on the coordinate plane
- Midpoint and distance formulas
- Coordinate geometry
- Summing it up

In this chapter, you'll review the fundamentals involving plane geometry, starting with the following:

- Relationships among angles formed by intersecting lines
- Characteristics of any triangle
- Characteristics of special right triangles
- The Pythagorean theorem
- Characteristics of squares, rectangles, and parallelograms
- Characteristics of circles

Then, you'll review the basics of coordinate geometry:

- The characteristics of the *xy*-plane
- Defining and plotting points and lines on the plane
- Applying the midpoint and distance formulas to problems involving line segments

When we've finished reviewing the basics, we'll take a look at the following advanced topics involving plane and coordinate geometry:

- Properties of isosceles and equilateral triangles
- Properties of trapezoids
- Properties of polygons (including those with more than four sides)
- Relationships between arcs and other features of circles
- Relationships between circles and tangent lines
- Relationships created by combining a circle with another geometric figure (such as a triangle or another circle)
- Properties of cubes, other rectangular solids, and cylinders
- Plotting and defining 2-dimensional figures (triangles, rectangles, and circles) on the xy-plane

LINES AND ANGLES

Lines and line segments are the basic building blocks for most GMAT geometry problems. A GMAT geometry question might involve nothing more than intersecting lines and the angles they form. To handle the question, just remember four basic rules about angles formed by intersecting lines:

1 Vertical angles (angles across the vertex from each other and formed by the same two lines) are equal in degree measure, or congruent ($\cong$). In other words, they're the same size.

2 If adjacent angles combine to form a straight line, their degree measures total 180. In fact, a straight line is actually a 180° angle.

3 If two lines are perpendicular ($\perp$) to each other, they intersect, forming right (90°) angles.

4 The sum of the measures of all angles where two or more lines intersect at the same point is 360° (regardless of how many angles are involved).

Note that the symbol ($\cong$) indicates that two geometric features are congruent, meaning that they are identical (the same size, length, degree measure, etc.). The equation $\overline{AB} \cong \overline{CD}$ means that line segment $\overline{AB}$ is *congruent* (equal in length) to line segment $\overline{CD}$. The two equations $\angle A \cong \angle B$ and $m\angle A = m\angle B$ are two different ways of symbolizing the same relationship: that the angle whose vertex is at point A is congruent (equal in degree measure, or size) to the angle whose vertex is at point B. (The letter m symbolizes degree measure.)

Angles Formed by Intersecting Lines

When two or more lines intersect at the same point, they form a "wheel-spoke" pattern with a "hub." On the GMAT, "wheel-spoke" questions require you to apply one or more of the preceding four rules.

1.

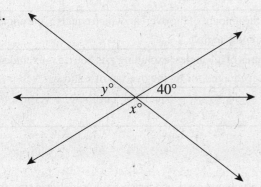

The figure above shows three intersecting lines. What is the value of $x + y$?

(A) 50

(B) 80

(C) 130

(D) 140

(E) 150

The angle vertical to the one indicated as 40° must also measure 40°. That 40° angle, together with the angles whose measures are x° and y°, combine to form a straight (180°) line. In other words, $40 + x + y = 180$. Thus, $x + y = 140$. **The correct answer is (D).**

A slightly tougher "wheel-spoke" question might focus on overlapping angles and require you to apply Rule 1 (about vertical angles) to determine the amount of the overlap. Look at this next "wheel-spoke" figure:

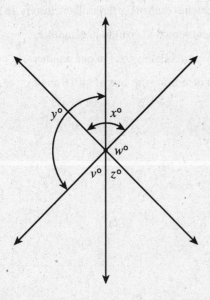

A GMAT question about the preceding figure might test your ability to recognize one of the following relationships:

$x + y - z = 180$	$x + y$ exceeds 180 by the amount of the overlap, which equals z, the angle vertical to the overlapping angle.
$x + y + v + w = 360$	The sum of the measures of all angles, excluding z, is 360°; z is excluded because it is already accounted for by the overlap of x and y.
$y - w = z$	w equals its vertical angle, so $y - w$ equals the portion of y vertical to angle z.

Parallel Lines and Transversals

GMAT problems involving parallel lines also involve at least one transversal, which is a line that intersects each of two (or more) lines. Look at this next figure, in which $l_1 \parallel l_2$ and $l_1 \parallel l_4$:

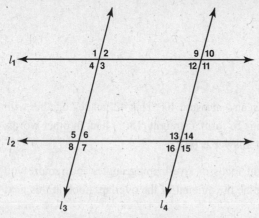

The upper-left "cluster" of angles 1, 2, 3, and 4 matches each of the three other clusters. In other words:

- All the odd-numbered angles are congruent (equal in size) to one another.
- All the even-numbered angles are congruent (equal in size) to one another.

If you know the size of just one angle, you can determine the size of all 16 angles.

2.

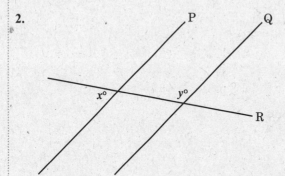

In the figure above, lines P and Q are parallel to each other. If m $\angle x = 75°$, what is the measure of $\angle y$?

(A) 75°

(B) 85°

(C) 95°

(D) 105°

(E) 115°

The angle "cluster" where lines P and R intersect corresponds to the cluster where lines Q and R intersect. Thus, $\angle x$ and $\angle y$ are supplementary (their measures add up to 180°). Given that $\angle x$ measures 75°, $\angle y$ must measure 105°. **The correct answer is (D).**

TRIANGLES

The *triangle* (a three-sided polygon) is the test-makers' favorite geometric figure. You'll need to understand triangles not only to solve "pure" triangle problems but also to solve certain problems involving four-sided figures, three-dimensional figures, and even circles. After a brief review of the properties of any triangle, you'll focus on right triangles (which include one right, or 90°, angle).

Properties of All Triangles

Here are four properties that all triangles share:

1. **Length of the sides.** Each side is shorter than the sum of the lengths of the other two sides. (Otherwise, the triangle would collapse into a line.)

2. **Angle measures.** The measures of the three angles total 180°.

3. **Angles and opposite sides.** Comparative angle sizes correspond to the comparative lengths of the sides opposite those angles. For example, a triangle's largest angle is opposite its longest side. (The sides opposite two congruent angles are also congruent.) Be careful not to take this rule too far: The ratio of angle sizes need not be identical to the ratio of lengths of sides. For example, if a certain triangle has angle measures of 30°, 60°, and 90°, the ratio of the angles is 1:2:3. But this doesn't mean that the ratio of the opposite sides is also 1:2:3.

4. **Area.** The area of any triangle is equal to one-half the product of its base and its height (or "altitude"): Area $= \dfrac{1}{2} \times$ base $\times$ height. You can use any side as the base to calculate area.

Right Triangles and the Pythagorean Theorem

In a right triangle, one angle measures 90° (and, of course, each of the other two angles measures less than 90°). The *Pythagorean theorem* expresses the relationship among the sides of any right triangle. In the following expression of the theorem, a and b are the two *legs* (the two shortest sides) that form the right angle, and c is the *hypotenuse*—the longest side, opposite the right angle:

$$a^2 + b^2 = c^2$$

For any right triangle, if you know the length of two sides, you can determine the length of the third side by applying the theorem. For example:

If the two shortest sides (the legs) of a right triangle are 2 and 3 units long, then the length of the triangle's third side (the hypotenuse) is $\sqrt{13}$ units:

$$2^2 + 3^2 = 13 = c^2; \; c = \sqrt{13}$$

If a right triangle's longest side (hypotenuse) is 10 units long and another side (one of the legs) is 5 units long, then the third side is $5\sqrt{3}$ units long:

$$a^2 + 5^2 = 10^2; \; a^2 = 75; \; a = \sqrt{75} = \sqrt{(25)(3)} = 5\sqrt{3}$$

ALERT!

Do not equate altitude (height) with any particular side. Instead, imagine the base on flat ground, and drop a plumb line straight down from the top peak of the triangle to define height or altitude. The only type of triangle in which the altitude equals the length of one side is the right triangle.

Pythagorean Triplets

A Pythagorean triplet is a specific ratio among the sides of a triangle that satisfies the Pythagorean theorem. In each of the following triplets, the first two numbers represent the comparative lengths of the two legs, whereas the third—and greatest—number represents the comparative length of the hypotenuse (on the GMAT, the first four appear far more frequently than the last two):

$1:1:\sqrt{2}$	$1^2 + 1^2 = \left(\sqrt{2}\right)^2$
$1:\sqrt{3}:2$	$1^2 + \left(\sqrt{3}\right)^2 = 2^2$
$3:4:5$	$3^2 + 4^2 = 5^2$
$5:12:13$	$5^2 + 12^2 = 13^2$
$8:15:17$	$8^2 + 15^2 = 17^2$
$7:24:25$	$7^2 + 24^2 = 25^2$

Each triplet above is expressed as a *ratio* because it represents a proportion among the triangle's sides. All right triangles with sides having the same proportion, or ratio, have the same shape. For example, a right triangle with sides of 5, 12, and 13 is smaller but exactly the same shape (proportion) as a triangle with sides of 15, 36, and 39.

3. Two boats leave the same dock at the same time, one traveling due east at 10 miles per hour and the other due north at 24 miles per hour. How many miles apart are the boats after 3 hours?

   (A) 68
   (B) 72
   (C) 78
   (D) 98
   (E) 110

TIP

To save valuable time on GMAT right-triangle problems, learn to recognize given numbers (lengths of triangle sides) as multiples of Pythagorean triplets.

The distance between the two boats after 3 hours forms the hypotenuse of a triangle in which the legs are the two boats' respective paths. The ratio of one leg to the other is 10:24, or 5:12. So you know you're dealing with a 5:12:13 triangle. The slower boat traveled 30 miles (10 mph × 3 hours). Thirty corresponds to the number 5 in the 5:12:13 ratio, so the multiple is 6 (5 × 6 = 30). 5:12:13 = 30:72:78. **The correct answer is (C).**

Pythagorean Angle Triplets

In two (and only two) of the unique triangles identified in the preceding section as Pythagorean side triplets, all degree measures are *integers*:

❶ The corresponding angles opposite the sides of a $1:1:\sqrt{2}$ triangle are 45°, 45°, and 90°.

❷ The corresponding angles opposite the sides of a $1:\sqrt{3}:2$ triangle are 30°, 60°, and 90°.

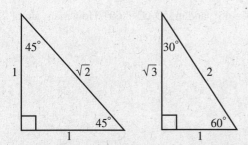

If you know that the triangle is a right triangle (one angle measures 90°) and that one of the other angles is 45°, then given the length of any side, you can determine the unknown lengths. For example:

- If one leg is 5 units long, then the other leg must also be 5 units long, while the hypotenuse must be $5\sqrt{2}$ units long.

- If the hypotenuse (the longest side) is 10 units long, then each leg must be $5\sqrt{2}$ units long. Divide hypotenuse by $\sqrt{2}$:

$$\frac{10}{\sqrt{2}} = \frac{10\sqrt{2}}{2} = 5\sqrt{2}$$

Similarly, if you know that the triangle is a right triangle (one angle measures 90°) and that one of the other angles is either 30° or 60°, then given the length of any side you can determine the unknown lengths. For example:

- If the shortest leg (opposite the 30° angle) is 3 units long, then the other leg (opposite the 60° angle) must be $3\sqrt{3}$ units long, and the hypotenuse must be 6 units long (3×2).

- If the longer leg (opposite the 60° angle) is 4 units long, then the shorter leg (opposite the 30° angle) must be $\frac{4\sqrt{3}}{3}$ units long (divide by $\sqrt{3}$: $\frac{4}{\sqrt{3}} = \frac{4\sqrt{3}}{3}$), while the hypotenuse must be $\frac{8\sqrt{3}}{3}$ (twice as long as the shorter leg).

- If the hypotenuse is 10 units long, then the shorter leg (opposite the 30° angle) must be 5 units long, while the longer leg (opposite the 60° angle) must be $5\sqrt{3}$ units long (the length of the shorter leg multiplied by $\sqrt{3}$).

4. In the figure below, $\overline{AC}$ is 5 units long, m$\angle ABD$ = 45°, and m$\angle DAC$ = 60°. How many units long is $\overline{BD}$?

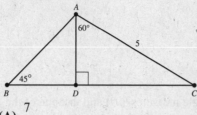

(A) $\dfrac{7}{3}$

(B) $2\sqrt{2}$

(C) $\dfrac{5}{2}$

(D) $\dfrac{3\sqrt{3}}{2}$

(E) $\dfrac{7}{2}$

To find the length of $\overline{BD}$, you first need to find $\overline{AD}$. Notice that $\angle ADC$ is a 30°-60°-90° triangle. The ratio among its sides is $1 : \sqrt{3} : 2$. Given that $\overline{AC}$ is 5 units long, $\overline{AD}$ must be $\dfrac{5}{2}$ units long. (The ratio 1:2 is equivalent to the ratio $\dfrac{5}{2} : 5$.) Next, notice that $\triangle ABD$ is a 45°-45°-90° triangle. The ratio among its sides is $1 : 1 : \sqrt{2}$. You know that $\overline{AD}$ is $\dfrac{5}{2}$ units long. Thus, $\overline{BD}$ must also be $\dfrac{5}{2}$ units long. **The correct answer is (C).**

ISOSCELES AND EQUILATERAL TRIANGLES

Isosceles Triangles

An isosceles triangle has the following two special properties:

1 Two of the sides are congruent (equal in length).

2 The two angles opposite the two congruent sides are congruent (equal in size, or degree measure).

If you know any two angle measures of a triangle, you can determine whether the triangle is isosceles.

5.

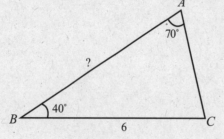

In the figure above, $\overline{BC}$ is 6 units long, m$\angle A = 70°$, and m$\angle B = 40°$. How many units long is $\overline{AB}$?

(A) 5

(B) 6

(C) 7

(D) 8

(E) 9

Since m$\angle A$ and m$\angle B$ add up to 110°, m$\angle C = 70°$ (70 + 110 = 180), and you know the triangle is isosceles. What's more, since m$\angle A =$ m$\angle C$, $\overline{AB} \cong \overline{BC}$. Given that $\overline{BC}$ is 6 units long, $\overline{AB}$ must also be 6 units long. **The correct answer is (B).**

The line bisecting the angle connecting the two congruent sides divides the triangle into two congruent right triangles. So if you know the lengths of all three sides of an isosceles triangle, you can determine the area of the triangle by applying the Pythagorean theorem.

6. Two sides of a triangle are each 8 units long, and the third side is 6 units long. What is the area of the triangle, expressed in square units?

(A) 14

(B) $12\sqrt{3}$

(C) 18

(D) 22

(E) $3\sqrt{55}$

Bisect the angle connecting the two congruent sides. The bisecting line is the triangle's height (h), and the triangle's base is 6 units long.

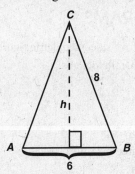

You can determine the triangle's height (h) by applying the Pythagorean theorem:

$3^2 + h^2 = 8^2$

$h^2 = 64 - 9$

$h^2 = 55$

$h = \sqrt{55}$

A triangle's area is half the product of its base and height. Thus, the area of $\triangle ABC = \frac{1}{2}(6)\sqrt{55} = 3\sqrt{55}$.

The correct answer is (E).

Equilateral Triangles

An equilateral triangle has the following three properties:

1 All three sides are congruent (equal in length).

2 The measure of each angle is 60°.

3 Area $= \dfrac{s^2\sqrt{3}}{4}$ (s = any side)

Any line bisecting one of the 60° angles divides an equilateral triangle into two right triangles with angle measures of 30°, 60°, and 90°; in other words, into two $1 : \sqrt{3} : 2$ triangles, as shown in the right-hand triangle in the next figure. (Remember that Pythagorean angle triplet?)

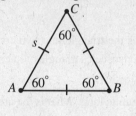 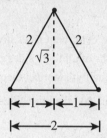

In the left-hand triangle, if $s = 6$, the area of the triangle $= 9\sqrt{3}$. To confirm this formula, bisect the triangle into two 30°-60°-90° $\left(1 : \sqrt{3} : 2\right)$ triangles (as in the right-hand triangle in the preceding figure). The area of this equilateral triangle is $\dfrac{1}{2}(2)\sqrt{3}$, or $\sqrt{3}$. The area of each smaller right triangle is $\dfrac{\sqrt{3}}{2}$.

RECTANGLES, SQUARES, AND PARALLELOGRAMS

Rectangles, squares, and parallelograms are types of *quadrilaterals*—four-sided geometric figures. Here are five characteristics that apply to all rectangles, squares, and parallelograms:

1 The sum of the measures of all four interior angles is 360°.

2 Opposite sides are parallel.

3 Opposite sides are congruent (equal in length).

4 Opposite angles are congruent (the same size, or equal in degree measure).

5 Adjacent angles are supplementary (their measures total 180°).

A rectangle is a special type of parallelogram in which all four angles are right angles (90°). A square is a special type of rectangle in which all four sides are congruent (equal in length). For the GMAT, you should know how to determine the perimeter and area of each of these three types of quadrilaterals. Referring to the next three figures, here are the formulas (l = length and w = width):

Rectangle

Perimeter = $2l + 2w$

Area = $l \times w$

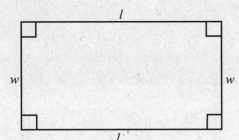

Square

Perimeter = $4s$ [s = side]

Area = s^2

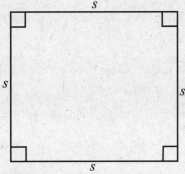

Parallelogram

Perimeter = $2l + 2w$

Area = base (b) × altitude (a)

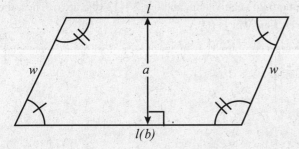

GMAT questions involving squares come in many varieties. For example, you might need to determine area, given the length of any side or either diagonal, or perimeter. Or, you might need to do just the opposite—find a length or perimeter given the area. For example:

The area of a square with a perimeter of 8 is 4.

($s = 8 \div 4 = 2$; $s^2 = 4$)

The perimeter of a square with an area of 8 is $8\sqrt{2}$.

$$(s = \sqrt{8} = 2\sqrt{2}; \; 4s = 4 \times 2\sqrt{2})$$

The area of a square with a diagonal of 6 is 18.

$$\left(A = \left(\frac{1}{2}\right)6^2 = \left(\frac{1}{2}\right)(36) = 18\right)$$

Or, you might need to determine a change in area resulting from a change in perimeter (or vice versa).

7. If a square's sides are each increased by 50%, by what percent does the square's area increase?

   (A) 75%

   (B) 100%

   (C) 125%

   (D) 150%

   (E) 200%

Letting s = the length of each side before the increase, area = s^2. If $\frac{3}{2}s$ = the length of each side after the increase, the new area = $\left(\frac{3}{2}s\right)^2 = \frac{9}{4}s^2$. The increase from s^2 to $\frac{9}{4}s^2$ is $\frac{5}{4}$, or 125%. **The correct answer is (C).**

GMAT questions involving non-square rectangles also come in many possible flavors. For example, a question might ask you to determine area based on perimeter, or vice versa.

8. The length of a rectangle with area 12 is three times the rectangle's width. What is the perimeter of the rectangle?

   (A) 10

   (B) 12

   (C) 14

   (D) 16

   (E) 20

The ratio of length to width is 3:1. The ratio 6:2 is equivalent, and $6 \times 2 = 12$ (the area). Thus, the perimeter = $(2)(6) + (2)(2) = 16$. **The correct answer is (D).**

Or, a question might require you to determine a combined perimeter or area of adjoining rectangles.

9.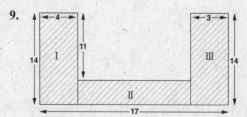

   In the figure above, all intersecting line segments are perpendicular. What is the area of the shaded region, in square units?

   (A) 84

   (B) 118

   (C) 128

   (D) 139

   (E) 238

The figure provides the perimeters you need to calculate the area. One way to find the area of the shaded region is to consider it as what remains when a rectangular shape is cut out of a larger rect-angle. The area of the entire figure without the "cut-out" is 14 × 17 = 238. The "cut-out" rectangle has a length of 11, and its width is equal to 17 − 4 − 3 = 10. Thus, the area of the cut-out is 11 × 10 = 110. Accordingly, the area of the shaded region is 238 − 110 = 128. **The correct answer is (C).**

Another way to solve the problem is to partition the shaded region into three smaller rectangles, as shown in the next figure, and sum up the area of each.

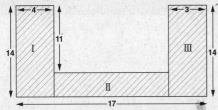

A GMAT question about a non-rectangular parallelogram might focus on angle measures. These questions are easy to answer. In any parallelogram, opposite angles are congruent, and adjacent angles are supplementary. (Their measures total 180°.) So if one of a parallelogram's angles measures 65°, then the opposite angle must also measure 65°, while the two other angles each measure 115°.

A more difficult question about a non-rectangular parallelogram might focus on area. To determine the parallelogram's altitude, you might need to apply the Pythagorean theorem (or one of the side or angle triplets).

10.

In the figure above, $\overline{AB} \parallel \overline{CD}$ and $\overline{AD} \parallel \overline{BC}$. If $\overline{BC}$ is 4 units long and $\overline{CD}$ is 2 units long, what is the area of quadrilateral $ABCD$?

(A) 4
(B) $4\sqrt{2}$
(C) 6
(D) 8
(E) $6\sqrt{2}$

TIP

A non-rectangular parallelogram in which all four sides are congruent (called a *rhombus*) has the following in common with a square: Perimeter = 4s; Area = one-half the product of the diagonals.

Since *ABCD* is a parallelogram, its area = base (4) × altitude (*a*). To determine altitude (*a*), draw a vertical line segment connecting point A to $\overline{BC}$, which creates a 45°-45°-90° triangle. The ratio of the triangle's hypotenuse to each leg is $\sqrt{2}$: 1. The hypotenuse $\overline{AB} = 2$. Thus, the altitude (*a*) of *ABCD* is $\dfrac{2}{\sqrt{2}}$, or $\sqrt{2}$. Accordingly, the area of *ABCD* = 4 × $\sqrt{2}$, or $4\sqrt{2}$. **The correct answer is (B).**

Trapezoids

A trapezoid is a special type of quadrilateral. The next figure shows a trapezoid. All trapezoids share these four properties:

1 Only one pair of opposite sides are parallel ($BC \parallel AD$).

2 The sum of the measures of all four angles is 360°.

3 Perimeter = $AB + BC + CD + AD$

4 Area = $\dfrac{BC + AD}{2}$ × altitude (that is, one-half the sum of the two parallel sides multiplied by the altitude).

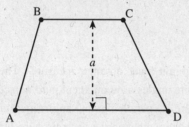

On the GMAT, a trapezoid problem might require you to determine the altitude, the area, or both.

11.

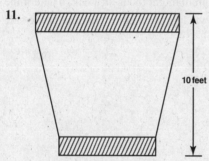

To cover the floor of an entry hall, a 1' × 12' strip of carpet is cut into two pieces, shown as the shaded strips in the figure above, and each piece is connected to a third carpet piece as shown. If the 1' strips run parallel to each other, what is the total area of the carpeted floor, in square feet?

(A) 46

(B) 48

(C) 52.5

(D) 56

(E) 60

The altitude of the trapezoidal piece is 8. The sum of the two parallel sides of this piece is 12' (the length of the 1' × 12' strip before it was cut). You can apply the trapezoid formula to determine the area of this piece:

$$A = 8 \times \frac{12}{2} = 48$$

The total area of the two shaded strips is 12 square feet, so the total area of the floor is 60 square feet. **The correct answer is (E).**

A GMAT trapezoid problem might require you to find the trapezoid's altitude by the Pythagorean theorem.

12.

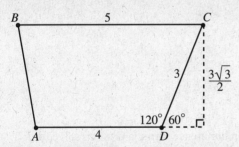

In the figure above, $BC \parallel AD$. What is the area of quadrilateral $ABCD$?

(A) $5\sqrt{2}$

(B) $\dfrac{9\sqrt{3}}{2}$

(C) $\dfrac{27\sqrt{3}}{4}$

(D) $\dfrac{27}{2}$

(E) 16

The figure shows a trapezoid. To find its area, first determine its altitude by creating a right triangle:

This right triangle conforms to the 30°-60°-90° Pythagorean angle triplet. Thus, the ratio of the three sides is $1 : \sqrt{3} : 2$. The hypotenuse is given as 3, so the trapezoid's altitude is $\dfrac{3\sqrt{3}}{2}$. Now you can calculate the area of the trapezoid:

$$\left(\frac{1}{2}\right)(4+5)\left(\frac{3\sqrt{3}}{2}\right) = \left(\frac{9}{2}\right)\left(\frac{3\sqrt{3}}{2}\right) = \frac{27\sqrt{3}}{4}$$

The correct answer is (C).

CIRCLES

For the GMAT, you'll need to know the following basic terminology involving circles:

- **Circumference:** The distance around the circle (its "perimeter")
- **Radius:** The distance from a circle's center to any point on the circle's circumference

- **Diameter:** The greatest distance from one point to another on the circle's circumference (twice the length of the radius)

- **Chord:** A line segment connecting two points on the circle's circumference (a circle's longest possible chord is its diameter, passing through the circle's center)

You'll also need to apply the two basic formulas involving circles (r = radius, d = diameter):

① Circumference = $2\pi r$, or πd

② Area = πr^2

Note that the value of π is approximately 3.14, or $\dfrac{22}{7}$. For the GMAT, you won't need to work with a value for π any more precise. In fact, in most circle problems, the solution is expressed in terms of π rather than numerically.

With the two formulas, all you need is one value—area, circumference, diameter, or radius—and you can determine all the others. For example:

Given a circle with a diameter of 6:

radius = 3

circumference = $(2)(3)\pi = 6\pi$

area = $\pi(3)^2 = 9\pi$

13. If a circle's circumference is 10π centimeters long, what is the area of the circle, in square centimeters?

   (A) 12.5

   (B) 5π

   (C) 22.5

   (D) 25π

   (E) 10π

First, determine the circle's radius. Applying the circumference formula C = $2\pi r$, solve for r:

$10\pi = 2\pi r$

$5 = r$

Then, apply the area formula, with 5 as the value of r:

$A = \pi(5)2 = 25\pi$

The correct answer is (D).

ADVANCED CIRCLE PROBLEMS

GMAT circle problems sometimes involve other geometric figures as well, so they're inherently tougher than average. The most common such "hybrids" involve triangles, squares, and other circles. In the next sections, you'll learn all you need to know to handle any hybrid problem.

Arcs and Degree Measures of a Circle

An arc is a segment of a circle's circumference. A *minor arc* is the shortest arc connecting two points on a circle's circumference. For example, in the next figure, minor arc *AB* is the one formed by the 60° angle from the circle's center (*O*).

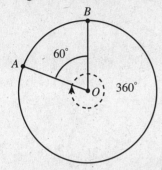

A circle, by definition, contains a total of 360°. The length of an arc relative to the circle's circumference is directly proportionate to the arc's degree measure as a fraction of the circle's total degree measure of 360°. For example, in the preceding figure, minor arc *AB* accounts for $\frac{60}{360}$, or $\frac{1}{6}$, of the circle's circumference.

14.

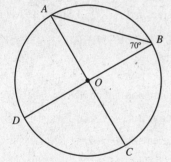

Circle *O*, as shown in the figure above, has diameters of $\overline{DB}$ and $\overline{AC}$ and a circumference of 9. What is the length of minor arc *BC*?

(A) 4

(B) $\frac{11}{3}$

(C) $\frac{7}{2}$

(D) $\frac{13}{4}$

(E) 3

Since $\overline{AO}$ and $\overline{OB}$ are both radii, we have isosceles $\angle AOB$ thus making m$\angle BAO = 70°$. From this we can find m$\angle AOB = 40°$. $\angle BOC$ is supplementary to $\angle AOB$, therefore m$\angle BOC = 140°$. (Remember: Angles from a circle's center are proportionate to the arcs they create.) Since m$\angle BOC$ accounts for $\frac{140}{360}$, or $\frac{7}{18}$, of the circle's circumference, we have the length of minor arc $BC = \left(\frac{7}{18}\right)(9) = \frac{7}{2}$. **The correct answer is (C).**

Circles and Inscribed Polygons

A polygon is *inscribed* in a circle if each vertex of the polygon lies on the circle's circumference. The next figure shows an inscribed square. The square is partitioned into four congruent triangles, each with one vertex at the circle's center (O).

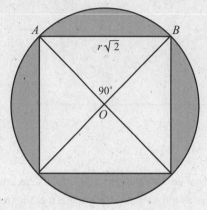

Look at any one of the four congruent triangles—for example, $\triangle ABO$. Notice that $\triangle AOB$ is a *right* triangle with the 90° angle at the circle's center. The length of each of the triangle's two legs ($\overline{AO}$ and $\overline{OB}$) equals the circle's radius (r). Accordingly, $\triangle ABO$ is a right isosceles triangle, m$\angle OAB$ = m$\angle OBA$ = 45°, and $AB = r\sqrt{2}$. (The ratio of the triangle's sides is $1:1:\sqrt{2}$.) Since $\overline{AB}$ is also the side of the square, the area of a square inscribed in a circle is $\left(r\sqrt{2}\right)^2$, or $2r^2$.

(The area of $\triangle ABO$ is $\dfrac{r^2}{2}$, or one fourth the area of the square.)

You can also determine relationships between the inscribed square and the circle:

- The ratio of the inscribed square's area to the circle's area is $2:\pi$.
- The *difference* between the two areas—the total shaded area—is $\pi r^2 - 2r^2$.
- The area of each crescent-shaped shaded area is $\dfrac{1}{4}\left(\pi r^2 - 2r^2\right)$.

The next figure shows a circle with an inscribed regular hexagon. (In a regular polygon, all sides are congruent.) The hexagon is partitioned into six congruent triangles, each with one vertex at the circle's center (O).

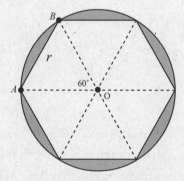

Look at any one of the six congruent triangles—for example, $\triangle ABO$. Since all six triangles are congruent, m$\angle AOB$ = 60°, (one sixth of 360°). You can see that the length of $\overline{AO}$ and $\overline{BO}$ each equals the circle's radius (r). Accordingly, m$\angle OAB$ = m$\angle OBA$ = 60°, ΔABO is an equilateral triangle, and length of $\overline{AB} = r$.

Applying the area formula for equilateral triangles: Area of $\Delta ABO = \dfrac{r^2\sqrt{3}}{4}$. The area of the hexagon is 6 times the area of ΔABO, or $\dfrac{3r^2\sqrt{3}}{2}$. You can also determine relationships between the inscribed hexagon and the circle. For example, the difference between the two areas—the total shaded area—is $\pi r^2 - \dfrac{3r^2\sqrt{3}}{2}$.

15.

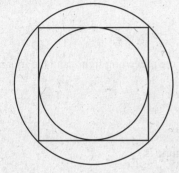

The figure above shows a square that is tangent to one circle at four points, and inscribed in another. If the diameter of the large circle is 10, what is the diameter of the smaller circle?

(A) $\dfrac{5\sqrt{3}}{2}$

(B) 5

(C) 2π

(D) $5\sqrt{2}$

(E) 7.5

The square's diagonal is equal in length to the large circle's diameter, which is 10. This diagonal is the hypotenuse of a triangle whose legs are two sides of the square. The triangle is right isosceles, with sides in the ratio $1:1\sqrt{2}$. The length of each side of the square $= \dfrac{10}{\sqrt{2}}$ or $5\sqrt{2}$. This length is also the diameter of the small circle. **The correct answer is (D).**

Tangents and Inscribed Circles

A circle is *tangent* to a line (or line segment) if they intersect at one and only one point (called the *point of tangency*). Here's the key rule to remember about tangents: A line that is tangent to a circle is *always* perpendicular to the line passing through the circle's center at the point of tangency.

The next figure shows a circle with center O inscribed in a square. Point P is one of four points of tangency. By definition, $\overline{OP} \perp \overline{AB}$.

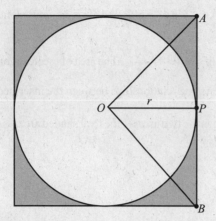

Also, notice the following relationships between the circle in the preceding figure and the square in which it is inscribed (r = radius):

- Each side of the square is $2r$ in length.

- The square's area is $(2r)^2$, or $4r^2$.

- The ratio of the square's area to that of the inscribed circle is $\dfrac{4}{\pi}$.

- The difference between the two areas—the total shaded area—is $4r^2 - \pi r^2$.

- The area of each separate (smaller) shaded area is $\dfrac{1}{4}\left(4r^2 - \pi r^2\right)$.

For *any* regular polygon (including squares) that inscribes a circle:

- The point of tangency between each line segment and the circle *bisects* the segment.

- Connecting each vertex to the circle's center creates an array of congruent angles, arcs, and triangles.

For example, the left-hand figure below shows a regular pentagon, and the right-hand figure shows a regular hexagon. Each polygon inscribes a circle. In each figure, the shaded region is one of five (or six) identical ones.

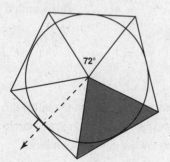
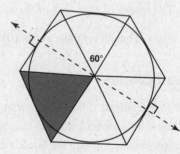

16.

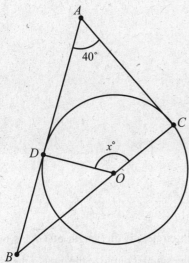

In the figure above, a circle with center O is tangent to $\overline{AB}$ at point D and tangent to $\overline{AC}$ at point C. If m $\angle A = 40°$, then $x =$

(A) 140

(B) 45

(C) 150

(D) 155

(E) 160

Since $\overline{AC}$ is tangent to the circle, $\overline{AC} \perp \overline{BC}$. Accordingly, $\triangle ABC$ is a right triangle, and m $\angle B = 50°$. Similarly, $\overline{AB} \perp \overline{DO}$, $\triangle DBO$ is a right triangle, and $\angle DOB = 40°$. $\angle DOC$ (the angle in question) is supplementary to $\angle DOB$. Thus, m $\angle DOC = 140°$ ($x = 140$). **The correct answer is (A).**

Comparing Circles

On the GMAT, questions asking you to compare circles come in two varieties:

1. Calculate the *difference* between radii, circumferences, and areas.

2. Determine *ratios* involving the two circles and their radii, circumferences, and areas.

To calculate a *difference* between the radii, circumferences, or areas, just calculate each area or circumference, then subtract. And if the question asks you for a difference between the areas of sectors of two concentric circles, first calculate the areas of each sector, then subtract the smaller area from the larger area.

To handle questions involving ratios, you need to understand that the relationship between a circle's radius or circumference and its area is *exponential*, not linear (because $A = \pi r^2$). For example, if one circle's radius is *twice* that of another, the ratio of the circles' areas is 1:4 $[\pi r^2 : \pi (2r)^2]$. If the larger circle's radius is *three* times that of the smaller circle, the ratio is 1:9 $[\pi r^2 : \pi (3r)^2]$. A 1:4 ratio between radii results in a 1:16 area ratio (and so forth).

TIP

The proportions noted on this page also apply if you compare circumferences and areas. If the circumference ratio is 2:1, then the area ratio is 4:1. If the circumference ratio is 4:1, then the area ratio is 16:1.

17.

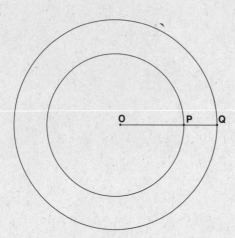

In the figure above, point O lies at the center of both circles. If the length of $\overline{OP}$ is 6 and the length of $\overline{PQ}$ is 2, what is the ratio of the area of the smaller circle to the area of the larger circle?

(A) $\dfrac{3}{8}$

(B) $\dfrac{7}{16}$

(C) $\dfrac{7}{16}$

(D) $\dfrac{9}{16}$

(E) $\dfrac{5}{8}$

The ratio of the small circle's radius to that of the large circle is 6:8, or 3:4. Since Area = πr^2, the area ratio is $\pi(3)^2 : \pi(4)^2$, or 9:16. **The correct answer is (D).**

POLYGONS

Polygons include all plane figures formed only by straight segments. Up to this point, we've focused on only two types of polygons: three-sided ones (triangles) and four-sided ones (quadrilaterals). Now take a quick look at the key characteristics of all polygons.

You can use the following formula to determine the sum of the measures of all interior angles of *any* polygon whose angles each measure less than 180° (n = number of sides):

$(n-2)(180°)$ = sum of interior angles

For *regular* polygons, the average angle measure is also the measure of every angle. But for any polygon (except for those with an angle exceeding 180°), you can find the average angle measure by dividing the sum of the measures of the angles by the number of sides. One way to shortcut the math is to memorize the angle sums and averages for polygons with 3–8 sides:

3 sides: $(3 - 2)(180°) = 180° \div 3 = 60°$

4 sides: $(4 - 2)(180°) = 360° \div 4 = 90°$

5 sides: $(5 - 2)(180°) = 540° \div 5 = 108°$

6 sides: $(6 - 2)(180°) = 720° \div 6 = 120°$

7 sides: $(7 - 2)(180°) = 900° \div 7 = 129°$

8 sides: $(8 - 2)(180°) = 1080° \div 8 = 135°$

A GMAT question might simply ask for the measure of any interior angle of a certain regular polygon; to answer it, just apply the preceding formula. If the polygon is not regular, you can add up known angle measures to find unknown angle measures.

18. If exactly two of the angles of the polygon shown below are congruent, what is the LEAST possible sum of the degree measures of two of the polygon's interior angles?

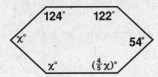

    (A) 162°

    (B) 174°

    (C) 176°

    (D) 204°

    (E) 216°

The figure shows a hexagon. The sum of the measures of six angles is 720°. Subtracting the measures of the three known angles from 720° leaves 420°, which is the sum of the measures of the three unknown angles. Set up an equation, then solve for x:

$$x + x + \frac{4}{5}x = 420$$

$$\frac{14}{5}x = 420$$

$$x = (420)\frac{5}{14} = (30)(5) = 150$$

Of the three unknown angles, two are 150° each. The other is 120°. The polygon's two smallest angles measure 54° and 120°. Their sum is 174°. **The correct answer is (B).**

Another, more difficult type of problem requires you to determine the area of a polygon, which might be either regular or irregular. To do so, you need to partition the polygon into an assemblage of smaller geometric figures.

19.

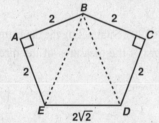

What is the area of polygon *ABCDE* shown above?

(A) $4 + 2\sqrt{3}$

(B) $3 + 3\sqrt{2}$

(C) $6\sqrt{3}$

(D) $2 + 6\sqrt{2}$

(E) $8\sqrt{2}$

Divide the polygon into three triangles as shown below. The area of each of the two outer triangles $= \frac{1}{2}bh = \frac{1}{2}(2)(2) = 2$. (Their combined area is 4.) Since the two outer triangles are both $1:1:\sqrt{2}$ right triangles, $\overline{BE} \cong \overline{BD}$, and both line segments are $2\sqrt{2}$ units long. Accordingly, the central triangle is equilateral. Calculate its area:

$$\frac{s^2\sqrt{3}}{4} = \frac{\left(2\sqrt{2}\right)^2\sqrt{3}}{4} = \frac{8\sqrt{3}}{4} = 2\sqrt{3}$$

Thus, the area of the polygon is $4 + 2\sqrt{3}$.

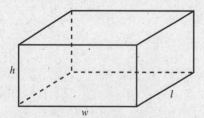

The correct answer is (A).

CUBES AND OTHER RECTANGULAR SOLIDS

GMAT questions about rectangular solids always involve one or both of two basic formulas (*l* = length, *w* = width, *h* = height):

Volume = *lwh*

Surface Area = $2lw + 2wh + 2lh = 2(lw + wh + lh)$

For *cubes*, the volume and surface-area formulas are even simpler than for other rectangular solids (let s = any edge):

Volume = s^3, or $s = \sqrt[3]{\text{Volume}}$

Surface Area = $6s^2$

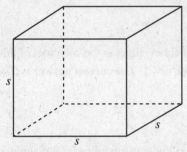

GMAT question might require you to apply any one of the formulas. Plug what you know into the formula, then solve for whatever characteristic the question asks for. Or, a question might require you to deal with the formulas for both surface area and volume.

20. A closed rectangular box with a square base is 5 inches in height. If the volume of the box is 45 square inches, what is the box's surface area in square inches?

   (A) 45
   (B) 66
   (C) 78
   (D) 81
   (E) 90

First, determine the dimensions of the square base. The box's height is given as 5. Accordingly, the box's volume (45) = $5lw$, and $lw = 9$. Since the base is square, the base is 3 inches long on each side. Now you can calculate the total surface area: $2lw + 2wh + 2lw = (2)(9) + (2)(15) + (2)(15) =$ 78. **The correct answer is (C).**

A variation on the preceding question might ask the number of smaller boxes you could fit, or "pack," into the box that the question describes. For instance, the number of cube-shaped boxes, each one 1.5 inches on a side, that you could pack into the $3 \times 3 \times 5$ box is 12 (3 levels of 4 cubes, with a half-inch space left at the top of the box).

A test question involving a cube might focus on the *ratios* among the cube's linear, square, and cubic measurements.

21. If the volume of one cube is 8 times greater than that of another, what is the ratio of the area of one square face of the larger cube to that of the smaller cube?

(A) 16:1

(B) 12:1

(C) 8:1

(D) 4:1

(E) 2:1

The ratio of the two volumes is 8:1. Thus, the linear ratio of the cubes' edges is the cube root of this ratio: $\sqrt[3]{8} : \sqrt[3]{1} = 2:1$. The area ratio is the square of the linear ratio, or 4:1. **The correct answer is (D).**

CYLINDERS

The only kind of cylinder the GMAT covers is a "right" circular cylinder (a tube sliced at 90° angles). The *surface area* of a right cylinder is the sum of the areas of:

- The circular base
- The circular top
- The rectangular surface around the cylinder's vertical face (visualize a rectangular label wrapped around a soup can)

The area of the vertical face is the product of the circular base's circumference (i.e., the rectangle's width) and the cylinder's height. Thus, given a radius r and height h of a cylinder:

Surface Area (SA) $= 2\pi r^2 + (2\pi r)(h)$

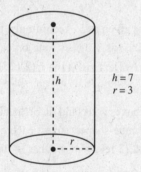

$h = 7$
$r = 3$

Given a cylinder's radius and height, you can determine its volume by multiplying the area of its circular base by its height:

Volume $= \pi r^2 h$

On the GMAT, a cylinder problem might require little more than a straightforward application of formula for either surface area or volume. As with rectangular-solid questions, just plug what you know into the formula, then solve for what the question asks. For example:

Given a radius of 3 and a height of 7, a right cylinder's volume $= \pi(3)^2(7) = 63\pi$.

A tougher cylinder problem might require you to apply other math concepts. It also might call for you to convert one unit of measure into another.

22. One hose dispenses water at the rate of 1 gallon per minute, and a second hose dispenses water at the rate of $1\frac{1}{2}$ gallons per minute. At the same time, the two hoses begin filling a cylindrical pail whose diameter is 14 inches and whose height is 10 inches. Which of the following most closely approximates the water level, measured in inches up from the pail's circular base, after $1\frac{1}{2}$ minutes? [231 cubic inches = 1 gallon]

   (A) 3.5
   (B) 4.2
   (C) 4.8
   (D) 5.6
   (E) 6.7

After $1\frac{1}{2}$ minutes, the two hoses have dispensed a total of 3.75 gallons. Set up a proportion in which 3.75 as a portion of the pail's volume equals the water level after $1\frac{1}{2}$ minutes as a portion of the pail's height:

$$\frac{3.75}{V} = \frac{x}{10}$$

The volume of the cylindrical pail is equal to the area of its circular base multiplied by its height:

$$V = \pi r^2 h \approx \left(\frac{22}{7}\right)(49)(10) \approx 1540$$

The gallon capacity of the pail = 1540 ÷ 231, or about 6.7. Plug this value into the proportion, then solve for x:

$$\frac{3.75}{6.7} = \frac{x}{10}$$
$$6.7x = 37.5$$
$$x = 5.6$$

The correct answer is (D).

COORDINATE SIGNS AND THE FOUR QUADRANTS

GMAT coordinate geometry questions involve the rectangular coordinate plane (or xy-plane) defined by two axes—a horizontal x-axis and a vertical y-axis. You can define any point on the coordinate plane by using two coordinates: an x-coordinate and a y-coordinate. A point's x-coordinate is its horizontal position on the plane, and its y-coordinate is its vertical position on the plane. You denote the coordinates of a point with (x,y), where x is the point's x-coordinate and y is the point's y-coordinate.

The center of the coordinate plane—the intersection of the x and y axes—is called the origin. The coordinates of the *origin* are (0,0). Any point along the x-axis has a y-coordinate of 0 $(x,0)$, and any point along the y-axis has an x-coordinate of 0 $(0,y)$. The coordinate signs (positive or negative) of points lying in the four Quadrants I–IV in this next figure are as follows:

Quadrant I (+,+)   Quadrant III (–,–)

Quadrant II (–,+)   Quadrant IV (+ ,–)

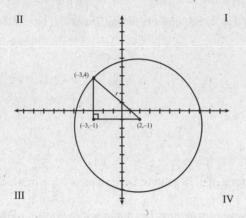

Notice that we've plotted three different points on this plane. Each point has its own unique coordinates. (Before you read on, make sure you understand why each point is identified by two coordinates.)

DEFINING A LINE ON THE COORDINATE PLANE

You can define any line on the coordinate plane by the equation:

$y = mx + b$

In this equation:

- The variable m is the slope of the line.
- The variable b is the line's y-intercept (where the line crosses the y-axis).
- The variables x and y are the coordinates of any point on the line. Any (xy) pair defining a point on the line can substitute for the variables x and y.

Determining a line's *slope* is often crucial to solving GMAT coordinate geometry problems. Think of the slope of a line as a fraction in which the numerator indicates the vertical change from one point to another on the line (moving left to right) corresponding to a given horizontal change, which the fraction's denominator indicates. The common term used for this fraction is "rise-over-run."

You can determine the slope of a line from any two pairs of (x,y) coordinates. In general, if (x_1, y_1) and (x_2, y_2) lie on the same line, calculate the line's slope as follows (notice that you can subtract either pair from the other):

$$\text{slope } (m) = \frac{y_2 - y_1}{x_2 - x_1} \text{ or } \frac{y_1 - y_2}{x_1 - x_2}$$

In applying the preceding formula, be sure to subtract corresponding values. For example, a careless test-taker calculating the slope might subtract y_1 from y_2 but subtract x_2 from x_1. Also, be sure to calculate "rise-over-run," and *not* "run-over-rise"—another careless but relatively common error.

As another example, here are two ways to calculate the slope of the line defined by the two points P(2,1) and Q(−3,4):

$$\text{slope (m)} = \frac{4-1}{-3-2} = \frac{3}{-5}$$

$$\text{slope (m)} = \frac{1-4}{2-(-3)} = \frac{-3}{5}$$

A GMAT question might ask you to identify the slope of a line defined by a given equation, in which case you simply put the equation in the standard form $y = mx + b$, and then identify the m-term. Or, it might ask you to determine the equation of a line, or just the line's slope (m) or y-intercept (b), given the coordinates of two points on the line.

23. On the xy-plane, at what point along the vertical axis (the y-axis) does the line passing through points (5,−2) and (3,4) intersect that axis?

    (A) −8

    (B) $-\dfrac{5}{2}$

    (C) 3

    (D) 7

    (E) 13

The question asks for the line's y-intercept (the value of b in the general equation $y = mx + b$). First, determine the line's slope:

$$\text{slope } m = \frac{y_2 - y_1}{x_2 - x_1} = \frac{4-(-2)}{3-5} = \frac{6}{-2} = -3$$

In the general equation ($y = mx + b$), $m = -3$. To find the value of b, substitute either (x,y) value pair for x and y, then solve for b. Substituting the (x,y) pair (3,4):

$$y = -3x + b$$
$$4 = -3(3) + b$$
$$4 = -9 + b$$
$$13 = b$$

The correct answer is (E).

To determine the point at which two nonparallel lines intersect on the coordinate plane, first determine the equation for each line. Then, solve for x and y by either substitution or addition-subtraction.

24. In the standard xy-coordinate plane, the xy-pairs (0,2) and (2,0) define a line, and the xy-pairs (−2,−1) and (2,1) define another line. At which of the following points do the two lines intersect?

    (A) $\left(\dfrac{4}{3}, \dfrac{2}{3}\right)$

    (B) $\left(\dfrac{3}{2}, \dfrac{4}{3}\right)$

    (C) $\left(-\dfrac{1}{2}, \dfrac{3}{2}\right)$

    (D) $\left(\dfrac{3}{4}, -\dfrac{2}{3}\right)$

    (E) $\left(-\dfrac{3}{4}, \dfrac{2}{3}\right)$

For each line, formulate its equation by determining slope (m), and then y-intercept (b). For the pairs (0,2) and (2,0):

$$y = \left(\frac{0-2}{2-0}\right)x + b \text{ (slope} = -1)$$

$$0 = -2 + b$$

$$2 = b$$

The equation for the line is $y = -x + 2$.

For the pairs (−2,−1) and (2,1):

$$y = \left(\frac{1-(-1)}{2-(-2)}\right)x + b \left(\text{slope} = \frac{1}{2}\right)$$

$$1 = \frac{1}{2}(2) + b$$

$$0 = b$$

The equation for the line is $y = \frac{1}{2}x$. To find the point of intersection, solve for x and y by substitution.

For example:

$$\frac{1}{2}x = -x + 2$$

$$\frac{3}{2}x = 2$$

$$x = \frac{4}{3}$$

$$y = \frac{2}{3}$$

The point of intersection is defined by the coordinate pair $\left(\frac{4}{3}, \frac{2}{3}\right)$. **The correct answer is (A).**

GRAPHING A LINE ON THE COORDINATE PLANE

You can graph a line on the coordinate plane if you know the coordinates of any two points on the line. Just plot the two points, and then draw a line connecting them. You can also graph a line from one point on the line, if you know either the line's slope or its y-intercept.

A GMAT question might ask you to recognize the value of a line's slope (m) based on a graph of the line. If the graph identifies the precise coordinates of two points, you can determine the line's precise slope (and the entire equation of the line). Even without any precise coordinates, you can still estimate the line's slope based on its appearance.

Lines that slope *upward* from left to right:

- A line sloping upward from left to right has a positive slope (m).

- A line with a slope of 1 slopes upward from left to right at a 45° angle in relation to the x-axis.

- A line with a fractional slope between 0 and 1 slopes upward from left to right but at less than a 45° angle in relation to the x-axis.

- A line with a slope greater than 1 slopes upward from left to right at more than a 45° angle in relation to the x-axis.

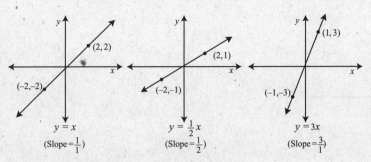

Lines that slope *downward* from left to right:

- A line sloping downward from left to right has a negative slope (*m*).

- A line with a slope of −1 slopes downward from left to right at a 45° angle in relation to the *x*-axis.

- A line with a fractional slope between 0 and −1 slopes downward from left to right but at less than a 45° angle in relation to the *x*-axis.

- A line with a slope less than −1 (for example, −2) slopes downward from left to right at more than a 45° angle in relation to the *x*-axis.

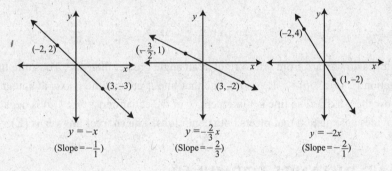

Horizontal and vertical lines:

- A horizontal line has a slope of zero ($m = 0$, and $mx = 0$).

- A vertical line has either an undefined or an indeterminate slope (the fraction's denominator is 0).

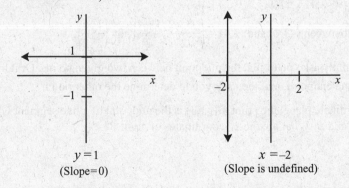

TIP

Parallel lines have the same slope (the same *m*-term in the general equation). The slope of a line perpendicular to another is the negative reciprocal of the other line's slope. (The product of the two slopes is −1.)

25.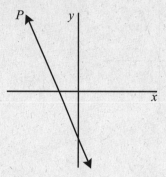

Referring to the xy-plane above, which of the following could be the equation of line P?

(A) $y = \dfrac{2}{5}x - \dfrac{5}{2}$

(B) $y = -\dfrac{5}{2}x + \dfrac{5}{2}$

(C) $y = \dfrac{5}{2}x - \dfrac{5}{2}$

(D) $y = \dfrac{2}{5}x + \dfrac{2}{5}$

(E) $y = -\dfrac{5}{2}x - \dfrac{5}{2}$

Notice that line P slopes downward from left to right at an angle greater than 45°. Thus, the line's slope (m in the equation $y = mx + b$) < -1. Also notice that line P crosses the y-axis at a negative y-value (that is, below the x-axis). The line's y-intercept (b in the equation $y = mx + b$) is negative. Only choice (E) provides an equation that meets both conditions. **The correct answer is (E).**

MIDPOINT AND DISTANCE FORMULAS

To be ready for GMAT coordinate geometry, you'll need to know these two formulas. To find the coordinates of the midpoint of a line segment, simply average the two endpoints' x-values and y-values:

$$x_M = \frac{x_1 + x_2}{2} \text{ and } y_M = \frac{y_1 + y_2}{2}$$

For example, the midpoint between $(-3,1)$ and $(2,4) = \left(\dfrac{-3+2}{2}, \dfrac{1+4}{2}\right)$, or $\left(\dfrac{1}{2}, \dfrac{5}{2}\right)$.

A GMAT question might simply ask you to find the midpoint between two given points. Or it might provide the midpoint and one endpoint, and then ask you to determine the other point.

26. In the standard xy-coordinate plane, the point $M(-1,3)$ is the midpoint of a line segment whose endpoints are $A(2,-4)$ and B. What are the xy-coordinates of point B?

    (A) $(-1,-2)$

    (B) $(-3,8)$

    (C) $(8,-4)$

    (D) $(5,12)$

    (E) $(-4,10)$

Apply the midpoint formula to find the x-coordinate of point B:

$$-1 = \frac{x+2}{2}$$
$$-2 = x+2$$
$$-4 = x$$

Apply the midpoint formula to find the y-coordinate of point B:

$$3 = \frac{y-4}{2}$$
$$6 = y-4$$
$$10 = y$$

The correct answer is (E).

To find the distance between two points that have the same x-coordinate (or y-coordinate), simply compute the difference between the two y-values (or x-values). Otherwise, the line segment is neither vertical nor horizontal, and you'll need to apply the distance formula, which is actually the Pythagorean theorem in thin disguise (it measures the length of a right triangle's hypotenuse):

$$d = \sqrt{\left(x_1 - x_2\right)^2 + \left(y_1 - y_2\right)^2}$$

For example, the distance between $(-3,1)$ and $(2,4)$ =

$$\sqrt{\left(-3-2\right)^2 + \left(1-4\right)^2} = \sqrt{25+9} = \sqrt{34}$$

A GMAT question might ask for the distance between two defined points (as in the example above). Or, it might provide the distance, and then ask for the value of a missing coordinate—in which case you solve for the missing x-value or y-value in the formula.

COORDINATE GEOMETRY

To handle GMAT questions involving the standard xy-coordinate plane, you must be able to perform the following five basic tasks:

1. Plot points on the coordinate plane
2. Determine the slope of a line (or line segment) on the plane
3. Interpret and formulate the equation of a line
4. Find the midpoint of a line segment
5. Find the distance between two points

Notice that all these tasks involve points and lines (line segments) only. In this section, you'll explore coordinate-geometry problems involving two-dimensional geometric figures, especially triangles and circles.

Triangles and the Coordinate Plane

On the GMAT, a question might ask you to find the perimeter or area of a triangle defined by three particular points. As you know, either calculation requires that you know certain information about the lengths of the triangle's sides. Apply the distance formula (or the standard form of the Pythagorean theorem) to solve these problems.

27. On the xy-plane, what is the perimeter of a triangle with vertices at points A $(-1,-3)$, B $(3,2)$, and C $(3,-3)$?

    (A) 12

    (B) $10+2\sqrt{3}$

    (C) $7+5\sqrt{2}$

    (D) 15

    (E) $9+\sqrt{41}$

The figure below shows the triangle on the coordinate plane:

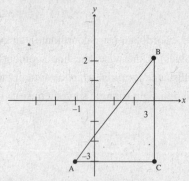

$AC = 4$ and $BC = 5$. Calculate AB (the triangle's hypotenuse) by the distance formula or, since the triangle is right, by the standard form of the Pythagorean theorem: $(AB)^2 = 4^2 + 5^2$; $(AB)^2 = 41$; $AB = \sqrt{41}$. The triangle's perimeter $= 4+5+\sqrt{41} = 9+\sqrt{41}$. **The correct answer is (E).**

Note that, since the triangle is right, had the preceding question asked for the triangle's area instead of perimeter, all you'd need to know are the lengths of the two legs ($\overline{AC}$ and $\overline{BC}$). The area is $\left(\dfrac{1}{2}\right)(4)(5)=10$.

To complicate these questions, the test-makers might provide vertices that do not connect to form a right triangle. (Answering this type of question requires the extra step of finding the triangle's altitude.) Or, they might provide only two points, and then require that you construct a triangle to meet certain conditions.

28. On the xy-plane, the xy-coordinate pairs $(-6,2)$ and $(-14,-4)$ define one line, and the xy-coordinate pairs $(-12,1)$ and $(-3,-11)$ define another line. What is the unit length of the longest side of a triangle formed by the y-axis and these two lines?

    (A) 15

    (B) 17.5

    (C) 19

    (D) 21.5

    (E) 23

For each line, formulate its equation by determining slope (m), and then y-intercept (b):

For the pairs (–6,2) and (–14,–4)	For the pairs (–12,1) and (–3,–11)
$y = \dfrac{6}{8}x + b \ \left(\text{slope} = \dfrac{3}{4}\right)$	$y = \dfrac{-12}{9}x + b \ \left(\text{slope} = -\dfrac{4}{3}\right)$
$2 = \dfrac{3}{4}(-6) + b$	$1 = -\dfrac{4}{3}(-12) + b$
$2 = -4\dfrac{1}{2} + b$	$1 = \dfrac{48}{3} + b$
$2 + 4\dfrac{1}{2} = b$	$1 - 16 = b$
$6\dfrac{1}{2} = b$	$-15 = b$

The two y-intercepts are $6\dfrac{1}{2}$ and –15. Thus the length of the triangle's side along the y-axis is 21.5. But is this the longest side? Yes. Notice that the slopes of the other two lines (l_1 and l_2) are negative reciprocals of each other: $\left(\dfrac{3}{4}\right)\left(-\dfrac{4}{3}\right) = -1$. This means that they're perpendicular, forming the two legs of a right triangle in which the y-axis is the hypotenuse (the longest side). **The correct answer is (D).**

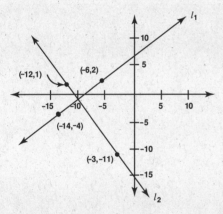

If the preceding question had instead asked for the point at which the two lines intersect, to answer the question you would formulate the equations for both lines, then solve for x and y with this system of two equations in two variables:

$$\frac{3}{4}x - y = -6\frac{1}{2}$$

$$\frac{4}{3}x + y = -15$$

The point of intersection is $(-10.32, -21.5)$.

Circles and the Coordinate Plane

GMAT question might ask you to find the circumference or area of a circle defined by a center and one point along its circumference. As you know, either calculation requires that you know the circle's radius. Apply the distance formula (or the standard form of the Pythagorean theorem) to find the radius and to answer the question.

29. On the *xy*-plane, a circle has center $(2,-1)$, and the point $(-3,3)$ lies along the circle's circumference. What is the square-unit area of the circle?

(A) 36π

(B) $\dfrac{81}{2}$

(C) 41π

(D) 48π

(E) 57π

The circle's radius is the distance between its center $(2,-1)$ and any point along its circumference, including $(-3,3)$. Hence, you can find r by applying the distance formula:

$$\sqrt{(-3-2)^2 + (3-(-1))^2} = \sqrt{25+16} = \sqrt{41}$$

The area of the circle $= \pi(\sqrt{41})^2 = 41\pi$. **The correct answer is (C).**

Here's something to watch out for: In any geometry problem involving right triangles, keep your eyes open for the Pythagorean triplet in which you'll see the correct ratio, but it's between the wrong two sides. For instance, in the preceding problem, the lengths of the two legs of a triangle whose hypotenuse is the circle's radius are 4 and 5. But the triangle does *not* conform to the 3:4:5 Pythagorean side triplet. Instead, the ratio is $4:5:\sqrt{41}$.

SUMMING IT UP

- Lines and line segments are the fundamental elements for most GMAT geometry problems, so it's essential to be familiar with the basic rules of angles formed by intersecting lines.

- Be certain you know the properties of all basic types of triangles. You'll not only encounter several problems involving triangles on the GMAT, but you'll also need to have the skills necessary for solving problems with four-sided figures, three-dimensional figures, and circles.

- GMAT circle problems typically involve other types of geometric figures as well, including triangles, squares, rectangles, and tangent lines. Learn the basics of circle problems and you'll be a step ahead in solving the most advanced geometric problems.

- GMAT coordinate geometry questions involve the xy-plane defined by the horizontal x-axis and the vertical y-axis. You will need to know how to determine the slope of a line, so remember to calculate it as "rise-over-run" and not "run-over-rise."

PART VI

GMAT VERBAL SECTION

Critical Reasoning

chapter 12

OVERVIEW

- **The 6-step plan**
- **Assumption questions**
- **Additional evidence questions**
- **Inference questions**
- **Strategy questions**
- **Hypothesis questions**
- **Necessary inference questions**
- **Parallel argument questions**
- **Summing it up**

In this chapter, you'll:

- Briefly review the basic terminology you need to know for GMAT Critical Reasoning

- Learn a step-by-step approach to handling any Critical Reasoning question

- Learn how to recognize and handle each of the three basic, and most common, types of Critical Reasoning questions

- Learn success keys for tackling Critical Reasoning questions

THE 6-STEP PLAN

The first task in this chapter is to learn the six basic steps for handling a GMAT Critical Reasoning question. Let's apply these steps to the following sample question:

> Among customers of breakfast restaurants, more order fresh fruit for breakfast than any other menu item. However, a recent health research report indicates that eating eggs does not pose so significant a health risk as previously thought. In response to this report, operators of breakfast restaurants should increase the number of eggs but decrease the amount of fresh fruit they order from their suppliers.

1. Which of the following, if true, would be the best reason to reject the recommendation made in the argument above?

   (A) Eating eggs still poses a substantial health risk, especially for males over age 50.

   (B) Most fresh fruits are available only seasonally, whereas eggs are available any time of the year.

   (C) Alternatives to breakfast egg dishes, such as pancakes and cereals, are growing in popularity at breakfast restaurants.

   (D) Many customers of breakfast restaurants who order eggs also order fresh fruit.

   (E) Compared to fresh fruits, pre-prepared fruit juices are growing in popularity among people who dine at breakfast restaurants.

Step One: Read the Question "Stem"

Reading the question stem (the actual question or prompt that follows the passage) first will tell you what you should think about as you read the passage. Be sure you understand the specific task that the question is asking you to perform.

Step Two: Read the Passage and Identify Its Key Elements

Identify the argument's conclusion (if any) and its premises. If the passage contains a conclusion (most Critical Reasoning passages do), try to follow the argument's line of reasoning from premise(s) to conclusion. To help yourself along, try reading the passage again, starting with the conclusion. (Critical Reasoning passages are brief, so a second reading won't take much time.)

Step Three: Try to Formulate Your Own Answer to the Question

Once you've determined exactly what the question is asking you, try to come up with your own answer before reading the given answer choices.

Step Four: Read the Five Answer Choices for the "Best" Response

Look for the answer choice that is similar to one of the "best" answers you've formulated. But don't assume that your home-grown best answer will look exactly the way you imagined it. Instead, look for a choice that conveys the same general idea. Also, keep an open mind to a possible "best" answer that hasn't yet occurred to you.

Step Five: If You're Still Not Sure, Eliminate Choices

Eliminate choices that make no sense to you, that don't seem directly relevant to the argument, or that accomplish just the opposite of what the question asks for.

Step Six: Compare the Quality of the Remaining Answer Choices

Try to determine which is qualitatively better than the others. Don't try to make ultrafine semantic distinctions, parse words, or second-guess the test-makers. The qualitative difference between the best and any runner-up choice will be clear enough—if your thinking is straight.

Now let's walk through the sample question about breakfast restaurants, using this 6-step approach.

Step 1: This question stem tells you quite a bit about the passage as well as what to look for in a viable answer choice. The stem essentially asks you to recognize how the argument can be weakened. Since it refers to the "argument above," you know that the passage will contain at least one premise (information that you should assume is factual) as well as a conclusion, which, in this case, will be in the form of a "recommendation."

Step 2: The passage's last sentence expresses the argument's conclusion, while the first two sentences indicate the premises on which the conclusion is based. So what's the line of reasoning here? In other words, what's the logical connection between the premises and the recommendation? Apparently, the passage's author thinks that breakfast restaurant customers now know that it's okay to eat eggs, so a significant number will begin ordering eggs *instead of* (as a substitute for) fresh fruit. Based on this reasoning, it would make sense for restaurants to get ready for the shift in demand toward eggs and away from fresh fruits—by adjusting their supplies accordingly. If you find this line of reasoning a bit questionable—in other words, if you think it's full of holes—you're on the right track. Proceed to Step 3.

Step 3: The question essentially asks how you'd weaken the argument. So now's the time to critique it—to shoot some big holes in it. Ask yourself what else is needed to justify the recommendation, based solely on the premises. Doesn't the logical leap from premises to conclusion rely on certain assumptions about a significant number of breakfast restaurant patrons? Here are three such assumptions (have any of these occurred to you?):

1. Customers are actually aware of the report (otherwise, why anticipate increased demand for eggs?).

2. Customers would prefer eggs over fresh fruit, even if they knew about the report (otherwise, why anticipate a shift in demand from fresh fruit to eggs?).

3. Customers consider eggs a suitable substitute for fresh fruit (otherwise, why decrease the supply of fresh fruit?).

Any one of these assumptions would form a good basis for a "best" answer to the question. To draft that best answer, all you'd need to do is *refute* any one of those assumptions—in other words, point out that any of the following is true:

- Customers are not aware of the report.
- Customers would not prefer eggs over fresh fruit (even if they knew about the report).
- Customers do not consider eggs a suitable substitute for fresh fruit.

Step 4: Notice that the statement in choice (D) (*Many customers of breakfast restaurants who order eggs also order fresh fruit*) is not quite the same as saying that eggs are not a substitute for fresh fruit (the last of our homegrown answers from Step 3). Yet, the essence of the critique is essentially the same: It's unfair to assume, without any supporting evidence, that a significant number of customers are going to switch from fruit to eggs. Notice that choice (D) uses the word "many," leaving open the possibility that for some customers these two choices might be mutually exclusive. So does that mean that there's probably a better answer choice? No; it's a pretty safe bet that (D) is the best choice. But go ahead and consider the other choices, anyway, just in case. Tentatively earmark choice (D) as your selection, then continue to Step 5.

Step 5: Consider each of the other four answer choices in turn:

Choice (A) also tends to weaken the argument. (If eating eggs is risky, this fact would tend to discourage, rather than encourage, people from eating them.) But if choice (A) is to significantly weaken the argument, we need to assume that a significant percentage of breakfast restaurant customers are males over the age of 50. Since choice (A) depends heavily on this additional assumption, it is not so effective as choice (D) in weakening the argument. Earmark it as a "runner-up."

Choice (B) is difficult to assess without more information, isn't it? The fact that fresh fruits are seasonal might have a bearing on whether owners should decrease their fruit supplies at a particular time. (For example, you could argue that, when fresh fruit is plentiful, lowering the supply might be safer than when it is not.) But what does that have to do with increasing egg supply? Absolutely nothing. As you can see, it's a real stretch to defend choice (B) as directly relevant to the argument at all, let alone as a statement that would clearly weaken the argument.

Choice (C) provides a reason why restaurant owners might want to decrease their supply of eggs. So choice (C) does tend to weaken the argument. But choice (C) helps refute only half of what the argument recommends. What about the recommendation to decrease fresh fruit supplies? Whether alternatives to eggs are gaining in popularity has no clear relationship on the demand for fresh fruit. So earmark choice (C) as another "runner-up."

Choice (E) provides a reason why restaurant owners might want to decrease their supply of fresh fruit—which is part of what the argument recommends. So choice (E) actually tends to support, or strengthen, the argument—just the opposite of what you're looking for in the best choice. Eliminate choice (E).

Step 6: Reflect again on the three most viable choices—the ones that tend to weaken the argument. Notice that choices (A) and (C), the two runners-up, both pale in comparison to choice (D) in terms of how seriously they weaken the argument. You can confidently confirm your selection. **The correct answer is (D).**

In this question, note that the difference between (D), the best choice, and the two runner-up choices, (A) and (C), is just the degree of qualitative difference that's typical of the GMAT. On the actual exam, you won't need to make judgment calls that are any closer than the ones we've made here.

ASSUMPTION QUESTIONS

In an assumption question, the passage will contain a series of premises and a conclusion. However, in order for the argument's conclusion to be probable, at least one additional premise must be *assumed*. In other words, the argument will rely on at least one *assumption*. Your task is to identify which of the five answer choices indicates an assumption. Think of the structure of the argument this way:

Argument: stated premise(s) + assumption → inference (conclusion)

You know you're dealing with an assumption question when the question stem looks something like one of the following (a question stem might refer to specific passage information as well):

"The argument in the passage depends on which of the following assumptions?"

"Which of the following is an assumption that enables the conclusion above to be properly drawn?"

"The conclusion drawn in the first sentence logically depends on which of the following assumptions?"

How to Identify an Argument's Assumptions

To identify an argument's assumptions, always ask yourself this question:

"In addition to the stated premises, what *must* be assumed as factual to justify the argument's logical leap from premises to conclusion—for the conclusion to be probable?"

Try asking and answering this question for Arguments 1 and 2 below. For each argument, try to think of at least one or two assumptions, then jot them down on paper. (On the GMAT, premises and conclusions are not labeled as they are here.)

Argument 1

Premise: More new Jupiter Motors automobiles were sold this year than any other brand.

Premise: Jupiter Motors automobiles have the lowest sticker prices, which are the manufacturers' suggested retail prices, of any new automobiles on the market.

Conclusion: Consumers rank low purchase price as the most important factor when purchasing new automobiles.

Argument 2

Premise: Three years ago a business tax credit for research and development was enacted into law for the purpose of stimulating these business activities.

Premise: Overall business profits have risen steadily since the enactment of this law.

Conclusion: The tax credit has failed to achieve its objective of stimulating research and development.

Now read the following assumptions. Think about each assumption until you understand the necessary link it provides in the argument's chain of reasoning—from premises to conclusion. Without the assumption the argument falls apart, doesn't it?

Assumption (Argument 1): Comparative sticker prices coincide with comparative prices consumers actually pay for new automobiles.

Assumption (Argument 2): New investment in research and development does not generally enhance business profits within a brief (three-year) period.

Did you identify these necessary assumptions, or did you instead jot down various propositions that merely lend additional support to the argument, such as the ones below? Any of these propositions, if factual, *might* lend support to the argument, rendering its conclusion more probable. Yet the argument would not fall apart without them, would it?

Additional supporting evidence (Argument 1):

- The supply of new automobiles other than Jupiter Motors automobiles is sufficient to meet demand for them.

- Jupiter Motors salespeople are no more adept at salesmanship than salespeople who sell other automobiles.

- Warranties, service contracts, and other purchase incentives besides sticker price are no more attractive for Jupiter Motors automobiles than those of other brands.

- Jupiter Motors automobiles provide no advantage over other brands with respect to features other than price—such as safety, functionality, and appearance.

Additional supporting evidence (Argument 2):

- The tax credit is small compared to the costs of new research and development.

- The general economic climate for business has remained at least as healthy as it was three years ago.

- Taxes on businesses have otherwise remained at current levels or declined during the same time period.

- Major corporate research initiatives begun prior to the enactment of the law began to enhance profits during the last three years.

Be sure you understand the qualitative difference between necessary assumptions and merely helpful additional evidence. Why? In any GMAT assumption question, the best answer choice will provide a necessary assumption.

A Typical Assumption Question

Now that you know how to identify and distinguish between necessary assumptions and other supporting evidence, attempt the following GMAT-style assumption question. (This one is a bit easier than average.) As you tackle the question, follow these five steps:

1. Identify the argument's conclusion and premises.

2. Try to identify at least one necessary assumption and jot it down—before reading the answer choices.

3. Scan the answer choices for that assumption—or one similar to it.

4. Earmark other choices you think provide supporting evidence.

5. For each remaining answer choice, ask yourself why it is not a viable choice. Then read the analysis of the question and of each answer choice.

For several consecutive years, poultry prices at each of three statewide grocery store chains have exceeded the national average by about 50 percent. Also, the per-pound difference in poultry prices among the three stores never amounted to more than a few pennies, while among grocery stores in other states, the prices varied by nearly a dollar over the same period. The three chains must have conspired to not compete among themselves and to fix their poultry prices at mutually agreed upon levels.

2. The claim that the three grocery store chains conspired to fix poultry prices rests on which of the following assumptions for the time period referred to above?

(A) No other grocery store charged higher prices for poultry than the three chains.

(B) Average poultry prices in the state where the three chains operate exceeded the national average.

(C) The price that grocery stores paid for poultry did not vary significantly from state to state.

(D) Consumers in the state where the three chains operate generally prefer poultry over other meats, even if poultry is more expensive than other meats.

(E) Other grocery stores operating in the same state as the three chains also sell poultry to consumers.

The argument relies on the assumption that all other possible factors in the price grocery stores charge for poultry were essentially the same in the state where the three chains operate as in other states. One such factor is wholesale price (the price grocery stores pay suppliers for poultry). A higher wholesale price generally leads to higher prices for consumers. Answer choice (C) expressly eliminates this factor. Admittedly, an "ideal" answer choice would provide a more sweeping statement—that all factors possibly affecting poultry price were the same from state to state. Nevertheless, choice (C) is the only answer choice that serves to affirm the assumption; thus (C) is the best choice. **The correct answer is (C).**

Choice (A) admittedly provides *some support* for the argument. Higher poultry prices at another store would weaken the argument that the three chains conspired to fix prices; thus given the inverse—that no other store charges higher poultry prices—the argument's conclusion becomes more probable. However, choice (A) is not a necessary assumption. Even if a certain grocery store charged higher prices for poultry during the period, this fact would probably not be statistically significant in light of the much lower national average— especially if that store were located in another state and therefore did not compete with the three chains.

Choice (B) actually serves to weaken the argument. Given choice (B), the greater the number of other grocery stores in the same state the more likely that these other stores also charged high prices for poultry. This fact would in turn help refute the claim that the three chains were motivated by any concern other than to compete effectively against other stores in the state.

Choice (D) is *not relevant* to the argument, which is concerned with poultry prices charged by the three chains compared to poultry prices in other states, *not* compared to prices of other meats.

Choice (E) actually *weakens* the argument. The more competitors, the less likely these three chains together hold a statewide poultry monopoly. (Monopolists are more likely to charge whatever price they wish for their products.)

Five Tips for Tackling Assumption Questions

1 Formulate your own "best" answer as you read the passage—by filling in the missing logical link between the arguments premises and its conclusion. If you know what to look for among the five answer choices, you'll be more likely to find it and less likely to fall prey to the test-maker's wrong-answer ploys.

2 Don't spend too much time brainstorming; if the missing link (a necessary assumption) doesn't occur to you within 10 or 15 seconds, go ahead and read the answer choices.

3 If a necessary assumption occurs to you as you read the passage, scan the answer choices quickly for it (or a statement similar to it). If you spot it, immediately select it (click on the button to the left of it) as your tentative choice.

4 If more than one answer choice seems viable to you, ask yourself whether each proposition provides a link in the argument's chain of reasoning. If it doesn't, eliminate that answer choice even if it lends support to the argument.

5 Look out for the following types of wrong answers (in addition to those that provide supporting but nonessential additional evidence):

- Additional information that serves to weaken the argument
- Superfluous information, which is not directly relevant to the argument

ADDITIONAL EVIDENCE QUESTIONS

In this type of question, the passage will look just like a passage for an assumption question; the passage will contain a series of premises, along with a conclusion whose probability depends on one or more assumptions. Here's the basic structure again:

Argument: stated premise(s) + assumption(s) → inference (conclusion)

In a weakening evidence question, however, your task is to identify which of the five answer choices *most seriously weakens* the argument. You know you're dealing with a weakening evidence question when the question stem looks similar to one of the following (a question stem might refer to specific passage information as well):

"Which of the following, if true, would most weaken the argument above?"

"The argument in the passage would be most seriously weakened if it were true that . . ."

"Which of the following, if true, is most damaging to the conclusion above?"

"Which of the following, if true, provides the best evidence that the reasoning in the argument above is flawed?"

"Each of the following, if true, raises a consideration against the conclusion above, EXCEPT:" (Your task here is to identify the only answer choice that does NOT weaken the argument.)

How to Weaken an Argument

To understand how an argument by inference can be weakened, consider Argument 1. Here it is again:

Argument 1

Premise: More new Jupiter Motors automobiles were sold this year than any other brand.

Premise: Jupiter Motors automobiles have the lowest sticker prices, which are the manufacturers suggested retail prices, of any new automobiles on the market.

Conclusion: Consumers rank low purchase price as the most important factor when purchasing new automobiles.

There are many ways to weaken an argument like the one above. One way is to essentially point out as a matter of fact that the conclusion is false, or that a stated premise needed for the conclusion to be probable is false. However, in a GMAT weakening evidence question, you're unlikely to find either method among the five choices—because both are a bit too obvious. Instead, the test-makers prefer the following two methods:

1 Directly refute a necessary assumption—in other words, provide evidence that the assumption is false as a matter of fact.

New automobiles with comparatively high sticker prices are often sold to consumers for less than automobiles with lower sticker prices.

2 Refute other possible supporting evidence—evidence that does not pertain directly to a necessary assumption but that, if true, would nevertheless increase the conclusion's probability.

Example A: Production at the plants of Jupiter Motors main competitor has been hampered by numerous labor strikes during the last three years.

Example B: Warranties and other nonprice purchase incentives vary widely among retailers of new automobiles.

Here's what you need to remember about these two methods when analyzing a GMAT weakening evidence question:

- A Method 1 answer choice is always better than a Method 2 choice, because the former is a *direct* attack on a *necessary* assumption.

- If no Method 1 proposition appears among the answer choices, then the best choice will be the best among the Method 2 propositions listed. (*Example A* above would be a better choice than *Example B*. Why? *Example B* leaves open the possibility that nonprice incentives at Jupiter retailers are less attractive than at other retailers, which would actually *strengthen* the Argument.)

A Typical Weakening Evidence Question

Now that you know how to weaken an argument and distinguish between propositions that merely weaken and those that completely undermine the argument, take another look at the GMAT-style question you encountered near the beginning of this chapter. (This question is average in difficulty level.) This time around, take the following five steps:

1 Identify the argument's conclusion and premises.

2 Try to identify at least one *necessary* assumption and jot it down—before reading the answer choices.

3 Scan the answer choices for a proposition that directly refutes, or contradicts, that assumption.

4 Earmark other choices you think serve to weaken the Argument—then rank them in quality (degree of damage to the conclusion).

5 For each remaining answer choice, ask yourself why it is not a viable choice. Then read the analysis of the question and of each answer choice.

Worldwide retail sales of home entertainment systems, which include a television and an audio system, increased 25 percent this year over last year. At the same time, worldwide retail sales of new automobiles declined by about the same percent. These statistics show that consumers can no longer afford to purchase both types of products during the same year.

TIP

In weakening evidence questions, don't expect any answer choice to directly refute or contradict the Argument's conclusion or one of its premises. Although either method is a great way to annihilate an Argument, the choice would be too easy to spot as the best one.

3. Which of the following, if true, would cast most serious doubt on the conclusion drawn above?

   (A) Fewer advertisements for new cars appeared on television during the most recent year than during the previous year.

   (B) Consumers are spending more money on home entertainment systems than on new cars.

   (C) People who own home entertainment systems do not drive their automobiles so often as other people.

   (D) Prices of home entertainment systems and new cars were higher during the most recent year than during the previous year.

   (E) The reliability of automobiles this year improved significantly over last year.

The argument relies on the assumption that all other possible factors influencing consumers buying decisions respecting the two products remained unchanged from last year to this year. An ideal "best" answer would directly refute or provide strong evidence against this assumption.

Choice (E) accomplishes this better than any other choice—by providing an alternative explanation for the fact that consumers are buying fewer new cars and more entertainment centers. Specifically, if a car is more reliable, then it is less likely to be replaced by a new one. By the same token, if people keep their cars longer and do not need to spend much money to repair them, then people can better afford to purchase other consumer items such as entertainment centers.

Choice (A) might explain why sales of new cars have declined. However, choice (A) does not explain increased sales of home entertainment centers.

Choice (B) reinforces the argument's premise, thereby *strengthening* the argument.

Choice (C) is irrelevant to the argument. Choice (C) provides a reason why people with home entertainment systems might replace their cars less often. However, even if this were the case, it would have no bearing on whether these people can afford both items.

Choice (D) does not explain why consumers have chosen one type of product over another. **The correct answer is (E).**

Six Tips for Tackling Weakening Evidence Questions

❶ As you read the passage, try to identify at least one necessary assumption. There are two general types of assumptions that are especially common in weakening evidence arguments: a) The assumption that all other factors are equal—if the argument seeks to explain certain differences between two phenomena; and b) the assumption that all other relevant conditions remain unchanged over time, if the argument seeks to explain or predict change from one point in time (or period of time) to another.

❷ Scan the answer choices for a proposition that directly refutes an assumption. If you spot one, immediately select it (click on the button to the left of it) as your tentative choice.

❸ In all likelihood, more than one answer choice will serve to weaken the argument. Always select a choice that directly addresses, and attacks, a necessary assumption over any other choice that weakens the argument.

❹ Before confirming your selection, ask yourself whether your choice serves to destroy a logical link needed for a convincing argument; if it doesn't, look for a better answer choice.

⑤ If no answer choice refutes a necessary assumption (it could happen), you'll need to weigh the comparative quality of all answer choices that serve to weaken the argument.

⑥ Look out for the following types of wrong answers:

- A statement that affirms a necessary assumption—in other words, that accomplishes just the opposite of what the question asks for
- A statement that serves to strengthen (rather than weaken) the argument in some other way
- A statement that could either strengthen or weaken the argument, depending on additional unknown facts
- A statement that contains superfluous information, which is not directly relevant to the argument

When handling a weakening evidence question, what if no answer choice hits directly on a key assumption behind the argument? Don't assume that your powers of reasoning have failed you. Perhaps the argument depends on other assumptions as well, or maybe the particular question wasn't designed to test you on recognizing assumptions.

Supporting the Argument

For a supporting evidence question, your task is to identify which of five propositions provides *the most support* for the argument—just the opposite of a weakening evidence question. You know you're dealing with a supporting evidence question when the question stem looks similar to one of the following (a question stem might refer to specific passage information as well):

"Which of the following, if true, most strongly supports the author's argument?"

"Which of the following statements, if true, would most strengthen the argument above?"

"Which of the following, if true, provides the best indication that the conclusion in the argument above was logically well supported?"

"Which of the following best completes the passage below?"

How to Strengthen an Argument

To understand how an argument by inference can be supported or strengthened, consider Argument 2. Here it is again:

Argument 2

Premise: Three years ago a business tax credit for research and development was enacted into law for the purpose of stimulating these business activities.

Premise: Overall business profits have risen steadily since the enactment of this law.

Conclusion: The tax credit has failed to achieve its objective of stimulating research and development.

There are two methods of strengthening an argument like this one (the first is more effective):

1 Provide a necessary assumption (assert it is factual) or provide strong evidence that it is factual.

Example: Investing in research and development does not generally enhance profitability until several years after the investment.

2 Provide evidence that adds weight or credibility to the argument but that does not affirm a necessary assumption.

Example A: Costs of certain raw materials used in many areas of research and development have increased since the law was enacted.

Example B: Many large corporations curtailed significant research and development shortly before the law was enacted.

Here's what you need to know about these two methods for analyzing a GMAT supporting evidence question:

- A proposition that affirms a necessary assumption (Method 1) provides better support for an argument than one that does not.

- If no Method 1 proposition appears among the answer choices, then the best choice will be the strongest Method 2 proposition listed. (*Example A* above would be a better choice than *Example B*. Why? The degree of support *Example B* lends to the argument depends entirely on our assumption that new research and development cannot enhance profits within three years; *Example A* lends support to the argument irrespective of this assumption.)

A Typical Supporting Evidence Question

Now that you know how to strengthen an argument and distinguish among propositions of varying degrees of support, attempt the following GMAT-style supporting evidence question. (This one is average in difficulty.) As you tackle the question, follow these five steps:

1 Identify the argument's conclusion and premises.

2 Try to identify at least one necessary assumption and jot it down—before reading the answer choices.

3 Scan the answer choices for a proposition that essentially provides that assumption.

4 Earmark other choices you think serve to strengthen the argument—then rank them in quality (degree of support).

5 For each remaining answer choice, ask yourself why it is not a viable choice. Then read the analysis of the question and of each answer choice.

In an experiment involving addicted cigarette smokers, each subject was unknowingly administered either the new drug Nico-Gone or a placebo. One year later, fewer than a third of the subjects who were administered Nico-Gone had resumed smoking, compared with about two thirds of the subjects who were administered a placebo. These reports confirm that Nico-Gone is effective in curing addiction to cigarette smoking.

TIP

The best way to strengthen an argument is to affirm an assumption; the best way to weaken it is to refute an assumption.

4. Which of the following, if true, most strongly supports the conclusion above?

(A) One year after the experiment, the percentage of the experiments subjects who were cigarette smokers was smaller than the percentage of the general population who were smokers.

(B) Other reliable studies indicate that cigarette smokers often falsely inform others that they are not smokers.

(C) During the year following the experiment, cigarettes were readily available to all of the subjects.

(D) One year after the experiment, the total number of subjects who were cigarette smokers was smaller than the number who were smokers one year prior to the experiment.

(E) During the year following the experiment, some of the subjects received other treatment to help them avoid cigarette smoking.

The argument relies on the major unstated assumption that no factor other than the experiment at issue was responsible for the reported result one year after the experiment. Choice (C) provides evidence that lends credence to this assumption. If cigarettes were unavailable to some of the subjects during the year, this fact would be the primary explanation for any decrease in the number of smokers among the subjects.

Choice (A) does lend *some* measure of support to the argument. However, choice (A) fails to provide the specific difference between the two percentages; a small percentage would not be statistically significant, especially if the number of subjects participating in the experiment was small. Thus, choice (A) is qualitatively not so strong as (C).

Choice (B) actually *weakens* the argument, by providing evidence that the results as reported by the subjects themselves might have been unreliable.

Choice (D) fails to provide sufficient information to support the argument. Specifically, choice (D) fails to distinguish between the subjects receiving Nico-Gone and those receiving the placebo. Choice (D) also fails to account for the possibility that the number of subjects who smoked might have changed significantly during the year immediately preceding the experiment.

Choice (E) actually *weakens* the argument by providing evidence that some factor other than Nico-Gone might have been responsible for the reported results.

The correct answer is (C).

Five Tips for Tackling Supporting Evidence Questions

1 As you read the passage, try to identify a *necessary* assumption. There are two general types of assumptions that are especially common in supporting evidence questions:

- The assumption that *all other factors are equal*—if the argument seeks to explain certain differences between two phenomena

- The assumption that *all other relevant conditions remain unchanged over time*—if the argument seeks to explain or predict some sort of change from one point in time (or period of time) to another

2 Scan the answer choices for a proposition that provides that assumption. If you spot it, immediately select it (click on the button to the left of it) as your tentative choice.

3 In all likelihood, more than one answer choice will serve to strengthen the argument. Always select a choice that directly affirms a necessary assumption over any other choice.

4 If no answer choice affirms a necessary assumption, you'll need to weigh the comparative quality of all answer choices that serve to strengthen the argument.

5 Look out for the following types of wrong answers:

- A statement that weakens rather than strengthens the argument
- A statement that could either strengthen or weaken the argument, depending on additional unknown facts
- A statement that contains superfluous information, which is not directly relevant to the argument

INFERENCE QUESTIONS

For a GMAT inference question, the passage will simply provide a series of premises—information that you are to accept as factual. Your task is to identify among the five answer choices the statement that provides the most reliable, or probable, conclusion from the passage information. Expect to encounter at least one or two questions of this type on the GMAT.

You know you're dealing with an inference question when the question stem looks similar to one of the following:

"Which of the following statements draws the most reliable conclusion from the information above?"

"Which of the following conclusions about . . . is best supported by the passage?"

"Which of the following can most properly be inferred from the information in the passage above?"

Notice that each of these question stems contains the word "most" or "best." These are important words. For an inference question, even the best answer choice will *not necessarily* follow from the premises; yet it will be more probable than any other answer choice.

How to Identify a Strong Inference

How do you recognize a probable, or reliable, inference among five answer choices and distinguish it from less reliable ones? The best way to answer this question is by example. Consider the following two GMAT-style passages. After reading each one, ask yourself: "Given this information, what else is probably true?" Try to think of at least one answer—then jot it down as if you were drafting your own best answer choice for a GMAT inference question. (Expect an easier time with Passage 1 than Passage 2.)

Passage 1

Many sociologists argue that science fiction television programs play a crucial role in fostering the belief that intelligent aliens have visited Earth. However, in countries where relatively few people have access to television, belief that intelligent aliens have visited Earth is at least as prevalent as in other countries.

Passage 2

To subsidize the profits of domestic farms that grow a certain crop, Country X imposes a tariff on exports of the crop. As a result, foreign food product manufacturers that must use the crop in their products find it more difficult to compete with Country X businesses that must use the same crop in their products.

Next, for each passage read the following conclusions (inferences). Think about each one until you understand that the one listed as a possible best answer choice *makes sense*; in other words, that it is *reasonably inferable* from the passage and *probable to some degree*. Then compare it to the ones listed as typical wrong-answer choices. Notice that each of these unreliable inferences depends on additional, unsubstantiated assumptions and is therefore far less probable.

Conclusions (inferences) from Passage 1

Reliable inference (potential "best" answer choice):

- Science fiction television programs are not the only factor in determining whether a person believes intelligent aliens have visited Earth.

Unreliable inferences (typical wrong answer choices):

- Science fiction television programs do not affect whether people believe that intelligent aliens have visited Earth.

- People who do not watch television are more likely to believe that intelligent aliens have visited Earth than people who do.

- Science fiction television programming is not realistic enough to persuade people that intelligent aliens have visited Earth.

Conclusions (inferences) from Passage 2

Reliable inference (potential "best" answer choice):

- Importing the crop from Country X is less costly for foreign businesses than if these businesses obtain the crop from another source.

Unreliable inferences (typical wrong-answer choices):

- The farms of Country X are the only sources of the crop.

- Other countries that produce the crop also impose export tariffs on the crop.

- The total demand for the crop produced in Country X declined as a result of the export tariff.

Compare the reliable inferences with the unreliable ones listed above. Notice that the unreliable ones either depend on additional assumptions that find no support in the passage and/or go too far—beyond the reliable inference to one that amounts to a sweeping, all-encompassing conclusion.

A Typical Inference Question

Now that you know how to identify and distinguish between reliable and unreliable inferences, attempt the following GMAT-style inference question, which is average in difficulty. As you tackle the question, follow these four steps:

① Try to answer the question "What else is probably true" after reading the passage but before reading the answer choices. If you think of an answer, jot it down.

② Scan the answer choices for your answer or one similar to it.

③ If there's no answer choice similar to the one you thought of, analyze each one in turn to determine how strongly the passage supports it.

④ For each statement you eliminated, be sure you can think of an additional assumption needed for the statement to make sense as a conclusion. Then, read the analysis of the question and of each answer choice..

During each of the last five years, both the demand for beverage containers and the quantity of beverage containers recycled to produce new beverage containers have increased steadily. At the same time, the number of freshly cut trees used to produce beverage containers has declined each year.

5. If the statements above are all true, they provide most support for which of the following conclusions about the last five years?

   (A) The number of new beverage containers not made of recycled materials has decreased.

   (B) More beverage containers have been recycled for producing new beverage containers than have not been recycled for this purpose.

   (C) Recycled beverage containers have been used only for making new beverage containers.

   (D) The number of beverage containers made of tree materials has decreased.

   (E) The number of used beverage containers not being recycled has decreased.

The fact that the number of recycled beverage containers has been increasing while the number of new trees used to make beverage containers has been declining lends considerable support to choice (A). Moreover, choice (A) allows for the possibility that some beverage containers are made of recycled materials other than tree materials. Admittedly, demand for beverage containers in general has increased recently, reducing the likelihood that choice (A) is true. On balance, however, choice (A) is more strongly supported than any of the other answer choices.

Choice (B) is not inferable from the statements, which provide information about *changes* in numbers from one year to the next, not *total* numbers. The passage provides no information that would permit a comparison between the total numbers of recycled beverage containers and nonrecycled beverage containers.

Choice (C) is not inferable. The passage provides no information permitting the sweeping inference that the increasing demand for beverage containers has been so great as to necessitate the use of *all* recycled beverage containers to meet this increased demand.

Choice (D) is not inferable. Although the decrease in the number of freshly cut trees each year tends to show that choice (D) might be true, the increase in demand for beverage containers and in the number of recycled beverage containers tend to show just the opposite. In any event, choice (D) also requires more information (additional assumptions) about the *percentage* of beverage containers, both new and recycled, made of tree products.

Choice (E) is not inferable. Just because the number of beverage containers being recycled has increased each year, it is unfair to conclude that the number of beverage containers not being recycled has been decreasing. In fact, given the increased demand for beverage containers in general, it is just as likely that consumers are recycling more beverage containers and discarding more beverage containers. **The correct answer is (A).**

Five Tips for Tackling Inference Questions

1 All statements in the passage are premises; thus, you should assume they are all factual (even if in real life they seem somewhat dubious).

2 Remember: Your task is not to recognize what must be true but rather to recognize what's most likely to be true among the five conclusions listed.

3 Formulating a possible "best" answer might help you zero in on the best answer choice. But don't expect this technique to work as reliably for inference questions as for the other question types covered in this chapter.

4 If an answer choice makes sense as a conclusion only if additional facts are assumed, you can safely eliminate it.

5 If an answer choice draws a sweeping conclusion—an all-encompassing generalization— you can probably eliminate it as the best answer choice. When in doubt, choose a narrower conclusion over a broader one.

STRATEGY QUESTIONS

In a GMAT strategy question, the passage sets up a scenario where a decision-maker must develop a plan, or *strategy*, for solving a "real-life" problem such as:

- An undesirable economic or sociological trend
- A decline in a certain business's revenue or profitability
- An increasingly serious public-health threat
- Declining performance levels among workers or students

Typically, the problem at hand is an undesirable trend or development that the decision-maker hopes to either halt or reverse. The question stem will indicate the decision-maker's objective. Your task is to identify, among the five answer choices, the strategy or course of action that would be *most effective, efficient,* or *appropriate* in achieving the stated objective. Expect to encounter no more than one question of this type on the GMAT.

You know you're dealing with a strategy question when the question stem looks similar to one of the following:

"Which of the following strategies would be most likely to reverse the decline in . . .?"

"To prevent the continued loss of . . ., it would be best for [the decision-maker] to . . ."

"Among the following proposals, which one, if implemented, is likely to be most effective in discouraging . . .?"

Notice that each of these question stems contains the word "most" or "best." These are important words. For a strategy question, even the best answer choice will *not necessarily* achieve the decision-maker's objective; yet, it will be *more likely* to achieve that objective than any other answer choice.

ALERT!

For GMAT strategy passages, think in terms of general strategy rather than specific actions. Any number of specific actions might help in achieving the stated goal, so your chances of coming up with one listed as the best answer choice are slim.

How to Identify the Best Strategy

How do you recognize the "best" strategy among five choices and distinguish it from less effective, efficient, or appropriate ones? To answer this question for yourself, consider the following GMAT-style passage:

> At Xenon Company, overall worker productivity, which depends primarily on the amount of time workers spend at their workstations, has been declining recently. Meanwhile, instead of either bringing lunch from home or eating lunch in the company's cafeteria, an increasing number of Xenon workers have been dining out for lunch, which usually takes more time than eating lunch at the Xenon premises.

Given the passage information, ask yourself: *How would I reverse the decline in worker productivity at Xenon?* Well, based on the passage, you know that eating out tends to reduce productivity because it takes more time away from actual work than does eating on the premises. So, to increase productivity, it would make sense to implement a plan that encourages workers to stay on the premises for lunch or, conversely, that discourages them from going out for lunch. Notice that the general strategy here is to encourage workers not just to eat in the cafeteria and not just to bring lunch from home, but, more generally, to remain on Xenon premises for lunch. This is an important distinction, as you're about to see.

Now read the following list of possible actions (i.e., answer choices). Think about each one until you understand why the one listed as the best course of action is more likely to discourage Xenon workers from leaving Xenon's premises for lunch than any of the others.

Alternative Courses of Action

Effective action (potential "best" answer choice):

- Impose stricter limits on the amount of time Xenon's workers are allowed for lunch breaks.

Actions that would have no clear, direct effect (typical wrong-answer choices):

- Allow Xenon workers greater flexibility in determining when they start and end their workdays.
- Establish free after-work nutrition and cooking classes for Xenon workers.

Actions that could either help or harm, depending on other facts (typical wrong-answer choices):

- Replace the vendor that currently provides Xenon's cafeteria food service with a different one.
- Begin charging workers a fee for parking in Xenon's employee parking lot.

Actions that would help but are too narrow (typical wrong-answer choices):

- Provide a greater variety of menu choices at the company cafeteria.
- Install a kitchenette on the premises for workers to prepare their own lunches.

Notice the three categories of typical wrong-answer choices. Actions that are unlikely to have any direct impact on worker productivity are the easiest to recognize as incorrect answers.

Actions that might be effective, depending on other circumstances, are a bit tougher to recognize as incorrect. Finally, actions that clearly help to achieve the objective, but not to as great an extent as the best choice, are the ones that lure most test-takers away from the correct choice.

A Typical Strategy Question

Now that you know how to identify and distinguish between effective and less effective strategies, attempt the following GMAT-style strategy question, which is more difficult than average due to the kinds of wrong-answer choices that follow it. In tackling the question, follow these three steps:

1 Before reading the answer choices, try to answer the question, "What general strategy would help achieve the objective?" If you think of a strategy, jot it down.

2 Scan the answer choices for a specific course of action that would implement that strategy effectively.

3 For each other answer choice, ask yourself why it's less effective than the one you selected. (Keep in mind the wrong-answer categories you just learned about.) Then, read the analysis of the question and of each answer choice.

Company Q, a manufacturer of consumer products, offers a manufacturer's rebate through retailers that sell its products. Retailers offer their own rebate as well on Company Q products, and Company Q reimburses the retailer for a portion of each such rebate. Both Company Q and its retailers are currently losing money on overall sales of Company Q products as a result of the rebate scheme.

6. Which of the following plans, if implemented, is most likely to be effective in reversing the losses that Company Q and its retailers are currently experiencing from overall sales of Company Q products?

(A) Restrict both types of rebates to purchases of products priced only below a certain amount.

(B) Restrict both types of rebates to purchases of certain higher-priced products only.

(C) Develop a new advertising campaign designed to boost retail sales of Company Q's newest products.

(D) Reduce the amount of the rebate that retailers offer on purchases of Company Q products.

(E) Discontinue reimbursement to retailers for any portion of rebates on Company Q products that retailers pay to consumers.

Notice that the objective is twofold: (1) decrease Company Q's losses *and* (2) decrease the retailers' losses. The most effective strategy would help achieve not just one but *both* objectives. The manufacturer and retailer currently share the cost of rebates that the retailer pays to consumers. Both can reduce their overall costs, thereby reducing losses, by lowering the amount of the retail rebate—as choice (D) provides—and continuing to share the rebate costs. Hence, the course of action that choice (D) suggests is likely to be effective in achieving both stated objectives.

Choice (A) suggests a plan that wouldn't necessarily reduce losses for either Company Q or its retailers. In fact, the plan is just as likely to increase those losses. How? If Company Q and its retailers discontinue rebate offers on certain items, then sales of those items are more likely to decline. Since the passage states that it is the rebate items that are responsible for current losses, sales of non-rebate items are less likely to generate losses and might even generate profits. A decline in sales of profitable items would only add to the overall losses for Company Q and its retailers.

Choice (B) is incorrect for essentially the same reason as choice (A). Restricting the rebate to purchases of only certain items might actually *increase* losses, especially if consumers buy fewer profit-generating (non-rebate) items as a result of the new rebate restrictions.

Choice (C) suggests a plan that is just as likely, if not more likely, to *increase* losses as decrease them. Why? First, the ad campaign will no doubt add to costs. Second, if the ads are effective, there's no reason to believe that consumers enticed by the ads would not take advantage of the rebate offers; the more money paid as rebates, the greater the losses for company Q and its retailers.

Choice (E) suggests a plan that would obviously help reduce Company Q's losses, since it would no longer need to reimburse its retailers. By the same token, however, the plan would *increase* losses for retailers, who would now pay the entire rebate. Since the stated objective is to reduce losses not just for Company Q but also for its retailers, choice (E) is too narrow to be the "best" plan.

In handling basic inference questions like the ones you encountered earlier in the chapter, we suggested that, when in doubt, you should choose a narrow conclusion over a broader one. This advice also applies to strategy questions—but with a twist. For instance, in answering the previous question, choice (E) suggests a course of action whose effect would be too narrow, which is exactly why choice (E) is not the best answer. **The correct answer is (D).**

Four Tips for Tackling Strategy Questions

1. All statements in the passage are premises, so you should assume they are all factual. Also, accept the scenario at face value, even though it oversimplifies real life.

2. Before you read the answer choices, try to formulate an effective general strategy rather than a specific course of action. (Otherwise, you might be frustrated by not finding your proposal listed as an answer choice.) Then scan the answer choices for a course of action that carries out the strategy.

3. Remember: Your job is to determine which plan is most likely to achieve the objective, not which one will do so. You won't find any bullet-proof plan that will work no matter what happens, so don't waste time looking for one. Improve your odds of picking the best answer choice by at least eliminating the most unlikely ones. Look for choices that "get it backwards" (that suggest plans that are sure to hurt the cause) or that strike you as nonsense (that aren't directly relevant to the objective).

4. Watch out for proposals that could either help or hinder, depending on other circumstances. If there's a possible "flip side" to a proposed course of action, eliminate it.

HYPOTHESIS QUESTIONS

In a GMAT hypothesis question, the passage provides two pieces of evidence (factual information) that seem inconsistent or in conflict with each other (paradoxical). The passage might involve a "real-world" scenario like one of these:

- An apparent discrepancy between results of different experiments or statistical studies
- Two seemingly contrary economic, business, or sociological trends
- Conflicting conclusions drawn by two different individuals based on the same set of facts
- A surprising difference between two things that are ostensibly similar in other ways

Your task is to recognize a logical explanation (hypothesis) for the apparent discrepancy, conflict, or difference. You know you're dealing with a hypothesis question when the question stem looks similar to one of the following:

"Which of the following best explains the apparent discrepancy between the . . .?"

"Which of the following, if true, would provide the best explanation for the seemingly contradictory results of the two studies described above?"

"Each of the following, if true, could help account for the simultaneous increase in . . . and . . . EXCEPT:"

How to Recognize an Effective Hypothesis

In tackling this question type, the best way to recognize an effective hypothesis is to first formulate a broader explanation for the apparent discrepancy or conflict. Let's do just that by analyzing three brief passages.

Passage 1

While on Diet X, most dieters reduce their daily calorie intake from previous levels. However, people who try Diet X generally gain rather than lose weight over the course of the diet.

What might explain the apparent discrepancy between reduced caloric intake and weight gain? One good general explanation is that calorie intake is only one of many factors that determines a person's body weight. (One or two such factors might come to your mind.)

Passage 2

A study comparing the benefits of different popular diets observed that dieters tend to lose more weight while on Diet Y than while on Diet X. However, Diet X calls for a lower daily-calorie intake than Diet Y.

What might explain the surprising comparative results of the two diets? One general explanation is that Diet X and Diet Y might differ in certain other respects—one of which might account for the counter-intuitive results. (One or two such differences might come to your mind.)

Passage 3

One independent study on the benefits of dieting observed that people on Diet X lost more weight, on average, than people on Diet Y. However, another such study observed just the opposite—that people on Diet X tended to lose less weight than people on Diet Y.

What might explain the apparent conflict between the results of the two studies? One general explanation is that studies often vary in methodology and that different methodologies can yield different results. (One or two possible differences in methodology might come to your mind.)

Now examine different hypotheses involving each passage. Notice that each hypothesis provides a specific scenario rather than a general explanation and that the effective hypotheses support the general explanations we just formulated. Also notice that each poor hypothesis falls into one of these four categories (try to determine which category each one belongs to):

1 It relies heavily on certain assumed facts.

2 It helps explain only one aspect of the discrepancy or conflict.

3 It's not directly relevant to the discrepancy or conflict.

4 It actually makes the discrepancy or conflict more inexplicable.

Hypotheses Based on Passage 1

Effective hypothesis (possible "best" answer choice):

- Diet X makes a person too tired to engage in the kinds of exercise that help a person lose weight.

Poor hypotheses (typical wrong-answer choices):

- Most people who try Diet X find it to be bland and lacking in variety.

- Most people who try Diet X have already tried other diets but failed to lose weight as a result of those diets.

Hypotheses Based on Passage 2

Effective hypothesis (possible "best" answer choice):

- Dieters find Diet X more restrictive than Diet Y and therefore more difficult to stay on.

Poor hypotheses (typical wrong-answer choices):

- Other diets are far more effective than either Diet X or Diet Y.

- More people on Diet Y than on Diet X are first-time dieters.

- Diet X is more effective than Diet Y in satisfying a dieter's appetite.

Hypotheses Based on Passage 3

Effective hypothesis (possible "best" answer choice):

- One of the studies observed only first-time dieters, while the other study observed only dieters who had previously lost weight on other diets.

Poor hypotheses (typical wrong-answer choices):

- Among dieters as a group, Diet X is currently more popular than Diet Y.

- Neither study continued to observe the dieters weight after discontinuing the diet.

- Although lower in calories than Diet Y, Diet X is more effective in satisfying a dieter's appetite.

In a typical hypothesis passage, the number of scenarios that would help explain the facts is virtually limitless. So if you happen to come up with a few good scenarios, keep an open mind: The answer choices may or may not list one of them.

A Typical Hypothesis Question

In each of the three passages you just analyzed, the discrepancy or conflict was relatively easy to identify and explain. Now that you've seen some easier passages, try tackling a more difficult GMAT-style hypothesis question. (What makes this question tricky is that it actually involves two paradoxes.) As you grapple with it, follow these three steps:

1 Before reading the answer choices, try to formulate a general explanation for both paradoxes. Jot down your idea.

2 Scan the answer choices for a scenario that supports your explanation.

3 For each other answer choice, ask yourself why it fails to adequately explain the paradox. (Keep in mind the wrong-answer categories you just learned about.) Then, read the analysis of the question and of each answer choice.

Kiki birds breed more effectively in some temperatures than in others. During the period from 2001 to 2005, the kiki bird population in a certain region increased, despite a moratorium, or official ban, on the hunting of the kiki bird's chief predator. During the period from 2006 to 2010, the kiki bird population in the same region declined, despite ideal breeding temperatures during that period.

7. Which of the following, if true, best explains why the kiki bird population increased during the period from 2001 to 2005, and then declined during the period from 2006 to 2010?

   (A) During the period from 2001 to 2005, temperatures in the region were ideally suited for kiki bird breeding.

   (B) The moratorium on the hunting of the kiki bird's chief predator was rigorously enforced only after 2005.

   (C) Ideal breeding temperatures for the kiki bird's chief predator differ from those for the kiki bird.

   (D) The kiki bird is only one of many animal species that is potential prey for the bird's chief predator.

   (E) During the period from 2006 to 2010, the population of the kiki bird's chief predator increased throughout the region.

The passage presents a double-paradox: How could the bird's population increase in the face of an ostensible threat to its survival, and then decrease when breeding conditions were ideal? A comprehensive explanation would need to account for both the increase and subsequent decrease in population. One explanation is that some other condition likely to have an impact on the kiki bird population changed from one time period to the other. Choice (B) provides such a condition—a specific scenario that supports this explanation. Without enforcement of the moratorium, a greater number of the kiki bird's predators might be killed, which would tend to stabilize and perhaps even result in an increase in the kiki bird population. Conversely, enforcing the moratorium would tend to increase the predator's population, thereby possibly decreasing the bird's population.

Choice (A) explains why the kiki bird population increased from 2001 to 2005, but not why the kiki bird population declined from 2006 to 2010.

Choice (C) actually makes the paradox more inexplicable by providing an additional reason why the kiki bird population should have *increased* during the period from 2006 to 2010.

Choice (D) is completely irrelevant to the paradox—it serves neither to explain nor reinforce it.

Choice (E) explains why the kiki bird population decreased from 2006 to 2010, but not why the kiki bird population increased from 2001 to 2005.

The correct answer is (B).

Four Tips for Tackling Hypothesis Questions

1 All statements in the passage are premises, so you should assume they are all factual.

2 Before you read the answer choices, try to formulate a *general* explanation for the discrepancy or conflict, rather than a *specific* scenario. (Otherwise, you might be frustrated by not finding your scenario listed as an answer choice.) Then scan the answer choices for a scenario that supports your explanation.

3 Remember: Your job is to zero in on an answer choice that *helps* explain the facts—that provides *one possible* explanation. No one hypothesis is going to cover all the bases; so don't waste time looking for it.

4 Watch out for the following types of wrong-answer choices:

- The incomplete or partial explanation (you're looking for a choice that helps explain all the facts)

- The choice that "gets it backward"—that makes the discrepancy or paradox even more inexplicable

- The choice that assumes too much—that helps explain only if certain additional facts are assumed

- The irrelevant scenario (it's on the topic but doesn't relate to the discrepancy or conflict)

NECESSARY INFERENCE QUESTIONS

In this type of GMAT question, an argument's conclusion will be *necessarily* inferable (or not inferable) from its premises—in other words, necessarily true (or false). Expect to encounter at least one necessary inference question on the GMAT.

GMAT necessary inference questions come in two varieties. In one type, the passage provides a series of premises, and your task is to determine which of the five answer choices must be true (or false) based on the premises. You know you're dealing with this type when the question stem looks similar to one of the following:

"If the statements above are true, which of the following statements can logically be derived from them?"

"Which of the following must be true on the basis of the statements above?"

"Which of the following can be correctly inferred from the statements above?"

"If the statements above are true, any of the following statements might also be true EXCEPT:"

In the second type of necessary inference question, the passage provides one or more premises along with a conclusion, and your task is to determine what additional premise is required for the conclusion to be necessarily inferable (true). You know you're dealing with this type when the question stem looks similar to one of the following:

"The passages conclusion is true only if which of the following statements is also true?"

"The conclusion of the argument above cannot be true unless which of the following is true?"

"Any of the following, if introduced into the argument as an additional premise, makes the argument above logically correct EXCEPT:"

Notice the absence of words such as *best, most,* and *least* in both groups of questions above. That's because, for this type of question, evaluating the argument does not involve a conclusion's probability but rather its certainty—whether it is true or false, valid or invalid, correct or incorrect, inferable or not inferable—based on the premises. So the mode of reasoning for necessary inference questions is entirely different from the question types we've covered up to this point. If you're ready to shift to this other mode, read on.

Here's something to keep in mind: Necessary inference questions involve deductive reasoning, which is actually a specific kind of inference. You'll see this term used often in the following pages. A logician might define deduction as the process of drawing specific inferences from general laws or propositions. Since the definition is a bit technical, the test-makers avoid using any form of the term in Critical Reasoning questions.

Forms and Fallacies of Deductive Reasoning

To master GMAT necessary inference questions, you need to recognize certain basic argument forms and fallacies. (A "fallacy" is simply an argument by deduction whose conclusion is incorrect—or whose *inference is invalid.*) The following series of forms are the ones you're most likely to encounter on the GMAT. The best way to identify a form is to first use symbols in premises and conclusions, and then analyze an example that matches the form.

Based on the following premise, there is only one valid inference. Notice that the valid inference switches A with B and negates both.

Argument 1

Premise: If A, then B.

Valid inference: If not B, then not A.

Invalid inference: If B, then A.

Invalid inference: If not A, then not B.

Example (Argument 1)

Premise: If I strike the window with a hammer, the window will break.

Valid inference: If the window is not broken, then I have not struck it with a hammer.

Invalid inference: If the window is broken, I have struck it with a hammer.

Invalid inference: If I do not strike the window with a hammer, the window will not break.

(Both invalid inferences overlook that the window might be broken for any number of reasons besides my having struck it with a hammer.)

The following argument form and accompanying fallacies are logically identical to the ones above.

Argument 2

Premise: All A are B.

Valid inference: All non-Bs are non-As. (No non-B is an A.)

Invalid inference: All B are A.

Invalid inference: No non-As are Bs.

Example (Argument 2)

Premise: All red gremlins are spotted.

Valid inference: No gremlin that is not spotted is red.

Invalid inference: All spotted gremlins are red.

Invalid inference: No gremlins that are not red are spotted.

(Both invalid inferences overlook that a spotted gremlin might be a color other than red.)

This next form involves two premises and a third symbol, (C), allowing inferences (and inviting fallacies) in addition to the ones covered in Arguments 1 and 2 above.

Argument 3

Premise: If A, then B.

Premise: If B, then C.

Valid inference: If A, then C.

Valid inference: If not C, then not A.

Invalid inference: If not A, then not B.

Invalid inference: If C, then A.

Example (Argument 3)

Premise: If I strike the window with a hammer, the window will break.

Premise: If the window is broken, the cold outside air will blow into the house.

Valid inference: If I strike the window with a hammer, then the cold outside air will blow into the house.

Valid inference: If the cold outside air has not blown into the house, then I have not struck the window with a hammer.

Invalid inference: If I do not strike the window with a hammer, the window will not break.

Invalid inference: If cold outside air has blown into the house, I have struck the window with a hammer.

The following argument is logically identical to Argument 3 above.

Argument 4

Premise: All A are B.

Premise: All B are C.

Valid inference: All A are C.

Valid inference: No non-C is an A.

Invalid inference: No non-A is a C.

Invalid inference: All C are A.

Example (Argument 4)

Premise: All red gremlins are spotted.

Premise: All spotted gremlins are female.

(*Assumption:* A gremlin must be either male or female but not both.)

Valid inference: All red gremlins are female.

Valid inference: No male gremlin is red.

Invalid inference: No gremlin that is not red is female.

Invalid inference: All female gremlins are red.

In Arguments 1–4, each statement is essentially an all-or-none assertion (signaled by words such as "all" and "no"). In this next series of arguments, the word "some" is introduced into a premise. For each form, try conjuring up your own example (perhaps involving red, spotted, and female gremlins).

Argument 5

Premise: Some A are B.

Valid inference: Some B are A.

Invalid inference: Some A are not B.

Invalid inference: Some B are not A.

(*In formal logic, the word "some" means at least one and possibly as many as all; thus the premise allows for the possibility that all A are B and that all B are A.*)

Argument 6

Premise: Some A are B.

Premise: Some B are C.

Valid inference: Some B are A.

Valid inference: Some C are B.

Invalid inference: Some A are C.

Invalid inference: Some C are A.

(*If a B is an A, it is not necessarily a C as well; in other words, the set of Bs that are also As does not necessarily overlap the set of Bs that are also Cs.*)

Argument 7

Premise: Some A are B.

Premise: All B are C.

Valid inference: Some B are A.

Valid inference: Some A are C.

Valid inference: Some C are A.

Invalid inference: All C are B.

Invalid inference: All C are A.

The following two arguments involve "either-or" forms:

Argument 8

Premise: Either A or B, but not both.

Valid inference: If A, then not B.

Valid inference: If B, then not A.

Valid inference: If not B, then A.

Valid inference: If not A, then B.

Argument 9

Premise: Either A or B, but not both.

Premise: Either B or C, but not both.

Valid inference: If B, then not C (and not A).

Valid inference: If A, then C (but not B).

Valid inference: If C, then A (but not B).

A Typical Necessary Inference Question

Now that you know how to recognize various forms of deductive reasoning and distinguish between valid and invalid inferences, attempt the following GMAT-style question, which is a bit more difficult than average for this question type. As you tackle the question, follow these four steps:

1. Try to reduce the passage to simple statements using symbols (letters). Jot down the premise and conclusion using those symbols.
2. Before reading the answer choices, try to determine the missing premise for yourself.
3. Scan the answer choices for your answer.
4. For each answer choice you eliminated, try to determine what valid conclusion (if any) would be inferable by adding the premise provided in the answer choice. Then read the analysis of the question and of each answer choice.

In the country of Xania, periods of political instability are always accompanied by a volatile Xania stock market and by volatility of Xania's currency compared to currencies of other countries. At the present time, Xania's currency is experiencing volatility. Hence, the Xania stock market must also be experiencing volatility.

8. Which of the following allows the conclusion above to be properly drawn?
   (A) Whenever Xania is politically stable, the Xania currency is stable as well.
   (B) Whenever the Xania currency is stable, Xania is politically stable as well.
   (C) Whenever the Xania stock market is unstable, Xania is politically unstable as well.
   (D) Whenever the Xania stock market is unstable, the Xania currency is unstable as well.
   (E) Whenever the Xania stock market is stable, the Xania currency is stable as well.

The argument boils down to the following:

Premise 1: If there is political instability, then the stock market is volatile (unstable).

Premise 2: If there is political instability, then the currency is volatile (unstable).

Premise 3: The currency is volatile (unstable).

Conclusion: The stock market is volatile (unstable).

To reveal the argument's structure, let's reduce it to symbols:

Premise 1: If A, then B.

Premise 2: If A, then C.

Premise 3: C.

Conclusion: B.

The conclusion above requires the following additional premise:

Premise 4: If the currency is volatile (unstable), then there is political instability.

Premise 4: If C, then A.

Only answer choice (A) provides this essential premise. Note that Premise 4 above is essentially the same proposition as answer choice (A). In other words, the following two propositions are logically identical:

Premise 4: If C, then A.

Answer choice (A): If not A, then not C.

Choice (B) merely reiterates Premise 2. In other words, the following two statements are essentially the same:

If X, then Y.

If not Y, then not X.

Choice (C) commits the following fallacy:

Premise: If X, then Y.

Conclusion: If Y, then X.

Choice (D) would lead to the conclusion that if the stock market is volatile (unstable), then the currency is volatile (unstable). In other words, choice (D) commits the same fallacy as choice (C):

Premise: If X, then Y.

Conclusion: If Y, then X.

Choice (E) merely reiterates the argument's conclusion. In other words, the following two statements are essentially the same:

If X, then Y.

If not Y, then not X.

The correct answer is (A).

Six Tips for Tackling Necessary Inference Questions

1 If the question asks for a missing premise, identify the premise(s) and conclusion in the passage.

2 If you're having trouble following the logic, reduce each part of the passage to simple statements using letters as symbols. Write down the form of the argument on paper.

3 Rephrase the answer to the question by determining the additional premise needed for the conclusion to be valid (or the conclusion that necessarily follows from the stated premises).

4 Express your answer using symbols.

5 If you're having trouble making sense of a particular statement in the passage, try to rephrase it so its logical meaning is clearer. Eliminating double-negatives can be particularly helpful.

Confusing: Only gremlins that are spotted are red.

Clear: All red gremlins are spotted.

Confusing: If a gremlin is not spotted, then it cannot be red.

Confusing: A gremlin is spotted only if it is red.

Clear: If a gremlin is red, then it must be spotted.

6 Look out for the following types of wrong answers:

- A statement that results in one of the logical fallacies identified in this chapter.

- A statement that merely reiterates a stated premise (or stated conclusion), expressing it in a slightly different way.

PARALLEL ARGUMENT QUESTIONS

In this type of question, the passage and the five answer choices each provide an argument (one or more premises and a conclusion). Your task is to determine which of the five choices provides the argument most similar *in its pattern of reasoning* to the pattern in the passage. Don't expect to encounter more than one question of this type on the GMAT.

You know you're dealing with a parallel argument question when the question stem looks similar to one of the following (notice that the first two are essentially the same, but the third one suggests a slightly different task):

"Which of the following is most like the argument above in its logical structure?"

"Which of the following illustrates a pattern of reasoning most similar to the pattern of reasoning in the argument above?"

"The flawed reasoning in the argument above is most similar to the reasoning in which of the following arguments?"

A Typical Parallel Argument Question

Attempt the following GMAT-style parallel argument question, which is average in difficulty. As you tackle the question, follow these three steps:

1 Try to reduce the passage to simple statements using symbols (letters). Jot down the premise and conclusion using these symbols.

2 Perform the same task (Step 1) for each answer choice.

3 Compare the pattern of reasoning in each answer choice to the pattern in the original passage. Then read the analysis of the question and of each answer choice.

Very few software engineers have left MicroFirm Corporation to seek employment elsewhere. Thus, unless CompTech Corporation increases the salaries of its software engineers to the same level as those of MicroFirm, these CompTech employees are likely to leave CompTech for another employer.

9. The flawed reasoning in the argument above is most similar to the reasoning in which of the following arguments?

(A) Robert does not gamble, and he has never been penniless. Therefore, if Gina refrains from gambling she will also avoid being penniless.

(B) If Dan throws a baseball directly at the window, the window pane will surely break. The window pane is not broken, so Dan has not thrown a baseball directly at it.

(C) If a piano sits in a humid room, the piano will need tuning within a week. This piano needs tuning. Therefore, it must have sat in a humid room for at least a week.

(D) Diligent practice results in perfection. Hence, one must practice diligently in order to achieve perfection.

(E) More expensive cars are stolen than inexpensive cars. Accordingly, owners of expensive cars should carry auto theft insurance, whereas owners of inexpensive cars should not.

The original argument's line of reasoning is essentially as follows:

Premise: The well-paid engineers at MicroFirm do not quit their jobs.

Conclusion: If CompTech engineers are not well-paid, they will quit their jobs.

To reveal the argument's logical structure, let's express it using letters as symbols:

Premise: All As are Bs.

Conclusion: If not A, then not B.

The reasoning is fallacious (flawed), because it fails to account for other possible reasons why MicroFirm engineers have not left their jobs. (Some Bs might not be As.)

Choice (D) is the only answer choice that demonstrates the same essential pattern of flawed reasoning. To recognize the similarity we can rephrase the argument's sentence structure to match the essence of the original argument:

Premise: All people who practice diligently (A) achieve perfection (B).

Conclusion: If one does not practice diligently (not A), one cannot achieve perfection (not B).

Choice (A) reasons essentially as follows: One certain A is B. Therefore, if A, then B. This reasoning is flawed, but in a different respect from the reasoning in the original argument.

Choice (B) reasons essentially as follows: If A, then B. Not B. Therefore, not A. This reasoning is sound (not flawed).

Choice (C) reasons essentially as follows: If A, then B. Therefore, if B, then A. This reasoning is flawed, but in a different respect from the reasoning in the original argument.

Choice (E) does not involve deductive reasoning and can't easily be expressed in symbols. Without additional evidence, it's impossible to determine the strength of the argument.

The correct answer is (D).

Four Tips for Tackling Parallel Argument Questions

1 Before reading the answer choices, reduce the original passage to its basic structure.

2 Express the argument in general terms—perhaps using letters as symbols—that incorporate the argument's logic but not its subject matter.

3 Don't equate logical structure with sequence. The passage might provide the conclusion first, while the best answer choice provides its conclusion last (or vice-versa). In other words, try to identify parallel logic—not parallel sequence.

4 Don't equate logical structure with subject matter. Be suspicious of any answer choice involving a topic that is similar to that of the passage. Although that answer choice might be the best one, more than likely it is not.

SUMMING IT UP

- Always read the question stem (or prompt) before reading the passage. It will contain useful clues about what to look for and think about as you read the passage.

- Assume that all premises are factual. Critical Reasoning questions are not designed to test your real-world knowledge of passage topics. Although the premises often resemble real-world facts, whether they are factual is beside the point.

- Most passages will contain a conclusion, which can appear at the beginning, in the middle, or at the end of the passage. If a passage confuses you, look for the conclusion, then try to follow the argument's line of reasoning from premises to conclusion.

- Read every answer choice before confirming your selection. The exam directions ask you to select the best among the five choices, and the difference between the best and second-best choices can be subtle. Unless you carefully consider all five answer choices, you might select the second-best one without even reading the best one.

- For most test-takers, Critical Reasoning questions require more thought than Sentence Correction and Reading Comprehension questions. Moreover, for all but the easiest Critical Reasoning questions, you'll probably need to read the passage and answer choices twice before deciding on an answer. So plan to devote a bit more time to Critical Reasoning questions than to other Verbal Ability questions.

- When in doubt, go with your initial hunch about whether an answer choice is viable or not. It's remarkably easy to overanalyze any Critical Reasoning question to the point that you second-guess your own judgment. Although you should carefully consider all five answer choices, don't disregard your instincts.

Sentence Correction

OVERVIEW

- **The 4-step plan**
- **Grammatical errors involving parts of speech**
- **Problems with a sentence's structural elements**
- **Redundancy, wordiness, awkwardness, and omissions**
- **Errors in parts of speech**
- **Problems in tense, voice, and mood**
- **Sentence structure and sense**
- **Summing it up**

In this chapter, you'll do the following:

- Learn a step-by-step approach to handling any Sentence Correction question
- Learn to recognize and fix basic grammatical errors and problems with sentence structure and verbosity
- Recognize and fix challenging grammatical problems involving parts of speech
- Distinguish between verb tenses
- Recognize and correct improper mixing and shifting of tense, voice, and mood
- Recognize and handle challenging problems involving sentence structure

THE 4-STEP PLAN

The first task in this chapter is to learn the four basic steps for handling a GMAT Sentence Correction question. Let's apply these steps to the following sample question:

1. <u>Despite sophisticated computer models for assessing risk, such a model is nevertheless</u> limited in their ability to define what risk is.

   (A) Despite sophisticated computer models for assessing risk, such a model is nevertheless

   (B) Sophisticated computer models, which assess risk, are nevertheless

   (C) Despite their sophistication, computer models for assessing risk are

   (D) Assessment of risk can be achieved with sophisticated computer models, but these models are

   (E) Assessing risk with sophisticated computer models is limited because such models are

chapter 13

Step One: Read the Original Sentence Carefully

As you do so, ask yourself:

- Does it sound odd or wrong to my ear?
- Do any errors in grammar jump out at me?
- Is the sentence confusing, and would I have to read it again to try to figure out what it means?

If your answer to any of these questions is "yes," you can confidently eliminate choice (A), the original underlined part, even if you're not sure why it's wrong.

Step Two: Plug in Your Remaining Choices

Plug your remaining choices, one at a time, into the original sentence, and read the entire revised sentence. As you do so, ask yourself the same three questions as in Step 1 and eliminate any choice for which your answer to any of those questions is "yes."

Step Three: If You're Still Not Sure, Compare the Remaining Choices

If you still haven't narrowed the choices down to a clear winner, compare the remaining candidates. Resolve close judgment calls in favor of:

- A briefer, more concise version
- A version that more accurately conveys the intended meaning of the sentence
- A less awkward version

Step Four: Verify Your Selection Before Confirming Your Response

Check your selection one more time by plugging it into the sentence. If it sounds right, confirm your response, and move on.

Now let's walk through the sample question about computer models, using this 4-step approach.

Step 1: Upon a first reading, doesn't "such a model" sound a bit awkward? That's a good clue that choice (A) is not the correct response. In fact, the original sentence contains two flaws. One is a grammatical error: The plural pronoun *their* is used to refer to the singular noun *model*. Either both should be plural or both should be singular, but they must match. The word *their* is not part of the underlined phrase, so look for an answer choice that uses *models* instead of *model*. (In grammatical terminology, the original sentence contains an error in "pronoun-antecedent agreement.") The other flaw is one of ineffective expression: the first clause (before the comma) is structured differently than the second clause, and the result is an awkward and confusing sentence. So you should look for an answer choice that renders the sentence clearer and perhaps a bit more concise—one that helps the sentence sound a bit sweeter and "flow" more smoothly.

Step 2: Substitute each answer choice in turn for the underlined part. Choice (B) does not contain any grammatical errors. But doesn't the phrase *which assess risk* appear to describe computer models in general rather than models for assessing risk? Surely, this isn't the intended meaning of the sentence. Choice (B) is a perfect example of an answer choice that is wrong because it either distorts, confuses, or obscures the intended meaning of the sentence. Eliminate choice (B). Choice (C) takes care of both problems with the original sentence. The plural noun *models* matches the plural pronoun *their*, and both clauses are now constructed in a similar way, making for a clearer and briefer sentence. Choice (C) is probably the correct answer, but read the remaining choices anyway. Choice (D) sounds pretty good when you read it as part of the sentence, doesn't it? No grammatical errors jump out at you. So is it a toss-up between choices (C) and (D)? Well, go on to choice (E) for now, then come back to the choice (C) versus choice (D) debate. Choice (E) incorrectly uses the phrase *is limited* to describe *assessing risk*. It is the computer model's ability, *not* assessing risk, that is limited. Eliminate choice (E).

Step 3: Go back to choices (C) and (D). Is one less awkward than the other? More concise? Closer in meaning to the original version? Perhaps you noticed that the first clause in choice (D) (*assessment of risk can be achieved*) sounds a bit awkward. So you've got a good reason to choose (C) over (D).

Step 4: Check choice (C) one more time by plugging it into the sentence: *Despite their sophistication, computer models for assessing risk are limited in their ability to define what risk is*. Sounds great. Confirm your response, and move on to the next question. **The correct answer is (C).**

GRAMMATICAL ERRORS INVOLVING PARTS OF SPEECH

In the remainder of this chapter, you'll examine basic kinds of grammatical errors and problems with sentence structure and written expression. These are the ones that, for most test-takers, are easiest to recognize and most straightforward to fix. In addition to learning how to fix these problems, you'll see how the GMAT might test you on each one.

We'll start with grammatical errors involving *parts of speech*—which include adjectives, adverbs, pronouns, and verbs. Here are the kinds of errors we'll cover in the pages ahead:

- Error in choice between adjective and adverb
- Error in choice of adjective for comparisons
- Error in choice of personal pronoun
- Error in pronoun-antecedent agreement
- Error in subject-verb agreement

By the way, immersing yourself in the rules of English grammar and the guidelines for effective written expression (as you're about to do) will help you not only for Sentence Correction questions but also for the Analytical Writing Assessment (AWA) section of the GMAT. So pay close attention; your efforts here will be doubly rewarded on exam day.

Error in Choice Between Adjective and Adverb

Adjectives describe nouns, while *adverbs* describe verbs, adjectives, and other adverbs. Adverbs generally end with *-ly*, while adjectives don't. Look for adjectives incorrectly used as adverbs (and vice versa).

ALERT!

Don't select an answer choice as the correct one just because it fixes every flaw in the original sentence. You can be certain that one or two of the answer choices may fix the flaw but create a new one.

incorrect: The movie ended *sudden*.

correct: The movie ended *suddenly*.

(The adverb *suddenly* describes the verb ended.)

Although adverbs generally end with *-ly*, some don't. Also, if you're dealing with two adverbs in a row, sometimes the *-ly* is dropped from the second adverb. There are no hard-and-fast rules here. Trust your ear as to what sounds correct.

incorrect: Risk-takers drive fastly, play hardly, and arrive lately for their appointments.

correct: Risk-takers drive *fast*, play *hard*, and arrive *late* for their appointments.

incorrect: The Canadian skater jumps *particularly highly*.

correct: The Canadian skater jumps *particularly high*.

Also keep in mind that adjectives, not adverbs, should be used to describe verbs involving the senses (sight, taste, smell, hearing, touch).

incorrect: Dinner tasted *deliciously*.

incorrect: Dinner tasted *awful* delicious.

correct: Dinner tasted *awfully* delicious.

(The adjective *delicious* is used to describe the verb *tasted*, while the adverb *awfully* is used to describe *delicious*.)

Now look at how the test-makers might try to slip one of these errors past you in a GMAT sentence. In the next question, the original sentence is flawed, so choice (A) is incorrect. Your choice is between (C) and (D).

To help you focus on the specific grammatical error at hand, we'll simplify the Sentence Correction format by listing just *three* answer choices, and by limiting the kinds of errors to one or two. Actual GMAT questions include five answer choices, of course.

2. A recent report from the Department of Energy suggests that over the next two decades demand for crude oil will *increase at an alarming fast rate, and greatly exceeds* most economists' previous forecasts.

   (A) increase at an alarming fast rate, and greatly exceeds
   (B) ***
   (C) increase at an alarmingly fast rate, greatly exceeding
   (D) be at an increasingly alarming rate and will greatly exceed
   (E) ***

The original sentence incorrectly uses the adjective *alarming* instead of the adverb *alarmingly* to describe the adjective *fast*. The original sentence also contains an additional, and more conspicuous, flaw. The phrase *and greatly exceeds* improperly suggests that the rate is increasing alarmingly at the present time. However, the sentence as a whole makes clear that this is a future event. Choice (C) corrects both of these problems. Although choice (D) also corrects both problems, it creates a new flaw. The use of the word *be* to refer to *demand* is an awkward and inappropriate expression of the idea that the sentence attempts to convey. The word *be* suggests one point in time, but the sentence intends to describe the changing demand over a period of time. **The correct answer is (C).**

Because this sort of error is generally easy to spot in a sentence, the GMAT test-makers will probably try to sneak it past you by including another (and possibly more conspicuous) flaw as well, in the hope that you'll carelessly overlook the incorrect adjective or adverb. Beat them at their own game by looking carefully at adjectives and adverbs, *especially when they appear in pairs* (as in the previous sample question).

Error in Choice of Adjective for Comparisons

As you read a GMAT sentence, pay close attention to any adjective ending in -*er*, -*ier*, -*est*, and -*iest*. Adjectives ending in -*er* and -*ier* should be used to compare *two* things, while adjectives ending in -*est* and -*iest* should be used when dealing with three or more things.

> **incorrect:** Frank is less intelligent than the other four students.

> **correct:** Frank is the *least* intelligent among the *five* students.

> **correct:** Frank is *less* intelligent than *any* of the other four students (The word *any* is singular, so the comparative form is proper.)

Another way of making a comparison is to precede the adjective with a word such as *more, less, most,* or *least*. But if both methods are used together, the sentence is incorrect.

> **incorrect:** Francis is *more healthier* than Greg.

> **correct:** Francis is *healthier* than Greg.

Now, look at a GMAT-style sentence involving the kinds of issues we just covered. The original version, choice (A), is faulty, so your choice is between the two alternative versions listed here.

3. <u>The more busier the trading floor at the stock exchange, the less opportunities</u> large institutional investors have to influence the direction of price by initiating large leveraged transactions.

   (A) The more busier the trading floor at the stock exchange, the less opportunities

   (B) ***

   (C) ***

   (D) The busier trading floor at the stock exchange results in less opportunities

   (E) The busier the trading floor at the stock exchange, the fewer opportunities

In the original sentence, the phrase *more busier* incorrectly uses both comparative methods. Choice (E) corrects this flaw by using *busier*. The original sentence includes another flaw as well. The phrase *less opportunities* is incorrect; the word *fewer* should be used instead of *less* in referring to numbers of things—as opposed to the amount of one thing. Choice (E) corrects this flaw. However, choice (D) does not. **The correct answer is (E).**

Error in Choice of Personal Pronoun

Personal pronouns are words such as *they, me, his,* and *itself*—words that refer to specific people, places, and things. Pronouns take different forms, called "cases," depending on how they are used in a sentence. Just for the record, you'll find all the various cases listed below.

You can generally trust your ear when it comes to detecting personal-pronoun errors. In some cases, however, your ear can betray you, so make sure you are "tuned in" to the following uses of pronouns.

incorrect: Either him or Trevor *would* be the best spokesman for our group.

incorrect: The best spokesperson for our group *would* be either him or Trevor.

correct: Either Trevor or *he would* be the best spokesperson for our group.

correct: The best spokesperson for our group *would be* either he or Trevor.

(Any form of the verb *to be* is followed by a subject pronoun, such as *he.*)

incorrect: One can't help admiring *them* cooperating with one another.

correct: One can't help admiring *their cooperating* with one another.

(The *possessive* form is used when the pronoun is part of a "noun clause," such as *their cooperating.*)

incorrect: In striving to understand others, *we* also learn more about *us.*

correct: In striving to understand others, *we* also learn more about *ourselves.* (A *reflexive* pronoun is used to refer to the sentence's subject.)

Now, look at a GMAT-style sentence involving the issue of pronoun case. The original version, choice (A), is faulty, so your choice is between the two alternative versions listed here.

4. <u>Those of the legislators opposing the swampland protection bill have only theirselves to blame</u> for the plight of the endangered black thrush bird.

   (A) Those of the legislators opposing the swampland protection bill have only theirselves to blame

   (B) ***

   (C) Those legislators, who opposed the swampland protection bill, have only themselves to blame

   (D) Those legislators who opposed the swampland protection bill have only themselves to blame

   (E) ***

The original sentence suffers from two flaws. First, *theirselves* is a nonword and should be replaced with the reflexive pronoun *themselves.* Second, the phrase *those of the legislators opposing,* while not grammatically incorrect, is awkward and confusing. Choice (D) provides a briefer and clearer alternative phrase and corrects the pronoun error. Choice (C) also corrects the pronoun error, but it creates a new problem by setting off a portion of the sentence with commas. In doing so, choice (C) implies that all of "those legislators" are opposed the bill, thereby distorting the intended meaning of the original sentence. **The correct answer is (D).**

Error in Pronoun-Antecedent Agreement

An *antecedent* is simply the noun to which a pronoun refers. In GMAT sentences, make sure that pronouns agree in *number* (singular or plural) with their antecedents.

singular: Studying other artists actually helps a young *painter* develop *his* or *her* own style.

plural: Studying other artists actually helps young *painters* develop *their* own style.

But what's the rule for pronouns that refer to nouns describing a group of people or things (called *collective nouns*)? The same rule applies here as for subject-verb agreement: the pronoun can either be singular or plural, depending on whether the collective noun is used in a singular or plural sense.

correct: The legislature hesitates to punish *its* own members for ethics violations. (*Legislature* used in the singular sense.)

correct: The planning *committee* recessed, but Jack continued to work without *them*. (*Committee* used in the plural sense.)

Singular pronouns are generally used in referring to antecedents such as *each, either, neither,* and *one*.

correct: *Neither* of the two countries imposes an income tax on *its* citizens.

correct: *One* cannot be too kind to *oneself*.

When it comes to antecedents such as *anyone, anybody, everybody, everyone,* or *a person*, the rules of English grammar get a bit fuzzy. For instance, any grammarian would agree that the first sentence below is correct, but whether the second one is correct is hotly debated.

correct: If *anyone* offends you, please don't confront *him* or *her*.

proper? If *anyone* offends you, please don't confront *them*.

Because the rule of grammar here is unsettled, rest assured that you will not encounter these words as pronoun antecedents on the GMAT.

Now, look at a GMAT-style sentence involving pronoun-antecedent agreement. The original version, choice (A), is faulty, so your choice is between the two alternative versions.

5. Many powerful leaders throughout history, such as President Nixon during the Watergate debacle, had become victimized by his own paranoia.

   (A) Many powerful leaders throughout history, such as President Nixon during the Watergate debacle, had become victimized by his own paranoia.

   (B) Many powerful leaders throughout history, such as President Nixon during the Watergate debacle, have become victims of their own paranoia.

   (C) Throughout history, many a powerful leader, such as President Nixon during the Watergate debacle, have by his or her own paranoia become a victim.

   (D) ***

   (E) ***

The original sentence intends to make the point that many leaders (plural) have (plural verb) become victimized by their (plural pronoun) own paranoia. However, by using the singular *had* and *his*, the original clause seems to refer to Nixon instead of to leaders. Choice (B) correctly uses the plurals *have* and *their*. In choice (C), the plural subject *leaders* has been transformed into a singular subject (many a powerful leader). This form is grammatically acceptable. However, the subject's verb, as well as any pronouns that refer to the subject, should now be singular as well. Although the singular *his* or *her* is correct, the plural verb *have* is incorrect. So choice (C) contains a subject-verb agreement error. Choice (C) also improperly separates the words *have* and *become*. The phrase *have become* is an example of an "infinitive" verb form. Have you ever heard the phrase "split infinitive"? Choice (C) provides a good example of one, and it's grammatically incorrect. **The correct answer is (B).**

Error in Subject-Verb Agreement

A verb should always "agree" in number—either singular or plural—with its subject. A singular subject takes a singular verb, while a plural subject takes a plural verb.

correct (singular): The *parade was* spectacular.

correct (plural): Both *parades were* spectacular.

correct (plural): The parade *and* the pageant *were* spectacular.

Don't be fooled by any words or phrases that might separate the verb from its subject. In each of the following sentences, the singular verb *was* agrees with its subject, the singular noun *parade*.

correct: The *parade* of cars *was* spectacular.

correct: The *parade* of cars and horses *was* spectacular.

An intervening clause set off by commas can serve as an especially effective "smokescreen" for a subject-verb agreement error. Pay careful attention to what comes immediately before and after the intervening clause. Reading the sentence without the clause often reveals a subject-verb agreement error.

incorrect: John, as well as his sister, *were* absent from school yesterday.

correct: *John*, as well as his sister, *was* absent from school yesterday.

Here's a GMAT-style sentence that raises a subject-verb agreement issue. The original version, choice (A), is faulty, so your choice is between the two alternative versions listed here.

6. Grade school instruction in ethical and social values, particularly the <u>values of respect and of tolerance, are</u> required for any democracy to thrive.
    (A) values of respect and of tolerance, are
    (B) value of respect, together with tolerance, is
    (C) values of respect and tolerance, is
    (D) ***
    (E) ***

TIP

Keep a keen eye out for GMAT sentences that separate verbs from their subjects. In every one of these sentences, it's a sure bet that the test-makers are testing you on subject-verb agreement.

In the original sentence, the subject of the plural verb are is the singular noun *instruction*. The correct answer choice must correct this subject-verb agreement problem. Also, the second *of* in the underlined phrase should be deleted because its use results in an awkward and nonsensical clause, which seems to suggest that *of tolerance* is a value. Both choices (B) and (C) correct the problem by changing *are* to *is* and by dropping the second *of*. However, choice (B) creates two new problems. First, using the word *value* instead of *values* distorts the meaning of the underlined phrase. Respect and tolerance are not referred to in choice (B) as *values*. However, the original sentence, considered as a whole, clearly intends to refer to respect and tolerance as examples of ethical and social values. Second, the phrase *together with tolerance* (set off by commas), adds an unnecessary clause and results in a sentence that is wordy and awkward. Choice (C) is clearer and more concise. **The correct answer is (C).**

PROBLEMS WITH A SENTENCE'S STRUCTURAL ELEMENTS

Now, let's move ahead to another broad area covered in GMAT Sentence Correction: sentence structure. Here are the specific kinds of structural problems we'll cover in this section:

- Sentence fragments (incomplete sentences)
- Two main clauses connected improperly
- Faulty parallelism involving a list or "string"
- Faulty parallelism involving correlatives

Sentence Fragments (Incomplete Sentences)

It was probably your fifth- or sixth-grade teacher who first informed you that a sentence must include both a subject and a predicate. Well, your teacher was right, and the GMAT is here to remind you. Grammarians call incomplete sentences "sentence fragments."

fragment: Expensive private colleges, generally out of financial reach for most families with college-aged children.

fragment: Without question, responsibility for building and maintaining safe bridges.

On the GMAT, you probably won't have any trouble recognizing a sentence fragment. However, an especially long fragment might escape your detection if you're not paying close attention.

Now, look at a GMAT-style example of a sentence fragment. The original version, choice (A), is faulty, so your choice is between the two alternative versions listed here.

7. One cannot deny that, even after the initial flurry of the feminist movement subsided, Congresswoman Bella Abzug, undeniably her female constituency's truest voice, <u>as well as its most public advocate.</u>

   (A) as well as its most public advocate.
   (B) who was her constituency's most public advocate.
   (C) ***
   (D) was also its most public advocate.
   (E) ***

If you use choice (D), the sentence can be distilled down to this: *One cannot deny that Bella Abzug was also its [her female constituency's] most public advocate.* Adding the verb *was* is the key to transforming the original fragment into a complete sentence. **The correct answer is (D).**

Two Main Clauses Connected Improperly

A main clause is any clause that can stand alone as a complete sentence. There's nothing wrong with combining two main clauses into one sentence—as long as the clauses are properly connected. On the GMAT, look for any of these three flaws:

❶ No punctuation between main clauses

❷ A comma between main clauses, but no connecting word (such as *and, or, but, yet, for, so*)

❸ A confusing or inappropriate connecting word

incorrect:

Dan ran out of luck Mike continued to win.

Dan ran out of luck, Mike continued to win.

Dan ran out of luck, or Mike continued to win.

correct:

Dan ran out of luck, *but* Mike continued to win.

Dan ran out of luck, *while* Mike continued to win.

Dan ran out of luck, *yet* Mike continued to win.

Here's a GMAT-style sentence that focuses on the comma-splice issue. The original version, choice (A), is faulty, so your choice is between the two alternative versions listed here.

8. The Aleutian Islands of Alaska include many islands near the mainland, <u>the majority of them are</u> uninhabited by humans.

   (A) the majority of them are
   (B) ***
   (C) so the majority of them are
   (D) ***
   (E) yet the majority of them are

Notice that choice (E) includes a connecting word (*yet*) that gives the sentence a reasonable meaning by underscoring the contrast between the mainland (which is populated) and the unpopulated nearby islands. Although choice (C) adds a connecting word (*so*), this word is inappropriate—inferring that the islands are unpopulated *because* they are near the mainland. The resulting sentence is nonsensical, so choice (C) can't be the best answer choice. (By the way, notice the appropriate use of *so* as a connector in the preceding sentence.) **The correct answer is (E).**

Faulty Parallelism Involving a List or "String"

Sentence elements that are grammatically equal should be constructed similarly. Otherwise the result will be what is referred to as *faulty parallelism*. For instance, whenever you see a list, or "string," of items in a sentence, look for inconsistent or mixed use of:

- Prepositions (such as *in, with,* or *on*)
- Gerunds (verbs with -*ing* added to the end)
- Infinitives (plural verb preceded by *to*)
- Articles (such as *a* and *the*)

faulty: Flight 82 travels first to Boise, then to Denver, then Salt Lake City. (*To* precedes only the first two of the three cities in this list.)

parallel: Flight 82 travels first to Boise, then Denver, then Salt Lake City.

parallel: Flight 82 travels first to Boise, then to Denver, then to Salt Lake City.

faulty: Being understaffed, lack of funding, and being outpaced by competitors soon resulted in the fledgling company's going out of business. (Only two of the three listed items begin with the gerund *being*.)

parallel: Understaffed, underfunded, and outpaced by competitors, the fledgling company soon went out of business.

parallel: As a result of understaffing, insufficient funding, and outpacing by its competitors, the fledgling company soon went out of business.

faulty: Among *the* mountains, *the* sea, and desert, we humans have yet to fully explore only the sea.

parallel: Among *the* mountains, sea, and desert, we humans have yet to fully explore only the sea.

parallel: Among *the* mountains, *the* sea, and *the* desert, we humans have yet to fully explore only the sea.

Now, look at a GMAT-style sentence involving lists and faulty parallelism. The original version, choice (A), is faulty, so your choice is between the two alternative versions listed here.

9. Long before the abolition of slavery, many freed indentured servants were able to acquire property, <u>to interact with people of other races, and maintain</u> their freedom.

   (A) to interact with people of other races, and maintain
   (B) interact with people of other races, and maintain
   (C) ***
   (D) to interact with people of other races, as well as maintaining
   (E) ***

Notice the string of three items in this sentence. In the original version, the second item repeats the preposition *to*, but the third item does not. Choice (B) corrects this faulty parallelism. Choice (D) improperly mixes the use of a prepositional phrase (beginning with *to*) with a construction that uses a gerund (*maintaining*) instead. **The correct answer is (B).**

Be careful: Just because all items in a string are parallel, don't assume that the string is problem-free. Repeating the same preposition, article, or other modifier before each item in a string can sometimes result in an awkward and unnecessarily wordy sentence. In other instances, repeating the modifier may be necessary to achieve clarity.

awkward: Some pachyderms can go for days at a time without water or without food or without sleep.

better: Some pachyderms can go for days at a time without water, food, or sleep.

unclear: Going for broke and broke usually carry identical consequences.

clear: Going for broke and going broke usually carry identical consequences.

Faulty Parallelism Involving Correlatives

You just saw how items in a list can suffer from faulty parallelism. Now look at how this grammatical error shows up in what are called *correlatives*. Here are the most commonly used correlatives:

- either . . . or . . .
- neither . . . nor . . .
- both . . . and . . .
- not only . . . but also . . .

Whenever you spot a correlative in a sentence, make sure that the element immediately following the first correlative term is parallel in construction to the element following the second term.

faulty: Those wishing to participate should *either* contact us by telephone or should send an e-mail to us.

parallel (but repetitive): Those wishing to participate *either should* contact us by telephone *or should* send an e-mail to us.

parallel: Those wishing to participate should *either* contact us by telephone *or* send an e-mail to us.

Now, look at how faulty parallelism in a correlative might appear in a GMAT sentence. The original version, choice (A), is faulty, so your choice is between the two alternative versions listed here.

10. Species diversity in the Amazon basin results <u>not from climate stability, as once believed, but</u> climate disturbances.

    (A) from climate stability, as once believed, but

    (B) only from climate stability, as once believed, but instead from

    (C) ***

    (D) ***

    (E) from climate stability, as once believed, but rather from

As it stands, the original sentence might carry one of two very different meanings: (1) stability and disturbances *both* contribute to species diversity, or (2) disturbances, *but not* stability, contribute to species diversity. The reason for the ambiguity is the use of an improper correlative as well as faulty parallelism (*from* appears only in the first correlative term). The correct answer choice must make the sentence's meaning clear, probably by using one of two correlatives: *not only . . . but also* or *not . . . but rather.* Also, the two correlative terms must be parallel. Choice (E) corrects the faulty parallelism (*from* appears in each correlative term) and clears up the sentence's meaning. Although choice (B) corrects the parallelism problem, it uses the nonsensical (and improper) correlative *not only . . . but instead.* **The correct answer is (E).**

REDUNDANCY, WORDINESS, AWKWARDNESS, AND OMISSIONS

In addition to covering grammar and sentence structure, GMAT Sentence Correction also tests you on your skill at recognizing and fixing the following types of problems involving written expression:

- Redundancy (repeating the same idea)
- Wordiness (using more words than needed to make the point)
- Awkwardness (using clumsy, confusing, or overly complicated wording)
- Omissions (omitting words that are needed for clarity or sentence sense)

The problems of wordiness and awkwardness will show up in the majority of the fourteen to fifteen Sentence Correction questions on the GMAT. So always be on the lookout for them in both the original sentences and in one or more of the answer choices.

Redundant Words and Phrases

Look for words and phrases that express the same idea twice. This syndrome is known as "redundancy." In many cases, correcting the problem is as simple as omitting one of the redundant phrases.

redundant: *The reason that we* stopped for the night was *because* we were sleepy.

redundant: *Because* we were sleepy, we *therefore* stopped for the night.

better: We stopped for the night because we were sleepy.

redundant: The *underlying* motive *behind* his seemingly generous offer was old-fashioned greed.

better: The motive behind his seemingly generous offer was old-fashioned greed.

better: The underlying motive for his seemingly generous offer was old-fashioned greed.

redundant: One of the fossils is 20,000 years old *in age*.

better: One of the fossils is 20,000 years old.

redundant: The German Oktoberfest takes place *each October of every year*.

better: The German Oktoberfest takes place every October.

redundant: *At the same time* that lightning struck, we *simultaneously* lost our electric power.

better: At the same time that lightning struck, we lost our electric power.

redundant: *Both* unemployment *as well* as interest rates can affect stock prices.

better: Both unemployment levels and interest rates can affect stock prices.

better: Unemployment levels as well as interest rates can affect stock prices.

redundant: Not only does dinner smell good, but it *also* tastes good *too*.

better: Not only does dinner smell good, but it tastes good too.

Now look at a GMAT-style sentence that raises the issue of redundancy. The original version, choice (A), is faulty, so your choice is between the two alternative versions listed here.

11. <u>Due to a negligible difference in Phase III results between patients using the drug and those using a placebo, the Food and Drug Administration refused to approve it on this basis.</u>

   (A) Due to a negligible difference in Phase III results between patients using the drug and those using a placebo, the Food and Drug Administration refused to approve the drug on this basis.

   (B) The Food and Drug Administration refused to approve the drug based upon a negligible difference in Phase III results between patients using it and those using a placebo.

   (C) Due to a negligible difference in Phase III results between patients using the drug and those using a placebo, the Food and Drug Administration refused to approve the drug.

   (D) ***

   (E) ***

There are three distinct problems with the original version. First, *due to* and *on this basis* serve the same function—to express that the FDA's refusal was based on the Phase III results. (The redundancy is easy to miss since one phrase begins the sentence while the other phrase ends it.) Second, the intended antecedent of *it* is the drug, but the intervening noun *placebo* obscures the reference. Third, the sentence is ambiguous. Did the FDA refuse to approve the drug, or did it approve the drug on some basis other than the one mentioned in the sentence? Choice (C) corrects all three problems, simply by omitting *on this basis* and by replacing it with the drug. Choice (B) corrects the first two problems by omitting *due to* and reconstructing the sentence. But choice (B) fails to clarify the meaning of the sentence. **The correct answer is (C).**

Be on the lookout for sentences having the following "themes" and keywords. Redundancies are most likely to spring up in these kinds of sentences:

- Words establishing cause-and-effect (*because, since, if, then, therefore*)
- References to time (*age, years, hours, days*)
- Words used as conjunctions (*both, as well, too, also*)

Superfluous (Unnecessary) Words

You just took a look at one variety of unnecessary verbiage: redundancy. Now look at some other kinds of sentences in which certain words can simply be omitted without affecting the meaning or effectiveness of the original sentence. Remember: Briefer is better.

Each sentence in the first group below contains an *ellipsis*: a word or phrase that can be omitted because it is clearly implied. (In the incorrect version, the ellipsis is italicized.)

superfluous: The warmer the weather *is*, the more crowded the beach *is*.

concise: The warmer the weather, the more crowded the beach.

superfluous: He looks exactly like Francis *looks*.

concise: He looks exactly like Francis.

superfluous: That shirt is the ugliest *shirt that* I have ever seen.

concise: That shirt is the ugliest I have ever seen.

Each sentence in the next group includes a superfluous preposition. (In the incorrect version, the preposition is italicized.)

superfluous: The other children couldn't help *from* laughing at the girl with mismatched shoes.

concise: The other children couldn't help laughing at the girl with mismatched shoes.

superfluous: One prominent futurist predicts a nuclear holocaust by the year *of* 2020.

concise: One prominent futurist predicts a nuclear holocaust by the year 2020.

superfluous: They made the discovery *in* around December of last year.

concise: They made the discovery around December of last year.

superfluous: The waiter brought half *of* a loaf of bread to the table.

concise: The waiter brought half a loaf of bread to the table.

Superfluous words can also appear in a series of parallel clauses. Both versions of the next sentence use proper parallelism, but briefer is better—as long as the meaning of the sentence is clear.

superfluous: My three goals in life are *to be* healthy, *to be* wealthy, and *to be* wise.

concise: My three goals in life are to be healthy, wealthy, and wise.

Here's a GMAT-style sentence that contains superfluous words. The original version, choice (A), is faulty, so your choice is between the two alternative versions listed here.

12. Only through a comprehensive, federally funded vaccination program can a new epidemic of tuberculosis be curbed, just like the spread of both cholera <u>as well as the spread of typhoid was curbed.</u>

    (A) as well as the spread of typhoid was curbed.

    (B) ***

    (C) ***

    (D) and typhoid.

    (E) as well as typhoid was curbed.

The original sentence suffers from no fewer than three distinct verbiage problems. First, the correlative *both . . . as well as* is redundant (and improper). Since *both* is not underlined, *as well as* should be replaced with *and*. Second, because the preposition *like* sets up an ellipsis, *were curbed* is implied and can be omitted. Third, the second occurrence of the *spread of* can be omitted since it is implied through the use of parallel construction. Choice (D) pares down the underlined phrase to its most concise form. Choice (E) fails to correct the redundant correlative *both . . . as well as.* Choice (E) also fails to omit the unnecessary *was curbed.* **The correct answer is (D).**

Wordy and Awkward Phrases

Just because a sentence is grammatically acceptable, you shouldn't assume that there is no room for improvement. You've already seen that unnecessary words can sometimes be omitted, thereby improving a GMAT sentence. Now, look at some phrases that can be replaced with clearer, more concise ones.

wordy: Failure can *some of the time* serve as a prelude to success.

concise: Failure can *sometimes* serve as a prelude to success.

wordy: *As a result of Greg's being* a compulsive overeater, *it is not likely that he will* live past the age of 50.

concise: *Because* Greg is a compulsive overeater, *he is unlikely* to live past the age of 50.

wordy: Before the mother eats, she feeds *each and every one* of her offspring.

concise: Before the mother eats, she feeds *each* of her offspring.

wordy: There are fewer buffalo on the plains today than *there ever were* before.

concise: There are fewer buffalo on the plains today than *ever* before.

wordy: Discipline is crucial to the *attainment* of one's objectives.

concise: Discipline is crucial to *attaining* one's objectives.

wordy: Her husband was waiting for her on the platform *at the time of the train's arrival*.

concise: Her husband was waiting for her on the platform *when the train arrived*.

awkward: Calcification *is when* (or *is where*) calcium deposits form around a bone.

concise: Calcification *occurs when* calcium deposits form around a bone.

awkward: *There are* eight cats in the house, *of which* only two have been fed.

concise: Of the eight cats in the house, only two have been fed.

awkward: The wind poses a serious threat to the old tree, and *so does* the snow.

concise: The wind and snow both pose a serious threat to the old tree.

Now, take a look at a wordy and awkward GMAT-style sentence. The original version, choice (A), is faulty, so your choice is between the two alternative versions listed here.

13. To avoid confusion between oral medications, <u>different pills' coatings should have different colors, and pills should be different in shape and size.</u>

   (A) different pills' coatings should have different colors, and pills should be different in shape and size.
   (B) pills should differ in color as well as in shape and size.
   (C) ***
   (D) pills should be able to be distinguished by their color, shape, and size.
   (E) ***

NOTE

The wordy and awkward phrases the GMAT can throw at you are limited in variety only by the collective imagination of test-makers. The phrases we've provided here are just a sampling.

There are several problems with the original sentence. The first is that *different pills' coatings* is very awkward. Second, the word *coatings* is probably superfluous here; *color* suffices to make the point. Third, *have different colors* is awkward (*differ in color* would be better). Fourth, the phrase *be different* is ambiguous (different from what?). Finally, a parallel series including color, shape, and size would be more concise and less awkward than the construction used in the sentence. Choice (B) corrects all these problems. In choice (D), the phrase *be able to be distinguished* is wordy and very awkward; the phrase *should be distinguishable* would be better. **The correct answer is (B).**

Omitting a Necessary Word

On the flip side of redundancy and wordiness is the error of *omission*. Excluding a necessary word can obscure or confuse the meaning of the sentence. Check especially for the omission of key "little" words—prepositions, pronouns, conjunctions, and especially the word *that*.

omission: The newscaster announced the voting results were incorrect. (What did the newscaster announce: the results or the fact that the results were incorrect?)

clearer: The newscaster announced that the voting results were incorrect.

Look out especially for an omission that results in an illogical comparison, as in the following sentences. It can easily slip past you if you're not paying close attention.

illogical: The color of the blouse is different from the skirt.

logical: The color of the blouse is different from *that* of the skirt.

illogical: China's population is greater than any country in the world. (This sentence draws an illogical comparison between a population and a country and illogically suggests that China is not a country.)

logical: China's population is greater than *that of* any *other* country in the world.

ERRORS IN PARTS OF SPEECH

Earlier in the chapter, we covered grammatical errors involving parts of speech that are the most basic and that the GMAT covers most frequently. Here you'll focus on the trickiest, most testworthy rules of grammar involving pronoun choice and subject-verb agreement:

- Error in choice of *relative* pronoun
- Error in subject-verb agreement (*pronoun* and *compound* subjects)

Error in Choice of Relative Pronoun

The English language includes only a handful of *relative* pronouns: *which, who, that, whose, whichever, whoever,* and *whomever.* Don't worry about what the term "relative pronoun" means. Instead, just remember the following rules about when to use each one:

- Use *which* to refer to things.
- Use either *who* or *that* to refer to people.

incorrect: Amanda, *which* was the third performer, was the best of the group.

correct: Amanda, *who* was the third performer, was the best of the group.

correct: The first employee *that* fails to meet his or her sales quota will be fired.

correct: The first employee *who* fails to meet his or her sales quota will be fired.

- Whether you should use *which* or *that* depends on what the sentence is supposed to mean.

one meaning: The third page, *which* had been earmarked, contained several typographical errors.

different meaning: The third page *that* had been earmarked contained several typographical errors.

(The first sentence describes the third page as earmarked and containing errors. The second sentence suggests that the page containing the errors was the third earmarked page.)

- Whether you should use *who* (*whoever*) or *whom* (*whomever*) depends on the grammatical function of the person (or people) being referred to. Confused? Don't worry; just take a look at the following sample sentences, and you shouldn't have any trouble deciding between *who* and *whom* on the GMAT.

incorrect: It was the chairman *whom* initiated the bill.

correct: It was the chairman *who* initiated the bill.

incorrect: First aid will be available to *whomever* requires it.

correct: First aid will be available to *whoever* requires it.

incorrect: The team members from East High, *who* the judges were highly impressed with, won the debate.

correct: The team members from East High, with *whom* the judges were highly impressed, won the debate.

On the GMAT, to make sure that *who* (*whoever*) and *whom* (*whomever*) are being used correctly, try substituting a regular pronoun, then rearrange the clause (if necessary) to form a simple sentence. If a subject-case pronoun works, then *who* (*whoever*) is the right choice. On the other hand, if an object-case pronoun works, then *whom* (*whomever*) is the right choice. Here's how it works with the foregoing sentences:

- It was the chairman whom initiated the bill.

  He initiated the bill.

  (*He* is a subject-case pronoun, so *whom* should be replaced with *who*.)

- First aid will be available to whomever requires it.

  She requires it.

  (*She* is a subject-case pronoun, so *whomever* should be replaced with *whoever*.)

- The team members from East High, who the judges were highly impressed with, won the debate.

  The judges were impressed with them.

  (*Them* is an object-case pronoun, so *who* should be replaced by *whom*.)

Now, look at a GMAT-style sentence that focuses on a relative-pronoun issue. The original version, choice (A), is faulty, so your choice is between the two alternative versions listed here.

14. The Civil War's <u>bloodiest battle was initiated on behalf of those, the indentured black slaves, for who life was most precious.</u>
    - **(A)** bloodiest battle was initiated on behalf of those, the indentured black slaves, for who life was most precious.
    - **(B)** indentured black slaves, for whom life was most precious, initiated the war's bloodiest battle.
    - **(C)** ***
    - **(D)** ***
    - **(E)** bloodiest battle was initiated on behalf of the indentured black slaves, for whom life was most precious.

The original sentence suffers from two flaws. First, the relative pronoun *who* should be replaced with *whom*. (Replace the last clause with: *Life was most precious for them*. The pronoun *them* is an object-case pronoun, so the correct choice is *whom*.) Second, the word *those*, probably intended to refer to the slaves, should be deleted because it is unnecessary and because it confuses the meaning of the sentence. The comma following *those* should also be omitted. Choice (E) corrects both flaws. Choice (B) also corrects both flaws, but it radically alters the sentence's meaning, improperly suggesting that the slaves initiated the bloodiest battle (rather than properly communicating that it was on the slaves' behalf that the battle was fought). **The correct answer is (E).**

Error in Subject-Verb Agreement (Pronoun and Compound Subjects)

Determining whether a sentence's subject is singular or plural isn't always as simple as you might think. You can easily determine whether a personal pronoun such as *he, they,* and *its* is singular or plural. But other pronouns are not so easily identified as either singular or plural. Here are two lists, along with sample sentences, to help you keep these pronouns straight in your mind.

Singular pronouns:

anyone, anything, anybody each either, neither every, everyone, everything, everybody nobody, no one, nothing what, whatever, who, whom, whoever, whomever

correct: *Every* possible cause *has* been investigated.

correct: *Each* one of the children here *speaks* fluent French.

correct: *Neither* of the pens *has* any ink remaining in it.

correct: *Whatever* he's doing *is* very effective.

correct: *Everything* she touches *turns* to gold.

Even when they refer to a "compound" subject joined by *and*, the pronouns listed above remain singular.

correct: *Each adult and child* here *speaks* fluent French.

correct: *Every* possible *cause and suspect was* investigated.

Plural pronouns:

both, several, few, some, many, others

correct: *Few* would *argue* with that line of reasoning.

correct: *Many claim* to have encountered alien beings.

correct: *Some thrive* on commotion, while *others need* quiet.

It's especially easy to overlook a subject-verb agreement problem in a sentence involving a compound subject (multiple subjects joined by connectors such as the word *and* or the word *or*). If joined by *and*, a compound subject is usually plural (and takes a plural verb). But if joined by *or, either . . . or,* or *neither . . . nor,* compound subjects are usually singular.

plural: The chorus *and* the introduction need improvement.

singular: *Either* the chorus *or* the introduction needs improvement.

singular: *Neither* the chorus *nor* the introduction needs improvement.

But what if one subject is singular and another is plural? Which form should the verb take? Here's the rule: Look to see which subject is *nearer* to the verb; the verb should agree with that subject.

plural: Either the rhythm or the *lyrics need* improvement.

singular: Either the lyrics or the *rhythm needs* improvement.

In some cases, you can't tell whether a subject is singular or plural without looking at how it's used in the sentence. This is true of so-called *collective* nouns and nouns of *quantity*. These might call for either a singular verb or a plural verb, depending on whether the noun is used in a singular or plural sense.

> **correct:** Four years *is* too long to wait. (*four years* used in singular sense)

> **correct:** Four years can *pass* by quickly. (*four years* used in plural sense)

> **correct:** The majority *favors* the Republican candidate. (*majority* used in singular sense)

> **correct:** The majority of the voters here *favor* the Republican candidate. (*majority* used in plural sense)

Here's a GMAT-style sentence that contains a compound subject. The original version, choice (A), is faulty, so your choice is between the two alternative versions listed here.

15. Neither his financial patron <u>or Copernicus himself were expecting the societal backlash resulting from him</u> denouncing the Earth-centered Ptolemaic model of the universe.

    (A) or Copernicus himself were expecting the societal backlash resulting from him
    (B) ***
    (C) nor Copernicus himself was expecting the societal backlash resulting from his
    (D) nor Copernicus were expecting the societal backlash resulting from him
    (E) ***

The original sentence actually contains three grammatical errors. First, *neither* should be paired with *nor* instead of *or*. Second, the singular verb *was* should be used instead of the plural *were* because *neither . . . nor* calls for a singular subject and because both parts of the subject (*patron* and *Copernicus*) are singular. Third, the phrase *him denouncing* (which grammarians call a "noun clause") is improper; *denouncing* is a gerund (a verb turned into a noun by adding *-ing*), and gerunds always take possessive pronouns (*his*, in this case). Choice (C) corrects all three errors without creating any new ones. Choice (D) corrects the first error, but not the other two. Also, notice that choice (D) deletes *himself* from the original sentence. In doing so, choice (D) obscures the intended meaning of the sentence, which makes it clear, through the use of *himself*, that the word "his" (appearing twice in the sentence) refers to Copernicus rather than to someone else. So choice (D) creates a new error. **The correct answer is (C).**

PROBLEMS IN TENSE, VOICE, AND MOOD

You've arrived at what some grammarians would consider the inner sanctum of Standard Written English: tense, voice, and mood. These three concepts are among the trickiest covered by GMAT Sentence Correction. In this section, you'll focus on the following types of problems involving these concepts (notice the similarities):

- Error in verb tense and improper tense shifting and mixing
- Awkward use of either the passive or active voice
- Improper use of the subjunctive mood

Error in Verb Tense and Improper Tense Shifting and Mixing

Tense refers to how a verb's form indicates the *time frame* (past, present, or future) of the sentence's action. You won't need to know the names of the tenses for the GMAT, of course. But here they are anyway (all six of them), in case you're interested. Notice that we've used the singular form of the confusing verb *to have* in order to illustrate how verb form differs among different tenses. All of these sentences are correct.

simple present: He *has* enough money to buy a new car.

simple past: He *had* enough money after he was paid to buy a new car.

simple future: He *will have* enough money after he is paid to buy a new car.

present perfect: He *has had* enough food but *has* continued to eat anyway.

past perfect: He *had had* enough food but *had* kept eating anyway.

future perfect: He *will have had* enough food once he *has* finished eating the dessert.

With many verbs, the same form is used for all tenses, except that *-ed* is added for the past tenses—as in *walk, walked*. However, other verbs use distinctive forms for different tenses—as in *see, saw, seen*. Use your ear to determine whether the form sounds correct.

incorrect: The pilot seen the mountain but was flying too low to avoid a collision.

correct: The pilot *saw* the mountain but was flying too low to avoid a collision.

An incorrect sentence might needlessly *mix* tenses or *shift* tenses from one time frame to another in a confusing manner.

incorrect: If it rains tomorrow, we cancel our plans.

correct: If it rains tomorrow, *we will* cancel our plans.

incorrect: When Bill arrived, Sal still did not begin to unload the truck.

correct: When Bill arrived, Sal still *had not begun* to unload the truck.

Our warning about mixing and shifting tenses also applies to sentences like these:

incorrect: *To go* to war is *to have traveled* to hell.

correct: *To go* to war is *to travel* to hell.

correct: *To have gone* to war is to *have traveled* to hell.

incorrect: *Seeing* the obstacle *would have allowed* him to alter his course.

correct: *Having seen* the obstacle *would have allowed* him to alter his course.

correct: *Seeing* the obstacle *would allow* him to alter his course.

By the way, verbs preceded by *to* (for example, *to go*) are called *infinitives*, and verbs turned into nouns by tacking an *-ing* at the end (for example, *seeing*) are called *gerunds*. Of course, you don't need to know that for the GMAT.

Now look at how a tense-shift problem might appear in a GMAT-style sentence. The original version, choice (A), is faulty, so your choice is between the two alternative versions listed here.

16. Companies that <u>fail in their making cost-of-living adjustments of salaries of workers could not</u> attract or retain competent employees.

(A) fail in their making cost-of-living adjustments of salaries of workers could not

(B) ***

(C) ***

(D) will fail to adjust worker salaries to reflect cost-of-living changes can neither

(E) fail to make cost-of-living adjustments in their workers' salaries cannot

The original sentence mixes present tense (*fail*) with past tense (*could not attract*). Also, the phrases *fail in their making* and of *salaries of workers* are awkward and unnecessarily wordy. Choice (E) renders the sentence consistent in tense by replacing *could* with *can*. Choice (E) is also more concise than the original sentence. Choice (D) improperly mixes future tense (*will fail*) with present tense *can . . . retain*. Choice (D) also uses neither to form the improper correlative pair *neither . . . or*. (The proper correlative pair is *neither . . . nor*.) **The correct answer is (E).**

Awkward Use of Either the Passive or Active Voice

In a sentence expressed in the active voice, the subject "acts upon" an object. Conversely, in a sentence expressed in the passive voice, the subject "is acted upon" by an object. The passive voice can sound a bit awkward, so the active voice is generally preferred.

passive (awkward): The book was read by the student.

active (better): The student read the book.

passive (awkward): Repetitive tasks are performed tirelessly by computers.

active (better): Computers perform repetitive tasks tirelessly.

Mixing the active and passive voices results in an even more awkward sentence.

mixed (awkward): Although the house was built by Gary, Kevin built the garage.

passive (less awkward): Although the house was built by Gary, the garage was built by Kevin.

active (best): Although Gary built the house, Kevin built the garage.

Although the active voice is usually less awkward than the passive voice, sometimes the passive voice is appropriate for emphasis or impact.

active (less effective): Yesterday a car hit me.

passive (more effective): Yesterday I was hit by a car.

active (less effective): Only the sun itself *surpasses* the sunrise over the Tetons in beauty.

passive (more effective): Sunrise over the Tetons *is surpassed* in beauty only by the sun itself.

Keep in mind that the passive voice is not grammatically wrong, so you need not eliminate an answer choice merely because it uses it. Check for grammatical errors among all five choices. If the one that uses the passive voice is the only one without a grammatical error, then it's the best choice.

Here's a GMAT-style sentence that focuses on the use of the passive voice. The original version, choice (A), is faulty, so your choice is between the two alternative versions listed here.

17. <u>It is actually a chemical in the brain that creates the sensation of eating enough, a chemical that is</u> depleted by consuming simple sugars.

   (A) It is actually a chemical in the brain that creates the sensation of eating enough, a chemical that is

   (B) ***

   (C) The sensation of having eaten enough is actually created by a chemical in the brain that is

   (D) A chemical actually creates the sensation in the brain of having eaten enough, and this chemical is

   (E) ***

The original sentence isn't terrible, but it includes two flaws. First, the awkward *eating enough* should be replaced; *having eaten enough* is the proper idiom here. Both choices (C) and (D) correct this flaw. Second, notice that *a chemical* appears twice in the sentence. A more effective sentence would avoid repetition. Only choice (C) avoids repeating this phrase by reconstructing the first clause. In doing so, choice (C) admittedly uses the passive voice. Nevertheless, choice (C) is more concise and less awkward overall than the original sentence. One more point about choice (D): It also creates a new problem. It separates *the sensation* from *of having eaten enough*, thereby creating an awkward and confusing clause. The phrase *in the brain* should be moved to either an earlier or later position in the sentence. **The correct answer is (C).**

Improper Use of the Subjunctive Mood

The *subjunctive mood* should be used to express a *wish* or a *contrary-to-fact* condition. These sentences should include words such as *if, had, were,* and *should*.

   incorrect: I wish it *was* earlier.

   correct: I wish it *were* earlier.

   incorrect: Suppose he speeds up suddenly . . .

   correct: Suppose he *were* to speed up suddenly . . .

   incorrect: If the college lowers its tuition, I would probably enroll.

   correct: *Should* the college lower its tuition, I *would* probably enroll.

   correct: *If* the college *were* to lower its tuition, I *would* probably enroll.

   incorrect: Had he driven slower, he will recognize the landmarks.

   correct: *Had* he driven slower, he *would* have recognized the landmarks.

   correct: *If* he *had* driven slower, he *would* have recognized the landmarks.

Just remember: If the sentence uses a regular verb tense (past, present, future, etc.) to express a wish or contrary-to-fact condition, then it is grammatically incorrect, even if the subjunctive verb form is also used. Look, for example, at the *incorrect* sample sentences from above.

TIP

The subjunctive mood can be tricky because it uses its own idiomatic verb forms and because you can't always trust your ear when it comes to catching an error.

- I wish it *was* earlier. (*It was earlier* uses past tense.)
- Suppose he speeds up suddenly. (*He speeds up suddenly* uses present tense.)
- If the college lowers its tuition, I would probably enroll. (The first clause uses present tense, while the second clause uses subjunctive form.)
- Had he driven slower, he will recognize the landmarks from now on. (The first clause uses subjunctive form, while the second clause uses future tense.)

The subjunctive mood is also used in clauses of recommendation, request, suggestion, or demand. These clauses should include the word *that*:

incorrect: Ann suggested we should go to the Chinese restaurant.

correct: Ann suggested that we go to the Chinese restaurant.

incorrect: I insist you be quiet.

correct: I *insist that* you be quiet.

incorrect: The supervisor prefers all workers wear uniforms from now on.

correct: The supervisor *prefers that* all workers wear uniforms from now on.

Now, look at a GMAT-style sentence designed to test you on the use of the subjunctive mood. The original version, choice (A), is faulty, so your choice is between the two alternative versions listed here.

18. The Environmental Protection Agency would be overburdened by its detection and enforcement duties <u>if it fully implemented all of its own regulations completely.</u>
    - **(A)** if it fully implemented all of its own regulations completely.
    - **(B)** if it was to implement all of its own regulations completely.
    - **(C)** were it to fully implement all of its own regulations.
    - **(D)** ***
    - **(E)** ***

The original sentence poses two problems. First, the sentence clearly intends to express a hypothetical or contrary-to-fact situation; yet the underlined phrase does not use the subjunctive *were*. Second, *fully* and *completely* are redundant; one of them should be deleted. Choice (C) corrects both problems without creating a new one. Choice (B) corrects the redundancy problem by deleting *fully*. However, it incorrectly uses was instead of the subjunctive *were*. **The correct answer is (C).**

SENTENCE STRUCTURE AND SENSE

Sentence structure refers to how sentence parts fit together as a whole. You know a sentence is poorly structured when its ideas are confusing, vague, ambiguous, or nonsensical—or even when its structure places undue emphasis (or de-emphasis) on certain ideas.

Problems involving sentence structure can be challenging to fix because there are no hard-and-fast rules of grammar to tell you what the best solution is. And since there are many acceptable ways to make any statement, the distinction between a highly effective structure and a less effective one can be subtle.

Here are the specific types of structural problems you'll examine in this section:

- Improper placement of modifiers
- Confusing pronoun references
- Dangling modifier errors
- Rhetorical imbalance between sentence parts
- Improper splitting of a grammatical unit
- Too many subordinate clauses in a row

Improper Placement of Modifiers

A *modifier* is a word or phrase that describes, restricts, or qualifies another word or phrase. Modifying phrases are typically set off with commas, and many such phrases begin with a relative pronoun (*which, who, that, whose,* and *whom*). Modifiers should generally be placed as close as possible to the word(s) they modify. Positioning a modifier in the wrong place can result in a confusing or even nonsensical sentence.

misplaced: His death shocked the entire family, which occurred quite suddenly.

better: His death, which occurred quite suddenly, shocked the entire family.

misplaced: *Nearly dead,* the police finally found the victim.

better: The police finally found *the victim, who was nearly dead.*

unclear: Bill punched Carl while wearing a mouth protector.

clear: While wearing a mouth protector, Bill punched Carl.

Modifiers such as *almost, nearly, hardly, just,* and *only* should immediately precede the word(s) they modify, even if the sentence sounds correct with the parts separated. For example:

misplaced: Their one-year-old child *almost* weighs *forty pounds*.

better: Their one-year-old child weighs *almost forty pound*s.

Note the position of *only* in the following sentences:

unclear: The assistant was only able to detect obvious errors.

clear: *Only the assistant* was able to detect obvious errors.

unclear: The assistant was able to *only* detect *obvious errors*.

clear: The assistant was able to detect *only obvious errors*.

Now, look at a GMAT-style sentence that misplaces a modifier. The original version, choice (A), is faulty, so your choice is between the two alternative versions listed here.

19. Exercising contributes frequently to not only a sense of well being but also to longevity.
    (A) Exercising contributes frequently to not only a sense of well being but also to longevity.
    (B) ***
    (C) Exercising frequently contributes not only to a sense of well being but to longevity.
    (D) ***
    (E) Frequent exercise contributes not only to a sense of well being but also to longevity.

In the original sentence, *frequently* is probably intended to describe (or modify) *exercising* (frequent exercise). But separating these words makes it appear as though *frequently* describes *contributing*, which makes no sense in the overall context of the sentence. The original sentence also contains a "parallelism" error. The phrase after *not only* should parallel the phrase after *but also,* so that the two phrases can be interchanged and still make sense grammatically. But in the original sentence, the two phrases are not parallel. Choice (E) corrects both problems. In choice (E), it is clear that what is "frequent" is *exercise* (rather than *contributing*). Also, the phrases following each part of the *not only . . . but also* pair are now parallel. (Notice that each phrase begins with *to.*) Choice (C) fails to clear up the confusion as to whether *frequently* describes *exercising* or *contributes*. Also, choice (C) improperly uses *not only . . . but* instead of the proper idiom *not only . . . but also*. **The correct answer is (E).**

The general rule about placing modifiers near the words they modify applies *most* of the time—but in some cases, trying to do so actually confuses the meaning of the sentence.

> **unclear:** Nathan can read the newspaper and *shave without his glasses*. (It is unclear whether *without his glasses* refers only to *shave* or to both *shave* and *read the newspaper.*)

> **unclear:** *Without his glasses, Nathan* can read the newspaper and can shave. (This sentence implies that these are the only two tasks Nathan can perform without his glasses.)

> **clear:** *Even without his glasses,* Nathan can read the newspaper and shave.

It is important not to apply the modifier rule mechanically. Instead, check to see whether the sentence as a whole makes sense.

Confusing Pronoun References

A pronoun (e.g., *she, him, their, its*) is a "shorthand" way of referring to an identifiable noun—person(s), place(s) or thing(s). Nouns to which pronouns refer are called *antecedents*. Make sure every pronoun in a sentence has a clear antecedent.

> **unclear:** Minutes before Kevin's meeting with Paul, *his* wife called with the bad news. (Whose wife called—Kevin's or Paul's?)

> **clear:** *Kevin's* wife called with the bad news minutes before *his* meeting with Paul.

> **clear:** Minutes before Kevin's meeting with Paul, *Kevin's* wife called with the bad news.

Pronoun reference errors are usually corrected in one of two ways:

❶ By placing the noun and pronoun as near as possible to each other without other nouns coming between them (second sentence above)

❷ By replacing the pronoun with its antecedent (third sentence above)

Also, look for the vague use of *it, you, that,* or *one*—without clear reference to a particular antecedent.

> **vague:** When one dives in without looking, *you* never know what will happen. (Does *you* refer to the diver or to the broader *one*?)

> **clear:** *One* never knows what will happen when *one* dives in without looking.

> **clear:** When *you* dive in without looking, *you* never know what will happen.

vague: When the planets are out of alignment, *it* can be disastrous. (*It* does not refer to any noun.)

clear: Disaster can occur when the planets are out of alignment.

The following GMAT-style sentence contains more than one confusing pronoun reference. The original version, choice (A), is faulty, so your choice is between the two alternative versions listed here.

20. E-mail accounts administered by <u>an employer belong to them, and they can be seized and used</u> as evidence against the employee.

   (A) an employer belong to them, and they can be seized and used

   (B) employers belong to them, who can seize and use it

   (C) an employer belong to the employer, who can seize and use the accounts

   (D) ***

   (E) ***

There are two pronoun problems in the original sentence. First, *them* is used vaguely, without clear reference to *employers*, which seems to be the intended antecedent. Adding to this confusion is that the pronoun *them* is plural, yet its intended antecedent *employer* is singular. In addition, the antecedent of *they* is unclear because it is separated from its intended antecedent, *accounts*, by two other nouns (*them* and *employer*). Choice (C) corrects the first problem by replacing the pronoun *them* with its (singular) antecedent employer. Choice (C) also corrects the second problem by using *who*, which clearly refers to *employer*, since the two words appear immediately next to each other. Choice (B) is riddled with problems. First, choice (B) does not correct the vague use of *them* (although the use of the plural *employers* is an improvement). Second, choice (B) leaves it unclear as to which noun *who* refers; presumably, *who* refers to *them*, yet the antecedent of *them* is uncertain. Third, although the pronoun *it* is intended to refer to *accounts*, the reference is unclear because the pronoun and antecedent are separated by other nouns. Finally, the pronoun it is singular, yet its antecedent *accounts* is plural (they should both be either singular or plural). **The correct answer is (C).**

Dangling Modifier Errors

A *dangling modifier* is a modifier that doesn't refer to any particular word(s) in the sentence. The best way to correct a dangling-modifier problem is to reconstruct the sentence.

   dangling: *Set by an arsonist*, firefighters were unable to save the burning building. (This sentence makes no reference to whatever was set by an arsonist.)

   better: Firefighters were unable to save the burning building from *the fire set by an arsonist*.

Despite the rule against dangling modifiers, certain dangling modifiers are acceptable because they're idiomatic.

   acceptable: *Judging* from the number of violent crimes committed every year, our nation is doomed. (Although the sentence makes no reference to whomever is judging, it is acceptable anyway.)

   acceptable: *Considering* that star's great distance from the Earth, its brightness is amazing. (Although this sentence makes no reference to whomever is considering, it is acceptable anyway.)

Now, look at a GMAT-style sentence that contains a dangling modifier. The original version, choice (A), is faulty, so your choice is between the two alternative versions listed here.

TIP

If you encounter a dangling modifier in a GMAT sentence that you've heard many times from well-educated people, then it's probably an idiomatic exception to the rule against such modifiers.

21. <u>By imposing artificial restrictions in price on oil suppliers, these suppliers will be forced</u> to lower production costs.

    (A) By imposing artificial restrictions in price on oil suppliers, these suppliers will be forced

    (B) Imposing artificial price restrictions on oil suppliers will force these suppliers

    (C) By imposing on oil suppliers artificial price restrictions, these suppliers will be forced

    (D) ***

    (E) ***

The original sentence includes a dangling modifier. The sentence makes no reference to whomever (or whatever) is imposing the price restrictions. Choice (B) corrects the problem by reconstructing the sentence. Choice (B) also improves on the original sentence by replacing *restrictions in price* with the more concise *price restrictions*. Choice (C) does not correct the dangling modifier problem. Also, the grammatical construction of the first clause in choice (C) is awkward and confusing. **The correct answer is (B).**

Rhetorical Imbalance Between Sentence Parts

An effective sentence gets its point across by placing appropriate emphasis on its different parts. If you're dealing with two equally important ideas, they should be separated as two distinct "main clauses," and they should be similar in length (to suggest equal importance).

> **unbalanced:** Julie and Sandy were the first two volunteers for the fundraising drive, *and* they are twins.

> **balanced:** Julie and Sandy, *who* are twins, were the first two volunteers for the fundraising drive.

> **commingled (confusing):** Julie and Sandy, *who* are twins, are volunteers.

> **separated (balanced):** Julie and Sandy are twins, *and* they are volunteers.

On the other hand, if you're dealing with only one main idea, be sure that it receives greater emphasis (as a main clause) than the other ideas in the sentence.

> **equal emphasis (confusing):** Jose and Victor were identical twins, *and* they had completely different ambitions.

> **emphasis on second clause (better):** *Although* Jose and Victor were identical twins, they had completely different ambitions.

Here's a GMAT-style example of a rhetorically challenged sentence. The original version, choice (A), is faulty, so your choice is between the two alternative versions listed here.

22. <u>Treating bodily disorders by noninvasive methods is generally painless, and these</u> methods are less likely than those of conventional Western medicine to result in permanent healing.

    (A) Treating bodily disorders by noninvasive methods is generally painless, and these methods

    (B) Treating bodily disorders by noninvasive methods is generally painless, but they

    (C) ***

    (D) ***

    (E) Although treating bodily disorders by noninvasive methods is generally painless, these methods

Notice that the original sentence contains two main clauses, connected by *and*. Two problems should have occurred to you as you read the sentence: (1) the connector *and* is inappropriate to contrast differing methods of treatment (it fails to get the point across), and (2) the second clause expresses the more important point but does not receive greater emphasis than the first clause. Choice (E) corrects both problems by transforming the first clause into a subordinate one and by eliminating the connecting word *and*. What about choice (B)? Replacing *and* with but is not as effective in shifting the emphasis to the second clause as the method used in choice (E). Moreover, by replacing *these methods* with *they*, choice (B) creates a pronoun-reference problem, making it unclear whether *they* refers to *disorders* or to *methods*. **The correct answer is (E).**

Improper Splitting of a Grammatical Unit

Splitting clauses or phrases (by inserting another clause between them) often results in an awkward and confusing sentence.

split: The value of the dollar *is not*, relative to other currencies, *rising* universally.

better: The value of the dollar *is not rising* universally relative to other currencies.

split: The government's goal this year *is to provide* for its poorest residents *an economic safety net*.

split: *The government's goal* is to provide an economic safety net *this year* for its poorest residents.

better: The government's goal this year is to provide an economic safety net for its poorest residents.

In GMAT sentences, look closely for *split infinitives*. An infinitive is the plural form of an action verb, preceded by the word "to." If to is separated from its corresponding verb, then you're dealing with a "split infinitive," and the sentence is grammatically incorrect.

improper (split): The executive was compelled *to*, by greed and ambition, *work* more and more hours each day.

correct: The executive was compelled by greed and ambition *to work* more and more hours each day.

improper (split): Meteorologists have been known *to* inaccurately *predict* snowstorms.

correct: Meteorologists have been known *to predict* snowstorms inaccurately.

Now, look at a GMAT-style sentence with a split personality. The original version, choice (A), is faulty, so your choice is between the two alternative versions listed here.

23. Typographer Lucian Bernhard was influenced, perhaps more so than any of his contemporaries, by Toulouse-Lautrec's emphasis on large, unharmonious lettering.

   (A) Typographer Lucian Bernhard was influenced, perhaps more so than any of his contemporaries, by Toulouse-Lautrec's emphasis on large, unharmonious lettering.

   (B) Perhaps more so than any of his contemporaries, typographer Lucian Bernhard was influenced by Toulouse-Lautrec's emphasis on large, unharmonious lettering.

   (C) ***

   (D) ***

   (E) Typographer Lucian Bernhard was influenced by Toulouse-Lautrec's emphasis on large, unharmonious lettering perhaps more so than any of his contemporaries.

TIP

Whenever you see a clause set off by commas in the middle of the sentence, check the words immediately before and after the clause. If keeping those words together would sound better to your ear or would more effectively convey the sentence's main point, then the sentence (answer choice) is wrong, and you can safely eliminate it.

The original sentence awkwardly splits the main clause with an intervening subordinate one (set off by commas). Both choices (B) and (E) keep the main clause intact. However, choice (E) creates a pronoun reference problem: It's unclear as to whom the pronoun *his* refers—Bernhard or Toulouse-Lautrec. **The correct answer is (B).**

Too Many Subordinate Clauses in a Row

A *subordinate clause* is one that does not stand on its own as a complete sentence. Stringing together two or more subordinate clauses can result in an awkward and confusing sentence.

awkward: Barbara's academic major is history, *which* is a very popular course of study among liberal arts students, who are also contributing to the popularity of political science as a major.

better: Barbara's academic major is history, which, along with political science, is a very popular course of study among liberal arts students.

Now, look at a GMAT-style sentence that suffers from this sort of error. The original version, choice (A), is faulty, so your choice is between the two alternative versions listed here.

24. By relying unduly on anecdotal evidence, which often conflicts with more reliable data, including data from direct observation and measurement, a scientist risks losing credibility among his or her peers.

   (A) By relying unduly on anecdotal evidence, which often conflicts with more reliable data, including data from direct observation and measurement, a scientist risks losing credibility among his or her peers.

   (B) ***

   (C) ***

   (D) A scientist, by relying unduly on anecdotal evidence, which often conflicts with more reliable data, including data from direct observation and measurement, risks losing credibility among his or her peers.

   (E) A scientist risks losing credibility among his or her peers by relying unduly on anecdotal evidence, which often conflicts with more reliable data, including data from direct observation and measurement.

The original sentence contains four clauses (separated by commas). The first three are all subordinate clauses. The result is that you are left in suspense as to who unduly relies on anecdotal evidence (first clause) until you reach the last (and main) clause. The solution is to rearrange the sentence to join the first and last clause, thereby minimizing the string of subordinate clauses and eliminating confusion. Choice (E) provides this solution. Choice (D) solves the problem only partially by moving only a section of the main clause (the scientist) to the beginning of the sentence. In fact, by doing so, (D) probably creates more confusion. **The correct answer is (E).**

Subordination of a dependent clause to a main clause can be achieved through the use of:

- Words modifying relative pronouns: *which, who, that*
- Words establishing time relationship: *before, after, as, since*
- Words establishing a causal relationship: *because, since*
- Words of admission or concession: *although, though, despite*
- Words indicating place: *where, wherever*
- Words of condition: *if, unless*

SUMMING IT UP

- Read the answer choices very carefully. The difference between answer choices can be subtle: perhaps one extra word or a word replaced by a different one. It's easy to overlook these differences if you rush through a question. Take your time and read carefully.

- For each choice, review the entire sentence, not just the underlined part. GMAT Sentence Correction questions are not nearly as time-consuming as other Verbal questions, so take your time. Plug each version into the sentence, then read the entire sentence. You may see an occasional answer choice that's grammatically incorrect apart from the rest of the sentence, but such cases are the exception, not the rule.

- Don't choose an answer just because it fixes every flaw in the original version. If the original version is flawed, it's a sure bet that one or two of the other answer choices will fix the flaw but create a new flaw.

- Trust your ear. If an answer choice doesn't sound right as you read it in the context of the sentence, eliminate it. There's no need to analyze it any further.

- Don't be thrown by a nonsensical answer choice. If an answer choice seems confusing or unclear, don't assume that you are at fault for not understanding the sentence. Some answer choices will simply not make much sense. Don't waste your time analyzing the answer choice to determine why it is wrong.

Reading Comprehension

OVERVIEW

- **"Interactive" reading: The key to reading comprehension**
- **The 7-step plan**
- **Techniques for interactive reading**
- **Sample reading passages and question types**
- **Top 10 wrong-answer ploys**
- **Keys to successful GMAT reading comprehension: The basics**
- **Keys to successful GMAT reading comprehension: Advanced techniques**
- **Summing it up**

In this Reading Comprehension section, you'll learn:

- The importance of reading GMAT passages "interactively"
- A step-by-step approach to handling Reading Comprehension questions
- Techniques for reading more effectively and efficiently

You'll also learn how to handle:

- Simple recall questions
- Recap questions
- Restatement questions
- Inference questions
- Method questions
- Application questions
- Logical continuation questions

"INTERACTIVE" READING: THE KEY TO READING COMPREHENSION

If you're like most GMAT test-takers, you'll experience at least one of the following problems as you tackle Reading Comprehension:

- Your concentration is poor—perhaps due to your lack of familiarity with or interest in the topic or perhaps due to general test anxiety.
- Your reading pace is slow—so you have trouble finishing the Verbal section in time.

- To answer each question, you find yourself searching the passage again and again to find the information you need.

- You have trouble narrowing down the answer choices to one that's clearly the best.

Believe it or not, all of these problems are due to the same bad habit: passive reading, by which you simply read the passage from start to finish, giving equal time and attention to every sentence without thought as to what particular information might be key in answering the questions. You might call this approach the "osmosis strategy," since you're hoping to absorb what you need to know by simply allowing your eyes to glaze over the words.

What's the likely result of this osmosis strategy? You might remember some scattered facts and ideas, which will help you respond correctly to some easier questions. But the passive mind-set won't take you very far when it comes to most of the questions, which measure your ability to *understand* the ideas in the passage rather than to simply *recall* information. Understanding a passage well enough to answer all the questions requires a highly active frame of mind—one in which you constantly *interact* with the text as you read, asking yourself questions such as these:

- What's the passage's main idea (or "thesis") and the author's overall concern or purpose?

- How does each part of the passage relate to the main idea and the author's overall purpose?

- What's the author's line of reasoning or "train of thought"?

THE 7-STEP PLAN

The first task in this chapter is to learn the seven basic steps for handling a GMAT Reading Comprehension passage and question set. Let's apply these steps to the following sample passage and three questions:

Passage 1

Line　　The encounter that a portrait records is most tangibly the sitting itself, which may be brief or extended, collegial or confrontational. Renowned photographer Cartier-Bresson has expressed his passion for portrait photography by characterizing it as "a duel without rules, a delicate rape." Such metaphors contrast quite sharply with Richard Avedon's conception of a sitting.

(5)　　While Cartier-Bresson reveals himself as an interloper and opportunist, Avedon confesses—perhaps uncomfortably—to a role as diagnostician and (by implication) psychic healer: not as someone who necessarily transforms his subjects, but as someone who reveals their essential nature. Both photographers, however, agree that the fundamental dynamic in this process lies squarely in the hands of the artist.

(10)　　A quite-different paradigm has its roots not in confrontation or consultation but in active collaboration between the artist and sitter. This very different kind of relationship was formulated most vividly by William Hazlitt in his essay entitled "On Sitting for One's Picture" (1823). To Hazlitt, the "bond of connection" between painter and sitter is most like the relationship between two lovers. Hazlitt fleshes out his thesis by recalling the career of Sir Joshua

(15)　　Reynolds. According to Hazlitt, Reynolds' sitters were meant to enjoy an atmosphere that was both comfortable for them and conducive to the enterprise of the portrait painter, who was simultaneously their host and their contractual employee.

1. The author of the passage quotes Cartier-Bresson in order to

    (A) refute Avedon's conception of a portrait sitting.

    (B) provide one perspective of the portraiture encounter.

    (C) support the claim that portrait sittings are, more often than not, confrontational encounters.

    (D) show that a portraiture encounter can be either brief or extended.

    (E) distinguish a sitting for a photographic portrait from a sitting for a painted portrait.

2. Which of the following characterizations of the portraiture experience as viewed by Avedon is most readily inferable from the passage?

    (A) A collaboration

    (B) A mutual accommodation

    (C) A confrontation

    (D) An uncomfortable encounter

    (E) A consultation·

3. Which of the following best expresses the passage's main idea?

    (A) The success of a portrait depends largely on the relationship between artist and subject.

    (B) Portraits, more than most other art forms, provide insight into the artist's social relationships.

    (C) The social aspect of portraiture sitting plays an important part in the sitting's outcome.

    (D) Photographers and painters differ in their views regarding their role in portrait photography.

    (E) The paintings of Reynolds provide a record of his success in achieving a social bond with his subjects.

Step One: Read the First Question and Answers Before Reading the Passage

Try to anticipate what the passage is about and what sort of information you should be on the lookout for in order to answer the first question.

Step Two: Read the Passage with a Possible Thesis in Mind

Begin reading the passage, actively thinking about a possible thesis (main idea) and how the author attempts to support that thesis. Also, begin your reading with an eye for information useful in answering the first question.

Step Three: Choose a Tentative Answer

When you think you've learned enough to take a stab at the first question, go ahead and choose a *tentative* answer. You probably won't have to read very far to at least take a reasoned guess at the first question. But don't confirm your selection yet.

Step Four: Begin to Develop an Outline

Read the remainder of the passage, formulating an outline as you go. As you read, try to (1) separate main ideas from supporting ideas and examples; (2) determine the basic structure of the passage (e.g., chronology of events, classification of ideas or things, comparison between two or more ideas, events, or things); and (3) determine the author's opinion or position on the subject. Make notes on your scratch paper as needed to see the flow of the passage and to keep the passage's details straight in your mind.

Step Five: Sum Up the Passage and Formulate a Thesis Statement

Sum up the passage; formulate a brief thesis (main idea) statement. Take a few seconds to review your outline. Then, in your own words, express the author's main point—in one sentence. Jot it down on your scratch paper. Your thesis statement should reflect the author's opinion or position (e.g., critical, supportive, neutral) toward the ideas presented in the passage.

Step Six: Confirm Your Selection for the First Question

Eliminate any answer choice that is inconsistent with your thesis statement, that doesn't respond to the question, or that doesn't make sense to you.

Step Seven: Move on to the Remaining Questions

Make sure you consider *all* of the answer choices for each question.

Now let's walk through Passage 1 (involving portraiture) and the sample questions about it, using this 7-step approach.

Step 1: The first question tells you a lot about what you might expect in the passage. In all likelihood, the passage will be primarily about the portraiture experience. The author will probably provide different viewpoints and insights on this experience from the perspective of particular artists.

Step 2: The first four sentences reinforce your initial prediction about the passage's content. Based on these initial lines, it appears that the author will indeed be comparing and contrasting different views of the portraiture experience. At this point, you don't know whether the passage will involve the views of any artists other than Cartier-Bresson and Richard Avedon, nor do you know whether the author has any opinion on the subject. But you should be on the lookout for answers to these unknowns during Step 4.

Step 3: Consider Question 1 based on what you've read so far. The author points out that Cartier-Bresson's conception is quite different from that of Avedon. Choices (A), (B), and (C) all appear to be viable choices. But whether the author's purpose here is to *refute* Avedon's view (choice (A)), *support* Cartier-Bresson's view (choice (C)), or simply *provide* one of at least two perspectives without taking sides (choice (B)) remains to be seen. You'll have to read on to find out. In any event, you can probably eliminate choices (D) and (E), since neither one seems relevant to the Cartier-Bresson quotation. Don't confirm a selection yet; go on to Step 4.

Step 4: Your goal in Step 4 is to formulate an informal outline of the passage as you read from start to finish. You might want to jot down some key words and phrases to help you see how the ideas flow and to keep the four individuals discussed in the passage straight in your mind. Here's a good outline of the passage:

Paragraph 1

Contrast:

— CB: confrontation (rape)

— Avedon: diagnosis (consultation)

— BUT agree artist is key

Paragraph 2

3rd view: Hazlitt (writer)

— collaboration (like lovers)

— e.g. Reynolds

Step 5: Now let's sum up the passage based on the outline you formulated in Step 4. It's a good idea to jot it down. Notice that the "thesis" is neutral; the author does not side with any viewpoint presented in the passage.

Thesis: Portraiture is a social experience, but artists disagree about their role in it.

Step 6: Having read the entire passage, return to the question. Nowhere in the passage does the author attempt to either refute or support any of the viewpoints presented. So you can eliminate choices (A) and (C).

Question 1: **The correct answer is (B).** Notice also that choice (B) is consistent with our thesis statement. Regardless of the particular question, you can eliminate any answer choice that is inconsistent with your thesis statement.

Step 7: Move ahead to Questions 2 and 3. In the following analysis, notice the qualitative difference (from best to worst) among the answer choices.

Question 2: In the first sentence of the second paragraph, the author distinguishes a "quite-different paradigm" (that is, the case of Reynolds) from the conceptions of Cartier-Bresson and Avedon in that the Reynolds paradigm "has its roots not in confrontation or consultation but in active collaboration between artist and sitter." The second sentence of the passage makes it clear that Cartier-Bresson conceives the encounter as "confrontational"; thus, you can *reasonably infer* that the author characterizes an Avedon sitting as a "consultation." **The correct answer is (E).**

Choice (B) is also a good response but nevertheless not as good as choice (E). Although the term "mutual accommodation," which does not appear in the passage, is not altogether inconsistent with Avedon's view, the term suggests a relationship in which both artist and sitter allow for the other's needs or desires. Such a description is closer to Hazlitt's analogy of two lovers than to Avedon's view of the artist as diagnostician and psychic healer.

Choice (A) also has merit, yet it is not as good a response as either choice (B) or choice (E). Admittedly, the idea of "a collaboration" is not in strong opposition to the idea of "a consultation." However, the author explicitly ascribes this characterization to the Reynolds paradigm, not to Avedon's view. Thus, choice (A) *confuses the passage's information.*

Choices (C) and (D) are qualitatively the worst choices among the five. Choice (C) *confuses the passage's information*. The quotation in the first paragraph makes it clear that Cartier-Bresson (not Avedon) conceives the encounter as "confrontational." (D) also *confuses the passage's information*. According to the passage, Avedon confesses "uncomfortably" to his role as diagnostician and psychic healer. It does not necessarily follow, however, that Avedon finds his encounters with his sitters to be uncomfortable.

Question 3: Although this passage doesn't seem to convey a strong central idea or thesis, the author seems to be most concerned with emphasizing that a portrait sitting is a social encounter, not just an artistic exercise, and that artists consider their relationship with their sitters to be somehow significant. For this reason, choice (C) is a good statement of the author's main point. **The correct answer is (C).**

Choice (A) also has merit. In fact, but for choice (C), choice (A) would be the best choice because it embraces the passage as a whole and properly focuses on the author's primary concern with exploring the relationship between artist and sitter. However, the passage does not discuss how or whether this relationship results in a "successful" portrait; thus, choice (A) *distorts the passage's information.*

Choice (D) has merit because the author does claim that the Reynolds paradigm (described in the second paragraph) is "quite different" from the two paradigms that the first paragraph discusses. The latter does indeed involve a painter (Reynolds) whereas the other two paradigms involve photographers (Cartier-Bresson and Avedon). However, the author does not generalize from this fact that a portrait artist's approach or view depends on whether the artist is a painter or a photographer. Thus, choice (D) is a bit *off focus* and calls for an *unwarranted generalization.*

Choices (B) and (E) are qualitatively the worst among the five choices. Choice (B) *distorts* the information in the passage and departs from the topic at hand. Although the passage does support the notion that a portrait might reveal something about the relationship between artist and sitter, the author neither states nor implies that a portrait reveals anything about the artist's other relationships. Moreover, nowhere in the passage does the author compare portraiture with other art forms.

Choice (E) is *too narrow* and refers to information *not mentioned* in the passage. The passage is not just about Reynolds but about the portraiture encounter in general. Also, the author does not comment on Reynolds' "success" or about how his relationship with his sitters might have contributed to his success.

TECHNIQUES FOR INTERACTIVE READING

During Step 4 of the 7-step approach you just learned, you read the passage and formulated an outline that revealed its basic structure and how its ideas flowed from one to the next. In this section, we'll focus more closely on this step, which lies at the heart of GMAT Reading Comprehension.

Think of any GMAT reading passage as a structure of ideas. Each passage is designed to convey a number of ideas that are connected to one another in some way. If you understand these ideas and the connections between them, then you truly understand the passage as a whole. Focusing on structure helps you in several ways:

- It makes it easy to see the "big picture"—what the passage is about as a whole.

- It tells you the purpose of the supporting details, even when you don't know what those details are.

- The logical structure organizes all the information in the passage, making it easy to locate any detail to which a particular question might refer.

- The structure explains how the author's main points are related to one another.

Focus on the Passage's Logical Structure

Although GMAT passages don't invariably have clear-cut, logical structures, a structure of some kind is almost always present. Here's a list of the most common types of logical structures found in GMAT passages. Either alone or in combination, these structures underlie most of the passages you'll encounter on the exam.

- A theory or idea illustrated by two (or more) detailed examples or illustrations or supported by two (or more) arguments (the passage might also critique the theory based on the examples or arguments)

- Two (or more) alternative theories, each of which seeks to explain a certain phenomenon (the passage might also argue for one theory over another)

- Pro and con arguments presented for both sides of a single issue

- A comparison and/or contrast between two (or more) events, ideas, phenomena, or people

- A cause-and-effect sequence showing how one event led to another (presented either in chronological order or via "flashback," with later events described before earlier ones)

- Two or three basic types, categories, or classes of a phenomenon identified and distinguished, beginning with main classes, and then possibly branching out to subclasses (this structure is most common in passages involving the natural sciences)

Now let's look at a couple of examples. Here's the passage about portraiture that you read earlier in this chapter. This time, key portions are underlined to help you see its structure. Notice how nicely it fits into the comparison-contrast structural pattern.

Passage 1 (comparison and contrast)

Line   The encounter that a portrait records is most tangibly the sitting itself, which may be brief or extended, collegial or confrontational. Renowned photographer Cartier-Bresson has expressed his passion for portrait photography by characterizing it as "a duel without rules, a delicate rape." Such metaphors contrast quite sharply with Richard Avedon's conception of a sitting.
(5)   While Cartier-Bresson reveals himself as an interloper and opportunist, Avedon confesses—perhaps uncomfortably—to a role as diagnostician and (by implication) psychic healer: not as someone who necessarily transforms his subjects, but as someone who reveals their essential nature. Both photographers, however, agree that the fundamental dynamic in this process lies squarely in the hands of the artist.
(10)   A quite-different paradigm has its roots not in confrontation or consultation but in active collaboration between the artist and sitter. This very different kind of relationship was formulated most vividly by William Hazlitt in his essay entitled "On Sitting for One's Picture" (1823). To Hazlitt, the "bond of connection" between painter and sitter is most like the relationship between two lovers. Hazlitt fleshes out his thesis by recalling the career of Sir Joshua

TIP

Each of the structures listed here requires paragraph breaks to turn from one theory, reason, example, or class to another, or to separate pros from cons or similarities from differences. But don't assume a passage's structure will reveal itself so neatly. In fact, a passage with a complex structure might contain only one paragraph. The moral: Use paragraph breaks as structural clues, but don't rely on them as crutches.

(15) Reynolds. <u>According to Hazlitt, Reynolds' sitters</u> were meant to enjoy an atmosphere that was both comfortable for them and conducive to the enterprise of the portrait painter, who was simultaneously their host and their contractual employee.

Here's a new passage. This one has a typical cause-and-effect structure. Again, some key phrases are underlined to help reveal the structure.

Passage 2 (cause-and-effect sequence)

Line   Scientists in the post-1917 Soviet Union occupied an ambiguous position—while the government encouraged and generally supported scientific research, it simultaneously thwarted the scientific community's ideal: freedom from geographic and political boundaries. A strong nationalistic <u>emphasis on science led at times to</u> the dismissal of all non-Russian scientific
(5) work as irrelevant to Soviet science. A 1973 article in *Literatunaya Gazeta*, a Soviet publication, insisted: "World science is based upon national schools, so the weakening of one or another national school inevitably leads to stagnation in the development of world science." According to the Soviet regime, socialist science was to be consistent with, and in fact grow out of, the Marxist-Leninist political ideology. <u>Toward this end,</u> some scientific theories or fields, such
(10) as relativity and genetics, were abolished. Where scientific work conflicted with political criteria, the work was often disrupted. <u>During the Stalinist purges</u> of the 1930s, many Soviet scientists simply disappeared. <u>In the 1970s,</u> Soviet scientists who were part of the refusenik movement lost their jobs and were barred from access to scientific resources. Nazi Germany during the 1930s and, more recently, Argentina imposed strikingly similar, though briefer,
(15) constraints on scientific research.

Although the structure of passage 2 is not quite so obvious as that of passage 1, the structure is nevertheless there, lying just beneath the details. Notice that the passage's opening describes the cause (Russia's insular political ideology), while the rest of the passage lists the effects (non-Russian work was deemed irrelevant, certain theories and fields were abolished, scientific work was disrupted, and scientists disappeared). The final two sentences (beginning with "in the 1970s") is a postscript that simply notes two similar cause-and-effect relationships in modern history.

Look for Structural Clues or "Triggers"

"Triggers" are key words and phrases that provide clues to the structure and organization of the passage and the direction in which the discussion is flowing. The lists below contain many common trigger words and phrases. Be on the lookout for trigger words as you read the passage. They'll help you see the structure of the passage and follow the author's train of thought.

These words precede an item in a list (e.g., examples, classes, reasons, or characteristics):

first, second, etc.

in addition, also, another

These words signal that the author is contrasting two phenomena:

alternatively, by contrast, however, on the other hand, rather than, while, yet

These words signal a logical conclusion based upon preceding material:

consequently, in conclusion, then, thus, therefore, as a result, accordingly

These words signal that the author is comparing (identifying similarities between) two phenomena:

similarly, in the same way, analogous, parallel, likewise, just as, also, as

These words signal evidence (factual information) used to support the author's argument:

because, since, in light of

These words signal an example of a phenomenon:

for instance, e.g., such as, . . . is an illustration of

Obviously, it's not possible to circle or underline key words or to otherwise annotate passages on the CAT computer screen as you could on the previous paper-based GMAT. To help make up for this, the GMAT test-makers shortened the length of Reading passages by about one half when they switched to computerized testing (under the theory that a briefer passage is easier to assimilate without annotating it).

The Art of Note-Taking and Outlining

As you're reading, make shorthand notes to summarize paragraphs or to indicate the flow of the passage's discussion. Notes can also help you locate details more quickly and recap the passage more effectively. Keep your notes as brief as possible—two or three words are enough in most cases to indicate a particular idea or component of the passage. For complicated or high-density passages, an outline is a good way to organize information and to keep particular details straight in your mind. The following three situations are ideal for outlining:

1 If the passage categorizes or classifies various things, use an outline to help you keep track of which belong in each category.

2 If the passage mentions numerous individual names (e.g., of authors, artists, political figures, etc.), use notes to link them according to influence, agreement or disagreement, and so forth.

3 If the passage describes a sequence of events, use a timeline outline to keep track of the major features of each event in the sequence. In chronological passages, mark historical benchmarks and divisions—centuries, years, decades, or historical periods—that help form the structure of the author's discussion.

Use arrows to physically connect words that signify ideas that link together; for example:

- To clarify cause and effect in the natural sciences or in the context of historical events
- To indicate who was influenced by whom in literature, music, psychology, etc.
- To connect names (philosophers, scientists, authors, etc.) with dates, events, other names, theories, or schools of thought, works, etc.
- To indicate the chronological order in which historical events occurred

To Preview . . . or Not to Preview

Many GMAT-prep books recommend that before reading a passage straight through from beginning to end, you *preview* the passage by reading the first (and perhaps the last) sentence of each paragraph. This technique supposedly provides clues about the scope of the passage, the author's thesis or major

TIP

The only situation in which you should preview is if you're running out of time. Some questions, especially the ones that refer to particular line numbers, you can answer quickly by reading just one paragraph or perhaps just a few sentences. And a quick scan of the first and last few sentences of the passage might provide clues about the passage's main idea or primary purpose, so you can at least take educated guesses at some questions.

conclusions, and the structure and flow of the discussion. Although these techniques make sense *in theory*, there are several reasons why in *practice* they are rarely helpful on the GMAT:

- Once immersed in the passage itself, you'll quickly forget most if not all of what you learned from previewing.

- These techniques call for you to read the same material twice. Does that sound efficient to you?

- Previewing takes time—time that you might not be able to afford under timed testing conditions.

- Previewing involves rapid vertical scrolling, which adds to eye strain.

- While reading the beginning and end of each paragraph may be helpful for some passages, for others this technique will be of little or no help—and there's no way to know whether you're wasting your time until you've already wasted it.

SAMPLE READING PASSAGES AND QUESTION TYPES

Most of the sample questions you'll analyze in this chapter are based on the following two passages. Read both passages now, and then earmark this page so you can more easily refer to it as you work through the chapter.

Passage 1

Line   The arrival of a nonindigenous plant or animal species in a new location may be either intentional or unintentional. Rates of species movement driven by human transformations of natural environments as well as by human mobility—through commerce, tourism, and travel— dwarf natural rates by comparison. While geographic distributions of species naturally expand

(5) or contract over historical time intervals (tens to hundreds of years), species' ranges rarely expand thousands of miles or across physical barriers such as oceans or mountains.

    A number of factors confound quantitative evaluation of the relative importance of various entry pathways. Time lags often occur between establishment of nonindigenous species and their detection, and tracing the pathway for a long-established species is difficult. Experts

(10) estimate that nonindigenous weeds are usually detected only after having been in the country for thirty years or having spread to at least ten thousand acres. In addition, federal port inspection, although a major source of information on nonindigenous species pathways, especially for agricultural pests, provides data only when such species enter via scrutinized routes. Finally, some comparisons between pathways defy quantitative analysis—for example, which is more

(15) "important": the entry pathway of one very harmful species or one by which many but less harmful species enter the country?

Passage 2

Line   Scientists have long claimed that, in order to flourish and progress, their discipline requires freedom from ideological and geographic boundaries, including the freedom to share new scientific knowledge with scientists throughout the world. In the twentieth century, however, increasingly close links between science and national life undermined these ideals. Although

(5) the connection facilitated large and expensive projects, such as the particle-accelerator program, that would have been difficult to fund through private sources, it also channeled the direction of scientific research increasingly toward national security (military defense).

    For example, scientists in the post-1917 Soviet Union found themselves in an ambiguous position. While the government encouraged and generally supported scientific research, it simul-

(10) taneously imposed significant restrictions on science and scientists. A strong nationalistic emphasis on science led at times to the dismissal of all non-Russian scientific work as irrelevant to Soviet science. A 1973 article in *Literatunaya Gazeta*, a Soviet publication, insisted: "World science is

based upon national schools, so the weakening of one or another national school inevitably leads
to stagnation in the development of world science." According to the Soviet regime, socialist
(15)   science was to be consistent with, and in fact grow out of, the Marxist-Leninist political ideology.
Toward this end, some scientific theories or fields, such as relativity and genetics, were abolished.
Where scientific work conflicted with political criteria, the work was often disrupted. During
the Stalinist purges of the 1930s, many Soviet scientists simply disappeared. In the 1970s, Soviet
scientists who were part of the refusenik movement lost their jobs and were barred from access
(20)   to scientific resources. Nazi Germany during the 1930s and, more recently, Argentina imposed
strikingly similar, though briefer, constraints on scientific research.

Simple Recall Questions

For these questions, your job is to identify which answer choice provides information that appears
in the passage and that the question asks about. The question stem might look something like one
of these:

"Which of the following does the author mention as an example of . . .?"

"According to the passage, . . . is caused by . . .?"

This is the most common question type, and it's the easiest type because all that's required to handle
it is to either remember or find the appropriate information in the passage.

Here's a good example, based on Passage 1:

  4.   According to the passage, the rate at which plant or animal species move naturally across land
   (A)   might depend on the prevalence of animals that feed on the species.
   (B)   is hindered by federal port inspectors.
   (C)   is often slower than the rate at which they move across water.
   (D)   is slower than human-assisted rates.
   (E)   varies according to the size of the species.

Only the first paragraph talks about the rate of species movement, so it's there that you'll find the
answer to this question. The author states that rates of species movement driven by human transformations and mobility "dwarf natural rates by comparison." In other words, natural rates are slower
than human-assisted rates, just as choice (D) provides. **The correct answer is (D)**.

Choice (A) might be true in the "real world," but the passage mentions nothing about predators, let
alone about their effect on movement rates. So you can easily eliminate it.

Choice (B) confuses the passage's details. It refers to information in the second paragraph, which
discusses problems in determining entry pathways. This paragraph has nothing to do with the rate
of species movement. Also, did you notice that choice (B) is a bit nonsensical? How could port
inspectors, who are located where ocean meets land, affect the rate at which a species moves *naturally* across land?

Choice (C) involves relevant information from the passage but distorts that information. The last
sentence in the first paragraph indicates that oceans and mountains are barriers that typically prevent
species movement. But choice (C) implies that mountains pose a greater barrier than oceans. Nowhere
in the passage does the author seek to compare rates across land with rates across water.

TIP

In handling a Simple
Recall question,
don't expect the
correct answer
choice to quote the
passage verbatim.
That's generally
not how the test-
makers write them.
Instead, they prefer
to paraphrase what's
in the passage. In
this question, for
instance, the precise
phrase "human-
assisted" movement
doesn't appear in
the passage, does it?
But that's no reason
to eliminate (D),
which turns out to be
the correct answer
choice.

Choice (E) is completely unsupported by the passage, which never mentions the size of a species in any context.

Notice the types of wrong-answer ploys built into the preceding question:

- Bringing in irrelevant details from elsewhere in the passage
- Distorting what the passage says
- Bringing in outside information (not found anywhere in the passage)
- Providing a nonsensical response to the question at hand

Always look for these ploys in a Simple Recall question. In addition, to complicate things, test-designers might turn the question around by asking you to identify an exception to what the passage provides (with a word such as "except" or "least" in upper-case letters).

"The author mentions all of the following as examples of . . . EXCEPT:"

"According to the passage, . . . could be caused by any of the following EXCEPT:"

To handle this variation, eliminate all choices that the passage covers and that are relevant to the question, and you'll be left with one choice—the correct one. The following question, based on Passage 1 is a typical example. Although this question is about as tough a Simple Recall question as you'll find on the GMAT, you'll probably agree that it's pretty easy. Here it is, along with an explanatory answer:

5. Whether the entry pathway for a particular nonindigenous species can be determined is LEAST likely to depend upon which of the following?

   (A) Whether the species is considered to be a pest
   (B) Whether the species gains entry through a scrutinized route
   (C) The rate at which the species expands geographically
   (D) How long the species has been established
   (E) The size of the average member of the species

Nowhere in the passage does the author state or imply that the physical size of a species' members affects whether the entry pathway for the species can be determined.

You can easily eliminate choices (B), (C), and (D). All three are mentioned explicitly in the second paragraph as factors affecting how precisely the entry pathway(s) of a species can be determined.

Choice (A) is a bit trickier, and it's the runner-up choice. Unlike the other incorrect choices, (A) is not *explicitly* supported by the passage. However, the author mentions in the final paragraph that federal port inspection is "a major source of information on nonindigenous species pathways, especially for agricultural pests." Accordingly, whether a species is an agricultural pest might have some bearing upon whether or not its entry is detected (by port inspectors). Hence choice (A) is not as good as choice (E), which finds no support in the passage whatsoever. **The correct answer is (E).**

ALERT!

In more difficult Simple Recall questions, one wrong-answer choice will be more tempting than the others because the passage will implicitly support it. Don't be fooled; you'll find a better choice among the five.

Recap Questions

For these questions, your job is to recognize either the main idea, or thesis, of the passage (or a particular paragraph) *as a whole,* or the author's primary purpose or concern in the passage (or in a particular paragraph) *as a whole.* In other words, your job is to *recap* what the passage or paragraph is about. The question stem will look like one of these:

"Which of the following best expresses the main idea of the passage?"

"Among the following characterizations, the passage is best viewed as . . ."

"Which of the following would be the most appropriate title of the passage?"

"The author's primary purpose in the passage [or "*in the third paragraph*"] is to . . ."

"The passage [or "*the first paragraph*"] is primarily concerned with . . ."

To handle this question type, you'll need to recognize the passage's (or paragraph's) overall scope and main emphasis. Most of the wrong-answer choices will fall into these categories:

- Too broad (embracing ideas outside the scope of the passage or paragraph)
- Too narrow (focusing on only a certain portion or aspect of the discussion)
- Distorted (an inaccurate reflection of the passage's ideas or the author's perspective on the topic)

To complicate a Recap question, the test-makers might include a runner-up answer choice that's just a bit off the mark. Here's a moderately difficult Recap question, based on Passage 2, that illustrates this tactic, along with an explanatory answer:

6. The author's primary purpose in the passage is to

   (A) examine the events leading up to the suppression of the Soviet refusenik movement of the 1970s.
   (B) define and dispel the notion of a national science as promulgated by the post-revolution Soviet regime.
   (C) describe specific attempts by the modern Soviet regime to suppress scientific freedom.
   (D) examine the major twentieth-century challenges to the normative assumption that science requires freedom and that it is inherently international.
   (E) point out the similarities and distinctions between scientific freedom and scientific internationalism in the context of the Soviet Union.

Notice that, with the exception of the very last sentence, the passage is entirely concerned with describing Soviet attempts to suppress scientific freedom. In the order mentioned, the attempts include thwarting science's ideals, emphasizing a national science, controlling scientific literature, and threatening and punishing renegade scientists. Choice (C) aptly expresses this overall concern. **The correct answer is (C).**

Choice (D) is the runner-up. Admittedly, the passage does mention, in the final sentence, two other twentieth-century attempts to suppress scientific freedom. Had the passage continued by describing these two other attempts, (D) would probably have been the best answer choice. But since it doesn't, choice (D) is a bit *too broad.*

Choice (A) *distorts* the author's primary purpose. The author does not actually discuss any specific events that might have caused the suppression of the refusenik movement; rather, this historical phenomenon is mentioned simply as another example of the Soviet regime's long-term pattern of suppression.

Choice (B) *distorts* the author's perspective on the topic. Although the author does define the concept of national science, nowhere does the author attempt to dispel or disprove the concept.

Choice (E) *distorts* the author's message and is *too narrow*. Although the author does imply that scientific freedom and scientific internationalism are related, the author makes no attempt to examine their differences.

Now here's a Recap question that focuses on just one paragraph, the second one in Passage 1. An easier question would provide wrong-answer choices that refer to information in the *first* paragraph. But this question is a bit tougher; it doesn't allow you such an easy way to rule out wrong choices.

TIP

The best answer to a Recap question must embrace the whole passage (or paragraph) better than any other choice but not exceed the passage's scope or concerns.

7. The second paragraph as a whole is concerned with
    (A) identifying the problems in assessing the relative significance of various entry pathways for nonindigenous species.
    (B) describing the events usually leading to the detection of a nonindigenous species.
    (C) discussing the role that time lags and geographic expansion of nonindigenous species play in species detection.
    (D) pointing out the inadequacy of the federal port inspection system in detecting the entry of nonindigenous species.
    (E) explaining why it is difficult to trace the entry pathways for long-established nonindigenous species.

In the first sentence of the second paragraph, the author claims that "A number of factors confound quantitative evaluation of the relative importance of various entry pathways." In the remainder of the paragraph, the author identifies three such problems: (1) the difficulty of early detection, (2) the inadequacy of port inspection, and (3) the inherent subjectivity in determining the "importance" of a pathway. Choice (A) provides a good "recap" of what the second paragraph accomplishes. **The correct answer is (A).**

Choice (B) is *too narrow*. Although the author does mention that a species is usually not detected until it spreads to at least 10,000 acres, the author mentions this single "event" leading to detection as part of the broader point that the unlikelihood of early detection contributes to the problem of quantifying the relative importance of entry pathways.

Choice (C) is a *distortion*. Although the author mentions these factors, they are not "discussed" in any detail, as choice (C) suggests. Also, the primary concern of the second paragraph is not with identifying the factors affecting species detection, but rather with identifying the problems in quantifying the relative importance of various entry pathways.

Choice (D) is *too narrow*. The author is concerned with identifying other problems as well as in determining the relative importance of various entry pathways.

Choice (E) is a *distortion*. Although the author asserts that it is difficult to trace an entry pathway once a species is well established, the author does not explain why this is so.

Restatement Questions

In handling a Restatement question, your job is to understand a specific idea the author is trying to convey in the passage. These questions are different from Simple Recall questions in that you won't find the answer explicitly in the text. And it's this feature that makes them more difficult. A Restatement question stem might look something like one of the following:

"Which of the following statements about . . . is most strongly supported by the passage's information?"

"With which of the following statements about . . . would the author most likely agree?"

"Which of the following best characterizes . . . as viewed by . . .?"

Here's a good example of a moderately difficult Restatement question, based on Passage 1. Notice that the wrong-answer choices are designed to confuse you by combining details from the passage that relate to the question but that don't add up.

8. Which of the following statements about species movement is best supported by the passage?
   (A) Species movement is affected more by habitat modifications than by human mobility.
   (B) Human-driven factors affect the rate at which species move more than they affect the long-term amount of such movements.
   (C) Natural expansions in the geographic distribution of species account for less species movement than natural contractions do.
   (D) Natural environments created by commerce, tourism, and travel contribute significantly to species movement.
   (E) Movement of a species within a continent depends largely upon the geographic extent of human mobility within the continent.

Choice (E) restates the author's point in the first paragraph that rates of species movement driven by human transformation of the natural environment and by human mobility dwarf natural rates by comparison. **The correct answer is (E).**

Choice (A) is the most tempting wrong-answer choice. Based on the passage, habitat modifications and human mobility can both affect species movement, as choice (A) implies. And the passage does make a comparison involving human-driven species movement. So choice (A) looks appealing. However, the comparison made in the passage is between natural species movement and human-driven movement, not between human modification of habitats and human mobility. So choice (A) *confuses the details* of the passage.

Choice (B) is easier to eliminate because it is completely *unsupported* by the passage, which makes no attempt to compare rate (interpreted either as frequency or speed) of species movement to total amounts of movement (distance).

Choice (C) is also easier to eliminate than choice (A). It is completely unsupported by the passage. The author makes no attempt to compare natural expansions to natural contractions.

Choice (D) is the easiest one to eliminate. You don't even need to read the passage to recognize that choice (D) is a *nonsensical* statement. Human mobility (commerce, tourism, and travel) do not create "natural" environments. It is human mobility itself, not the "natural environment" created by it, that contributes significantly to species movement.

The following is a good example of how the test-makers might further boost the difficulty level of a Restatement question. As you read this question, which is based on Passage 2, notice that most of the wrong answer choices appear to respond to the question because they describe an "ambiguous position." What's more, most of the answer choices contain information that the passage supports. The use of these two wrong-answer ploys makes this question tougher than average.

9. Which of the following best characterizes the "ambiguous position" in which Soviet scientists were placed during the decades that followed the Bolshevik Revolution?

   (A) The Soviet government demanded that their research result in scientific progress, although funding was insufficient to accomplish this goal.

   (B) They were exhorted to strive toward scientific advancements, while at the same time the freedoms necessary to make such advancements were restricted.

   (C) While they were required to direct research entirely toward military defense, most advancements in this field were being made by non-Soviet scientists with whom the Soviet scientists were prohibited contact.

   (D) They were encouraged to collaborate with Soviet colleagues but were prohibited from any discourse with scientists from other countries.

   (E) The Soviet government failed to identify those areas of research that it deemed most worthwhile, but punished those scientists with whose work it was not satisfied.

According to the passage, the ambiguous position of Soviet scientists was that the Soviet government encouraged and generally supported scientific research, while at the same time imposing significant restrictions upon its scientists. Choice (B) restates this idea.

Choice (C) is the easiest one to eliminate. Choice (C) is wholly *unsupported* by the passage, which neither states nor suggests either assertion made in choice (C), which in any case does not describe an ambiguous situation.

Choice (A) is *unsupported* by the passage. The author neither states nor suggests that the Soviets lacked sufficient funding. If true, choice (A) would indicate an ambiguous position for scientists, although that ambiguity is not the kind referred to in the passage.

Choice (E) is also *unsupported*. Although some Soviet scientists were indeed punished by the government, the author neither states nor implies that the government failed to identify those areas of research that it deemed most worthwhile. If true, choice (E) would indicate an ambiguous position for scientists, but, as with choice (A), the ambiguity described in choice (E) is not the sort referred to in the passage.

Choice (D) is the most tempting wrong-answer choice. It's a better choice than either choice (A) or (E) because the passage supports it, at least implicitly. What's more, choice (D), if true, would present an ambiguous position for Soviet scientists. However, as with choices (A) and (E), the ambiguity that choice (D) describes doesn't reflect the nature of the ambiguity referred to in the passage. **The correct answer is (B).**

Inference Questions

Inference questions test your ability to recognize what the author implies but does not state explicitly. In other words, you are tested on your ability to "read between the lines." To make the inference, you'll need to see a logical connection between two bits of information in the passage (usually in two consecutive sentences) and draw a reasonable conclusion from them.

Inference questions resemble Critical Reading questions: To answer them, you need to distinguish a reasonable, well-supported conclusion from an unreasonable, poorly supported one. But don't expect them to look exactly the same or require the same level of inferential reasoning as Critical Reading questions.

Look for two basic types of Inference questions on the GMAT. One type focuses just on the passage's ideas. Your job is to infer a specific idea from what's stated. The question stem will probably contain some form of the word "infer," as in these examples:

"It can be inferred from the passage that the reason for . . . is that . . ."

"The discussion about . . . most reasonably infers which of the following?"

A second type of Inference question asks you to infer the author's purpose in mentioning a specific idea. Look for a question stem like one of these:

"The author mentions . . . (lines X–X) most probably in order to . . ."

"The example discussed in lines X–X is probably intended to illustrate . . ."

In designing either type of Inference question, the test-makers will often include a runner-up answer choice in which the inference is a bit more speculative than the inference in the best choice. Both of the following questions, based on Passage 2, incorporate this wrong-answer ploy.

10. Which of the following is most reasonably inferable from the passage's first paragraph?
    (A) Expensive research projects such as the particle-accelerator program apply technology that can also be applied toward projects relating to national security.
    (B) Scientific knowledge had become so closely linked with national security that it could no longer be communicated to scientific colleagues without restriction.
    (C) Without free access to new scientific knowledge, scientists in different countries are less able to communicate with one another.
    (D) Governments should de-emphasize scientific projects related to military defense and emphasize instead research that can be shared freely within the international scientific community.
    (E) Government funding of scientific research undermines the ideal of scientific freedom to a greater extent than private funding.

The first two sentences establish that the link between science and national life undermined scientists' freedom to communicate with other scientists. The next sentence points to the channeling of scientific research toward protecting national security as a manifestation of that link. Notice the almost unavoidable inference here—that national security concerns were part of the "national life" that took precedence over scientific freedoms. **The correct answer is (B).**

Choice (E) is the runner up. An argument can be made from the information in the first paragraph that government-funded research is more likely than privately funded research to relate to matters affecting the national security (i.e., military defense). However, this inference is hardly as unavoidable as the one that choice (B) provides, is it? To compete with choice (B), the inference would need additional supporting evidence.

Choice (A) is unsupported. The author implies no connection between the particle-accelerator program and national security.

Choice (C) is nonsensical. Ready access to new scientific knowledge would require ready communication among scientists—not the other way around.

Choice (D) is unsupported. The author neither states nor suggests which areas of scientific research should be emphasized.

11. The author quotes an article from *Literatunaya Gazeta* most probably to
    (A) illustrate the general sentiment among members of the international scientific community during the time period.
    (B) support the point that only those notions about science that conformed to the Marxist-Leninist ideal were sanctioned by the Soviet government.
    (C) show the disparity of views within the Soviet intellectual community regarding the proper role of science.
    (D) underscore the Soviet emphasis on the notion of a national science.
    (E) support the author's assertion that the Marxist-Leninist impact on Soviet scientific freedom continued through the decade of the 1970s.

TIP

For Inference questions, you need to know the difference between a reasonable inference, which no rational person could dispute based on the passage's information, and mere speculation, which requires additional information to hold water.

This part of the passage is concerned exclusively with pointing out evidence of the Soviet emphasis on a national science; given the content of the excerpt from *Literatunaya Gazeta*, you can *reasonably infer* that the author is quoting this article as one such piece of evidence. **The correct answer is (D).**

Choice (A) is easy to rule out because it distorts the nature of the quoted article and runs *contrary* to the passage. The article illustrates the official Soviet position and possibly the sentiment among some members of the Soviet intellectual or scientific community. However, the article does not necessarily reflect the views of scientists from other countries.

Choice (C) is not likely to be the author's purpose in quoting the article, because the author does not discuss disagreement and debate among Soviet intellectuals.

Choice (E) is a bit tempting because it might in fact be true and because it is indeed supported by the information in the passage. But the author gives no indication as to when the article was written or published; thus, the article itself lends no support to choice (E).

Choice (B) is the runner-up choice that helps make this question tougher than it would be otherwise. The quoted article does indeed reflect the Marxist-Leninist ideal (at least as interpreted and promulgated by the government) and may in fact have been published only because it was sanctioned (approved) by the Soviet government. However, since this conclusion would require *speculation* and since the quoted excerpt makes no mention of government approval or disapproval of certain scientific notions, it is not likely that choice (B) expresses the author's purpose in quoting the article.

Method Questions

Method questions ask you to recognize *how* the author goes about making his points—rather than focusing on the points themselves. Some Method questions ask for the author's overall approach in the passage, while others ask how a specific point is made or about the structure of a particular paragraph. In Method questions, the answer choices are usually stated very generally, and it's up to you to connect the general wording of the choices with what's going on in the passage.

A Method question can appear in many different forms. Here are just a few examples of what the question stem might look like:

"Which of the following best describes the approach of the passage?"

"In the last paragraph (lines X–X), the author proceeds by . . ."

"How does the second paragraph function in relation to the first paragraph?"

"Which of the following most accurately describes the organization of the second paragraph (lines X–X)?"

"Which of the following techniques is used in the second paragraph (lines X–X)?"

When you see a Method question, first let the question guide you to the appropriate area of the passage. Your notes or outline might suffice to determine how the author proceeds in making her points there. If not, reread that section carefully. Focus on what the author is doing; don't get bogged down in details. Again, Method questions concern how the author makes points, not what those points are.

Here's the last paragraph of a passage about Francis Bacon, a sixteenth-century philosopher of science. (As a whole, the passage explores the link between his thinking and the modern-day scientific establishment.) Read the paragraph, and then answer the Method question based on it.

No one questions the immense benefits already conferred by science's efficient methodology. However, since individual scientists must now choose between improving standards of living and obtaining financial support for their research, there is cause for concern. In light of current circumstances, we must ask certain questions about science that Francis Bacon, from a sixteenth-century perspective, could not possibly have put to himself.

12. Which of the following most accurately describes the technique that the author employs in the last paragraph of the passage?
   (A) An assertion is made and is backed up by evidence.
   (B) A viewpoint is expressed and an opposing viewpoint is stated and countered.
   (C) An admission is offered and is followed by a warning and recommendation.
   (D) Contradictory claims are presented and then reconciled.
   (E) A problem is outlined and a solution is proposed and defended.

The notion that no one questions the benefits of science does qualify as an admission in the context of the paragraph; that is, the author admits that science has given mankind enormous benefits. The author then goes on to voice his concern regarding the current state of the scientific enterprise. Note how the contrast signal word *however* flags us that some kind of change must come after the author admits that science has conferred immense benefits. Indeed, what comes next is, as choice (C) puts it, a warning: there is cause for concern. A recommendation appears in the final sentence, highlighted by the words "we must ask certain questions . . . ." Every element in choice (C) is present and accounted for, so it aptly describes the technique used in the paragraph. **The correct answer is (C).**

Choice (A) indicates that the paragraph begins with an assertion, and we can surely accept the assertion that no one questions the benefits of science. Is this then backed up by evidence? No. The contrast signal word *however* tells us that some kind of change is coming, but does not provide evidence for the statement in the first sentence. And indeed, the paragraph does go in a different direction.

Choice (B) doesn't reflect what's going on in the paragraph. Choice (B) claims that the final paragraph begins with a viewpoint, which it does. But does an opposing viewpoint follow—that is, an argument against the benefits of science? No; instead, concern is expressed about the way science is now conducted.

Choice (D) is incorrect because there are no contradictory claims here. The author admits that science has given humankind enormous benefits but then goes on to voice his concern regarding the current state of the scientific enterprise. These things aren't contradictory, and nothing in the paragraph reconciles them, so choice (D) can't be the best choice.

As for choice (E), it's fair to say that a problem is outlined. (The problem is that securing financial support for scientific work might get in the way of scientists improving standards of living.) But does the author propose a solution? No. He recommends that serious questions be asked about the problem but offers no solution of his own. And the passage ends before any kind of defense of his recommendation is offered.

Application Questions

These questions, which require you to apply the author's ideas to new situations, usually involve relatively broad inferences. You might be asked to interpret how the author's ideas apply to, or are affected by, other situations. To do this requires you to make logical connections between the author's stated ideas and other ideas not explicitly discussed in the passage. Or, you might be asked to assess the author's attitude (agreement or disagreement) toward some new situation.

Application questions often add or refer to new information, so there's no predictable question stem to look for. But the stem might look something like one of these:

"If it were determined that . . ., what effect would this fact have on the author's assessment of . . . as presented in the passage?"

"Which of the following new discoveries, if it were to occur, would most strongly support the author's theory about . . .?"

"Which of the following is most analogous to the situation of . . . described in the passage?"

In dealing with Application questions:

- Be on the lookout for wrong-answer choices that require you to make an inference not supported by the passage.

- Eliminate answer choices that contradict the author's main idea or position.

- Eliminate answer choices that distort the passage's ideas.

Here's another brief excerpt from a passage about Francis Bacon (the sixteenth-century philosopher of science), along with an Application question based on the excerpt.

Francis Bacon contributed to the scientific enterprise a prophetic understanding of how science would one day be put to use in the service of technology and how this symbiotic relationship between the two would radically impact both man and his surroundings. As inseparable as they are today, it is hard to imagine science and technology as inhabiting separate domains.

13. As discussed in the passage, the relationship between science and technology is best illustrated by which of the following scenarios?

  (A) A biologist writes an article documenting a new strain of influenza that is subsequently published and taught in medical schools around the world.

  (B) A breakthrough in the field of psychology enables psychoanalysts to diagnose patients with greater accuracy.

  (C) An engineering firm hires a public relations agency to advertise the benefits of a labor-saving mechanical device.

  (D) A physics discovery leads to the development of a machine that helps researchers view previously uncharted areas of the ocean floor.

  (E) The development of a new software application helps research scientists isolate genes that are responsible for certain diseases.

If you're not sure what "symbiotic" means, you can figure it out by its context. We're told that science is used to help develop and contribute to technology and that technology also contributes to science. So we need to find the choice that illustrates the same sort of link. Choice (D) fits the bill: A scientific discovery in one area (physics) leads to the invention of a machine (technology) that helps scientists in another field (oceanography) make new discoveries. The interplay between science and technology in this example is a good application of the author's description of "symbiotic relationship." **The correct answer is (D).**

Neither choice (A) nor choice (B) accounts for technology; each involves only science. Since there's nothing in either choice about the interplay between science and technology, neither is as good a choice as (D).

As for choice (C), if there's a symbiotic relationship at work at all in (C), it's between technology (a new mechanical device) and marketing. There's nothing about science here, so this choice doesn't illustrate the interplay between science and technology.

Choice (E) is the runner-up choice. It illustrates how science (genetic research) can benefit from technology (a computer application). But it does not illustrate the reverse relationship—how technology can also benefit from science. So choice (E) does not illustrate as completely as (D) the symbiotic relationship the author describes.

Logical Continuation Questions

In this question type, the test-maker gauges your ability to determine the flow of the discussion and anticipate where it will go beyond the end of the passage—were the passage to continue. A Logical Continuation question stem might look something like one of the following:

  "Which of the following would be the most logical continuation of the passage?"

  "The author would probably continue the discussion by . . ."

To answer a question of this type, it helps to have a general outline of the passage so that you know how it flows and therefore how it would continue to flow. However, just the final few sentences probably provide enough information for you to eliminate some of the wrong-answer choices—and possibly even zero in on the best choice.

In dealing with Logical Continuation questions:

- Focus on the operative word (probably the first word) in each answer choice. This can help you narrow down the choices.

- Be on the lookout for wrong-answer choices that rehash what's already been covered in the passage. Although the discussion is unlikely to reverse course, don't automatically rule out this possibility.

Here's the final paragraph of a passage about the geography of a South American mountain range. Based only on this paragraph, you can narrow down the choices—and probably even hone in on the best one.

> At the regional or macroscale level, vegetation patterns in the Northern and Central Andes tend to reflect climatic zones determined by latitude and altitude. At the local or mesoscale level, however, this correspondence becomes less precise, as local variations in soil type, slope, drainage, climate, and human intervention come into play.

14. Among the following, the passage would most logically continue by
    - **(A)** describing the climate and topography of the portions of the Andean cordillera other than the Northern and Central regions.
    - **(B)** discussing how high- and low-pressure systems affect the climate of the Amazon.
    - **(C)** exploring how proximity to the equator affects vegetation in the Andean cordillera.
    - **(D)** identifying problems in determining the relation between soil type and vegetation in the Andean cordillera.
    - **(E)** examining the effects of vegetation patterns on the topography of the Andean cordillera.

In this paragraph, the author asserts that altitude as well as latitude (proximity to the equator) determines climatic zones as reflected by vegetation patterns. Accordingly, a more detailed discussion about why different forms of vegetation appear at different latitudes is a logical continuation. **The correct answer is (C).**

Choice (D) is the runner-up; it's consistent with the content of the final paragraph, and the author does suggest a relationship between soil type and vegetation (presumably, soil type determines what forms of vegetation will thrive). However, the paragraph neither indicates nor suggests any potential problems in determining such a relationship.

Choices (A) and (B) both ignore the direction of the paragraph.

Choice (E) appears at first glance to be a viable answer because it includes the same subject matter (i.e., vegetation) as the paragraph. However, choice (E) is a bit nonsensical—it is unlikely that vegetation would have much effect upon topography; even if it did, nothing in the paragraph indicates that this is the direction in which the discussion is likely to turn.

Beware: In handling a Logical Continuation question, the passage's final few sentences are sure to help you narrow down the answer choices. But don't ignore the rest of the passage. Check your notes or outline for the flow of ideas from the passage's beginning to its end. The best answer choice should correspond with the overall flow.

TOP 10 WRONG-ANSWER PLOYS

If you read the analysis of each sample question in this chapter carefully, you learned a lot about how the test-makers design wrong-answer choices. Now here's a review of the types they resort to most often:

1. The response distorts the information in the passage. It might understate, overstate, or twist the passage's information or the author's point in presenting that information.

2. The response uses information from the passage but does not answer the question. The information cited from the passage isn't useful to respond to the question at hand.

3. The response relies on speculation or an unsupported inference. It calls for some measure of speculation in that the statement is not readily inferable from the information given.

4. The response is contrary to what the passage says. It contradicts the passage's information or runs contrary to what the passage implies.

5. The response gets something in the passage backwards. It reverses the logic of an idea in the passage, confuses cause with effect, or otherwise turns information in the passage around.

6. The response confuses one opinion or position with another. It incorrectly represents the viewpoint of one person (or group) as that of another.

7. The response is too narrow or specific. It focuses on particular information in the passage that is too specific or narrowly focused in terms of the question posed.

8. The response is too broad (general). It embraces information or ideas that are too general or widely focused in terms of the question posed.

9. The response relies on information that the passage does not mention. It brings in information not found anywhere in the passage.

10. The response is utter nonsense. It makes almost no logical sense in the context of the question; it's essentially gibberish.

KEYS TO SUCCESSFUL GMAT READING COMPREHENSION: THE BASICS

We've covered a lot of ground in this chapter. To help you assimilate it all, here's a checklist of the most salient advice for improving your reading efficiency and comprehension as you read GMAT passages. Apply them to the Practice Tests in Part VII and then review them again just before exam day.

Take Notes and Make Outlines

As you're reading, make notes to summarize paragraphs or indicate the flow of the passage's discussion. Keep your notes brief, jotting down just enough key words to remind you of the particular idea. For complicated or high-density passages, an outline is a good way to organize information and to keep details straight in your mind.

Pause Occasionally to Sum Up and Anticipate

After you read each logical "block" (perhaps after each paragraph), pause briefly to evaluate the paragraph as a whole. Try to recapitulate or summarize the paragraph as two or three basic ideas. After each paragraph, answer the following questions for yourself:

- How would I sum up the discussion to this point?
- At what point is the discussion now?
- What basic points is the author trying to get across in this paragraph? Do these ideas continue a line of thought or do they begin a new one?
- Where is the discussion likely to go from here?

Pay Attention to the Overall Structure of the Passage

Different types of reading passages are organized in various ways. The passage might be organized as a chronology of events, a critique of a theory, a comparison of two or more things, or a classification system. Understanding how the passage is organized—in other words, recognizing its structure—will help you to articulate the passage's main idea and primary purpose, understand the author's purpose in mentioning various details, and distinguish between main points and minor details. And all of these will in turn help you answer the questions.

Look for Structural Clues or "Triggers"

As you read a passage, be on the lookout for trigger words. They'll help you see the passage's structure and follow the author's train of thought.

Don't Get Bogged Down in Details

GMAT reading passages are packed with details: lists, statistics and other numbers, dates, titles, and so forth. Don't try to absorb all of the details as you read; you'll not only lose sight of the main points, but you'll also lose reading speed. On your scratch paper, note where particular examples, lists, and other details are located. Then, if a particular question involving those details is included, you can quickly and easily locate them and read them more carefully.

Sum Up the Passage After You Read It

After reading the entire passage, take a few seconds to recap it. What was the author's main point and what were the major supporting points? Remind yourself of the flow of the discussion without thinking about all the details. Chances are you'll be able to answer at least one or two of the questions based just on your recap.

Don't Bother Previewing Unless You're Short on Time

So-called previewing (skimming a passage or reading just the first and last few sentences of the passage) might allow you to make educated guesses and to answer certain detail questions, but use this strategy only if you're running out of time.

Try to Minimize Vertical Scrolling

You'll need to scroll to read the entire passage. But scrolling to reread the passage uses up valuable time and contributes to eyestrain and fatigue. The best way to minimize rereading (and scrolling) is to take good notes.

KEYS TO SUCCESSFUL GMAT READING COMPREHENSION: ADVANCED TECHNIQUES

Here are a few more tips for successfully applying advanced techniques to solving Reading Comprehension problems. As with the basic tips, try to apply them when you take the Practice Tests in Part VII of this book; then review them again just before exam day.

Don't Second-Guess the Test-Maker

The directions for the GMAT Reading Comprehension sets instruct you to choose the "best" among the five answer choices. While there is an element of subjective judgment involved in reading comprehension, GMAT questions are reviewed, tested, and revised several times before they appear as scored questions on an actual GMAT. If you think there are two or more viable "best" choices, it's likely that you—and not the test-designers—have misread or misinterpreted the passage, the question, or the answer choices.

Read Every Answer Choice in Its Entirety

As you know, you're looking for the "best" answer choice. Often, more than one choice will be viable. Don't hastily select or eliminate answer choices without reading them all. GMAT test-takers miss more questions for this reason than for any other.

Don't Overanalyze Questions or Second-Guess Yourself

If you believe you understood the passage fairly well but a particular answer choice seems confusing or a bit nonsensical, do not assume that it's your fault. Many wrong-answer choices simply don't make sense. If an answer choice strikes you this way, don't examine it further; eliminate it. Similarly, if you've read and considered all five choices, and one strikes you as the best one, more often than not your initial hunch will be correct.

Don't Overlook the Obvious

Reading Comprehension questions vary in difficulty level, and this means that many of the questions are rather easy. If a particular choice seems obviously correct or incorrect, don't assume that you are missing something. You might simply have come across a relatively easy question.

Eliminate Answer Choices That Are Inconsistent with the Main Idea

Regardless of the type of question you are dealing with, keep in mind the overall thesis, main idea, or point that the author is making in the passage as a whole. You can safely eliminate any answer choice that runs contrary to or is inconsistent with that thesis. You may be surprised how many questions can be answered correctly using only this guideline.

Be Alert to the Test-Makers' Favorite Wrong-Answer Ploys

Keep a mental list of the wrong-answer ploys you learned about in this chapter. When you have trouble narrowing down the answer choices, review this list in your mind. The remaining wrong answers should reveal themselves.

SUMMING IT UP

- With Reading Comprehension questions, ask yourself what the passage's main thesis is; how each part of the passage relates to the main idea and author's overall purpose; and what the author's line of reasoning is. Keeping an "active" mindset while reading will help you understand questions better and score higher.

- To get a good handle on what you need to answer the GMAT Reading Comprehension questions, first try to figure out the basic structure of the passage and how it conveys its main ideas.

- Take notes and make outlines—you'll save time in the long run and the notes will help you organize your thoughts.

- Watch for wrong-answer ploys that may throw you off the track. Your clues are responses that distort the information in the passage, cite information that doesn't answer the question at hand, rely on speculation, run contrary to or reverse what the passage says, confuse opinions, are too broad or too narrow, rely on outside information, or are nonsensical.

PART VII

FIVE PRACTICE TESTS

ANSWER SHEET PRACTICE TEST 2

ANALYTICAL WRITING ASSESSMENT

_____

_____

_____

_____

_____

_____

_____

_____

_____

_____

_____

_____

_____

_____

_____

_____

_____

_____

_____

_____

_____

_____

answer sheet

answer sheet

INTEGRATED REASONING

1.1 Ⓐ Ⓑ Ⓒ Ⓓ Ⓔ Ⓕ   4.1 Ⓐ Ⓑ Ⓒ Ⓓ Ⓔ Ⓕ   7.1 Ⓐ Ⓑ   10.1 Ⓐ Ⓑ Ⓒ Ⓓ
1.2 Ⓐ Ⓑ Ⓒ Ⓓ Ⓔ Ⓕ   4.2 Ⓐ Ⓑ Ⓒ Ⓓ Ⓔ Ⓕ   7.2 Ⓐ Ⓑ   10.2 Ⓐ Ⓑ Ⓒ
2.1 Ⓐ Ⓑ   5.1 Ⓐ Ⓑ Ⓒ Ⓓ Ⓔ Ⓕ   7.3 Ⓐ Ⓑ   11.1 Ⓐ Ⓑ Ⓒ Ⓓ
2.2 Ⓐ Ⓑ   5.2 Ⓐ Ⓑ Ⓒ Ⓓ Ⓔ Ⓕ   8. Ⓐ Ⓑ Ⓒ Ⓓ Ⓔ   11.2 Ⓐ Ⓑ Ⓒ Ⓓ
2.3 Ⓐ Ⓑ   6.1 Ⓐ Ⓑ   9.1 Ⓐ Ⓑ   12.1 Ⓐ Ⓑ Ⓒ Ⓓ
3.1 Ⓐ Ⓑ Ⓒ Ⓓ Ⓔ   6.2 Ⓐ Ⓑ   9.2 Ⓐ Ⓑ   12.2 Ⓐ Ⓑ Ⓒ Ⓓ
3.2 Ⓐ Ⓑ Ⓒ Ⓓ Ⓔ   6.3 Ⓐ Ⓑ   9.3 Ⓐ Ⓑ

QUANTITATIVE SECTION

1. Ⓐ Ⓑ Ⓒ Ⓓ Ⓔ   9. Ⓐ Ⓑ Ⓒ Ⓓ Ⓔ   17. Ⓐ Ⓑ Ⓒ Ⓓ Ⓔ   25. Ⓐ Ⓑ Ⓒ Ⓓ Ⓔ   33. Ⓐ Ⓑ Ⓒ Ⓓ Ⓔ
2. Ⓐ Ⓑ Ⓒ Ⓓ Ⓔ   10. Ⓐ Ⓑ Ⓒ Ⓓ Ⓔ   18. Ⓐ Ⓑ Ⓒ Ⓓ Ⓔ   26. Ⓐ Ⓑ Ⓒ Ⓓ Ⓔ   34. Ⓐ Ⓑ Ⓒ Ⓓ Ⓔ
3. Ⓐ Ⓑ Ⓒ Ⓓ Ⓔ   11. Ⓐ Ⓑ Ⓒ Ⓓ Ⓔ   19. Ⓐ Ⓑ Ⓒ Ⓓ Ⓔ   27. Ⓐ Ⓑ Ⓒ Ⓓ Ⓔ   35. Ⓐ Ⓑ Ⓒ Ⓓ Ⓔ
4. Ⓐ Ⓑ Ⓒ Ⓓ Ⓔ   12. Ⓐ Ⓑ Ⓒ Ⓓ Ⓔ   20. Ⓐ Ⓑ Ⓒ Ⓓ Ⓔ   28. Ⓐ Ⓑ Ⓒ Ⓓ Ⓔ   36. Ⓐ Ⓑ Ⓒ Ⓓ Ⓔ
5. Ⓐ Ⓑ Ⓒ Ⓓ Ⓔ   13. Ⓐ Ⓑ Ⓒ Ⓓ Ⓔ   21. Ⓐ Ⓑ Ⓒ Ⓓ Ⓔ   29. Ⓐ Ⓑ Ⓒ Ⓓ Ⓔ   37. Ⓐ Ⓑ Ⓒ Ⓓ Ⓔ
6. Ⓐ Ⓑ Ⓒ Ⓓ Ⓔ   14. Ⓐ Ⓑ Ⓒ Ⓓ Ⓔ   22. Ⓐ Ⓑ Ⓒ Ⓓ Ⓔ   30. Ⓐ Ⓑ Ⓒ Ⓓ Ⓔ
7. Ⓐ Ⓑ Ⓒ Ⓓ Ⓔ   15. Ⓐ Ⓑ Ⓒ Ⓓ Ⓔ   23. Ⓐ Ⓑ Ⓒ Ⓓ Ⓔ   31. Ⓐ Ⓑ Ⓒ Ⓓ Ⓔ
8. Ⓐ Ⓑ Ⓒ Ⓓ Ⓔ   16. Ⓐ Ⓑ Ⓒ Ⓓ Ⓔ   24. Ⓐ Ⓑ Ⓒ Ⓓ Ⓔ   32. Ⓐ Ⓑ Ⓒ Ⓓ Ⓔ

VERBAL SECTION

1. Ⓐ Ⓑ Ⓒ Ⓓ Ⓔ   9. Ⓐ Ⓑ Ⓒ Ⓓ Ⓔ   17. Ⓐ Ⓑ Ⓒ Ⓓ Ⓔ   25. Ⓐ Ⓑ Ⓒ Ⓓ Ⓔ   33. Ⓐ Ⓑ Ⓒ Ⓓ Ⓔ
2. Ⓐ Ⓑ Ⓒ Ⓓ Ⓔ   10. Ⓐ Ⓑ Ⓒ Ⓓ Ⓔ   18. Ⓐ Ⓑ Ⓒ Ⓓ Ⓔ   26. Ⓐ Ⓑ Ⓒ Ⓓ Ⓔ   34. Ⓐ Ⓑ Ⓒ Ⓓ Ⓔ
3. Ⓐ Ⓑ Ⓒ Ⓓ Ⓔ   11. Ⓐ Ⓑ Ⓒ Ⓓ Ⓔ   19. Ⓐ Ⓑ Ⓒ Ⓓ Ⓔ   27. Ⓐ Ⓑ Ⓒ Ⓓ Ⓔ   35. Ⓐ Ⓑ Ⓒ Ⓓ Ⓔ
4. Ⓐ Ⓑ Ⓒ Ⓓ Ⓔ   12. Ⓐ Ⓑ Ⓒ Ⓓ Ⓔ   20. Ⓐ Ⓑ Ⓒ Ⓓ Ⓔ   28. Ⓐ Ⓑ Ⓒ Ⓓ Ⓔ   36. Ⓐ Ⓑ Ⓒ Ⓓ Ⓔ
5. Ⓐ Ⓑ Ⓒ Ⓓ Ⓔ   13. Ⓐ Ⓑ Ⓒ Ⓓ Ⓔ   21. Ⓐ Ⓑ Ⓒ Ⓓ Ⓔ   29. Ⓐ Ⓑ Ⓒ Ⓓ Ⓔ   37. Ⓐ Ⓑ Ⓒ Ⓓ Ⓔ
6. Ⓐ Ⓑ Ⓒ Ⓓ Ⓔ   14. Ⓐ Ⓑ Ⓒ Ⓓ Ⓔ   22. Ⓐ Ⓑ Ⓒ Ⓓ Ⓔ   30. Ⓐ Ⓑ Ⓒ Ⓓ Ⓔ   38. Ⓐ Ⓑ Ⓒ Ⓓ Ⓔ
7. Ⓐ Ⓑ Ⓒ Ⓓ Ⓔ   15. Ⓐ Ⓑ Ⓒ Ⓓ Ⓔ   23. Ⓐ Ⓑ Ⓒ Ⓓ Ⓔ   31. Ⓐ Ⓑ Ⓒ Ⓓ Ⓔ   39. Ⓐ Ⓑ Ⓒ Ⓓ Ⓔ
8. Ⓐ Ⓑ Ⓒ Ⓓ Ⓔ   16. Ⓐ Ⓑ Ⓒ Ⓓ Ⓔ   24. Ⓐ Ⓑ Ⓒ Ⓓ Ⓔ   32. Ⓐ Ⓑ Ⓒ Ⓓ Ⓔ   40. Ⓐ Ⓑ Ⓒ Ⓓ Ⓔ
   41. Ⓐ Ⓑ Ⓒ Ⓓ Ⓔ

answer sheet

Practice Test 2

ANALYTICAL WRITING ASSIGNMENT

Analysis of an Argument

1 Question • 30 Minutes

Directions: Using a word processor, compose an essay for the following argument and directive. Do not use any spell-checking or grammar-checking functions.

The following appeared as part of an article in a national business publication:

> "In order to prevent a decline of Oak City's property values and in rents that Oak City property owners can command, the residents of Oak City must speak out against the approval of a new four-year private college in their town. After all, in the nearby town of Mapleton the average rent for apartments has decreased by ten percent since its new community college opened last year, while the average value of Mapleton's single-family homes has declined by an even greater percentage over the same time period."

Discuss how well reasoned you find this argument. In your discussion be sure to analyze the line of reasoning and the use of evidence in the argument. For example, you may need to consider what questionable assumptions underlie the thinking and what alternative explanations or counterexamples might weaken the conclusion. You can also discuss what sort of evidence would strengthen or refute the argument, what changes in the argument would make it more logically sound, and what, if anything, would help you better evaluate its conclusion.

INTEGRATED REASONING

12 Questions • 30 Minutes

1. During a lottery, several lots are to be selected. *A* is the event that a certain subset of these lots is selected, and *B* is the event that another subset of these lots is selected, such that:

- the probability of event *A* occurring is $\dfrac{2}{5}$.

- the probability of event *B* occurring is $\dfrac{4}{5}$.

- the probability of the union of events *A* and *B* occurring is 1.

- the intersection of events *A* and *B* is an event with four desirable outcomes.

In the following table, identify the total number of lots and the number of desirable outcomes in event *B*. Make only one selection in each column.

1.1	Number of lots	1.2	Desirable outcomes in *B*	
(A)	○	(A)	○	15
(B)	○	(B)	○	16
(C)	○	(C)	○	17
(D)	○	(D)	○	18
(E)	○	(E)	○	19
(F)	○	(F)	○	20

2. The table gives information about a state's ski resorts. The "% Beginner" and "% Expert" columns refer to each resort's runs. Omitted is the percent of each resort's runs that are rated "Intermediate," which is all runs that are rated neither "Beginner" nor "Expert."

Sort By: Select ▼

Resort	Base Elevation (meters)	Summit Elevation (meters)	Number of Runs	% Beginner	% Expert	Number of Lifts	Total Lift Capacity (skiers/ hour)	Hours of Operation, Daily
Bald Eagle	2118	3094	102	19	33	16	31,300	9 a.m.– 4 p.m.
Brenton	2791	3438	81	23	34	8	11,300	9 a.m.– 4 p.m.
Condor	2444	3612	94	23	35	12	18,100	9 a.m.– 4:30 p.m.
Emperor	1958	2939	119	24	30	19	37,700	9 a.m.– 5 p.m.
Foxx	2863	3950	161	14	49	29	38,400	9 a.m.– 4:30 p.m.
Gentle Giant	2668	3352	109	23	32	9	14,300	9 a.m.– 4:30 p.m.
Olympian	2257	2814	141	21	40	10	9750	9 a.m.– 5 p.m.
Powder Peak	2151	2719	54	21	47	6	8200	9 a.m.– 4 p.m.
Slopes	2026	3138	174	14	46	24	34,650	9 a.m.– 4 p.m.

For each of the following statements, select *Yes* if the statement is true based on the information in the table. Otherwise, select *No*.

	(A) Yes	(B) No	
2.1	○	○	The resort with the greatest vertical rise (defined as the difference between summit elevation and base elevation) also has the most runs.
2.2	○	○	The resort with the greatest percentage of Expert runs has the smallest number of Beginner runs.
2.3	○	○	The maximum number of skiers who can use Emperor resort's lifts during a full day is greater than the number for any other resort.

(On the computer test, this will be the end of the question prompt and statements. For this paper test and your convenience, we are providing the various other ways you may sort the data.)

Sort By: | Base Elevation ▼ |

Resort	Base Elevation (meters)	Summit Elevation (meters)	Number of Runs	% Beginner	% Expert	Number of Lifts	Total Lift Capacity (skiers/ hour)	Hours of Operation, Daily
Emperor	1958	2939	119	24	30	19	37,700	9 a.m.– 5 p.m.
Slopes	2026	3138	174	14	46	24	34,650	9 a.m.– 4 p.m.
Bald Eagle	2118	3094	102	19	33	16	31,300	9 a.m.– 4 p.m.
Powder Peak	2151	2719	54	21	47	6	8200	9 a.m.– 4 p.m.
Olympian	2257	2814	141	21	40	10	9750	9 a.m.– 5 p.m.
Condor	2444	3612	94	23	35	12	18,100	9 a.m.– 4:30 p.m.
Gentle Giant	2668	3352	109	23	32	9	14,300	9 a.m.– 4:30 p.m.
Brenton	2791	3438	81	23	34	8	11,300	9 a.m.– 4 p.m.
Foxx	2863	3950	161	14	49	29	38,400	9 a.m.– 4:30 p.m.

Sort By: | Summit Elevation ▼ |

Resort	Base Elevation (meters)	Summit Elevation (meters)	Number of Runs	% Beginner	% Expert	Number of Lifts	Total Lift Capacity (skiers/ hour)	Hours of Operation, Daily
Powder Peak	2151	2719	54	21	47	6	8200	9 a.m.– 4 p.m.
Olympian	2257	2814	141	21	40	10	9750	9 a.m.– 5 p.m.
Emperor	1958	2939	119	24	30	19	37,700	9 a.m.– 5 p.m.
Bald Eagle	2118	3094	102	19	33	16	31,300	9 a.m.– 4 p.m.
Slopes	2026	3138	174	14	46	24	34,650	9 a.m.– 4 p.m.
Gentle Giant	2668	3352	109	23	32	9	14,300	9 a.m.– 4:30 p.m.
Brenton	2791	3438	81	23	34	8	11,300	9 a.m.– 4 p.m.

Condor	2444	3612	94	23	35	12	18,100	9 a.m.–4:30 p.m.
Foxx	2863	3950	161	14	49	29	38,400	9 a.m.–4:30 p.m.

Sort By: Number of Runs ▼

Resort	Base Elevation (meters)	Summit Elevation (meters)	Number of Runs	% Beginner	% Expert	Number of Lifts	Total Lift Capacity (skiers/hour)	Hours of Operation, Daily
Powder Peak	2151	2719	54	21	47	6	8200	9 a.m.–4 p.m.
Brenton	2791	3438	81	23	34	8	11,300	9 a.m.–4 p.m.
Condor	2444	3612	94	23	35	12	18,100	9 a.m.–4:30 p.m.
Bald Eagle	2118	3094	102	19	33	16	31,300	9 a.m.–4 p.m.
Gentle Giant	2668	3352	109	23	32	9	14,300	9 a.m.–4:30 p.m.
Emperor	1958	2939	119	24	30	19	37,700	9 a.m.–5 p.m.
Olympian	2257	2814	141	21	40	10	9750	9 a.m.–5 p.m.
Foxx	2863	3950	161	14	49	29	38,400	9 a.m.–4:30 p.m.
Slopes	2026	3138	174	14	46	24	34,650	9 a.m.–4 p.m.

Sort By: % Beginner ▼

Resort	Base Elevation (meters)	Summit Elevation (meters)	Number of Runs	% Beginner	% Expert	Number of Lifts	Total Lift Capacity (skiers/hour)	Hours of Operation, Daily
Slopes	2026	3138	174	14	46	24	34,650	9 a.m.–4 p.m.
Foxx	2863	3950	161	14	49	29	38,400	9 a.m.–4:30 p.m.
Bald Eagle	2118	3094	102	19	33	16	31,300	9 a.m.–4 p.m.

Powder Peak	2151	2719	54	21	47	6	8200	9 a.m.–4 p.m.
Olympian	2257	2814	141	21	40	10	9750	9 a.m.–5 p.m.
Brenton	2791	3438	81	23	34	8	11,300	9 a.m.–4 p.m.
Condor	2444	3612	94	23	35	12	18,100	9 a.m.–4:30 p.m.
Gentle Giant	2668	3352	109	23	32	9	14,300	9 a.m.–4:30 p.m.
Emperor	1958	2939	119	24	30	19	37,700	9 a.m.–5 p.m.

Sort By: % Expert ▼

Resort	Base Elevation (meters)	Summit Elevation (meters)	Number of Runs	% Beginner	% Expert	Number of Lifts	Total Lift Capacity (skiers/hour)	Hours of Operation, Daily
Emperor	1958	2939	119	24	30	19	37,700	9 a.m.–5 p.m.
Gentle Giant	2668	3352	109	23	32	9	14,300	9 a.m.–4:30 p.m.
Bald Eagle	2118	3094	102	19	33	16	31,300	9 a.m.–4 p.m.
Brenton	2791	3438	81	23	34	8	11,300	9 a.m.–4 p.m.
Condor	2444	3612	94	23	35	12	18,100	9 a.m.–4:30 p.m.
Olympian	2257	2814	141	21	40	10	9750	9 a.m.–5 p.m.
Slopes	2026	3138	174	14	46	24	34,650	9 a.m.–4 p.m.
Powder Peak	2151	2719	54	21	47	6	8200	9 a.m.–4 p.m.
Foxx	2863	3950	161	14	49	29	38,400	9 a.m.–4:30 p.m.

Sort By: | Number of Lifts ▼ |

Resort	Base Elevation (meters)	Summit Elevation (meters)	Number of Runs	% Beginner	% Expert	Number of Lifts	Total Lift Capacity (skiers/ hour)	Hours of Operation, Daily
Powder Peak	2151	2719	54	21	47	6	8200	9 a.m.– 4 p.m.
Brenton	2791	3438	81	23	34	8	11,300	9 a.m.– 4 p.m.
Gentle Giant	2668	3352	109	23	32	9	14,300	9 a.m.– 4:30 p.m.
Olympian	2257	2814	141	21	40	10	9750	9 a.m.– 5 p.m.
Condor	2444	3612	94	23	35	12	18,100	9 a.m.– 4:30 p.m.
Bald Eagle	2118	3094	102	19	33	16	31,300	9 a.m.– 4 p.m.
Emperor	1958	2939	119	24	30	19	37,700	9 a.m.– 5 p.m.
Slopes	2026	3138	174	14	46	24	34,650	9 a.m.– 4 p.m.
Foxx	2863	3950	161	14	49	29	38,400	9 a.m.– 4:30 p.m.

Sort By: | Total Lift Capacity ▼ |

Resort	Base Elevation (meters)	Summit Elevation (meters)	Number of Runs	% Beginner	% Expert	Number of Lifts	Total Lift Capacity (skiers/ hour)	Hours of Operation, Daily
Powder Peak	2151	2719	54	21	47	6	8200	9 a.m.– 4 p.m.
Olympian	2257	2814	141	21	40	10	9750	9 a.m.– 5 p.m.
Brenton	2791	3438	81	23	34	8	11,300	9 a.m.– 4 p.m.
Gentle Giant	2668	3352	109	23	32	9	14,300	9 a.m.– 4:30 p.m.
Condor	2444	3612	94	23	35	12	18,100	9 a.m.– 4:30 p.m.
Bald Eagle	2118	3094	102	19	33	16	31,300	9 a.m.– 4 p.m.

Slopes	2026	3138	174	14	46	24	34,650	9 a.m.–4 p.m.
Emperor	1958	2939	119	24	30	19	37,700	9 a.m.–5 p.m.
Foxx	2863	3950	161	14	49	29	38,400	9 a.m.–4:30 p.m.

Sort By: Hours of Operation ▼

Resort	Base Elevation (meters)	Summit Elevation (meters)	Number of Runs	% Beginner	% Expert	Number of Lifts	Total Lift Capacity (skiers/hour)	Hours of Operation, Daily
Powder Peak	2151	2719	54	21	47	6	8200	9 a.m.–4 p.m.
Brenton	2791	3438	81	23	34	8	11,300	9 a.m.–4 p.m.
Bald Eagle	2118	3094	102	19	33	16	31,300	9 a.m.–4 p.m.
Slopes	2026	3138	174	14	46	24	34,650	9 a.m.–4 p.m.
Gentle Giant	2668	3352	109	23	32	9	14,300	9 a.m.–4:30 p.m.
Condor	2444	3612	94	23	35	12	18,100	9 a.m.–4:30 p.m.
Foxx	2863	3950	161	14	49	29	38,400	9 a.m.–4:30 p.m.
Olympian	2257	2814	141	21	40	10	9750	9 a.m.–5 p.m.
Emperor	1958	2939	119	24	30	19	37,700	9 a.m.–5 p.m.

3. A prominent entertainment analyst has predicted that the family drama film *Prime Meridian* will have weak box office revenue during its theatrical run. On the one hand, it will open the same weekend as two big-budget films: the highly anticipated action-adventure *Blowtorch* and the sequel to the very successful comedy *Animal Pleasures*. On the other, on its opening week it is scheduled to be shown on only half as many movie screens as *Animal Pleasures*, so its earning potential is limited.

Select *Strengthen* for the statement that, if true, would most strengthen the analyst's argument, and select *Weaken* for the statement that, if true, would most weaken the analyst's argument. Make only two selections, one in each column.

3.1 Strengthen	3.2 Weaken	
(A)	(A)	Family dramas have historically not performed well at the box office when competing against big-budget action-adventures.
(B)	(B)	*Blowtorch* is expected to have higher box office revenues than *Animal Pleasures*.
(C)	(C)	The last two films by the *Prime Meridian* lead actor did very well in DVD sales, rentals, and online downloads.
(D)	(D)	After the first week, the number of movie screens on which *Prime Meridian* is shown will be doubled.
(E)	(E)	Sequels do not always match the box office success of the original films.

4. *Wildlife expert:* Cheetahs face many threats. They have poor immune systems and low fertility rates. They have evolved great speed, but at the expense of muscle and stamina, so they often cannot defend their kill or their young against other large predators, such as lions and hyenas. Meanwhile, the greatest danger for adult cheetahs comes from farmers, who view the cats as a threat to their livestock, so they have been killing them in great numbers over the past few decades. As a result, cheetah populations have been decreasing precipitously, and the species will be extinct in the wild within a few years.

Indicate two different statements as follows: one statement identifies an *assumption required* by the wildlife expert's argument, and the other identifies a *possible fact* that, if true, would provide significant logical support for the required assumption.

4.1 Assumption	4.2 Fact	
(A)	(A)	A viral disease will decimate the remaining cheetah population in the coming years.
(B)	(B)	The Thomson's gazelle, which is one of the cheetah's favorite prey animals, has had its grazing territory diminished by the expansion of farmland.
(C)	(C)	Farmers have resisted efforts by wildlife experts to get the farmers not to kill cheetahs, but rather protect their livestock by using guard dogs to scare cheetahs away.
(D)	(D)	Lion populations have been declining steadily over the past few decades.
(E)	(E)	Conservation efforts will not succeed in reversing the decline of cheetah populations in the wild.
(F)	(F)	Efforts to breed cheetahs in captivity will not be successful.

5. Marcel is taking a trip, driving at a constant speed of X miles per hour for the first 2 hours of his trip, and at a constant speed of Y miles per hour after the first 2 hours.

In terms of X and Y, select the expression that represents Marcel's average speed if he drives for a total of 5 hours, and select the expression that represents Marcel's average speed if he drives for a total of $5X$ miles. Make only one selection in each column.

5.1 Average speed over 5 hours	5.2 Average speed over $5X$ miles	
(A)	(A)	$\dfrac{3Y}{5}$
(B)	(B)	$\dfrac{3X + 2Y}{5}$
(C)	(C)	$\dfrac{2X + 3Y}{5}$
(D)	(D)	$\dfrac{5XY}{2Y + 3X}$
(E)	(E)	$\dfrac{5XY}{2X + 3Y}$
(F)	(F)	$\dfrac{5XY}{3X}$

6. The table shows the number of U.S. workers 25 years and older in terms of their level of education for the years 2006 and 2010, as well as the median earnings of these workers for the years 2006 to 2010.

Sort By: [Select   ▼]

Group, by Educational Attainment	Number (in thousands)		Median Earnings (in 2010 dollars)				
	2006	2010	2006	2007	2008	2009	2010
Less than 9th grade	1596	1417	$15,632	$15,220	$13,760	$14,187	$13,509
9th to 12th grade, nongraduate	3219	2615	$16,396	$16,166	$14,893	$15,934	$15,650
High school graduate	17,751	16,165	$23,368	$23,510	$22,580	$22,839	$22,452
Some college, no degree	11,557	11,301	$28,407	$28,574	$26,778	$27,276	$26,615
Associate's degree	7071	7774	$31,459	$32,126	$31,255	$31,103	$31,537
Bachelor's degree or more	21,219	23,096	$45,156	$44,554	$44,927	$45,224	$45,232

For each of the following statements, select *Yes* if the statement can be shown to be true based on the information in the table. Otherwise, select *No*.

	(A)	(B)	
	Yes	No	
6.1	○	○	In 2010, more workers had not attended college as workers had a bachelor's degree or more.
6.2	○	○	The probability that a group's median earnings decreased between 2006 and 2010 is lower than 70%.
6.3	○	○	The group that experienced the greatest percentage change (increase or decrease) in number of earners between 2006 and 2010 was the "High school graduate" group.

(On the computer test, this will be the end of the question prompt and statements. For this paper test and your convenience, we are providing you the various other ways you may sort the data.)

Sort By: | Number with Earnings ▼ |

Group, by Educational Attainment	Number (in thousands)		Median Earnings (in 2010 dollars)				
	2006	2010	2006	2007	2008	2009	2010
Less than 9th grade	1596	1417	$15,632	$15,220	$13,760	$14,187	$13,509
9th to 12th grade, nongraduate	3219	2615	$16,396	$16,166	$14,893	$15,934	$15,650
Associate's degree	7071	7774	$31,459	$32,126	$31,255	$31,103	$31,537
Some college, no degree	11,557	11,301	$28,407	$28,574	$26,778	$27,276	$26,615
High school graduate	17,751	16,165	$23,368	$23,510	$22,580	$22,839	$22,452
Bachelor's degree or more	21,219	23,096	$45,156	$44,554	$44,927	$45,224	$45,232

Sort By: | Median Earnings ▼ |

Group, by Educational Attainment	Number (in thousands)		Median Earnings (in 2010 dollars)				
	2006	2010	2006	2007	2008	2009	2010
Less than 9th grade	1596	1417	$15,632	$15,220	$13,760	$14,187	$13,509
9th to 12th grade, nongraduate	3219	2615	$16,396	$16,166	$14,893	$15,934	$15,650
High school graduate	17,751	16,165	$23,368	$23,510	$22,580	$22,839	$22,452
Some college, no degree	11,557	11,301	$28,407	$28,574	$26,778	$27,276	$26,615
Associate's degree	7071	7774	$31,459	$32,126	$31,255	$31,103	$31,537
Bachelor's degree or more	21,219	23,096	$45,156	$44,554	$44,927	$45,224	$45,232

7.

| Class Agent | Financial Aid |

Letter by Class Agent.

Dear fellow alumni,

As we approach the 10th anniversary of our college graduation, I am reminded of all the things that made our time in college special: our idyllic campus, the academic rigor fostered by our exceptional faculty, and, above all, the excellence and diversity of the student body.

As you know, the College is committed to maintaining this diversity and the rigorous education its students receive, even in the face of rising costs. While other institutions, in order to combat these costs, have expanded their student classes so that they could increase their overall tuition revenues, our alma mater has resisted such student growth, choosing instead to safeguard its preciously low student-to-faculty ratio—which is a great benefit for students. With a total enrollment of 1600 students in 2010, the College remains one of the smallest liberal arts schools of its kind. Furthermore, the College has increased its average financial aid package every year over the past 25 years, and has offered this aid to an increasing percentage of its student population, in order to ensure that all deserving students can afford to attend, regardless of their financial circumstances.

This commitment to the students must be financed somehow. This is where we come in: the Alumni Fund directly supports student financial aid. In 2010, 46% of our class of 320 members contributed to the fund, and the total donations were enough to finance exactly two-thirds of one financial aid package. This year we have set a goal of 55% participation. Will you join me in helping today's bright students afford the same excellent education that we received?

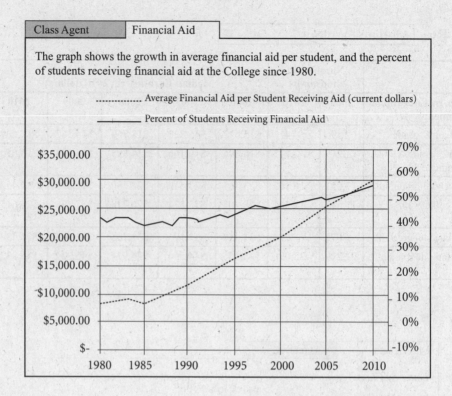

| Class Agent | Financial Aid |

The graph shows the growth in average financial aid per student, and the percent of students receiving financial aid at the College since 1980.

·············· Average Financial Aid per Student Receiving Aid (current dollars)

————— Percent of Students Receiving Financial Aid

For each of the following statements, select *Yes* if the statement is reasonably inferable from the information provided. Otherwise, select *No*.

	(A) Yes	(B) No	
7.1	○	○	If in 2011 the average financial aid package is the same as it was in 2010, the class of '02 will fund a full scholarship if half the members of the class contribute at least $187.50 on average.
7.2	○	○	The total amount that the class of '02 contributed to the Annual Fund in 2010 would have been sufficient to fund one full scholarship in 2000.
7.3	○	○	165 of the members of the class of '02 contributed to the Alumni Fund in 2010.

8.

| Class Agent | Financial Aid |

Letter by Class Agent.

Dear fellow alumni,

As we approach the 10th anniversary of our college graduation, I am reminded of all the things that made our time in college special: our idyllic campus, the academic rigor fostered by our exceptional faculty, and, above all, the excellence and diversity of the student body.

As you know, the College is committed to maintaining this diversity and the rigorous education its students receive, even in the face of rising costs. While other institutions, in order to combat these costs, have expanded their student classes so that they could increase their overall tuition revenues, our alma mater has resisted such student growth, choosing instead to safeguard its preciously low student-to-faculty ratio—which is a great benefit for students. With a total enrollment of 1600 students in 2010, the College remains one of the smallest liberal arts schools of its kind. Furthermore, the College has increased its average financial aid package every year over the past 25 years, and has offered this aid to an increasing percentage of its student population, in order to ensure that all deserving students can afford to attend, regardless of their financial circumstances.

This commitment to the students must be financed somehow. This is where we come in: the Alumni Fund directly supports student financial aid. In 2010, 46% of our class of 320 members contributed to the fund, and the total donations were enough to finance exactly two-thirds of one financial aid package. This year we have set a goal of 55% participation. Will you join me in helping today's bright students afford the same excellent education that we received?

| Class Agent | Financial Aid |

The graph shows the growth in average financial aid per student, and the percent of students receiving financial aid at the College since 1980.

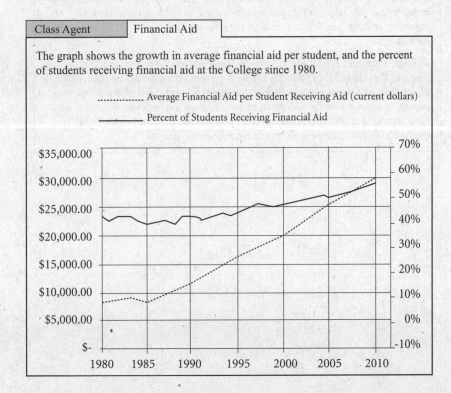

- Average Financial Aid per Student Receiving Aid (current dollars)
- Percent of Students Receiving Financial Aid

Approximately what was the total amount of financial aid that the College offered to its students in 2010?

(A) 1.6 million

(B) 2.5 million

(C) 21.6 million

(D) 26.9 million

(E) 48 million

9.

| Class Agent | Financial Aid |

Letter by Class Agent.

Dear fellow alumni,

As we approach the 10th anniversary of our college graduation, I am reminded of all the things that made our time in college special: our idyllic campus, the academic rigor fostered by our exceptional faculty, and, above all, the excellence and diversity of the student body.

As you know, the College is committed to maintaining this diversity and the rigorous education its students receive, even in the face of rising costs. While other institutions, in order to combat these costs, have expanded their student classes so that they could increase their overall tuition revenues, our alma mater has resisted such student growth, choosing instead to safeguard its preciously low student-to-faculty ratio—which is a great benefit for students. With a total enrollment of 1600 students in 2010, the College remains one of the smallest liberal arts schools of its kind. Furthermore, the College has increased its average financial aid package every year over the past 25 years, and has offered this aid to an increasing percentage of its student population, in order to ensure that all deserving students can afford to attend, regardless of their financial circumstances.

This commitment to the students must be financed somehow. This is where we come in: the Alumni Fund directly supports student financial aid. In 2010, 46% of our class of 320 members contributed to the fund, and the total donations were enough to finance exactly two-thirds of one financial aid package. This year we have set a goal of 55% participation. Will you join me in helping today's bright students afford the same excellent education that we received?

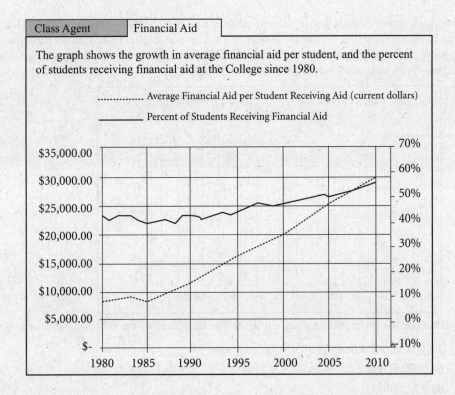

Class Agent | Financial Aid

The graph shows the growth in average financial aid per student, and the percent of students receiving financial aid at the College since 1980.

.... Average Financial Aid per Student Receiving Aid (current dollars)

————— Percent of Students Receiving Financial Aid

For each of the following statements, select *Yes* if it can be inferred from the given information that the College has chosen to support its student body by the method described in the statement. Otherwise, select *No*.

	(A)	(B)	
	Yes	No	
9.1	○	○	Increasing its average financial aid package each year over the past 25 years
9.2	○	○	Not charging higher tuition
9.3	○	○	Maintaining a low student-to-faculty ratio

10. The graph shows the number of student-athletes who participated during the 2010–11 school year in four team sports at certain schools in a six-school league. Each student participated in no more than one of these sports. The combined number of student-athletes who participated in these four sports at all six schools in 2010–11 was 425.

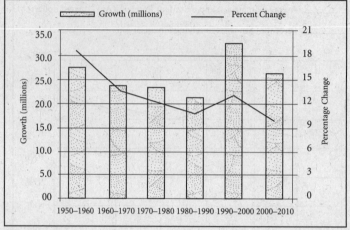

Based on the given information, fill in the blanks in each of the following statements.

10.1. The U.S. population in 1960 was approximately _____.

    (A) 107 million

    (B) 151 million

    (C) 179 million

    (D) 210 million

10.2. The percentage change in the U.S. population between 1960 and 1980 was _____.

    (A) 11

    (B) 26

    (C) 48

11. The income-to-poverty ratio determines how close someone's income is to the poverty threshold. For the United States in 2010, the graph shows the percent of all people and the percent of people age 65 years and over whose income-to-poverty ratio was 2.00 or lower. For each income-to-poverty ratio in the graph, the corresponding percentage is of people with income-to-poverty ratios below that ratio.

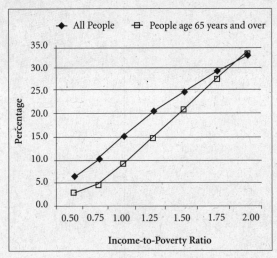

Based on the given information, fill in the blanks in each of the following statements.

11.1. The income of approximately _____ of all people was between 1 time and 1.5 times the poverty threshold.

(A) 9.5

(B) 14.1

(C) 19.8

(D) 24.6

11.2. If in 2010, 3.5 million people over the age of 65 had incomes below the poverty threshold in the United States, then the total number of people over the age of 65 in the United States was approximately _____.

(A) 10 million

(B) 23 million

(C) 39 million

(D) 78 million

12. The chart shows the breakdown of the stock holdings in one investor's portfolio, by number of company stocks held, each company's market capitalization type (Large, Mid, or Small), and the type of stock (Growth, Core, or Value).

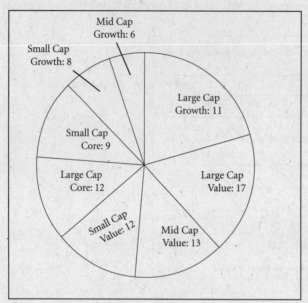

Based on the given information, fill in the blanks in each of the following statements.

12.1. The Growth stocks in the investor's portfolio represent _____% of the total portfolio.

(A) 20.83

(B) 32

(C) 35.42

(D) 50

12.2. The investor has _____ times as many Large Cap stocks in her portfolio as Small Cap stocks.

(A) 0.60

(B) 1.28

(C) 1.66

(D) 2.18

QUANTITATIVE SECTION

37 Questions • 75 Minutes

Directions for Problem Solving Questions: *(These directions will appear on your screen before your first Problem Solving question.)*

Solve this problem and indicate the best of the answer choices given.

Numbers: All numbers used are real numbers.

Figures: A figure accompanying a Problem Solving question is intended to provide information useful in solving the problem. Figures are drawn as accurately as possible EXCEPT when it is stated in a specific problem that its figure is not drawn to scale. Straight lines may sometimes appear jagged. All figures lie on a plane unless otherwise indicated.

To review these directions for subsequent questions of this type, click on HELP.

Directions for Data Sufficiency Questions: *(These directions will appear on your screen before your first Data Sufficiency question.)*

This Data Sufficiency problem consists of a question and two statements, labeled (1) and (2), in which certain data are given. You have to decide whether the data given in the statements are *sufficient* for answering the question. Using the data given in the statements *plus* your knowledge of mathematics and everyday facts (such as the number of days in July or the meaning of *counterclockwise*), you must indicate whether:

(A) Statement (1) ALONE is sufficient, but Statement (2) alone is not sufficient to answer the question asked;

(B) Statement (2) ALONE is sufficient, but Statement (1) alone is not sufficient to answer the question asked;

(C) BOTH Statements (1) and (2) TOGETHER are sufficient to answer the question asked, but NEITHER statement ALONE is sufficient;

(D) EACH statement ALONE is sufficient to answer the question asked;

(E) Statements (1) and (2) TOGETHER are NOT sufficient to answer the question asked, and additional data specific to the problem are needed.

Numbers: All numbers used are real numbers.

Figures: A figure accompanying a Data Sufficiency problem will conform to the information given in the question, but will not necessarily conform to the additional information in Statements (1) and (2).

Lines shown as straight can be assumed to be straight and lines that appear jagged can also be assumed to be straight.

You may assume that positions of points, angles, regions, etc., exist in the order shown and that angle measures are greater than zero.

All figures lie in a plane unless otherwise indicated.

Note: In Data Sufficiency problems that ask you for the value of a quantity, the data given in the statements are sufficient only when it is possible to determine exactly one numerical value for the quantity.

To review these directions for subsequent questions of this type, click on HELP.

1. What is $\frac{1}{3}$% of 54?
   - (A) 0.0018
   - (B) 0.018
   - (C) 0.18
   - (D) 1.8
   - (E) 18

2. If the value of *XYZ* Company stock drops from $25 per share to $21 per share, what is the percent of decrease?
   - (A) 4%
   - (B) 8%
   - (C) 12%
   - (D) 16%
   - (E) 20%

3. How many buses are required to transport 175 students to the museum?
   - (1) No two buses have the same carrying capacity.
   - (2) The average capacity of a bus is 55 students.

4. The storage capacity of disk drive A is 85% that of disk drive B. What percentage of drive B's storage capacity is currently used?
   - (1) Disk drive B holds 3 more gigabytes than disk drive A.
   - (2) 8.5 gigabytes of disk drive B's storage capacity is currently used.

5. Eight square window panes of equal size are to be pieced together to form a rectangular French door. What is the perimeter of the door, excluding framing between and around the panes?
   - (1) The area of each pane is 1 square foot.
   - (2) The area of the door, excluding framing between and around the panes, is 8 square feet.

6. The denominator of a certain fraction is twice as great as the numerator. If 4 were added to both the numerator and denominator, the new fraction would be $\frac{5}{8}$. What is the denominator of the fraction?

   - (A) 3
   - (B) 6
   - (C) 9
   - (D) 12
   - (E) 13

7. If $36 = 169x^2$, then x could equal which of the following?
   - (A) $-\frac{13}{6}$
   - (B) $-\frac{6}{14}$
   - (C) $-\frac{6}{13}$
   - (D) $\frac{6}{14}$
   - (E) $\frac{13}{6}$

8. **AREA OF WAREHOUSE UNITS A, B, C, AND D (AS PORTIONS OF TOTAL WAREHOUSE AREA)**

   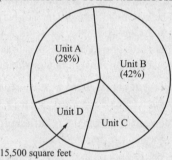

   Total: 140,000 square feet

   By approximately how many square feet does the size of Unit A exceed that of Unit C?
   - (A) 9000
   - (B) 11,000
   - (C) 12,600
   - (D) 15,500
   - (E) 19,000

9. Which of the following is the point at which the graphs of the functions $f(x) = x^2 + 2$ and $g(x) = 1 - 2x$ intersect?
   - (A) $(-1, -3)$
   - (B) $(-1, 3)$
   - (C) $(1, -3)$
   - (D) $(-1, 2)$
   - (E) $(1, 3)$

10. If $n \triangle m = \dfrac{m^2}{n-m}$, then what is the value of $(3 \triangle 4) \triangle 4$?

(A) $-\dfrac{81}{5}$

(B) $-\dfrac{64}{5}$

(C) $-\dfrac{16}{13}$

(D) $-\dfrac{4}{5}$

(E) $\dfrac{64}{5}$

11.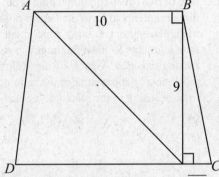

In the figure above, if the length of $\overline{DC}$ is 12, what is the area of $ABCD$?

(A) 99

(B) 108

(C) 112

(D) 120

(E) $50\sqrt{3}$

12. $\dfrac{\sqrt[3]{81x^7}}{\sqrt{9x^4}} - \dfrac{\sqrt{162x^5}}{\sqrt[3]{27x^6}} =$

(A) $3x^3 - \dfrac{1}{3}$

(B) $\sqrt[3]{2x} - 3$

(C) $\sqrt[3]{3x} - 3\sqrt{2x}$

(D) $3x^2 - \sqrt{2}$

(E) $9x - \sqrt{3}$

13. If the average (arithmetic mean) of the first sixteen positive integers is subtracted from the average (arithmetic mean) of the next sixteen positive integers, what is the result?

(A) 0

(B) 16

(C) 32

(D) 64

(E) 128

14. If $a > b$, and if $c > d$, then

(A) $a - b > c - d$

(B) $a - c > b - d$

(C) $c + d < a - b$

(D) $a - c < b + d$

(E) $b + d < a + c$

15.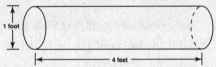

A closed cardboard box is to be designed for packing the cylindrical tube shown above. Will the entire tube fit inside the box?

(1) The empty box contains 3 cubic feet.

(2) The total surface area of the box is 14 square feet.

16. If x and y are negative integers, and if $x - y = 1$, what is the least possible value of xy?

(A) 0

(B) 1

(C) 2

(D) 3

(E) 4

17. A certain jar contains 20 jellybeans; each jellybean is either black, pink, or yellow. Does the jar contain more pink jellybeans than yellow jellybeans?

(1) The jar contains more black jellybeans than pink jellybeans.

(2) The jar contains 6 pink jellybeans.

18. Is the value of $a^2 - b^2$ greater than the value of $(3a + 3b)(2a - 2b)$?

(1) $b < a$

(2) $a < 1$

19. In ten years, Rob will be twice as old as his son. Six years ago, Rob's son was 16 years-old. How old is Rob now?

(A) 22

(B) 32

(C) 48

(D) 54

(E) 64

20.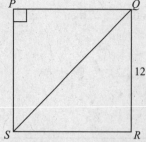

In the figure above, if *PQRS* is a rectangle, and if the length of $\overline{QR}$ is 12, is *PQRS* a square?

(1) The length of $\overline{SQ}$ is $12\sqrt{2}$.

(2) The length of $\overline{PS}$ is 12.

21. If a computer dealer bought a particular computer system for $10,000 and sold the computer system to a customer, how much did the customer pay for the computer system?

(1) The dealer's profit from the sale was 50%.

(2) The amount that the dealer paid for the computer system was two thirds the amount that the customer paid for the computer system.

22. Which of the following distribution of numbers has the greatest standard deviation?

(A) {−3,1,2}

(B) {−2,−1,1,2}

(C) {3,5,7}

(D) {1,2,3,4}

(E) {0,2,4}

23. Patrons at a certain restaurant can select two of three appetizers—fruit, soup, and salad—along with two of three vegetables—carrots, squash, and peas. What is the statistical probability that any patron will select fruit, salad, squash, and peas?

(A) $\dfrac{1}{12}$

(B) $\dfrac{1}{9}$

(C) $\dfrac{1}{6}$

(D) $\dfrac{1}{3}$

(E) $\dfrac{1}{2}$

24. If bin *A* contains exactly twice as many potatoes as bin *B*, and if bin *A* contains exactly 11 more potatoes than bin *C*, does bin *B* contain more potatoes than bin *C*?

(1) The difference between the number of potatoes in bin *A* and the number in bin *C* is greater than the number of potatoes in bin *B*.

(2) If one potato were added to bin *A* and to bin *C*, bin *A* would contain exactly twice as many potatoes as bin *C*.

25. One of two ropes equal in length is cut into three segments to form the largest possible triangular area. The other rope is cut into four segments to form the largest possible rectangular area. Which of the following most closely approximates the ratio of the triangle's area to the rectangle's area?

(A) 1:2

(B) 2:3

(C) 3:4

(D) 1:1

(E) 4:3

26. Code letters *X*, *Y*, and *Z* each represent one digit in the three-digit prime number *XYZ*. If neither *X* nor *Y* is an odd integer, what is the number represented by *XYZ*?

(1) The sum of the three digits is 7.

(2) $X − Y > 2$

27. If *abcd* ≠ 0, and if $0 < c < b < a < 1$, is it true that $\dfrac{a^4bc}{d^2} < 1$?

(1) $a = \sqrt{d}$

(2) $d > 0$

28. If *x* > 0, and if *x* + 3 is a multiple of 3, which of the following is NOT a multiple of 3?

(A) *x*

(B) *x* + 6

(C) 3*x* + 5

(D) 2*x* + 6

(E) 6*x* + 18

29. If one dollar can buy *m* pieces of paper, how many dollars are needed to buy *p* reams of paper? (Note: 1 ream = 500 pieces of paper.)

(A) $\dfrac{p}{500m}$

(B) $\dfrac{m}{500p}$

(C) $\dfrac{500}{p+m}$

(D) $\dfrac{500p}{m}$

(E) $500m(p-m)$

QUESTIONS 30 AND 31 REFER TO THE FOLLOWING FIGURE.

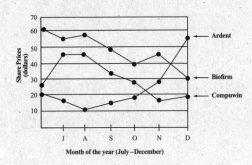

SHARE PRICES OF COMMON STOCK
(ARDENT, BIOFIRM AND COMPUWIN CORPORATIONS)

Month of the year (July–December)

30. At the end of September, the combined share price of Ardent stock and Biofirm stock exceeded the share price of Compuwin stock by approximately

(A) 20%

(B) 35%

(C) 50%

(D) 100%

(E) 150%

31. During which of the following months did the aggregate share price of stock in all three companies change the LEAST?

(A) July

(B) August

(C) October

(D) November

(E) December

32.

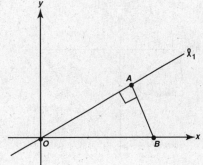

On the xy-plane above, if the equation of l_1 is $y = \dfrac{1}{2}x$ and if point B is defined by the xy-coordinate pair (5,0), what is the area of $\triangle OAB$?

(A) 4

(B) $3\sqrt{2}$

(C) $2\sqrt{5}$

(D) 5

(E) 7

33. In a group of 30 students, 18 are enrolled in an English class and 16 are enrolled in an Algebra class. How many students are enrolled in both an English and Algebra class?

(1) 20 are enrolled in exactly one of these two classes.

(2) 3 are not enrolled in either of these classes.

34. Total revenue from the sale of adult and student tickets was $180. If twice as many student tickets as adult tickets were sold, and if 27 tickets were sold altogether, what was the total revenue from the sale of student tickets?

(1) The price of each adult ticket was $10.

(2) The price of each student ticket was 50% of the price of each adult ticket.

35. If $a, b, c,$ and d are integers, is the sum of ab and cd an odd integer?

(1) a and c are both even integers.

(2) b is an even integer and d is an odd integer.

36.

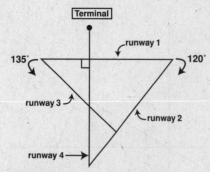

As shown in the figure above, from runway 1, airplanes must turn either 120° to the right onto runway 2 or 135° to the left onto runway 3. Which of the following does NOT indicate a complete turn from one runway to another?

(A) 30°

(B) 55°

(C) 60°

(D) 75°

(E) 105°

37. A legislature passed a bill into law by a 5:3 margin. No legislator abstained. What part of the votes cast were cast in favor of the motion?

(A) $\dfrac{3}{8}$

(B) $\dfrac{2}{5}$

(C) $\dfrac{8}{15}$

(D) $\dfrac{3}{5}$

(E) $\dfrac{5}{8}$

VERBAL SECTION

41 Questions • 75 Minutes

Directions for Sentence Correction Questions: *(These directions will appear on your screen before your first Sentence Correction question.)*

This question presents a sentence, all or part of which is underlined. Beneath the sentence you will find five ways of phrasing the underlined part. The first of these repeats the original; the other four are different. If you think the original is best, choose the first answer; otherwise choose one of the others.

This question tests correctness and effectiveness of expression. In choosing your answer, follow the requirements of Standard Written English; that is, pay attention to grammar, choice of words, and sentence construction. Choose the answer that produces the most effective sentence; this answer should be clear and exact, without awkwardness, ambiguity, redundancy, or grammatical error.

Directions for Critical Reasoning Questions: *(These directions will appear on your screen before your first Critical Reasoning question.)*

For this question, select the best of the answer choices given.

Directions for Reading Comprehension Questions: *(These directions will appear on your screen before your first group of Reading Comprehension questions.)*

The questions in this group are based on the content of a passage. After reading the passage, choose the best answer to each question. Answer all the questions following the passage on the basis of what is stated or implied in the passage.

1. Either the museum curator must order the use of an interventive methodology, including but not limited to <u>varnish removal and the securing of the flaking paint, or they must</u> fully document and justify the current non-interventive stance at once.

   (A) varnish removal and the securing of the flaking paint, or they must

   (B) varnish removal and securing flaking paint, or they must

   (C) removing varnish and securing flaking paint, or they must

   (D) removing varnish and the securing of the flaking paint, or he must

   (E) removing varnish and securing flaking paint, or he must

2. <u>In the cross-section of the molar, the widening of the periodontal ligament and adjacent bone loss was shown.</u>

   (A) In the cross-section of the molar, the widening of the periodontal ligament and adjacent bone loss was shown.

   (B) The cross-section of the molar showed widening of the periodontal ligament and adjacent bone loss.

   (C) In the cross-section of the molar, the widening of the periodontal ligament and adjacent bone loss were shown.

   (D) Both the widening of the periodontal ligament and adjacent bone loss was shown in the cross-section of the molar.

   (E) The cross-section of the molar having shown widening of the periodontal ligament and adjacent bone loss.

3. Using the microscope, Anton von Leewun-hoek observed the process of <u>parthenogenesis; it stunned and amazed him.</u>

    (A) parthenogenesis; it stunned and amazed him

    (B) parthenogenesis, it stunned and amazed him

    (C) parthenogenesis, which stunned and amazed him

    (D) parthenogenesis; a stunning and amazing process

    (E) parthenogenesis, stunning and amazing him

4. According to life-insurance company statistics, nine out of ten alcoholics die before the age of seventy-five, as opposed to seven out of ten non-alcoholics. A recent report issued by the State Medical Board recounts these statistics and concludes that alcohol addiction increases a person's susceptibility to life-threatening diseases, thereby reducing life expectancy.

    The conclusion drawn by the State Medical Board depends on which of the following assumptions?

    (A) People who are predisposed to life-threatening diseases are more likely than other people to become alcoholic.

    (B) The statistics cited exclude deaths due to other alcohol-related events such as automobile accidents.

    (C) Alcoholism does not also increase a person's susceptibility to diseases that are not life-threatening.

    (D) The life expectancy of that portion of the general population not characterized by alcoholism increases over time.

    (E) The author of the report is not biased in his or her personal opinion about the morality of alcohol consumption.

5. For the purpose of stimulating innovation at TechCorp, one of the company's long-standing goals has been to obtain at least 50 percent of its annual revenues from sales of products that are no more than three years old. Last year, TechCorp achieved this goal, despite the fact that the company introduced no new products during the year.

    Which of the following, if true, best explains the results described above?

    (A) None of the company's competitors introduced any new products during the last year.

    (B) Scientists at the company report that they are close to breakthroughs that should result in several new products during the coming year.

    (C) Sales of some of the company's older products were discontinued during that last year.

    (D) The company has introduced very few new products during the last three years.

    (E) Company spending on research and development has increased sharply over the past five years.

QUESTIONS 6–8 ARE BASED ON THE FOLLOWING PASSAGE.

Line   The Pan-American land bridge, or isthmus, connecting North and South America was formed volcanically long after dinosaurs became extinct. The isthmus
(5) cleaved populations of marine organisms, creating sister species. These twin species, called "geminates," then evolved independently. Scientists observe, for example, that Pacific pistol shrimp no longer mate with
(10) those from the Atlantic Ocean. Yet the two oceans had already begun to form their distinctive personalities long before the isthmus was fully formed. As the seabed rose, Pacific waters grew cooler, their
(15) upswelling currents carrying rich nutrients, while the Atlantic side grew shallower, warmer, and nutrient poor. In fact, it was these new conditions, and not so much the fully formed isthmus, that spawned changes
(20) in the shrimp population.

     For terrestrial life, the impact of the isthmus was more immediate. Animals traversed the newly formed bridge in both directions, although North American
(25) creatures proved better colonizers—more than half of South America's mammals trace direct lineage to this so-called Great American Biotic Exchange. Only three animals—the armadillo, opossum, and
(30) hedgehog—survive as transplants in the north today.

6. Which of the following statements finds the LEAST support in the passage?

  (A) Population divergences resulting from the formation of the Pan-American isthmus were more a process than an event.

  (B) The divergence in ocean temperature during the formation of the Pan-American isthmus resulted in a divergence in the ocean's nutrient value.

  (C) Genetic differences among pistol shrimp have grown to the point that there are now at least two distinct species of these shrimp.

  (D) The part of the ocean that is now the Pacific grew deeper due to the geologic forces that created the Pan-American isthmus.

  (E) Not until the Pan-American isthmus was fully formed did geminate marine organisms begin to develop in that area of the ocean.

7. The author mentions the mating habits of pistol shrimp in order to show that

  (A) some species of marine organisms inhabiting the Pacific Ocean are now entirely distinct from those in the Atlantic Ocean.

  (B) twin species of marine organisms can each survive even though one species can no longer mate with the other.

  (C) since the formation of the Pan-American isthmus, some marine geminates no longer mate with their sister species.

  (D) geminate species that do not mate with one another are considered separate species.

  (E) the evolutionary impact of the Pan-American isthmus was greater for marine organisms than for land animals.

8. Which of the following statements is most readily inferable from the information in the passage?

  (A) Species of marine organisms in the Atlantic Ocean number fewer today than before the formation of the Pan-American isthmus.

  (B) The number of terrestrial animal species in South America today exceeds the number prior to the formation of the Pan-American isthmus.

  (C) Of the indigenous North American species that migrated south across the Pan-American isthmus, more than three survive to this day.

  (D) Since the formation of the Pan-American isthmus, fewer terrestrial animals have traveled north across the isthmus than south.

  (E) As the Pan-American isthmus began to form, most pistol shrimp migrated west to what is now the Pacific Ocean.

9. That which is self-evident cannot be disputed, and that in itself is self-evident is an example, I believe, of one definition of the word *tautology*.

   (A) That which is self-evident cannot be disputed, and that in

   (B) That that is self-evident cannot be disputed, of which

   (C) It is self-evident that which cannot be disputed, and this fact

   (D) The self-evident cannot be disputed, and this fact

   (E) That which is self-evident cannot be disputed, a fact which

10. People who discontinue regular exercise typically claim that exercising amounted to wasted time for them. But this claim is born of laziness, in light of the overwhelming evidence that regular exercise improves one's health.

    Which of the following statements, if true, would most seriously weaken the argument above?

    (A) Exercise has been shown to not only improve one's health, but also to increase longevity, or life span.

    (B) People who have discontinued regular exercise now make productive use of the time they formerly devoted to exercise.

    (C) People who are in good health are more likely to exercise regularly than people who are in poor health.

    (D) A person need not exercise every day to experience improved health from the exercise.

    (E) People who are in poor health are less likely to exercise than other people.

11. Very few software engineers have left Micro-Firm Corporation to seek employment elsewhere. Thus, unless CompTech Corporation increases the salaries of its software engineers to the same level as those of MicroFirm's, these CompTech employees are likely to leave CompTech for another employer.

    The flawed reasoning in the argument is most similar to the reasoning in which of the following arguments?

    (A) Robert does not gamble, and he has never been penniless. Therefore, if Gina refrains from gambling she will also avoid being penniless.

    (B) If Dan throws a baseball directly at the window, the window pane will surely break. The window pane is not broken, so Dan has not thrown a baseball directly at it.

    (C) If a piano sits in a humid room, the piano will need tuning within a week. This piano needs tuning; therefore, it must have sat in a humid room for at least a week.

    (D) Diligent practice results in perfection. Thus, one must practice diligently in order to achieve perfection.

    (E) More expensive cars are stolen than inexpensive cars. Accordingly, owners of expensive cars should carry auto theft insurance, whereas owners of inexpensive cars should not.

12. The doctoral student provided a brief summary of her advance planning for her thesis.

    (A) a brief summary of her advance planning for her thesis

    (B) a summary of her thesis plans

    (C) a summary of her advance planning for her thesis

    (D) a summary of her advance planning steps for her thesis

    (E) a brief summary of her planning for her thesis

13. The Tonkin Gulf Resolution stating that the President, as Commander in Chief, could take "all necessary measures" to repel any armed attack and to prevent future aggression.

    (A) The Tonkin Gulf Resolution stating that

    (B) The Tonkin Gulf Resolution was stating that

    (C) The Tonkin Gulf Resolution stated that

    (D) The Tonkin Gulf Resolution having stated that

    (E) Stating that the Tonkin Gulf Resolution

14. In 19th-century Europe, a renewed interest in Middle Eastern architecture was kindled <u>not only by increased trade but also by</u> increased tourism and improved diplomatic relations.

(A) not only by increased trade but also by

(B) by not only increased trade but also by

(C) not only by increased trade but also

(D) not only by increased trade but

(E) by increased trade and also by

QUESTIONS 15–17 ARE BASED ON THE FOLLOWING PASSAGE.

Line　　Historians sometimes forget that no matter how well they might come to know a particular historical figure, they are not free to claim a godlike knowledge of the
(5)　figure or of the events surrounding the figure's life. Richard III, one of England's monarchs, is an apt case because we all think we "know" what he was like. In his play *Richard III,* Shakespeare provided a
(10)　portrait of a monster of a man, twisted in both body and soul. Shakespeare's great artistry and vivid depiction of Richard has made us accept this creature for the man. We are prepared, therefore, to interpret all
(15)　the events around him in such a way as to justify our opinion of him.

　　We accept that Richard executed his brother Clarence, even though the records of the time show that Richard pleaded for
(20)　his brother's life. We assume that Richard supervised the death of King Henry VI, overlooking that there is no proof that Henry was actually murdered. And we recoil at Richard's murdering his two
(25)　nephews, children of his brother's wife Elizabeth; yet we forget that Elizabeth had spent her time on the throne plotting to replace her husband's family in power with her own family. Once we appreciate the
(30)　historical context, especially the actions of Richard's opponents, we no longer see his actions as monstrous. Richard becomes, if not lovable, at least understandable. What's more, when we account for the
(35)　tone of the times during which Richard lived, as illuminated in literary works of

that era such as Machiavelli's *The Prince*, Richard's actions seem to us all the more reasonable.

15. With which of the following statements would the author of the passage most likely agree?

(A) In *Richard III*, Shakespeare portrays the king as more noble than he actually was.

(B) The deeds of Elizabeth were even more evil than those of Richard III.

(C) Richard III may have been innocent of some of the crimes that Shakespeare leads us to believe he committed.

(D) Richard III may have had a justifiable reason for killing Henry VI.

(E) Shakespeare was unaware of many of the historical facts about the life of Richard III.

16. The author of the passage refers to Shakespeare's "great artistry and vivid depiction of Richard" most probably in order to

(A) make the point that studying *Richard III* is the best way to understand Richard as a historical figure.

(B) explain why *Richard III* is widely acclaimed as one of Shakespeare's greatest works.

(C) contrast Shakespeare's depiction of Richard with how Richard might have described himself.

(D) illustrate how historians might become prejudiced in their view of historical figures.

(E) point out that historians should never rely on fictional works to understand and interpret historical events.

17. It can be inferred from the passage information that Machiavelli's *The Prince* helps show

(A) that, in his play *Richard III*, Shakespeare's depiction of the king was historically accurate.

(B) that Richard's actions were an accurate reflection of the times in which he lived.

(C) that different authors often depict the same historical figures in very different ways.

(D) that Machiavelli was more astute than Shakespeare as an observer of human nature.

(E) that Richard's actions as a king are not surprising in light of his earlier actions as a prince.

18. PharmaCorp, which manufactures the drug Aidistan, claims that Aidistan is more effective than the drug Betatol in treating Puma Syndrome. To support its claim, PharmaCorp cites the fact that one of every two victims of Puma Syndrome is treated successfully with Aidistan alone, as opposed to one out of every three treated with Betatol alone. However, PharmaCorp's claim cannot be taken seriously in light of the fact that the presence of Gregg's Syndrome has been known to render Puma Syndrome more resistant to any treatment.

Which of the following, if true, would most support the allegation that PharmaCorp's claim cannot be taken seriously?

(A) Among people who suffer from both Puma Syndrome and Gregg's Syndrome, fewer are treated with Aidistan than with Betatol.

(B) Among people who suffer from both Puma Syndrome and Gregg's Syndrome, fewer are treated with Betatol than with Aidistan.

(C) Gregg's Syndrome reduces Aidistan's effectiveness in treating Puma Syndrome more than Betatol's effectiveness in treating the same syndrome.

(D) Betatol is less effective than Aidistan in treating Gregg's Syndrome.

(E) Neither Aidistan nor Betatol is effective in treating Gregg's Syndrome.

19. *City official:* In order to revitalize our city's downtown business district, we should increase the number of police officers who patrol the district during business hours. Three years ago, the city reduced the total size of its police force by nearly 20 percent.

Since then, retail businesses in the district have experienced a steady decline in revenue.

Any of the following, if true, would be an effective criticism of the city official's recommendation EXCEPT:

(A) Two years ago, the city established more rigorous standards for the retention and hiring of its police officers.

(B) New businesses offering products or services similar to those in the district have emerged outside the district recently.

(C) The number of people who reside in the district has not changed significantly over the last three years.

(D) Businesses operating in the city but outside the district have experienced declining revenues during the last three years.

(E) Some of the city's police officers patrol areas outside as well as inside the district.

20. Which of the following provides the most logical completion of the passage below?

More and more consumers are being attracted to sport utility vehicles because they are safer to drive than regular cars and because of the feeling of power a person experiences when driving a sport utility vehicle. In its current advertising campaign, Jupiter Auto Company emphasizes the low price of its new sport utility vehicle compared to the price of other such vehicles. However, this marketing strategy is unwise because _____.

(A) Jupiter's sport utility vehicle is not so safe as those produced by competing automobile manufacturers.

(B) if Jupiter reduces the price of its sport utility vehicle even further, Jupiter would sell even more of these vehicles.

(C) the retail price of Jupiter's most expensive luxury car is less than that of its new sport utility vehicle.

(D) most consumers who purchase sport utility vehicles are also concerned about the reliability of their vehicle.

(E) consumers who purchase sport utility vehicles associate affordability with lack of safety.

21. Since City X reduced the frequency with which its service vehicles pick up recyclable materials from residences for transport to its recycling center, the volume of material that its service vehicles transport to land-fills for permanent disposal has increased to unmanageable levels. However, the city cannot increase the frequency of either its trash pickup or its recycling pickup at city residences.

Based only on the information above, which of the following strategies seems most appropriate for City X in the interest of reducing the volume of material that the city's service vehicles transport to landfills?

(A) Provide larger recycling containers to the residents of the city.

(B) Establish a community program to increase awareness of the benefits of recycling.

(C) Establish additional recycling centers as near as possible to the city's residential areas.

(D) Provide incentives to the city's residents to reuse, rather than discard for pickup by the city's service vehicles, whatever they can.

(E) Ease restrictions on the types of materials the city's service vehicles will pick up for transport to its recycling center.

22. The pesticide Azocide, introduced to central valley farms three summers ago, has proven ineffective because other pesticides' chemical compositions already in wide use neutralizing its desired effect.

(A) because other pesticides' chemical compositions already in wide use

(B) because of the chemical compositions of the pesticides already in wide use

(C) due to other pesticides already in wide use, whose chemical compositions have been

(D) since, due to the chemical compositions of other pesticides already in use, those pesticides have been

(E) because of other pesticides and their chemical compositions already in use, which have been

23. To relieve anxiety, moderate exercise can be equally effective as, and less addictive than, most sedatives and one should not discount the value of a good diet and enough sleep.

(A) effective as, and

(B) as effective as, while being

(C) effectively equal to, but

(D) as effective as, and

(E) effective, and

24. The government's means of disposal of war surplus following World War II met with vociferous objections by industrialists, prominent advisors, and many others.

(A) of disposal of

(B) in disposing

(C) for the disposition of

(D) used in disposing

(E) of disposing

25. No nation in the world has experienced so significant a decline in its Yucaipa tree population as our nation. Yet only our nation imposes a law prohibiting the use of Yucaipa tree-bark oil in cosmetics. The purpose of this law in the first place was to help maintain the Yucaipa tree population, at least in this nation. But the law is clearly unnecessary and therefore should be repealed.

Which of the following, if true, would most seriously weaken the conclusion drawn in the passage?

(A) This nation contains more Yucaipa trees than any other nation.

(B) Yucaipa tree-bark oil is not used for any consumer goods other than cosmetics.

(C) The demand for cosmetics containing Yucaipa tree-bark oil is expected to decline in the future in other nations while continuing unabated in this nation.

(D) In other countries, labor used to harvest Yucaipa trees for cosmetics is less expensive than comparable labor in this nation.

(E) In this nation, some wild animals eat Yucaipa tree bark, thereby contributing to their destruction.

26. Some official Web sites of regionally accredited colleges have received the highest possible rating from the Federal Department of Education. However, all official Web sites of nationally accredited colleges have received the highest possible rating from the same department.

Which of the following, if added to the statements above, would provide most support for the conclusion that all Web sites administered by individuals holding advanced degrees in educational technology have received the highest possible rating from the Federal Department of Education?

(A) Only official Web sites of nationally accredited colleges are administered by individuals holding advanced degrees in educational technology.

(B) All Web sites of nationally accredited colleges are administered by individuals holding advanced degrees in educational technology.

(C) Only Web sites that have not received the highest possible rating from the Federal Department of Education are administered by individuals not holding advanced degrees in educational technology.

(D) All official Web sites of nationally accredited colleges are administered by individuals holding advanced degrees in educational technology.

(E) No Web site administered by individuals holding advanced degrees in educational technology is an official Web site of a regionally accredited college.

27. The time it takes for a star to change its brightness is directly related to <u>the luminosity of it,</u> a fact that has not been in dispute for some time among astronomers and astrophysicists.

(A) the luminosity of it,

(B) the luminosity of its brightness,

(C) the luminosity of a star,

(D) luminosity of it,

(E) its luminosity,

QUESTIONS 28–30 ARE BASED ON THE FOLLOWING PASSAGE.

Line   Diseases associated with aging in women are difficult to correlate explicitly with estrogen deficiency because aging and genetics are important influences in
(5) the development of such diseases. A number of studies, however, indicate a profound effect of estrogen deficiency in syndromes such as cardiovascular disease (including atherosclerosis and stroke) and
(10) osteoporosis—the loss and increasing fragility of bone in aging individuals.

    The amount of bone in the elderly skeleton—a key determinant in its susceptibility to fractures—is believed to be a
(15) function of two major factors. The first is the peak amount of bone mass attained, determined to a large extent by genetic inheritance. The marked effect of gender is obvious—elderly men experience only
(20) one-half as many hip fractures per capita as elderly women. However, African American women have a lower incidence of osteoporotic fractures than Caucasian women. Other important variables include
(25) diet, exposure to sunlight, and physical activity. The second major factor is the rate of bone loss after peak bone mass has been attained. While many of the variables that affect peak bone mass also affect rates
(30) of bone loss, additional factors influencing bone loss include physiological stresses such as pregnancy and lactation. It is hormonal status, however, reflected primarily by estrogen and progesterone levels,
(35) that may exert the greatest effect on rates of decline in skeletal mass.

28. Based upon the passage, which of the following is LEAST clearly a factor affecting the rate of decline in bone mass?

    (A) Gender
    (B) Exposure to sunlight
    (C) Progesterone levels
    (D) Age
    (E) Estrogen levels

29. In discussing the "marked effect of gender", the author assumes all of the following EXCEPT:

    (A) the difference in incidence of hip fractures is not due instead to different rates of bone loss.
    (B) the incidence of hip fractures among elderly men as compared to elderly women is representative of the total number of bone fractures among elderly men as compared to elderly women.
    (C) elderly women are not more accident-prone than elderly men.
    (D) the population upon which the cited statistic is based includes both African Americans and Caucasians.
    (E) men achieve peak bone mass at the same age as women.

30. It can be inferred from the passage that the peak amount of bone mass in women

    (A) is not affected by either pregnancy or lactation.
    (B) is determined primarily by diet.
    (C) depends partly upon hormonal status.
    (D) may play a role in determining the rate of decrease in estrogen and progesterone levels.
    (E) is not dependent upon genetic makeup.

31. Vining University's teacher credential program should be credited for the high grade-point averages of high school students who enroll in classes taught by Vining graduates. More new graduates of Vining's credential program accept entry-level positions at Franklin High School than at any other high school. And during the most recent academic year, just prior to which many of Franklin's teachers transferred to Valley View High School, the median grade point average of the students at Franklin has declined while at Valley View it has increased. The argument above depends on which of the following assumptions?

    (A) The two high schools employ different methods of computing student grade point averages.
    (B) Neither high school has a peer tutoring program that would afford the school an advantage over the other in terms of student academic performance.
    (C) Just prior to last year, more teachers transferred from Franklin to Valley View than from Valley View to Franklin.
    (D) The teachers who transferred from Franklin to Valley View were replaced with teachers who are also graduates of Vining University's teacher credential program.
    (E) The teachers who transferred from Franklin to Valley View last year were graduates of Vining's teacher credential program.

32. More airplane accidents are caused by pilot error than any other single factor. The military recently stopped requiring its pilots to obtain immunization shots against chemical warfare agents. These shots are known to cause unpredictable dizzy spells, which can result in pilot error. Since many military pilots also pilot commercial passenger airliners, the reason for the military's decision must have been to reduce the number of commercial airline accidents. Which of the following, if true, provides most support for the conclusion drawn above?

    (A) Recently, more pilots have been volunteering for the immunization shots.
    (B) All commercial airline flights are piloted by two co-pilots, whereas military flights are usually piloted by only one.
    (C) Chemical warfare is likely to escalate in the future.

(D) Military pilots are choosing to resign rather than obtain the immunization shots.

(E) Recently, the number of military pilots also piloting commercial airliners has declined.

33. While few truly great artists consider themselves visionary, many lesser talents boast about their own destiny to lead the way to higher artistic ground.

(A) While few truly great artists consider themselves visionary, many lesser talents boast about their own destiny to lead the way to higher artistic ground.

(B) While many lesser talents boast about their own destinies to lead the way to higher ground, few truly great artists consider themselves as visionary.

(C) Many lesser talents boast about their own destiny to lead the way to higher artistic ground while few truly great artists consider themselves as being visionary.

(D) Few truly great artists consider himself or herself a visionary while many lesser talents boast about their own destinies to lead the way to higher artistic ground.

(E) While many lesser talents boast about their own destiny, few truly great artists consider themselves visionary, to lead the way to higher artistic ground.

34. History shows that while simultaneously attaining global or even regional dominance, a country generally succumbs to erosion of its social infrastructure.

(A) History shows that while simultaneously attaining

(B) History would show that, while attaining

(C) History bears out that, in the course of attaining

(D) During the course of history, the attainment of

(E) Throughout history, during any country's attaining

35. *Connie:* This season, new episodes of my favorite television program are even more entertaining than previous episodes; so the program should be even more popular this season than last season.

Karl: I disagree. After all, we both know that the chief aim of television networks is to maximize advertising revenue by increasing the popularity of their programs. But this season the television networks that compete with the one that shows your favorite program are showing reruns of old programs during the same time slot as your favorite program. Which of the following, if true, would provide the most support for Karl's response to Connie's argument?

(A) What Connie considers entertaining does not necessarily coincide with what most television viewers consider entertaining.

(B) Entertaining television shows are not necessarily popular as well.

(C) Television networks generally schedule their most popular shows during the same time slots as their competitors' most popular shows.

(D) Certain educational programs that are not generally considered entertaining are nevertheless among the most popular programs.

(E) The most common reason for a network to rerun a television program is that a great number of television viewers request the rerun.

QUESTIONS 36–39 ARE BASED ON THE FOLLOWING PASSAGE.

Line   In periods when there are more qualified candidates than job openings, human resource departments may develop employee retention myopia, discounting
(5)   the effect of their shortsightedness on everything from daily product sales to effective succession planning. In addition, despite conflicting evidence about whether demographic trends related to baby boomer
(10)   retirements may or may not constitute a code red, every human resource department does face a potential threat from that

Line phenomenon, and should continue to focus sharply on the retention of its most talented
(15) and productive employees.

While some issues in employee retention, such as defined expectations and clear supervision, now seem codified, the landscape appears to shift more elusively
(20) and continuously in the area of benefits. As noted in the influential tenth annual MetLife study of benefits, employee level of engagement in the issue of benefits has burgeoned. Ten years ago, according to
(25) the study, employees were far less likely to consider, let alone calculate, the true value of benefits when assessing an employment offer. Currently, they are more likely to appreciate what their employer
(30) provides, even if they personally have to incur some portion of the cost of those benefits. Finally, the keen interest in benefits and the attribution of a quantifiable value to them is now common among
(35) younger workers as well as older ones.

The study also suggests that while wage and salary issues continue to rate as the pre-eminent factor in employee loyalty, medical and retirement benefits are a close
(40) second and third and rank above the opportunity for advancement. More stunningly—or perhaps soberingly—employees rate nonmedical benefits such as vision, life, and disability insurances
(45) on a par with the importance of opportunity for advancement.

Study data also suggest the increasing value of voluntary benefits in achieving human capital goals. Increasingly, person-
(50) alized benefits, geared to the needs of particular age groups, have come to the fore as a factor in employee satisfaction and retention. Particularly in those companies where a serious talent or skills
(55) shortage prevails, and in those positions where long-term, costly training is needed, personalized benefits may tip the human capital balance.

36. In the passage, the author's chief concern is to

(A) suggest that benefits may be more important than ever in employee retention.

(B) analyze the influential tenth annual MetLife study of benefits.

(C) suggest the often overlooked role of personalized benefits in employee retention.

(D) stress the need for continuity of benefits in periods of high unemployment.

(E) urge employers to continue to offer the same benefits as always.

37. It can be inferred that the author

(A) is an expert in employee benefits.

(B) may be relying too heavily on a single source.

(C) has wide-ranging knowledge of the benefits field.

(D) is most likely employed by a benefits company.

(E) believes baby boomer retirements are not a problem.

38. Which of the following is NOT mentioned in the passage as a reason for focusing on benefits as a method of employee retention?

(A) the importance of employee retention to effective succession planning

(B) the costs of training new employees

(C) the continuous change in what employees want and value in terms of benefits

(D) predominance of benefits in the hiring discussion

(E) a new desire among employees for personalized benefits

39. With which of the following statements would the author most likely agree?

(A) Younger workers paid less attention to benefits in the past.

(B) The amount of employee interest in benefits has wavered in recent years.

(C) Most employees are not willing to take on additional co-pays for most benefits.

(D) Having life and disability insurance is less important than the opportunity for advancement.

(E) Voluntary benefits must be personalized to the ages and life stages of employees.

40. Currently, the supply of office buildings in this state far exceeds demand, while demand for single-family housing far exceeds supply. As a result, real estate developers have curtailed office building construction until demand meets supply and have stepped up construction of single-family housing. The state legislature recently enacted a law eliminating a state income tax on corporations whose primary place of business is this state. In response, many large private employers from other states have already begun to relocate to this state and, according to a reliable study, this trend will continue during the next five years.

Which of the following predictions is best supported by the information above?

(A) During the next five years, fewer new office buildings than single-family houses will be constructed in the state.

(B) Five years from now, the available supply of single-family housing in the state will exceed demand.

(C) Five years from now, the per capita income of the state's residents will exceed current levels.

(D) During the next five years, the cost of purchasing new single-family residential housing will decrease.

(E) During the next five years, the number of state residents working at home as opposed to working in office buildings will decrease.

41. Humans naturally crave to do good, act reasonably, and to think decently, these urges must have a global purpose in order to have meaning.

(A) to think decently, these

(B) think decently, yet these

(C) to decently think, and these

(D) thinking decently, but these

(E) think decent, these

ANSWER KEY AND EXPLANATIONS

See Appendix B for score conversion tables to determine your score. Be sure to keep a tally of correct and incorrect answers for each test section.

Analysis of an Argument—Evaluation and Scoring

Evaluate your Argument-Analysis essay on a scale of 1 to 6 (6 being the highest score) according to the following five criteria:

❶ Does your essay identify the key features of the argument and analyze each one in a thoughtful manner?

❷ Does your essay support each point of its critique with insightful reasons and examples?

❸ Does your essay develop its ideas in a clear, organized manner, with appropriate transitions to help connect ideas?

❹ Does your essay demonstrate proficiency, fluency, and maturity in its use of sentence structure, vocabulary, and idiom?

❺ Does your essay demonstrate command of the elements of Standard Written English, including grammar, word usage, spelling, and punctuation?

The following series of questions, which serve to identify the Argument's five distinct problems, will help you evaluate your essay in terms of criteria 1 and 2. To earn a score of 4 or higher, your essay should identify at least three of these problems and, for each one, provide at least one example or counterexample that supports your critique. (Your examples need not be the same as the ones below.) Identifying and discussing at least four of the problems would help earn you an even higher score.

❶ Does the Argument draw *a questionable analogy* between Oak City's circumstances and Mapleton's? (Perhaps the percentage of students needing off-campus housing, which might affect property values, is significantly greater in one town than the other.)

❷ Does the Argument draw a *questionable analogy* between four-year colleges and community colleges? (Perhaps a four-year college would bring greater prestige or higher culture to the town.)

❸ Is the presence of Mapleton's new community college necessarily the actual cause of the decline in Mapleton's property values and rents? (Perhaps some other recent development is responsible instead.)

❹ Is it *necessary* to refuse the new college in order to prevent a decline in property values and rents? (Perhaps Oak City can counteract downward pressure on property values and rents through some other means.)

INTEGRATED REASONING SECTION

1. F, B	4. E, C	7.1 A	9.2 B	11.1 A
2.1 B	5. C, D	7.2 A	9.3 A	11.2 C
2.2 B	6.1 B	7.3 B	10.1 C	12.1 C
2.3 A	6.2 A	8. D	10.2 B	12.2 C
3. A, D	6.3 B	9.1 A		

1. **The correct answers are (F)** (*Number of lots*) **and (B)** (*Desirable outcomes in B*). The probability of the union of events A and B occurring equals the probability of event A occurring, plus the probability of event B occurring, minus the probability of the intersection of events A and B occurring. You know the value of all of these probabilities except the last one. The probability of the intersection of events A and B equals the number of desirable outcomes in the intersection of A and B, which is 4, over the number of total outcomes in the lottery—let's call that t. Thus, you have:

$$P(A \cup B) = P(A) + P(B) - P(A \cap B)$$
$$1 = \frac{2}{5} + \frac{4}{5} - \frac{4}{t}$$
$$1 = \frac{2t + 4t - 20}{5t}$$
$$5t = 6t - 20$$
$$t = 20$$

So the correct answer in the first column is F: the total number of lots is 20.

Next, let the number of desirable outcomes in event B be b. In that case, you have:

$$P(B) = \frac{b}{20}$$
$$\frac{4}{5} = \frac{b}{20}$$
$$4 = \frac{b}{4}$$
$$b = 16$$

So the correct answer in the second column is B: the number of desirable outcomes in event B is 16.

2.1. **The correct answer is (B).** Sort the table by the "Base Elevation" column and compare each resort's base elevation with its summit elevation. It looks like only a few resorts have a vertical rise of more than 1,000 meters, so scan through the rows and focus only on those that do. These are Slopes, Condor, and Foxx. Do the math on those three resorts, and you'll find that Condor has the greatest vertical rise, at 1,168 meters. Now, does Condor have the most runs? Not at all: Condor has only 94 runs, while several resorts have more than 100 of them. Thus, the statement is false.

2.2. **The correct answer is (B).** The resort with the greatest percentage of Expert runs is Foxx, 49% of whose runs are Expert. Fourteen percent of Foxx's 161 runs are Beginner, so that number is 23 (rounding to the nearest integer). Scan through the other resorts to see whether one appears likely to have fewer than 23 Beginner runs. Powder Peak is a good possibility: 21% of its 54 runs are Beginner, so it has 11 Beginner runs—fewer than Foxx does. Thus, the statement is false.

2.3. The correct answer is (A). Re-sort by Total Lift Capacity. Emperor resort can accommodate 37,700 skiers per hour, which is the second-most among all resorts. However, Emperor operates for a half-hour longer each day than does Foxx, which can accommodate the most skiers per hour. If you multiply Emperor's 37,700 skiers per hour by its 8 hours of operation daily, you see that the maximum number of skiers who can use its lifts during a full day is 301,600. For Foxx, that number is 288,000. All other resorts can accommodate fewer skiers daily than that, so the statement is correct.

3. **The correct answers are (A) (*Strengthen*) and (D) (*Weaken*).** The analyst concludes that *Prime Meridian* will not do well at the box office because of its competition and the limited number of screens on which it will be shown the first week of its release. The statement that weakens the argument would undermine at least some of the evidence. Choice (D) does so: If the film will be shown on more screens after the first week, then its earning potential will increase later in its theatrical run and, thus, the analyst's prediction of poor revenues for the entire run is weakened. Choice (A) says that history is not on the side of family dramas, such as *Prime Meridian*, when they go up against big-budget action-adventures, such as *Blowtorch*. This statement describes the situation that *Prime Meridian* is in, thus reinforcing the analyst's conclusion. Choice (B) offers an irrelevant comparison between the other two films. Choice (C) refers to revenues after the theatrical run is over, so it, too, is irrelevant. Choice (E) does possibly weaken the argument (if the *Animal Pleasures* sequel may not have a strong showing at the box office, then it may not pose so formidable a competition for *Prime Meridian* as the analyst suggests), but not enough to be a better answer over choice (D).

4. **The correct answers are (E) (*Assumption*) and (C) (*Fact*).** The wildlife expert gives many reasons why cheetahs are vulnerable. She states that cheetah populations have been declining, and concludes that the species will soon be extinct in the wild. Her argument assumes that nothing will change in the near future in order to stem the downward trend of cheetah populations. In particular, since the main threat to cheetahs is humans, this failed change will probably be related to human behavior toward the cats. Choice (E) identifies this assumption: Conservation efforts will not alter the current trend. A fact suggesting this is supplied by choice (C): Farmers, who are the biggest threat to cheetahs, have resisted such conservation efforts. The statement in choice (A), if true, would certainly go a long way toward spelling the extinction of cheetahs; however, it neither is assumed by the argument nor supports the argument's assumption. Statement (B) suggests that one type of cheetah prey may have trouble of its own. If this leads to diminished populations of Thomson's gazelles, it could be trouble for cheetahs as well—but again, this is a possible fact that does not address an assumption made by the wildlife expert, and it is not an assumption made by her, either. Choice (D) would seem to help cheetahs, not hurt them: fewer lions would mean fewer threats for cheetahs. Finally, choice (F) refers to cheetah populations in captivity, while the argument discusses cheetahs in the wild.

5. **The correct answers are (C) (*Over 5 hours*) and (D) (*Over 5X miles*).** The first question is easier to answer. If Marcel drives for 5 hours, then he goes at a constant speed of X for 2 hours and at a constant speed of Y for the remaining 3 hours. Thus, his average speed is $\frac{2X + 3Y}{5}$.

Now, if Marcel travels a total of $5X$ miles, then over the first 2 hours he covers $2X$ miles, so he has $3X$ miles left to travel at a speed of Y miles per hour:

$$\frac{Y \text{ miles}}{1 \text{ hours}} = \frac{3X \text{ miles}}{? \text{ hours}}$$

$$? = \frac{3X}{Y}$$

So he covers the remaining $3X$ miles in $\dfrac{3X}{Y}$ hours. Therefore, in total his trip lasts $2 + \dfrac{3X}{Y}$ hours. You can now find his average speed for the trip:

$$S = \frac{\text{Total Distance}}{\text{Total Time}}$$

$$S = \frac{5X}{2 + \dfrac{3X}{Y}}$$

$$S = \frac{5X}{\dfrac{2Y + 3X}{Y}}$$

$$S = \frac{5XY}{2Y + 3X}$$

6.1. The correct answer is (B). You do not need to re-sort the table for any of the statements in this set. Regarding the first statement, the figures are as follows: The number of workers with a bachelor's degree or more in 2010 was 23,096. The number of workers in the "Less than 9th grade" category was 1,417, in the "9th to 12th grade, nongraduate" category it was 2,615, and in the "High school graduate" category it was 16,165. These figures add up to 20,197, but you could also see that their sum would be less than 23,000 without calculating precisely. In any event, the statement is false.

6.2. The correct answer is (A). Four of the six groups had a lower median earnings figure in 2010 than in 2006. Therefore, the probability that a group's median earnings decreased between 2006 and 2010 is 67%, which is lower than 70%.

6.3. The correct answer is (B). You do not need to calculate the percentage change for each group. Rather, calculate this change for the "High school graduate" group and then try to find one other group that may have had a greater change. In 2006, 17,751 earners were in the "High school graduate" category; in 2010, that figure was 16,165. The percentage change was:

$$\frac{17,751 - 16,165}{17,751}(100\%) = 8.93\%$$

The "9th to 12th grade" group seems as though it may have experienced a greater percentage change between 2006 and 2010: the numerical change is certainly smaller than that for high school graduates, but the initial number is considerably smaller. For "9th to 12th graders", the percentage change was:

$$\frac{3,219 - 2,615}{3,219}(100\%) = 18.76\%$$

This is a significantly greater percentage change, so the statement is false.

7.1. The correct answer is (A). The average financial aid package in 2010 was $30,000, as you can tell from the graph. The Class Agent mentions that the class of '02 has 320 members. If half of them contribute in 2011, they'll have to contribute $\dfrac{\$30,000}{160}$, or $187.50, on average in order to cover one full financial aid package.

7.2. The correct answer is (A). In 2010, the class of '02 contributed enough for exactly two-thirds of one financial aid package. The average financial aid package in 2010 was $30,000, so the class contributed $20,000. This is the amount of the average financial aid package in 2000.

7.3. The correct answer is (B). Forty-six percent of the 320 members of the class contributed to the fund in 2010. That number is 147, not 165.

8. The correct answer is (D). You can tell from the graph that in 2010 the College offered $30,000 on average to about 56% of its students. The Class Agent tells you that there were 1,600 students in total in 2010. Thus, the total amount of the financial aid that the College offered was approximately:

$$56\%(1600)\$30,000 = 26,880,000$$

9.1. The correct answer is (A). The graph and the Class Agent's letter show that the College has increased its average financial aid package each year over the past 25 years—and the Class Agent says the College has done so as part of its commitment to its students.

9.2. The correct answer is (B). This is unclear. All you know is that "our alma mater has resisted such student growth." You don't know whether it has or has not increased its tuition.

9.3. The correct answer is (A). The Class Agent does list the college's "safeguarding its preciously low student-to-faculty ratio" as a key benefit for students.

10.1. The correct answer is (C). Between 1960 and 1970, the U.S. population grew by approximately 24 million. This growth is represented on the graph by the second bar from the left. The 24 million was approximately 13.5% of the U.S. population in 1960. This percentage is represented by the value of the line at the middle of the 1960–1970 interval. Let X be the U.S. population in 1960. Then,

$$24,000,000 = 13.5\%X$$
$$24 \times 10^6 = 13.5\%X$$
$$X = \frac{24 \times 10^6}{13.5\%}$$
$$X = \frac{24 \times 10^8}{13.5}$$
$$X \approx 1.78 \times 10^8$$
$$X \approx 178,000,000$$

You calculated the U.S. population in 1960 as "approximately" 178 million. Only one answer choice is close enough to this figure, and that's choice (C).

10.2. The correct answer is (B). Pick numbers: Let 100 stand for the U.S. population in 1960. Between 1960 and 1970, the U.S. population grew by approximately 13.5%, so in 1970 it was 113.5. Between 1970 and 1980 the U.S. population grew by approximately 11.5%, so in 1980 it was approximately 1.115 times 113.5, which equals 126.5525. That comes to a growth of approximately 27% compared to the 1960 population of 100. Again, the approximation was not perfect, but the correct answer is clear: choice (B).

11.1. The correct answer is (A). The top line in the graph represents "All People." The percent of all people with an income-to-poverty ratio below 1.5 is slightly less than 25 percent, and the percent of all people with income-to-poverty ratio over 1.0 is slightly more than 15 percent. Therefore, the percent of all people with an income-to-poverty ratio between 1 and 1.5 is slightly less than 25 minus slightly more than 15, which equals somewhat less than 10. Choice (A), 9.5, is the best answer.

11.2.   The correct answer is (C). In 2010, approximately 9% of people over the age of 65 had income below the poverty threshold. If there were 3.5 million such people, then you can find the total number, x, of people over the age of 65:

$$3.5 = 9\%(x)$$
$$x = \frac{3.5}{9\%}$$
$$x = \frac{3.5}{9}(100)$$
$$x \approx 39$$

12.1.   The correct answer is (C). The investor has 20 Large Cap Growth stocks, 8 Small Cap Growth stocks, and 6 Mid Cap Growth stocks, for a total of 34 Growth stocks. In total, the investor has 96 stocks in her portfolio. Therefore, the percentage of growth stocks in the portfolio is:

$$\frac{34}{96}100\% = 35.42\%$$

12.2.   The correct answer is (C). The investor has 20 Large Cap Growth, 17 Large Cap Value, and 11 Large Cap Core stocks, for a total of 48 Large Cap stocks. She has 12 Small Cap Value, 9 Small Cap Core, and 8 Small Cap Growth stocks, for a total of 29 Small Cap stocks. If the investor has n times as many Large Cap stocks in her portfolio as Small Cap stocks, then:

$$48 = 29n$$
$$n = 1.66$$

QUANTITATIVE SECTION

1. C	9. B	17. E	25. C	33. D
2. D	10. D	18. C	26. E	34. D
3. B	11. A	19. D	27. A	35. A
4. C	12. C	20. A	28. C	36. B
5. E	13. B	21. D	29. D	37. E
6. D	14. E	22. A	30. D	
7. C	15. D	23. B	31. B	
8. C	16. C	24. D	32. D	

1. **The correct answer is (C).** Evaluate the expression:

$$\left(\frac{1}{3}\%\right)54 = \frac{\frac{1}{3}\times 54}{100} = \frac{18}{100} = 0.18$$

2. **The correct answer is (D).** The amount of the decrease is $4. The percent of the decrease is $\frac{4}{25}$ or $\frac{16}{100}$, or 16%.

3. **The correct answer is (B).** Statement (2) provides an average of 55 students per bus. Thus, since $(55)(4) = 220 > 175$, this means that 4 buses would be required.

4. **The correct answer is (C).** To answer the question, you need to know drive B's total capacity as well as the amount (number of gigabytes) of drive B's capacity currently used. Statement (1), together with the information given in the question stem, provides the former, while Statement (2) provides the latter. [The storage capacities of drives A and B are 17 and 20, respectively. Of drive B's 20 gigabyte capacity, 42.5% (8.5 gigabytes) is currently used.]

5. **The correct answer is (E).** You could piece together the panes into either a single column (or row) of 8 panes or into 2 adjacent columns (or rows) of 4 panes each. In the first case, the door's perimeter would be 18. In the second case, the door's perimeter would be 12. Thus, Statement (1) alone is insufficient to answer the question. Statement (2) alone is insufficient for the same reason. Both statements together still fail to provide sufficient information to determine the shape (or perimeter) of the door.

6. **The correct answer is (D).** One way to solve this problem is to substitute each answer choice in turn into the given fraction. You can also solve the problem algebraically. Let $\dfrac{x}{2x}$ represent the original fraction. Add 4 to both the numerator and denominator, then cross-multiply to solve for x:

$$\frac{x+4}{2x+4} = \frac{5}{8}$$
$$8x + 32 = 10x + 20$$
$$12 = 2x$$
$$6 = x$$

The original denominator is $2x$, or 12.

7. **The correct answer is (C).** The best way to proceed is to note that you can rewrite the equation as a difference of two squares:

$$36 = 169x^2$$
$$169x^2 - 36 = 0$$
$$(13x)^2 - 6^2 = 0$$
$$(13x + 6)(13x - 6) = 0$$

$$13x + 6 = 0 \qquad 13x - 6 = 0$$
$$x = -\frac{6}{13} \;\; \text{OR} \qquad x = \frac{6}{13}$$

Only choice (C) lists one of these two solutions, so it is the correct answer.

8. **The correct answer is (C).** To determine the size of Unit C, first determine the size of Unit D as a percentage of the total warehouse size. Unit D occupies 15,500 square feet, or approximately 11%, of the total 140,000 square feet in the warehouse. Thus, Unit C occupies 19% of that total ($100\% - 28\% - 42\% - 11\% = 19\%$). The question asks for the difference in size between Unit A (28%) and Unit D (19%). That difference is 9% of the 140,000 total square feet, or 12,600 square feet.

9. **The correct answer is (B).** If $f(x)$ and $g(x)$ intersect at the point (a,b), then when x equals a, $f(x)$ equals $g(x)$. Set $f(x)$ equal to $g(x)$ and solve for x:

$$x^2 + 2 = 1 - 2x$$
$$x^2 + 2x + 1 = 0$$
$$(x+1)^2 = 0$$
$$x + 1 = 0$$
$$x = -1$$

Substitute this value of x into either equation in order to find the y-coordinate: $f(-1) = (-1)^2 + 2 = 3$. So, the graphs of the two functions intersect at the point $(-1,3)$.

10. **The correct answer is (D).** Apply the defined operation substituting 3 for n and 4 for m:

$$3_\triangle 4 = \frac{4^2}{3-4}$$

$$3_\triangle 4 = -16$$

Next, apply the defined operation again, this time substituting -16 for n and 4 for m:

$$-16_\triangle 4 = \frac{4^2}{-16-4}$$

$$-16_\triangle 4 = \frac{16}{-20}$$

$$-16_\triangle 4 = -\frac{4}{5}$$

11. **The correct answer is (A).** Because of the two right angles indicated in the figure, $AB \parallel DC$, $ABCD$ is a trapezoid. The area of a trapezoid $= \frac{1}{2}h(b_1 + b_2)$, where h is the height and each b is a parallel base (side):

$$A = \frac{1}{2}(9)(10+12) = 99$$

12. **The correct answer is (C).** Simplify all four terms by removing perfect squares or cubes. Then, for each fraction, divide common factors:

$$\frac{\sqrt[3]{81x^7}}{\sqrt{9x^4}} - \frac{\sqrt{162x^5}}{\sqrt[3]{27x^6}} = \frac{(3x^2)\sqrt[3]{3x}}{3x^2} - \frac{(9x^2)\sqrt{2x}}{3x^2} = \sqrt[3]{3x} - 3\sqrt{2x}$$

13. **The correct answer is (B).** Since each of the two series is strictly arithmetic (all terms are evenly spaced), for each series the mean is the same as the median: exactly midway between the least and greatest numbers.

Mean of first series: $\dfrac{1+16}{2} = \dfrac{17}{2}$

Mean of second series: $\dfrac{17+32}{2} = \dfrac{49}{2}$

Now, do the subtraction: $\dfrac{49}{2} - \dfrac{17}{2} = \dfrac{32}{2}$, or 16

14. **The correct answer is (E).** If unequal quantities (c and d) are added to unequal quantities of the same order (a and b), the result is an inequality of the same order. Choice (E) essentially states this rule.

15. **The correct answer is (D).** First, you need to determine the volume of the cylindrical tube. The tube's radius (r) is $\dfrac{1}{2}$ and its length is 4. Apply the formula for the volume of a right cylinder ($V = \pi r^2 h$):

$$V = \pi \left(\frac{1}{2}\right)^2 (4) = \pi \left(\frac{1}{4}\right)(4) = \pi$$

The tube's volume is *pi* (approximately 3.1) cubic feet. Regardless of its shape, the tube will not fit into a box containing only 3 cubic feet. Thus, given statement (1) alone, you can answer the question. (The answer is *no*.) Statement (2) alone allows for an infinite variety of box shapes. However, no shape with a surface area of 14 will accommodate the tube. How do you know this? Assume that the box's dimensions are $3 \times 1 \times 1$. It's total surface area is exactly 14, yet it's too short (only 3 feet long) to accommodate the tube, which is 4 feet long. Visualize altering the box's shape (making it either "fatter" or "skinnier") while maintaining a surface area of 14. To increase its length, you must sacrifice surface area of the base (and vice versa). In any case, a box with surface area of 14 cannot accommodate the tube. Thus, Statement (2) alone suffices to answer the question. (Again, the answer is *no*.)

16. **The correct answer is (C).** Using negative integers with the least absolute value yields the least product. Start with -1, then decrease the values of x and y if necessary. The first two values that satisfy the equation are: $y = -2$, $x = -1[-1 - (-2) = 1]$. Accordingly, $xy = 2$.

17. **The correct answer is (E).** Neither Statement (1) nor (2) alone provides any information about the number of yellow jellybeans. Considering both statements together, however, we know that the jar must contain 1 or more black jellybeans (along with exactly 6 pink jellybeans). Accordingly, the jar can contain a maximum of 1 yellow jellybean. If the jar contains either 6 or 1 yellow jellybeans, the answer to the question is *no*. However, if the jar contains 5 or fewer yellow jellybeans, the answer to the question is *yes*.

18. **The correct answer is (C).** The expression $a^2 - b^2$ can also be expressed in its factored form: $(a + b)(a - b)$. Notice the similarity between this form and the binomial expression given in the question. Factor out the constants (numbers) in the binomial so that it more closely resembles the factored form of $a^2 - b^2$:

$$(3a + 3b)(2a - 2b) = 6(a + b)(a - b) = 6(a^2 - b^2)$$

So the question is asking: Is $a^2 - b^2$ greater than $6(a^2 - b^2)$? Considering Statement (1) alone, $(a^2 - b^2)$ might be either positive or negative, depending on whether the absolute value of b is less than a or greater than a. Accordingly, $(6)(a^2 - b^2)$ might be either greater or less than $(a^2 - b^2)$, and Statement (1) alone does not suffice to answer the question. Considering Statement (2) alone, whether $(a^2 - b^2)$ is positive or negative depends on the value of b, and therefore (6)$(a^2 - b^2)$ might be either greater or less than $(a^2 - b^2)$. Thus, Statement (2) alone does not suffice to answer the question. However, both statements together do suffice to answer the question. Given that $b < a < -1$, $(a^2 - b^2)$ must be a negative number. Multiplying this negative number by 6 yields an even lesser number (to the left on the real number line). Therefore, $6(a^2 - b^2) < a^2 - b^2$. (The answer to the question is *yes*.)

19. **The correct answer is (D).** If six years ago Rob's son was 16 years-old, then ten years from now, he will be $16 + 6 + 10$, that is 32 years old. At that point, Rob will be twice as old as his son, so he will be 64 years old. Therefore, he is currently 54 years old.

20. **The correct answer is (A).** Given Statement (1) alone, ΔQRS must be a $1:1:\sqrt{2}$ triangle. Accordingly, $\overline{QR} \cong \overline{SR}$. Since $PQRS$ is a rectangle, $\overline{QR}$ and $\overline{SR}$ are congruent to their respec-

tive opposite sides. Thus, all four sides are congruent, and *PQRS* must be a square. Statement (2) alone provides no new information. We already know that *PQRS* is a rectangle and, accordingly, that the length of $\overline{PS}$ is 12. $\overline{PQ}$ and $\overline{SR}$ could be any length, so the rectangle might, but need not, be a square.

21. **The correct answer is (D).** Consider Statement (1) alone. If the dealer earned a 50% profit from the sale to the customer, determining the amount the customer paid is a simple matter of adding 50% of $10,000 to $10,000. Thus, Statement (1) alone suffices to answer the question. Consider Statement (2) alone. If the dealer's cost was two-thirds the amount the customer paid, then the customer paid $\frac{3}{2}$ of dealer's cost. Determining how much the customer paid is a simple matter of multiplying $10,000 by $\frac{3}{2}$. Thus, Statement (2) alone suffices to answer the question.

22. **The correct answer is (A).** Computing standard deviation involves these steps:

Step 1: Compute the arithmetic mean (simple average) of all terms in the set.

Step 2: Compute the difference between the mean and each term.

Step 3: Square each difference you computed in Step 2.

Step 4: Compute the mean of the squares you computed in Step 3.

Step 5: Compute the non-negative square root of the mean you computed in Step 5.

Applying Steps 1–4 to each of the five answer choices yields the following results:

(A) $\frac{14}{3}$

(B) $\frac{5}{2}$

(C) $\frac{8}{3}$

(D) $\frac{7}{2}$

(E) $\frac{8}{3}$

Choice (A) is the only fraction that exceeds 4. [There's no need to compute the square roots of any of these fractions (Step 5), since their relative values would remain the same.]

23. **The correct answer is (B).** In each set are three distinct member pairs. Thus the probability of selecting any pair is one in three, or $\frac{1}{3}$. Accordingly, the probability of selecting fruit and salad from the appetizer menu along with squash and peas from the vegetable menu is $\frac{1}{3} \times \frac{1}{3} = \frac{1}{9}$.

24. **The correct answer is (D).** Statement (1) says essentially: $A - C > B$. Given that bin *A* contains exactly twice as many potatoes as bin *B*, you can substitute $2B$ for *A* in the inequality, then determine the relationship between the number of potatoes in bins *B* and *C*:

$$A - C > B$$
$$2B - C > B$$
$$B - C > 0$$
$$B > C$$

Thus, Statement (1) alone suffices to answer the question. (The answer is *yes*.) Given Statement (2) alone, C must be less than $\frac{1}{2}A$. (If you're not certain of this, use a few simple numbers to confirm it.) Given that $B = \frac{1}{2}A$, you can conclude from Statement (2) alone that $B > C$. Statement (2) alone also suffices to answer the question. (Notice that you can answer the question with either statement alone without the additional fact that bin A contains exactly 11 more potatoes than bin C. This additional information appears to make the problem more complicated than it really is.)

25. **The correct answer is (C).** The largest possible rectangular area is formed by a square, the area of which is the square of any side. (The length of each side is one-fourth the rope's length.) The largest possible triangular area is formed by an equilateral triangle, the area of which is defined as follows ($s =$ the length of any side):

$$Area = \frac{s^2\sqrt{3}}{4}$$

One way to compare the two areas is to substitute a hypothetical value for the length of the ropes. Assume the length of each rope before it was cut was 12. The length of each of the triangle's sides is 4, while the length of the square's sides is 3:

The triangle's area $= \dfrac{4^2\sqrt{3}}{4} = 4\sqrt{3} \approx 4(1.7) \approx 6.8$

The triangle's area $= 3^2 = 9$

The ratio of 6.8 to 9 is approximately 3 to 4.

26. **The correct answer is (E).** Any multiple-digit prime number must end in an odd digit other than 5 (1, 3, 7, or 9). Considering Statement (1) alone, Z must be either 1 or 3, and five possibilities emerge:

    601

    421

    241

    403

    223

Statement (2) alone allows for many possibilities, since Z can be either 1, 3, 7 or 9. Statements (1) and (2) together eliminate only three of the possibilities, leaving more than one answer.

27. **The correct answer is (A).** Given Statement (1), $a^2 = d$. Substituting a^2 for d in the fraction: $\dfrac{a^4bc}{a^4}$, or simply bc. Given that b and c are both positive but less than 1, $bc < 1$, and Statement (1) alone suffices to answer the question. (The answer to the question is *yes*.) However, Statement (2) alone is insufficient to answer the question. Even if d is greater than zero, Statement (2) fails to provide sufficient information to determine the relative values of the numerator and denominator. A sufficiently small d-value relative to the values of a, b, and c results in a quotient greater than 1, whereas a sufficiently greater relative d-value results in a quotient less than 1.

28. **The correct answer is (C).** $3x$ is a multiple of 3; thus, adding 5 to that number yields a number that is not a multiple of 3. None of the other choices fits the bill. Choice (A) is incorrect because $x > 0$ and therefore must equal 3 or some multiple of 3. Choices (B), (D), and (E) are incorrect because any integer multiplied by 3 is a multiple of 3, and any multiple of 3 (such as 6 or 18) added to a multiple of 3 is also a multiple of 3.

29. **The correct answer is (D).** The number of dollars increases proportionately with the number of pieces of paper. The question is essentially asking: "1 is to m as what is to p?" First, set up a proportion (equate two ratios, or fractions). Then convert pieces of paper to reams (divide m by 500) or reams to pieces (multiply p by 500). (The second conversion method is used below.) Cross-multiply to solve for x:

$$\frac{1}{m} = \frac{x}{500p}$$
$$mx = 500p$$
$$x = \frac{500p}{m}$$

30. **The correct answer is (D).** At the end of September the approximate share prices of the three companies' stocks were as follows:

Ardent stock: $15

Biofirm stock: $49

Compuwin stock: $34

The aggregate price of Ardent stock and Biofirm stock was $64, which exceeds the price of Compuwin stock ($34) by approximately 100%.

31. **The correct answer is (B).** During August, the price of Biofirm stock and Compuwin stock increased by a combined amount of about $5. During the same month the price of Ardent stock decreased by about $6. The net aggregate change is nearly zero.

32. **The correct answer is (D).** The key to this problem involves perpendicular lines and the concept of slope. The slope of l_1 is $\frac{1}{2}$, which means that every 2 units from left to right (the line's "run") corresponds to 1 unit upward (vertically) on the plane (the line's "rise"). Since the angle at point A is a right angle, the slope of $\overline{AB}$ must be -2 (a "drop" or "negative rise" of 2 units for every 1 unit from left to right). Drawing a plumb line down from point A reveals that, in order to attain these slopes, the height (altitude) of ΔOAB must be 2:

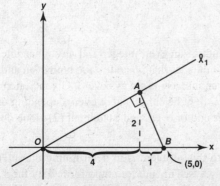

The area of any triangle is defined as one-half the product of its base and height (altitude). Given a base ($\overline{OB}$) of 5 and an altitude of 2, the area of ΔOAB must equal 5.

33. The correct answer is (D). Using the variables to represent portions of these intersecting circles, we know that $x + y = 18$ and $y + z = 16$. Through subtraction, we get $x - z = 2$. Using Statement (1) only, $x + z = 20$, and combined with $x - z = 2$, we find that $x = 11$ and $z = 9$. We know that $y = 7$ by substituting into $x + y = 18$ or $y + z = 16$. Using Statement (2) only, $w = 3$, so $x + y + z = 27$. Combine this equation with $x + y = 18$, and $y + z = 16$. If $x + y = 18$, then $x = 18 - y$. If $y + z = 16$, then $z = 16 - y$. Substitute into $x + y + z = 27$ to get $18 - y + y + 16 - y = 27$, so $y = 7$. Thus, Statements (1) and (2) are each sufficient to establish that 7 students are enrolled in both English and Algebra classes.

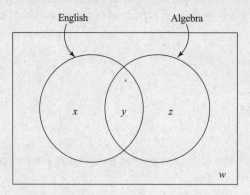

34. The correct answer is (D). Given that twice as many student tickets as adult tickets were sold, two thirds (18) of the 27 tickets sold were student tickets, while one third (9) were adult tickets. You can express the ticket sales revenue by way of the following equation (A = adult ticket price, S = student ticket price):

$$9A + 18S = \$180$$

Statement (1) provides the value of A, which allows you to determine the value of S (the answer to the question):

$$9(10) + 18S = 180$$
$$18S = 90$$
$$S = 5$$

Statement (2) allows you to substitute $2S$ for A in the equation above, thereby allowing you to determine the value of S (the answer to the question):

$$9(2S) + 18S = \$180$$
$$36S = \$180$$
$$S = \$5$$

35. The correct answer is (A). The product of an even integer and any other integer is always even. Therefore, Statement (1) alone establishes that ab and cd are both even and, accordingly, that $ab + cd$ is even (the sum of two even integers is always even). Given Statement (2) alone, however, although ab must be even, cd might be either odd or even, depending on the value of c. Accordingly, $ab + cd$ might be either odd or even, and Statement (2) alone does not suffice to answer the question.

36. The correct answer is (B). The key to this problem is in determining the interior angles of the various triangles formed by the runways. The interior angle formed by the 120° turn from runway 1 to 2 is 60° (a 180° turn would reverse the airplane's direction). Similarly, the interior angle formed by the 135° turn from runway 1 to 3 is 45° (180° − 135°). Two triangle "angle triplets" emerge: a 45°-45°-90° triplet and a 30°-60°-90° triplet, as shown in the next figure. Since the sum of the measures of any triangle's interior angles is 180°, the remaining angles can also be determined:

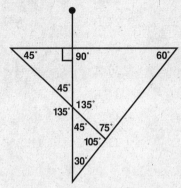

The only angle measure listed among the answer choices that does not appear in the figure above is 55°.

37. **The correct answer is (E).** You can answer this question without knowing the total number of legislators who voted, because the question involves ratios only. Think of the legislature as containing 8 voters divided into two parts: $\frac{5}{8} + \frac{3}{8} = \frac{8}{8}$. For every 5 votes in favor, 3 were cast against the motion. Thus, 5 out of every 8 votes, or $\frac{5}{8}$, were cast in favor of the motion.

VERBAL SECTION

1. E	10. B	18. A	26. A	34. C
2. B	11. D	19. C	27. E	35. E
3. C	12. B	20. E	28. B	36. A
4. B	13. C	21. D	29. E	37. B
5. C	14. A	22. C	30. A	38. D
6. E	15. C	23. D	31. E	39. A
7. A	16. D	24. E	32. C	40. A
8. C	17. B	25. D	33. A	41. B
9. D				

1. **The correct answer is (E).** The original answer is faulty in three ways: the phrases "varnish removal" and "the securing of the flaking paint" are not parallel, the phrase "the securing of the flaking paint" is wordy, and the plural pronoun *they* does not agree with its singular antecedent *museum curator*. Choice (E) remedies all three problems by making the phrase parallel, eliminating the pronoun-antecedent error, and eliminating extra words.

2. **The correct answer is (B).** The original sentence suffers from two distinct faults: the subject and verb do not agree, and the passive voice creates wordiness. Choice (B) eliminates the passive voice, thus correcting the subject-verb agreement problem and streamlining the sentence.

3. **The correct answer is (C).** The original answer is passable, but it coordinates information that should be subordinated in order to show its proper relationship to the independent clause. Choice (C) is the best choice because it correctly creates a relative clause that describes the effects of observing parthenogenesis on von Leeuwenhoek.

4. **The correct answer is (B).** The argument relies on the assumption that alcoholics die relatively young only because alcoholism increases a person's susceptibility to life-threatening diseases and not for other reasons as well. Choice (B) provides explicitly that those other possible reasons were ruled out in compiling the insurance statistics cited in the report.

5. **The correct answer is (C).** Choice (C) helps explain last year's sales results by suggesting that sales of products three years old and older could have fallen sharply during the year. Thus, the proportion of sales produced by newer products could have grown, even without popular new products.

6. **The correct answer is (E).** It can reasonably be inferred that the "new conditions" that sparked the divergence in pistol shrimp are an aspect of the two oceans' "distinctive personalities," which the author states began to emerge "long before the isthmus was fully formed." Choice (E) contradicts the inference.

7. **The correct answer is (A).** The author discusses pistol shrimp as an example of twin species or geminates. Thus, choice (A) expresses the author's immediate purpose in mentioning the mating habits of pistol shrimp.

8. **The correct answer is (C).** The second paragraph provides ample support for this inference. The author states that the terrestrial species migrating south were "better colonizers" than the ones migrating north, that *more than half* of those in the south today came from the north, and that *only three* animal species migrating north across the isthmus survive today. It is readily inferable, then, that more than three species that migrated south across the isthmus survive today.

9. **The correct answer is (D).** The original sentence contains a vague pronoun reference. It is unclear as to what the second *that* refers. Choice (D) restates the idea of the first clause of the original sentence more succinctly and clearly, as well as making it clear by the use of the phrase *and this fact* that the latter part of the sentence refers to the earlier part.

10. **The correct answer is (B).** The conclusion of the argument is that the claim made by those who have discontinued regular exercise is born of laziness; in other words, these people are making this claim because they are lazy. One effective way to refute the argument is to provide convincing evidence that directly contradicts the conclusion. Choice (B) provides just such evidence, by showing that these people are not in fact lazy.

11. **The correct answer is (D).** The original argument's line of reasoning is essentially as follows:

Premise: The well-paid engineers at CompTech do not quit their jobs.

Conclusion: If MicroFirm engineers are not well-paid, they will quit their jobs.

You can express this argument symbolically as follows:

Premise: All As are Bs.

Conclusion: If not A, then not B.

The reasoning is fallacious (flawed), because it fails to account for other possible reasons why MicroFirm engineers have not left their jobs. (Some Bs might not be As.) Choice (D) is the only answer choice that demonstrates the same essential pattern of flawed reasoning. To recognize the similarity, rephrase the argument's sentence structure to match the essence of the original argument:

Premise: All people who practice diligently (A) achieve perfection (B).

Conclusion: If one does not practice diligently (not A), one cannot achieve perfection (not B).

12. **The correct answer is (B).** The original sentence is redundant. Choice (B) corrects these problems by choosing *summary* over "brief summary" (all summaries are brief relative to the whole) and *planning* over "advance planning" (all planning is advance planning). Choice (B) also reduces wordiness by collapsing the prepositional phrase "for her thesis" into a single modifier.

13. **The correct answer is (C).** The original sentence is a fragment because it substitutes an incomplete verb form for a complete verb. Choice (C) is a complete verb; it also correctly places the action in the past and forms a correct sequence of tenses with the verb *could take*.

14. **The correct answer is (A).** The original sentence properly uses the correlative *not only . . . but also.* The two modifying phrases (*not only by increased* and *but also by increased*) are grammatically parallel.

15. **The correct answer is (C).** Shakespeare depicts Richard III as a monster with a twisted soul—a depiction that leads us to believe that Richard could well have been responsible for the deaths of both his brother Clarence and Henry VI. However, the author of the passage tells us that there is historical evidence that Richard did not kill his brother and that there is no proof that Henry VI was actually murdered.

16. **The correct answer is (D).** In the passage, the author first tells us that historians sometimes think they know a historical figure better than they really do. Then the passage's author explains how this can happen by providing an illustrative example—a biographical work (*Richard III*) that is so compelling in its development of the main character that even a historian can be unduly influenced by it.

17. **The correct answer is (B).** According to the passage, Machiavelli's *The Prince* provides information about the tone of the times in which Richard lived. The passage's final sentence tells us that Richard's actions seem "reasonable" in light of the tone of the times—in other words, that his actions reflected the times.

18. **The correct answer is (A).** This argument relies on the assumption that Gregg's Syndrome is more prevalent among Puma Syndrome victims who take Betatol than among those who take Aidistan. Choice (A) essentially affirms this assumption, although it expresses it in a somewhat different way. Given that Gregg's Syndrome renders any Puma Syndrome treatment less effective, if victims who have both syndromes are treated with Betatol while victims who have only Puma Syndrome are treated with Aidistan, then Aidistan will appear to be more effective, although the absence of Gregg's Syndrome might in fact be the key factor that explains the differing results.

19. **The correct answer is (C).** In all likelihood, the district's residents contribute to the revenues of businesses there by purchasing goods and services from them. A net loss in the number of district residents would provide an alternative explanation for the loss of revenue. Choice (C) rules out this possibility, thereby *strengthening* the claim that the loss in revenue was due to the city's reduction in its police force and, accordingly, that increasing the size of the force will reverse the decline in revenues.

20. **The correct answer is (E).** The passage boils down to the following:

    Premise: People buy sport utility vehicles because they believe these vehicles are safe.

    Conclusion: To sell a vehicle, a manufacturer should not emphasize affordability.

    Choice (E) provides the assumption needed to render the argument logically convincing:

    Premise: People buy sport utility vehicles because they believe these vehicles are safe.

    Premise (E): People do not believe that affordable vehicles are safe.

    Conclusion: To sell a sport utility vehicle, a manufacturer should not emphasize its affordability.

21. **The correct answer is (D).** Regardless of the reason for the increase in the volume of material transported to landfills, reducing the volume of material available for transport to landfills would serve the stated objective. Choice (D) suggests a plan of action that, if successful, would help.

22. **The correct answer is (C).** The original sentence is faulty in two respects. First, it improperly uses *because* instead of *because of.* Second, the construction leaves it unclear as to whether the modifying phrase *already in wide use* refers to *other pesticides* or to *chemical compositions.* Choice (C) corrects the misuse of *because* by replacing it with *due to* (an alternative to *because of*).

23. **The correct answer is (D).** Instead of using the proper idiom *equal . . . to* or the proper correlative pair *as . . . as*, the original version attempts to make a comparison by using the improper *equal . . . as.* Choice (D) corrects this error with the correlative pair *as . . . as.*

24. **The correct answer is (E).** The original sentence uses *of* twice; the result is wordy and awkward. Choice (E) is idiomatically proper and more concise than the original version.

25. **The correct answer is (D).** Choice (D) weakens the argument by providing some evidence that in this nation it would be comparatively expensive to produce cosmetics with Yucaipa tree-bark oil and, accordingly, that the tree population in this nation might not be significantly depleted even if the law were repealed.

26. **The correct answer is (A).** You can rephrase choice (A) as follows: *All* Web sites administered by individuals holding advanced degrees in educational technology are official Web sites of nationally accredited colleges. In other words, the following two symbolic statements are logically equivalent:

Only A are B.

All B are A.

Given that all Web sites of nationally accredited colleges have received the highest possible rating from the Department, and given that all Web sites administered by individuals holding advanced degrees in educational technology are official Web sites of nationally accredited colleges, it follows logically that all Web sites administered by individuals holding advanced degrees in educational technology have received the highest possible rating from the Department. To follow the logical steps, it helps to express the premises and conclusion symbolically:

Premise: All A are C.

Premise: All B are A.

Conclusion: All B are C.

27. **The correct answer is (E).** The original version is grammatically correct, but the pronoun reference is vague. (To what does it refer?) Choice (E) clarifies the pronoun reference by using the possessive *its luminosity*.

28. **The correct answer is (B).** Exposure to sunlight was mentioned as one factor determining peak bone mass. Although the passage states that "many of the factors that affect the attainment of peak bone mass also affect rates of bone loss," it is unwarranted to infer that exposure to sunlight is one such factor.

29. **The correct answer is (E).** As long as the population upon which the cited statistic was based excluded those who had not yet achieved peak bone mass, it does not make a difference whether the men in the group achieved their peak bone mass at a different age from the women.

30. **The correct answer is (A).** The author lists various factors affecting peak bone mass, then asserts that many of these factors also affect the rate of bone loss. In mentioning pregnancy and lactation as "additional factors" affecting bone loss, the author implies that these two factors do not also affect peak bone mass.

31. **The correct answer is (E).** The argument relies on two important assumptions. One is that the teachers who transferred from Franklin to Valley View were Vining graduates; the other is that teachers who transferred from Valley View to Franklin were not Vining graduates. If neither or only one were the case, then it would be unreasonable to conclude that Vining graduates are responsible for high academic performance. Admittedly, these assumptions involve a matter of degree; for example, the greater the percentage of Vining alumni among the teachers transferring from Franklin to Valley View, the stronger the argument's conclusion. And admittedly, choice (E) does not acknowledge this fact. Nevertheless, choice (E) provides the essence of one of these two crucial assumptions.

32. **The correct answer is (C).** The argument concludes that the reason for the military's decision was to reduce pilot error during commercial flights. Choice (C) is the only answer choice that supports this conclusion. Given that chemical warfare is likely to escalate in the future, it would

seem that the military would *continue* to require immunization shots. But the military stopped requiring the shots. So the military's decision must have been based on some factor outweighing the potential danger of chemical warfare to pilots. One such possible factor is the increased danger of commercial airline accidents resulting from the immunization shots.

33. **The correct answer is (A).** The original sentence contains no grammatical errors, ambiguous references, or idiomatically improper words or phrases. The word *visionary*, used as an adjective here, is proper, although you could use the word *visionaries* (a noun) instead.

34. **The correct answer is (C).** The original sentence is unclear in meaning; the use of the word *simultaneously* suggests that two or more items are attained. If the sentence had continued with the phrase *global and regional dominance,* the use of the word *simultaneously* would have made more sense. Choice (C) excludes the confusing word *simultaneously* and properly sets off the prepositional phrase beginning with *in the course* with commas to clarify the sentence's meaning.

35. **The correct answer is (E).** Karl's response relies on two alternative but interrelated assumptions: (1) the reruns are likely to be popular enough to compete with Connie's favorite program, and (2) Connie's favorite program will not in fact be popular. Choice (E) provides evidence that helps affirm both of these assumptions by suggesting that the reruns might very well be popular enough to draw the viewing audience away from Connie's favorite program, thus rendering it less popular. Admittedly, choice (E) would provide even greater support if it explicitly indicated that one popular program can draw viewers away from another. Nevertheless, choice (E) is the best among the five answer choices.

36. **The correct answer is (A).** Choice (A) presents the focus of the entire first paragraph. Furthermore, all points made in the article have to do with the relationship between benefits and what employees want or value. Choice (B) is not correct. The author does rely heavily on information from this study to make his or her point; indeed, the study may inform the entire passage, though that is not certain. Nevertheless, the study is used in the service of making a larger point: That benefits may be more important than ever in retaining employees. Choice (C) is tempting; the author does mention this, but it is the focus of a single paragraph, the last paragraph, and not the entire passage. Choice (D) is incorrect because the passage never says that. Instead, it makes the point that human resource departments may undervalue the importance of benefits at times when hiring is easier, presumably as a result of high unemployment. Choice (E) should be eliminated because the author suggests a shifting landscape of benefits; therefore, while benefits remain as important as ever, if not more important, the desired benefits themselves have changed.

37. **The correct answer is (B).** Choice (B) is the correct answer because the writer refers to the MetLife study specifically three times and also suggests no other source for facts or claims beyond the MetLife study. Choice (A) must be ruled out because nothing in the passage suggests this nor is any such claim made. Choice (C) must be ruled out because nothing in the passage suggests this and there are no facts that could lead to this conclusion. Choice (D) presents a tempting possibility; this answer constitutes a reasonable conjecture but is, nevertheless, not supported by any fact in the passage. Choice (E) should be eliminated because the author makes it clear in the first paragraph that baby boomer retirements are at least a "potential threat" if not a code red.

38. **The correct answer is (D).** Choice (D) is the only reason not mentioned in the passage. Choice (A) is mentioned in paragraph 1 as a reason to focus on retention. Choice (B) is mentioned as a reason to focus on retention in the final paragraph. Choice (C) is incorrect because the change in employee wants and values is mentioned in paragraph 2, where the author implies that human resource departments must keep up with such change. Choice (E) should be eliminated because the author does mention this desire and implies that a competent human resources department will keep up with it in order to retain employees.

39. **The correct answer is (A).** At the end of paragraph 2, the author mentions that a keen interest in benefits is now common among younger workers, which suggests this wasn't the case in the past. Choice (B) is not correct. The author says in paragraph 2 that the level of employee interest in benefits has burgeoned, that is, increased dramatically. Choice (C) is incorrect because the author makes it clear that employees appreciate their benefits even when they have to come up with some portion of the cost. Choice (D) is incorrect because the author states that employees now rate life and disability benefits on a par with opportunity for advancement. Choice (E) should be eliminated because the author concludes by noting the "increasing value" of voluntary or personalized benefits and their value in creating employee satisfaction and contributing to retention.

40. **The correct answer is (A).** The passage indicates that developers have curtailed construction of new office buildings until demand grows to meet supply, while stepping up construction of single-family houses. This evidence in itself strongly supports choice (A). Admittedly, it is possible that an influx of businesses from other states will deplete the current oversupply of office buildings and create sufficient demand for new ones. Nevertheless, choice (A) is the best of the five choices.

41. **The correct answer is (B).** The original sentence lacks proper parallelism; *to* should be omitted. Also, the original sentence is composed of two main clauses (each of which could stand on its own as a complete sentence) separated only by a comma. This comma splice should be corrected by inserting an appropriate connecting word, such as *but, yet,* or *although.* Choice (B) corrects both problems.

ANSWER SHEET PRACTICE TEST 3

ANALYTICAL WRITING ASSESSMENT

_____

_____

_____

_____

_____

_____

_____

_____

_____

_____

_____

_____

_____

_____

_____

_____

_____

_____

_____

_____

_____

_____

_____

_____

_____

answer sheet

answer sheet

INTEGRATED REASONING

1.1 Ⓐ Ⓑ Ⓒ Ⓓ Ⓔ Ⓕ   4.1 Ⓐ Ⓑ Ⓒ Ⓓ Ⓔ   7.1 Ⓐ Ⓑ   10.1 Ⓐ Ⓑ Ⓒ Ⓓ
1.2 Ⓐ Ⓑ Ⓒ Ⓓ Ⓔ Ⓕ   4.2 Ⓐ Ⓑ Ⓒ Ⓓ Ⓔ   7.2 Ⓐ Ⓑ   10.2 Ⓐ Ⓑ Ⓒ Ⓓ
2.1 Ⓐ Ⓑ   5.1 Ⓐ Ⓑ Ⓒ Ⓓ Ⓔ Ⓕ   7.3 Ⓐ Ⓑ   11.1 Ⓐ Ⓑ Ⓒ Ⓓ
2.2 Ⓐ Ⓑ   5.2 Ⓐ Ⓑ Ⓒ Ⓓ Ⓔ Ⓕ   8.1 Ⓐ Ⓑ   11.2 Ⓐ Ⓑ Ⓒ Ⓓ
2.3 Ⓐ Ⓑ   6.1 Ⓐ Ⓑ   8.2 Ⓐ Ⓑ   12.1 Ⓐ Ⓑ Ⓒ Ⓓ
3.1 Ⓐ Ⓑ Ⓒ Ⓓ Ⓔ Ⓕ   6.2 Ⓐ Ⓑ   8.3 Ⓐ Ⓑ   12.2 Ⓐ Ⓑ Ⓒ Ⓓ Ⓔ
3.2 Ⓐ Ⓑ Ⓒ Ⓓ Ⓔ Ⓕ   6.3 Ⓐ Ⓑ   9.   Ⓐ Ⓑ Ⓒ Ⓓ Ⓔ

QUANTITATIVE SECTION

1. Ⓐ Ⓑ Ⓒ Ⓓ Ⓔ   9. Ⓐ Ⓑ Ⓒ Ⓓ Ⓔ   17. Ⓐ Ⓑ Ⓒ Ⓓ Ⓔ   25. Ⓐ Ⓑ Ⓒ Ⓓ Ⓔ   33. Ⓐ Ⓑ Ⓒ Ⓓ Ⓔ
2. Ⓐ Ⓑ Ⓒ Ⓓ Ⓔ   10. Ⓐ Ⓑ Ⓒ Ⓓ Ⓔ   18. Ⓐ Ⓑ Ⓒ Ⓓ Ⓔ   26. Ⓐ Ⓑ Ⓒ Ⓓ Ⓔ   34. Ⓐ Ⓑ Ⓒ Ⓓ Ⓔ
3. Ⓐ Ⓑ Ⓒ Ⓓ Ⓔ   11. Ⓐ Ⓑ Ⓒ Ⓓ Ⓔ   19. Ⓐ Ⓑ Ⓒ Ⓓ Ⓔ   27. Ⓐ Ⓑ Ⓒ Ⓓ Ⓔ   35. Ⓐ Ⓑ Ⓒ Ⓓ Ⓔ
4. Ⓐ Ⓑ Ⓒ Ⓓ Ⓔ   12. Ⓐ Ⓑ Ⓒ Ⓓ Ⓔ   20. Ⓐ Ⓑ Ⓒ Ⓓ Ⓔ   28. Ⓐ Ⓑ Ⓒ Ⓓ Ⓔ   36. Ⓐ Ⓑ Ⓒ Ⓓ Ⓔ
5. Ⓐ Ⓑ Ⓒ Ⓓ Ⓔ   13. Ⓐ Ⓑ Ⓒ Ⓓ Ⓔ   21. Ⓐ Ⓑ Ⓒ Ⓓ Ⓔ   29. Ⓐ Ⓑ Ⓒ Ⓓ Ⓔ   37. Ⓐ Ⓑ Ⓒ Ⓓ Ⓔ
6. Ⓐ Ⓑ Ⓒ Ⓓ Ⓔ   14. Ⓐ Ⓑ Ⓒ Ⓓ Ⓔ   22. Ⓐ Ⓑ Ⓒ Ⓓ Ⓔ   30. Ⓐ Ⓑ Ⓒ Ⓓ Ⓔ
7. Ⓐ Ⓑ Ⓒ Ⓓ Ⓔ   15. Ⓐ Ⓑ Ⓒ Ⓓ Ⓔ   23. Ⓐ Ⓑ Ⓒ Ⓓ Ⓔ   31. Ⓐ Ⓑ Ⓒ Ⓓ Ⓔ
8. Ⓐ Ⓑ Ⓒ Ⓓ Ⓔ   16. Ⓐ Ⓑ Ⓒ Ⓓ Ⓔ   24. Ⓐ Ⓑ Ⓒ Ⓓ Ⓔ   32. Ⓐ Ⓑ Ⓒ Ⓓ Ⓔ

VERBAL SECTION

1. Ⓐ Ⓑ Ⓒ Ⓓ Ⓔ   9. Ⓐ Ⓑ Ⓒ Ⓓ Ⓔ   17. Ⓐ Ⓑ Ⓒ Ⓓ Ⓔ   25. Ⓐ Ⓑ Ⓒ Ⓓ Ⓔ   33. Ⓐ Ⓑ Ⓒ Ⓓ Ⓔ
2. Ⓐ Ⓑ Ⓒ Ⓓ Ⓔ   10. Ⓐ Ⓑ Ⓒ Ⓓ Ⓔ   18. Ⓐ Ⓑ Ⓒ Ⓓ Ⓔ   26. Ⓐ Ⓑ Ⓒ Ⓓ Ⓔ   34. Ⓐ Ⓑ Ⓒ Ⓓ Ⓔ
3. Ⓐ Ⓑ Ⓒ Ⓓ Ⓔ   11. Ⓐ Ⓑ Ⓒ Ⓓ Ⓔ   19. Ⓐ Ⓑ Ⓒ Ⓓ Ⓔ   27. Ⓐ Ⓑ Ⓒ Ⓓ Ⓔ   35. Ⓐ Ⓑ Ⓒ Ⓓ Ⓔ
4. Ⓐ Ⓑ Ⓒ Ⓓ Ⓔ   12. Ⓐ Ⓑ Ⓒ Ⓓ Ⓔ   20. Ⓐ Ⓑ Ⓒ Ⓓ Ⓔ   28. Ⓐ Ⓑ Ⓒ Ⓓ Ⓔ   36. Ⓐ Ⓑ Ⓒ Ⓓ Ⓔ
5. Ⓐ Ⓑ Ⓒ Ⓓ Ⓔ   13. Ⓐ Ⓑ Ⓒ Ⓓ Ⓔ   21. Ⓐ Ⓑ Ⓒ Ⓓ Ⓔ   29. Ⓐ Ⓑ Ⓒ Ⓓ Ⓔ   37. Ⓐ Ⓑ Ⓒ Ⓓ Ⓔ
6. Ⓐ Ⓑ Ⓒ Ⓓ Ⓔ   14. Ⓐ Ⓑ Ⓒ Ⓓ Ⓔ   22. Ⓐ Ⓑ Ⓒ Ⓓ Ⓔ   30. Ⓐ Ⓑ Ⓒ Ⓓ Ⓔ   38. Ⓐ Ⓑ Ⓒ Ⓓ Ⓔ
7. Ⓐ Ⓑ Ⓒ Ⓓ Ⓔ   15. Ⓐ Ⓑ Ⓒ Ⓓ Ⓔ   23. Ⓐ Ⓑ Ⓒ Ⓓ Ⓔ   31. Ⓐ Ⓑ Ⓒ Ⓓ Ⓔ   39. Ⓐ Ⓑ Ⓒ Ⓓ Ⓔ
8. Ⓐ Ⓑ Ⓒ Ⓓ Ⓔ   16. Ⓐ Ⓑ Ⓒ Ⓓ Ⓔ   24. Ⓐ Ⓑ Ⓒ Ⓓ Ⓔ   32. Ⓐ Ⓑ Ⓒ Ⓓ Ⓔ   40. Ⓐ Ⓑ Ⓒ Ⓓ Ⓔ
                                                                                 41. Ⓐ Ⓑ Ⓒ Ⓓ Ⓔ

answer sheet

Practice Test 3

ANALYTICAL WRITING ASSIGNMENT

Analysis of an Argument

1 Question • 30 Minutes

Directions: Using a word processor, compose an essay for the following argument and directive. Do not use any spell-checking or grammar-checking functions.

The following appeared in a speech by a prominent state politician:

> "At Giant Industries, our state's largest private business, the average production worker is now 42 years old. Recently, Giant's revenue from the sale of textiles and paper, which together account for the majority of Giant's manufacturing business, has declined significantly. Since an increasing percentage of new graduates from our state's colleges and universities are finding jobs in other states, our state will soon face a crisis in which the size of our workforce will be insufficient to replace our current workers as they retire, in turn resulting in widespread business failure and a reduced quality of life in our state."

Discuss how well reasoned you find this argument. In your discussion be sure to analyze the line of reasoning and the use of evidence in the argument. For example, you may need to consider what questionable assumptions underlie the thinking and what alternative explanations or counterexamples might weaken the conclusion. You can also discuss what sort of evidence would strengthen or refute the argument, what changes in the argument would make it more logically sound, and what, if anything, would help you better evaluate its conclusion.

INTEGRATED REASONING

12 Questions • 30 Minutes

1. An amusement park has enough space on its ground to add one more roller coaster. It is considering two options: a roller coaster based on a popular action film and one based on a popular children's television series. However, studies show that only young children are fans of the television series, so the amusement park will be better served by building the roller coaster based on the action film.

   Indicate two different statements as follows: one statement identifies an *assumption required* by the argument, and the other identifies a *possible fact* that, if true, would provide significant logical support for the required assumption.

1.1 Assumption	1.2 Fact	
(A)	(A)	The film will not lose popularity once its sequel is released.
(B)	(B)	Most young children are not tall enough to ride on roller coasters.
(C)	(C)	Movie attendance has declined significantly since the 1960s.
(D)	(D)	Most of the people who will consider riding on the new roller coaster are not young children.
(E)	(E)	Children spend increasing amounts of time on the Internet and decreasing amounts of time watching television.
(F)	(F)	The park already has a roller coaster based on a children's show.

2. The table shows a wine critic's ratings of the 2006 through 2010 vintages of wines from several wine regions. The critic considers Outstanding the vintages that received a grade of 96 or higher; Excellent, the vintages that received a grade between 91 and 95, inclusive; Very Good, the vintages that received a grade between 86 and 90, inclusive; Good, the vintages that received a grade between 81 and 85, inclusive; Average, the vintages that received a grade between 71 and 80, inclusive; and Below Average, the vintages that received a grade of 70 or lower. "N/A" refers to vintages that have not been rated.

Sort By: Select ▼

Region	Country	2010	2009	2008	2007	2006
Bordeaux – Haut Médoc	France	N/A	92	92	83	86
Bordeaux – Margaux	France	94	97	91	84	85
Bordeaux – Pomerol	France	93	94	92	84	87
Bordeaux – Sauternes	France	91	95	88	91	85
Bordeaux – St. Emilion	France	92	91	93	84	89
Burgundy – Beaujolais	France	89	94	81	85	87
Burgundy – Côte de Beaune	France	91	92	88	80	81
Burgundy – Côte de Nuits	France	90	93	84	85	90
California, Central Coast (Pinot Noir)	U.S.A.	85	87	90	93	93
California, North Coast (Merlot)	U.S.A.	N/A	86	81	84	82
California, North Coast (Cabernet Sauvignon)	U.S.A.	91	92	95	95	89

California, North Coast (Pinot Noir)	U.S.A.	90	91	87	93	85
California, North Coast (Zinfandel)	U.S.A.	84	82	77	86	81
Languedoc – Roussillon	France	96	90	88	90	91
Piemonte – Barbaresco	Italy	N/A	N/A	91	89	92
Piemonte – Barbera	Italy	N/A	87	88	83	87
Piemonte – Barolo	Italy	N/A	N/A	94	96	98
Rhone – Châteauneuf du Pape	France	96	94	87	95	88
Rhone – Côte Rôtie	France	93	97	82	87	90
Rhone – Gigondas	France	92	94	81	86	89
Tuscany – Brunello di Montalcino	Italy	N/A	N/A	91	94	97
Tuscany – Chianti	Italy	N/A	92	89	93	94
Tuscany – Vino Nobile di Montepulciano	Italy	N/A	91	92	91	93

For each of the following statements, select *Yes* if the statement is true based on the information in the table. Otherwise, select *No*.

	(A) Yes	**(B)** No	
2.1	○	○	Of all the regions and vintages that were rated, a 2006 vintage was less likely to receive an Average rating than was a 2007 vintage.
2.2	○	○	Of all the regions and vintages that were rated, a 2010 vintage was more likely to receive an Outstanding rating than was the vintage of any other year.
2.3	○	○	Among the 2006 vintages from California's North Coast that were rated, none received a grade higher than 89.

(On the computer test, this will be the end of the question prompt and statements. For this paper test and your convenience, we are providing the various other ways you may sort the data.)

Sort By: | Country ▼ |

Region	Country	2010	2009	2008	2007	2006
Languedoc – Roussillon	France	96	90	88	90	91
Bordeaux – St. Emilion	France	92	91	93	84	89
Burgundy – Côte de Beaune	France	91	92	88	80	81
Bordeaux – Haut Médoc	France	N/A	92	92	83	86
Burgundy – Côte de Nuits	France	90	93	84	85	90
Burgundy – Beaujolais	France	89	94	81	85	87
Rhone – Gigondas	France	92	94	81	86	89
Bordeaux – Pomerol	France	93	94	92	84	87
Rhone – Châteauneuf du Pape	France	96	94	87	95	88
Bordeaux – Sauternes	France	91	95	88	91	85
Rhone – Côte Rôtie	France	93	97	82	87	90

Bordeaux – Margaux	France	94	97	91	84	85
Piemonte – Barbera	Italy	N/A	87	88	83	87
Tuscany – Vino Nobile di Montepulciano	Italy	N/A	91	92	91	93
Tuscany – Chianti	Italy	N/A	92	89	93	94
Piemonte – Barbaresco	Italy	N/A	N/A	91	89	92
Piemonte – Barolo	Italy	N/A	N/A	94	96	98
Tuscany – Brunello di Montalcino	Italy	N/A	N/A	91	94	97
California, North Coast (Zinfandel)	U.S.A.	84	82	77	86	81
California, North Coast (Merlot)	U.S.A.	N/A	86	81	84	82
California, Central Coast (Pinot Noir)	U.S.A.	85	87	90	93	93
California, North Coast (Pinot Noir)	U.S.A.	90	91	87	93	85
California, North Coast (Cabernet Sauvignon)	U.S.A.	91	92	95	95	89

Sort By: [2010 ▼]

Region	Country	2010	2009	2008	2007	2006
California, North Coast (Zinfandel)	U.S.A.	84	82	77	86	81
California, Central Coast (Pinot Noir)	U.S.A.	85	87	90	93	93
Burgundy – Beaujolais	France	89	94	81	85	87
Burgundy – Côte de Nuits	France	90	93	84	85	90
California, North Coast (Pinot Noir)	U.S.A.	90	91	87	93	85
Bordeaux – Sauternes	France	91	95	88	91	85
Burgundy – Côte de Beaune	France	91	92	88	80	81
California, North Coast (Cabernet Sauvignon)	U.S.A.	91	92	95	95	89
Bordeaux – St. Emilion	France	92	91	93	84	89
Rhone – Gigondas	France	92	94	81	86	89
Bordeaux – Pomerol	France	93	94	92	84	87
Rhone – Côte Rôtie	France	93	97	82	87	90
Bordeaux – Margaux	France	94	97	91	84	85
Languedoc – Roussillon	France	96	90	88	90	91
Rhone – Châteauneuf du Pape	France	96	94	87	95	88
Bordeaux – Haut Médoc	France	N/A	92	92	83	86
California, North Coast (Merlot)	U.S.A.	N/A	86	81	84	82
Piemonte – Barbaresco	Italy	N/A	N/A	91	89	92
Piemonte – Barbera	Italy	N/A	87	88	83	87
Piemonte – Barolo	Italy	N/A	N/A	94	96	98
Tuscany – Brunello di Montalcino	Italy	N/A	N/A	91	94	97
Tuscany – Chianti	Italy	N/A	92	89	93	94
Tuscany – Vino Nobile di Montepulciano	Italy	N/A	91	92	91	93

Sort By: | 2009 ▼

Region	Country	2010	2009	2008	2007	2006
California, North Coast (Zinfandel)	U.S.A.	84	82	77	86	81
California, North Coast (Merlot)	U.S.A.	N/A	86	81	84	82
California, Central Coast (Pinot Noir)	U.S.A.	85	87	90	93	93
Piemonte – Barbera	Italy	N/A	87	88	83	87
Languedoc – Roussillon	France	96	90	88	90	91
California, North Coast (Pinot Noir)	U.S.A.	90	91	87	93	85
Bordeaux – St. Emilion	France	92	91	93	84	89
Tuscany – Vino Nobile di Montepulciano	Italy	N/A	91	92	91	93
Burgundy – Côte de Beaune	France	91	92	88	80	81
California, North Coast (Cabernet Sauvignon)	U.S.A.	91	92	95	95	89
Bordeaux – Haut Médoc	France	N/A	92	92	83	86
Tuscany – Chianti	Italy	N/A	92	89	93	94
Burgundy – Côte de Nuits	France	90	93	84	85	90
Burgundy – Beaujolais	France	89	94	81	85	87
Rhone – Gigondas	France	92	94	81	86	89
Bordeaux – Pomerol	France	93	94	92	84	87
Rhone – Châteauneuf du Pape	France	96	94	87	95	88
Bordeaux – Sauternes	France	91	95	88	91	85
Rhone – Côte Rôtie	France	93	97	82	87	90
Bordeaux – Margaux	France	94	97	91	84	85
Piemonte – Barbaresco	Italy	N/A	N/A	91	89	92
Piemonte – Barolo	Italy	N/A	N/A	94	96	98
Tuscany – Brunello di Montalcino	Italy	N/A	N/A	91	94	97

Sort By: | 2008 ▼

Region	Country	2010	2009	2008	2007	2006
California, North Coast (Zinfandel)	U.S.A.	84	82	77	86	81
California, North Coast (Merlot)	U.S.A.	N/A	86	81	84	82
Burgundy – Beaujolais	France	89	94	81	85	87
Rhone – Gigondas	France	92	94	81	86	89
Rhone – Côte Rôtie	France	93	97	82	87	90
Burgundy – Côte de Nuits	France	90	93	84	85	90
California, North Coast (Pinot Noir)	U.S.A.	90	91	87	93	85
Rhone – Châteauneuf du Pape	France	96	94	87	95	88
Piemonte – Barbera	Italy	N/A	87	88	83	87
Languedoc – Roussillon	France	96	90	88	90	91

Region	Country					
Burgundy – Côte de Beaune	France	91	92	88	80	81
Bordeaux – Sauternes	France	91	95	88	91	85
Tuscany – Chianti	Italy	N/A	92	89	93	94
California, Central Coast (Pinot Noir)	U.S.A.	85	87	90	93	93
Bordeaux – Margaux	France	94	97	91	84	85
Piemonte – Barbaresco	Italy	N/A	N/A	91	89	92
Tuscany – Brunello di Montalcino	Italy	N/A	N/A	91	94	97
Tuscany – Vino Nobile di Montepulciano	Italy	N/A	91	92	91	93
Bordeaux – Haut Médoc	France	N/A	92	92	83	86
Bordeaux – Pomerol	France	93	94	92	84	87
Bordeaux – St. Emilion	France	92	91	93	84	89
Piemonte – Barolo	Italy	N/A	N/A	94	96	98
California, North Coast (Cabernet Sauvignon)	U.S.A.	91	92	95	95	89

Sort By: [2007   ▼]

Region	Country	2010	2009	2008	2007	2006
Burgundy – Côte de Beaune	France	91	92	88	80	81
Piemonte – Barbera	Italy	N/A	87	88	83	87
Bordeaux – Haut Médoc	France	N/A	92	92	83	86
California, North Coast (Merlot)	U.S.A.	N/A	86	81	84	82
Bordeaux – Margaux	France	94	97	91	84	85
Bordeaux – Pomerol	France	93	94	92	84	87
Bordeaux – St. Emilion	France	92	91	93	84	89
Burgundy – Beaujolais	France	89	94	81	85	87
Burgundy – Côte de Nuits	France	90	93	84	85	90
California, North Coast (Zinfandel)	U.S.A.	84	82	77	86	81
Rhone – Gigondas	France	92	94	81	86	89
Rhone – Côte Rôtie	France	93	97	82	87	90
Piemonte – Barbaresco	Italy	N/A	N/A	91	89	92
Languedoc – Roussillon	France	96	90	88	90	91
Bordeaux – Sauternes	France	91	95	88	91	85
Tuscany – Vino Nobile di Montepulciano	Italy	N/A	91	92	91	93
California, North Coast (Pinot Noir)	U.S.A.	90	91	87	93	85
Tuscany – Chianti	Italy	N/A	92	89	93	94
California, Central Coast (Pinot Noir)	U.S.A.	85	87	90	93	93
Tuscany – Brunello di Montalcino	Italy	N/A	N/A	91	94	97
Rhone – Châteauneuf du Pape	France	96	94	87	95	88
California, North Coast (Cabernet Sauvignon)	U.S.A.	91	92	95	95	89
Piemonte – Barolo	Italy	N/A	N/A	94	96	98

Sort By: | 2006 | ▼

Region	Country	2010	2009	2008	2007	2006
Burgundy – Côte de Beaune	France	91	92	88	80	81
California, North Coast (Zinfandel)	U.S.A.	84	82	77	86	81
California, North Coast (Merlot)	U.S.A.	N/A	86	81	84	82
Bordeaux – Margaux	France	94	97	91	84	85
Bordeaux – Sauternes	France	91	95	88	91	85
California, North Coast (Pinot Noir)	U.S.A.	90	91	87	93	85
Bordeaux – Haut Médoc	France	N/A	92	92	83	86
Piemonte – Barbera	Italy	N/A	87	88	83	87
Bordeaux – Pomerol	France	93	94	92	84	87
Burgundy – Beaujolais	France	89	94	81	85	87
Rhone – Châteauneuf du Pape	France	96	94	87	95	88
Bordeaux – St. Emilion	France	92	91	93	84	89
Rhone – Gigondas	France	92	94	81	86	89
California, North Coast (Cabernet Sauvignon)	U.S.A.	91	92	95	95	89
Burgundy – Côte de Nuits	France	90	93	84	85	90
Rhone – Côte Rôtie	France	93	97	82	87	90
Languedoc – Roussillon	France	96	90	88	90	91
Piemonte – Barbaresco	Italy	N/A	N/A	91	89	92
Tuscany – Vino Nobile di Montepulciano	Italy	N/A	91	92	91	93
California, Central Coast (Pinot Noir)	U.S.A.	85	87	90	93	93
Tuscany – Chianti	Italy	N/A	92	89	93	94
Tuscany – Brunello di Montalcino	Italy	N/A	N/A	91	94	97
Piemonte – Barolo	Italy	N/A	N/A	94	96	98

practice test

3. A prep school in Europe is soliciting donations from its alumni for its scholarship fund. The total number of the school's alumni is A, and a donation of €1 per month for one year from each alumnus will fund exactly S full tuition scholarships for the upcoming school year.

In terms of A and S, select the expression that represents how many full-tuition scholarships will be funded if half the alumni donate €1.50 per month each for one year, and select the expression that represents how many alumni must donate €1.50 per month each for one year in order to fund collectively exactly $1.5S$ full-tuition scholarships for the upcoming school year. Make only one selection in each column.

3.1 Scholarships funded	3.2 Alumni donating	
(A)	(A)	$\dfrac{3S}{4A}$
(B)	(B)	$\dfrac{4A}{3S}$
(C)	(C)	$\dfrac{3}{4}S$
(D)	(D)	A
(E)	(E)	$\dfrac{4}{3}S$
(F)	(F)	$\dfrac{3}{4}A$

4. Passengers enrolled in an airline's frequent flyer program can qualify for free reward flights by earning a certain number of miles over a two-year period. Any miles earned that have not been redeemed two years after they were earned expire (no longer qualify for reward flight consideration). Passengers earn one mile for each mile traveled on a flight with the airline, for all paid flights (reward flights do not earn miles). The number of miles that must be earned for the various reward flights is as follows:

Free reward flight between:	Number of miles required
Any two cities in the U.S. or Canada	25,000
Between the U.S. or Canada and Central America	30,000
Between the U.S. or Canada and Europe or South America	40,000
Between the U.S. or Canada and Asia	50,000

The table contains a complete list of the trips that 5 people took with the airline between 2008 and 2011. Unless otherwise noted, these were paid flights, not reward flights. Select a flyer who, on the date of her last trip, had earned enough miles to qualify for a reward flight between any two cities in the United States or Canada, but not enough for any other reward flight, and select a flyer who, on the date of his last trip, had earned enough miles to qualify for a reward flight between the United States and Europe, but not enough for a reward flight between the United States and Asia.

4.1 Within the U.S. or Canada	4.2 U.S. and Europe	
(A)	**(A)**	4070 miles on Jan. 7, 2008, and 4070 miles on Jan. 19, 2008; 2510 miles on Aug. 13, 2008, and 2510 miles on Aug. 19, 2008; 5380 miles on Sep. 13, 2009, and 5380 miles on Sep. 23, 2009
(B)	**(B)**	9940 miles on Feb. 23, 2009, and 9940 miles on Mar 14, 2009; 5610 miles on Aug. 17, 2009, and 5610 miles on Sep. 1, 2009; 6750 miles on June 10, 2010, and 6750 miles on July 7, 2010
(C)	**(C)**	7350 miles on Oct. 6, 2008, and 7350 miles on Oct. 21, 2008; 5330 miles on May 23, 2009, and 5330 miles on Aug. 16, 2009; 7350 miles on Sep. 13, 2010, and 7350 miles on Dec. 9, 2010
(D)	**(D)**	10,200 miles on a reward flight on Mar. 23, 2008; 10,200 miles on Apr. 7, 2008; 10,200 miles on Sep. 17, 2008, and 10,200 miles on Oct, 12, 2008
(E)	**(E)**	6790 miles on Mar. 9, 2010, and 6790 miles on Mar. 21, 2010; 6790 miles on Oct. 14, 2010, and 6790 miles on Oct. 27, 2010

5. The sum of the first n terms of a geometric sequence is 255, and the sum of the reciprocals of these n terms is $\frac{255}{128}$. The ratio, r, of the sequence is a positive integer greater than 1, and the first term of the sequence is 1. The sum, S_n, of the first n terms of a geometric sequence is given by $S_n = \dfrac{a_1\left(1 - r^n\right)}{1 - r}$, where a_1 is the first term of the sequence.

In the table, select the number that equals the ratio, r, of the sequence, and the number that equals the number, n, of the terms. Make only one selection in each column.

5.1	r	5.2	n	
(A)	○	**(A)**	○	2
(B)	○	**(B)**	○	4
(C)	○	**(C)**	○	6
(D)	○	**(D)**	○	8
(E)	○	**(E)**	○	10
(F)	○	**(F)**	○	12

6. The Springfield Symphony Orchestra (SSO) is planning three performances in the spring: Performance A, B, and C. The table shows the compositions included in the program for each performance as well as the number of instruments of each instrument group needed for each composition. The number of instruments required for each composition also equals the number of musicians for that composition: No musician will play more than one instrument in each piece. Each musician will be contracted for the entire spring season, even though he or she may not need to play on all compositions.

Sort By: | Select   ▼ |

Composition	Composer	Performance	Instrument Groups				
			Woodwinds	Brass	Percussion	Strings	Solo Instrument
Concerto for 3 Violins	Kwan	B	16	15	2	62	3
Concerto for Cello	Sanford, M.	C	8	6	1	21	1
Concerto for Clarinet	Sanford, M.	A	9	6	1	21	1
Concerto for Piano #4	Baranko	B	8	4	1	51	1
Phaedra Overture	Sanford, L.	A	8	12	1	45	0
Romance for Strings	Zlatan	B	0	0	0	21	0
Serenade for Strings	Mysel	C	0	0	0	31	0
Symphony #2	Baranko	A	14	14	2	51	0
Symphony #7	Limoges	C	16	16	3	54	0

For each of the following statements, select *Yes* if the statement can be shown to be true based on the information in the table. Otherwise, select *No*.

	(A)	(B)	
	Yes	No	
6.1	o	o	The total number of musicians, not counting soloists, whom the SSO must contract for the entire spring season is 97.
6.2	o	o	The average number of strings required by the compositions in the program for Performance C is smaller than the average number of strings required by the compositions in the program of either of the other two performances.
6.3	o	o	If a composition requires 8 woodwinds, the probability that it was not composed by Sanford, M. is 33%.

(On the computer test, this will be the end of the question prompt and statements. For this paper test and your convenience, we are providing you the various other ways you may sort the data.)

Sort By: Composer ▼

Composition	Composer	Instrument Groups					Solo Instrument
		Performance	Woodwinds	Brass	Percussion	Strings	
Concerto for Piano #4	Baranko	B	8	4	1	51	1
Symphony #2	Baranko	A	14	14	2	51	0
Concerto for 3 Violins	Kwan	B	16	15	2	62	3
Symphony #7	Limoges	C	16	16	3	54	0
Serenade for Strings	Mysel	C	0	0	0	31	0
Phaedra Overture	Sanford, L.	A	8	12	1	45	0
Concerto for Cello	Sanford, M.	C	8	6	1	21	1
Concerto for Clarinet	Sanford, M.	A	9	6	1	21	1
Romance for Strings	Zlatan	B	0	0	0	21	0

Sort By: Performance ▼

Composition	Composer	Instrument Groups					Solo Instrument
		Performance	Woodwinds	Brass	Percussion	Strings	
Symphony #2	Baranko	A	14	14	2	51	0
Phaedra Overture	Sanford, L.	A	8	12	1	45	0
Concerto for Clarinet	Sanford, M.	A	9	6	1	21	1
Concerto for Piano #4	Baranko	B	8	4	1	51	1
Concerto for 3 Violins	Kwan	B	16	15	2	62	3
Romance for Strings	Zlatan	B	0	0	0	21	0
Symphony #7	Limoges	C	16	16	3	54	0
Serenade for Strings	Mysel	C	0	0	0	31	0
Concerto for Cello	Sanford, M.	C	8	6	1	21	1

practice test

Sort By: Woodwinds ▼

Composition	Composer	Performance	Instrument Groups				Solo Instrument
			Woodwinds	Brass	Percussion	Strings	
Romance for Strings	Zlatan	B	0	0	0	21	0
Serenade for Strings	Mysel	C	0	0	0	31	0
Phaedra Overture	Sanford, L.	A	8	12	1	45	0
Concerto for Piano #4	Baranko	B	8	4	1	51	1
Concerto for Cello	Sanford, M.	C	8	6	1	21	1
Concerto for Clarinet	Sanford, M.	A	9	6	1	21	1
Symphony #2	Baranko	A	14	14	2	51	0
Concerto for 3 Violins	Kwan	B	16	15	2	62	3
Symphony #7	Limoges	C	16	16	3	54	0

Sort By: Brass ▼

Composition	Composer	Performance	Instrument Groups				Solo Instrument
			Woodwinds	Brass	Percussion	Strings	
Romance for Strings	Zlatan	B	0	0	0	21	0
Serenade for Strings	Mysel	C	0	0	0	31	0
Concerto for Piano #4	Baranko	B	8	4	1	51	1
Concerto for Cello	Sanford, M.	C	8	6	1	21	1
Concerto for Clarinet	Sanford, M.	A	9	6	1	21	1
Phaedra Overture	Sanford, L.	A	8	12	1	45	0
Symphony #2	Baranko	A	14	14	2	51	0
Concerto for 3 Violins	Kwan	B	16	15	2	62	3
Symphony #7	Limoges	C	16	16	3	54	0

Sort By: [Percussion   ▼]

| Composition | Composer | Performance | Instrument Groups | | | | Solo Instrument |
			Woodwinds	Brass	Percussion	Strings	
Romance for Strings	Zlatan	B	0	0	0	21	0
Serenade for Strings	Mysel	C	0	0	0	31	0
Concerto for Piano #4	Baranko	B	8	4	1	51	1
Concerto for Cello	Sanford, M.	C	8	6	1	21	1
Concerto for Clarinet	Sanford, M.	A	9	6	1	21	1
Phaedra Overture	Sanford, L.	A	8	12	1	45	0
Symphony #2	Baranko	A	14	14	2	51	0
Concerto for 3 Violins	Kwan	B	16	15	2	62	3
Symphony #7	Limoges	C	16	16	3	54	0

Sort By: [Strings   ▼]

| Composition | Composer | Performance | Instrument Groups | | | | Solo Instrument |
			Woodwinds	Brass	Percussion	Strings	
Romance for Strings	Zlatan	B	0	0	0	21	0
Concerto for Cello	Sanford, M.	C	8	6	1	21	1
Concerto for Clarinet	Sanford, M.	A	9	6	1	21	1
Serenade for Strings	Mysel	C	0	0	0	31	0
Phaedra Overture	Sanford, L.	A	8	12	1	45	0
Concerto for Piano #4	Baranko	B	8	4	1	51	1
Symphony #2	Baranko	A	14	14	2	51	0
Symphony #7	Limoges	C	16	16	3	54	0
Concerto for 3 Violins	Kwan	B	16	15	2	62	3

practice test

Sort By: | Solo Instrument ▼ |

| Composition | Composer | Instrument Groups | | | | | Solo Instrument |
		Performance	Woodwinds	Brass	Percussion	Strings	
Romance for Strings	Zlatan	B	0	0	0	21	0
Serenade for Strings	Mysel	C	0	0	0	31	0
Phaedra Overture	Sanford, L.	A	8	12	1	45	0
Symphony #2	Baranko	A	14	14	2	51	0
Symphony #7	Limoges	C	16	16	3	54	0
Concerto for Cello	Sanford, M.	C	8	6	1	21	1
Concerto for Clarinet	Sanford, M.	A	9	6	1	21	1
Concerto for Piano #4	Baranko	B	8	4	1	51	1
Concerto for 3 Violins	Kwan	B	16	15	2	62	3

7.

Lyric Poetry   Lyric Poets

A team of classicists is examining some newly discovered manuscripts of ancient Greek lyric poetry, keeping in mind the following background information:

Lyric poetry is a broad term, used to describe the poems that were not epics or drama, and which were composed from roughly the 7th century BCE through the middle of the 5th century BCE.

The content of these poems spanned a wide range. While the Greek epics and tragedies dealt almost exclusively with the myths of Greece's past, lyric poetry, though at times using a mythic background, kept its focus mostly on the present.

Stylistically, lyric poetry had a wide variety, as well. Choral songs, such as eulogies, dithyrambs, dirges, and victory odes, were performed by a chorus and an accompanying instrument, usually on public occasions. Solo songs, also accompanied by an instrument, were typically of a more personal nature, with love as their chief subject. Alcaeus' poetry provided a partial exception as solo songs go, for he also composed songs about politics as well as hymns to the gods.

Besides choral and solo songs, lyric poetry included elegiac and iambic poems, which may or may not have been performed to music. Elegiac poems are defined by meter, and the elegiac couplet, and were usually political or ethical exhortations. Iambic poems were usually polemics, or monologues of a satirical or salacious nature, often, but not always, composed in the iambic meter. Archilochus used iambics and trochaics for his poetry, whereas Hipponax was unique in his use of the choliambic meter.

Lyric Poetry	Lyric Poets

The table has brief information on the major lyric poets—though many poets composed poems of types not listed here.

Poet	Time (estimate)	Primary Type of Poetry
Archilochus	7th Century	Iambic, Elegiac
Callinus	7th Century	Elegiac
Tyrtaeus	7th Century	Elegiac
Semonides	7th Century	Iambic
Alcman	7th Century	Choral (earliest known composer of choral poetry)
Mimnermus	7th Century	Elegiac
Solon	7th–6th Century	Elegiac
Stesichorus	7th–6th Century	Choral
Sappho	7th–6th Century	Solo Song
Alcaeus	7th–6th Century	Solo Song
Ibycus	6th Century	Solo Song, Choral
Anacreon	6th Century	Solo Song, Choral
Xenophanes	6th Century	Elegiac
Theognis	6th Century	Elegiac
Hipponax	6th Century	Iambic
Simonides	6th–5th Century	Choral, Elegiac
Bacchylides	5th Century	Choral
Pindar	5th Century	Choral

For each of the following statements about the newly discovered manuscripts, select *Yes* if it can be reasonably inferred from the given information. Otherwise, select *No*.

	(A)	(B)	
	Yes	No	
7.1	○	○	The poems in the manuscripts were most likely composed in 700 BCE or later.
7.2	○	○	A poem referring to Greece's mythical past could not have been composed by any of the major lyric poets.
7.3	○	○	The love poems discovered in the manuscripts were probably not composed in the 5th century BCE.

8.

| Lyric Poetry | Lyric Poets |

A team of classicists is examining some newly discovered manuscripts of ancient Greek lyric poetry, keeping in mind the following background information:

Lyric poetry is a broad term, used to describe the poems that were not epics or drama, and which were composed from roughly the 7th century BCE through the middle of the 5th century BCE.

The content of these poems spanned a wide range. While the Greek epics and tragedies dealt almost exclusively with the myths of Greece's past, lyric poetry, though at times using a mythic background, kept its focus mostly on the present.

Stylistically, lyric poetry had a wide variety, as well. Choral songs, such as eulogies, dithyrambs, dirges, and victory odes, were performed by a chorus and an accompanying instrument, usually on public occasions. Solo songs, also accompanied by an instrument, were typically of a more personal nature, with love as their chief subject. Alcaeus' poetry provided a partial exception as solo songs go, for he also composed songs about politics as well as hymns to the gods.

Besides choral and solo songs, lyric poetry included elegiac and iambic poems, which may or may not have been performed to music. Elegiac poems are defined by meter, and the elegiac couplet, and were usually political or ethical exhortations. Iambic poems were usually polemics, or monologues of a satirical or salacious nature, often, but not always, composed in the iambic meter. Archilochus used iambics and trochaics for his poetry, whereas Hipponax was unique in his use of the choliambic meter.

| Lyric Poetry | Lyric Poets |

The table has brief information on the major lyric poets—though many poets composed poems of types not listed here.

Poet	Time (estimate)	Primary Type of Poetry
Archilochus	7th Century	Iambic, Elegiac
Callinus	7th Century	Elegiac
Tyrtaeus	7th Century	Elegiac
Semonides	7th Century	Iambic
Alcman	7th Century	Choral (earliest known composer of choral poetry)
Mimnermus	7th Century	Elegiac
Solon	7th–6th Century	Elegiac
Stesichorus	7th–6th Century	Choral
Sappho	7th–6th Century	Solo Song
Alcaeus	7th–6th Century	Solo Song
Ibycus	6th Century	Solo Song, Choral
Anacreon	6th Century	Solo Song, Choral
Xenophanes	6th Century	Elegiac
Theognis	6th Century	Elegiac
Hipponax	6th Century	Iambic
Simonides	6th–5th Century	Choral, Elegiac
Bacchylides	5th Century	Choral
Pindar	5th Century	Choral

For each of the following statements about a newly discovered poem that was composed in the choliambic meter, select *Yes* if it can be reasonably inferred from the given information. Otherwise, select *No*.

	(A) Yes	(B) No	
8.1	○	○	It is probably not a love song.
8.2	○	○	It was probably not composed in the 7th century.
8.3	○	○	It would not have been performed to musical accompaniment.

9.

Lyric Poetry	Lyric Poets

A team of classicists is examining some newly discovered manuscripts of ancient Greek lyric poetry, keeping in mind the following background information:

Lyric poetry is a broad term, used to describe the poems that were not epics or drama, and which were composed from roughly the 7th century BCE through the middle of the 5th century BCE.

The content of these poems spanned a wide range. While the Greek epics and tragedies dealt almost exclusively with the myths of Greece's past, lyric poetry, though at times using a mythic background, kept its focus mostly on the present.

Stylistically, lyric poetry had a wide variety, as well. Choral songs, such as eulogies, dithyrambs, dirges, and victory odes, were performed by a chorus and an accompanying instrument, usually on public occasions. Solo songs, also accompanied by an instrument, were typically of a more personal nature, with love as their chief subject. Alcaeus' poetry provided a partial exception as solo songs go, for he also composed songs about politics as well as hymns to the gods.

Besides choral and solo songs, lyric poetry included elegiac and iambic poems, which may or may not have been performed to music. Elegiac poems are defined by meter, and the elegiac couplet, and were usually political or ethical exhortations. Iambic poems were usually polemics, or monologues of a satirical or salacious nature, often, but not always, composed in the iambic meter. Archilochus used iambics and trochaics for his poetry, whereas Hipponax was unique in his use of the choliambic meter.

Lyric Poetry	Lyric Poets

The table has brief information on the major lyric poets—though many poets composed poems of types not listed here.

Poet	Time (estimate)	Primary Type of Poetry
Archilochus	7th Century	Iambic, Elegiac
Callinus	7th Century	Elegiac
Tyrtaeus	7th Century	Elegiac
Semonides	7th Century	Iambic
Alcman	7th Century	Choral (earliest known composer of choral poetry)
Mimnermus	7th Century	Elegiac
Solon	7th–6th Century	Elegiac
Stesichorus	7th–6th Century	Choral
Sappho	7th–6th Century	Solo Song
Alcaeus	7th–6th Century	Solo Song
Ibycus	6th Century	Solo Song, Choral
Anacreon	6th Century	Solo Song, Choral
Xenophanes	6th Century	Elegiac
Theognis	6th Century	Elegiac
Hipponax	6th Century	Iambic
Simonides	6th–5th Century	Choral, Elegiac
Bacchylides	5th Century	Choral
Pindar	5th Century	Choral

The poetry of which of the following is most likely to have been performed with musical accompaniment?

(A) Callinus

(B) Semonides

(C) Solon

(D) Stesichorus

(E) Hipponax

10. Springfield Middle School has 600 students in total, 200 in each class. The graph shows the percentage of students in each grade who do or do not read on grade level.

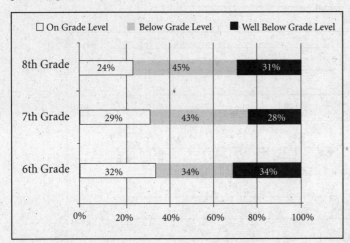

Based on the given information, fill in the blanks in each of the following statements.

10.1. The total number of 7th-grade students who do not read on grade level is _____.

(A) 56

(B) 71

(C) 86

(D) 142

10.2. If a Springfield middle school student is selected at random, there is a _____ probability that he or she reads on grade level.

(A) 0.24

(B) 0.28

(C) 0.29

(D) 0.32

11. The graph shows the stock price and the earnings per share for a number of companies in the same sector. A company's price-to-earnings (P/E) ratio is the ratio of the company's stock price to the company's earnings per share.

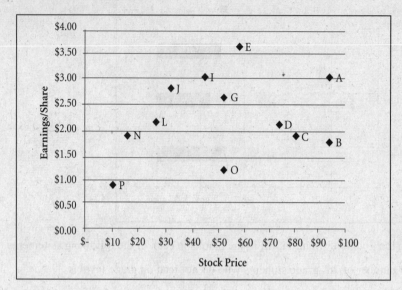

Based on the given information, fill in the blanks in each of the following statements.

11.1. Of the companies whose stock price is greater than $60, _____ have a P/E ratio greater than 40.

(A) 1
(B) 2
(C) 3
(D) 4

11.2. The number of companies that have a P/E ratio less than 10 is _____.

(A) 1
(B) 2
(C) 3
(D) 4

12. The graph shows a family's monthly electricity consumption, in kWh, over the course of two years.

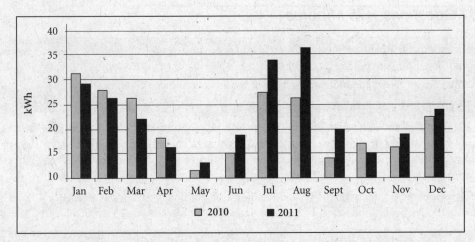

Based on the given information, fill in the blanks in each of the following statements.

12.1. The family's electricity consumption in January 2011 was approximately _____% of its consumption in December 2010.

(A) 74

(B) 79

(C) 126

(D) 135

12.2. If the family paid a constant rate of $x per kWh between June 2010 and November 2010, inclusive, then it paid _____ as much between June 2010 and August 2010, inclusive, as it did between September 2010 and November 2010, inclusive.

(A) 0.45

(B) 1.45

(C) 145

(D) 0.45x

(E) 1.45x

QUANTITATIVE SECTION

37 Questions • 75 Minutes

Directions for Problem Solving Questions: *(These directions will appear on your screen before your first Problem Solving question.)*

Solve this problem and indicate the best of the answer choices given.

Numbers: All numbers used are real numbers.

Figures: A figure accompanying a Problem Solving question is intended to provide information useful in solving the problem. Figures are drawn as accurately as possible EXCEPT when it is stated in a specific problem that its figure is not drawn to scale. Straight lines may sometimes appear jagged. All figures lie on a plane unless otherwise indicated.

To review these directions for subsequent questions of this type, click on HELP.

Directions for Data Sufficiency Questions: *(These directions will appear on your screen before your first Data Sufficiency question.)*

This Data Sufficiency problem consists of a question and two statements, labeled (1) and (2), in which certain data are given. You have to decide whether the data given in the statements are *sufficient* for answering the question. Using the data given in the statements *plus* your knowledge of mathematics and everyday facts (such as the number of days in July or the meaning of *counterclockwise*), you must indicate whether:

(A) Statement (1) ALONE is sufficient, but Statement (2) alone is not sufficient to answer the question asked;

(B) Statement (2) ALONE is sufficient, but Statement (1) alone is not sufficient to answer the question asked;

(C) BOTH Statements (1) and (2) TOGETHER are sufficient to answer the question asked, but NEITHER statement ALONE is sufficient;

(D) EACH statement ALONE is sufficient to answer the question asked;

(E) Statements (1) and (2) TOGETHER are NOT sufficient to answer the question asked, and additional data specific to the problem are needed.

Numbers: All numbers used are real numbers.

Figures: A figure accompanying a Data Sufficiency problem will conform to the information given in the question, but will not necessarily conform to the additional information in Statements (1) and (2).

Lines shown as straight can be assumed to be straight and lines that appear jagged can also be assumed to be straight.

You may assume that positions of points, angles, regions, etc., exist in the order shown and that angle measures are greater than zero.

All figures lie in a plane unless otherwise indicated.

Note: In Data Sufficiency problems that ask you for the value of a quantity, the data given in the statements are sufficient only when it is possible to determine exactly one numerical value for the quantity.

To review these directions for subsequent questions of this type, click on HELP.

1. If $\dfrac{a}{b} \cdot \dfrac{b}{c} \cdot \dfrac{c}{d} \cdot \dfrac{d}{e} \cdot x = 1$, then $x =$

   (A) $\dfrac{a}{e}$

   (B) $\dfrac{e}{a}$

   (C) e

   (D) $\dfrac{1}{a}$

   (E) $\dfrac{be}{a}$

2. Three of four women—A, B, C, and D—are to be selected randomly to serve on a certain committee. Two of three men—X, Y, and Z—are to be selected randomly to serve on the same committee. What is the probability that the committee will consist of B, C, D, Y, and Z?

   (A) $\dfrac{1}{12}$

   (B) $\dfrac{1}{9}$

   (C) $\dfrac{1}{6}$

   (D) $\dfrac{3}{16}$

   (E) $\dfrac{2}{9}$

3. Which of the following is in the domain of function $f(x) = \dfrac{\sqrt{x-3}}{x-4}$?

   (A) -4

   (B) -3

   (C) 0

   (D) 3

   (E) 4

4. A theater sells only two types of tickets: a full-price ticket of $100 and a discounted-price ticket of $60. If, for a given performance, the theater sold 350 full-price tickets, which of the following could be the total ticket revenue the theater received for that performance?

   (A) $65,080

   (B) $65,100

   (C) $65,120

   (D) $65,140

   (E) $65,160

5. What is the minimum value of $|a + b|$?

   (1) $|a| = 3$

   (2) $|a - b| = 1$

6.

   In the simple light show pictured above, a light starts at the center (white) at time zero and moves once every second in the following pattern: from white (W) to blue (B), back to white, then to green (G), back to white, then to red (R), and back to white—in a *counterclockwise* direction. If the light continues to move in this way, what will be the color sequence from the 208th second to the 209th second?

   (A) White to green

   (B) White to blue

   (C) White to red

   (D) Red to white

   (E) Green to white

7. What is the value of x?

   (1) $x > 0$

   (2) $x^2 - 6x + 9 = 0$

8. If $\blacktriangleleft\ u\ \blacktriangleright = u^2 - u$, what is the value of $\blacktriangleleft \dfrac{2}{3} \blacktriangleright + \blacktriangleleft -\dfrac{2}{3} \blacktriangleright$?

   (A) $-\dfrac{2}{3}$

   (B) 0

   (C) $\dfrac{2}{3}$

   (D) $\dfrac{4}{9}$

   (E) $\dfrac{8}{9}$

9.

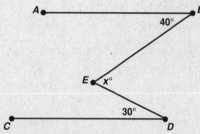

In the figure above, if $AB \parallel CD$, then $x =$

(A) 40

(B) 50

(C) 60

(D) 70

(E) 80

10. A call center representative made 35 outbound sales calls one day. Eleven of these calls resulted in a sale, while the rest did not. If the representative spent on average x minutes on each call that resulted in a sale and if he spent on average y minutes on all calls, which of the following equals the number of minutes the representative spent on average on calls that did not result in a sale?

(A) $35y - 11x$

(B) $35x - 11y$

(C) $\dfrac{35x - 11y}{24}$

(D) $\dfrac{24y - 11x}{35}$

(E) $\dfrac{35y - 11x}{24}$

11. If $x + y = a$, and if $x - y = b$, then $x =$

(A) $\dfrac{1}{2}(a+b)$

(B) $a + b$

(C) $a - b$

(D) $\dfrac{1}{2}ab$

(E) $\dfrac{1}{2}(a-b)$

12. At which point do the graphs of the equations $x - y = 4$ and $2y = 3x - 1$ intersect?

(A) $(-7, -11)$

(B) $(7, -11)$

(C) $(-11, -7)$

(D) $(-3, -1)$

(E) $(11, -7)$

13. A certain animal shelter houses two different types of animals—dogs and cats. If d represents the number of dogs and c the number of cats, which of the following expresses the portion of animals at the shelter that are dogs?

(A) $\dfrac{d}{c+d}$

(B) $\dfrac{c}{c+d}$

(C) $\dfrac{c}{d}$

(D) $\dfrac{d}{c}$

(E) $d + \dfrac{c}{d}$

14.

HARVESTED CROP REVENUES (YEAR X)
(Percent of total revenue among four counties)

	non-subsidized farms	subsidized farms
Willot County	7%	
Tilson County		12%
Stanton County		
Osher County	8%	
(Total Percentages)	30%	

Based on the table above, if the total harvested crop revenues for Willot and Tilson Counties combined equaled those for Stanton and Osher Counties combined, then Stanton County's subsidized farm revenues accounted for what percentage of the total harvested crop revenues for all four counties?

(1) During year X, Osher County's total harvested crop revenues totaled twice those of Tilson County.

(2) During year X, Tilson County's farms contributed 18% of all harvested crop revenues for the four counties.

15.

In the figure above, the centers of all three circles lie on the same line. The radius of the middle-sized circle is twice that of the smallest circle. If the radius of the smallest circle is 1, what is the length of the boundary of the shaded region?

(A) 9

(B) 3π

(C) 12

(D) 6π

(E) 12π

16. If $a^m = b^n$, and if $a \neq b \neq m \neq n$, what is the value of $a + b + m + n$?

(1) a, b, m, and n are all non-negative integers less than 10.

(2) $b^n = 81$.

17. M college students agree to rent an apartment for D dollars per month, sharing the rent equally. If the rent is increased by \$100, what amount must each student contribute?

(A) $\dfrac{D+100}{M}$

(B) $\dfrac{D}{M}+100$

(C) $\dfrac{D}{M}$

(D) $\dfrac{M}{D+100}$

(E) $\dfrac{M+100}{D}$

18. If n is a positive even integer, and if $n \div 3$ results in a quotient with a remainder of 1, which of the following expressions is NOT divisible by 3?

(A) $n + 2$

(B) $n + 5$

(C) $n - 1$

(D) $n \times 2$

(E) $n \times 3$

19. $\sqrt{\dfrac{a^2}{b^2}+\dfrac{a^2}{b^2}} =$

(A) $\dfrac{a^2}{b^2}$

(B) $\dfrac{a}{b}$

(C) $\dfrac{a^4}{b^4}$

(D) $\dfrac{a}{b}\sqrt{\dfrac{a}{b}}$

(E) $\dfrac{|a|\sqrt{2}}{|b|}$

20. Is it true that $\sqrt[3]{a} < a$?

(1) $a < 0$

(2) $a > -1$

21. The lengths of two sides of a triangle are 15 inches and 7 inches, respectively. Which of the following could not be the length, in inches, of the third side?

(A) 9

(B) 10

(C) 20

(D) 21

(E) 22

22.

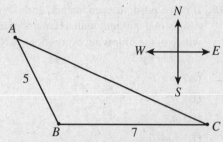

Once a month, a crop duster sprays a triangular area defined by three farm houses—*A*, *B*, and *C*—as indicated in the figure. Farmhouse *B* lies due west of Farmhouse *C*. Given the compass directions and distances (in miles) indicated in the figure, what is the total area that the crop duster sprays?

(1) Farmhouse *C* is located 4 miles farther south than Farmhouse *A*.

(2) Farmhouse *C* is located 10 miles farther east than Farmhouse *A*.

23. Each computer system in a graphic arts classroom is equipped with a scanner or a printer or both. What percentage of the computer systems are equipped with scanners but not printers?

(1) 20 percent of the computer systems are equipped with both scanners and printers.

(2) 25 percent of the computer systems are equipped with printers but not with scanners.

24. Daniel, Carl, and Todd working together can load a moving van in 8 hours. How long would it take Daniel working alone to load the van?

(1) Working alone, Carl can load the van in 15 hours.

(2) Carl and Todd working together can load the van in 12 hours.

25. What is the unit area of circle *O* on the standard *xy*-coordinate plane?

(1) Point *R* (7,–3) and point *S* (7,7) both lie along the circumference of circle *O*.

(2) *R* and *S* are the endpoints of the longest possible chord of circle *O*.

26. If A and B denote the digits of a three-digit number BAB, is BAB divisible by 4?

(1) The product of A and B is divisible by 4.

(2) The sum of B, A, and B is divisible by 4.

27. If a total of 55 books were sold at a community book fair and if each book was either hardback or paperback, how many hardback books were sold at the book fair?

(1) The proceeds from the sale of paperback books, each of which was sold for 75 cents, totaled $19.50.

(2) The proceeds from the book fair totaled $48.50.

QUESTIONS 28 AND 29 REFER TO THE FOLLOWING FIGURE.

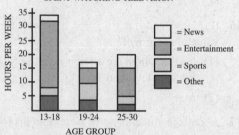

28. According to the graph, the two age groups, other than the group that spent the greatest number of hours per week watching sports on television, accounted for approximately what percent of the total hours spent watching television among all three age groups?

(A) 27

(B) 36

(C) 60

(D) 76

(E) 85

29. Which of the following is the approximate ratio of the average number of hours per week that the youngest age group spent watching entertainment on television to the average number of hours that the other two groups combined spent watching the same type of programming?

(A) 3:4

(B) 1:1

(C) 5:4

(D) 4:3

(E) 5:3

30. If a portion of $10,000 is invested at 6% and the remaining portion is invested at 5%, and if x represents the amount invested at 6%, what is the annual income in dollars from the 5% investment?

(A) $0.05(10,000 - x)$

(B) $0.05(x + 10,000)$

(C) $5(x - 10,000)$

(D) $5(10,000 - x)$

(E) $0.05(x - 10,000)$

31. In a geometric series, each term is a constant multiple of the preceding one. If the first three terms in a geometric series are -2, x, and -8, which of the following could be the sixth term in the series?

(A) -128

(B) -17

(C) 64

(D) 256

(E) 512

32. What is the maximum number of rectangular boxes, each measuring 2 inches by 3 inches by 5 inches, that can be packed into a rectangular packing box measuring 18 inches by 19 inches by 35 inches, if all of the smaller boxes are aligned in the same direction?

(A) 296

(B) 356

(C) 378

(D) 412

(E) 424

33. If J is a set of six integers, what is the median value of those integers?

(1) The difference between the least and greatest integers in Set J is 40.

(2) The arithmetic mean (average) of the six integers in Set J is 15.

34.

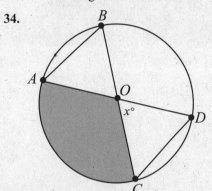

In the circle with center O above, is the area of the shaded region less than the combined area of the two triangles?

(1) $x = 60$.

(2) The length of chord $\overline{AB}$ equals the circle's radius.

35. Two buses are 515 miles apart. At 9:30 a.m., they start traveling toward each other at rates of 48 and 55 miles per hour. At what time will they pass each other?

(A) 1:30 p.m.

(B) 2:00 p.m.

(C) 2:30 p.m.

(D) 3:00 p.m.

(E) 3:30 p.m.

36. $\dfrac{7^{77} - 7^{76}}{6} =$

(A) 7

(B) $7^{\frac{77}{76}}$

(C) 49

(D) 7^{75}

(E) 7^{76}

37. An investor can sell her MicroTron stock for $36 per share and her Dynaco stock for $52 per share. If she sells 300 shares altogether, some of each stock, at an average price per share of $40, how many shares of Dynaco stock has she sold?

(A) 52

(B) 75

(C) 92

(D) 136

(E) 184

VERBAL SECTION

41 Questions • 75 Minutes

Directions for Sentence Correction Questions: *(These directions will appear on your screen before your first Sentence Correction question.)*

This question presents a sentence, all or part of which is underlined. Beneath the sentence you will find five ways of phrasing the underlined part. The first of these repeats the original; the other four are different. If you think the original is best, choose the first answer; otherwise choose one of the others.

This question tests correctness and effectiveness of expression. In choosing your answer, follow the requirements of Standard Written English; that is, pay attention to grammar, choice of words, and sentence construction. Choose the answer that produces the most effective sentence; this answer should be clear and exact, without awkwardness, ambiguity, redundancy, or grammatical error.

Directions for Critical Reasoning Questions: *(These directions will appear on your screen before your first Critical Reasoning question.)*

For this question, select the best of the answer choices given.

Directions for Reading Comprehension Questions: *(These directions will appear on your screen before your first group of Reading Comprehension questions.)*

The questions in this group are based on the content of a passage. After reading the passage, choose the best answer to each question. Answer all the questions following the passage on the basis of what is stated or implied in the passage.

1. Edward Lear was not only the author of nonsense verses and limericks that have charmed generations of <u>children, but he is also meticulously illustrating living animals</u> in precise, scientific sketches that were lauded by contemporary luminaries Charles Darwin and James Audubon.

   (A) children, but he is also meticulously illustrating living animals

   (B) children, but he was also illustrating meticulously living animals

   (C) children, but he was also the meticulous illustrator of living animals

   (D) children; but he also was meticulously illustrating living animals

   (E) children, having meticulously illustrated living animals

2. By that time, <u>Adam Smith having published</u> *An Inquiry into the Nature and Causes of the Wealth of Nations*, based on the then-radical premise that goods and services create wealth.

   (A) Adam Smith having published

   (B) Adam Smith having had published

   (C) Adam Smith had been published

   (D) Adam Smith had published

   (E) Adam Smith having to publish

3. Although this may frankly seem impossible to those uninitiated in the lives of birds, some varieties of parrots live <u>as long as the age of one hundred years.</u>

   (A) as long as the age of one hundred years.

   (B) as long as one hundred.

   (C) as long as one hundred years old.

   (D) as long as one hundred years.

   (E) to be one hundred years old in age.

4. Two years ago, a court found a certain cigarette manufacturer legally liable for the deaths of several thousand people who smoked the company's cigarettes and ordered the company to pay a large sum to the families of those victims. The next year, the company's profits increased to record levels. The lesson for other large corporations is clear: Produce products that are unsafe or unhealthy for consumers and your company will become more profitable.

Which of the following, if true, would provide the best reason for rejecting the conclusion drawn in the last sentence above?

(A) Publicity resulting from court judgments against large businesses often affects their profitability.

(B) Manufacturers of potentially unsafe or unhealthy products are required by law to provide appropriate warnings to consumers.

(C) Manufacturers of dangerous products are often held liable for injuries to consumers resulting from the use of those products.

(D) The risks involved in using any product are just one of many types of factors consumers consider when buying a product.

(E) Compared to cigarettes, most consumer products pose insignificant risks to the health or safety of those who use them.

5. *John:* If a person believes in the inevitability of success, then that person will surely succeed.

Jolanda: I disagree. According to a recent magazine article entitled "The 100 Most Successful Women in History," most of these 100 women did not believe they would ever become successful.

Which of the following would be John's most logically convincing response to Jolanda's counterargument above?

(A) Success does not depend on whether a person believes in its inevitability.

(B) Successful people are often viewed by others as unsuccessful.

(C) Success is inevitable for some people but not for others.

(D) Society's definition of success might have changed throughout history.

(E) None of the successful people listed in the magazine article were men.

QUESTIONS 6–8 ARE BASED ON THE FOLLOWING PASSAGE.

Line   The decline of the Iroquois Indian nations began during the American Revolution of 1776, when disagreement among them as to whether they should become
(5) involved in the war began to divide the Iroquois. Because of the success of the revolutionaries and the encroachment upon Iroquois lands that followed, many Iroquois resettled in Canada, while those who
(10) remained behind lost the respect they had enjoyed among other Indian nations. The introduction of distilled spirits resulted in widespread alcoholism, leading in turn to the rapid decline of both the culture and
(15) population. The influence of the Quakers impeded, yet in another sense contributed, to this decline. By establishing schools for the Iroquois and by introducing them to modern technology for agriculture and
(20) husbandry, the Quakers instilled in the Iroquois some hope for the future yet undermined the Iroquois' sense of national identity. Ironically, it was Handsome Lake who can be credited with reviving the
(25) Iroquois culture. Lake, the alcoholic half-brother of Seneca Cornplanter, perhaps the most outspoken proponent among the Iroquois for assimilation of white customs and institutions, was a former member of
(30) the Great Council of Iroquois nations. Inspired by a near-death vision in 1799, Lake established a new religion among the Iroquois, which tied the more useful aspects of Christianity to traditional Indian
(35) beliefs and customs.

6. The passage mentions all of the following events as contributing to the decline of the Iroquois culture EXCEPT:

(A) new educational opportunities for the Iroquois people.

(B) divisive power struggles among the leaders of the Iroquois nations.

(C) introduction of new farming technologies.

(D) territorial threats against the Iroquois nations.

(E) discord among the nations regarding their role in the American Revolution.

7. Among the following reasons, it is most likely that the author considers Handsome Lake's leading a revival of the Iroquois culture to be "ironic" because

(A) he was a former member of the Great Council.

(B) he was not a full-blooded relative of Seneca Cornplanter.

(C) he was related by blood to an important proponent of assimilation.

(D) Seneca Cornplanter was Lake's alcoholic half-brother.

(E) his religious beliefs conflicted with traditional Iroquois beliefs.

8. Assuming that the reasons asserted by the author for the decline of the Iroquois culture are historically representative of the decline of cultural minorities, which of the following developments would most likely contribute to the demise of a modern-day ethnic minority?

(A) A bilingual education program in which children who are members of the minority group learn to read and write in both their traditional language and the language prevalent in the present culture.

(B) A tax credit for residential-property owners who lease their property to members of the minority group.

(C) Increased efforts by local government to eradicate the availability of illegal drugs.

(D) The declaration of a national holiday commemorating a past war in which the minority group played an active role.

(E) A government-sponsored program to assist minority-owned businesses in using computer technology to improve efficiency.

9. <u>Completely engulfed in the flames, screams for help were heard from the burning house</u> at the corner of Valencia Drive.

(A) Completely engulfed in the flames, screams for help were heard from the burning house

(B) Completely engulfed in the flames, from the burning house were heard screams for help

(C) Engulfed in the flames, screams for help were heard from the burning house.

(D) Screams for help were heard from the burning house, which was completely engulfed in flames

(E) Screams for help were heard from the house that was engulfed in flames

10. Babies who are breast fed instead of bottle fed until at least their first birthday are 70 percent less likely to become obese children than babies who are bottle fed but not breast fed. A child is obese if the ratio of the child's weight to height is among the highest 3 percent of all children. But breast feeding instead of bottle feeding during the first three months of a baby's life also reduces the likelihood that the baby will become an obese child.

Which of the following can be most properly inferred from the information in the passage?

(A) Genetic propensity for obesity is not significant in determining whether a baby will become an obese child.

(B) Bottle feeding is more likely than breast feeding to result in obesity in children.

(C) Unless a baby is breast fed instead of bottle fed until at least its first birthday, the baby is likely to become an obese child.

(D) If a child is obese, there is a 70 percent likelihood that, as a baby, the child was bottle fed but not breast fed.

(E) Breast feeding is ineffective to prevent obesity unless it is continued until at least the baby's first birthday.

11. When people are worried about general economic conditions, they tend to spend less on consumer goods. Official government figures show that retail inventory levels throughout the economy have been increasing in recent months. However, consumer-confidence levels are currently the highest they've been in several years.

Any of the following, if true, would help to explain the apparent discrepancy described above EXCEPT:

(A) High interest rates tend to discourage consumers from buying products on credit that they otherwise could not afford.

(B) Businesses often increase production of consumer goods in anticipation of improving economic conditions.

(C) Consumer-spending levels tend to follow seasonal patterns.

(D) When the domestic currency's value increases compared to that of foreign currencies, foreign products become less expensive for domestic consumers.

(E) Increased business spending generally precedes a decline in consumer-confidence levels.

12. Ignorance of the law does not preclude <u>one being arrested for violating it,</u> nor from going to trial, being convicted, and paying a fine or going to prison.

(A) one being arrested for violating it,

(B) arrest for one's violation of it,

(C) one's violation and arrest for it,

(D) one from being arrested for violating that law,

(E) one from an arrest for having violated the law,

13. In his testimony, <u>Eugene Debs asserted that the Espionage Law, which</u> had abridged free speech, was a violation of the Constitution.

(A) Eugene Debs asserted that the Espionage Law, which

(B) it was asserted by Eugene Debs that the Espionage Law that

(C) Eugene Debs asserting that the Espionage Law, which

(D) Eugene Debs having asserted that the Espionage Law, which

(E) Eugene Debs asserted that the Espionage Law that

14. Cambodia <u>remains being</u> a largely underdeveloped country because virtually all educated citizens were slaughtered during the regime of Pol Pot.

(A) remains being

(B) is still remaining

(C) is being

(D) remains

(E) remains still

QUESTIONS 15–17 ARE BASED ON THE FOLLOWING PASSAGE.

Line For absolute dating of archeological artifacts, the radiocarbon method emerged during the latter half of the twentieth century as the most reliable and precise
(5) method. The results of obsidian (volcanic glass) dating, a method based on the belief that newly exposed obsidian surfaces absorb moisture from the surrounding atmosphere at a constant rate, proved
(10) uneven. It was initially thought that the thickness of the hydration layer would provide a means of calculating the time elapsed since the fresh surface was made. But this method failed to account for the
(15) chemical variability in the physical and chemical mechanism of obsidian hydration. Moreover, each geographic source presented unique chemical characteristics, necessitating a trace element
(20) analysis for each such source. Yet, despite its limitations, obsidian dating helped archeologists identify the sources of many obsidian artifacts and to identify in turn ancient exchange networks for the flow of
(25) goods. Nor were ceramic studies and fluoride analysis supplanted entirely by the radiocarbon method, which in use allows for field labeling and laboratory errors, as well as sample contamination.
(30) In addition, in the 1970s dendrochronological (tree-ring) studies on the bristlecone pine showed that deviation from radiocarbon values increases as one moves back in time. Eventually, calibration curves were

(35) developed to account for this phenomenon; but in the archeological literature, we still find dual references to radiocarbon and sidereal, or calendar, time.

15. Based on the information in the passage, which of the following is LEAST likely to have been a means of dating archeological artifacts?

    (A) Ceramics studies

    (B) Radiocarbon dating

    (C) Dendrochronological studies

    (D) Fluoride analysis

    (E) Obsidian hydration-layer analysis

16. In the passage, the author mentions all of the following as problems with radiocarbon dating EXCEPT:

    (A) disparities with the calendar dating system.

    (B) deterioration of samples.

    (C) identification errors by archeological field workers.

    (D) contamination of artifacts.

    (E) mistakes by laboratory workers.

17. With which of the following statements would the passage's author most likely agree?

    (A) The greater the time that has elapsed since exposure of obsidian surface to moisture, the less reliable the results of obsidian dating.

    (B) The hydration layer accumulating through obsidian moisture absorption varies in thickness depending on the amount of surface area exposed to moisture.

    (C) The unpredictability of the obsidian hydration process renders the obsidian dating method problematic as a means of determining historical trade routes.

    (D) The results of obsidian dating are as reliable and precise as those of fluoride analysis only if trace element analysis is performed for the geographic source of the obsidian.

    (E) An obsidian artifact can be reliably dated using the obsidian method only

if certain environmental conditions where the artifact was found are considered.

18. When inhaled, asbestos fibers are known to significantly increase the likelihood of lung cancer and other respiratory ailments. Thousands of buildings in this state, especially apartment houses, are insulated with asbestos. Some local governments in the state have initiated massive and costly efforts to remove this asbestos.

    Which of the following, if true, taken together with the information above, best supports the conclusion that the health of those who occupy the buildings would be better preserved by leaving the asbestos in place than by removing it?

    (A) In removing the asbestos, millions of fibers are likely to be dislodged and sent into circulation in the air.

    (B) Asbestos removal is a hazardous procedure, posing significant health dangers to those who perform it.

    (C) Fewer than one person in a hundred who breathes asbestos-contaminated air is likely to contract a respiratory ailment as a result.

    (D) Apartment dwellers typically move from one residence to another more frequently than people who live in single family homes.

    (E) Most people who live in apartment buildings insulated with asbestos are aware of that fact.

19. Over the last year, the price that toy manufacturer FunTime charges for each toy it produces and sells directly to consumers has, on average, nearly doubled, prompting complaints to the company by many consumers. To combat this problem, FunTime's management must make every effort to improve relations with its union workers in order to help prevent them from striking, as these workers did for several weeks during the past year.

    Which of the following, if true, would cast the most doubt on the effectiveness of the proposal suggested above?

(A) Despite the complaints from consumers, sales of FunTime toys directly to consumers have increased steadily over the last year.

(B) FunTime's union workers are likely to be skeptical of any attempt by management to improve its relations with them.

(C) Some consumers who buy FunTime toys don't mind paying more for them because they are the highest quality toys available.

(D) FunTime's union workers are likely to strike again in the near future, regardless of management's efforts to improve relations with them.

(E) Most of the increase in the prices of FunTime toys is attributable to an increase in the cost of the raw materials the company uses to manufacture its toys.

20. The emission of fluorocarbons into the Earth's atmosphere has been shown to deplete the ozone layer in the atmosphere. Therefore, if we were to eliminate all sources of fluorocarbon emission, we could successfully halt ozone layer depletion.

Which of the following demonstrates a pattern of reasoning that is most similar to the flawed reasoning in the argument above?

(A) When challenged to prove their psychic abilities, several of the world's most celebrated so-called psychics were unable to do so, clearly proving that the psychic phenomenon is fiction rather than fact.

(B) The theory that the Earth's temperature would be shown to be cyclical if measured over millions of years is convincing, in light of the fact that the extinction of the dinosaurs occurred due to changes in the Earth's temperature.

(C) Flag burning is ultimately in the state's interest as well as the individual's interest, because the First Amendment right to free expression was created for the purpose of preserving our democratic way of life.

(D) Any person suffering from phlebitis must take the drug Anatol in order to prevent the condition from worsening, as evidenced by the fact that doctors have used Anatol successfully for many years to treat and control phlebitis.

(E) Autopsies of the residents of Huiki Island killed by a recent volcanic eruption have shown excessive bone deterioration, which leads to my conclusion that the Huikan culture encourages a diet that promotes bone marrow disease.

21. *Advertising executive:* Those who oppose the use of humor in advertising, whether print or television, either lack a sense of humor or fail to understand the advantage of using humor to advertise a product or service. After all, numerous surveys show that ordinary consumers are almost twice as likely to recall a humorous commercial as they are to recall a serious commercial.

Which of the following, if true, would cast the most serious doubt on the accuracy of the advertising executive's contention?

(A) Although most consumers surveyed were able to recall viewing humorous commercials, many said they enjoyed the serious commercials more.

(B) For certain types of products, humorous advertising would be inappropriate and potentially offensive.

(C) Although most consumers surveyed were able to recall viewing humorous commercials, most failed to recall the name of the product advertised.

(D) The consumers surveyed about humorous commercials included people considered unlikely to buy the particular product advertised.

(E) The use of humorous television commercials by advertisers has been declining over the last few years.

22. Upon man-made toxins' invading the human body, special enzymes are deployed, rebuilding any damaged DNA strands that result.

    (A) Upon man-made toxins' invading the human body, special enzymes are deployed, rebuilding any damaged DNA strands that result.

    (B) Upon man-made toxins, invasion of the human body, special enzymes are deployed that rebuild any damaged DNA strands resulting from the invasion.

    (C) When man-made toxins invade the human body, special enzymes are deployed to rebuild any DNA strands damaged as a result.

    (D) Special enzymes are deployed whenever man-made toxins invade the human body; they rebuild any damage that results to DNA strands.

    (E) Damage to DNA strands that results when man-made toxins invade the human body are repaired by deployed special enzymes.

23. The fact that the tie between the Manchus and the Chinese was cultural rather than racial helps to account for the homogeneity of the Chinese people.

    (A) cultural rather than racial helps to account for

    (B) not racial but cultural in nature helps explain

    (C) a cultural tie but not racial helps explain

    (D) cultural rather than a racial one helps to explain

    (E) cultural rather than a racial tie helps to account for

24. Even if her name was placed on the ballot in November, the third-party candidate would face overwhelming odds not only against the incumbent, but also against the mainstream opposition party.

    (A) Even if her name was placed on the ballot in November, the third-party candidate would

    (B) Even if, in November, her name was placed on the ballot, the third-party candidate will

    (C) Even if her name was to be placed on the ballot in November, the third-party candidate will

    (D) Even if being placed on the ballot in November, the third-party candidate would

    (E) Even if her name were placed on the ballot in November, the third-party candidate would

25. Although the use of fertilizers tends to diminish the flavor of fruits, the use of pesticides makes virtually no difference in flavor, assuming the fruit is washed thoroughly. Moreover, the use of pesticides repels insects that would otherwise leave unsightly blemishes on the fruit. Therefore, in the interest of appealing to consumer tastes, fruit growers would be well advised to use pesticides but not artificial fertilizers.

    Which of the following, if true, could proponents of the argument most appropriately cite as evidence for the soundness of the advice to fruit growers given in the last sentence?

    (A) The use of natural fertilizer results in larger, more colorful fruit than the use of artificial fertilizer.

    (B) The use of pesticides and fertilizers increases fruit growers' costs, which the growers generally pass on to consumers in the form of higher fruit prices.

    (C) Consumers generally consider a fruit's flavor to be important but consider a fruit's appearance to be less important.

    (D) Chemicals in artificial fertilizers pose a health threat to consumers who eat fruits produced using artificial fertilizers.

    (E) The use of artificial fertilizers in growing fruit has no effect on the appearance of the fruit.

26. A recent research study of a particular state's prison systems indicates that prisoners participating in the weekend furlough program are less likely to become repeat offenders after they are released than prisoners who do not participate in the program. The study confirms the researchers' hypothesis that weekend furlough programs at the state's prisons are an effective means of reducing crime.

Which of the following, if true, would cast the most serious doubt on the hypothesis to which the last sentence above refers?

(A) The furlough program was available only to prisoners who had demonstrated good behavior while in prison.

(B) The crime rate in other states with similar furlough programs is lower overall than the crime rate in states without furlough programs.

(C) Whether the weekend furlough program is effective depends on how greatly one values the reform of any one prisoner.

(D) Less than half of the prisoners not involved in the furlough program become repeat offenders after they are released.

(E) Less than half of all the prisoners studied participated in the furlough program.

27. Too many naive consumers <u>hasty and happily provide</u> credit information to unscrupulous merchants, who provide nothing in exchange but a credit fraud nightmare.

(A) hasty and happily provide

(B) hastily and happily provide

(C) hasty and happy providing

(D) hastily and happily providing

(E) providing hastily and happily

QUESTIONS 28–30 ARE BASED ON THE FOLLOWING PASSAGE.

Line   Modern containerization was born with the concept of intermodalism, the efficient transfer between modes of transportation (i.e., truck, train, ship). When international
(5) standards for containers were agreed on in 1961, the ground was laid not only for the dramatic reduction of import and export costs, but for the container industry and its contribution to global trade. Expo-
(10) nential, explosive growth in each soon followed. Today, the ubiquity of containerization over bulk is unchallenged.

In "The Containerization of Commodities," Jean-Paul Rodrigue and Theo
(15) Notteboom argue that despite the current saturation of containerization in some commodities, opportunities for growth still remain in niche markets. In fact, the global ubiquity of containerization has, they
(20) contend, created more opportunity for containerization by virtue of factors that range from economies of scale to the availability of empty containers.

Clearly, the niche is the key, and areas
(25) of current trade imbalances are cited by Rodrigue and Notteboom as obvious opportunities. Nevertheless, they add a cautionary note: Factors relating to complex logistics and ranging from the
(30) load units of available containers to transloading and terminal issues must be considered.

While Rodrigue and Notteboom suggest there is little competition between existing
(35) global containerized and bulk commodity chains, Bloomberg News has reported a "decline in the fortunes of dry-bulk and tanker operators." Bloomberg also notes a concomitant surge in some areas of
(40) containerization.

28. In responding to the summary of the Rodrigue/Notteboom analysis of global containerized and bulk chains, the author implies that

(A) the expected and dramatic reduction of import and export costs never occurred.

(B) Rodrigue and Notteboom are less interested in this issue than in the issue of niche markets.

(C) some market trends may suggest a counterargument to the Rodrigue/Notteboom claim.

(D) most shipping operators now accept that the containerization market is saturated.

(E) the ubiquity of containerization over bulk is, in fact, challenged after all.

29. Based on passage information, which of the following statements is LEAST likely to be true?

(A) The concept of intermodalism is the basis of efficient containerization.

(B) Transloading and terminal issues may prove barriers to efficient containerization.

(C) The availability of empty containers and other factors may facilitate the growth of the containerization market.

(D) Containerization is widespread and has saturated some commodities.

(E) Current market trends suggest great competition between existing global containerized and bulk commodity chains.

30. It can be inferred that

(A) bulk transfer will eventually disappear entirely.

(B) containerization often competes with bulk.

(C) containerization has a 100% saturation.

(D) some commodities cannot easily be containerized.

(E) dry-bulk and tanker operators continue to flourish.

31. Many individuals take antihistamine medications to alleviate the symptoms of allergies. Although all antihistamines are essentially similar, there is sufficient variation among the available formulas to make some more effective than others for any particular individual. Therefore, by trying different antihistamine formulations, any allergy sufferer can eventually find one that is effective.

Which of the following, if true, would most strengthen the conclusion drawn in the argument above?

(A) Antihistamines are the only types of medications proven effective in treating allergy symptoms.

(B) At least one antihistamine will relieve any individual's allergy symptoms.

(C) The effectiveness of an antihistamine is partially determined by the drug's specific formulation.

(D) The specific formulation used most often by allergy sufferers is not the one that would be most effective for the greatest number of allergy sufferers.

(E) Most allergy sufferers experience allergy symptoms that are typical of many different types of allergies.

32. All college students read either literary classics or current best-selling books as a habit, but some avid readers of current best-selling books do not read literary classics as a habit because they do not appreciate these books. People who enjoy classical music do not find current best-selling books interesting, and therefore do not read them as a habit. Since Javier is a college student who enjoys classical music, he must appreciate literary classics.

Which of the following must be true for the conclusion drawn above to be logically correct?

(A) Literary classics are more interesting than current best-selling books.

(B) All college students who appreciate literary classics read them as a habit.

(C) Literary classics are more interesting than classical music.

(D) All avid readers of literary classics appreciate this type of book.

(E) All college students who find classical music enjoyable also read current best-selling books as a habit.

33. Due to racial discrimination, some of the most gifted and influential jazz musicians were prohibited from dining <u>at the venues they have performed in.</u>

(A) at the venues they have performed in.

(B) at the very same venues they have performed in.

(C) where they have performed.

(D) at the same venues at which they performed.

(E) in venues, which were where they performed.

34. In asserting that a thing is honorable, <u>a favorable distinction is bestowed upon it,</u> which, after further reflection, we may find was not deserved.

(A) a favorable distinction is bestowed upon it,

(B) we bestow a distinction upon it favorably,

(C) we bestow upon it a favorable distinction,

(D) a favorable distinction upon it is bestowed,

(E) bestowing a favorable distinction upon it,

35. A proposed law would prohibit any individual who has been employed as a lobbyist on behalf of a particular industry from serving as the director of a government agency charged with regulating that same industry. The purpose of the proposed law is to prevent conflicts of interest. However, if passed, the law would prove counterproductive because it would prevent individuals who are knowledgeable about industries from serving as government regulators.

The argument above depends most directly on which of the following assumptions?

(A) The individuals in government who hold the power to enact the proposed law are susceptible to influence on the part of industry lobbyists.

(B) Government has a legitimate role to play in the regulation of most industries.

(C) Only individuals who have served as lobbyists on behalf of an industry are knowledgeable about that industry.

(D) Those who have served as lobbyists on behalf of an industry are capable of objective, unbiased decisions as regulators.

(E) The primary objective of government regulation of industry should be to strengthen and support that industry.

QUESTIONS 36–39 ARE BASED ON THE FOLLOWING PASSAGE.

Line　In 1930, a century after the birth of Victorian poetess Christina Rossetti, writer and scholar Virginia Woolf identified her as "one of Shakespeare's more recent
(5)　sisters" whose life had been reclusively Victorian but whose artistic achievement was enduring. Woolf remembered Rossetti for the explosive originality, vivid imagery, and emotional energy of her poems. "A
(10)　Birthday," for instance, is no typical Victorian poem and is certainly unlike predictable works of the era's best-known women poets. Rossetti's most famous poem, "Goblin Market," is at once
(15)　Christian, psychological, and pro-feminist. Like many of Rossetti's works, it is extraordinarily original, risky in subject matter, and unorthodox in form. Its Christian allusions are obvious but grounded in
(20)　opulent images whose lushness borders on the erotic.

　From Rossetti's work emerge not only emotional force, frequently ironic playfulness, and intellectual vigor, but also an
(25)　intriguing, enigmatic quality. "Winter: My

Secret," for example, combines these traits along with a very high (and un-Victorian) level of poetic self-consciousness. "How does one reconcile the aesthetic sensuality (30) of Rossetti's poetry with her repressed, ascetic lifestyle?" Woolf wondered. That Rossetti did indeed withhold a "secret" both from those intimate with her and from posterity is Lorna Packer's thesis in her (35) 1963 biography of Rossetti. Packer's claim that Rossetti's was a secret of the heart has since been disproved through the discovery of hundreds of letters by Rossetti, which reinforce the conventional image of her as (40) pious, scrupulously abstinent, and semi-reclusive.

Yet the passions expressed in Rossetti's love poems do expose the "secret" at the heart of both her life and art: a willingness (45) to forego worldly pleasures in favor of an aestheticized Christian version of transcendent fulfillment in heaven. The world, for Rossetti, is a fallen place, and her work is pervasively designed to convey this (50) inescapable truth. The beauty of her poetry must be seen, therefore, as an artistic strategy, a means toward a moral end.

36. All of the following are mentioned in the passage as qualities that emerge from Rossetti's work EXCEPT:

(A) lush imagery

(B) ironic playfulness

(C) stark realism

(D) unorthodox form

(E) intellectual vigor

37. Which of the following statements is most reasonably inferable from the passage?

(A) "Winter: My Secret" is Rossetti's best-known poem.

(B) Rossetti was not among the best-known poets during her era.

(C) The accounts of Rossetti's life contained in Packer's biography of Rossetti differ from those included in Woolf's biography of Rossetti.

(D) Rossetti's display of poetic self-consciousness drew criticism from her contemporaries.

(E) "Goblin Market" was published later than "A Birthday."

38. The author discusses Packer's thesis and its flaws in order to

(A) contrast the sensuality of Rossetti's poetry with the relative starkness of her devotional commentary.

(B) reveal the secret to which Rossetti alludes in "Winter: My Secret."

(C) call into question the authenticity of recently discovered letters written by Rossetti.

(D) compare Woolf's understanding of Rossetti with a recent, more enlightened view.

(E) provide a foundation for the author's own theory about Rossetti's life and work.

39. Which of the following best expresses the main idea of the passage?

(A) Newly discovered evidence suggests that Rossetti's works were misinterpreted by earlier critics and scholars.

(B) Rossetti can be compared to Shakespeare both in her private life and in the enduring quality of her work.

(C) Victorian poetry can be properly interpreted only by considering the personal life of the particular poet.

(D) The apparent inconsistency between Rossetti's personal life and literary work are explained by Rossetti's poems themselves.

(E) Rossetti's artistic integrity served as a model for later women poets.

40. Everyone agrees that current licensing requirements for child-care facilities are reasonably necessary to ensure public safety. Current licensing requirements for handgun ownership are far less stringent than those for operating child-care facilities. Yet the recent flurry of school shootings by young children using their parents' handguns shows that handgun ownership poses a significant potential threat to public safety.

The author is arguing that

(A) the recent school shootings would not have occurred were it not for lenient handgun ownership laws.

(B) parents of young children should not be allowed to own handguns.

(C) the legal requirements for obtaining a license for operating a child-care facility are more stringent than those for handgun ownership.

(D) unlicensed child care and unlicensed handgun ownership both pose a potential threat to public safety.

(E) it would be reasonable to impose more stringent requirements for handgun ownership.

41. The ancient Greek states boasted that <u>within their domains word and speech were free;</u> however, they seem to have forgotten the presence of slaves among them as well as that of women who also had no rights.

(A) within their domains word and speech were free;

(B) within its domain word and speech were free;

(C) word and speech were within their domains free;

(D) within their domains both word as well as speech were free;

(E) free word and speech were within their domains;

ANSWER KEY AND EXPLANATIONS

See Appendix B for score conversion tables to determine your score. Be sure to keep a tally of correct and incorrect answers for each test section.

Analysis of an Argument—Evaluation and Scoring

Evaluate your Argument-Analysis essay on a scale of 1 to 6 (6 being the highest score) according to the following five criteria:

❶ Does your essay identify the key features of the argument and analyze each one in a thoughtful manner?

❷ Does your essay support each point of its critique with insightful reasons and examples?

❸ Does your essay develop its ideas in a clear, organized manner, with appropriate transitions to help connect ideas?

❹ Does your essay demonstrate proficiency, fluency, and maturity in its use of sentence structure, vocabulary, and idiom?

❺ Does your essay demonstrate command of the elements of Standard Written English, including grammar, word usage, spelling, and punctuation?

The following series of questions, which serve to identify the Argument's five distinct problems, will help you evaluate your essay in terms of criteria 1 and 2. To earn a score of 4 or higher, your essay should identify at least three of these problems and, for each one, provide at least one example or counterexample that supports your critique. (Your examples need not be the same as the ones below.) Identifying and discussing at least four of the problems would help earn you an even higher score.

❶ Are key characteristics of one group member (Giant Industries) also characteristics of the group as a whole (all employers in a certain state)? (Perhaps Giant is not typical of the state's employers, as a group, with respect to either its financial strength or the average age of its workforce.)

❷ Does the term "largest private business" necessarily mean that Giant employs more workers than any other business in the state? (The smaller the workforce at Giant, the less likely that Giant is representative of the state's employers as a group.)

❸ Doesn't the prediction's accuracy require that other future conditions remain unchanged? (For example, the argument ignores a possible influx of workers from other states.)

❹ Would a reduced workforce necessarily result in business failure? (Perhaps businesses will be more profitable by trimming their workforce.)

❺ What is the definition of "quality of life"? (The argument's ultimate prediction depends on this missing definition.)

INTEGRATED REASONING SECTION

1. D, B	4. E, B	7.1 A	8.3 B	11.1 B
2.1 A	5. A, D	7.2 B	9. D	11.2 A
2.2 A	6.1 A	7.3 A	10.1 D	12.1 C
2.3 A	6.2 A	8.1 A	10.2 B	12.2 B
3. C, D	6.3 B	8.2 A		

1. **The correct answers are (D) (*assumption*) and (B) (*fact*).** The argument concludes that a roller coaster based on the film will be a better investment than one based on the children's show, because only children are fans of the show. For this conclusion to be sound, it must be assumed that children will not be the ones riding the new roller coaster. Choice (D) identifies this assumption. Choice (B) lends it support by stating that young children wouldn't even be able to ride on the new roller coaster, due to minimum height requirements.

2.1. **The correct answer is (A).** A vintage is considered Average if it receives a grade between 71 and 80, inclusive. Sort the table by the 2006 column and then by the 2007 column. No 2006 vintage received such a grade; however, the 2007 Côte de Beaune did. Since the same number of wines were rated in 2006 and 2007, the statement is correct.

2.2. **The correct answer is (A).** This statement is also correct. The 2010 vintages from 15 regions were rated, and two received an Outstanding rating (96 or higher). Two 2009 vintages and two 2006 vintages also received an Outstanding rating, but that was from a larger number of regions rated (20 of them in 2009 and 23 in 2006). Thus, the probability of an Outstanding rating was greater for a 2010 vintage than for any other vintage.

2.3. **The correct answer is (A).** This statement is correct as well. Four different wines from California's north coast were rated in 2006, and all of them received a grade of 89 or lower. Note that the one 2006 vintage from the United States that received a higher grade came from California's central coast, not its north coast.

3. **The correct answers are (C) (*scholarships funded*) and (D) (*alumni donating*).** If each of the school's A alumni donates €1 per month, that is, €12 for one year, then all the alumni collectively will donate €12A. Now, if half the alumni donate €1.50 per month each for one year, that means that $\frac{A}{2}$ alumni will donate each for the full year, for a total alumni donation of €9A. Set up and solve a proportion in order to find how many scholarships that amount will fund:

$$\frac{€12A}{S \text{ scholarships}} = \frac{€9A}{? \text{ scholarships}}$$

$$? = \frac{€9AS}{€12A}$$

$$? = \frac{3}{4}S$$

Next, let x be the number of alumni who must donate €1.50 per month each for one year (€18 each, in total) in order to fund collectively exactly $1.5S$ full-tuition scholarships. Set up a new proportion in order to find x:

$$\frac{€12A}{S \text{ scholarships}} = \frac{€18x}{1.5S \text{ scholarships}}$$

$$\frac{2A}{1} = \frac{3x}{1.5}$$

$$x = A$$

4. **The correct answers are (E) (*within the U.S. or Canada*) and (B) (*U.S. and Europe*).** The last passenger, choice (E), earned a total of 27,160 miles between Mar. 9, 2010, and Oct. 27, 2010, so she met the threshold for a reward flight between any two U.S. or Canadian cities, but not the threshold for any other reward flight. Thus, she's the correct answer in the first column. The second passenger, choice (B), earned a total of 44,600 between Feb. 23, 2009, and July 7, 2010, so he met the threshold for a reward flight between the United States and Europe, but not between the United States and Asia. Thus, he's the correct answer in the second column. The first passenger, choice (A), earned fewer than 25,000 miles. Choice (C) earned 40,060 miles, but her last trip (Dec. 9, 2010) was more than two years after her first trip (Oct. 6, 2008), so by that time the first trip's miles had expired. Finally, the fourth passenger, choice (D), flew for a total of 40,800 miles, but 10,200 of those were on a reward flight, so they don't count toward his total earned miles for reward consideration. Without them, he qualifies for a reward flight between the United States or Canada and Central America—which is not what you're looking for in either column.

5. **The correct answers are (A) (*r*) and (D) (*n*).** The first n terms of the sequence are $1, r, r^2, r^3, \ldots, r^n$. The reciprocals of these terms are $1, \dfrac{1}{r}, \dfrac{1}{r^2}, \dfrac{1}{r^3}, \ldots, \dfrac{1}{r^n}$. These terms form a geometric sequence, as well, with ratio $\dfrac{1}{r}$. Now, apply the formula for the sum of terms of a geometric sequence twice, for the original sequence and for the sequence of the inverses. First, the sum of the terms of the original sequence:

$$S_n = \frac{a_1\left(1 - r^n\right)}{1 - r}$$

$$255 = \frac{1\left(1 - r^n\right)}{1 - r}$$

$$255 = \frac{1 - r^n}{1 - r}$$

Next, the sum of the terms of the sequence of inverses:

$$S_n = \frac{1\left[1 - \left(\frac{1}{r}\right)^n\right]}{1 - \frac{1}{r}}$$

$$\frac{255}{128} = \frac{1\left[1 - \left(\frac{1}{r}\right)^n\right]}{1 - \frac{1}{r}}$$

$$\frac{255}{128} = \frac{\frac{r^n - 1}{r^n}}{\frac{r - 1}{r}}$$

$$\frac{255}{128} = \frac{r^n - 1}{r^{n-1}(r - 1)}$$

Substitute $\frac{1 - r^n}{1 - r}$ for 255 in the last expression:

$$\frac{\frac{1 - r^n}{1 - r}}{128} = \frac{r^n - 1}{r^{n-1}(r - 1)}$$

$$\frac{\frac{r^n - 1}{r - 1}}{128} = \frac{r^n - 1}{r^{n-1}(r - 1)}$$

$$\frac{r^n - 1}{128(r - 1)} = \frac{r^n - 1}{r^{n-1}(r - 1)}$$

$$\frac{1}{128} = \frac{1}{r^{n-1}}$$

$$r^{n-1} = 128$$

$$r^{n-1} = 2^7$$

Clearly, if r equals 2 and $n - 1$ equals 7 (that is, n equals 8), the above expression is correct. These two values are in the answer choices, so they have to be the right answers.

6.1. **The correct answer is (A).** The most woodwinds players that the SSO needs is 16, for Kwan's Concerto for 3 Violins and for Limoges' Symphony #7. The most brass players that it needs is 16, also for Limoges' Symphony #7. The most percussion players that it needs is 3, again for Limoges' Symphony #7. The most string players it needs is 62, for Kwan's Concerto for 3 Violins. The total number of musicians, not counting soloists, whom the SSO must contract for the entire spring season is the sum of these four numbers, which is 97.

6.2. **The correct answer is (A).** Sort by "Performance." You don't need to calculate the averages: rather, eyeball the table and save some time. One of the compositions in each program requires 21 strings, so these compositions cancel one another out. The other two compositions for each performance require 51 and 45 strings (Performance A), 51 and 62 strings (Performance B), and 54 and 31 (Performance C). It is clear that the 31 strings required by Performance C's Serenade for Strings bring the average number of strings for Performance C down considerably, compared to those averages for the other two performances.

6.3. **The correct answer is (B).** Three compositions require 8 woodwinds, and two of them were not composed by Sanford, M.; one was composed by Sanford, L. and the other by Baranko.

Thus, if a composition requires 8 woodwinds, the probability that it was not composed by Sanford, M. is 67%, not 33%.

7.1. **The correct answer is (A).** The statement is inferable: lyric poetry was composed in the 7th century BCE or later, so it comes after the year 700 BCE.

7.2. **The correct answer is (B).** The statement is not inferable. Though concerned with the present, lyric poems did at times use Greece's mythical past as their backdrop. Thus, a poem referring to Greece's mythical past could have been composed by one of the major lyric poets.

7.3. **The correct answer is (A).** The given information tells you that love poems were mainly (if not exclusively) written as solo songs. The table of poets does not list any poet who wrote solo songs after the 6th century. Thus, the newly discovered love songs were probably not composed in the 5th century.

8.1. **The correct answer is (A).** Hipponax is mentioned as perhaps the only composer of choliambics, and he was a composer of iambic poetry, which is not love poetry. Thus, this statement can be inferred.

8.2. **The correct answer is (A).** This statement is inferable: Hipponax lived in the 6th century.

8.3. **The correct answer is (B).** This statement cannot be inferred. The given information says that iambic poetry may or may not have been performed to music, and since this choliambic poem was probably by Hipponax, who was a composer of iambic poetry, this poem may or may not have been performed to music.

9. **The correct answer is (D).** All of these poets except Stesichorus composed mainly elegiac or iambic poems, which did not necessarily make use of musical accompaniment. Stesichorus, on the other hand, composed mainly choral songs, which were always performed to music. Thus, his poetry is the most likely to have been performed with musical accompaniment.

10.1. **The correct answer is (D).** There are 200 students in the 7th grade. Of them, 43% (that is, 86 students) read below grade level, and 28% (that is, 56 students) read well below grade level. Thus, 142 students in the 7th grade (86 plus 56) do not read on grade level.

10.2. **The correct answer is (B).** The probability for a 6th grader is 32%, or 0.32; for a 7th grader it is 29%, or 0.29; and for an 8th grader it is 24%, or 0.24. Since the three classes have the same number of students as one another, the probability for a student of any grade is the average of the three probabilities:

$$\frac{0.32 + 0.29 + 0.24}{3} = 0.28\overline{3} \approx 0.28$$

11.1. **The correct answer is (B).** Companies A, B, C, and D have a stock price greater than $60. Company A's P/E ratio is 90-something over 3, which is roughly 30. Company B's P/E ratio is 90-something over (less than 2), which is greater than 45. Company C's P/E ratio is 80-ish over (less than 2), which is slightly greater than 40. Finally, company D's P/E ratio is 70-something over (more than 2), which is less than 40. Thus, two of the four companies have a P/E ratio over 40.

11.2. **The correct answer is (A).** The easiest way to figure out this answer is to realize that a P/E ratio of 10 requires the numerator to be 10 times greater than the denominator. For instance, if the company's share price is $10 and the company's earnings per share are $1, then its P/E ratio is 10. Similarly, a P/E ratio of 10 comes from the value pairs ($20, $2), ($30, $3), and so on. So, examine the graph with this in mind. First of all, you can eliminate all companies whose stock price is greater than $40, because no company earned more than $4 per share. That leaves only four companies: J, L, N, and P. Company J's stock price is greater than $30, but its earnings per share are less than $3, so its P/E ratio is greater than 10. Company L's stock price is greater than $25, but its earnings per share are less than $2.50, so its P/E ratio is greater than 10. Company N's stock price is about $15, and its earnings per share are almost $2, so its P/E ratio is less than 10. Finally, company P's stock price is greater than $10, but its earnings per share are less than $1, so its P/E ratio is greater than 10. Thus, only one company has a P/E ratio less than 10.

12.1. **The correct answer is (C).** In January 2011, the family consumed 29 kWh of electricity. In December 2010, it consumed 23 kWh. Thus, if 29 is $x\%$ of 23, then:

$$29 = x\%(23)$$

$$x = \frac{29}{23\%}$$

$$x = \frac{29}{23}(100)$$

$$x = 126$$

12.2. **The correct answer is (B).** Between June 2010 and August 2010, the family consumed 15, 27, and 26 kWh, respectively, for a total of 68 kWh. Between September 2010 and November 2010, it consumed 14, 17, and 16 kWh, respectively, for a total of 47 kWh. Thus, it spent $68x$ and $47x$ during the two periods. Let $68x$ equal y times $47x$. Then:

$$68x = y47x$$

$$y = \frac{68}{47}$$

$$y = 1.45$$

QUANTITATIVE SECTION

1. B	9. D	17. A	25. C	33. E
2. A	10. E	18. D	26. E	34. D
3. D	11. A	19. E	27. A	35. C
4. C	12. A	20. C	28. D	36. E
5. C	13. A	21. E	29. E	37. B
6. C	14. C	22. D	30. A	
7. B	15. D	23. C	31. C	
8. E	16. C	24. B	32. C	

1. **The correct answer is (B).** In combining fractions, you can cancel across fractions all variables except a (in the numerator) and e (in the denominator), leaving $\dfrac{a}{e} \bullet x = 1$.

   Then, to isolate x on one side of the equation, multiply both sides by $\dfrac{e}{a}$:

   $$\frac{e}{a} \bullet \frac{a}{e} \bullet x = 1 \bullet \frac{e}{a}$$

   $$x = \frac{e}{a}$$

2. **The correct answer is (A).** Any one of four distinct groups of three women might be selected: *ABC, ABD, ACD,* or *BCD.* The probability that the selections will result in any particular one of these groupings is 1 in 4, or $\dfrac{1}{4}$. Similarly, any one of three distinct pairs of two men might be selected: *XY, XZ,* and *YZ.* The probability that the selections will result in any particular one of these pairs is 1 in 3, or $\dfrac{1}{3}$. To determine the combined probability, multiply one individual probability by the other: $\dfrac{1}{4} \times \dfrac{1}{3} = \dfrac{1}{12}$.

3. **The correct answer is (D).** Recall that the domain of a function is the set of numbers for which the function is defined. For the function in this question, the quantity under the square root must be nonnegative, so x must be greater than or equal to 3. Additionally, the denominator cannot be zero, so x cannot equal 4. The only answer choice that satisfies both of these conditions is choice (D).

4. **The correct answer is (C).** The theater sold 350 full-price tickets, so its revenue from those tickets was $35,000. Now, look at the answer choices. All of them are of the form $65,*xxx*. If you subtract $35,000 from $65,*xxx*, you are left with $30,*xxx*. This number has to be divisible by 60, since it represents the total revenue from the $60 tickets sold. Note that 30,000 is divisible by 60, so essentially you need to identify the answer choice for which the portion to the right of the comma (that is, the numbers 080, 100, 120, 140 or 160) is divisible by 60. Only 120 is divisible by 60, so the correct answer is (C).

5. **The correct answer is (C).** Statement (1) alone provides no information about b and is therefore insufficient to answer the question. Statement (2) alone is also insufficient because it provides two distinct equations in two variables: $a - b = 1$ and $a - b = -1$. Now consider both statements together. Given Statement (1), $a = 3, -3$. Substituting 3 and -3 for a into each of the two equations that Statement (2) suggests yields four possible values for b: 2, -4, 4, and -2. Since you now know all possible values for a and b, you can determine the minimum value of $|a + b|$. (The answer to the question is 5.)

6. **The correct answer is (C).** Here's the sequence up to the 12th second:

    0 *W*   1 *B*   2 *W*   3 *G*   4 *W*   5 *R*   6 *W*

    7 *B*   8 *W*   9 *G*   10 *W*   11 *R*   12 *W*

    Every time you reach a time divisible by 6, the sequence starts over with W and proceeds: $W\text{-}B\text{-}W\text{-}G\text{-}W\text{-}R$. 204 is divisible by 6; hence, starting at the 204th second, here are the lights' movements through the 209th second:

    204 *W*   205 *B*   206 *W*

    207 *G*   208 *W*   209 *R*

    As you can see, the movement from the 208th to the 209th second is from white (W) to red (R).

7. **The correct answer is (B).** Statement (1) alone is obviously insufficient to answer the question. Considering Statement (2) alone, the factored form of the quadratic expression $x^2 - 6x + 9$ is $(x - 3)(x - 3)$. As you can see, the two roots of the equation in Statement (2) are the same. The only possible value of x is 3. Thus, Statement (2) alone suffices to answer the question.

8. **The correct answer is (E).** Substitute $\frac{2}{3}$ and $\frac{-2}{3}$ individually for u in the defined operation

    $$\blacktriangleleft u \blacktriangleright = u^2 - u:$$

    $$\blacktriangleleft \frac{2}{3} \blacktriangleright = \frac{4}{9} - \frac{2}{3} = \frac{4}{9} - \frac{6}{9} = \frac{-2}{9}$$

    $$\blacktriangleleft -\frac{2}{3} \blacktriangleright = \frac{4}{9} + \frac{2}{3} = \frac{4}{9} + \frac{6}{9} = \frac{10}{9}$$

    Then add the two results together:

    $$-\frac{2}{9} + \frac{10}{9} = \frac{8}{9}$$

9. **The correct answer is (D).** Extend $\overline{BE}$ to F (as in the diagram below). m$\angle EFD$ = m $\angle ABE$ = 40°. m $\angle FED$ must be 110° because a triangle's angle measures sum to 180°. Since $\angle BED$ and $\angle FED$ are supplementary, m$\angle BED$ = 70°.

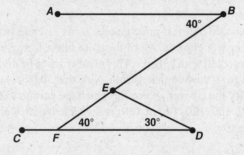

10. **The correct answer is (E).** The representative made 35 calls in total spending on average y minutes on each of these calls, so he spent $35y$ minutes on all calls. He made 11 calls that resulted in a sale spending on average x minutes on each of these calls, so he spent $11x$ minutes on all calls that resulted in a sale. Let z be the number of minutes he spent on average on calls that did not result in a sale—the number the question is asking for. He made 24 such calls, so he spent a total of $24z$ minutes on all calls that did not result in a sale. The total number of minutes he spent on all calls equals the sum of the total number of minutes he spent on calls that resulted in a sale and the total number of minutes he spent on calls that did not result in a sale:

$$35y = 11x + 24z$$
$$24z = 35y - 11x$$
$$z = \frac{35y - 11x}{24}$$

11. **The correct answer is (A).** Add the two equations:

$$x + y = a$$
$$\underline{x - y = b}$$
$$2x = a + b$$
$$x = \frac{1}{2}(a + b)$$

12. **The correct answer is (A).** To find the point of intersection of the two graphs, you have to solve the system of these two equations. First, solve the first equation for x: $x - y = 4 \Rightarrow x = y + 4$. Now, substitute this expression of x into the second equation:

$$2y = 3x - 1$$
$$2y = 3(y + 4) - 1$$
$$2y = 3y + 12 - 1$$
$$2y = 3y + 11$$
$$-11 = y$$

Next, substitute $y = -11$ into the first equation: $x = y + 4 \Rightarrow x = -11 + 4 \Rightarrow x = -7$. So the graphs of the two equations intersect at the point $(-7, -11)$.

13. **The correct answer is (A).** The shelter houses $d + c$ animals altogether. Of these animals, d are dogs. That portion can be expressed as the fraction $\frac{d}{c + d}$.

14. **The correct answer is (C).** The information in the question establishes the total contributions of Willot and Tilson Counties relative to those of Stanton and Osher Counties. Statement (1) provides information about the total crop revenues of Osher County relative to those of Tilson County, but the statement provides no additional information about Stanton County's specific percentage contribution. Statement (1) alone is therefore insufficient to answer the question. Based on Statement (2) alone, Tilson County's nonsubsidized farms must have accounted for 6% of all revenues (18% – 12%). Accordingly, Stanton County's nonsubsidized farms must have accounted for 9% of all revenues. (The percentages in the leftmost column must total 30.) However, this information is insufficient to determine Stanton County's subsidized farm contribution. With Statements (1) and (2) together, Osher County's revenues must total 36% [because Statement (2) stipulates that Osher County contributed twice the revenues of Tilson County, which you now know contributed 18% of all revenues]. At this point, you've partially completed the table:

	non-subsidized farms	subsidized farms		
Willot County	7%			} 50%
Tilson County	(6%)	12%	(18%)	
Stanton County	(9%)			} 50%
Osher County	8%	(28%)	(36%)	
(Total Percentages)	30%	(70%)		

Now you can see that Stanton County's subsidized farms contributed 5% of the total revenues. (Stanton and Osher revenues must account for 50% of the total.) Thus, Statements (1) and (2) together suffice to answer the question.

15. **The correct answer is (D).** Since the smallest circle has a radius of 1, the medium circle has a radius of 2, and, therefore, the diameter of the large circle must be 6, which makes its radius 3. The arc of a semicircle is half the circle's circumference—that is, πr. So, the length of the boundary of the shaded region is the sum of the arcs of the three semicircles:

$$\pi + 2\pi + 3\pi = 6\pi$$

16. **The correct answer is (C).** Statement (1) alone is insufficient because you can make several possible equations using the integers 0 through 9. Statement (2) alone is insufficient for the same reason. Considering Statements (1) and (2) together leaves you with only two possibilities for b^n: 3^4 or 9^2. Given that $a^m = b^n$, you can now answer the question. The sum of the four integers is $3 + 4 + 9 + 2$, or 18.

17. **The correct answer is (A).** The total rent is $D + 100$, which must be divided by the number of students (M).

18. **The correct answer is (D).** Start with 2, then 4, then 6, and so forth (positive even integers), as the value of n. Test each value in turn. You'll find that only the numbers in the following sequence leave a remainder of 1 when divided by 3: {4, 7, 10, . . .}. Notice that the numbers increase by 3 in sequence. Next, try a few of these numbers as the value of n in each of the five expressions. You'll find that all but ($n \times 2$) are divisible by 3.

19. **The correct answer is (E).** First combine the two terms inside the radical using the common denominator b^2. Then, remove perfect squares from the radical:

$$\sqrt{\frac{a^2}{b^2} + \frac{a^2}{b^2}} = \sqrt{\frac{a^2 + a^2}{b^2}} = \sqrt{\frac{2a^2}{b^2}} = \frac{|a|}{|b|}\sqrt{2}$$

20. **The correct answer is (C).** First, consider Statement (1) alone. If $a = -1$, then the two quantities are equal, while if a has any other value less than 0, the two quantities are unequal. Thus, you can easily dismiss Statement (1) as insufficient to answer the question. Consider Statement (2) alone. If $-1 < a < 0$, then $\sqrt[3]{a} < a$ (and the answer to the question is *yes*). For example, $\sqrt[3]{-\frac{1}{8}} = -\frac{1}{2}$, which is less than $-\frac{1}{8}$. But, if $0 < a < 1$, then $\sqrt[3]{a} > a$ (and the answer to the question is *no*). For example, $\sqrt[3]{\frac{1}{8}} = \frac{1}{2}$, which is greater than $\frac{1}{8}$. Thus, Statement (2) does not suffice.

Considering both statements together, $-1 < a < 0$. As already noted, under this constraint, the answer to the question is always *yes*.

21. **The correct answer is (E).** According to the triangle inequality, the length of any side of a triangle is less than the sum of the lengths of the other two sides, and it is greater than the positive

difference of the lengths of the other two sides. If a is the length of the third side of the triangle in question, you can express this property as:

$$a < 15 + 7$$
$$a > 15 - 7$$

Solving these inequalities you get:

$$a < 15 + 7 \Rightarrow a < 22$$
$$a > 15 - 7 \Rightarrow a > 8$$

In other words, a can take any value greater than 8 and less than 22. Note that a cannot equal either 8 or 22. The only answer choice that violates this result is choice (E).

22. The correct answer is (D). The area of any triangle equals $\frac{1}{2} \times base \times height$. Using 7 miles as the base of the triangle in this problem, the triangle's height is the north-south (vertical) distance from A to an imaginary line extending west from B. Statement (1) explicitly provides the triangle's height. Statement (2) also provides sufficient information to determine this height.

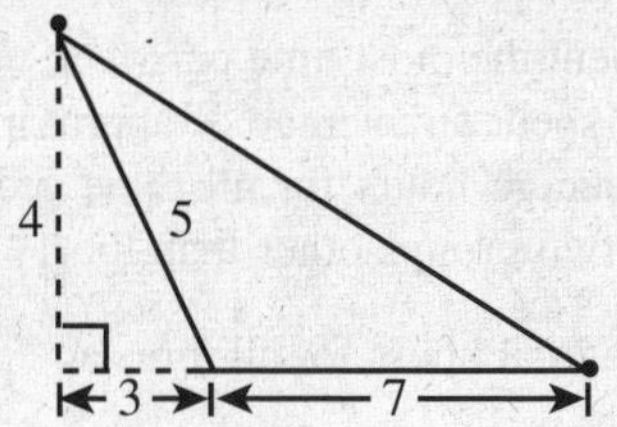

As indicated in the figure above, the triangle's height is 4 miles ($3^2 + 4^2 = 5^2$, per the Pythagorean theorem). Accordingly, either statement alone suffices to determine the triangle's area.

(The area $= \frac{1}{2} \times 7 \times 4 = 14$.)

23. The correct answer is (C). Neither Statement (1) nor Statement (2) alone suffices to answer the question. You still do not know what portion of the remaining computer systems is equipped only with scanners. However, both statements together establish that 55% (100% – 20% – 25%) are equipped only with scanners.

24. The correct answer is (B). To answer the question, you need to compare Daniel's rate of work with that of Carl and Todd working together. Statement (1) provides Carl's rate, but not Todd's; therefore, Statement (1) alone is insufficient to answer the question. Statement (2) provides Carl's and Todd's combined rate. By comparing this combined rate with the rate of all three working together, you can determine Daniel's rate. Statement (2) alone suffices to answer the question. Although you don't have to do the math, here's how you would answer the question. All three workers can load $\frac{1}{8}$ of the van in one hour. Similarly, Carl and Todd can load $\frac{1}{12}$ of the van in one hour. Subtract $\frac{1}{12}$ from $\frac{1}{8}$ to obtain Daniel's rate: $\frac{1}{8} - \frac{1}{12} = \frac{3}{24} - \frac{2}{24} = \frac{1}{24}$.

Daniel can do $\frac{1}{24}$ of the job (loading the van) in one hour, so it would take Daniel 24 hours to load the van.

25. **The correct answer is (C).** By definition, the longest possible chord of a circle is equal in length to the circle's diameter. Thus, the coordinates of R and S allow you to calculate the circle's diameter and, in turn, its area. Statements (1) and (2) together suffice to answer the question.

26. **The correct answer is (E).** This problem requires a bit of trial and error. Given Statement (1), a bit of experimenting with a few numbers—e.g., AB = 43 and AB = 24—quickly reveals that Statement (1) alone is insufficient to answer the question: $4 \times 3 = 12$ (divisible by 4), but BAB (343) is not divisible by 4. $2 \times 4 = 8$ (divisible by 4), and BAB (424) is also divisible by 4. Similarly, given Statement (2), substituting a few different value pairs for A and B that satisfy Statement (2) quickly reveals that Statement (2) alone is insufficient to answer the question. $3 + 6 + 3 = 12$ (divisible by 4), but 363 (BAB) is not divisible by 4. $4 + 0 + 4 = 8$ (divisible by 4), and 404 is divisible by 4. Even considered together, Statements (1) and (2) are insufficient to answer the question. For example, the number 242 satisfies both Statements (1) and (2) but is not divisible by 4, whereas the number 484 satisfies both Statements (1) and (2) and is divisible by 4.

27. **The correct answer is (A).** Given Statement (1), you can determine the total number of paperbacks sold: $(\$0.75)(P) = \$19.50$, or $P = 26$. Given that 55 books were sold altogether, 29 hardback books were sold, and Statement (1) alone suffices to answer the question. Statement (2) provides no information about the price of either type of book, and therefore alone is insufficient to answer the question.

28. **The correct answer is (D).** The age group that spent the most time per week watching sports on television was the 19–24-year-old group (who spent an average of approximately 6 hours per week watching sports programming). The average hours for all three groups totals approximately 71 ($34 + 17 + 20$). Of that total, the two groups other than the 19–24 age group accounted for 54 hours, or about 76% $\left(\dfrac{54}{71}\right)$ of the total hours for all three age groups.

29. **The correct answer is (E).** Your task here is to compare the size of the entertainment portion of the left-hand bar to the combined sizes of the same portion of the other two bars. Size up the ratio visually. The portion on the first chart is just a bit larger than the other two combined, isn't it? So you're looking for a ratio that's greater than 1:1. You can rule out answer choices (A) and (B). Approximate the height of each of the three portions:

> 13–18 age group: 25 hours
>
> 19–24 age group: 5 hours
>
> 25–30 age group: 10 hours

The ratio in question is 25:15, or 5:3.

30. **The correct answer is (A).** The amount invested at 5% is $(10,000 - x)$ dollars. Thus, the income from that amount is $0.05(10,000 - x)$ dollars.

31. **The correct answer is (C).** Based on the definition of a geometric series in the question, all pairs of successive terms must have the same ratio. Thus, $\dfrac{x}{-2} = \dfrac{-8}{x}$. Cross-multiplying, $x^2 = 16$; hence $x = \pm 4$. The constant multiple is either 2 or –2. If the second term is +4, the sixth term would be $(-2)(-2)^{(6-1)} = (-2)(-2)^5 = 64$. If the second term is –4, the sixth term would be $(-2)(2)^5 = -64$.

32. **The correct answer is (C).** This question requires a bit of intuition. The objective is to minimize the unused space in the packing box by turning the smaller boxes on their appropriate sides. Align the 2-inch edge of each box along the 18-inch edge of the packing box (9 boxes make up a row). Align the 5-inch side of each box along the 35-inch edge of the packing box (7 boxes make up a row). Arranged in this manner with the 18-inch by 35-inch face of the packing box

as the base, one layer of small boxes 3 inches high includes 63 boxes (9×7). Given that the packing box's third dimension is 19 inches, 6 layers of boxes, each 3 inches high, will fit into the packing box, for a total of 378 boxes. An unused 1-inch layer remains at the top of the box. (You could reverse the alignment of the 2- and 3-inch sides and arrive at the same result.)

33. **The correct answer is (E).** A median is the number that ranks exactly in the middle of the set. To know the median here, you would need to know what the six specific values are, not just their range and/or average.

34. **The correct answer is (D).** Statement (1) alone suffices to answer the question. Given that $x = 60$, the area of each of the two triangles must be less than $\frac{60}{360}$ (or $\frac{1}{6}$) of the area of the circle (the difference is the region between each triangle and the circle's circumference). So, the combined area of the two triangles is less than $\frac{1}{3}$ the area of the circle. Given that $x = 60$, m$\angle AOC = 120$, and the area of the shaded region is exactly $\frac{120}{360}$ (or $\frac{1}{3}$) that of the circle.

Statement (2) alone also suffices to answer the question. Given that the length of $\overline{AB}$ equals the radius, each of the two triangles must be equilateral, and all angles measure 60°. You can now apply the same reasoning as with Statement (1) to answer the question.

35. **The correct answer is (C).** The total distance is equal to the distance that one bus traveled plus the distance that the other bus traveled (to the point where they pass each other). Letting x equal the number of hours traveled, you can express the distances that the two buses travel in that time as $48x$ and $55x$. Equate the sum of these distances with the total distance and solve for x:

$$48x + 55x = 515$$
$$103x = 515$$
$$x = 5$$

The buses will pass each other five hours after 9:30 a.m.—at 2:30 p.m.

36. **The correct answer is (E).** The expression involves subtraction, so neither the base numbers nor the exponents can be combined. Only choice (E) is equivalent to the original expression. To confirm this without using a calculator, factor 7^{76} from both terms:

$$\frac{7^{77} - 7^{76}}{6} = \frac{7^{76}\left(7^1 - 1\right)}{6} = \frac{7^{76}\left(6\right)}{6} = 7^{76}$$

37. **The correct answer is (B).** The value of Dynaco shares sold plus the value of MicroTron shares sold must be equal to the value of all shares sold. Letting x represent the number of Dynaco shares sold, you can represent the number of MicroTron shares sold by $300 - x$. Set up an equation in which the value of Dynaco shares sold plus the value of MicroTron shares sold equals the total value of all shares sold. Then solve for x:

$$52x + 36\left(300 - x\right) = 40\left(300\right)$$
$$52x + 10,800 - 36x = 12,000$$
$$16x = 1200$$
$$x = 75$$

The investor has sold 75 shares of Dynaco stock.

VERBAL SECTION

1. C	10. B	18. A	26. A	34. C
2. D	11. E	19. E	27. B	35. C
3. D	12. D	20. D	28. C	36. C
4. D	13. A	21. C	29. E	37. B
5. A	14. D	22. C	30. D	38. E
6. B	15. C	23. A	31. B	39. D
7. C	16. B	24. E	32. D	40. E
8. E	17. E	25. C	33. D	41. A
9. E				

1. **The correct answer is (C).** The original sentence is not parallel. Choice (C) makes the sentence parallel by repeating the same form of the verb *to be* (was) and by making "illustrator of living animals" parallel to "author of nonsense verses."

2. **The correct answer is (D).** The original answer is a fragment because "having published" is not a predicate; it is a verbal, which is sometimes also called a non-finite verb. Choice (D) remedies this problem by using the correct and complete verb, *had published.*

3. **The correct answer is (D).** The original version contains superfluous words; either *the age of* or *years* should be omitted. Choice (D) corrects the original version by omitting *the age of.* Choice (E) is redundant; either *old* or *in age* should be omitted.

4. **The correct answer is (D).** The argument suggests that the company's improved profitability the year after the court judgment was attributable to that judgment. However, the mere fact that one event follows the other does not necessarily mean that it was *caused* by the other event. Choice (D) points out this critical flaw in the argument by recognizing that consumer buying decisions and, in turn, the profitability of product manufacturers, can depend on a variety of possible factors.

5. **The correct answer is (A).** John's statement does *not* logically imply, as Jolanda seems to infer, that a person must believe in the inevitability of success in order to be successful. Choice (A) is an effective rebuttal for John because it points out Jolanda's apparent reasoning error.

6. **The correct answer is (B).** Nowhere in the passage does the author mention any power struggles among the leaders of the Iroquois nations. Although the first paragraph does refer to a dispute among the Iroquois leaders, the dispute involved the role that the Iroquois should play in the American Revolution. Thus, choice (B) confuses the information in the passage by referring to unrelated details.

7. **The correct answer is (C).** The passage states that Cornplanter was an outspoken proponent of assimilation and that Handsome Lake was related to Cornplanter as a half-brother. The fact that Lake was responsible for the Iroquois reasserting their national identity is ironic, then, in light of Lake's blood relationship to Cornplanter.

8. **The correct answer is (E).** According to the author, the Quakers' introduction of new technology to the Iroquois was partly responsible for the decline of the Iroquois culture in that it contributed to the tribe's loss of national identity. Choice (E) presents a similar situation.

9. **The correct answer is (E).** The original sentence suffers from both a misplaced, or dangling modifier and redundancy. Choice (E) corrects these problems by eliminating the modification

of *screams* by the participial phrase "completely engulfed in flames." It also eliminates redundancy: *engulfed* suggests something that is entirely or completely swallowed up, immersed in, or taken in; furthermore, there is no need to say both *burning* and *in flames*. Note that the use of the passive voice is appropriate here, as it is in all sentences where the specific doer of the action is not known or is not important.

10. **The correct answer is (B).** The first and third sentences, considered together, strongly imply the conclusion expressed by choice (B). Admittedly, the passage does not rule out the possibility that babies who are breast fed during some portion of the first year other than the first three months are more likely than other babies to become obese. However, this possible scenario runs completely contrary to the passage information. Thus, despite this remote possibility, choice (B) is the best answer.

11. **The correct answer is (E).** The passage's first sentence implies that a high level of consumer confidence leads to increased consumer spending, which in turn leads to depletion of retail inventories. However, the passage indicates that, at a time when consumer confidence is great, retail inventories are *increasing* instead. Each answer except choice (E) provides a logical explanation for this apparent discrepancy. However, choice (E) suggests that an increase in consumer confidence levels should be preceded by decreased business spending, which would tend to *decrease*, rather than increase, retail inventory levels. Thus, choice (E) actually renders the discrepancy more inexplicable.

12. **The correct answer is (D).** In the original version, *one being arrested* should be replaced either with *one from being arrested* or with *one's arrest* or with the noun clause *one's being arrested*. (Noun clauses take the possessive verb form.) Also, *it* would more clearly refer to its antecedent *the law* if it were positioned closer to the antecedent or replaced with the antecedent. Choice (D) corrects both problems with the original version. An even better version would include *one's arrest* instead of *one from being arrested*; nevertheless, choice (D) is the best of the five choices.

13. **The correct answer is (A).** The original sentence correctly uses the active voice, a complete verb, and a nonrestrictive clause that begins with *which*.

14. **The correct answer is (D).** The original version uses the awkward (and improper) *remains being*. Either *is still* or simply *remains* should be used instead. Choice (D) corrects the problem.

15. **The correct answer is (C).** As the passage indicates, dendrochronological studies involve analyzing tree rings. Although the wood from trees might have been used to create items that are now considered archeological artifacts, the author does not indicate explicitly that tree rings are studied for the purpose of dating such artifacts.

16. **The correct answer is (B).** In the second paragraph, the author mentions choices (A), (C), (D), and (E) as problems with radiocarbon dating. Nowhere in the passage, however, does the author mention any problem involving sample deterioration.

17. **The correct answer is (E).** In mentioning that a trace element analysis is needed for the geographic source of an obsidian artifact, the author strongly implies that an accounting for specific conditions of the geographic area is needed in order to determine the age of the obsidian artifact by measuring its hydration layer.

18. **The correct answer is (A).** Choice (A), if true, suggests that the removal of the asbestos could endanger the health of the building's occupants by sending dangerous fibers into the atmosphere. Since it is possible that this health risk outweighs the health risk of leaving the asbestos in place, the statement provides strong support for the conclusion that the asbestos should be left in place in the interest of the occupants' health.

19. **The correct answer is (E).** The argument assumes that union-relations problems are the major cause of the price increase. Choice (E) undermines the logic of the proposed solution by suggesting that another factor—the cost of raw materials—may be more important.

20. **The correct answer is (D).** The original argument essentially demonstrates the following reasoning:

    Premise: If fluorocarbons are emitted, then ozone depletion will occur.

    Conclusion: If fluorocarbons are not emitted, then ozone depletion will not occur.

    You can express this reasoning symbolically as follows:

    Premise: If A, then B.

    Conclusion: If not A, then not B.

    The reasoning is fallacious (flawed), because it fails to account for other possible causes of ozone depletion. (B might occur whether or not A occurs.)

    Choice (D) is the only answer choice that demonstrates the same essential pattern of flawed reasoning.

    Premise: If a person with phlebitis takes Anatol, the phlebitis will be controlled.

    Conclusion: If a person does not take Anatol, the phlebitis will not be controlled.

    Note that choice (D) begins with the conclusion, whereas the original argument begins with the premise. This fact makes no difference, however, in assessing the reasoning itself.

21. **The correct answer is (C).** The argument relies on the assumption that consumers are more likely to buy a particular product (or service) if they remember a particular advertisement for it than if they don't remember. Choice (C) undermines this crucial assumption. Even if consumers remember an advertisement, unless they also remember the particular product advertised, they're no more likely to buy that product than had they not remembered the advertisement at all.

22. **The correct answer is (C).** In the original sentence, the antecedent of *that result* is unclear. Is it DNA strands or damage to those strands that result from the deployment of enzymes? Also, the use of the noun clause *man-made toxins' invading* in a prepositional phrase here is somewhat awkward, albeit grammatically correct. Choice (B) improperly uses *that* instead of *which*. Also, it is unclear what "resulting" refers to here—DNA strands or damage to the DNA strands. Choice (C) improves on the awkward use of a noun clause in the first part of the original sentence. The infinitive *to rebuild* and the phrase *as a result* clarify the meaning of the second part of the sentence. In spite of its use of the passive voice (*enzymes are deployed*), choice (C) is the best version.

23. **The correct answer is (A).** The original version is correct. By omitting *rather*, choice (B) obscures the meaning of the sentence; the original version is clearer. Choice (C) sets up a faulty parallel between *cultural tie* and *racial*. Choice (D) also sets up a faulty parallel—between *cultural* and *a racial one*. Choice (E) also sets up a faulty parallel—between *cultural* and *a racial tie*.

24. **The correct answer is (E).** The original sentence presents a condition contrary to fact but does not use the subjunctive mood. Choice (E) corrects this problem by replacing *was* with *were*, thus employing the subjunctive.

25. **The correct answer is (C).** The argument recommends that fruit growers not use artificial fertilizers if they wish to appeal to consumer tastes because these fertilizers diminish flavor. This recommendation depends on the assumption that flavor enhances a fruit's appeal to consumers. Choice (C) helps substantiate this assumption. (Presumably, flavorful fruit is more appealing than flavorless fruit.)

26. **The correct answer is (A).** The argument relies on the assumption that the furlough program is responsible for, or at least contributes to, a prisoner's refraining from committing crimes after release. One effective way of weakening the argument is to refute this assumption by providing evidence that the program does *not* contribute to the reform of prisoners. Choice (A) provides strong evidence to this effect—specifically, that program participants are less likely than non-participants to commit crimes upon their release.

27. **The correct answer is (B).** The original sentence improperly uses the adjective *hasty* instead of the adverb *hastily* to modify the verb provide. Choice (B) remedies the problem.

28. **The correct answer is (C).** Choice (C) is the correct answer because the Rodrigue/Notteboom claim is that there is little competition between existing global containerized and bulk commodity chains. But the Bloomberg News report suggests that market trends are the contrary to this claim. Choices (A) and (B) must be ruled out because nothing of the kind is stated or implied; furthermore, this information does not appear within the context of the Rodrigue/Notteboom claim that there is little competition between existing global containerized and bulk commodity chains. Choice (D) is incorrect because the author does not imply saturation so much as state it outright; furthermore, the concept of saturation is outside the context of the Rodrigue/Notteboom claim about competition. Choice (E) should be eliminated because nothing in the passage states or implies this; in fact, the last sentence of paragraph 1 says just the opposite.

29. **The correct answer is (E).** Choice (E) is the correct answer because there is nothing in the article to suggest the information from Bloomberg News is current. Choice (A) must be ruled out because the statement is logical and nothing in the passage suggests anything to the contrary. Choices (B) and (C) are incorrect because the suggestion itself is reasonable and because no facts in the passage contradict it. Choice (D) should be eliminated because these facts are the basis of the passage and form the support on which other claims are laid.

30. **The correct answer is (D).** Choice (D) is the correct answer because everything in the passage points to the efficiency of containerization. Therefore, if some commodities are still being transported as bulk, the likely reason is that they cannot be easily containerized. Choice (A) is incorrect; nothing in the passage suggests this. Rather, facts in the passage point to the idea that there are logistical problems with containerizing some commodities and, therefore, bulk remains the best option for them. Choice (B) is incorrect because the main ideas of the passage suggest that most commodities lend themselves to containerization, and that others are bulk. While a few opportunities still exist for more containerization in niche markets, probably not every bulk commodity can be containerized. Choice (C) is the most obviously wrong answer among these choices. The passage suggests in many places that containerization cannot be used for all commodities. Choice (E) should be eliminated not only because the Bloomberg News report suggests a situation to the contrary, but also because the article is about expanding containerization to more niche markets.

31. **The correct answer is (B).** The argument relies on the assumption that every allergy sufferer can be helped by one or another antihistamine. Choice (B) substantiates this necessary assumption.

32. **The correct answer is (D).** Based on the passage's premise, we can conclude that Javier reads literary classics. In order to also conclude that Javier appreciates literary classics, we must assume that all readers of literary classics appreciate these types of books. Choice (D) provides the additional premise needed to draw that conclusion.

33. **The correct answer is (D).** The original version incorrectly mixes the past tense (were prohibited) with the present perfect tense (*have performed*), resulting in confusion as to the proper time frame. Also, ending the sentence with a preposition (*in*), although not grammatically incorrect, is somewhat awkward and should be avoided if possible. Choice (D) corrects both problems, as well as clarifying the meaning of the sentence by adding the word *same*. Choice (E) is awkward and distorts the meaning of the original sentence by suggesting that these musicians were prohibited from dining at any "venue" and that "venues" were the only places they performed.

34. The correct answer is (C). The original version includes a dangling modifier. The sentence fails to refer to whoever is doing the asserting. The original version also uses the awkward passive voice. Choice (C) corrects both problems. The first clause now refers clearly to *we*, and the underlined clause has been reconstructed using the active voice.

35. The correct answer is (C). The argument's conclusion, stated in the passage's final sentence, is true only if it is also true that the government has no other choice but to turn to former industry lobbyists if it wants to find knowledgeable regulators. [This is the assumption that choice (C) provides.] If such people are available elsewhere—for example, among university professors— then the conclusion is faulty.

36. The correct answer is (C). In describing Rossetti's work, the author never uses the words "stark" or "realism," nor does the author describe her work in any way that might be expressed by either of these terms. (The term "vivid imagery," appearing in line 9, does not carry the same meaning as "stark realism.")

37. The correct answer is (B). The author states that "'A Birthday' is no typical Victorian poem and is certainly unlike predictable works of the era's best-known women poets." It is reasonably inferable that Rossetti was not among the era's best-known women poets, at least during her time.

38. The correct answer is (E). The author's threshold purpose in discussing Packer's biography is to affirm that Rossetti's style of writing was not a reflection of her personal lifestyle. Having dismissed the theory that Rossetti was keeping secrets about her life, the author goes on (in the final paragraph) to offer a better explanation for the apparent contradiction between Rossetti's lifestyle and the emotional, sensual style of her poetry.

39. The correct answer is (D). In the passage, the author's first concern is to point out that Rossetti's work conflicts with her apparently conservative personal life. The author's own impressions of Rossetti's work are corroborated by those of Woolf. Then, in the second paragraph, the author asks how to reconcile this apparent conflict. (The newly discovered letters discussed in that paragraph only reinforce the inconsistency between her personal life and literary work.) In the last paragraph, the author attempts to explain the inconsistency by way of Rossetti's love poems. Choice (D) nicely embraces all these ideas.

40. The correct answer is (E). The argument boils down to the following:

> *Premise:* Child-care license requirements are reasonable because they ensure public safety.

> *Premise:* Handgun ownership laws are not so stringent as child-care license laws.

> *Intermediate Conclusion:* Current handgun ownership laws do not ensure public safety.

> *Final conclusion:* More stringent handgun ownership laws would be reasonable.

Choice (E) expresses the argument's final conclusion.

41. The correct answer is (A). The original version is clear and grammatically correct. Choice (B) incorrectly uses the singular form *its*; the verb should agree in number with its plural subject *states*. Choice (C) awkwardly splits the grammatical element *were free*. Choice (D) uses the redundant and improper correlative *both . . . as well as . . . .* Choice (E) confuses the meaning of the sentence; the construction unfairly suggests that free word and speech could be found *only* in the Greek states.

ANSWER SHEET PRACTICE TEST 4

ANALYTICAL WRITING ASSESSMENT

_____

_____

_____

_____

_____

_____

_____

_____

_____

_____

_____

_____

_____

_____

_____

_____

_____

_____

_____

_____

_____

_____

_____

_____

_____

_____

_____

_____

answer sheet

answer sheet

INTEGRATED REASONING

1.1 Ⓐ Ⓑ Ⓒ Ⓓ Ⓔ Ⓕ   4.1 Ⓐ Ⓑ Ⓒ Ⓓ Ⓔ Ⓕ   7.1 Ⓐ Ⓑ   10.1 Ⓐ Ⓑ Ⓒ
1.2 Ⓐ Ⓑ Ⓒ Ⓓ Ⓔ Ⓕ   4.2 Ⓐ Ⓑ Ⓒ Ⓓ Ⓔ Ⓕ   7.2 Ⓐ Ⓑ   10.2 Ⓐ Ⓑ Ⓒ Ⓓ
2.1 Ⓐ Ⓑ   5.1 Ⓐ Ⓑ Ⓒ Ⓓ Ⓔ   7.3 Ⓐ Ⓑ   11.1 Ⓐ Ⓑ Ⓒ Ⓓ Ⓔ
2.2 Ⓐ Ⓑ   5.2 Ⓐ Ⓑ Ⓒ Ⓓ Ⓔ   8. Ⓐ Ⓑ Ⓒ Ⓓ Ⓔ   11.2 Ⓐ Ⓑ Ⓒ Ⓓ Ⓔ
2.3 Ⓐ Ⓑ   6.1 Ⓐ Ⓑ   9.1 Ⓐ Ⓑ   12.1 Ⓐ Ⓑ Ⓒ
3.1 Ⓐ Ⓑ Ⓒ Ⓓ Ⓔ   6.2 Ⓐ Ⓑ   9.2 Ⓐ Ⓑ   12.2 Ⓐ Ⓑ Ⓒ Ⓓ
3.2 Ⓐ Ⓑ Ⓒ Ⓓ Ⓔ   6.3 Ⓐ Ⓑ   9.3 Ⓐ Ⓑ

QUANTITATIVE SECTION

1. Ⓐ Ⓑ Ⓒ Ⓓ Ⓔ   9. Ⓐ Ⓑ Ⓒ Ⓓ Ⓔ   17. Ⓐ Ⓑ Ⓒ Ⓓ Ⓔ   25. Ⓐ Ⓑ Ⓒ Ⓓ Ⓔ   33. Ⓐ Ⓑ Ⓒ Ⓓ Ⓔ
2. Ⓐ Ⓑ Ⓒ Ⓓ Ⓔ   10. Ⓐ Ⓑ Ⓒ Ⓓ Ⓔ   18. Ⓐ Ⓑ Ⓒ Ⓓ Ⓔ   26. Ⓐ Ⓑ Ⓒ Ⓓ Ⓔ   34. Ⓐ Ⓑ Ⓒ Ⓓ Ⓔ
3. Ⓐ Ⓑ Ⓒ Ⓓ Ⓔ   11. Ⓐ Ⓑ Ⓒ Ⓓ Ⓔ   19. Ⓐ Ⓑ Ⓒ Ⓓ Ⓔ   27. Ⓐ Ⓑ Ⓒ Ⓓ Ⓔ   35. Ⓐ Ⓑ Ⓒ Ⓓ Ⓔ
4. Ⓐ Ⓑ Ⓒ Ⓓ Ⓔ   12. Ⓐ Ⓑ Ⓒ Ⓓ Ⓔ   20. Ⓐ Ⓑ Ⓒ Ⓓ Ⓔ   28. Ⓐ Ⓑ Ⓒ Ⓓ Ⓔ   36. Ⓐ Ⓑ Ⓒ Ⓓ Ⓔ
5. Ⓐ Ⓑ Ⓒ Ⓓ Ⓔ   13. Ⓐ Ⓑ Ⓒ Ⓓ Ⓔ   21. Ⓐ Ⓑ Ⓒ Ⓓ Ⓔ   29. Ⓐ Ⓑ Ⓒ Ⓓ Ⓔ   37. Ⓐ Ⓑ Ⓒ Ⓓ Ⓔ
6. Ⓐ Ⓑ Ⓒ Ⓓ Ⓔ   14. Ⓐ Ⓑ Ⓒ Ⓓ Ⓔ   22. Ⓐ Ⓑ Ⓒ Ⓓ Ⓔ   30. Ⓐ Ⓑ Ⓒ Ⓓ Ⓔ
7. Ⓐ Ⓑ Ⓒ Ⓓ Ⓔ   15. Ⓐ Ⓑ Ⓒ Ⓓ Ⓔ   23. Ⓐ Ⓑ Ⓒ Ⓓ Ⓔ   31. Ⓐ Ⓑ Ⓒ Ⓓ Ⓔ
8. Ⓐ Ⓑ Ⓒ Ⓓ Ⓔ   16. Ⓐ Ⓑ Ⓒ Ⓓ Ⓔ   24. Ⓐ Ⓑ Ⓒ Ⓓ Ⓔ   32. Ⓐ Ⓑ Ⓒ Ⓓ Ⓔ

VERBAL SECTION

1. Ⓐ Ⓑ Ⓒ Ⓓ Ⓔ   9. Ⓐ Ⓑ Ⓒ Ⓓ Ⓔ   17. Ⓐ Ⓑ Ⓒ Ⓓ Ⓔ   25. Ⓐ Ⓑ Ⓒ Ⓓ Ⓔ   33. Ⓐ Ⓑ Ⓒ Ⓓ Ⓔ
2. Ⓐ Ⓑ Ⓒ Ⓓ Ⓔ   10. Ⓐ Ⓑ Ⓒ Ⓓ Ⓔ   18. Ⓐ Ⓑ Ⓒ Ⓓ Ⓔ   26. Ⓐ Ⓑ Ⓒ Ⓓ Ⓔ   34. Ⓐ Ⓑ Ⓒ Ⓓ Ⓔ
3. Ⓐ Ⓑ Ⓒ Ⓓ Ⓔ   11. Ⓐ Ⓑ Ⓒ Ⓓ Ⓔ   19. Ⓐ Ⓑ Ⓒ Ⓓ Ⓔ   27. Ⓐ Ⓑ Ⓒ Ⓓ Ⓔ   35. Ⓐ Ⓑ Ⓒ Ⓓ Ⓔ
4. Ⓐ Ⓑ Ⓒ Ⓓ Ⓔ   12. Ⓐ Ⓑ Ⓒ Ⓓ Ⓔ   20. Ⓐ Ⓑ Ⓒ Ⓓ Ⓔ   28. Ⓐ Ⓑ Ⓒ Ⓓ Ⓔ   36. Ⓐ Ⓑ Ⓒ Ⓓ Ⓔ
5. Ⓐ Ⓑ Ⓒ Ⓓ Ⓔ   13. Ⓐ Ⓑ Ⓒ Ⓓ Ⓔ   21. Ⓐ Ⓑ Ⓒ Ⓓ Ⓔ   29. Ⓐ Ⓑ Ⓒ Ⓓ Ⓔ   37. Ⓐ Ⓑ Ⓒ Ⓓ Ⓔ
6. Ⓐ Ⓑ Ⓒ Ⓓ Ⓔ   14. Ⓐ Ⓑ Ⓒ Ⓓ Ⓔ   22. Ⓐ Ⓑ Ⓒ Ⓓ Ⓔ   30. Ⓐ Ⓑ Ⓒ Ⓓ Ⓔ   38. Ⓐ Ⓑ Ⓒ Ⓓ Ⓔ
7. Ⓐ Ⓑ Ⓒ Ⓓ Ⓔ   15. Ⓐ Ⓑ Ⓒ Ⓓ Ⓔ   23. Ⓐ Ⓑ Ⓒ Ⓓ Ⓔ   31. Ⓐ Ⓑ Ⓒ Ⓓ Ⓔ   39. Ⓐ Ⓑ Ⓒ Ⓓ Ⓔ
8. Ⓐ Ⓑ Ⓒ Ⓓ Ⓔ   16. Ⓐ Ⓑ Ⓒ Ⓓ Ⓔ   24. Ⓐ Ⓑ Ⓒ Ⓓ Ⓔ   32. Ⓐ Ⓑ Ⓒ Ⓓ Ⓔ   40. Ⓐ Ⓑ Ⓒ Ⓓ Ⓔ
                                                                                                              41. Ⓐ Ⓑ Ⓒ Ⓓ Ⓔ

answer sheet

Practice Test 4

ANALYTICAL WRITING ASSIGNMENT

Analysis of an Argument

1 Question • 30 Minutes

Directions: Using a word processor, compose an essay for the following argument and directive. Do not use any spell-checking or grammar-checking functions.

The following appeared in a memo from the principal of Harper Elementary School to the school's faculty and staff:

"To raise the level of reading skills of our students to a level that at least represents the national average for students in the same age group, we should adopt the 'Back to Basics' reading program. After all, according to the company that created the program and provides it directly to elementary schools throughout the country, Back to Basics has a superior record for improving reading skills among youngsters nationwide. By adopting Back to Basics, the parents of Harper Elementary School students would be assured that their children will develop the reading skills they will need throughout their lives."

Discuss how well reasoned you find this argument. In your discussion be sure to analyze the line of reasoning and the use of evidence in the argument. For example, you may need to consider what questionable assumptions underlie the thinking and what alternative explanations or counterexamples might weaken the conclusion. You can also discuss what sort of evidence would strengthen or refute the argument, what changes in the argument would make it more logically sound, and what, if anything, would help you better evaluate its conclusion.

INTEGRATED REASONING

12 Questions • 30 Minutes

1. In the table, select an equation whose graph is a line perpendicular to the graph of the equation $2x + 3y - 5 = 0$, and an equation whose graph is a line parallel to the graph of the equation $2x + 3y - 5 = 0$. Make only one selection in each column.

	1.1 Perpendicular	1.2 Parallel	
(A)	○	○	$y = (x + 2)(x - 3)$
(B)	○	○	$3x = 8 + 2y$
(C)	○	○	$y = \dfrac{x + 2}{x}$
(D)	○	○	$y = \dfrac{2}{3}x + \dfrac{5}{3}$
(E)	○	○	$3y = -2x - 12$
(F)	○	○	$3x + 2y - 2 = 0$

2. The table shows all the mutual funds in a fund family. Each fund invests in a combination of assets, such as stocks and bonds, according to the fund's investment philosophy. Each fund's *total return* for a given year shows the total performance of the assets in the fund's portfolio during that year, minus the fund's expenses. A fund's expenses are reflected in the fund's Expense Ratio. So, if a fund's portfolio gained 5.00% in one year and the fund's expense ratio was 1.00%, then the fund's total return for the year was 4.00%. In the table, the 1-Year, 3-Year, 5-Year, and 10-Year columns show each fund's average annual *total returns* over the corresponding number of years. This average does not imply the same return for every year in that span.

Sort By: | Select ▼ |

Mutual Fund	Category	Expense Ratio	Average Annual Return			
			1-Year	3-Year	5-Year	10-Year
Charles I	Large-Cap Value	1.50%	4.28%	18.74%	1.01%	4.36%
Charles II	Large-Cap Value	1.20%	3.57%	13.61%	−0.19%	2.39%
Edward I	Large-Cap Blend	1.50%	4.13%	16.72%	−1.03%	4.44%
Edward II	Large-Cap Blend	1.75%	3.66%	18.13%	2.07%	5.36%
Elizabeth	Municipal Bond	0.75%	11.92%	6.13%	4.62%	3.94%
Henry III	Mid-Cap Blend	1.50%	0.37%	21.14%	1.76%	3.68%
Henry IV	Mid-Cap Blend	1.40%	2.20%	17.71%	2.03%	N/A
Henry V	Mid-Cap Growth	1.75%	6.39%	23.39%	6.41%	7.37%
Henry VI	Mid-Cap Growth	1.80%	3.11%	16.12%	5.13%	5.88%
James I	Commodities	1.40%	4.58%	21.20%	−3.13%	9.39%
James II	International	1.90%	−2.86%	19.97%	0.28%	N/A

Richard I	Large-Cap Growth	1.20%	14.13%	29.06%	4.48%	6.13%
Richard II	Large-Cap Growth	1.50%	12.09%	22.74%	5.31%	6.47%
Victoria	Municipal Bond	0.90%	8.13%	3.89%	4.17%	3.65%
William	Taxable Bond	1.65%	9.47%	13.73%	8.27%	N/A

For each of the following statements, select *Inferable* if the statement is reasonably inferable from the given information. Otherwise, select *Not inferable*.

	(A) Inferable	(B) Not inferable	
2.1	○	○	If today an investor invests $10,000 in Edward I and the fund's portfolio gains 10% over the next year, then in one year the value of the investor's assets in the fund will be $10,850.
2.2	○	○	If three years ago an investor invested a certain amount in Charles II, then the current value of his assets is greater than it would be if he had invested the same amount in William.
2.3	○	○	The range of 10-Year Average Annual Returns is greater for Mid-Cap funds than for Large-Cap funds.

(On the computer test, this will be the end of the question prompt and statements. For this paper test and your convenience, we are providing the various other ways you may sort the data.)

Sort By: [Category ▼]

Mutual Fund	Category	Expense Ratio	Average Annual Return			
			1-Year	3-Year	5-Year	10-Year
James I	Commodities	1.40%	4.58%	21.20%	−3.13%	9.39%
James II	International	1.90%	−2.86%	19.97%	0.28%	N/A
Edward I	Large-Cap Blend	1.50%	4.13%	16.72%	−1.03%	4.44%
Edward II	Large-Cap Blend	1.75%	3.66%	18.13%	2.07%	5.36%
Richard I	Large-Cap Growth	1.20%	14.13%	29.06%	4.48%	6.13%
Richard II	Large-Cap Growth	1.50%	12.09%	22.74%	5.31%	6.47%
Charles I	Large-Cap Value	1.50%	4.28%	18.74%	1.01%	4.36%
Charles II	Large-Cap Value	1.20%	3.57%	13.61%	−0.19%	2.39%
Henry III	Mid-Cap Blend	1.50%	0.37%	21.14%	1.76%	3.68%
Henry IV	Mid-Cap Blend	1.40%	2.20%	17.71%	2.03%	N/A
Henry V	Mid-Cap Growth	1.75%	6.39%	23.39%	6.41%	7.37%
Henry VI	Mid-Cap Growth	1.80%	3.11%	16.12%	5.13%	5.88%
Elizabeth	Municipal Bond	0.75%	11.92%	6.13%	4.62%	3.94%
Victoria	Municipal Bond	0.90%	8.13%	3.89%	4.17%	3.65%
William	Taxable Bond	1.65%	9.47%	13.73%	8.27%	N/A

Sort By: [Expense Ratio ▼]

Mutual Fund	Category	Expense Ratio	Average Annual Return			
			1-Year	3-Year	5-Year	10-Year
Elizabeth	Municipal Bond	0.75%	11.92%	6.13%	4.62%	3.94%
Victoria	Municipal Bond	0.90%	8.13%	3.89%	4.17%	3.65%
Richard I	Large-Cap Growth	1.20%	14.13%	29.06%	4.48%	6.13%
Charles II	Large-Cap Value	1.20%	3.57%	13.61%	−0.19%	2.39%
James I	Commodities	1.40%	4.58%	21.20%	−3.13%	9.39%
Henry IV	Mid-Cap Blend	1.40%	2.20%	17.71%	2.03%	N/A
Edward I	Large-Cap Blend	1.50%	4.13%	16.72%	−1.03%	4.44%
Richard II	Large-Cap Growth	1.50%	12.09%	22.74%	5.31%	6.47%
Charles I	Large-Cap Value	1.50%	4.28%	18.74%	1.01%	4.36%
Henry III	Mid-Cap Blend	1.50%	0.37%	21.14%	1.76%	3.68%
William	Taxable Bond	1.65%	9.47%	13.73%	8.27%	N/A
Edward II	Large-Cap Blend	1.75%	3.66%	18.13%	2.07%	5.36%
Henry V	Mid-Cap Growth	1.75%	6.39%	23.39%	6.41%	7.37%
Henry VI	Mid-Cap Growth	1.80%	3.11%	16.12%	5.13%	5.88%
James II	International	1.90%	−2.86%	19.97%	0.28%	N/A

Sort By: [1-Year ▼]

Mutual Fund	Category	Expense Ratio	Average Annual Return			
			1-Year	3-Year	5-Year	10-Year
James II	International	1.90%	−2.86%	19.97%	0.28%	N/A
Henry III	Mid-Cap Blend	1.50%	0.37%	21.14%	1.76%	3.68%
Henry IV	Mid-Cap Blend	1.40%	2.20%	17.71%	2.03%	N/A
Henry VI	Mid-Cap Growth	1.80%	3.11%	16.12%	5.13%	5.88%
Charles II	Large-Cap Value	1.20%	3.57%	13.61%	−0.19%	2.39%
Edward II	Large-Cap Blend	1.75%	3.66%	18.13%	2.07%	5.36%
Edward I	Large-Cap Blend	1.50%	4.13%	16.72%	−1.03%	4.44%
Charles I	Large-Cap Value	1.50%	4.28%	18.74%	1.01%	4.36%
James I	Commodities	1.40%	4.58%	21.20%	−3.13%	9.39%
Henry V	Mid-Cap Growth	1.75%	6.39%	23.39%	6.41%	7.37%
Victoria	Municipal Bond	0.90%	8.13%	3.89%	4.17%	3.65%
William	Taxable Bond	1.65%	9.47%	13.73%	8.27%	N/A
Elizabeth	Municipal Bond	0.75%	11.92%	6.13%	4.62%	3.94%
Richard II	Large-Cap Growth	1.50%	12.09%	22.74%	5.31%	6.47%
Richard I	Large-Cap Growth	1.20%	14.13%	29.06%	4.48%	6.13%

Sort By: 3-Year ▼

Mutual Fund	Category	Expense Ratio	Average Annual Return			
			1-Year	3-Year	5-Year	10-Year
Victoria	Municipal Bond	0.90%	8.13%	3.89%	4.17%	3.65%
Elizabeth	Municipal Bond	0.75%	11.92%	6.13%	4.62%	3.94%
Charles II	Large-Cap Value	1.20%	3.57%	13.61%	−0.19%	2.39%
William	Taxable Bond	1.65%	9.47%	13.73%	8.27%	N/A
Henry VI	Mid-Cap Growth	1.80%	3.11%	16.12%	5.13%	5.88%
Edward I	Large-Cap Blend	1.50%	4.13%	16.72%	−1.03%	4.44%
Henry IV	Mid-Cap Blend	1.40%	2.20%	17.71%	2.03%	N/A
Edward II	Large-Cap Blend	1.75%	3.66%	18.13%	2.07%	5.36%
Charles I	Large-Cap Value	1.50%	4.28%	18.74%	1.01%	4.36%
James II	International	1.90%	−2.86%	19.97%	0.28%	N/A
Henry III	Mid-Cap Blend	1.50%	0.37%	21.14%	1.76%	3.68%
James I	Commodities	1.40%	4.58%	21.20%	−3.13%	9.39%
Richard II	Large-Cap Growth	1.50%	12.09%	22.74%	5.31%	6.47%
Henry V	Mid-Cap Growth	1.75%	6.39%	23.39%	6.41%	7.37%
Richard I	Large-Cap Growth	1.20%	14.13%	29.06%	4.48%	6.13%

Sort By: 5-Year ▼

Mutual Fund	Category	Expense Ratio	Average Annual Return			
			1-Year	3-Year	5-Year	10-Year
James I	Commodities	1.40%	4.58%	21.20%	−3.13%	9.39%
Edward I	Large-Cap Blend	1.50%	4.13%	16.72%	−1.03%	4.44%
Charles II	Large-Cap Value	1.20%	3.57%	13.61%	−0.19%	2.39%
James II	International	1.90%	−2.86%	19.97%	0.28%	N/A
Charles I	Large-Cap Value	1.50%	4.28%	18.74%	1.01%	4.36%
Henry III	Mid-Cap Blend	1.50%	0.37%	21.14%	1.76%	3.68%
Henry IV	Mid-Cap Blend	1.40%	2.20%	17.71%	2.03%	N/A
Edward II	Large-Cap Blend	1.75%	3.66%	18.13%	2.07%	5.36%
Victoria	Municipal Bond	0.90%	8.13%	3.89%	4.17%	3.65%
Richard I	Large-Cap Growth	1.20%	14.13%	29.06%	4.48%	6.13%
Elizabeth	Municipal Bond	0.75%	11.92%	6.13%	4.62%	3.94%
Henry VI	Mid-Cap Growth	1.80%	3.11%	16.12%	5.13%	5.88%
Richard II	Large-Cap Growth	1.50%	12.09%	22.74%	5.31%	6.47%
Henry V	Mid-Cap Growth	1.75%	6.39%	23.39%	6.41%	7.37%
William	Taxable Bond	1.65%	9.47%	13.73%	8.27%	N/A

Sort By: | 10-Year ▼ |

Mutual Fund	Category	Expense Ratio	Average Annual Return			
			1-Year	3-Year	5-Year	10-Year
Charles II	Large-Cap Value	1.20%	3.57%	13.61%	–0.19%	2.39%
Victoria	Municipal Bond	0.90%	8.13%	3.89%	4.17%	3.65%
Henry III	Mid-Cap Blend	1.50%	0.37%	21.14%	1.76%	3.68%
Elizabeth	Municipal Bond	0.75%	11.92%	6.13%	4.62%	3.94%
Charles I	Large-Cap Value	1.50%	4.28%	18.74%	1.01%	4.36%
Edward I	Large-Cap Blend	1.50%	4.13%	16.72%	–1.03%	4.44%
Edward II	Large-Cap Blend	1.75%	3.66%	18.13%	2.07%	5.36%
Henry VI	Mid-Cap Growth	1.80%	3.11%	16.12%	5.13%	5.88%
Richard I	Large-Cap Growth	1.20%	14.13%	29.06%	4.48%	6.13%
Richard II	Large-Cap Growth	1.50%	12.09%	22.74%	5.31%	6.47%
Henry V	Mid-Cap Growth	1.75%	6.39%	23.39%	6.41%	7.37%
James I	Commodities	1.40%	4.58%	21.20%	–3.13%	9.39%
James II	International	1.90%	–2.86%	19.97%	0.28%	N/A
Henry IV	Mid-Cap Blend	1.40%	2.20%	17.71%	2.03%	N/A
William	Taxable Bond	1.65%	9.47%	13.73%	8.27%	N/A

3. Two call centers, Call Center A and Call Center B, receive a similar number of calls daily. Call Center A's current service level goal is to answer 90% of incoming calls within 10 seconds, while Call Center B's current goal is to answer 70% of incoming calls within 30 seconds. Both call centers have been meeting these goals, and report agent idle times (the percentage of time their telephone representatives spend not talking to customers or doing post-call follow-up work) of 30% and 10%, respectively.

Given a certain amount of incoming calls, the more aggressive service level goals (i.e., a higher percentage of calls answered in a shorter amount of time) require more employees and a higher agent idle time, while less aggressive goals can be met with fewer employees and a less agent idle time. If idle time is too high, then a company is wasting too much money on idle employees, while if idle time is too low, then a company risks burning out its employees.

Assuming any new service level goal between answering 70% of incoming calls within 30 seconds and answering 90% of incoming calls within 10 seconds would be acceptable to both companies, select an action that Company A could take in order to decrease its agent idle time, and an action that Company B could take in order to lower its risk of employee burn-out. Make only one selection in each column.

	3.1 Call Center A	**3.2** Call Center B	
(A)	○	○	Maintain its service level goal and decrease its staffing level.
(B)	○	○	Increase its service level goal and maintain its staffing level.
(C)	○	○	Maintain its service level goal and increase its staffing level.
(D)	○	○	Lower its service level goal and maintain its staffing level.
(E)	○	○	Lower its service level goal and decrease its staffing level.

4. During a clearance sale, a men's formalwear store is selling its remaining suits at a discount. Ten percent of the suits have a flawed jacket, 20% of the suits have flawed trousers, and 5% of the suits have both flawed jacket and trousers.

   A man buys a suit at random. In the table, indicate what the probability is that the suit will have no flaw, and what the probability is that the suit will have a flawed jacket only.

	4.1 No flaw	**4.2** Flawed jacket	
(A)	○	○	0.05
(B)	○	○	0.1
(C)	○	○	0.2
(D)	○	○	0.25
(E)	○	○	0.5
(F)	○	○	0.75

5. Vermiculite is a mineral used in insulation and other products. One particular vermiculite mine is the source of the majority of vermiculite sold in the United States from 1919 to 1990. The mine also has a deposit of asbestos (another mineral that was also used in insulation), so the vermiculite extracted from that site was contaminated with asbestos. When asbestos-containing materials are damaged or disturbed, microscopic fibers become airborne and, if inhaled, can cause significant health problems. It is strongly recommended that homeowners not disturb any asbestos or asbestos-contaminated material.

   Indicate which statement in the table the given information above most strongly suggests is *true*, and which statement in the table the given information above most strongly suggests is *false*. Make only two selections, one in each column.

	5.1 True	**5.2** False	
(A)	○	○	Any insulation material that has been disturbed or damaged poses a health risk.
(B)	○	○	Vermiculite insulation sold after 1990 does not pose a health risk.
(C)	○	○	The majority of vermiculite insulation sold between 1919 and 1990 is a health risk if damaged or disturbed.
(D)	○	○	Vermiculite insulation sold between 1919 and 1990 that came from other mines does not pose a health risk.
(E)	○	○	Homeowners are advised to open their walls in order to check for vermiculite.

6. The table shows a city's 10-day weather forecast.

Day	Temperature (degrees Fahrenheit)		Chance of Rain	Wind Speed (mph)
	High	Low		
31-May	80°	59°	10%	9
1-Jun	79°	66°	30%	17
2-Jun	77°	63°	20%	13
3-Jun	75°	62°	10%	11
4-Jun	71°	60°	10%	10
5-Jun	73°	61°	30%	8
6-Jun	74°	60°	30%	6
7-Jun	76°	62°	20%	6
8-Jun	82°	64°	20%	7
9-Jun	81°	62°	20%	6

For each of the following statements, select *Yes* if the statement can be shown to be true based on the information in the table. Otherwise, select *No*.

	(A) Yes	**(B)** No	
6.1	○	○	The mean Chance of Rain equals the mode of the set of Chance of Rain values.
6.2	○	○	If the high temperature is less than 80°F, then the low temperature is greater than 60°F.
6.3	○	○	The median high temperature is 11° higher than the highest low temperature.

(On the computer test, this will be the end of the question prompt and statements. For this paper test and your convenience, we are providing you the various other ways you may sort the data.)

Sort By: | High   ▼ |

	Temperature (degrees Fahrenheit)			
Day	High	Low	Chance of Rain	Wind Speed (mph)
4-Jun	71°	60°	10%	10
5-Jun	73°	61°	30%	8
6-Jun	74°	60°	30%	6
3-Jun	75°	62°	10%	11
7-Jun	76°	62°	20%	6
2-Jun	77°	63°	20%	13
1-Jun	79°	66°	30%	17
31-May	80°	59°	10%	9
9-Jun	81°	62°	20%	6
8-Jun	82°	64°	20%	7

Sort By: | Low   ▼ |

	Temperature (degrees Fahrenheit)			
Day	High	Low	Chance of Rain	Wind Speed (mph)
31-May	80°	59°	10%	9
4-Jun	71°	60°	10%	10
6-Jun	74°	60°	30%	6
5-Jun	73°	61°	30%	8
3-Jun	75°	62°	10%	11
7-Jun	76°	62°	20%	6
9-Jun	81°	62°	20%	6
2-Jun	77°	63°	20%	13
8-Jun	82°	64°	20%	7
1-Jun	79°	66°	30%	17

Sort By: Chance of Rain ▼

Day	Temperature (degrees Fahrenheit)		Chance of Rain	Wind Speed (mph)
	High	Low		
31-May	80°	59°	10%	9
4-Jun	71°	60°	10%	10
3-Jun	75°	62°	10%	11
7-Jun	76°	62°	20%	6
9-Jun	81°	62°	20%	6
2-Jun	77°	63°	20%	13
8-Jun	82°	64°	20%	7
6-Jun	74°	60°	30%	6
5-Jun	73°	61°	30%	8
1-Jun	79°	66°	30%	17

Sort By: Wind Speed ▼

Day	Temperature (degrees Fahrenheit)		Chance of Rain	Wind Speed (mph)
	High	Low		
31-May	80°	59°	10%	9
4-Jun	71°	60°	10%	10
6-Jun	74°	60°	30%	6
5-Jun	73°	61°	30%	8
3-Jun	75°	62°	10%	11
7-Jun	76°	62°	20%	6
9-Jun	81°	62°	20%	6
2-Jun	77°	63°	20%	13
8-Jun	82°	64°	20%	7
1-Jun	79°	66°	30%	17

7.

Greenhouse Gas Emissions	CO_2 from Fossil Fuels

The global warming potential (GWP) of a greenhouse gas is measured in teragrams (or million metric tons) of carbon dioxide (CO_2) equivalent (Tg CO_2 Eq.). In 2010, total U.S. greenhouse gas emissions were 6821.8 Tg CO_2 Eq. The primary greenhouse gas emitted by human activities in the United States was CO_2, representing approximately 83.6% of total greenhouse gas emissions. Overall, from 1990 to 2010, total emissions of CO_2 increased by 605.9 Tg CO_2 Eq. (11.9%). The largest source of CO_2, and of overall greenhouse gas emissions, was fossil fuel combustion.

Within the United States, fossil fuel combustion accounted for 94.4% of CO_2 emissions in 2010. Globally, approximately 30,313 Tg of CO_2 were added to the atmosphere through the combustion of fossil fuels in 2010, of which the United States accounted for about 18%.

CO_2 emissions result both directly—from the combustion of fossil fuels for use in one of four end-use sectors (Transportation, Industrial, Residential, and Commercial)—and indirectly—from the generation of electricity that is consumed by these sectors.

Greenhouse Gas Emissions	CO_2 from Fossil Fuels

The table shows the CO_2 emissions by fuel-consuming end-use sector (Tg CO_2 Eq.) from fossil fuel combustion, in terms of direct combustion and also combustion for electricity

End-Use Sector	1990	2005	2006	2007	2008	2009	2010
Transportation	**1488.9**	**1901.3**	**1882.6**	**1899.0**	**1794.5**	**1732.4**	**1750.0**
Direct Combustion	1485.9	1896.6	1878.1	1893.9	1789.8	1727.9	1745.5
Electricity Generation	3.0	4.7	4.5	5.1	4.7	4.5	4.5
Industrial	**1533.2**	**1553.4**	**1560.1**	**1559.8**	**1503.8**	**1328.6**	**1415.4**
Direct Combustion	846.4	816.4	848.1	844.4	806.5	726.6	777.8
Electricity Generation	686.8	737.0	712.0	715.4	697.3	602.0	637.6
Residential	**931.3**	**1214.6**	**1152.3**	**1205.1**	**1192.2**	**1125.5**	**1183.7**
Direct Combustion	338.3	357.9	321.5	341.6	349.3	339.0	340.2
Electricity Generation	593.0	856.7	830.8	863.5	842.9	786.5	843.5
Commercial	**757.0**	**1027.2**	**1007.6**	**1047.7**	**1041.1**	**978.1**	**997.1**
Direct Combustion	219.0	223.5	208.6	218.9	225.1	224.6	224.2
Electricity Generation	538.0	803.7	799.0	828.8	816.0	753.5	772.9
U.S. Territories	**27.9**	**50.0**	**50.3**	**46.1**	**39.8**	**41.7**	**41.6**
Total	**4738.3**	**5746.5**	**5652.9**	**5757.7**	**5571.4**	**5206.3**	**5387.8**

For each of the following statements, select *Yes* if it can be reasonably inferred from the given information. Otherwise, select *No*.

	(A) Yes	(B) No	
7.1	○	○	In 2010, total U.S. CO_2 emissions were approximately 5707.4 Tg.
7.2	○	○	In 2010, U.S. greenhouse gas emissions, not counting CO_2 emissions from fossil fuel combustion for electricity generation, were 4563.3 Tg CO_2 Eq.
7.3	○	○	In 2010, methane emissions in the U.S. were less than 6% of total U.S. greenhouse gas emissions.

8.

Greenhouse Gas Emissions	CO₂ from Fossil Fuels

The global warming potential (GWP) of a greenhouse gas is measured in teragrams (or million metric tons) of carbon dioxide (CO_2) equivalent (Tg CO_2 Eq.). In 2010, total U.S. greenhouse gas emissions were 6821.8 Tg CO_2 Eq. The primary greenhouse gas emitted by human activities in the United States was CO_2, representing approximately 83.6% of total greenhouse gas emissions. Overall, from 1990 to 2010, total emissions of CO_2 increased by 605.9 Tg CO_2 Eq. (11.9%). The largest source of CO_2, and of overall greenhouse gas emissions, was fossil fuel combustion.

Within the United States, fossil fuel combustion accounted for 94.4% of CO_2 emissions in 2010. Globally, approximately 30,313 Tg of CO_2 were added to the atmosphere through the combustion of fossil fuels in 2010, of which the United States accounted for about 18%.

CO_2 emissions result both directly—from the combustion of fossil fuels for use in one of four end-use sectors (Transportation, Industrial, Residential, and Commercial)—and indirectly—from the generation of electricity that is consumed by these sectors.

| Greenhouse Gas Emissions | | CO_2 from Fossil Fuels | | | | | |

The table shows the CO_2 emissions by fuel-consuming end-use sector (Tg CO_2 Eq.) from fossil fuel combustion, in terms of direct combustion and also combustion for electricity

End-Use Sector	1990	2005	2006	2007	2008	2009	2010
Transportation	**1488.9**	**1901.3**	**1882.6**	**1899.0**	**1794.5**	**1732.4**	**1750.0**
Direct Combustion	1485.9	1896.6	1878.1	1893.9	1789.8	1727.9	1745.5
Electricity Generation	3.0	4.7	4.5	5.1	4.7	4.5	4.5
Industrial	**1533.2**	**1553.4**	**1560.1**	**1559.8**	**1503.8**	**1328.6**	**1415.4**
Direct Combustion	846.4	816.4	848.1	844.4	806.5	726.6	777.8
Electricity Generation	686.8	737.0	712.0	715.4	697.3	602.0	637.6
Residential	**931.3**	**1214.6**	**1152.3**	**1205.1**	**1192.2**	**1125.5**	**1183.7**
Direct Combustion	338.3	357.9	321.5	341.6	349.3	339.0	340.2
Electricity Generation	593.0	856.7	830.8	863.5	842.9	786.5	843.5
Commercial	**757.0**	**1027.2**	**1007.6**	**1047.7**	**1041.1**	**978.1**	**997.1**
Direct Combustion	219.0	223.5	208.6	218.9	225.1	224.6	224.2
Electricity Generation	538.0	803.7	799.0	828.8	816.0	753.5	772.9
U.S. Territories	**27.9**	**50.0**	**50.3**	**46.1**	**39.8**	**41.7**	**41.6**
Total	**4738.3**	**5746.5**	**5652.9**	**5757.7**	**5571.4**	**5206.3**	**5387.8**

In 2010, CO_2 emissions from fossil fuel combustion in the United States accounted for what percent of total greenhouse gas emissions in the United States?

(A) 57.8%

(B) 78.9%

(C) 83.6%

(D) 94.4%

(E) 100%

9.

Greenhouse Gas Emissions | CO$_2$ from Fossil Fuels

The global warming potential (GWP) of a greenhouse gas is measured in teragrams (or million metric tons) of carbon dioxide (CO$_2$) equivalent (Tg CO$_2$ Eq.). In 2010, total U.S. greenhouse gas emissions were 6821.8 Tg CO$_2$ Eq. The primary greenhouse gas emitted by human activities in the United States was CO$_2$, representing approximately 83.6% of total greenhouse gas emissions. Overall, from 1990 to 2010, total emissions of CO$_2$ increased by 605.9 Tg CO$_2$ Eq. (11.9%). The largest source of CO$_2$, and of overall greenhouse gas emissions, was fossil fuel combustion.

Within the United States, fossil fuel combustion accounted for 94.4% of CO$_2$ emissions in 2010. Globally, approximately 30,313 Tg of CO$_2$ were added to the atmosphere through the combustion of fossil fuels in 2010, of which the United States accounted for about 18%.

CO$_2$ emissions result both directly—from the combustion of fossil fuels for use in one of four end-use sectors (Transportation, Industrial, Residential, and Commercial)—and indirectly—from the generation of electricity that is consumed by these sectors.

Greenhouse Gas Emissions | CO$_2$ from Fossil Fuels

The table shows the CO$_2$ emissions by fuel-consuming end-use sector (Tg CO$_2$ Eq.) from fossil fuel combustion, in terms of direct combustion and also combustion for electricity

End-Use Sector	1990	2005	2006	2007	2008	2009	2010
Transportation	**1488.9**	**1901.3**	**1882.6**	**1899.0**	**1794.5**	**1732.4**	**1750.0**
Direct Combustion	1485.9	1896.6	1878.1	1893.9	1789.8	1727.9	1745.5
Electricity Generation	3.0	4.7	4.5	5.1	4.7	4.5	4.5
Industrial	**1533.2**	**1553.4**	**1560.1**	**1559.8**	**1503.8**	**1328.6**	**1415.4**
Direct Combustion	846.4	816.4	848.1	844.4	806.5	726.6	777.8
Electricity Generation	686.8	737.0	712.0	715.4	697.3	602.0	637.6
Residential	**931.3**	**1214.6**	**1152.3**	**1205.1**	**1192.2**	**1125.5**	**1183.7**
Direct Combustion	338.3	357.9	321.5	341.6	349.3	339.0	340.2
Electricity Generation	593.0	856.7	830.8	863.5	842.9	786.5	843.5
Commercial	**757.0**	**1027.2**	**1007.6**	**1047.7**	**1041.1**	**978.1**	**997.1**
Direct Combustion	219.0	223.5	208.6	218.9	225.1	224.6	224.2
Electricity Generation	538.0	803.7	799.0	828.8	816.0	753.5	772.9
U.S. Territories	**27.9**	**50.0**	**50.3**	**46.1**	**39.8**	**41.7**	**41.6**
Total	**4738.3**	**5746.5**	**5652.9**	**5757.7**	**5571.4**	**5206.3**	**5387.8**

For each of the following sectors, select > *5.00%* if the sector accounted for more than *5.00%* of the world's CO_2 emissions in 2010. Otherwise, select < *5.00%*.

	(A)	**(B)**	
	> 5.00%	< 5.00%	
9.1	○	○	U.S. Transportation sector
9.2	○	○	U.S. Residential sector
9.3	○	○	U.S. Commercial sector

10. The graph is a frequency distribution of the earned run averages (ERA) of 92 qualifying pitchers at the end of the 2011 Major League Baseball season. The data are plotted separately for pitchers in the two leagues (the National League and the American League) that make up Major League Baseball. So, for example, 2 American League pitchers and 3 National League pitchers had an ERA between 2.00 and 2.49, inclusive, for a total of 5 Major League Baseball pitchers with an ERA between 2.00 and 2.49.

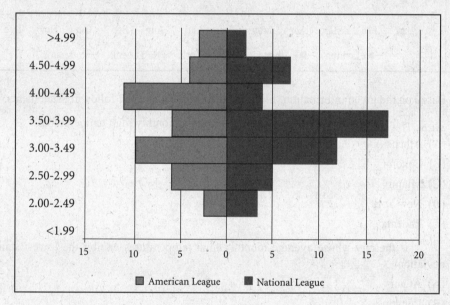

Based on the given information, fill in the blanks in each of the following statements.

10.1. Among the qualifying pitchers, the probability that an American League pitcher had an ERA between 2.00 and 2.49 is _____ the probability that a National League pitcher had an ERA greater than 4.99.

(A) less than

(B) equal to

(C) greater than

10.2. If a pitcher had an ERA between 2.00 and 2.99 inclusive, then the probability that he was a National League pitcher is _____.

(A) 0.09

(B) 0.16

(C) 0.5

(D) 0.6

11. The chart shows the average monthly high temperatures for five cities.

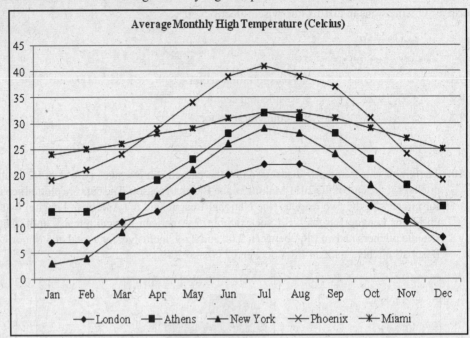

Based on the given information, fill in the blanks in each of the following statements.

11.1. _____ is the city with the greatest range of average monthly high temperatures.

(A) Athens

(B) London

(C) Miami

(D) New York

(E) Phoenix

11.2. _____ is the city whose average monthly high temperatures exhibit the lowest standard deviation.

(A) Athens

(B) London

(C) Miami

(D) New York

(E) Phoenix

12. The graph shows estimated annual user expenditures on pesticides by pesticide type in the United States between 1988 and 2007.

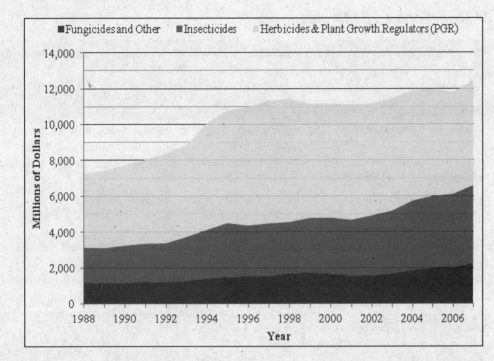

Based on the given information, fill in the blanks in each of the following statements.

12.1. The pesticide type that experienced the greatest percentage growth in user expenditures between 1988 and 2007 was _____.

(A) Herbicides & PGR

(B) Insecticides

(C) Fungicides and Other

12.2. In 1994, user expenditures on Insecticides accounted for _____ of total user expenditures on pesticides.

(A) between 20% and 25%

(B) between 25% and 30%

(C) between 30% and 35%

(D) between 35% and 40%

QUANTITATIVE SECTION

37 Questions • 75 Minutes

Directions for Problem Solving Questions: *(These directions will appear on your screen before your first Problem Solving question.)*

Solve this problem and indicate the best of the answer choices given.

Numbers: All numbers used are real numbers.

Figures: A figure accompanying a Problem Solving question is intended to provide information useful in solving the problem. Figures are drawn as accurately as possible EXCEPT when it is stated in a specific problem that its figure is not drawn to scale. Straight lines may sometimes appear jagged. All figures lie on a plane unless otherwise indicated.

To review these directions for subsequent questions of this type, click on HELP.

Directions for Data Sufficiency Questions: *(These directions will appear on your screen before your first Data Sufficiency question.)*

This Data Sufficiency problem consists of a question and two statements, labeled (1) and (2), in which certain data are given. You have to decide whether the data given in the statements are *sufficient* for answering the question. Using the data given in the statements *plus* your knowledge of mathematics and everyday facts (such as the number of days in July or the meaning of *counterclockwise*), you must indicate whether:

(A) Statement (1) ALONE is sufficient, but Statement (2) alone is not sufficient to answer the question asked;

(B) Statement (2) ALONE is sufficient, but Statement (1) alone is not sufficient to answer the question asked;

(C) BOTH Statements (1) and (2) TOGETHER are sufficient to answer the question asked, but NEITHER statement ALONE is sufficient;

(D) EACH statement ALONE is sufficient to answer the question asked;

(E) Statements (1) and (2) TOGETHER are NOT sufficient to answer the question asked, and additional data specific to the problem are needed.

Numbers: All numbers used are real numbers.

Figures: A figure accompanying a Data Sufficiency problem will conform to the information given in the question, but will not necessarily conform to the additional information in Statements (1) and (2).

Lines shown as straight can be assumed to be straight and lines that appear jagged can also be assumed to be straight.

You may assume that positions of points, angles, regions, etc., exist in the order shown and that angle measures are greater than zero.

All figures lie in a plane unless otherwise indicated.

Note: In Data Sufficiency problems that ask you for the value of a quantity, the data given in the statements are sufficient only when it is possible to determine exactly one numerical value for the quantity.

To review these directions for subsequent questions of this type, click on HELP.

1. A seven-day tennis tournament has a goal of earning $6.3 million in total ticket revenue. If its average daily ticket revenue for the first three days was $740,000, how much ticket revenue must it earn on average during the remaining four days in order to reach its goal?

   (A) $740,000

   (B) $900,000

   (C) $1,020,000

   (D) $2,220,000

   (E) $4,080,000

2. Which costs more: a can of corn or a can of beets?

   (1) Canned corn sells at three cans for a dollar.

   (2) Canned beets have been discounted by 10%.

3. If the cold-water tap and the hot-water tap running together can fill a bathtub in 30 minutes, how long would it take the hot-water tap alone to fill the tub?

   (1) The cold-water tap alone could fill the tub in 45 minutes.

   (2) The hot-water tap can fill a 10-gallon tank in 10 minutes.

4.

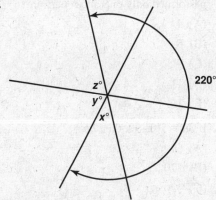

   In the figure above, $x =$

   (A) $30°$

   (B) $35°$

   (C) $40°$

   (D) $45°$

   (E) $50°$

5. If $(x - 1)$ is a prime number between 40 and 50, what is the greatest possible prime factor of x?

   (A) 2

   (B) 3

   (C) 7

   (D) 11

   (E) 13

6. A player selects at random one card from a regular deck of 52 playing cards. Then, without replacing the first card, she selects at random a second card. What is the probability that both cards selected are aces?

   (A) $\dfrac{1}{221}$

   (B) $\dfrac{1}{169}$

   (C) $\dfrac{4}{221}$

   (D) $\dfrac{1}{26}$

   (E) $\dfrac{30}{221}$

7. $\dfrac{2}{3} \times \dfrac{3}{4} + \dfrac{3}{2} \times \dfrac{5}{3} - \dfrac{3}{4} \times \dfrac{4}{5} =$

   (A) $\dfrac{9}{5}$

   (B) $\dfrac{12}{5}$

   (C) $\dfrac{8}{3}$

   (D) $\dfrac{14}{5}$

   (E) $\dfrac{31}{10}$

8. What is the value of x^2?

   (1) $(x - 3)^2 = (x + 7)^2$

   (2) $2x + 5 = 1$

9. An ice cream sundae consists of two ice cream scoops, one flavor per scoop, and one topping. How many different types of sundaes can be prepared if four ice cream flavors and two toppings are available?

   (A) 12

   (B) 14

   (C) 16

   (D) 18

   (E) 20

QUESTIONS 10–11 REFER TO THE FOLLOWING CHART.

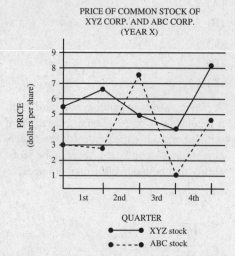

PRICE OF COMMON STOCK OF
XYZ CORP. AND ABC CORP.
(YEAR X)

10. During year X, the greatest dollar amount by which the share price of ABC common stock exceeded the share price of XYZ common stock was approximately

   (A) $1.80

   (B) $2.60

   (C) $3.00

   (D) $3.60

   (E) $3.80

11. Which of the following investments, if held through the 4th quarter of year X, would have appreciated most in dollar value?

   (A) A purchase of 500 shares of ABC stock at the beginning of the 1st quarter

   (B) A purchase of $500 in XYZ stock at the end of the 3rd quarter

   (C) A purchase of $1000 in ABC stock at the end of the 2nd quarter

   (D) A purchase of 200 shares of XYZ stock at the beginning of the 1st quarter

   (E) A purchase of $150 in ABC stock at the end of the 3rd quarter

12. What is the slope of a line L appearing on the xy-plane?

   (1) Line L contains the point P (0,2).

   (2) The y-intercept of line L is 2.

13. If $xy \neq 0$, is $x > y$?

   (1) $|x| > |y|$

   (2) $x = 1$

14. If x, y, and z are non-negative integers, is $5(x + y) + z$ divisible by 5?

   (1) $(x + y)$ is a multiple of 5.

   (2) z is divisible by 5.

15. A rectangular door measures 5 feet in width by 6 feet, 8 inches in height. What is the distance from one corner of the door to the diagonally opposite corner?

   (A) 8 feet, 3 inches

   (B) 8 feet, 4 inches

   (C) 9 feet

   (D) 9 feet, 4 inches

   (E) 9 feet, 6 inches

16. A classical singer gave 20 concerts during one year. Twenty percent of these were joint concerts with another singer, while the rest were solo concerts. In nine of the concerts she performed only operatic repertoire, while in the rest, none of which was a joint concert, she performed only art songs. How many solo concerts did she give during which she performed only operatic repertoire?

   (A) 4

   (B) 5

   (C) 9

   (D) 11

   (E) 16

17. If $3a = 5b = 90$, then $ab =$

   (A) 60

   (B) 270

   (C) 420

   (D) 540

   (E) 775

18. What is the arithmetic mean (simple average) of a, b, and c?

   (1) The mean of a and b is 5.

   (2) $c = 9$

19.

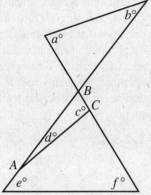

Referring to the figure above, what is the sum of c and d?

(1) $b + f = 80$

(2) $a + b = 110$

20. If $2 < \frac{x}{2} - 1 \le 9$, then which of the following must be true?

(A) $4 < x \le 20$

(B) $6 < x \le 10$

(C) $6 < x < 20$

(D) $6 < x \le 20$

(E) $6 > x \ge 20$

21. If a circle whose radius is x has an area of 4 square units, what is the unit area of a circle whose radius is $3x$?

(A) 24

(B) 28

(C) 36

(D) 40

(E) 42

22. Five executives earn $150,000 each per year, three executives earn $170,000 each per year, and one executive earns $180,000 per year. What is the average salary of these nine executives?

(A) $156,250

(B) $160,000

(C) $164,480

(D) $166,670

(E) $170,000

23. $\sqrt{\dfrac{x^2}{36} + \dfrac{x^2}{25}} =$

(A) $\dfrac{|x|}{30}\sqrt{61}$

(B) $\dfrac{x^2\sqrt{61}}{61}$

(C) $\dfrac{11x}{30}$

(D) $\dfrac{x^2}{15}\sqrt{\dfrac{x}{2}}$

(E) $\dfrac{x^2}{11}$

24. If 14 sculptors at a craft fair are also painters, how many painters are at the fair?

(1) The number of painters and the number of sculptors add up to 44.

(2) 7 of the sculptors are not painters.

25. Dan has $10,000 to invest. He invests some of the money in an account that pays 5% annual interest and the rest in an account that pays 6% annual interest. If, at the end of one year, he has earned $560 in interest, how much money did he invest at 5%?

(A) $3000

(B) $4000

(C) $5000

(D) $6000

(E) $7000

26. Is the area of Quadrilateral R greater than the area of Quadrilateral S?

(1) The perimeter of R is greater than the perimeter of S.

(2) R and S are both squares.

27. If $x \square y = x(x - y)$, then $(-1 \square -2) \square (1 \square 2) =$

(A) -2

(B) -1

(C) 0

(D) 1

(E) 2

28.

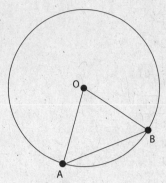

In the figure above, if O lies at the center of the circle, what is the degree measure of minor arc AB?

(1) The length of line segment $\overline{AB}$ equals the radius of the circle.

(2) $\angle OAB$ measures $60°$.

29. In a horse show, nine of the horses competing were awarded ribbons. The show's judge never awards ribbons to fewer than 15% of the horses and never to more than 30% of the horses. If h is the number of horses competing, how many different values of h are possible?

(A) 15

(B) 16

(C) 24

(D) 30

(E) 31

30. Distribution Q {15,10,x,7,12,10} has a median of 11. Which of the following describes all possible values of x?

(A) $x \geq 10$

(B) $x = 11$

(C) $x = 12$

(D) $x = 10$ or 12

(E) $x \geq 12$

31. Machine X, Machine Y, and Machine Z produce widgets. Machine Y's rate of production is one third that of Machine X, and Machine Z's production rate is twice that of Machine Y. If Machine Y can produce 35 widgets per day, how many widgets can the three machines produce per day working simultaneously?

(A) 105

(B) 164

(C) 180

(D) 210

(E) 224

32. On the xy-plane, what is the unit area of the quadrilateral defined by the (xy) coordinate pairs $(-1,-1)$, $(-5,3)$, $(2,-1)$, and $(2,3)$?

(A) $12\sqrt{2}$

(B) $11\sqrt{3}$

(C) 18

(D) 20

(E) 25

33. A bag contains 185 cards: 160 "Try Again" cards and 25 "Winner" cards. How many "Try Again" cards must be removed for the probability of selecting a "Winner" card among 25 such cards to be $\frac{1}{6}$?

(A) 35

(B) 40

(C) 42

(D) 48

(E) 64

34. What is the fifth number in a particular series of numbers, if the tenth number in the series is 450?

(1) The ninth number in the series is 150.

(2) Each number in the series is three times the previous number.

35. If $\dfrac{x+y}{x-y} = \dfrac{x+y}{x}$, which of the following

expresses the value of x in terms of y?

$(y \neq 0,\, x \neq y)$

(A) $-y$

(B) y^2

(C) $\dfrac{y}{2}$

(D) $y - 1$

(E) $2y$

37. By what percent has the price of a gallon of gasoline decreased since January 1 of this year?

(1) The price of gasoline has decreased by 20 cents per gallon since January 1 of this year.

(2) The current price of gasoline is $1.90 per gallon.

36.

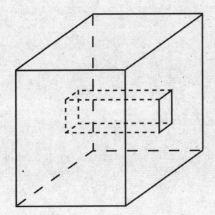

The figure above shows a solid cube 3 inches on a side but with a 1-inch square hole cut through it. How many square inches is the total surface area of the resulting solid figure?

(A) 24

(B) 42

(C) 52

(D) 58

(E) 64

practice test

VERBAL SECTION

41 Questions • 75 Minutes

> **Directions for Sentence Correction Questions:** *(These directions will appear on your screen before your first Sentence Correction question.)*
>
> This question presents a sentence, all or part of which is underlined. Beneath the sentence you will find five ways of phrasing the underlined part. The first of these repeats the original; the other four are different. If you think the original is best, choose the first answer; otherwise choose one of the others.
>
> This question tests correctness and effectiveness of expression. In choosing your answer, follow the requirements of Standard Written English; that is, pay attention to grammar, choice of words, and sentence construction. Choose the answer that produces the most effective sentence; this answer should be clear and exact, without awkwardness, ambiguity, redundancy, or grammatical error.

> **Directions for Critical Reasoning Questions:** *(These directions will appear on your screen before your first Critical Reasoning question.)*
>
> For this question, select the best of the answer choices given.

> **Directions for Reading Comprehension Questions:** *(These directions will appear on your screen before your first group of Reading Comprehension questions.)*
>
> The questions in this group are based on the content of a passage. After reading the passage, choose the best answer to each question. Answer all the questions following the passage on the basis of what is stated or implied in the passage.

1. To facilitate the flow of traffic, the plan for <u>the new northbound connection with I-80 westbound and 190 northbound highways include replacement</u> of the cloverleaf with a trumpet interchange that will require extensive changes to the earth foundation, embankment, subgrade, and base course.

   (A) the new northbound connection with I-80 westbound and 190 northbound highways include replacement

   (B) the new Northbound connection with I-80 Westbound and 190 Northbound highways include replacement

   (C) the new northbound connection with I-80 westbound, and 190 northbound highways, include replacement

   (D) the new northbound connection with I-80 westbound and 190 northbound highways includes replacement

   (E) the new northbound connection with I-80 westbound and 190 northbound highways will be including replacement

2. Neologisms often arise through the creation of lexemes from old ones, a process that may involve adding affixes to existing words, combining words or word forms, <u>or by conversion of a word's part of speech</u>.

   (A) or by conversion of a word's part of speech

   (B) or by converting of a word's part of speech

   (C) or converting of a word's part of speech

   (D) or converting a word's part of speech

   (E) or conversion of a word's part of speech

3. To save money, many manufacturers of chemical products decide to emit harmful chemicals into the environment instead of disposing of them safely. Often, these emissions are the obvious cause of health problems for people who live near the source of the emissions. Eventually, many manufacturers engaging in these activities are compelled by the courts to compensate their victims for these health problems.

Which of the following is most readily inferable from the information above?

(A) Emitting harmful chemicals to reduce costs ultimately results in lower profitability levels than if the manufacturer refrains from emitting the chemicals.

(B) Manufacturers of chemical products place a higher value on saving money than on public health.

(C) These manufacturers will eventually discontinue emitting harmful chemicals into the environment.

(D) The courts consider the rights of those harmed by the emissions to be more important than the rights of chemical manufacturers.

(E) Those harmed by the emissions deserve to be compensated for the resulting health problems.

4. Plunging momentarily down into the yawning abyss was not the rock climber's idea of a thrill—no matter how carefully she had secured her ropes.

(A) Plunging momentarily down into the yawning abyss

(B) Plunging momentarily into the abyss

(C) Plunging momentarily, down into the yawning abyss

(D) To plunge momentarily down into the abyss

(E) Having plunged momentarily down into the yawning abyss

5. Last year, more job-seekers applied for jobs with companies that regularly investigate their employees' personal medical histories than for jobs with companies that rarely do so. As a group, last year's job applicants were obviously unconcerned about the privacy of their medical records.

Which of the following, if true, would most seriously weaken the argument above?

(A) A common reason employers review employee medical files is to check for health problems that disqualify employees from receiving health-insurance benefits.

(B) Job applicants have no way of knowing whether a prospective employer investigates its employees' medical histories.

(C) A certain proposed law, if enacted, would make it easier for employers to gain access to the medical histories of their employees.

(D) Information about which companies investigate their employees' medical histories, and which do not, is widely available to job seekers.

(E) The number of people applying for jobs last year was significantly greater than during most years.

6. Only one pie can win first place at the annual pie-baking contest held at the county fair. Pies will be judged for flavor, freshness of ingredients, proper "doneness," and distinctness among the pies entered in the contest. The contest rules provide that only fruit-filled pies may be entered.

Which of the following would best support a prediction that the winning pie at the pie-baking contest will be a cherry pie?

(A) More cherry pies than any other type of pie have been entered in the contest.

(B) Achieving proper doneness is more difficult with fresh cherries than with other pie ingredients.

(C) Fresh fruits are not available to any of the pie-baking contestants.

(D) Judges prefer the flavor of cherry pies over the flavors of other pies.

(E) Baking fresh cherries to their proper doneness results in overbaking the pie's crust.

QUESTIONS 7–9 ARE BASED ON THE FOLLOWING PASSAGE.

Line   Dorothea Lange was perhaps the most notable of the photographers commissioned during the 1930s by the Farm Security Administration (FSA), part of a
(5)   federal plan to revitalize the nation's economy and to communicate its human and social dimensions. The value of Lange's photographs as documents for social history is enhanced by her technical
(10)   and artistic mastery of the medium. Her well-composed, sharp-focus images reveal a wealth of information about her subjects and show historical evidence that would scarcely be known but for her camera. Her
(15)   finest images … portray people who appear indomitable, unvanquished by their reverses. "Migrant Mother," for example, portrays a sense of the innocent victim, of perseverance, of destitution as a temporary
(20)   aberration calling for compassion, solutions, and politics to alter life for the better. The power of that photograph, which

became the symbol of the photographic file of the FSA, endures today.
(25)   The documentary book was a natural genre for Lange and her husband Paul Taylor, whose narrative accompanied Lange's FSA photographs. In *An American Exodus*, produced by Lange and Taylor, a
(30)   sense of the despair of Lange's subjects is heightened by the captioned quotations of the migrants. Taken from 1935 to 1940, the *Exodus* pictures became the accepted vision of the migration of Dust Bowl farm
(35)   workers into California.

7. According to the passage, the photograph entitled "Migrant Mother"

(A) appeared in the documentary book *An American Exodus*.

(B) was accompanied by a caption written by Lange's husband.

(C) was taken by Lange in 1935.

(D) portrays the mother of a Dust Bowl farm worker.

(E) is considered by the author to be one of Lange's best photographs.

8. The passage provides information for responding to all of the following questions EXCEPT:

(A) What was the FSA's purpose in compiling the photographic file to which Lange contributed?

(B) How did the FSA react to the photographs taken by Lange under its commission?

(C) In what areas of the United States did Lange take her photographs appearing in *An American Exodus*?

(D) Why did Lange agree to work under the commission of the FSA?

(E) What qualities make Lange's photographs noteworthy?

9. Among the following characterizations, the passage is best viewed as a/an

(A) survey of the great photographers of the Depression era.

(B) examination of the photographic techniques of Dorothea Lange.

(C) argument for the power of pictures to enact social change.

(D) discussion of the goals and programs of the FSA's photographic department.

(E) explanation of Lange's interest in documenting the plight of Depression victims.

10. Most people know what an eclipse is and have heard the terms "solar eclipse" and "lunar eclipse"; yet, most people could not explain how their different.

(A) how their different.

(B) them differently to others.

(C) the difference between them.

(D) why the difference.

(E) how their different from each other.

11. Freshmen college students are typically surprised to discover that even an introductory course in English literature can be challenging in that it requires a great deal of reading.

(A) it requires a great deal

(B) it is necessary to do large amounts

(C) you need to do a lot

(D) they all require large amounts

(E) one requirement is a large quantity

12. Engineering teams monitor over a hundred former nuclear test sites for radiation levels, the civilian populace is banned from any area with sufficiently high levels.

(A) for radiation levels, the civilian populace is

(B) to measure radiation levels, yet the civilian populace is

(C) for their radiation levels, the civilian populace are

(D) for their levels of radiation, and the civilian populace is

(E) to determine radiation levels, and the civilian populace are

13. Everybody agrees that a decline in the quality of television programming invariably results in a decrease in television viewership. Members of the Television Writers Union are threatening to go on strike this season to compel the television studios to meet certain demands. Clearly, the movie studios whose movies are shown in theaters should hope that the television writers will indeed decide to go on strike.

Each of the following must be assumed to be true in order for the conclusion above to be properly drawn EXCEPT:

(A) Television writers are not the same writers who write screenplays for movies shown in movie theaters.

(B) An increase in movie theater attendance will result in increased profits for movie theaters.

(C) A television writers' strike would result in a decline in the quality of television programming.

(D) Movie studio profits are directly correlated to the profits of the movie theaters themselves.

(E) When people watch less television their movie theater attendance increases.

14. Six weekends each year, Alpha Show-grounds are used exclusively for public horse shows. During all other weekends, the grounds are used exclusively as a public market. For its revenues, Alpha depends entirely on admission fees, and revenue from a typical weekend horse show is far greater than from a typical weekend market. However, Alpha's annual revenues from the market far exceed its annual revenues from horse shows.

Which of the following strategies is likely to provide the greatest boost to Alpha's revenues?

(A) Increase the fee for admission to the public market, but leave the admission fees for horse shows unchanged.

(B) Increase the fees for admission to the horse shows, but leave the admission fee for the public market unchanged.

(C) Discontinue use of the grounds for horse shows, and schedule the public market for each and every weekend of the year.

(D) Schedule some horse shows for weekdays instead of weekends and, during those weekends, use the grounds as a public market instead.

(E) Schedule some weekend markets for weekdays instead of weekends and, during those weekends, use the grounds for horse shows instead.

QUESTIONS 15–17 ARE BASED ON THE FOLLOWING PASSAGE.

Line   Viewing the undersea world from a land-based perspective, it is easy to consider a colony of coral to be something similar to a bed of flowers: Many species
(5)   of both display brilliant markings and have intricate, visually appealing shapes. Yet, their relationship is predominantly aesthetic, as the basic composition of a coral *polyp*, an animal, differs markedly from
(10)   that of a self-photosynthesizing plant like a rose or zinnia.

It could even be argued that *lichen*, a fungus, bears more in common with corals than flowers do, since both lichen and
(15)   corals are typified by mutually beneficial relationships with photosynthesizing algae. While there are some species of coral that can exist solely by capturing food, most corals receive energy by hosting
(20)   millions of single-celled organisms known as *zooxanthellae*. The *zooxanthellae* are provided safety from predation as well as certain by-products of the coral's metabolism, such as ammonia, which *zooxan-*
(25)   *thellae* require to grow and reproduce. In return, the coral uses a portion of the energy *zooxanthellae* produce through photosynthesis for its own sustenance, growth, and reproduction.

15. The author compares coral to a bed of flowers to illustrate

(A) how human perceptions of other habitats are influenced by their own environment.

(B) the zoological similarities that exist between corals and flowers.

(C) why a better understanding of corals is needed to preserve endangered forms.

(D) how plants and animals have more in common than most people realize.

(E) the ability of underwater life to mimic that of the land-based world.

16. In the passage's second paragraph, the author suggests that

(A) lichen uses *zooxanthellae* algae for use in photosynthesizing.

(B) lichen provides some form of photosynthesizing algae with the same basic nutrients that corals provide to *zooxanthellae*.

(C) *zooxanthellae* serve a function with corals that is served by some photosynthesizing organisms in lichen.

(D) corals are not so dependent as lichen on their photosynthesizing partners.

(E) corals and lichen are both able to capture food for themselves if necessary.

17. According to the passage, corals provide *zooxanthellae* with

    (A) lichens needed for sustenance and growth.

    (B) enzymes that immunize them from harmful bacteria.

    (C) metabolic by-products needed for reproduction.

    (D) brilliant coloration usually associated with flowering plants.

    (E) a certain fungus that camouflages them from predators.

18. In the city of Ocean View, escalating prices of single-family homes are forcing more and more people who work in Ocean View and wish to purchase a home to move inland, where homes are more affordable. This trend is unhealthy for Ocean View, both economically and socially. But the city can reverse the trend by providing economic incentives for home-building companies to build houses that are affordable to a greater percentage of Ocean View residents.

    Which of the following, if true, would provide the most support for the argument above?

    (A) Workers who commute a short distance to work are more productive, on average, than workers who commute further.

    (B) Most of Ocean View's workers would rather reside in Ocean View than in other areas.

    (C) The supply of rental housing in Ocean View currently exceeds the demand for such housing.

    (D) At present, there are a significant number of lots in Ocean View on which it is possible to build new single-family homes.

    (E) Home builders generate a greater profit from building expensive homes than less expensive ones.

19. Some of this year's Faimount College graduates are eligible for the internship program with the district attorney's office. Any person meeting the eligibility requirements for this program is likely to gain admission to the local law school if he or she applies, whether or not that person actually participates in the internship program. However, only this year's Faimount College graduates are eligible to participate in the internship program.

    If the information provided is true, which of the following must on the basis of it also be true?

    (A) Any of this year's Faimount College graduates who apply for admission to the local law school are likely to gain admission.

    (B) Some people likely to gain admission to the local law school would not have been eligible for the internship program.

    (C) Some of this year's Faimount College graduates are likely to gain admission to the local law school if they apply.

    (D) Everyone who is eligible for the internship program graduated from Faimount College this year.

    (E) Unless a person is among this year's Faimount College graduates, he or she cannot gain admission to the local law school.

20. Considered to be the most unforgiving course in the world, cyclists must train especially hard to meet the challenge.

(A) Considered to be the most unforgiving course in the world, cyclists must train especially hard to meet the challenge.

(B) Considered as the most unforgiving course in the world, the challenge is be met only by cyclists training especially hard.

(C) Cyclists must train especially hard to meet the challenge of the course considered more unforgiving than any other course in the world.

(D) The most unforgiving course in the world, the challenge for cyclists is to train especially hard for it.

(E) Meeting the challenge requires cyclists to train especially hard for the most unforgiving course in the world.

21. Based on controlled experiments involving laboratory animals, any new drug which is proved to be a cause of cancer will subsequently be denied approval by the Food and Drug Administration.

(A) which is proved to be a cause of

(B) proven to cause

(C) that is proved to cause

(D) which proves that it causes

(E) proved to cause

22. Because people are living longer, they are developing more new types of ailments. Pharmaceutical companies are responding by developing new prescription drugs that prevent these new ailments. But elderly people of modest financial means must essentially choose among ailments because our federal health-insurance program for the elderly does not cover prescription drugs. Thus, to promote health among our elderly citizens the federal government should force pharmaceutical companies to lower their prices for these new drugs.

Each of the following, if true, weakens the conclusion above EXCEPT:

(A) If forced to reduce their prices for the new drugs, pharmaceutical companies could not afford to develop drugs for the prevention of more new ailments.

(B) The new drugs prevent not only new types of ailments but also ailments already common among elderly people.

(C) Other new drugs are available to treat, but not prevent, the same new ailments.

(D) None of the new drugs has been shown to prolong an elderly person's life.

(E) The federal health-insurance program for the elderly covers all medical expenses of the elderly other than prescription drugs.

23. This county's current dumping ordinance, which requires that all refuse be hauled at least ten miles outside the city limits for dumping, should be repealed in the interest of public health. The purpose of the ordinance in the first place was to prevent the spread of Smith's Disease, which has been found to be most prevalent in regions near outdoor dumps. But the county funds used to maintain the roads to the dumping sites have been diverted from a proposed countywide education program for Smith's Disease awareness, which would have been more effective than the dumping ordinance in preventing the disease.

Which of the following, if true, would best support the assertion that the dumping ordinance should be repealed?

(A) The geographic area within the city limits is more heavily populated than the area outside the city limits.

(B) Treating Smith's Disease is more expensive on average than preventing it in the first place.

(C) The roads to the dumping sites are of no practical use other than for transport between the city limits and the dumping sites.

(D) The proposed education program would have been available to all county residents.

(E) The most effective means of preventing Smith's disease is an expensive vaccine that is not readily available.

24. One manifestation of the so-called "information age" is a feedback effect in which, <u>as faster and faster means of access to information are devised,</u> the sheer amount of new information generated grows exponentially.

    (A) as faster and faster means of access to information are devised,

    (B) by devising ever-increasingly fast access,

    (C) as they devise means of access that are faster and faster,

    (D) as faster and faster access becomes devised,

    (E) as faster and faster means of access is devised,

25. Contrary to earlier physicists, all of whom shared the assumption that time is constant, <u>expressing a radically different idea was Einstein, who believed</u> that time is relative in that it varies with distance and motion.

    (A) expressing a radically different idea was Einstein, who believed

    (B) Einstein was expressing a radically different idea, believing

    (C) expressing a radically different idea was Einstein, believing

    (D) Einstein's idea was radically different, expressing a belief

    (E) Einstein expressed the radically different idea

QUESTIONS 26–29 ARE BASED ON THE FOLLOWING PASSAGE, WHICH WAS WRITTEN IN 1985.

Line　　The steady growth of the world's population has clearly created a food production and distribution crisis. The time has arrived when government development agencies,
(5)　agronomists, and even bankers must borrow the environmentalists' slogan, "Small is beautiful." They need to scale back grandiose development projects— vast irrigation systems, power dams, new
(10)　industrial establishments, and huge loans for "economic growth" and for food imports to the poorest nations—and turn toward simpler, but politically less popular, approaches to world hunger that help
(15)　promote self-sufficiency.

　　It remains to be seen whether donor countries will willingly discontinue massive gifts bestowed ostensibly upon the poor. To curtail subsidized exports of
(20)　surplus foodstuffs, except in response to natural disasters or famine, would be politically inexpedient since such exports are extremely popular among powerful agribusiness interests. Persuading financial
(25)　institutions to restrain their eagerness to extend credit to poor nations, many already in debt, may prove equally difficult. A considerable percentage of these loan dollars ultimately purchase industrial-
(30)　world products for middle- or upper-income customers abroad, doing little to assuage hunger. Similarly, Third World– facilities of multinational corporations, which lure the poor from the land and into
(35)　city slums in search of bare subsistence wages or even nonexistent jobs, produce products primarily for affluent consumers. Exporting simple agricultural technology, by way of services as well as implements,
(40)　would be far more helpful.

　　Also needed are reforms on the part of the underdeveloped societies themselves: more equitable distribution of land and access to water, effective control of corrupt
(45)　marketing practices, and an end to the exploitation of labor. Ultimately, however, means must be found to make it contrary to anyone's interest to keep others poor. Movement in this direction may occur only
(50)　as the earth's resources become more scarce, population pressures increase, and the starving become more desperate and articulate.

26. According to the passage, all of the following have a stake in continuing the current forms of aid to hungry nations EXCEPT:

    (A) Members of environmental groups

    (B) Upper-income groups in poverty-stricken countries

    (C) Large corporate-run farms in industrial nations

    (D) International corporations operating in the Third World

    (E) Financial institutions in donor countries

27. Based on the passage, the author would be most likely to favor an aid program to an impoverished nation if the program included

   (A) the building of a large irrigation system.

   (B) a provision of credit for purchasing consumer goods.

   (C) development of a hydroelectric plant.

   (D) shipment of agricultural tools.

   (E) construction of an automobile factory.

28. The author develops the central idea of the passage primarily by

   (A) attacking the powerful oligarchies that have perpetuated hunger among Third World people.

   (B) contrasting hunger relief programs that have proven effective with those that have proven ineffective.

   (C) listing a series of recommended changes to the current approach to world hunger.

   (D) recounting the history of failed attempts to alleviate world hunger.

   (E) critically examining arguments for and against the most common approaches to the world hunger crisis.

29. In the last paragraph, the author implies that

   (A) developed countries are not ultimately responsible for the hunger problem in Third World countries.

   (B) developed countries are unwilling to make true sacrifices to help feed the hungry people of the Third World.

   (C) multinational corporations are largely to blame for a lack of self-sufficiency among Third World countries.

   (D) change in political leadership in Third World countries is needed to solve the hunger problem in those countries.

   (E) as the global population continues to grow, effective solutions to the world hunger problem will become more elusive.

30. When a new chain is installed on a competitive cyclist's bicycle, the cyclist typically experiences immediate improvement in racing performance, and then within three weeks, on average, performance reverts to the level just prior to installation of the new chain. Based on this observation, a sports-performance researcher hypothesized that installing a new component, such as a chain, gives a competitive cyclist a psychological boost, which helps motivate that cyclist during a race.

Which of the following investigations is most likely to yield information that would be useful in evaluating the researcher's hypothesis?

   (A) Determine if amateur and professional cyclists experience a similar performance boost when new chains are installed on their bicycles.

   (B) Determine if the materials used to make bicycle chains vary from one manufacturer to another.

   (C) Determine how often a bicycle chain must be cleaned and oiled to maintain it in new condition.

   (D) Determine if a competitive cyclist can tell merely by riding a bicycle whether it has a new chain or an older chain.

   (E) Determine if a new chain exerts less gear friction, which in turn requires the cyclist to exert less effort, than a used chain.

31. Cigarette smoking, which is widely accepted to be the leading cause of lung cancer, is less popular today than ever before. Therefore, we can expect the incidence of lung cancer to decline in the future.

Which of the following, if true, would most seriously weaken the argument above?

   (A) A major cigarette manufacturer will soon introduce a new type of cigarette pack that contains fewer cigarettes than its other types of packs.

   (B) Cigarette smoking is gaining in popularity compared to cigar smoking, which is also known to cause lung cancer.

(C) People rarely develop lung cancer within a few years after they begin smoking cigarettes.

(D) The nation that leads the world in exporting tobacco used in cigarettes is expected to place limits on the amount of tobacco it exports.

(E) An increasing number of people are developing lung cancer as a result of causes other than cigarette smoking.

32. Cleopatra's extraordinary education was the result of many <u>factors, not the least of which was her proximity and access to</u> the library of Alexandria, indubitably the greatest library in the world at the time.

(A) factors, not the least of which was her proximity and access to

(B) factors; not the less of which was her proximity and access to

(C) factors; not the least of which being her proximity to and access to

(D) factors not the least of which was her proximity and access to

(E) factors. Not the least of which being her proximity to and access to

33. While Marcus Garvey had proposed ideas similar to those voiced by black power advocates Stokeley Carmichael and Malcolm X, <u>they never created the same dynamic force that they would</u> later create.

(A) they never created the same dynamic force that they would

(B) Garvey never created the dynamic force that Carmichael and Malcolm X would

(C) they never created the same dynamic force that he would

(D) he never created the same dynamic force that he would

(E) Garvey's message never having created the same dynamic force that they will

34. The practice of drawing voting-district boundaries <u>on the basis of how people are likely to vote is known as "gerrymandering"</u> and has consistently been held by the federal courts to be unconstitutional.

(A) on the basis of how people are likely to vote is known as "gerrymandering"

(B) is, based on how people vote, known as "gerrymandering"

(C) based upon how likely people are to vote is called "gerrymandering"

(D) is likely to be called "gerrymandering" when based on how people vote

(E) is known, based on how people are likely to vote, as "gerrymandering"

35. According to the school's principal, no teacher refusing to participate in the afternoon conference was allowed to attend the buffet dinner immediately after the conference. Brett, who is one of the school's teachers, is not the sort of person to refuse a buffet dinner; yet I'm certain Brett was not at the dinner. I can only conclude that Brett refused to participate in the conference.

Which of the following demonstrates a pattern of reasoning most like the flawed reasoning in the argument above?

(A) All attentive students are rewarded with high grades in school. Alan is not attentive as a student. Therefore, he will not be rewarded with high grades in school.

(B) Every person seated in the front row can hear the coach's instructions to his players. Ursula can hear the coach's instructions. Therefore, Ursula must be seated in the front row.

(C) Anyone who claims to have been abducted by aliens is either not being truthful or is mistaken about whether he or she has been abducted by aliens. Sandy is always truthful. Therefore, she has not been abducted by aliens.

(D) Every legislator is in favor of the bill. Martha is not in favor of the bill. Therefore, she must not be a legislator.

(E) This sculpture is either priceless or a worthless fake. This sculpture is not a worthless fake. Therefore, it is priceless.

QUESTIONS 36–38 ARE BASED ON THE FOLLOWING PASSAGE.

Line   The nub of the restorationist critique of environmental preservationism is the claim that it rests on an unhealthy dualism that conceives nature and humankind as
(5)   radically distinct and opposed to each other. The crucial question about the restorationist outlook has to do with the degree to which the restorationist program is itself faithful to its first principle: that nature
(10)   and humanity are fundamentally united rather than separate.

Rejecting the old domination model, which sees humans as over nature, restoration theory champions a model of com-
(15)   munity participation. Yet, some of the descriptions of what restorationists are actually up to—for example, Turner's description of humans as "the lords of creation," or Jordan's statement that "the
(20)   fate and well being of the biosphere depend ultimately on us and our relationship with it"—do not cohere well with the community-participation model. Another holistic model—namely, that of nature as
(25)   an organism—might be more serviceable to the restorationists. As with the community model, the "organic" model pictures nature as a system of interconnected parts. A fundamental difference, however,
(30)   is that in an organism the parts are wholly subservient to the life of the organism.

36. Which of the following best expresses the author's primary criticism of the restorationists?

(A) They fail to recognize any limits as to the scope of legitimate human manipulation of nature.

(B) They assign to humans a controlling role in the world.

(C) They reject the most workable model for the relationship between humans and nature.

(D) Their critique of preservationism is not well supported.

(E) Their program does not coincide with their principles.

37. By asserting that the organic model "might be more serviceable to the restorationists," the author implies that

(A) the descriptions by Turner and Jordan of the restorationists' program conform more closely to the organic model than to the community participation model.

(B) the organic model is more consistent than the community participation model with the principle of restoration.

(C) the organic model is more consistent with the restorationists' agenda than with the preservationists' program.

(D) holistic models are more useful than the dualist model to the restorationists.

(E) the organic model, unlike the community participation model, represents nature as a system of interconnected parts.

38. Which of the following best expresses the function of the first paragraph in relation to the second one?

(A) To establish the parameters of an ensuing debate

(B) To identify a problem with a school of thought, which is then explored in detail

(C) To discuss a secondary issue as a prelude to a more detailed examination of a primary issue

(D) To provide a historical backdrop for a discussion of a modern-day issue

(E) To introduce opposing viewpoints, which are then evaluated

39. Hydrogen is widely touted as the energy source of the future. But making hydrogen requires fuel, which otherwise could be used to generate electricity, heat, or mechanical power directly. To run our hybrid cars and light our homes, for example, we can generate electricity in small, efficient plants fueled by natural gas. Consuming natural gas to produce hydrogen, which is then converted into electricity, lowers overall efficiency and increases the emission of harmful greenhouse gases into the environment.

    The passage is structured to lead to which of the following conclusions?

    (A) Natural gas is the most efficient source of energy and should be used instead of hydrogen for this purpose.

    (B) To reduce greenhouse gas emissions, we should drive hybrid cars because they are powered partly by electricity.

    (C) Generating hydrogen is prohibitively expensive to be worthwhile as a way to provide for our energy needs.

    (D) Using hydrogen as an energy source is not the most environmentally sound means of meeting our energy needs.

    (E) Producing hydrogen requires the consumption of fuels such as natural gas, which are in too short supply to accommodate our energy needs.

40. Many consider Warren Buffett's multibillion-dollar gift to the Gates Foundation more significant than the endowments of Andrew Carnegie, <u>who was a philanthropist around</u> the turn of the previous century.

    (A) who was a philanthropist around

    (B) a philanthropist about

    (C) who was a philanthropist who lived around

    (D) who was a philanthropist living at

    (E) a philanthropist from around

41. The recent privatization of five public high schools in our state has clearly enhanced their educational effectiveness. The private firm that has assumed responsibility for administering these schools has done so at no additional cost to taxpayers. Moreover, last year, the number of graduating senior students as a percentage of the entire senior class was greater than ever before.

    The argument's claim that privatization of the five high schools has enhanced their educational effectiveness relies on which of the following assumptions?

    (A) As a group, last year's graduating senior students deserved the academic grades that permitted them to graduate.

    (B) High school teachers are more effective when they are paid higher salaries.

    (C) Operating these five privatized schools costs taxpayers less per school, on average, than operating one of the state's public high schools.

    (D) The percentage of senior-class students that graduated from these five schools was greater than the percentage that graduated from the state's public high schools.

    (E) The tardiness and absentee rates among students at these five schools have declined since the schools were privatized.

ANSWER KEY AND EXPLANATIONS

See Appendix B for score conversion tables to determine your score. Be sure to keep a tally of correct and incorrect answers for each test section.

Analysis of an Argument—Evaluation and Scoring

Evaluate your Argument-Analysis essay on a scale of 1 to 6 (6 being the highest score) according to the following five criteria:

1. Does your essay identify the key features of the argument and analyze each one in a thoughtful manner?

2. Does your essay support each point of its critique with insightful reasons and examples?

3. Does your essay develop its ideas in a clear, organized manner, with appropriate transitions to help connect ideas?

4. Does your essay demonstrate proficiency, fluency, and maturity in its use of sentence structure, vocabulary, and idiom?

5. Does your essay demonstrate command of the elements of Standard Written English, including grammar, word usage, spelling, and punctuation?

The following series of questions, which serve to identify the Argument's five distinct problems, will help you evaluate your essay in terms of criteria 1 and 2. To earn a score of 4 or higher, your essay should identify at least three of these problems and, for each one, provide at least one example or counterexample that supports your critique. (Your examples need not be the same as the ones below.) Identifying and discussing at least four of the problems would help earn you an even higher score.

1. Doesn't the recommendation assume that Back to Basics is *necessary* to improve the students' reading skills to the desired level? (Perhaps some other reading program or, for that matter, some other alternative—such as encouraging parents to read with their children or simply devoting more time during school to reading—would be as effective as Back to Basics or possibly even more effective.)

2. Would adopting the Back to Basics program, in itself, be *sufficient* to improve the students' reading skills to the desired extent? (Unless the students are sufficiently attentive and motivated and unless the teachers are sufficiently competent, the program might not be effective.)

3. Was the Back to Basics program the *true* reason for the improved reading skills that the company cites? (Perhaps the improved reading skills observed among children nationwide are attributable instead to a general increase in teacher salaries or to a new national children's literacy campaign, to list just a few possibilities.)

4. Is Harper *representative* of the elementary schools throughout the nation that have adopted the program? (Perhaps this school's students would not respond so well to the program's methods as most other students, for whatever reason.)

5. Is the evidence of the program's effectiveness *credible* and *unbiased*? (The nationwide results of the Back to Basics program were reported by the program's provider, who probably stands to profit by overstating the program's effectiveness.)

INTEGRATED REASONING SECTION

1.1 B	3.2 C	6.2 B	8. B	10.2 C
1.2 E	4.1 F	6.3 B	9.1 A	11.1 D,
2.1 A	4.2 A	7.1 A	9.2 B	11.2 C
2.2 B	5.1 C	7.2 A	9.3 B	12.1 B
2.3 B	5.2 E	7.3 B	10.1 C	12.2 B
3.1 E	6.1 A			

1.1. **The correct answer is (B).** Write the equation $2x + 3y - 5 = 0$ in slope-intercept form ($y = mx + b$):

$$2x + 3y - 5 = 0$$
$$3y = -2x + 5$$
$$y = -\frac{2}{3}x + \frac{5}{3}$$

So the equation's slope is $-\frac{2}{3}$. Perpendicular to this line will be any line with slope $\frac{3}{2}$ (because the product of the slopes of perpendicular lines equals -1). Answer choice (B) lists such an equation:

$$3x = 8 + 2y$$
$$2y = 3x - 8$$
$$y = \frac{3}{2}x - 4$$

Choices (A) and (C) can be eliminated easily because they do not contain linear equations—that is, equations of the first degree: Choice (A) contains an x^2-term, and choice (C) contains an xy-term. Choice (D) is already written in slope-intercept form, so you can see that its slope is not what it needs to be as the answer. Choice (E) is the correct answer in the second column (see the explanation for Question 1.2, below). Finally, when you write the equation in choice (F) in slope-intercept form, you see that it has a slope of $-\frac{3}{2}$, which is also not correct.

1.2. **The correct answer is (E).** Here you're looking for an equation with the same slope as the given equation. The equation in choice (E) is that equation:

$$3y = -2x - 12$$
$$y = -\frac{2}{3}x - 4$$

For the remaining answer choices, see the explanation for Question 1.1, above.

2.1. **The correct answer is (A).** Edward I has a 1.5% expense ratio, so the 10% gain in the portfolio will become an 8.5% total return, which, for a $10,000 investment, is $850. Thus, in one year the value of the investor's assets in the fund will be $10,850.

2.2. **The correct answer is (B).** You cannot infer that this statement is correct because you do not know how the returns were distributed over the 3 years in each fund. For instance, an annual return of 0%, 0%, and 30% over three years produces an average of 10% for the 3-year period, as does an annual return of 10% in each of the three years. If you invested $100 and received the 0/0/30 return, your total would be $130 after the 3 years, but if you invested $100 and received the 10/10/10 return, your total would be $133.10 after the 3 years.

2.3. The correct answer is (B). The 10-Year Average Annual Returns of the Large-Cap funds range from 6.47% to 2.39%, or 4.08 points. The 10-Year Average Annual Returns of the Mid-Cap funds range from 7.37% to 3.68%, or 3.69 points. Thus, the range is greater for Large-Cap, not Mid-Cap, funds.

3.1. The correct answer is (E). According to the information in the prompt, Call Center A cannot maintain its current aggressive service level goal without having many employees and high idle times. For Call Center A, the key phrase in the prompt is "less aggressive goals can be met with fewer employees and less agent idle time." Since Call Center A wishes to lower its idle time, it should lower its service level goal (within the acceptable range of 70/30 to 90/10), in which case it will also be able to decrease its staffing level somewhat. This action appears as choice (E).

Choices (A) and (B) are not really feasible for Call Center A according to the prompt because aggressive goals require high idle times and more employees. Choices (C) and (D) would exacerbate Call Center A's idleness problem.

3.2. The correct answer is (C). Call Center B needs more employees so it won't burn out its employees. As a result, it must increase its staffing level—and either maintain its goal or increase it (which may be possible, given the increased number of employees). Choice (C) describes the former of these two choices, so it is the correct answer.

Choices (A) and (B) would exacerbate Call Center B's potential burn-out problem. Choices (D) and (E) would take the call center out of acceptable service level goal.

4.1. The correct answer is (F). Let A be the event of a flawed jacket and B be the event of flawed trousers. Then, you are given the following probabilities:

$$P(A) = 0.1$$
$$P(B) = 0.2$$
$$P(A \cap B) = 0.05$$

Given these three probabilities, you can find the probability that a suit has either a flawed jacket or flawed trousers (the union of A and B):

$$P(A \cup B) = P(A) + P(B) - P(A \cap B)$$
$$= 0.25$$

The probability that the suit will have no flaw equals 1 minus the probability that it will have either a flawed jacket or flawed trousers:

$$P(\text{no flaw}) = 1 - P(A \cup B) = 0.75$$

4.2. The correct answer is (A). To find the probability that a suit has a flawed jacket only, subtract from the probability of Event A (flawed jacket) the probability of event "A union B" (flawed jacket and trousers):

$$P(\text{jacket only}) = P(A) - P(A \cap B) = 0.1 - 0.05 = 0.05$$

5.1. The correct answer is (C). Statement (C) is true. The prompt says that the majority of vermiculite sold in the United States from 1919 to 1990 came from one mine, and that the vermiculite extracted from that mine was contaminated with asbestos. Therefore, the majority of vermiculite insulation sold between 1919 and 1990 was contaminated with asbestos. Further, the prompt says that asbestos, if damaged or disturbed, can cause significant health problems. Thus, the majority of vermiculite insulation sold between 1919 and 1990 can cause significant health problems if damaged or disturbed.

Choice (A) refers to any insulation material—but the passage only discusses vermiculite and asbestos. Therefore, you cannot tell whether any insulation material (regardless of what it is) that has been disturbed or damaged poses a health risk, or not. Similarly, the passage does not comment either way about vermiculite after 1990 or about vermiculite from other mines, so you cannot determine the veracity of Statements (B) or (D).

5.2. The correct answer is (E). Statement (E) is the one that the passage most strongly suggests is false. Asbestos is dangerous if damaged or disturbed. Thus, the best thing to do is not to damage it. If there is any asbestos in wall insulation, then opening the walls could disturb it. Homeowners are advised not to disturb any asbestos, so they should not open any walls.

6.1. The correct answer is (A). Simply eyeballing the ten values, you can tell that the mean value is 20%, since 3 values are exactly 10% less than 20% and 3 values are exactly 10% greater than 20%, while the remaining 4 values are all 20%. The mode of the set is the value that occurs in the set the most, which is also 20%. Thus, the set's mean and mode are equal to each other.

6.2. The correct answer is (B). This statement is incorrect: June 4th and June 6th are forecast to have a high temperature less than 80°F, but a low temperature of exactly 60°F—thus, not greater than 60°F.

6.3. The correct answer is (B). The median high temperature is 76.5°F (the average between June 7's 76°F and June 2's 77°F), which is 10.5°F higher than 66°F, the highest low temperature.

7.1. The correct answer is (A). In 2010, fossil fuel combustion accounted for 94.4% of CO_2 emissions in the United States (Tab 1), and total CO_2 emissions from fossil fuel combustion were 5387.8 Tg (Tab 2). Thus, if x were the total CO_2 emissions, then:

$$5387.8 = 94.4\%x$$
$$x = \frac{5387.8}{94.4} \times 100$$
$$x = 5707.4$$

7.2. The correct answer is (A). In 2010, total U.S. greenhouse gas emissions were 6,821.8 Tg CO_2 Eq. (Tab 1). Total CO_2 emissions from fossil fuel combustion for electricity generation equaled the sum of CO_2 emissions from fossil fuel combustion for electricity generation for each of the four end-use sectors. This sum is:

$$(4.5 + 637.6 + 843.5 + 772.9) \text{ Tg } CO_2 \text{ Eq.} = 2258.5 \text{ Tg } CO_2 \text{ Eq.}$$

The difference between 6821.8 and 2258.5 is 4563.3, which is the number of Tg CO_2 Eq. of U.S. greenhouse gas emissions, not counting CO_2 emissions from fossil fuel combustion for electricity generation.

7.3. The correct answer is (B). You only know that CO_2 represented approximately 83.6% of total greenhouse gas emissions. You do not know how the remaining 16.4% was distributed among the other greenhouse gases. Thus, this statement cannot be reasonably inferred.

8. **The correct answer is (B).** From Tab 1 you know that fossil fuel combustion accounted for 94.4% of CO_2 emissions in 2010, and that CO_2 represented approximately 83.6% of total greenhouse gas emissions. Therefore, CO_2 emissions from fossil fuel combustion accounted for 83.6% times 94.4% of total greenhouse gas emissions in the United States. That figure is 78.9%.

9.1. **The correct answer is (A).** From Tab 1 you know that "globally, approximately 30,313 Tg of CO_2 were added to the atmosphere through the combustion of fossil fuels in 2010." Tab 2 gives you the figures for the CO_2 emissions from fossil fuel combustion by each end-use sector. Transportation emitted 1750.0 Tg of CO_2. If this number is x percent of 30,313, then:

$$1750 = x\%(30,313)$$
$$x = \frac{1750}{30,313}(100)$$
$$x = 5.77$$

In other words, the U.S. Transportation sector emitted approximately 5.77% of the world's CO_2 emissions through the combustion of fossil fuels in 2010.

9.2. **The correct answer is (B).** Follow the same process as in Question 9.1, and you'll find that the 1183.7 Tg of CO_2 that the U.S. Residential sector emitted in 2010 was 3.90% of the world's CO_2 emissions through the combustion of fossil fuels in 2010.

9.3. **The correct answer is (B).** Follow the same process as in Question 9.1, and you'll find that the 997.1 Tg of CO_2 that the U.S. Commercial sector emitted in 2010 was 3.29% of the world's CO_2 emissions through the combustion of fossil fuels in 2010.

10.1. **The correct answer is (C).** Two American League pitchers had an ERA between 2.00 and 2.49, and two National League pitchers had an ERA greater than 4.99. However, it looks like more National League pitchers than American League pitchers are included in the graph and, if you count you'll find 50 National League pitchers and 42 American League pitchers. So, the probability that an American League pitcher had an ERA between 2.00 and 2.49 is 2 out of 42, which is greater than 2 out of 50, the probability that a National League pitcher had an ERA greater than 4.99.

10.2. **The correct answer is (C).** Two American League pitchers and three National League pitchers had an ERA between 2.00 and 2.49. Six American League pitchers and five National League pitchers had an ERA between 2.50 and 2.99. In total, 16 pitchers—eight in each league—had an ERA between 2.00 and 2.99, so the probability that a pitcher with an ERA between 2.00 and 2.99 was a National League pitcher is 0.5.

11.1. **The correct answer is (D).** The range of a city's average monthly high temperatures equals the difference between its highest and lowest such temperatures. By taking this difference for each of the five cities, you'll find that New York's temperatures have the greatest range: its highest temperature is 29°C and its lowest is 3°C, for a range of 26°C.

11.2. **The correct answer is (C).** Standard deviation is a measure of the dispersion of the data points in a set from the mean value of these data points. You could compute the standard deviation for each of the five cities, but you don't have to. It is clear that Miami has the lowest standard deviation, since all its temperatures in the graph are close to their mean value, something that is not the case with any of the other cities.

12.1. The correct answer is (B). In 1988, total user expenditures were approximately $7200. On the graph, expenditures on Herbicides extend from approximately $3200 up to $7200, so they were approximately $4000. Expenditures on Insecticides extend from approximately $1200 to $3200, so they were approximately $2000. And expenditures on Fungicides were approximately $1200. In 2007, the corresponding values are $5900 (Herbicides), $4400 (Insecticides) and $2200 (Fungicides). Without figuring out the exact percentage changes, you can tell that the greatest was for expenditures on Insecticides, since these more than doubled from 1988 to 2007, while the others less than doubled.

12.2. The correct answer is (B). In 1994, total user expenditures were approximately $10,000. Of that amount, roughly $2700 ($4100 minus $1400) was spent on Insecticides. This $2700 is 27% of $10,000.

QUANTITATIVE SECTION

1. C	9. E	17. D	25. B	33. A
2. E	10. B	18. C	26. C	34. B
3. A	11. A	19. B	27. C	35. A
4. C	12. E	20. D	28. D	36. E
5. D	13. C	21. C	29. E	37. C
6. A	14. B	22. B	30. E	
7. B	15. B	23. A	31. D	
8. D	16. B	24. C	32. D	

1. **The correct answer is (C).** Let N represent the ticket revenue the tournament must earn on average during the remaining four days in order to reach its goal. Then, N times four (the total revenue it must earn during the remaining four days) plus $740,000 times 3 (the total revenue it has earned so far) equals $6.3 million. Solve for N:

$$N \times 4 + 740,000 \times 3 = 6,300,000$$
$$4N + 2,220,000 = 6,300,000$$
$$4N = 4,080,000$$
$$N = 1,020,000$$

2. **The correct answer is (E).** From Statement (1), we know only the cost of corn. From Statement (2) alone, we know that beets have been discounted, but from what price we do not know, so we do not know the cost of beets. Even taken together, the statements tell us only the price of one item; we cannot compare them.

3. **The correct answer is (A).** This question focuses on the formula $\frac{1}{W_1} + \frac{1}{W_2} = \frac{1}{A}$, in which W_1

and W_2 represent the time it takes two different workers to complete a task independent of each other, and A represents the time it takes them to complete the task working together. As you can see, if you know any two of the three terms, you can calculate the third. Thus, Statement (1) alone suffices to answer the question. In one minute, the two taps together will fill $\frac{1}{30}$ of the

tub. From Statement (1), the cold-water tap will fill $\frac{1}{45}$ of the tub in one minute. That means

that the hot-water tap must be filling $\frac{1}{30} - \frac{1}{45} = \frac{1}{90}$ of the tub in one minute. (In other words,

it would take 90 minutes to fill the tub.) Statement (2) alone tells us how fast the water runs into the tub, but since we do not know its capacity, we cannot tell how long it will take to fill.

4. **The correct answer is (C).** The sum of the measures of all six angles formed by the intersecting lines in the figure is 360°. Given that the sum of the measures of all angles other than y and z is 220°, $y + z$ must equal 140 (360 − 220). Since angles x, y, and z form a straight line (180°), x must equal 40.

5. **The correct answer is (D).** A prime number is a positive integer greater than 1 that is divisible only by 1 and the number itself. The quantity $(x - 1)$ could be either 41, 43, or 47 (all the different prime numbers between 40 and 50). Accordingly, the integer x could be either 42, 44, or 48. Now, apply some common sense. Since the question asks for the greatest prime factor, look first at choice (E), which provides the greatest of the five numbers, to see if it gives a factor of either 42, 44, or 48. Since 13 is not a factor of any of these numbers, try choice (D). $11 \times 4 = 44$, and so the correct answer must be choice (D). You can also solve the problem by using prime factorization, as follows:

$$42 = 2 \times 3 \times 7$$
$$44 = 2 \times 2 \times 11$$
$$48 = 2 \times 2 \times 2 \times 2 \times 3$$

As you can see, the greatest of these prime factors is 11.

6. **The correct answer is (A).** This is a conditional probability question. The probability that both cards are aces equals the probability that the first card is an ace times the probability that the second card is an ace. The deck has 52 cards, four of which are aces, so the probability that the first card selected is an ace equals $\frac{4}{52}$. Once an ace is selected, three aces are left in the remaining 51 cards, so the probability that the second card is an ace equals $\frac{3}{51}$. Thus, the probability that both cards are aces equals:

$$\frac{4}{52} \times \frac{3}{51} = \frac{1}{13} \times \frac{1}{17} = \frac{1}{221}$$

7. **The correct answer is (B).** First, cancel common factors, then perform the multiplication. Next, find the lowest common denominator, then combine numerators over it. Express your solution in lowest terms:

$$\left(\frac{1}{1}\right)\left(\frac{1}{2}\right) + \left(\frac{1}{2}\right)\left(\frac{5}{1}\right) - \left(\frac{3}{1}\right)\left(\frac{1}{5}\right) = \frac{1}{2} + \frac{5}{2} - \frac{3}{5}$$
$$= \frac{5}{10} + \frac{25}{10} - \frac{6}{10}$$
$$= \frac{5 + 25 - 6}{10}$$
$$= \frac{24}{10}, \text{ or } \frac{12}{5}$$

8. **The correct answer is (D).** To answer the question, there's no way around doing some pencil-work. You need to solve for x in each equation, then square it. Let's start with Statement (2), which is a bit easier to work with:

$$2x + 5 = 1$$
$$2x = -4$$
$$x = -2$$
$$x^2 = 4$$

Now let's tackle Statement (1), which presents a more complex equation:

$$(x-3)^2 = (x+7)^2$$
$$(x-3)(x-3) = (x+7)(x+7)$$
$$x^2 - 6x + 9 = x^2 + 14x + 49$$
$$20x = -40$$
$$x = -2$$
$$x^2 = 4$$

As you can see, both statements provide essentially the same information about x. With either statement, you can answer the question. Hence the correct answer is choice (D).

9. **The correct answer is (E).** Referring to the ice cream flavors as A, B, C, and D, there are 10 possible two-scoop combinations:

A + either A, B, C, or D

B + either B, C, or D

C + either C or D

D + D

For each of these 10 combinations, either of two toppings can be used. Thus, the total number of different types of sundaes is 20.

10. **The correct answer is (B).** You're looking for the point at which the dotted line (ABC's stock price) is farthest above the solid line (XYZ's stock price). The dotted line lies above the solid line only during the second half of the 2nd quarter and the first half of the 3rd quarter; the end of the 2nd quarter marks the greatest difference between prices during that period. At that time, ABC stock was priced at approximately $7.60, while XYZ stock was priced at approximately $5.00 per share. The difference between those two prices is $2.60.

11. **The correct answer is (A).** For each investment, calculate the dollar increase in value (approximating percent gains in share price will suffice):

(A) The investment amount was $1500 (500 shares at $3 per share). The share price increased by about 50%, for about a $750 gain.

(B) The investment amount was $500. The share price increased by about 100%, for about a $500 gain.

(C) The investment amount was $1000. The share price decreased (by about 35%).

(D) The investment amount was $1100 (200 shares at $5.50 per share). The share price increased by almost 50%, for nearly a $550 gain.

(E) The investment amount was $150. The share price increased by just under 400%, for nearly a $600 gain.

12. **The correct answer is (E).** The two statements provide identical information—that the point defined by the xy-pair (0,2) lies on line L. Knowing only one point on a line is insufficient to define the line.

13. **The correct answer is (C).** Statement (1) alone does not suffice to answer the question; x and y could each be either positive or negative. Nor does Statement (2) alone suffice, since no information about the value of y is provided. Statements (1) and (2) together establish that $-1 < y < 1$, and hence that $x > y$.

14. **The correct answer is (B).** By definition, $5(x + y)$ is divisible by 5, but you also need to know whether z is divisible by 5. Statement (1) provides no additional information. However, Statement (2) alone is sufficient to answer the question. A quantity that is divisible by 5 added to another quantity, z, divisible by 5 results in a sum that is divisible by 5. (If x and y both equal 0, then $5(x + y) + z = z$.)

15. **The correct answer is (B).** The width of the door is 60 inches (5 feet), and its length is 80 inches (6 feet, 8 inches). This is a 6:8:10 triangle (conforming to the 3:4:5 Pythagorean triplet), with a diagonal of 100 inches, or 8 feet 4 inches.

16. **The correct answer is (B).** Create a table in order to solve this overlapping set question, jotting down the most basic information at first:

	Opera	Art Song	Total
Solo			
Joint			20%(20)
Total	9		20

You can easily deduce the following:

- Twenty percent of the total number of concerts was joint concerts, so 4 concerts were joint and 16 concerts were solo.

- In nine concerts she performed operatic repertoire, so in 11 concerts she performed art songs.

- No art song concert was joint, so all 11 of them were solo.

Your table now looks like this:

	Opera	Art Song	Total
Solo		11	16
Joint		0	4
Total	9	11	20

From here you can subtract the number of art song solo concerts (11) from the total number of solo concerts (16) to arrive at the number of opera solo concerts. Thus, the answer to the question is 5.

17. **The correct answer is (D).** Since $3a = 90$, $a = 30$. Since $5b = 90$, $b = 18$. Thus, $ab = (30)(18) = 540$.

18. **The correct answer is (C).** You can determine the average of a, b, and c if you know their sum. Statement (1) alone tells you that the sum of a and b is 10, but it provides no information to help you determine the value of c. Statement (2) alone tells you nothing about the value of either a or b, but it provides the value of c. Together, the two statements allow you to determine the sum of the three terms $(10 + 9)$ and in turn their mean: $\frac{10+9}{3} = \frac{19}{3}$

19. **The correct answer is (B).** Although Statement (1) tells us the sum of b and f, it tells us nothing about their individual values or the size of the other angles. Now consider Statement (2) alone. In any triangle, the sum of the measures of the three angles is $180°$. Thus, the bottom angle of the top triangle must measure $70°$. Notice that $\angle ABC$ is vertical to that $70°$ angle, which means that $\angle ABC$ also measures $70°$. Now you have the information you need to answer the question. Referring to $\triangle ABC$, we know that $c + d + 70 = 180$. Accordingly, the sum of c and d must be 110.

20. **The correct answer is (D).** Solve the double inequality, remembering to take the same action on all three sides of the inequality as you proceed:

$$2 < \frac{x}{2} - 1 \le 9$$

$$3 < \frac{x}{2} \le 10$$

$$6 < x \le 20$$

21. **The correct answer is (C).** The area of a circle is πr^2. The area of a circle with a radius of x is πx^2, which is given as 4. The area of a circle with radius $3x$ is $\pi(3x)^2 = 9\pi x^2$. Therefore, the area of the larger circle is 9 times the area of the smaller circle, or 36.

22. **The correct answer is (B).** Assign a "weight" to each of the three salary figures (to save time, express all numbers in thousands):

$$5(150) = 750$$

$$3(170) = 510$$

$$1(180) = 180$$

Then determine the weighted average of the nine salaries (again, express all numbers in thousands):
$$750 + 510 + 180 = 1440$$

$$\frac{1440}{9} = 160$$

23. **The correct answer is (A).** First, combine the two terms inside the radical. Then, remove perfect squares from inside the radical:

$$\sqrt{\frac{x^2}{36} + \frac{x^2}{25}} = \sqrt{\frac{25x^2 + 36x^2}{(36)(25)}} = \sqrt{\frac{61x^2}{(36)(25)}} = \frac{|x|}{(6)(5)}\sqrt{\frac{61}{1}} = \frac{|x|}{30}\sqrt{61}$$

24. **The correct answer is (C).** Statement (1) alone provides no information about the number of painters in relation to the number of sculptors. Statement (2) alone provides no information about the total number of painters and sculptors. However, both statements together tell you the number of painters at the fair. Why? The 14 sculptors who are also painters along with the 7 that are not adds up to 21. Thus, there must be 37 painters at the fair (23 of whom are not sculptors).

25. **The correct answer is (B).** You can solve this problem algebraically. But it's quicker and easier to work backward from the answer choices. First, test choice (A): $3000 at a 5% rate earns $150 interest. The remainder of the $10,000 is $7000. At a 6% rate, that amount will earn $420. The total interest earned would be $570, which does not match the $560 figure given in the question. Next, try choice (B): $4000 × 0.05 = $200, and $6000 × 0.06 = $360. Total earned interest = $200 + $360 = $560, which matches the figure given in the question.

26. **The correct answer is (C).** Statement (1) alone is insufficient to answer the question. A quadrilateral with a longer perimeter than another might have a greater area than the other. But a longer perimeter does not necessarily create a larger area. For example, visualize a rectangle with width approaching zero (0) and length approaching infinity. The rectangle's perimeter is great, while its area approaches zero (0). Statement (2) alone provides no information for

comparing the size of the two quadrilaterals, and thus is obviously insufficient to answer the question. Considered together, however, the two statements do suffice to answer the question. The larger a square's perimeter, the larger its area.

27. **The correct answer is (C).** First apply the defined operation □ to each parenthesized pair:

    $(-1 \square -2) = -1(-1 - [-2]) = -1(1) = -1$

    $(1 \square 2) = 1(1 - 2) = 1(-1) = -1$

    Then apply the defined operation again, substituting –1 for both x and y:

    $(-1 \square -1) = -1(-1 - [-1]) = -1(0) = 0$

28. **The correct answer is (D).** The degree measure of minor arc AB is the same as the degree measure of the central angle that forms it ($\angle AOB$). The key to this problem is that $\overline{OA} \cong \overline{OB}$. (Each of these two line segments is the circle's radius.) Given Statement (1) alone, $\triangle OAB$ must be equilateral, and all angle measures are 60°. Now, consider Statement (2) alone. Since $\overline{OA} \cong \overline{OB}$, the angles opposite those sides are also congruent—that is, m$\angle OAB$ = m$\angle OBA$. Based on Statement (2), both angles measure 60° and, accordingly, so does $\angle AOB$—the central angle that defines minor arc AB.

29. **The correct answer is (E).** To determine the maximum value of h, answer the question: "9 is 15% of what number?" To find the answer, divide 9 by 0.15 (or 900 by 15). The quotient is 60. (This is the maximum number of horses that competed.) Similarly, to determine the minimum value of h, answer the question: "9 is 30% of what number?" To find the answer, divide 9 by 0.3. The quotient is 30. (This is the minimum number of horses that competed.) Including the greatest and least possible values of h (60 and 30), there are 31 possible values of h.

30. **The correct answer is (E).** First, order the numbers you know from least to greatest: $\{7,10,10,12,15\}$. Since distribution Q contains an even number of terms (including x), the median is the arithmetic mean (simple average) of the two middle terms. Thus, if $x = 12$, the median would be 11 (the average of 10 and 12). The same would be true for any value of x greater than 12. However, if $x < 12$, then the median of Q must be less than 11 (the average of 10 and some number less than 12).

31. **The correct answer is (D).** The key to handling this question is to convert ratios to fractional parts that add up to 1. The ratio of X's rate to Y's rate is 3 to 1, and the ratio of Y's rate to Z's rate is 1 to 2. You can express the ratio among all three as 3:1:2 ($X:Y:Z$).

    Accordingly, Y's production accounts for $\frac{1}{6}$ of the total widgets that all three machines can produce per day. Given that Y can produce 35 widgets per day, all three machines can produce $(35)(6) = 210$ widgets per day.

32. **The correct answer is (D).** Points $(-1,-1)$ and $(2,-1)$ connect to form a horizontal line segment of length 3. Similarly, points $(2,3)$ and $(-5,3)$ connect to form a horizontal line segment of length 7. Since the two segments are parallel, the resulting quadrilateral is a trapezoid. The vertical distance between the two parallel segments is 4. Apply the formula for a trapezoid's area (AB and CD represent the two parallel segments, and h is the quadrilateral's height):

    $$A = \frac{AB + CD}{2} \times h$$
    $$A = \frac{3 + 7}{2} \times 4$$
    $$A = 20$$

You can also plot the quadrilateral on the grid, divide it into a right isosceles triangle and one rectangle, then calculate the area of each one. (The rectangle's area is 12, and the triangle's area is 8.)

33. **The correct answer is (A).** Solve this problem using the basic probability formula:

$$\frac{\text{winner card}}{\text{total cards}} = \frac{1}{6}$$

In this case, total cards (the fraction's denominator) equal 25 + 160, less the number of "Try Again" cards to be removed (let x equal this number):

$$\frac{\text{winner card}}{\text{total cards}} = \frac{25}{25 + (160 - x)} = \frac{1}{6}$$

Solve for x (use the cross-product method to clear fractions):

$$\frac{25}{25 + (160 - x)} = \frac{1}{6}$$
$$25 + 160 - x = 150$$
$$185 - x = 150$$
$$-x = -35$$
$$x = 35$$

34. **The correct answer is (B).** Statement (1) alone establishes no clear pattern for the series. For example, each successive number might exceed the previous number by 300, or it might be a multiple of the previous number. Statement (2) alone establishes the pattern—a constant multiple of three from one number to the next in the series. (The ninth number must be 150, the eighth number must be 50, and so on.)

35. **The correct answer is (A).** Apply the cross-product method to eliminate fractions. Rewrite the equation in unfactored form. (If you recognize the difference of two squares, you'll rewrite more quickly.) Simplify, and then solve for x:

$$x(x + y) = (x - y)(x + y)$$
$$x^2 + xy = x^2 - y^2$$
$$xy = -y^2$$
$$x = -y$$

36. **The correct answer is (E).** Each of the four outer surfaces of the cube is 9 square inches with the other two being 8 (subtract one for the hole), and so the cube contains a total of 52 square inches of outer surface area. Each of the four inner surfaces (inside the hole) accounts for an additional 3 square inches—for a total of 12 square inches of inner surface area. The solid's total surface area = 52 + 12 = 64 square inches.

37. **The correct answer is (C).** Statement (1) alone provides no information about actual price. Statement (2) alone provides no information about the change in price. Together, however, the two statements establish that the price was $2.10 on January 1, and, with this information, you can determine the percent decrease. (The answer to the question is the percent equivalent of the fraction $\frac{20}{210}$.)

VERBAL SECTION

1. D	10. C	18. D	26. A	34. A
2. D	11. A	19. C	27. D	35. B
3. B	12. D	20. C	28. C	36. E
4. B	13. A	21. B	29. B	37. A
5. B	14. E	22. D	30. E	38. B
6. D	15. A	23. C	31. E	39. D
7. E	16. C	24. A	32. C	40. E
8. D	17. C	25. E	33. D	41. A
9. C				

1. **The correct answer is (D).** The original answer is correctly punctuated and capitalized. It is flawed in only one way: the predicate *include* does not agree with the singular subject *plan*. Choice (D) creates the correct subject-verb agreement.

2. **The correct answer is (D).** The original answer is not parallel because the first two items in the series contain gerund phrases; furthermore, the final item in the series could be more directly stated. Choice (D) remedies both problems by creating a third gerund phrase, eliminating the superfluous *by*, and tightening "of a word's part of speech" to "a word's part of speech."

3. **The correct answer is (B).** The passage's first two sentences, considered together, suggest that the manufacturers probably knew about the risk to public health but, to save money, decided to emit the harmful chemicals anyway. In all likelihood, then, it's more important to them that they save money than help ensure that their chemicals do not harm the neighboring public.

4. **The correct answer is (B).** The original sentence suffers from redundancy. Something that plunges goes down; therefore, the adverb *down* is redundant. There is also no need to modify an abyss as "yawning"; the word already denotes something immeasurably deep. Choice (B) corrects these problems by eliminating excess modifiers.

5. **The correct answer is (B).** The argument relies on the assumption that job applicants know which employers regularly investigate employee medical histories and which ones don't—but disregard this distinction in deciding to which companies they'll apply. Choice (B) directly refutes this assumption.

6. **The correct answer is (D).** One of the judging criteria is flavor. If the judges prefer the flavor of cherry pie over other flavors, this fact would increase the likelihood that a cherry pie will win the contest. Admittedly, flavor is only one judging criterion. Nevertheless, choice (D) is the best of the five answer choices.

7. **The correct answer is (E).** The author cites "Migrant Mother" as an example of "[h]er finest images," i.e., as an example of one of her best photographs.

8. **The correct answer is (D).** The passage provides absolutely no information about Lange's motives or reasons for accepting her FSA commission.

9. **The correct answer is (C).** Admittedly, choice (C) is not an ideal characterization of the passage, which seems more concerned with Lange's work than with making a broader argument about the power of pictures. Nevertheless, the author does allude to Lange's ability to convey a need for social change through her photographs. Accordingly, the passage can be characterized as presenting one example (Lange) to support the broader point suggested by choice (C).

10. **The correct answer is (C).** The original version incorrectly uses *their* instead of *they're* (*they are*). Choice (C) rephrases the idea in a clear manner. Choice (B) alters the meaning of the original sentence. In choice (D), *explain why the difference* is not idiomatic (*why* should be omitted). Choice (E) commits the same usage error as the original version.

11. **The correct answer is (A).** The original sentence is perfectly fine. The singular pronoun *it* refers properly to the singular *course*. And *a great deal* is idiomatic.

12. **The correct answer is (D).** In the original sentence, two main clauses are incorrectly separated only by a comma, without an appropriate connecting word after the comma. Choice (D) inserts the word *and*, which makes sense in context—providing an appropriate rhetorical balance between the ideas in the two clauses. Although *their levels of radiation* is a bit wordier than *radiation levels*, the phrase is clear and grammatically correct.

13. **The correct answer is (A).** Choice (A) is irrelevant to the argument, without certain additional assumptions. Even if the same writers who write for television also write for movies, the passage provides no information about whether these writers would also strike against movie studios. Even if they would, we are not informed how the impending strike might affect the quality of new movie screenplays, if at all, and how this outcome might in turn affect movie-theater attendance and profits, if at all. (All of the other answer choices are necessary assumptions.)

14. **The correct answer is (E).** A typical weekend horse show generates more revenue than a typical weekend market. Hence, increasing the number of weekend horse shows is the surest way, among the five choices, for Alpha to maximize revenue—especially if the number of days per year that the grounds are used as a market would at least remain the same, as choice (E) suggests.

15. **The correct answer is (A).** In the first paragraph, the author points out how a land-based perspective can lead to the wrong conclusion about corals—stated more generally, how people's perceptions of other habitats (the ocean) are influenced by their own environment (the land). Choice (A) expresses this broad point of the paragraph.

16. **The correct answer is (C).** In the second paragraph, the author tells us that there's a functional relationship between lichen and its photosynthesizing organism (which the author does not identify or discuss) that is similar to the functional relationship between corals and *zooxanthellae*.

17. **The correct answer is (C).** The passage's second paragraph indicates that corals provide *zooxanthellae* "certain by-products of the coral's metabolism . . . which *zooxanthellae* require to grow and reproduce."

18. **The correct answer is (D).** Choice (D) is the best answer because it substantiates an assumption that is necessary for the argument. Unless it is possible to build more new homes in Ocean View to begin with, the argument's proposal—to build new homes that are affordable—would be impossible to implement. Choice (C) tends to show that Ocean View workers, as a group, prefer home ownership over renting. To this extent, choice (C) strengthens the argument that if Ocean View homes were more affordable, then Ocean View workers would buy them. But the argument does not depend on an oversupply of rental housing; hence, choice (D) is a better answer.

19. **The correct answer is (C).** According to the argument, *any* person eligible for the internship program is likely to gain admission to the local law school if he or she applies, and *some* people eligible for the program are among this year's Faimount College graduates. It follows logically that *some* of this year's Faimount College graduates are likely to gain admission to law school if they apply. To follow these logical steps, it helps to express the premises and conclusion symbolically, as follows (E = eligible for the program, A = likely to gain admission to law school, F = Faimount College graduate this year):

    Premise: All E are A.

    Premise: Some E are F.

    Conclusion: Some F are A.

    Choice (C) provides the above conclusion. None of the other choices provides a valid conclusion.

20. **The correct answer is (C).** The first clause in the original version is a dangling modifier; what is considered *the most unforgiving course* is never mentioned in the sentence. The sentence should be reconstructed to eliminate this problem. Only choice (C) corrects this problem without creating another one.

21. **The correct answer is (B).** There are two problems with the original version. First, *is proved* is an improper verb form (*is proven* is the correct present-perfect form). Also, *be a cause of* is wordy. Choice (B) corrects both problems. So does choice (D); however, the resulting sentence is nonsensical, suggesting that drugs (rather than researchers) do the proving.

22. **The correct answer is (D).** Choice (D) actually *strengthens* the argument, insofar as by prolonging life the new drugs would make it possible for the elderly to develop even more new ailments. (The argument does not equate health with prolonged life.)

23. **The correct answer is (C).** The argument relies on the unstated assumption that the funds used to maintain the roads would be available for the education program should the ordinance be repealed. Choice (C) provides evidence that this assumption is a reasonable one; if the roads are of no other practical use, then there would be no need to continue to spend county funds to maintain them. Choice (D) does admittedly lend some measure of support to the argument. Common sense tells us that the education program would be effective only if the group of individuals whom it is designed to benefit actually benefit from it. However, we are not informed whether the entire population is in fact susceptible to Smith's Disease. Without this additional information, it is impossible to assess the degree to which choice (D) strengthens the argument.

24. **The correct answer is (A).** Although the original version uses the passive voice, the sentence contains no grammatical or diction errors. Choices (B) and (C) both create dangling modifiers. In choice (B), who is it that devises? In choice (C), who are *they*? Choice (C) is also wordy. In choice (D), *access becomes devised* is very awkward. Choice (E) replaces the plural verb *are* with the singular form *is*. However, the noun *means* is plural in context and therefore should take the plural form *are*.

25. **The correct answer is (E).** The sentence begins with the modifying phrase *Contrary to earlier physicists* . . . . The main clause should begin by indicating who it is that is "contrary." Choices (B) and (E) both reconstruct the underlined part to clarify the reference. However, choice (E) is more graceful and concise.

26. **The correct answer is (A).** The passage explains how and why the various groups named in choices (B) through (E) have a stake in the current forms of aid. Environmentalists are not among them. In fact, in the first paragraph, the passage indicates that bankers, governments, and others should adopt the environmentalist philosophy of "small is better" in order to combat poverty more effectively. The implication here, if any, is that environmental groups would be philosophically opposed to the current forms of aid.

27. **The correct answer is (D).** In the second paragraph, the author strongly recommends programs that provide "simple agricultural technology" including "implements"—which means agricultural tools. The other answers are examples of the massive development projects the author rejects as ineffective.

28. **The correct answer is (C).** Throughout the passage, the author describes the current ineffective programs and explains how, in his opinion, they ought to be changed in order to have a greater impact on the hunger problem. Choice (C) essentially provides this recap of the passage.

29. **The correct answer is (B).** In stating, "Ultimately, however, means must be found to make it contrary to anyone's interest to keep others poor," the author strongly implies that developed countries are unlikely to implement the various reforms suggested in the preceding paragraphs unless and until those reforms are in their own economic self-interest—rather than in the interest of alleviating hunger. In other words, developed countries are unwilling to make "true sacrifices."

30. **The correct answer is (E).** Any information that helps determine the actual cause of the immediate performance boost will help evaluate the researcher's hypothesis. Of the five avenues of investigation listed, only choice (E) will yield this type of information. If it turns out that a new chain reduces gear friction, thereby allowing the cyclist to ride just as fast but with less effort, then this fact would help disprove the researcher's hypothesis—especially if friction increases materially during the first three weeks of use.

31. **The correct answer is (E).** This argument relies on the general assumption that all other factors in the incidence of lung cancer will remain unchanged in the near future. Choice (E) provides information that, if true, directly refutes this assumption.

32. **The correct answer is (A).** The original sentence correctly adds on nonrestrictive information by treating it as a dependent clause, not an independent clause; by using the superlative *least*, not the comparative *less*; and by using the correct, complete verb form.

33. **The correct answer is (B).** The original sentence is marred by unclear or ambiguous pronoun reference: the initial use of *they* is meant to refer to ideas, but it technically refers to Carmichael and Malcolm X. Furthermore, the second use of *they* is unclear because the first use is ambiguous. Choice (B) makes the intended meaning clear by replacing both uses of the pronoun *they* with precise nouns.

34. **The correct answer is (A).** The original version is correct. Choices (B) and (E) awkwardly split the grammatical element *is known as*. Choice (C) alters the meaning of the original sentence, suggesting that gerrymandering involves determining voting districts based on *whether* people vote rather than on *how* they vote. Choice (D) distorts the meaning of the word *gerrymandering*.

35. **The correct answer is (B).** The original argument boils down to the following:

    Premise: If a teacher refuses to attend the conference, then the teacher will not attend the buffet.

    Premise: Brett did not attend the buffet.

    Conclusion: Brett refused to attend the conference.

    To reveal the argument's structure (and its flawed reasoning), express the argument using symbols:

    Premise: If A, then B.

    Premise: X is B.

    Conclusion: X is A.

    This reasoning is fallacious (flawed), and choice (B) demonstrates the same basic pattern:

    Premise: If a person is seated in the front row, then the person can hear the coach. (If A, then B.)

    Premise: Ursula can hear the coach. (X is B.)

    Conclusion: Ursula is seated in the front row. (X is A.)

36. **The correct answer is (E).** The "crucial" (primary) question for the author involves the degree to which the restorationists are true to their "first principle." The author claims that they are not so true in that their program "does not cohere well" with their principle. Since this issue is "crucial" to the author, it is reasonable to assert that this criticism is the author's primary one.

37. **The correct answer is (A).** In the preceding sentence, the author asserts that Turner's and Jordan's descriptions of restorationist activities "do not cohere well with the community participation model." By following this assertion with the suggestion that another model might be more serviceable, the author suggests that restorationists' activities are more consistent with this other model than with the community participation model.

38. **The correct answer is (B).** In the first paragraph, the author refers to the "crucial question about"—or key problem with—the restorationists' program, which the author then elucidates in the second paragraph.

39. **The correct answer is (D).** The passage points out that producing electricity from hydrogen results in the emission of a greater amount of greenhouse gases (which is harmful to the environment) than producing electricity directly from natural gas. Based on this premise, the former method is not so environmentally sound as the latter method.

40. **The correct answer is (E).** The underlined part is ambiguous: Is the point that Carnegie *lived* at that time or that he *engaged in philanthropy* at that time? Choices (C), (D), and (E) all clarify the meaning, but choice (E) is more concise than choices (C) or (D). Although choice (B) is even briefer, the word *about* is not idiomatic here. (The idiom *at about* would have been correct.)

41. **The correct answer is (A).** The argument relies on an increase in graduation rates to conclude that the five privatized schools are "educationally effective." But if the schools' administration arbitrarily allows students to graduate, regardless of academic achievement, then any increase in graduation rates would not be meaningful. In other words, the argument depends on the assumption that the students deserved to graduate.

ANSWER SHEET PRACTICE TEST 5

ANALYTICAL WRITING ASSESSMENT

_____

_____

_____

_____

_____

_____

_____

_____

_____

_____

_____

_____

_____

_____

_____

_____

_____

_____

_____

_____

_____

_____

_____

_____

_____

_____

_____

_____

answer sheet

answer sheet

INTEGRATED REASONING

1.1 Ⓐ Ⓑ Ⓒ Ⓓ Ⓔ Ⓕ   4.1 Ⓐ Ⓑ Ⓒ Ⓓ Ⓔ Ⓕ   7.1 Ⓐ Ⓑ   10.1 Ⓐ Ⓑ Ⓒ Ⓓ Ⓔ
1.2 Ⓐ Ⓑ Ⓒ Ⓓ Ⓔ Ⓕ   4.2 Ⓐ Ⓑ Ⓒ Ⓓ Ⓔ Ⓕ   7.2 Ⓐ Ⓑ   10.2 Ⓐ Ⓑ Ⓒ Ⓓ
2.1 Ⓐ Ⓑ   5.1 Ⓐ Ⓑ Ⓒ Ⓓ Ⓔ   7.3 Ⓐ Ⓑ   11.1 Ⓐ Ⓑ Ⓒ
2.2 Ⓐ Ⓑ   5.2 Ⓐ Ⓑ Ⓒ Ⓓ Ⓔ   8.1 Ⓐ Ⓑ   11.2 Ⓐ Ⓑ Ⓒ
2.3 Ⓐ Ⓑ   6.1 Ⓐ Ⓑ   8.2 Ⓐ Ⓑ   12.1 Ⓐ Ⓑ Ⓒ Ⓓ
3.1 Ⓐ Ⓑ Ⓒ Ⓓ Ⓔ Ⓕ   6.2 Ⓐ Ⓑ   8.3 Ⓐ Ⓑ   12.2 Ⓐ Ⓑ Ⓒ Ⓓ
3.2 Ⓐ Ⓑ Ⓒ Ⓓ Ⓔ Ⓕ   6.3 Ⓐ Ⓑ   9.1 Ⓐ Ⓑ
9.2 Ⓐ Ⓑ
9.3 Ⓐ Ⓑ

QUANTITATIVE SECTION

1. Ⓐ Ⓑ Ⓒ Ⓓ Ⓔ   9. Ⓐ Ⓑ Ⓒ Ⓓ Ⓔ   17. Ⓐ Ⓑ Ⓒ Ⓓ Ⓔ   25. Ⓐ Ⓑ Ⓒ Ⓓ Ⓔ   33. Ⓐ Ⓑ Ⓒ Ⓓ Ⓔ
2. Ⓐ Ⓑ Ⓒ Ⓓ Ⓔ   10. Ⓐ Ⓑ Ⓒ Ⓓ Ⓔ   18. Ⓐ Ⓑ Ⓒ Ⓓ Ⓔ   26. Ⓐ Ⓑ Ⓒ Ⓓ Ⓔ   34. Ⓐ Ⓑ Ⓒ Ⓓ Ⓔ
3. Ⓐ Ⓑ Ⓒ Ⓓ Ⓔ   11. Ⓐ Ⓑ Ⓒ Ⓓ Ⓔ   19. Ⓐ Ⓑ Ⓒ Ⓓ Ⓔ   27. Ⓐ Ⓑ Ⓒ Ⓓ Ⓔ   35. Ⓐ Ⓑ Ⓒ Ⓓ Ⓔ
4. Ⓐ Ⓑ Ⓒ Ⓓ Ⓔ   12. Ⓐ Ⓑ Ⓒ Ⓓ Ⓔ   20. Ⓐ Ⓑ Ⓒ Ⓓ Ⓔ   28. Ⓐ Ⓑ Ⓒ Ⓓ Ⓔ   36. Ⓐ Ⓑ Ⓒ Ⓓ Ⓔ
5. Ⓐ Ⓑ Ⓒ Ⓓ Ⓔ   13. Ⓐ Ⓑ Ⓒ Ⓓ Ⓔ   21. Ⓐ Ⓑ Ⓒ Ⓓ Ⓔ   29. Ⓐ Ⓑ Ⓒ Ⓓ Ⓔ   37. Ⓐ Ⓑ Ⓒ Ⓓ Ⓔ
6. Ⓐ Ⓑ Ⓒ Ⓓ Ⓔ   14. Ⓐ Ⓑ Ⓒ Ⓓ Ⓔ   22. Ⓐ Ⓑ Ⓒ Ⓓ Ⓔ   30. Ⓐ Ⓑ Ⓒ Ⓓ Ⓔ
7. Ⓐ Ⓑ Ⓒ Ⓓ Ⓔ   15. Ⓐ Ⓑ Ⓒ Ⓓ Ⓔ   23. Ⓐ Ⓑ Ⓒ Ⓓ Ⓔ   31. Ⓐ Ⓑ Ⓒ Ⓓ Ⓔ
8. Ⓐ Ⓑ Ⓒ Ⓓ Ⓔ   16. Ⓐ Ⓑ Ⓒ Ⓓ Ⓔ   24. Ⓐ Ⓑ Ⓒ Ⓓ Ⓔ   32. Ⓐ Ⓑ Ⓒ Ⓓ Ⓔ

VERBAL SECTION

1. Ⓐ Ⓑ Ⓒ Ⓓ Ⓔ   9. Ⓐ Ⓑ Ⓒ Ⓓ Ⓔ   17. Ⓐ Ⓑ Ⓒ Ⓓ Ⓔ   25. Ⓐ Ⓑ Ⓒ Ⓓ Ⓔ   33. Ⓐ Ⓑ Ⓒ Ⓓ Ⓔ
2. Ⓐ Ⓑ Ⓒ Ⓓ Ⓔ   10. Ⓐ Ⓑ Ⓒ Ⓓ Ⓔ   18. Ⓐ Ⓑ Ⓒ Ⓓ Ⓔ   26. Ⓐ Ⓑ Ⓒ Ⓓ Ⓔ   34. Ⓐ Ⓑ Ⓒ Ⓓ Ⓔ
3. Ⓐ Ⓑ Ⓒ Ⓓ Ⓔ   11. Ⓐ Ⓑ Ⓒ Ⓓ Ⓔ   19. Ⓐ Ⓑ Ⓒ Ⓓ Ⓔ   27. Ⓐ Ⓑ Ⓒ Ⓓ Ⓔ   35. Ⓐ Ⓑ Ⓒ Ⓓ Ⓔ
4. Ⓐ Ⓑ Ⓒ Ⓓ Ⓔ   12. Ⓐ Ⓑ Ⓒ Ⓓ Ⓔ   20. Ⓐ Ⓑ Ⓒ Ⓓ Ⓔ   28. Ⓐ Ⓑ Ⓒ Ⓓ Ⓔ   36. Ⓐ Ⓑ Ⓒ Ⓓ Ⓔ
5. Ⓐ Ⓑ Ⓒ Ⓓ Ⓔ   13. Ⓐ Ⓑ Ⓒ Ⓓ Ⓔ   21. Ⓐ Ⓑ Ⓒ Ⓓ Ⓔ   29. Ⓐ Ⓑ Ⓒ Ⓓ Ⓔ   37. Ⓐ Ⓑ Ⓒ Ⓓ Ⓔ
6. Ⓐ Ⓑ Ⓒ Ⓓ Ⓔ   14. Ⓐ Ⓑ Ⓒ Ⓓ Ⓔ   22. Ⓐ Ⓑ Ⓒ Ⓓ Ⓔ   30. Ⓐ Ⓑ Ⓒ Ⓓ Ⓔ   38. Ⓐ Ⓑ Ⓒ Ⓓ Ⓔ
7. Ⓐ Ⓑ Ⓒ Ⓓ Ⓔ   15. Ⓐ Ⓑ Ⓒ Ⓓ Ⓔ   23. Ⓐ Ⓑ Ⓒ Ⓓ Ⓔ   31. Ⓐ Ⓑ Ⓒ Ⓓ Ⓔ   39. Ⓐ Ⓑ Ⓒ Ⓓ Ⓔ
8. Ⓐ Ⓑ Ⓒ Ⓓ Ⓔ   16. Ⓐ Ⓑ Ⓒ Ⓓ Ⓔ   24. Ⓐ Ⓑ Ⓒ Ⓓ Ⓔ   32. Ⓐ Ⓑ Ⓒ Ⓓ Ⓔ   40. Ⓐ Ⓑ Ⓒ Ⓓ Ⓔ
41. Ⓐ Ⓑ Ⓒ Ⓓ Ⓔ

answer sheet

Practice Test 5

ANALYTICAL WRITING ASSIGNMENT

Analysis of an Argument

1 Question • 30 Minutes

Directions: Using a word processor, compose an essay for the following argument and directive. Do not use any spell-checking or grammar-checking functions.

The following editorial appeared in a recent issue of a national business journal:

"Five years ago, MegaCorp switched from a monitoring system for detecting employee pilfering to an honor system. During the following year, the number of reported pilfering incidents at MegaCorp was 40 percent less than during the previous year; and during the most recent year, the number of such incidents was even lower. These statistics should not be surprising; in responding to a recent company-wide survey, MegaCorp employees indicated that they would be less likely to pilfer under an honor system than if they were closely monitored. All businesses can learn from MegaCorp's example and reduce employee pilfering by adopting a similar honor code."

Discuss how well reasoned you find this argument. In your discussion be sure to analyze the line of reasoning and the use of evidence in the argument. For example, you may need to consider what questionable assumptions underlie the thinking and what alternative explanations or counterexamples might weaken the conclusion. You can also discuss what sort of evidence would strengthen or refute the argument, what changes in the argument would make it more logically sound, and what, if anything, would help you better evaluate its conclusion.

INTEGRATED REASONING

12 Questions • 30 Minutes

1. A sock drawer contains 36 pairs of socks, which are colored white, brown, or black, in some combination as follows:

   - 5 pairs are colored with all three colors;
   - 25 pairs have some white;
   - 28 pairs have some brown;
   - 20 pairs have some black.

   In the table, select the number of pairs that have only one color and the number of pairs that have exactly two colors. Make only two selections, one in each column.

	1.1 One color	1.2 Two colors	
(A)	○	○	3
(B)	○	○	4
(C)	○	○	5
(D)	○	○	20
(E)	○	○	27
(F)	○	○	32

2. The table gives aggregate information about the hotels in a cluster of six neighboring small towns in a tourist area. Two of the towns are large enough that they are subdivided into two regions each. The other four towns comprise one region each. Hotels are rated on a scale of 1 star to 5 stars.

Sort By: [Select ▼]

Town Region	Number of Hotels	Average Hotel Rating	Average Number of Rooms per Hotel
Aphrodite, North	8	4.31	20
Aphrodite, South	6	4.25	18
Apollo	9	4.22	26
Ares	5	3.9	16
Artemis, East	8	4.25	17
Artemis, West	7	4	13
Hermes	4	4.25	9
Poseidon	12	3.88	22

For each of the following statements, select *Yes* if the statement is true based on the information in the table. Otherwise, select *No*.

	(A)	(B)	
	Yes	No	
2.1	o	o	The town with the most hotel rooms is Poseidon.
2.2	o	o	The average rating of all the hotels in the town of Artemis is greater than 4.125.
2.3	o	o	If in all the towns there are only two hotels with a 3-star rating, and if both of those hotels are in the same town, then that town is not Hermes.

(On the computer test, this will be the end of the question prompt and statements. For this paper test and your convenience, we are providing the various other ways you may sort the data.)

Sort By: [Number of Hotels ▼]

Town Region	Number of Hotels	Average Hotel Rating	Average Number of Rooms per Hotel
Hermes	4	4.25	9
Ares	5	3.9	16
Aphrodite, South	6	4.25	18
Artemis, West	7	4	13
Aphrodite, North	8	4.31	20
Artemis, East	8	4.25	17
Apollo	9	4.22	26
Poseidon	12	3.88	22

Sort By: [Average Hotel Rating ▼]

Town Region	Number of Hotels	Average Hotel Rating	Average Number of Rooms per Hotel
Poseidon	12	3.88	22
Ares	5	3.9	16
Artemis, West	7	4	13
Apollo	9	4.22	26
Hermes	4	4.25	9
Aphrodite, South	6	4.25	18
Artemis, East	8	4.25	17
Aphrodite, North	8	4.31	20

Sort By: | Average Number of Rooms per Hotel ▼ |

Town Region	Number of Hotels	Average Hotel Rating	Average Number of Rooms per Hotel
Hermes	4	4.25	9
Artemis, West	7	4	13
Ares	5	3.9	16
Artemis, East	8	4.25	17
Aphrodite, South	6	4.25	18
Aphrodite, North	8	4.31	20
Poseidon	12	3.88	22
Apollo	9	4.22	26

3. In an arithmetic sequence, the sum, S_n of the first n terms of the sequence equals $n + 3n^2$ for all n.

   In the table, select a value for the first term, a_1, of the sequence, and a value for the difference, d, between successive terms of the sequence.

3.1 a_1	3.2 d	
(A)	(A)	2
(B)	(B)	4
(C)	(C)	6
(D)	(D)	8
(E)	(E)	10
(F)	(F)	12

4. A jazz band will play two one-hour sets at a jazz festival. In the band's repertoire are a number of standards and original songs. The festival producers have requested that each set have more standards than originals. The band members will play five songs per set, and have already planned what some of these songs will be, as follows:

Set 1

"Giant Steps" (standard, up-tempo)

"Autumn Leaves" (standard, ballad)

"Marylou" (original, ballad)

"Phillip Buster" (original, up-tempo)

Set 2

"St. Thomas" (standard, up-tempo)

"Bye Bye Blackbird" (standard, ballad)

"Night in Tunisia" (standard, up-tempo)

The band members are considering what two other songs to perform, keeping in mind that they want to perform more up-tempo tunes than ballads in each set, and that they want to perform as many original songs as possible.

In the table, select one pair of songs, each of which the band could perform in either set, and one pair of songs, each of which the band could perform only in Set 1.

4.1 Either Set	4.2 Only Set 1	
(A)	(A)	"It Never Entered My Mind" (standard, ballad) and "Collard Greens" (original, up-tempo)
(B)	(B)	"Billie's Bounce" (standard, up-tempo) and "It Never Entered My Mind" (standard, ballad)
(C)	(C)	"Billie's Bounce" (standard, up-tempo) and "Straight, No Chaser" (standard, up-tempo)
(D)	(D)	"Simple Thoughts" (original, ballad) and "Collard Greens" (original, up-tempo)
(E)	(E)	"Collard Greens" (original, up-tempo) and "Grandma" (original, up-tempo)
(F)	(F)	"Billie's Bounce" (standard, up-tempo) and "Simple Thoughts" (original, ballad)

5. *Analyst:* Two companies, Company X and Company Y, have just released competing products. Company X's product is considered to be of higher quality, but Company Y's product sells for a lower price. As a result, we expect Company Y's product to have strong sales, unlike Company X's product.

In the table, select *Strengthen* for the statement that, if true, would most strengthen the analyst's argument, and select *Weaken* for the statement that, if true, would most weaken the analyst's argument. Make only two selections, one in each column.

5.1 Strengthen	5.2 Weaken	
(A)	(A)	Company X is well-known for high-quality products.
(B)	(B)	In a recent poll, most consumers rated both quality and price as important considerations when they purchase products of this type.
(C)	(C)	Both products have received higher ratings for quality than the current best-selling product.
(D)	(D)	Company X has a large and loyal customer base.
(E)	(E)	A third company will introduce a competing product later in the year.

6. A gallery displayed and sold works of art by five different artists. The table gives a list of all the pieces that were displayed.

Sort By: [Select ▼]

Piece	Artist	Material	Sale Price
Alley	Brooks	Watercolor on Paper	$3100
Conspire	Alenka	Ink on Paper	$1300
Flop	Masterson	Acrylic Paint on Canvas	$1900
Guarmy	Brooks	Acrylic Paint on Canvas	$1700
Inspire	Alenka	Chalk on Paper	$1900
Monsoul	Brooks	Chalk on Paper	$2200
Morgue	Masterson	Oil on Canvas	$2300
Past Mast	Fabiano	Collage	Not sold
Perspire	Alenka	Chalk on Paper	$1600
Sane	Masterson	Oil on Canvas	$2100
Shuffle #2	Julien	Ink on Paper	$1400
Shuffle #6	Julien	Ink on Paper	$1400
Spear Lear	Julien	Acrylic Paint on Canvas	$2500
Tender Mist	Fabiano	Watercolor on Paper	$1800
Untitled #26	Julien	Collage	$1700
Wispy Clouds	Fabiano	Acrylic Paint on Canvas	$1400

For each of the following statements, select *Yes* if the statement is true based on the information in the table. Otherwise, select *No*.

	(A)	(B)	
	Yes	No	
6.1	○	○	The median sale price among the pieces that sold was $1850.
6.2	○	○	If a piece sold for more than $2000, the probability that it was by Masterson was 33%.
6.3	○	○	Works on canvas sold for a higher average price than did works on paper.

(On the computer test, this will be the end of the question prompt and statements. For this paper test and your convenience, we are providing you the various other ways you may sort the data.)

Sort By: Artist ▼

Piece	Artist	Material	Sale Price
Conspire	Alenka	Ink on Paper	$1300
Inspire	Alenka	Chalk on Paper	$1900
Perspire	Alenka	Chalk on Paper	$1600
Alley	Brooks	Watercolor on Paper	$3100
Guarmy	Brooks	Acrylic Paint on Canvas	$1700
Monsoul	Brooks	Chalk on Paper	$2200
Past Mast	Fabiano	Collage	Not sold
Tender Mist	Fabiano	Watercolor on Paper	$1800
Wispy Clouds	Fabiano	Acrylic Paint on Canvas	$1400
Shuffle #2	Julien	Ink on Paper	$1400
Shuffle #6	Julien	Ink on Paper	$1400
Spear Lear	Julien	Acrylic Paint on Canvas	$2500
Untitled #26	Julien	Collage	$1700
Flop	Masterson	Acrylic Paint on Canvas	$1900
Morgue	Masterson	Oil on Canvas	$2300
Sane	Masterson	Oil on Canvas	$2,100

Sort By: Material ▼

Piece	Artist	Material	Sale Price
Guarmy	Brooks	Acrylic Paint on Canvas	$1700
Wispy Clouds	Fabiano	Acrylic Paint on Canvas	$1400
Spear Lear	Julien	Acrylic Paint on Canvas	$2500
Flop	Masterson	Acrylic Paint on Canvas	$1900
Inspire	Alenka	Chalk on Paper	$1900
Perspire	Alenka	Chalk on Paper	$1600
Monsoul	Brooks	Chalk on Paper	$2200
Past Mast	Fabiano	Collage	Not sold
Untitled #26	Julien	Collage	$1700
Conspire	Alenka	Ink on Paper	$1300
Shuffle #2	Julien	Ink on Paper	$1400
Shuffle #6	Julien	Ink on Paper	$1400
Morgue	Masterson	Oil on Canvas	$2300
Sane	Masterson	Oil on Canvas	$2100
Alley	Brooks	Watercolor on Paper	$3100
Tender Mist	Fabiano	Watercolor on Paper	$1800

practice test

Sort By: [Sale Price   ▼]

Piece	Artist	Material	Sale Price
Conspire	Alenka	Ink on Paper	$1300
Wispy Clouds	Fabiano	Acrylic Paint on Canvas	$1400
Shuffle #2	Julien	Ink on Paper	$1400
Shuffle #6	Julien	Ink on Paper	$1400
Perspire	Alenka	Chalk on Paper	$1600
Guarmy	Brooks	Acrylic Paint on Canvas	$1700
Untitled #26	Julien	Collage	$1700
Tender Mist	Fabiano	Watercolor on Paper	$1800
Flop	Masterson	Acrylic Paint on Canvas	$1900
Inspire	Alenka	Chalk on Paper	$1900
Sane	Masterson	Oil on Canvas	$2100
Monsoul	Brooks	Chalk on Paper	$2200
Morgue	Masterson	Oil on Canvas	$2300
Spear Lear	Julien	Acrylic Paint on Canvas	$2500
Alley	Brooks	Watercolor on Paper	$3100
Past Mast	Fabiano	Collage	Not sold

7.

Expenditures	Amount

The EPA has put together a report on the U.S. pesticide industry for the year 2007.

The table below shows estimates for the world and U.S. user expenditures on pesticides, by pesticide type, in 2007. The "Other" pesticide type includes nematicides, fumigants, and other miscellaneous conventional pesticides, plus other chemicals used as pesticides (e.g., sulfur and petroleum oil).

Pesticide Type	World Market Millions of $	%	U.S. Market Millions of $	%	U.S. Percentage of World Market
Herbicides	15,512	39	5856	47	38
Insecticides	11,158	28	4337	35	39
Fungicides	9216	23	1375	11	15
Other	3557	9	886	7	25
Total	**39,443**	**100**	**12,454**	**100**	**32**

Note that totals may not add up correctly due to rounding.

Expenditures	Amount

This table shows estimates for the world and U.S. amount of pesticide used, by pesticide type, in 2007.

Pesticide Type	World Market Millions of $	%	U.S. Market Millions of $	%	U.S. Percentage of World Market
Herbicides	2096	40	531	47	25
Insecticides	892	17	93	8	10
Fungicides	518	10	70	6	14
Other	1705	33	439	39	26
Total	5211	100	1133	100	22

For each of the following pesticide types, select *Yes* if the U.S. expenditures on this pesticide type accounted for more than 10% of the world's total expenditures on pesticides. Otherwise, select *No*.

	(A)	(B)	
	Yes	No	
7.1	○	○	Herbicides
7.2	○	○	Insecticides
7.3	○	○	Fumigants

8.

Expenditures	Amount

The EPA has put together a report on the U.S. pesticide industry for the year 2007.

The table below shows estimates for the world and U.S. user expenditures on pesticides, by pesticide type, in 2007. The "Other" pesticide type includes nematicides, fumigants, and other miscellaneous conventional pesticides, plus other chemicals used as pesticides (e.g., sulfur and petroleum oil).

Pesticide Type	World Market Millions of $	%	U.S. Market Millions of $	%	U.S. Percentage of World Market
Herbicides	15,512	39	5856	47	38
Insecticides	11,158	28	4337	35	39
Fungicides	9216	23	1375	11	15
Other	3557	9	886	7	25
Total	39,443	100	12,454	100	32

Note that totals may not add up correctly due to rounding.

Expenditures			Amount		

This table shows estimates for the world and U.S. amount of pesticide used, by pesticide type, in 2007.

Pesticide Type	World Market Millions of $	%	U.S. Market Millions of $	%	U.S. Percentage of World Market
Herbicides	2096	40	531	47	25
Insecticides	892	17	93	8	10
Fungicides	518	10	70	6	14
Other	1705	33	439	39	26
Total	**5211**	**100**	**1133**	**100**	**22**

Assuming that all U.S. pesticide expenditures in 2007 refer to pesticide used in 2007, and also that all expenditures for pesticide used in 2007 were made in 2007, for each of the following pesticide types, select *Yes* if the U.S. spent less per pound on this pesticide type than did the rest of the world. Otherwise, select *No*.

	(A)	(B)	
	Yes	No	
8.1	○	○	Herbicides
8.2	○	○	Insecticides
8.3	○	○	Fumigants

9.

Expenditures			Amount		

The EPA has put together a report on the U.S. pesticide industry for the year 2007.

The table below shows estimates for the world and U.S. user expenditures on pesticides, by pesticide type, in 2007. The "Other" pesticide type includes nematicides, fumigants, and other miscellaneous conventional pesticides, plus other chemicals used as pesticides (e.g., sulfur and petroleum oil).

Pesticide Type	World Market Millions of $	%	U.S. Market Millions of $	%	U.S. Percentage of World Market
Herbicides	15,512	39	5856	47	38
Insecticides	11,158	28	4337	35	39
Fungicides	9216	23	1375	11	15
Other	3557	9	886	7	25
Total	**39,443**	**100**	**12,454**	**100**	**32**

Note that totals may not add up correctly due to rounding.

Expenditures	Amount

This table shows estimates for the world and U.S. amount of pesticide used, by pesticide type, in 2007.

Pesticide Type	World Market Millions of $	%	U.S. Market Millions of $	%	U.S. Percentage of World Market
Herbicides	2096	40	531	47	25
Insecticides	892	17	93	8	10
Fungicides	518	10	70	6	14
Other	1705	33	439	39	26
Total	5211	100	1133	100	22

For each of the following statements, select *Yes* if it can be reasonably inferred from the given information. Otherwise, select *No*.

	(A)	(B)	
	Yes	No	
9.1	o	o	The United States spent less per pound of fumigant used than did the rest of the world.
9.2	o	o	The United States spent more on insecticides than the world did on petroleum oil.
9.3	o	o	If the U.S. agricultural sector accounted for 72% of U.S. expenditures on herbicides, then it accounted for approximately 10.67% of the world's expenditures on pesticides.

10. The graph shows the annual percent change in U.S. greenhouse gas emissions.

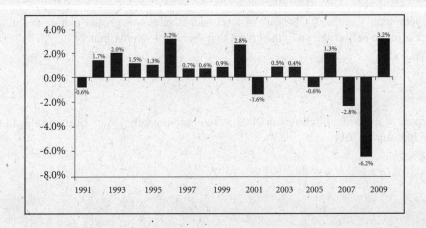

Based on the given information, fill in the blanks in each of the following statements.

10.1. U.S. emissions in 1996 were _____ of U.S. emissions in 1993.

    (A) 102.82%

    (B) 104.54%

    (C) 104.88%

    (D) 106.00%

    (E) 106.11%

10.2. U.S. emissions in 1993 were _____ of U.S. emissions in 1996.

    (A) 94.00%

    (B) 94.24%

    (C) 95.50%

    (D) 95.66%

11. The graph shows the sales of the only three widget-producing companies.

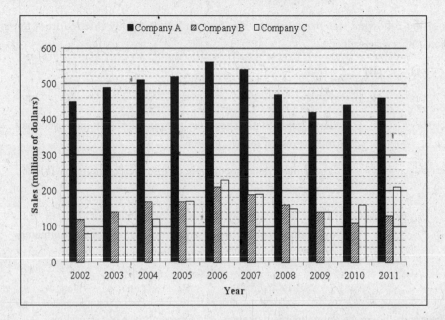

Based on the given information, fill in the blanks in each of the following statements.

11.1. In the year when Company C's share of total widget sales was greater than it was in any other year in the period shown in the graph, that share was approximately _____.

    (A) 21%

    (B) 23%

    (C) 26%

11.2. Total sales in the widget industry in 2002 were approximately _____ of total sales in the widget industry in 2011.

    (A) 81%

    (B) 92%

    (C) 123%

12. The chart shows the percentage (rounded to the nearest integer) of students at an international high school who come from different continents. The number of European students at the school is 177.

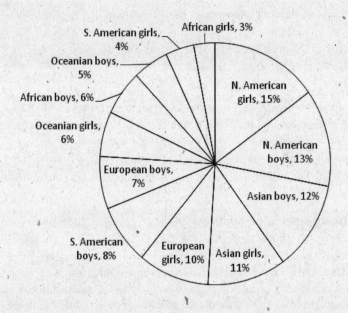

Based on the given information, fill in the blanks in each of the following statements.

12.1. The total number of students attending the school is _____.

   (A) 1041
   (B) 1475
   (C) 1770
   (D) 2529

12.2. _____ times as many North American girls as African students attend the school.

   (A) 1.7
   (B) 2.5
   (C) 3.1
   (D) 5

QUANTITATIVE SECTION

37 Questions • 75 Minutes

Directions for Problem Solving Questions: *(These directions will appear on your screen before your first Problem Solving question.)*

Solve this problem and indicate the best of the answer choices given.

Numbers: All numbers used are real numbers.

Figures: A figure accompanying a Problem Solving question is intended to provide information useful in solving the problem. Figures are drawn as accurately as possible EXCEPT when it is stated in a specific problem that its figure is not drawn to scale. Straight lines may sometimes appear jagged. All figures lie on a plane unless otherwise indicated.

To review these directions for subsequent questions of this type, click on HELP.

Directions for Data Sufficiency Questions: *(These directions will appear on your screen before your first Data Sufficiency question.)*

This Data Sufficiency problem consists of a question and two statements, labeled (1) and (2), in which certain data are given. You have to decide whether the data given in the statements are *sufficient* for answering the question. Using the data given in the statements *plus* your knowledge of mathematics and everyday facts (such as the number of days in July or the meaning of *counterclockwise*), you must indicate whether:

(A) Statement (1) ALONE is sufficient, but Statement (2) alone is not sufficient to answer the question asked;

(B) Statement (2) ALONE is sufficient, but Statement (1) alone is not sufficient to answer the question asked;

(C) BOTH Statements (1) and (2) TOGETHER are sufficient to answer the question asked, but NEITHER statement ALONE is sufficient;

(D) EACH statement ALONE is sufficient to answer the question asked;

(E) Statements (1) and (2) TOGETHER are NOT sufficient to answer the question asked, and additional data specific to the problem are needed.

Numbers: All numbers used are real numbers.

Figures: A figure accompanying a Data Sufficiency problem will conform to the information given in the question, but will not necessarily conform to the additional information in Statements (1) and (2).

Lines shown as straight can be assumed to be straight and lines that appear jagged can also be assumed to be straight.

You may assume that positions of points, angles, regions, etc., exist in the order shown and that angle measures are greater than zero.

All figures lie in a plane unless otherwise indicated.

Note: In Data Sufficiency problems that ask you for the value of a quantity, the data given in the statements are sufficient only when it is possible to determine exactly one numerical value for the quantity.

To review these directions for subsequent questions of this type, click on HELP.

1. If $a > b$ and $c > d$, which of the following is true?

   (A) $b - c < a - d$

   (B) $a + d > b - c$

   (C) $b - d > a - c$

   (D) $a + c > b + d$

   (E) $a + b > c + d$

2. Which of the following is nearest in value to $\sqrt{664} + \sqrt{414}$?

   (A) 16

   (B) 33

   (C) 40

   (D) 46

   (E) 68

3. In a group of 20 singers and 40 dancers, 20% of the singers are less than 25 years old, and 40% of the entire group are less than 25 years old. What percent of the dancers are less than 25 years old?

   (A) 20

   (B) 40

   (C) 50

   (D) 60

   (E) 80

4. How many ounces of coffee remain in a cup that has a 14-ounce capacity?

   (1) Originally, the cup contained 12 ounces of coffee.

   (2) The cup is currently filled to 50 percent of the cup's capacity with coffee.

5. If $0 < N < 30$, is N a factor of 30?

   (1) N is a factor of 12.

   (2) N is a multiple of 3.

6.

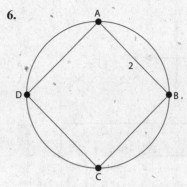

   In the figure above, which shows rectangle *ABCD* tangent to a circle at each corner, $\overline{AB}$ is 2 units in length. Is rectangle *ABCD* a square?

   (1) The length of minor arc *AB* is exactly half the length of arc *ABC*.

   (2) The length of minor arc *AD* is $\frac{\pi\sqrt{2}}{2}$.

7. What is 150% of the product of $\frac{1}{8}$ and 0.4?

   (A) 0.025

   (B) 0.075

   (C) 0.25

   (D) 0.75

   (E) 2.5

8. A recipe calls for $\frac{2}{3}$ cup of butter to make a batch of cookies. How big is the batch?

   (1) If each of six people wanted to eat five cookies, $\frac{5}{3}$ cup of butter would be needed.

   (2) Three batches would require 2 cups of butter.

9. What is the sum of five numbers?

   (1) The arithmetic mean (simple average) of the five numbers is 9.

   (2) The difference between the greatest and least of the five numbers is 9.

10.

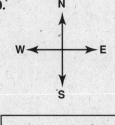

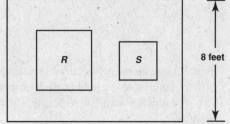

Two square rugs, R and S, have a combined area of 20 square feet and are placed on a floor whose area is 112 square feet, as shown above. Measured east to west, each rug is placed the same distance from the other rug as from the nearest east or west edge of the floor. If the area of rug R is four times the area of rug S, how far apart are the rugs?

(A) 1 foot, 6 inches

(B) 2 feet

(C) 2 feet, 8 inches

(D) 3 feet

(E) 3 feet, 4 inches

11. If $p = (3)(5)(6)(9)(q)$, and if q is a positive integer, then p must be divisible, with no remainder, by all the following EXCEPT:

(A) 27

(B) 36

(C) 45

(D) 54

(E) 90

12. $\dfrac{\sqrt{10}}{\sqrt{2}} \times \dfrac{\sqrt{5}}{\sqrt{2}} =$

(A) $\dfrac{\sqrt{10}}{2}$

(B) $\dfrac{5\sqrt{2}}{2}$

(C) $2\sqrt{5}$

(D) 10

(E) $\dfrac{25}{2}$

13. For all integers a and b, where $b \neq 0$, subtracting b from a must result in a positive integer if

(A) $|a - b|$ is a positive integer

(B) $(a + b)$ is a positive integer

(C) $\left(\dfrac{a}{b}\right)$ is a positive integer

(D) (ab) is a positive integer

(E) $(b - a)$ is a negative integer

14.

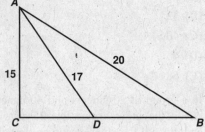

Note: Figure not drawn to scale

In the figure above, m$\angle ACB = 90°$. What is the length of $\overline{DB}$?

(A) $3\sqrt{21} - 8$

(B) 8

(C) $5\sqrt{7} - 8$

(D) $5\sqrt{5}$

(E) $18 - 5\sqrt{6}$

15. Let $\{2,3,3,9,10,n\}$ be a set of measurements, where n is a positive integer. If the median of the set is also an integer, which of the following is a list of all possible values the median may take?

(A) $\{2,3,4\}$

(B) $\{3,4,6\}$

(C) $\{3,4,5,6\}$

(D) $\{2,3,4,5,6\}$

(E) $\{3,4,5,6,7\}$

16. What is the equation of the line that is the perpendicular bisector of the line segment connecting points $(-1,1)$ and $(3,5)$ on the xy-plane?

(A) $y = 2x + 1$

(B) $y = x - 2$

(C) $y = -x + 4$

(D) $y = -3x + 2$

(E) $y = x + 3$

17. If $2x + 1$ is a positive multiple of 5, and if $2x + 1 \leq 100$, how many possible values of x are integers?

(A) 5

(B) 10

(C) 11

(D) 15

(E) 20

18. An empty swimming pool can be filled to capacity through an inlet pipe in 3 hours, and it can be completely drained by a drainpipe in 6 hours. If both pipes are fully open at the same time, in how many hours will the empty pool be filled to capacity?

(A) 4

(B) 4.5

(C) 5

(D) 5.5

(E) 6

QUESTIONS 19–20 REFER TO THE FOLLOWING TABLE.

WORLDWIDE SALES OF XYZ MOTOR COMPANY
(2008-09 Model Year)

Purchaser Category	Automobile Model		
	Basic	Standard	Deluxe
U.S. institutions	3.6	8.5	1.9
U.S. consumers	7.5	11.4	2.0
Foreign institutions	1.7	4.9	2.2
Foreign consumers	1.0	5.1	0.8

Note: All numbers are in thousands.

19. Which of the following most nearly describes sales totaling 9000 automobiles for the 2008–2009 model year?

(A) All U.S. institution sales of the standard and deluxe models

(B) All foreign sales of the standard model

(C) All foreign-institution sales

(D) All consumer sales of the basic model

(E) All institution sales of the standard model

20. Of the total number of automobiles sold to the institutions during the 2008–2009 model year, which of the following most closely approximates the percentage that were NOT standard models?

(A) 24%

(B) 36%

(C) 41%

(D) 59%

(E) 68%

21. What is Michael's monthly salary?

(1) If Michael's monthly salary were cut by 25 percent while Sam's monthly salary were raised by 25 percent, they would earn the same salary.

(2) Michael's monthly salary is $1000 more than Sam's.

22. In a room are five chairs to accommodate 3 people, one person to a chair. How many seating arrangements are possible?

(A) 45

(B) 60

(C) 72

(D) 90

(E) 120

23. N is $83\frac{1}{3}\%$ of what number?

(A) $\dfrac{6}{5N}$

(B) $\dfrac{7N}{8}$

(C) $\dfrac{5N}{4}$

(D) $\dfrac{6N}{5}$

(E) $N + \dfrac{50}{3}$

24. Mona has $2.05 in quarters and dimes. How many quarters does she have?

(1) She has more quarters than dimes.

(2) She has a total of ten coins.

25. If $f(x) = \frac{x}{2} - 1$, what is $f(f(x))$?

    (A) $2x + 2$

    (B) $\frac{x}{4} - \frac{3}{2}$

    (C) $\frac{x}{4} - 1$

    (D) $\frac{x}{4} - \frac{1}{2}$

    (E) $\frac{x^2}{4} - x + 1$

26. Four people plan to rent a summer cottage, apportioning the rent equally among themselves. What is the total amount of rent for the cottage?

    (1) If one additional person were to join in renting the cottage, each person would pay 20 percent of the total rent.

    (2) Three of the four people would pay a total of $2400 in rent.

27.

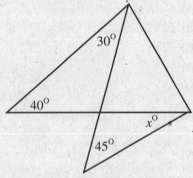

    In the figure above, what is the value of x?

    (A) 25

    (B) 30

    (C) 40

    (D) 45

    (E) 65

28. In a geometric sequence, each term is a constant multiple of the preceding one. If the first three terms in a geometric sequence are -2, x, and -8, which of the following could be the sixth term in the series?

    (A) -4096

    (B) -1024

    (C) 64

    (D) 1024

    (E) 2048

29. How long does it take Sam to eat an entire large pizza?

    (1) Thomas can eat the same large pizza in 8 minutes.

    (2) Sam and Thomas together can eat the same large pizza in $6\frac{1}{2}$ minutes.

30. If $y > 0$, is $x > y$?

    (1) $5x - 4y = 3$

    (2) $4y - 5x = 3$

31. Which of the following equals 1.33%?

    (A) 0.00133

    (B) 0.0133

    (C) 0.133

    (D) 13.3

    (E) 13.33

32. What is the one, unique value of x?

    (1) $x^2 - 4x + 3 = 0$

    (2) $x^2 - 2x + 1 = 0$

33.

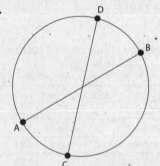

    If the length of arc ACB in the circle above is 5π, is the length $\overline{AB}$ of greater than the length of $\overline{CD}$?

    (1) The length of $\overline{AB}$ equals the circle's diameter.

    (2) The length of $\overline{CD}$ is 5.

34. A passenger train and a freight train leave from the same station at the same time. Over 3 hours, the passenger train travels 45 miles per hour faster, on average, than the freight train. Which of the following expresses the combined distance the two trains have traveled after 3 hours, where x represents the number of miles the freight train traveled per hour, on average?

(A) $3x + 45$

(B) $6x + 45$

(C) $3x + 120$

(D) $3x + 135$

(E) $6x + 135$

35. If the total price of five grocery items is $6.05, what is the price of the most expensive of these items?

(1) The price of the most expensive item is exactly 50 percent greater than the price of each of the other four items.

(2) The price of each item (except the most expensive item) is $1.10.

36. If s is an integer greater than 1, how many 1-inch cubes can be packed into a rectangular box having sides s, $s + \dfrac{3}{2}$, and $s - 1$, measured in inches?

(A) $s^3 - s$

(B) $s^3 + \dfrac{s^2}{2} + \dfrac{s}{2}$

(C) $s^3 - 2s + s$

(D) $s^3 + s^2 - s$

(E) s^3

37. In a certain card game, two specialty decks of cards are used. Each deck contains twelve cards, which are numbered 1 through 12. If a player picks at random one card from each deck, what is the probability that the sum of the numbers on the two selected cards will be either 3 or 7?

(A) $\dfrac{1}{1,728}$

(B) $\dfrac{1}{72}$

(C) $\dfrac{1}{24}$

(D) $\dfrac{1}{18}$

(E) $\dfrac{1}{12}$

VERBAL SECTION

41 Questions • 75 Minutes

Directions for Sentence Correction Questions: *(These directions will appear on your screen before your first Sentence Correction question.)*

This question presents a sentence, all or part of which is underlined. Beneath the sentence you will find five ways of phrasing the underlined part. The first of these repeats the original; the other four are different. If you think the original is best, choose the first answer; otherwise choose one of the others.

This question tests correctness and effectiveness of expression. In choosing your answer, follow the requirements of Standard Written English; that is, pay attention to grammar, choice of words, and sentence construction. Choose the answer that produces the most effective sentence; this answer should be clear and exact, without awkwardness, ambiguity, redundancy, or grammatical error.

Directions for Critical Reasoning Questions: *(These directions will appear on your screen before your first Critical Reasoning question.)*

For this question, select the best of the answer choices given.

Directions for Reading Comprehension Questions: *(These directions will appear on your screen before your first group of Reading Comprehension questions.)*

The questions in this group are based on the content of a passage. After reading the passage, choose the best answer to each question. Answer all the questions following the passage on the basis of what is stated or implied in the passage.

1. Capitalized words and erratic punctuation, especially dashes, in places that often surprise—if not momentarily halt—the reader, are hallmarks of Dickinson's poetry.

   (A) surprise—if not momentarily halt—the reader, are

   (B) surprise—if not momentarily halting—the reader, are

   (C) surprise—if not momentarily halt—the reader, being

   (D) surprise if not momentarily halt the reader, are

   (E) surprises if not momentarily halts the reader, are

2. Most likely an editorial reconstruction, the line "a plague on both your houses" from *Romeo and Juliet,* Act 3, scene 1, originally rendered as "a' both your houses" and "of both the houses."

   (A) originally rendered as "a' both your houses" and "of both the houses."

   (B) was originally rendered as "a' both your houses" and "of both the houses."

   (C) originally being rendered as "a' both your houses" and "of both the houses."

   (D) originally rendered not only as "a' both your houses" but also as "of both the houses."

   (E) originally having been rendered as "a' both your houses" and "of both the houses."

3. A reliable survey indicates that college graduates change employers four times on average during the first ten years after college graduation. Therefore, in order to avoid employee turnover, business administrators in charge of hiring new employees should favor job applicants who obtained college degrees at least ten years earlier.

The advice about how to avoid employee turnover rests on which of the following assumptions?

(A) Employee turnover among businesses that hire employees without college degrees is greater than among businesses that hire only employees with college degrees.

(B) Job changes within the same company are less common than job changes from one employer to another.

(C) Employees who graduated from college at least ten years ago change employers less frequently on average than other employees.

(D) Most employees who leave their jobs do so upon either request or demand of their employers rather than by their own initiative.

(E) The survey excluded college graduates who interrupted their vocational careers to pursue advanced academic degrees.

4. The economist pored carefully over the two sets of data, trying hard to discern not only which had preceded the other, but also which seemed <u>more conclusive; then he chose the best one.</u>

(A) more conclusive; then he chose the best one.

(B) most conclusive; then he chose the best one.

(C) more conclusive, then he chose the best one.

(D) more conclusive and then he chose the best one.

(E) more conclusive; then he chose the better one.

5. Driving excessively fast has been demonstrated to decrease the number of miles one can drive per gallon of fuel. Gary has recently been experiencing a decrease in mileage per gallon of fuel while driving his car. This clearly proves that Gary has been driving excessively fast lately.

Which of the following statements, if true, would most seriously weaken the conclusion about Gary's driving?

(A) Recently Gary's speedometer has been indicating the speed of his car as lower than the car's actual speed.

(B) Recently Gary has been driving more miles per day on average than before he began experiencing a decrease in fuel mileage.

(C) Other tests have shown that a car's speed affects fuel mileage more than any other single factor.

(D) Before Gary began driving excessively fast, his speedometer over-represented his car's actual speed.

(E) Recently the tires on Gary's car have been losing air pressure, and low tire air pressure is known to lower fuel mileage.

6. Expensive television advertising campaigns clearly help political candidates win elections, as evidenced by the fact that, in most political elections, the candidate with the most campaign money ultimately wins.

Which of the following, if true, would provide most support for the argument above?

(A) Endorsements from minor political office-holders generally have no effect on a candidate's chances of winning an election.

(B) In most cases, candidates who currently hold the office for which they seek re-election have more available campaign money than their competitors.

(C) Expensive television advertising campaigns are waged most frequently by candidates who have more available campaign money than their competitors.

(D) When it comes to choosing among candidates, the voting public tends to disregard how a candidate is portrayed in television advertisements.

(E) Nearly any political candidate can afford to wage some type of television advertising campaign.

QUESTIONS 7–9 ARE BASED ON THE FOLLOWING PASSAGE.

Line   The twentieth-century discovery of *Archaeans*, which did not fit into the *kingdom* classification scheme for biological life, led to the creation of the domain
(5)   classification level, above the kingdom level. This new level included the new domain *Archaean*. Prior to the discovery of Archaeans, it had been generally accepted that no life could exist in tem-
(10)   peratures much hotter than 60 degrees centigrade. This limit was set because it was thought that the molecular integrity of vital cellular components could not be maintained beyond such temperatures. The
(15)   thermal capacity of cellular life, it was believed, was a fixture across all biological organisms. Archaeans, in recent decades, have repeatedly demonstrated that the previously maintained thermal threshold
(20)   for life was far too low. So-called extremo-philic Archaeans have been discovered to thrive in temperatures as high as 160 degrees centigrade. Such discoveries have required a broadening of biology's concep-
(25)   tions concerning what environments are hospitable to life.

7. The author of the passage implies that extremophilic Archaeans

(A) are able to maintain molecular integrity of cellular components past what was formerly accepted as the thermal threshold of life.

(B) have been known to exist in moderate environments for some years, but their extremophilic properties have only recently been discovered.

(C) are able to live and thrive in temperatures higher than 160 degrees centigrade.

(D) were responsible for the development of a distinct kingdom in the classification scheme for biological life.

(E) are the oldest known form of multi-cellular biologic life.

8. The passage's author suggests that the "thermal threshold" is

(A) the thermal capacity of extremophiles.

(B) the critical point temperature at which the metabolic pathways of extremophiles become functional.

(C) an environmental extremity indicator.

(D) the temperature at which the molecular integrity of cellular components of an organism are compromised.

(E) a biological constant across all of nature.

9. In the passage, the author's chief concern is to

(A) acknowledge an error in mainstream science.

(B) explain the reason for a modification of a system.

(C) describe an anomalous biological phenomenon.

(D) trace the development of a scientific theory.

(E) outline a system of scientific classification.

10. The disposition of Poland and Saxony and conflicting borders of German states were <u>between the most contentious of the decisions</u> at the Congress of Vienna.

(A) between the most contentious of the decisions

(B) between the more contentious of the decisions

(C) among the most contentious of the decisions

(D) among the most contentious decisions

(E) the most contentious of all the decisions

11. Max Ernst's painting called *Europe After the Rain*, that Robert Hughes calls "a valediction to Europe," was begun in 1940 during a time of political dictatorships and assaults on democracies.

    (A) Max Ernst's painting called *Europe After the Rain*, that Robert Hughes calls

    (B) Max Ernst's painting, called *Europe After the Rain*, that Robert Hughes describes as

    (C) Max Ernst's painting *Europe After the Rain*, which Robert Hughes calls

    (D) Max Ernst's painting called *Europe After the Rain*, that Robert Hughes describes as

    (E) Max Ernst's painting *Europe After the Rain* called by Robert Hughes

12. Airplanes departing in a timely manner can some times be prevented by any one of a variety of factors, such as severe weather or a security threat.

    (A) Airplanes departing in a timely manner can some times be prevented by any one of a variety of factors, such as severe weather or a security threat.

    (B) Any one of a variety of factors, such as severe weather or a security threat, some times can prevent airplanes from their timely departing.

    (C) Any one of a variety of factors, such as severe weather or a security threat, can sometimes prevent the timely departure of airplanes.

    (D) The severity of the weather or a security threat, among a variety of other factors, can some of the time prevent airplanes departing on time.

    (E) Timely departures of airplanes are prevented as a result of severe weather, a security threat, or various other factors.

13. For large pharmaceutical companies, the profit motive has long been a deterrent to the preparation of medicines that treat illnesses afflicting primarily people who cannot easily afford to pay for medicines. While diseases such as cholera and malaria claim millions of lives every year, medicines that the companies have developed and that can prevent these deaths are simply not made available for this purpose. Pharmaceutical companies have expressed essentially the same attitude toward preparing antidotes in the event of germ warfare.

    The passage is structured to lead to which of the following conclusions?

    (A) Large pharmaceutical companies fail to appreciate the potential dangers of germ warfare.

    (B) The government must subsidize the preparation of germ-war antidotes in order to prevent a large-scale catastrophe.

    (C) Potential victims of germ warfare cannot rely on large pharmaceutical companies for antidotes that might be needed during war.

    (D) A victim of cholera or malaria is more likely to die from germ warfare than a person who has not contracted either disease.

    (E) Large pharmaceutical companies do not have sufficient resources to develop antidotes for use in the event of germ warfare.

14. Bayside Aquarium plans to capture a great white shark and to display it at the aquarium, in the hope that doing so will help raise public awareness that this species of shark is in danger of extinction. But few such sharks have ever survived in captivity for more than one month. In all likelihood, then, this plan would amount to a waste of the aquarium's financial resources, which would be better directed toward other efforts to preserve the great white shark.

    Which of the following, if true, would most seriously weaken the argument above?

    (A) Bayside Aquarium's shark habitat would resemble the species' natural environment far more closely than the shark habitats provided previously at other facilities.

(B) Most visitors to the aquarium are already aware that the great white shark is an endangered species.

(C) Certain other species of sharks are at greater risk of extinction than the great white shark.

(D) The expense involved in capturing a great white shark is difficult to predict.

(E) Bayside Aquarium's popularity is due primarily to its large variety of sea life.

QUESTIONS 15–17 ARE BASED ON THE FOLLOWING PASSAGE.

Line   The eighteenth-century literary work Encyclopedie, which coincided with nascent industrialization, distinguished itself from its predecessors with its mix of
(5)   the theoretical with the practical. While twenty pages were devoted to metaphysical speculation about the human soul, nearly as many were devoted to the machine manufacture of stockings, a principal
(10)   industrial product of the day. In fact, seventeen volumes of text were accompanied by eleven volumes of illustrations, at the insistence of chief editors Denis Diderot and Jean d'Alembert, known as the
(15)   "Encyclopedists."

Prior to the mid-eighteenth century, scholars had not dared to publicly assert the intellectual freedom to reason about the mundane tools of daily life with the
(20)   same seriousness as the human soul. Understandably, in 1759, Pope Clement XIII listed Encyclopedie in the Church's Index of Prohibited Books, and the French government refused to license its printing.
(25)   But due in part to the surreptitious assistance of an enlightened government official and in part to greedy booksellers, the work quickly became a best-seller throughout Europe.

15. The author mentions the machine manufacture of stockings most likely in order to

(A) show that for the Encyclopedists illustrations were just as important as text.

(B) underscore the Encyclopedists' skepticism about prevailing metaphysical notions.

(C) demonstrate the Encyclopedists' concern for the practical realm of human endeavor.

(D) point out the Encyclopedists' great attention to detail.

(E) explain why it was necessary to include eleven volumes of illustrations in the work.

16. In the context of the passage, which of the following is the most reasonable explanation for the author's characterization of government suppression of *Encyclopedie* as understandable?

(A) Pope Clement XIII had already called for the suppression of the work.

(B) The same government official who aided the Encyclopedists also refused to grant a license to print the work.

(C) The work's entry about Christianity was briefer than its entry about certain other religions.

(D) In challenging the general status quo, the work might incite readers to question political authority.

(E) The government had previously banned similar works.

17. The author suggests that the commercial success of *Encyclopedie*

(A) was the product of illegal printing operations.

(B) brought fame to the work's chief editors.

(C) spawned more volumes than were originally planned.

(D) was largely due to a publicity campaign by one individual.

(E) owed to the work's extensive use of illustrations.

18. Human exposure to even low levels of nuclear radiation dramatically increases the likelihood of contracting some form of cancer. According to a research study involving a town near a former nuclear testing site, no person who resided in the town during the testing—which occurred more than sixty years ago—and who was under the age of 10 during the testing lived beyond 50 years of age. However, some of the town's former residents who are now over 50 years old are cancer survivors who resided in the town during the nuclear testing.

If the information provided is true, which of the following must on the basis of it also be true about the town that is the subject of the research study?

(A) Some people who resided in the town during the nuclear testing do not remember the testing.

(B) The cancers contracted by the town's cancer survivors were not caused by exposure to nuclear radiation.

(C) Some of the town's former residents living today were over 10 years of age during the nuclear testing.

(D) The nuclear testing resulted in the emission of lower levels of radiation than initially believed.

(E) Some of the town's residents died before turning 50 years of age due to causes other than cancer.

19. Since the release of MicroTeam Corporation's newest version of its ActiveWeb software, more copies of this new version have been sold than any software product that competes with ActiveWeb. Therefore, MicroTeam Corporation's marketing campaign to promote the new version of ActiveWeb was highly effective.

Which of the following, if true, provides the best indication that the conclusion in the argument above is logically well supported?

(A) The number of potential purchasers of ActiveWeb and of products that compete with it has increased since the release of the new version of ActiveWeb.

(B) The number of products competing with ActiveWeb has diminished since the release of the new version of ActiveWeb.

(C) The new version of ActiveWeb corrected every known operational problem with previous versions.

(D) More copies of the new version of ActiveWeb have been sold than of any earlier version of ActiveWeb.

(E) Shortly after the release of the new version of ActiveWeb, a popular and influential magazine recommended a competing product over the new version of ActiveWeb.

20. A pluralistic democracy, <u>in greater degree than any</u> system of government, diffuses power away from a center.

(A) in greater degree than any

(B) which more than any

(C) to a greater extent than any

(D) as opposed to any other

(E) more than any other

21. During her internship at the hospital, Dr. Paulson observed that through careful examination, competent <u>diagnosing and successful treatment, patients can grow to trust their physicians.</u>

(A) diagnosing and successful treatment, patients can grow to trust their physicians.

(B) diagnosis and treatment, if successful, can lead patients to trust their physicians.

(C) and successful diagnosing and treatment, physicians can develop trust in their patients.

(D) diagnosis and successful treatment, physicians can help their patients grow to trust them.

(E) diagnosis and successful treatment, physicians can develop in their patients growing trust.

22. Topical application of oil from the bark of aoli trees, which are quite rare and grow only in certain regions of South America, has been shown to be the only effective means of treating certain skin disorders. At the current rate of harvesting bark for aoli

oil, however, aoli trees will become extinct within fifty years. Clearly, measures must be taken soon to reduce the demand for aoli oil; otherwise, fifty years from now it will no longer be possible to treat these skin disorders effectively.

Which of the following, if true, would most seriously weaken the argument above?

(A) One of the skin disorders for which aoli oil is an effective treatment is caused by exposure to chemicals used in a manufacturing process that is quickly becoming obsolete.

(B) The bark of newly planted aoli trees can be harvested for oil within twenty years after the new trees are planted.

(C) The cause of skin disorders treatable with aoli oil is also the cause of certain other health problems, which are treated effectively by ingesting aoli oil.

(D) In South America aoli tree bark is widely used in making a variety of decorative craft items and utensils.

(E) Only people who live in the regions of South America where aoli trees are found suffer from skin disorders treatable with aoli oil.

23. A child's conception of whether certain behavior is right or wrong, referred to as "behavioral pre-disposition," is fully developed by the age of 10. During a person's teenage years, other teenagers with whom the person associates regularly have a significant influence on whether the person later acts in accordance with his or her predisposition. In other words, teenagers tend to mimic their peers' behavior. It is interesting to note that the vast majority of adult criminals also committed crimes as teenagers and associated primarily with other teenagers who later became adult criminals.

Which of the following conclusions can most properly be drawn from the information above?

(A) A child's conception of whether certain behavior is right or wrong can change during the child's teenage years.

(B) Until a child becomes a teenager it is impossible to predict whether the child will eventually become an adult criminal.

(C) Law-abiding adults are unlikely to have developed a predisposition for adult criminal behavior.

(D) An adult criminal is likely to have been predisposed as a child to criminal behavior.

(E) Pre-teen children who are not predisposed to criminal behavior are unlikely to become adult criminals.

24. The game of Rugby began in the Middle Ages as a daylong free-for-all between neighboring villages, <u>without limit of the numbers of players on a side or of the boundaries</u> to the playing field.

(A) without limit of the numbers of players on a side or of the boundaries

(B) with no limit on the number of players on a side and with no boundaries

(C) without limitation as to how many players on each side or as to boundaries

(D) and it was without a limit on the number of players on a side or on boundaries

(E) with no limits on the numbers of players or boundaries

25. Rather than approving the rebuilding of oceanfront houses destroyed by the hurricane, land-use authorities are considering <u>alternative ways to utilize</u> the land on which the houses once sat, acknowledging that the region will always be vulnerable to nature's fury.

(A) alternative ways to utilize

(B) alternative ways of utilization of

(C) alternatives to using

(D) using alternatives as for

(E) alternative utilizations for

QUESTIONS 26–29 ARE BASED ON THE FOLLOWING PASSAGE.

Line   In the past century, Irish painting has changed from a British-influenced lyrical tradition to an art that evokes the ruggedness and roots of an Irish Celtic past.
(5)   At the turn of the twentieth century, Irish painters—including notables Walter Frederick Osborne and Sir William Orpen—looked elsewhere for influence. Osborne's exposure to "plein air" painting deeply
(10)   affected his stylistic development, and Orpen allied himself with a group of English artists, while at the same time participating in the French avant-garde experiment, both as painter and teacher.
(15)   However, nationalist energies were beginning to coalesce, reviving interest in Irish culture, including Irish visual arts. Beatrice Elvery's Eire (1907), a landmark achievement, merged the devotional sim-
(20)   plicity of fifteenth-century Italian painting with the iconography of Ireland's Celtic past, linking the history of Irish Catholicism with the still-nascent Irish republic. And, although also captivated by the
(25)   French plein air school, Sir John Lavery invoked the mythology of his native land for a 1928 commission to paint the central figure for the bank note of the new Irish Free State. Lavery chose as this figure
(30)   Eire, with her arm on a Celtic harp, the national symbol of independent Ireland.
    In Irish painting from about 1910, memories of Edwardian romanticism coexisted with a new sense of realism,
(35)   exemplified by the paintings of Paul Henry and Sean Keating, a student of Orpen. Realism also crept into the work of Edwardians Lavery and Orpen, both of whom made paintings depicting World
(40)   War I, Lavery with a distanced Victorian nobility, Orpen closer to the front, revealing a more sinister and realistic vision. Meanwhile, counterpoint to the Edwardians and realists came Jack B. Yeats, whose travels
(45)   throughout the rugged and more authentically Irish West led him to depict subjects ranging from street scenes in Dublin to boxing matches and funerals. Fusing close observations of Irish life and icons with
(50)   an Irish identity in a new way, Yeats

changed the face of Irish painting and became the most important Irish artist of his century.

26. With respect to which of the following painters does the passage provide LEAST support for the assertion that the painter was influenced by the contemporary art of France?
    (A) Walter Frederick Osborne
    (B) Sir William Orpen
    (C) Beatrice Elvery
    (D) Sean Keating
    (E) Sir John Lavery

27. Which of the following best explains the author's use of the word "counterpoint" in referring to Yeats?
    (A) Yeats' paintings differed significantly in subject matter from those of his contemporaries in Ireland.
    (B) Yeats reacted to the realism of his contemporary artists by invoking nineteenth-century naturalism in his own painting style.
    (C) Yeats avoided religious and mythological themes in favor of mundane portrayals of Irish life.
    (D) Yeats' paintings suggested that his political views departed radically from those of the Edwardians and the realists.
    (E) Yeats built upon the realism painting tradition, elevating it to unprecedented artistic heights.

28. The author points out the coexistence of romanticism and realism most probably in order to show that
    (A) Irish painters of the early twentieth century often combined elements of realism with those of romanticism into a single painting.
    (B) Irish painters of the early twentieth century tended to romanticize the harsh reality of war.
    (C) for a time painters from each school influenced painters from the other school.

(D) Yeats was influenced by both the romantic and realist schools of Irish painting.

(E) the transition in Irish painting from one predominant style to the other was not an abrupt one.

29. Which of the following is the most likely title of a longer article in which the passage might have appeared?

   (A) "Twentieth-Century Irish Masterpieces: A Coalescence of Painting Styles"

   (B) "Among Irish Painters, who Deserves Credit for the Preeminence of Yeats?"

   (C) "Realism vs. Romanticism: Ireland's Struggle for National Identity"

   (D) "Irish Paintings: Reflections of an Emerging Independent State"

   (E) "The Role of Celtic Mythology in Irish Painting"

30. Newspaper publishers earn their profits primarily from advertising revenue, and potential advertisers are more likely to advertise in newspapers with a wide circulation—a large number of subscribers and other readers—than with other newspapers. However, the circulation of the newspaper that is currently the most profitable one in this city has steadily declined during the last two years, while the circulation of one of its competitors has steadily increased.

   Any of the following, if true, would help explain the apparent discrepancy between the two statements above EXCEPT:

   (A) Advertisers generally switch from the most widely circulated newspaper to another one only when the other one becomes the most widely circulated newspaper instead.

   (B) The number of newspapers competing viably with the most profitable newspaper in the city has increased during the last two years.

   (C) The most profitable newspaper in the city receives revenue from its subscribers as well from advertisers.

   (D) The circulation of the most profitable newspaper in the city is still greater than of any of its competitors.

   (E) Advertising rates charged by the most profitable newspaper in the city are significantly higher than those charged by its competitors.

31. The purpose of the proposed law requiring a doctor's prescription for obtaining hypodermic needles is to lower the incidence of drug-related deaths, both accidental and intentional, involving hypodermic needles. But even knitting needles can be lethal if they fall into the wrong hands; yet everyone would agree that imposing legal restrictions on obtaining knitting needles would be preposterous. Hence the proposed law involving hypodermic needles makes no sense and should not be enacted.

   Which of the following, if true, would provide most support for the argument above?

   (A) Knitting needles have been known to cause injury and death.

   (B) The benefits of hypodermic needles outweigh those of knitting needles.

   (C) The proposed law would not deter the sort of activity known to result in drug-related deaths.

   (D) The proposed law could not be effectively enforced.

   (E) Knitting needles are not readily available to anybody who wants to obtain them.

32. The celestial equator divides an imagined celestial globe into two hemispheres just as Earth's equator does, and <u>the center of Earth's own galaxy, the Milky Way, lies</u> to the south of the celestial equator.

   (A) the center of Earth's own galaxy, the Milky Way, lies

   (B) the center of the Milky Way, the galaxy where Earth is located, lies

   (C) Earth's own galaxy, which lies at the Milky Way's center, lies

   (D) the Milky Way's center of Earth's own galaxy is located

   (E) the Milky Way, which is located at Earth's galaxy's center, lies

33. <u>Neither result of the two experiments involving Alzheimer's patients were what the researchers have expected.</u>

   (A) Neither result of the two experiments involving Alzheimer's patients were what the researchers have expected.

   (B) Of the two experiments involving Alzheimer's patients, neither result was expected by the researchers.

   (C) Neither of the two experiments involving Alzheimer's patients result in what the researchers expected.

   (D) Neither of the two experiments involving Alzheimer's patients resulted in what the researchers had expected.

   (E) What the researchers have expected was the result of neither of the two experiments involving Alzheimer's patients.

34. <u>Were empty space</u> nothing real, then any two atoms located in this "nothingness" would contact each other since nothing would be between them.

   (A) Were empty space

   (B) In the event that empty space is

   (C) If empty space is

   (D) That empty space were

   (E) If empty space was

35. During the past year, nationwide membership in health and fitness clubs has declined by about 7 percent. Over the same time period, sales of fastfood products widely known to contribute to health problems have risen by about the same percent. These statistics clearly show that consumers have become decreasingly concerned about their health and level of fitness during the past year.

   The argument that consumers have become decreasingly concerned about their health and fitness over the most recent one-year period depends most heavily on which of the following assumptions?

   (A) Concern about health is a major reason that consumers join fitness clubs and maintain their memberships.

   (B) The overall level of health and fitness among consumers declined over the most recent one-year period.

   (C) Consumers spent less money on health- and fitness-club memberships than on fast food during the past year.

   (D) Fitness equipment designed for home use has become increasingly affordable over the past year.

   (E) Consumers who have a low level of health and fitness tend to spend more money than other consumers on fast food.

QUESTIONS 36–38 ARE BASED ON THE FOLLOWING PASSAGE.

Line The Andean *cordillera* is made up of many interwoven mountain ranges, which include high intermontane plateaus, basins, and valleys. The Northern Andes contains
(5) several broad ecosystems falling into four altitudinal belts. Its northern subregion is distinguished from the rest of the region by higher relative humidity and greater climatic symmetry between the eastern
(10) and western flanks of the range. The Central Andes are characterized by a succession of agricultural zones with varied climatic conditions along the mountains' flanks and by large, high-altitude plateaus,
(15) variously called *puna* or *altiplano*, which are not present in the Northern Andes. The soil fertility of the northern *altiplano* is generally good. The western Central Andean ranges are relatively arid with
(20) desert-like soils, whereas the eastern ranges are more humid and have more diverse soils. The eastern slopes of the Central Andes in many ways are similar to the wet forests of the Northern Andes.
(25) Unlike the Northern Andes, however, these slopes have a dry season.

   Extreme topography and climate make regional weather projections in the Andean *cordillera* difficult. For example, while air
(30) temperature generally decreases with increasing altitude, variability of mountain topography can produce much lower than expected air temperatures. Vegetation can also be unpredictable, although certain
(35) general patterns are discernible. At the regional or macroscale level, vegetation patterns in the Northern and Central Andes tend to reflect climatic zones determined

Line by latitude and altitude. At the local or
(40) mesoscale level, however, this correspondence becomes less precise, as local variations in soil type, slope, drainage, climate,
and human intervention come into play.

36. Based on the passage information, which of
the following characterizes the northern part
of the Central Andes' high-altitude plateaus?

    (A) High relative humidity

    (B) Fertile soil

    (C) A succession of agricultural zones

    (D) Extremes in air temperature

    (E) An arid climate

37. Based only upon the information in the
passage, which of the following is a characteristic of the Central Andean *cordillera* that
clearly distinguishes it from the Northern
Andean *cordillera*?

    (A) An arid climate

    (B) A sparse human population

    (C) Wet forests

    (D) A humid climate

    (E) A dry season

38. Which of the following statements about
vegetation patterns in the Andean *cordillera*
is most strongly supported by the passage?

    (A) Local vegetation patterns are
    determined by the same factors as
    regional vegetation patterns.

    (B) Vegetation patterns vary more widely
    at the macroscale level than at the
    mesoscale level.

    (C) Vegetation patterns are affected by
    more factors at the mesoscale level
    than at the local level.

    (D) Some factors affecting vegetation
    patterns have only a local impact,
    whereas others have a broader
    impact.

    (E) Human intervention has a greater
    effect than either altitude or latitude
    upon vegetation patterns.

39. *Theme-park spokesperson:* We regret that
four visitor fatalities occurred last year in
separate accidents at our company's theme
parks. All four deaths involved roller coasters on which riders stand rather than sit, and
all victims were children under age 12. We
have since closed down all of our "stand-
ing" roller coasters, and our new policies
prohibit any child under age 12 from riding
any of our coasters. I can confidently state
that all coasters currently operating at our
parks are perfectly safe for any person age
12 or older.

Which of the following investigations would
be most useful in evaluating the spokesperson's safety assessment of the roller coasters
currently operating at the company's parks?

    (A) Surveying park visitors to determine
    the extent to which they are
    concerned about their safety when
    riding roller coasters

    (B) Determining the specific cause of
    death in the case of each of the four
    roller-coaster accidents

    (C) Comparing industry-wide safety
    records for "standing" roller coasters
    to safety records for coasters in
    which riders sit

    (D) Scrutinizing the repair and
    maintenance records for the roller
    coasters involved in the fatal
    accidents

    (E) Determining the incidence of non-
    fatal accidents involving all roller
    coasters at the company's parks that
    are currently in operation

40. In his new biography, author Martin Grier sees Abraham Lincoln as a thoughtful person who nevertheless knew instinctively that <u>only when its people obey and revere the law can a democracy flourish.</u>

(A) only when its people obey and revere the law can a democracy flourish.

(B) democracies flourish when laws are obeyed and revered only by their people.

(C) only when the law is obeyed and revered by its people can a democracy flourish.

(D) a democracy can flourish only when its people obey and revere the law.

(E) only when a democracy flourishes can its people obey and revere the law.

41. It is the policy of SubStop Sandwiches to give discretionary raises only to employees who demonstrate a strong commitment to their jobs and have worked at SubStop for more than six months. However, a state labor law requires SubStop to provide annual cost-of-living raises to all employees who have been continuously employed for at least six months. Last year, SubStop complied fully with its own policy and with the state's labor laws. Yet, two—and only two—of SubStop Sandwiches' eight employees received any wage raise whatsoever last year.

If the information provided is true, which of the following must on the basis of it also be true about SubStop last year?

(A) Two of its employees demonstrated a strong commitment to their jobs.

(B) None of its employees received a discretionary raise.

(C) Six of its employees failed to demonstrate a strong commitment to their jobs.

(D) Two of its employees worked at SubStop continuously for at least six months.

(E) It claimed to provide wage raises in compliance with the state's labor law but in fact did not.

ANSWER KEY AND EXPLANATIONS

See Appendix B for score conversion tables to determine your score. Be sure to keep a tally of correct and incorrect answers for each test section.

Analysis of an Argument—Evaluation and Scoring

Evaluate your Argument-Analysis essay on a scale of 1 to 6 (6 being the highest score) according to the following five criteria:

1. Does your essay identify the key features of the argument and analyze each one in a thoughtful manner?

2. Does your essay support each point of its critique with insightful reasons and examples?

3. Does your essay develop its ideas in a clear, organized manner, with appropriate transitions to help connect ideas?

4. Does your essay demonstrate proficiency, fluency, and maturity in its use of sentence structure, vocabulary, and idiom?

5. Does your essay demonstrate command of the elements of Standard Written English, including grammar, word usage, spelling, and punctuation?

The following series of questions, which serve to identify the Argument's five distinct problems, will help you evaluate your essay in terms of criteria 1 and 2. To earn a score of 4 or higher, your essay should identify at least three of these problems and, for each one, provide at least one example or counterexample that supports your critique. (Your examples need not be the same as the ones below.) Identifying and discussing at least four of the problems would help earn you an even higher score.

1. Does the argument confuse cause-and-effect with mere temporal (time) sequence? (Pilfering might usually go unnoticed by other employees, who in any event often look the other way whenever they do observe it; if so, the decline in pilfering cannot be attributed to the honor code.)

2. Does the argument assume that past conditions affecting the reported incidence of pilfering have remained unchanged? (Such conditions include the number of MegaCorp employees and the overall integrity of those employees; to the extent such conditions have changed over the five-year period, the reported decrease in pilfering might not be attributable to the honor code.)

3. Are MegaCorp employees representative of "all businesses"? (Perhaps under an honor system, MegaCorp employees are less likely to either pilfer or report pilfering than the typical employee, for whatever reason.)

4. Is the company-wide survey on which the recommendation depends potentially biased and therefore not credible? (The survey results are meaningful only to the extent that the people surveyed responded honestly, which is doubtful.)

5. Does the recommendation rely on a potentially unrepresentative statistical sample? (The author fails to assure us that the survey's respondents are representative of all MegaCorp employees.)

6. Are the survey responses a reliable indicator about the future behavior of the respondents? (Hypothetical predictions about one's future behavior are inherently less reliable than reports of proven behavior.)

INTEGRATED REASONING

1.1 B	4.2 C	7.3 B	10.1 E
1.2 E	5.1 C	8.1 B	10.2 B
2.1 B	5.2 D	8.2 B	11.1 C
2.2 A	6.1 B	8.3 B	11.2 A
2.3 A	6.2 B	9.1 B	12.1 A
3.1 B	6.3 A	9.2 A	12.2 A
3.2 C	7.1 A	9.3 A	
4.1 E	7.2 A		

1.1. **The correct answer is (B).** Let x be the number of pairs that are colored white and brown, y be the number of pairs that are colored white and black, and z be the number of pairs that are colored brown and black. Therefore, the number of pairs that have exactly two colors equals the sum of x, y, and z. Next:

• The number of pairs that are solid white is 25 minus the number of white/brown pairs minus the number of white/black pairs minus the 5 pairs that have all three colors. In other words:

$$White = 25 - x - y - 5 = 20 - x - y$$

• Similarly, the number of pairs that are solid brown is:

$$Brown = 28 - x - z - 5 = 23 - x - z$$

• The number of pairs that are solid black is:

$$Black = 20 - y - z - 5 = 15 - y - z$$

Now, the sum of these three expressions gives the total number of pairs of socks that have exactly one color:

$$Solid\ Color = (20 - x - y) + (23 - x - z) + (15 - y - z)$$
$$= 58 - 2x - 2y - 2z$$

So, you have expressions for the solid and two-color pairs, and you also know the number of tri-color pairs and the total number of pairs. Thus:

$$Solid\ Color + Two\text{-}Color + Tri\text{-}Color = 36$$
$$(58 - 2x - 2y - 2z) + (x + y + z) + 5 = 36$$
$$58 - x - y - z = 31$$
$$x + y + z = 27$$

Thus, the number of two-color pairs is 27. It is now a simple matter to find the number of solid-colored pairs:

$$\text{Solid} = 36 - \text{Two-Color} - \text{Tri-Color}$$
$$= 36 - 27 - 5$$
$$= 4$$

1.2. The correct answer is (E). See the explanation above.

2.1. The correct answer is (B). Poseidon has 12 hotels with 22 rooms per hotel, for a total of 264 rooms. The town of Aphrodite has two regions: Aphrodite, North, which has 8 hotels with 20 rooms per hotel, for a total of 160 rooms, and Aphrodite, South, which has 6 hotels with 18 rooms per hotel, for a total of 108 rooms. In all, the town of Aphrodite has 268 rooms, which is more than the number of rooms that the town of Poseidon has. Thus, the statement is false.

2.2. The correct answer is (A). This statement is true. The hotels in Artemis' two regions are rated on average 4.25 and 4, respectively, and the average of 4.25 and 4 is 4.125. However, this is not the correct average for all the hotels in Artemis, because the two regions do not have the same number of hotels. The 8 hotels from Artemis, East (rated 4.25 on average), will weigh more heavily on the average than the 7 hotels from Artemis, West (rated 4 on average), thus pushing the overall average a little higher than 4.125. Once you've realized this, you do not need to calculate the actual average: All that matters is that it is greater than 4.125.

2.3. The correct answer is (A). Assume to the contrary that both 3-star-rated hotels are in Hermes. In total, Hermes has 4 hotels, with an average rating of 4.25. Is it possible for the average rating of these four hotels to be 4.25 if two of the four ratings are 3 and the other two cannot be greater than 5? The maximum possible average in this scenario would occur if the other two ratings are both 5:

$$A = \frac{3 + 3 + 5 + 5}{4}$$
$$A = 4$$

So it is not possible to arrive at Hermes' 4.25 average hotel rating if two of Hermes' hotels have a 3-star rating. Thus, the statement is true.

3.1. The correct answer is (B). For n equal to 1, S_n is S_1 which equals a_1. Thus:

$$S_1 = 1 + 3(1)^2$$
$$a_1 = 1 + 3$$
$$a_1 = 4$$

3.2. The correct answer is (C). You know what the first term is, so you can find the second term:

$$S_2 = a_1 + a_2$$
$$2 + 3(2)^2 = a_1 + a_2$$
$$14 = 4 + a_2$$
$$a_2 = 10$$

Now that you know the first two terms, you can calculate their difference:

$$d = a_2 - a_1 = 10 - 4 = 6$$

4.1. **The correct answer is (E).** First examine the tunes they have already scheduled. Set 1 already has two ballads, so its remaining two songs must be up-tempo, in order that the set have more up-tempo songs than ballads. Also, only one of the remaining two songs in Set 1 can be an original because the festival producers have requested more standards than originals per set.

Next, Set 2 has only one ballad, so the remaining song can be up-tempo or ballad. However, it has to be an original because the band wants to maximize the number of originals it is allowed to perform in each set.

One consequence of these observations is that a standard ballad cannot be performed in either set (in Set 1 because it's a ballad, and in Set 2 because it's a standard). Thus, you can eliminate choices (A) and (B), which list the standard ballad "It Never Entered My Mind."

So, the songs that can be performed in either set can only be original (because of the need for an original in Set 2) and up-tempo (because the need for up-tempo in Set 1). Choice (E) lists two such tunes, and it is thus the correct answer.

4.2. **The correct answer is (C).** The right choice for Column 2 will be the one that lists two up-tempo standards: these can be performed only in Set 1. Note that these cannot be performed together in Set 1—rather, they have to be paired with an up-tempo original—but that's not what the question is asking. Choice (C) lists two songs that can be performed only in Set 1.

Note that choice (F) lists one up-tempo standard, which can be performed only in Set 1, and one up-tempo original, which can be performed only in Set 2.

5.1. **The correct answer is (C).** First, for conciseness, from here on let's call the products Product X and Product Y, rather than Company X's product and Company Y's product.

The analyst's argument could be vulnerable to customer concerns over the quality of Product Y. Choice (C) addresses this point in a way that strengthens the argument. If both products are of higher quality than the current best-selling product, then it is reasonable to assume that Product Y is of sufficiently high quality. Thus, quality concerns should not hurt its sales, and its lower price should help them.

That Company X is known for high-quality products, choice (A), need not imply that Product X will sell well. Choice (B) does not help you determine which product will sell better, since both quality and price appear to be significant to consumers. Finally, you do not know anything about the third company mentioned in choice (E), so you cannot judge how its product will affect the sales of Products X and Y.

5.2. **The correct answer is (D).** Part of the analyst's argument is that Company X's product will not sell very well. Choice (D) undermines that point. If Company X's customers are loyal, then it is reasonable to expect that most of them will buy the new product; and if there are many of these customers, it is reasonable to expect Company X's product sales to be high.

6.1. **The correct answer is (B).** Fifteen of the 16 pieces sold. The eighth highest sale price is the median of the set of sale prices. This price is $1800.

6.2. **The correct answer is (B).** The probability that a piece by Masterson sold for more than $2000 is 33%, but that's not what the question is asking. Five pieces in total sold for more than $2000, and two of them were by Masterson, so the probability is 2 out of 5, or 40%.

6.3. **The correct answer is (A).** This will take some doing, since there's no neat way to sort the table in order to get all the canvas and paper works grouped neatly together. It is also not easy to eyeball the table and judge whether paper or canvas works had a higher average sale price so you should calculate the actual averages. Sorting by material helps a little. Six pieces were on canvas. Their average sale price was:

$$\frac{\$1400 + \$1700 + \$1900 + \$2500 + \$2100 + \$2300}{6} \approx \$1983.33$$

Eight pieces were on paper and their average sale price was:

$$\frac{\$1600 + \$1900 + \$2200 + \$1300 + \$1400 + \$1400 + \$1800 + \$3100}{8} = \$1837.50$$

So the works on canvas did sell for a higher average price than did those on paper.

7.1. The correct answer is (A). The table in the first tab tells you that U.S. expenditures on pesticides accounted for 32% of the world's expenditures on pesticides. Of the total U.S. pesticide expenditures, 47% went toward herbicides, 35% went toward insecticides, and less than 7% went towards fumigants (which are part of the "Other" category). The United States spent on herbicides 47% of the 32% of the total world expenditures on pesticides: this equals 15% of total world expenditures.

7.2. The correct answer is (A). The United States spent on insecticides 35% of the 32% of the total world expenditures on pesticides: this equals 11% of total world expenditures.

7.3. The correct answer is (B). The United States spent on fumigants less than 7% of the 32% of the total world expenditures on pesticides: this equals less than 2.24% of total world expenditures.

8.1. The correct answer is (B). Think of this in terms of the percentages of the world's usage and expenditure that belonged to the United States. For example, if the United States used 50% of the world's pesticide X and spent 50% of what the world spent, then the United States spent the same amount per pound of X as did the rest of the world. On the other hand, if the United States used 10% of the world's pesticide X and spent 90% of what the world spent, then the United States spent more per pound of X than did the rest of the world.

Now, in 2007, the United States used 25% of the total amount of herbicides used in the world (Tab 2), and spent 38% of the total amount the world spent on them (Tab 1). Thus, the United States spent more per pound on herbicides than did the rest of the world.

8.2. The correct answer is (B). In 2007, the United States used 10% of the total amount of insecticides used in the world (Tab 2), and spent 39% of the total amount the world spent on them (Tab 1). Thus, the United States spent more per pound on insecticides than did the rest of the world.

8.3. The correct answer is (B). In 2007, the United States used 14% of the total amount of fungicides used in the world (Tab 2), and spent 15% of the total amount the world spent on them (Tab 1). Thus, the United States spent (slightly) more per pound on insecticides than did the rest of the world.

9.1. The correct answer is (B). This is unclear. Fumigants are part of the "Other" category of pesticides. U.S. expenditures on "Other" pesticides were 25% of the world's expenditures, and the United States used 26% of the "Other" pesticides used by the world. However, since "Other" pesticides includes not only fumigants, but also other types of pesticide, you do not know how many pounds of fumigants the United States and the world used, or how much they spent on them.

9.2. The correct answer is (A). This is clear: Tab 1 tells you that the United States spent $4337 million on insecticides, while the world spent no more than $3557 million on petroleum oil (since petroleum oil is part of the "Other" category).

9.3. The correct answer is (A). U.S. expenditures on herbicides were 38% of the world's expenditures on herbicides. Additionally, the world's expenditures on herbicides were 39% of the world's total expenditures on pesticides. Thus, if the U.S. agricultural sector accounted for 72% of the U.S. expenditures on herbicides, then it accounted for 72% times 38% times 39% of the world's expenditures on pesticides. This equals 10.67% of the world's expenditures on pesticides.

10.1. The correct answer is (E). Pick the number 100 to represent the value of U.S. emissions in 1993. Then, in 1994, U.S. emissions were:

$$100 + 100 \times 1.5\% = 101.5$$

Next, the 1995 emissions were:

$$101.5 + 101.5 \times 1.3\% = 102.8195$$

The 1996 emissions were:

$$102.8195 + 102.8195 \times 3.2\% = 106.109724$$

So, rounded to two decimal places, emissions in 1996 were 106.11% of emissions in 1993. Note that it's best not to round until the very end in a question like this.

10.2. The correct answer is (B). You did much of the work already in Question 10.1 when you calculated that, if emissions in 1993 were 100, then emissions in 1996 were 106.1097. Now, let the 1993 emissions be x percent of the 1996 emissions. Thus:

$$100 = x\%(106.1097)$$
$$x = \frac{100}{106.1097}(100)$$
$$x \approx 94.24$$

Again, do not round until the very end.

11.1. The correct answer is (C). The years 2006 and 2011 appear good candidates for the years when Company C's shares of total widget sales were greatest. In 2006, the company had greater sales, in absolute terms, than in 2011, but the industry's overall sales that year were greater, as well. So, it's a good idea to start by calculating Company C's share of total widget sales in 2011. In 2011, Company C's sales were $210 million and the industry's were $800 million ($460 plus $130 plus $210). Let x be the percentage of those total sales that were Company C's. Then:

$$210 = x\%(800)$$
$$x = \frac{210}{800\%}$$
$$x = \frac{210}{800}(100)$$
$$x = 26.25 \approx 26$$

Sure enough, 26% is the greatest percentage among the answer choices, so there's no reason to check any other year.

11.2. **The correct answer is (A).** In 2002, the widget industry had total sales of $650 million ($450 plus $120 plus $80). In 2011, it had total sales of $800, as you've calculated in Question 11.1 already. If the 2002 sales were $x\%$ of the 2011 sales, then:

$$650 = x\%(800)$$
$$x = \frac{650}{800\%}$$
$$x = \frac{650}{800}(100)$$
$$x = 81.25 \approx 81$$

12.1. **The correct answer is (A).** You know that 177 students are from Europe, and that the European boys and girls together make up 17% of the student population. Thus, if X is the total number of students, then:

$$17\%(X) = 177$$
$$X = \frac{177}{17\%}$$
$$X \approx 1,041$$

12.2. **The correct answer is (A).** North American girls make up 15% of the student population. African boys and girls make up 9% of the student population. Thus, if there are x times as many North American girls as African students, then:

$$15 = x(9)$$
$$x = \frac{15}{9}$$
$$x \approx 1.7$$

QUANTITATIVE SECTION

1. D	9. A	17. B	25. A	33. C
2. D	10. C	18. E	26. B	34. E
3. C	11. B	19. C	27. A	35. D
4. B	12. B	20. C	28. C	36. A
5. E	13. E	21. C	29. C	37. D
6. D	14. C	22. B	30. B	
7. B	15. A	23. D	31. A	
8. A	16. C	24. D	32. B	

1. **The correct answer is (D).** If the same number were added to both sides of the inequality $a > b$, the inequality would still hold. In other words, $a + c > b + c$. It follows that if d, a lower number than c, is added to b instead, the inequality must still hold. In other words, $a + c > b + d$.

2. **The correct answer is (D).** Since the question asks for an approximation, there's no need to calculate either root to solve the problem. 664 is slightly greater than 625, which is 25^2. 414 is slightly greater than 400, which is 20^2. Thus the sum of the terms is just over 45 (approximately 46).

3. **The correct answer is (C).** To answer the question, you need to know (1) the total number of dancers and (2) the *number* of dancers less than 25 years old. The question provides the first number: 40. To find the second number, start with what the question provides, and figure out what else you know. Keep going, and eventually you'll arrive at your destination. Of the whole group of 60, 24 are under 25 years old. (40 percent of 60 is 24.) 20 percent of the 20 singers, or 4 singers, are under 25 years old. Hence, the remaining 20 people under 25 must be dancers. That's the second number you needed to answer the question. 20 is 50 *percent* of 40.

4. **The correct answer is (B).** Statement (1) provides no information about how much coffee is in the cup *now* and is therefore insufficient alone to answer the question. Statement (2) alone, however, does suffice to answer the question: it establishes that the cup now contains 7 ounces of coffee (half the 14-ounce capacity).

5. **The correct answer is (E).** Considering Statement (1) alone, the possible values of N are: 1, 2, 3, 4, 6, and 12. Four of these six factors—1, 2, 3, and 6—are each a factor of 30. However, neither the number 4 nor the number 12 is a factor of 30. Thus, Statement (1) alone is insufficient to answer the question. Considering Statement (2) alone, if $N = 3$, 6, or 15, then N is a factor of 30. However, for all other multiples of 3 less than 30, N is not a factor of 30. Thus, Statement (2) alone is insufficient to answer the question. Considering the two statements together narrows down the possible values of N to three numbers: 3, 6, and 12. Of these three numbers, only two—3 and 6—are factors of 30. Thus, the two statements together are still insufficient to answer the question, and the correct answer is choice (E).

6. **The correct answer is (D).** Statement (1) alone suffices to answer the question. Given Statement (1), side AB must be the same length as side BC. (The arc lengths are proportionate to the side lengths.) Thus, all four sides of the rectangle are congruent, and the rectangle is a square. Statement (2) alone also suffices to answer the question. Assume hypothetically that $ABCD$ is a square. Given that $\overline{AB} = 2$, the circle's radius is $\sqrt{2}$, and the circle's circumference is $2\pi\sqrt{2}$.

Statement (2) provides that minor arc *AD* is exactly one-fourth that circumference, so all four sides of the rectangle must be congruent—that is, *ABCD* must be a square.

7. **The correct answer is (B).** One way to solve the problem is to first express $\frac{1}{8}$ as its decimal equivalent 0.125, then multiply: $0.125 \times 0.4 = 0.05$. Then, express 150% as the decimal number 1.5, and calculate the percentage: $1.5 \times 0.05 = 0.075$.

8. **The correct answer is (A).** What you need to know to answer the question is, essentially, how many cookies can be made per a given unit of butter or, conversely, how much butter per cookie is needed. Statement (1) essentially provides this information. It tells you that $\frac{5}{3}$ cup butter is needed for 30 cookies; from this information, you can easily calculate the number of cookies per $\frac{2}{3}$ cup—which answers the question. You could simply set up the following proportion, then solve for *B* (batch size in terms of number of cookies):

$$\frac{\frac{5}{3}}{30} = \frac{\frac{2}{3}}{B}$$

As you can plainly see without doing the math, you can solve for *B* and therefore answer the question. Just for the record, $B = 12$. (That's the answer to the question.) Statement (2) alone tells us nothing we did not already know; it merely says that tripling the desired output is achieved by tripling the quantity of each ingredient; that is, $3 \times \frac{2}{3} = 2$.

9. **The correct answer is (A).** Statement (1) alone suffices to answer the question. You can determine the sum of the numbers in a set by multiplying their average by the number of terms in the set. The information in Statement (1) allows you to calculate the sum: $9 \times 5 = 45$. Statement (2) alone provides no information about the values of the three middle terms and thus is insufficient alone to determine the sum.

10. **The correct answer is (C).** Given that Rug *R* has four times the area of Rug *S* and that their combined area is 20 square feet, Rug *R* must be $4' \times 4'$, and rug S must be $2' \times 2'$. Also, since the floor's area is 112 and its length is 8, the floor's width = 14, which in turn equals the sum of the following five lengths (let *x* = the distance between the two rugs, as well as from each rug to the nearest east or west edge):

$$x + 4 + x + 2 + x = 14$$

$$3x + 6 = 14$$

$$3x = 8$$

$$x = \frac{8}{3} \text{ or } 2\frac{2}{3}$$

$$x = 2 \text{ ft } 8 \text{ in}$$

11. **The correct answer is (B).** Multiplying together any combination of the factors of *p* will result in a product that is also a factor of *p*. The only number among the choices listed that is not a product of any of these combinations is 36.

12. **The correct answer is (B).** Multiply numerators together, and multiply denominators together. When combining, apply the rule $\sqrt{x}\sqrt{y} = \sqrt{xy}$ to the numerators. Then, factor and simplify:

$$\frac{\sqrt{10}}{\sqrt{2}} \times \frac{\sqrt{5}}{\sqrt{2}} = \frac{\sqrt{(10)(5)}}{\left(\sqrt{2}\right)^2} = \frac{\sqrt{50}}{2} = \frac{\sqrt{(25)(2)}}{2} = \frac{5\sqrt{2}}{2}$$

13. **The correct answer is (E).** If $b - a$ is a negative integer, then $a > b$, in which case $a - b$ must be a positive integer. (When you subtract one integer from another, the result is always an integer.)

14. **The correct answer is (C).** To find the length of DB, you subtract length CD from length CB. Thus, you need to find those two lengths first. $\triangle ACD$ is a right triangle with sides 8, 15, and 17 (one of the Pythagorean triplets). Thus, the length of CD is 8. CB is one of the legs of $\triangle ABC$. Determine the length of CB by applying the theorem:

$$15^2 + (CB)^2 = 20^2$$
$$225 + (CB)^2 = 400$$
$$(CB)^2 = 175$$
$$CB = \sqrt{(25)(7)}, \text{ or } 5\sqrt{7}$$

Accordingly, the length of $DB = 5\sqrt{7} - 8$.

15. **The correct answer is (C).** The set has six terms, so its median equals the average of the two middle terms (the third and fourth terms) when the terms are listed in ascending or descending order. Since the set contains two 3s, and since it contains at least one term less than 3 and at least two terms greater than 3, one of the 3s will be the third term of the set regardless of what n is. Therefore, the median will equal the average of 3 and one other number. In order to see what values this other number may take, you can reorder the terms as follows:

Case I: $\{n,2,3,3,9,10\}$ or $\{2,n,3,3,9,10\}$, if $n \le 3$

Case II: $\{2,3,3,n,9,10\}$, if $3 < n \le 9$

Case III: $\{2,3,3,9,10,n\}$, if $n > 9$

In either of the two options in Case I, the two middle terms are 3, so 3 is the median of the set. In Case II, the median will be 4 if n equals 5, it will be 5 if n equals 7, and it will be 6 if n equals 9. In Case III, the median equals 6, the average of 3 and 9. Therefore, the possible values that the median may take are 3, 4, 5, and 6.

16. **The correct answer is (C).** The segment connecting points $(-1,1)$ and $(3,5)$ has a slope of $m = \dfrac{5 - (1)}{3 - (-1)} = \dfrac{4}{4} = 1$. Hence, the slope of the segment's perpendicular bisector must be the negative reciprocal of 1, which is -1. Thus, the bisector's equation must be $y = -x + b$. Since the line bisects the segment, it must pass through its midpoint. Find this midpoint by averaging the coordinates of the endpoints: $\left(\dfrac{-1+3}{2}, \dfrac{1+5}{2}\right)$ or $(1,3)$. To determine the value of b, substitute $(1,3)$ for (x,y) in the line's equation: $3 = -1 + b$; $b = 4$. Hence, the line's equation is $y = -x + 4$.

17. **The correct answer is (B).** Plug in numbers for x until you see a pattern that allows you to get to the answer as quickly as possible. Positive multiples of 5 include 5, 10, 15, 20, and so on. To check for a pattern, start scratching out some equations, working your way up from the lowest possible value for x:

$$2(2) + 1 = 5$$
$$2(4.5) + 1 = 10$$
$$2(7) + 1 = 15$$
$$2(9.5) + 1 = 20$$
$$2(12) + 1 = 25$$

Notice that every other possible *x*-value is an integer, for which the sums increase from 5 to 15 to 25. The question asks us to account for all sums up to 100. So count the integers ending in the number 5 up to this limit: 5, 15, 25, 35, 45, ... You'll find that the total number of possibilities is 10.

18. **The correct answer is (E).** You can answer this question without resorting to formal algebra. The drainpipe empties the pool at half the rate that the inlet pipe fills the pool. So it makes sense that if both pipes are fully open, after 3 hours the pool will only be half full. (The inlet pipe fills the pool, but at the same time the drainpipe empties half the pool.) It follows that it takes 6 hours to fill the pool to capacity with both pipes fully open. You can also solve this problem algebraically. Letting *x* equal the number of hours, subtract the drainpipe's rate from the inlet pipe's rate (subtract because the drainpipe works against the inlet pipe), using the "work" formula:

$$\frac{x}{3} - \frac{x}{6} = 1$$

Multiply both sides by 6, then solve for *x*:

$$2x - x = 6$$
$$x = 6$$

19. **The correct answer is (C).** The question asks you to select the choice that most nearly describes sales totaling 9000 automobiles. Of the five choices, choice (C) comes closest to describing 9000 total automobiles sold. You need to calculate all five totals, as follows:

    (A) describes 8.5K + 1.9K = 10.4K sales.
    (B) describes 4.9K + 5.1K = 10.0K sales.
    (C) describes 1.7K + 4.9K + 2.2K = 8.8K sales.
    (D) describes 7.5K + 1.0K = 8.5K sales.
    (E) describes 8.5K + 4.9K = 13.4K sales.

20. **The correct answer is (C).** Answering this question requires two steps. First, the total number of product units sold to institutions = (3.6 + 8.5 + 1.9) + (1.7 + 4.9 + 2.2) = 22.8. The number of these units that were not standard versions = (3.6 + 1.9) + (1.7 + 2.2) = 9.4. Now go on to the second step. Ask yourself: "9.4 is approximately what percent of 22.8?" This question is the same as asking the percent equivalent of $\frac{9.4}{22.8}$. Here's a quick way to approximate the percentage: Round down both the numerator and denominator to give you the fraction $\frac{8}{20}$. It's now clear that you're looking for an answer choice that's around 40 percent $\left(\frac{8}{20} = \frac{40}{100}\right)$.

    Only choice (C) fills the bill.

21. **The correct answer is (C).** Statement (1) alone essentially provides one linear equation in two variables: $0.75M = 1.25S$. In this equation, you cannot solve for either *M* or *S*. An infinite number of value pairs are possible. Statement (2) alone presents a similar situation: one equation in two variables $(M - \$1000 = S)$. Together, however, the two statements provide a system of two distinct equations in two variables, which you can solve. Although there's no need to find the solution, one way to do so is to simply substitute $(M - 1000)$ for *S* in the equation derived from Statement (1), then solve for *M*:

$$0.75M = 1.25(M - 1000)$$
$$0.75M = 1.25M - 1250$$
$$-0.5M = -1250$$
$$M = 2500$$

22. **The correct answer is (B).** To solve this problem without resorting to listing possibilities, you need to apply the factorial formula as well as a bit of logic. If you think of each of the two empty chairs (C_1 and C_2) as a distinct object along with each of the 3 people (X, Y, and Z), the number of permutations is $5! = 5 \times 4 \times 3 \times 2 \times 1 = 120$. However, each permutation is coupled with another in which the two empty chairs are reversed—for example:

$$X, Y, Z, C_1, C_2$$
$$X, Y, Z, C_2, C_1$$

Since the question makes no distinction between the chairs, reduce the number of permutations by 50 percent, to 60.

23. **The correct answer is (D).** The answer choices provide a clue that you should first convert the percent to a fraction: $83\frac{1}{3}\% = \frac{5}{6}$. Next, express the question algebraically, then solve for x:

$$N = \frac{5}{6}x$$
$$6N = 5x$$
$$\frac{6N}{5} = x$$

24. **The correct answer is (D).** Let Q and D equal the number of quarters and dimes, respectively. The premise allows you to write the equation $\$0.25Q + \$0.10D = \$2.05$. As you can see, you'll need another equation in the two variables Q and D to find the value of either variable. Statement (2) obviously provides what you need: $Q + D = 10$. There's no need to actually answer the question by solving for Q. What about Statement (1) alone? It might strike you initially as insufficient to answer the question, since it does not allow you to write an equation. But a bit of trial-and-error reveals only one possibility. Let's start by assuming Mona has six quarters ($\$1.50$); that leaves fewer than 6 dimes (to be precise, 5.5 dimes) to account for the balance of her $\$2.05$. So she must have at least 7 quarters. If she has 7 quarters ($\$1.75$), then she has 3 dimes. (That's one possibility.) If she has 8 quarters, she must have 0.5 dime, which makes no sense, and any more quarters puts us over the $\$2.05$ limit. Thus, given Statement (1) only, there's only one possibility: Mona has 7 quarters and 3 dimes.

25. **The correct answer is (B).** This is a functions question, but let's look it as a question about a regular equation in terms of x and y. The equation becomes $y = \frac{x}{2} - 1$, where y is "a function of x", that is, y is a dependent variable whose value is determined by the value of x, the independent variable. You can think of it is as follows:

$$\text{Dependent Variable} = \frac{\text{Independent Variable}}{2} - 1$$

In order to find out the equation for $f(f(x))$, treat $f(x)$ as the independent variable, that is, replace x in the initial equation with $f(x)$ and $f(f(x))$ as the dependent variable:

$$f\left(f\left(x\right)\right)=f\left(\frac{x}{2}-1\right)$$

$$=\frac{\left(\frac{x}{2}-1\right)}{2}-1$$

$$=\frac{\frac{x-2}{2}}{2}-1$$

$$=\frac{x-2}{4}-1$$

$$=\frac{x-2-4}{4}$$

$$=\frac{x-6}{4}$$

$$=\frac{x}{4}-\frac{3}{2}$$

26. **The correct answer is (B).** Statement (1) provides absolutely no additional information. It merely reiterates that the rent is shared equally. Statement (2) alone suffices to answer the question; it establishes that each person pays $800 in rent and hence that the total rent = $800 × 4 = $3200.

27. **The correct answer is (A).** The number of degrees in the three interior angles of a triangle add up to 180. Thus, you can calculate the third, unmarked angle in the upper-left triangle: it must measure 110°. Since the vertical angles are congruent, the "top" angle in the bottom triangle must also measure 110°. Since 110° + 45° = 155°, there are just 25° left for x—the third angle of the triangle.

28. **The correct answer is (C).** All pairs of successive terms must have the same ratio, $\frac{-2}{x}=\frac{x}{-8}$.

    Cross-multiplying, $x^2 = 16$, and hence $x = \pm 4$. For +4, the sixth term would be $(-2)(-2)^5 = 64$, while for –4 it would be –64.

29. **The correct answer is (C).** Given one worker's rate and the aggregate rate of both workers, you can solve for the other worker's rate by applying the "work" formula:

    $$\frac{A}{8}+\frac{A}{S}=1$$

    In this equation, $A=6\frac{1}{2}$ minutes. You don't need to answer the question; in other words, you don't need to solve for S.

30. **The correct answer is (B).** Statement (1), restated, is $y=\frac{5}{4}x-\frac{3}{4}$. This line crosses the x-axis at $x=\frac{3}{5}$. So all positive values of y occur when $x>\frac{3}{5}$. Between $x=\frac{3}{5}$ and $x=3$, all values of x on the line are less than y. At $x = 3$, $y=\left(\frac{5}{4}\right)(3)-\frac{3}{4}=\frac{15}{4}-\frac{3}{4}=\frac{12}{4}=3$. So, for $y > 0$,

x is sometimes less than y, sometimes equal to y, and sometimes greater than y: Statement (1) is insufficient to determine if $x > y$. Eliminate choices (A) and (D). Statement (2), restated, is $y = \frac{5}{4}x + \frac{3}{4}$. This line crosses the x-axis at $x = -\frac{3}{5}$, so $y > 0$ on this line for all values of x such that $x > -\frac{3}{5}$. For all values of $x = -\frac{3}{5}$, each point on the line has a value of y that is greater than x. For example, at $x = 1$, the point on the line has a value of $y = \frac{5}{4}(1) + \frac{3}{4} = \frac{8}{4} = 2$. So, if Statement (2) is true, then for $y > 0$, the answer to the question "Is $x > y$?" is no. Statement (2) is sufficient. Eliminate choices (C) and (E); choice (B) is the correct answer.

31. **The correct answer is (B).** Finding the percent of a number is equivalent to dividing the number by 100. To divide 1.33 by 100, move the decimal point two places to the left, to arrive at the answer 0.0133.

32. **The correct answer is (B).** Statement (1) provides a factorable quadratic equation with two different roots: $(x - 1)(x - 3) = 0$; $x = 1, 3$. Since there are two roots (possible values of x), Statement (1) alone is insufficient to answer the question. Statement (2) also provides a factorable quadratic equation, but the two roots are the same: $(x - 1)(x - 1) = 0$; $x = 1$. Since the only possible value of x is 1, Statement (2) alone suffices to answer the question.

33. **The correct answer is (C).** Statement (1) alone is insufficient because it provides no information about $\overline{CD}$. Statement (2) alone is insufficient because it provides no information about $\overline{AB}$. Together, however, Statements (1) and (2) suffice to answer the question. Given Statement (1), you can determine the circle's circumference, which is twice the length of two arcs created by a diameter chord. From the circumference you can determine the circle's diameter and compare it to the length of $\overline{CD}$, which Statement (2) indicates is 5. (Although you don't need to do the calculations or actually answer the question, the circle's circumference is twice the length of arc ACB, or 10π, and its diameter is 10. Given that the length of $\overline{CD} = 5$, the length of $\overline{AB} >$ the length of $\overline{CD}$, and the answer to the question is yes.)

34. **The correct answer is (E).** Since x equals the rate (speed) of the freight train, you can express the rate of the passenger train as $x + 45$. Substitute these values for time and rate into the formula for each train:

    Formula: rate × time = distance

    Passenger: $(x + 45)(3) = 3x + 135$

    Freight: $(x)(3) = 3x$

The combined distance that the two trains covered is $3x + (3x + 135) = 6x + 135$.

35. **The correct answer is (D).** Statement (1) focuses on the weighted-average concept. Given a sum as well as the relative weight of all members in the set (all five grocery items), you can determine each member (the price of each item). Statement (1) provides all the information you need. Statement (2) alone suffices to answer the question: $\$6.05 - (4)(\$1.10) =$ the price of the most expensive item. (For the record, given either statement alone, the price of the most expensive item is \$1.65.)

36. **The correct answer is (A).** The edge $\left(s + \frac{3}{2}\right)$ only accommodates $(s + 1)$ 1-inch cubes along its edge. The additional half-inch is unused space. Thus, the number of 1-inch cubes that can be packed into the box is the product of the three edges: $(s)(s + 1)(s - 1) = s(s^2 - 1) = s^3 - s$.

37. The correct answer is (D). There are 12 cards in each deck, so the number of possible combinations of two cards is 12×12; in other words, there are 144 possible outcomes for the two cards selected. Next, consider the cases of the two cards adding up to 3 and adding up to 7 separately. There are two ways of getting a sum of 3: $1 + 2$ or $2 + 1$. Thus, the probability that the two cards will add up to 3 is $\frac{2}{144}$. There are six ways of getting a sum of 7: $1 + 6, 2 + 5, 3 + 4, 4 + 3, 5 + 2,$ or $6 + 1$. Thus, the probability that the two cards will add up to 7 is $\frac{6}{144}$.

These two events are mutually exclusive, so the probability of getting either a sum of 3 or a sum of 7 is the sum of the two probabilities:

$$\frac{2}{144} + \frac{6}{144} = \frac{8}{144} = \frac{1}{18}$$

VERBAL SECTION

1. A	10. D	19. E	28. E	37. E
2. B	11. C	20. E	29. D	38. D
3. C	12. C	21. D	30. B	39. E
4. E	13. C	22. B	31. A	40. D
5. E	14. A	23. D	32. B	41. D
6. C	15. C	24. B	33. D	
7. A	16. D	25. A	34. A	
8. D	17. A	26. C	35. A	
9. B	18. B	27. A	36. B	

1. **The correct answer is (A).** The original sentence correctly uses both commas to set off a non-restrictive phrase and dashes to interrupt the flow of words for effect. It also correctly uses *are* to agree with the compound subject joined by *and*.

2. **The correct answer is (B).** Correctness here hinges on diction. In this sentence, *rendered* must take a helping verb; otherwise, its meaning could relate to melting down or rendering fat from something. Choice (B) is the only choice that creates a complete sentence with the meaning of "took the form of."

3. **The correct answer is (C).** The argument fails to explicitly provide that employees who are at least ten years out of college change employers less frequently on average than other employees. This premise is essential to the argument's conclusion, and choice (C) supplies this additional premise.

4. **The correct answer is (E).** The original sentence incorrectly uses a superlative adjective: when comparing two things, use the comparative form. Choice (E) is correct because it uses the comparative form *better* instead of the superlative form *best*.

5. **The correct answer is (E).** The argument relies on the unstated assumption that no factor other than Gary's driving speed might be responsible for the recent decrease in his fuel mileage; in other words, no other circumstances that might affect fuel mileage have changed recently. One effective way to weaken the argument would be to refute this assumption. Choice (E) accomplishes this by providing a convincing alternative explanation for the decrease.

6. **The correct answer is (C).** Of the five choices, choice (C) is the best because it substantiates an assumption needed for the argument's conclusion to be reasonable. Unless the winning candidate actually wages an expensive television ad campaign, it makes no sense to conclude that this type of campaign contributed to the candidate's victory.

7. **The correct answer is (A).** The passage indicates that prior to the discovery of extremophiles the thermal threshold was set at 60 degrees centigrade "because it was thought that the molecular integrity of vital cellular components could not be maintained beyond such temperatures." It can be inferred that if extremophiles can live and thrive past 60 degrees centigrade, they can maintain molecular integrity past the previous thermal threshold. Hence, choice (A) is the correct answer. [The passage does not mention extremophiles existing in moderate environments, so choice (B) cannot be inferred from the passage.]

8. **The correct answer is (D).** Based on the context, it is clear that the author considers *thermal threshold* to mean "the temperature at which biological organisms begin to break down due to heat." Choice (D) best expresses this meaning.

9. **The correct answer is (B).** In the first sentence, the author describes the modification made to an existing system for classifying biological life forms. Then, in the rest of the passage, the author provides the reason for the modification.

10. **The correct answer is (D).** The original sentence uses *between* incorrectly. Choice (D) is the best answer not only because it correctly replaces *between* with *among*, but also because it is the most succinct and direct of all the answers. Furthermore, it does not change the meaning of the original sentence, as Choice (E) does.

11. **The correct answer is (C).** The original sentence contains two problems: repetition of forms of *call* (*calls* and *called*) and misuse of *that*. Choice (C) eliminates both forms of *call* and correctly replaces *that* with *which*.

12. **The correct answer is (C).** In the original sentence, the two-word phrase *some times* is improper in context and should be replaced with a word such as *occasionally* or *sometimes*. Also, the original sentence employs the passive voice—the subject (airplanes departing) is acted upon by (prevented by) its object (severe weather). The result is awkward and confusing. Choice (C) corrects both problems, replacing *some times* with *sometimes* and using the active voice instead.

13. **The correct answer is (C).** The passage's first two sentences point out that large pharmaceutical companies are motivated primarily by profit, even to the extent that they trade off millions of cholera- and malaria-related deaths every year to ensure their own profitability. In light of these premises, the next premise (the passage's final sentence) leads strongly to the conclusion that these companies are willing to make a similar trade-off when it comes to saving victims of germ warfare.

14. **The correct answer is (A).** The argument depends on the assumption that a great white shark would not survive at Bayside Aquarium long enough to have any significant impact on public awareness. Choice (A) provides evidence that helps refute this assumption. (Common sense tells us that a captive animal is more likely to survive in an environment similar to its natural habitat than in a different environment.)

15. **The correct answer is (C).** The sentence to which this question refers parallels the preceding sentence, in which the author indicates the Encyclopedists' concern for both the theoretical and the practical. The author appears to provide one example of each—the subject of the human soul is theoretical while the subject of stocking production is practical.

16. **The correct answer is (D).** Notice that in the preceding sentence the author uses the phrase "dared to publicly assert the intellectual freedom . . . ." This phrase suggests a challenge to political authority. Although the inference in choice (D) is not self-evident, choice (D) is nevertheless a more reasonable explanation than any of the other four choices for the author's use of the word "understandably."

17. **The correct answer is (A).** Although the French government refused to license its printing, the work was nevertheless printed and sold extensively throughout Europe. The clear implication is that its printing (as well as distribution) was illegal.

18. **The correct answer is (B).** The passage posits the following simple argument: If both of two conditions (exposure to the nuclear testing at an age less than 10 years) are true, then a particular result (death before age 50) is certain. Given that this argument is true, any person alive today who resided in the town during the testing (and therefore was exposed to the resulting radiation) must have been at least 10 years old at the time. Here's the essence of the reasoning:

Premise: If both A and B, then C.

Premise: Not C.

Conclusion: Not both A and B.

19. **The correct answer is (E).** The argument asserts essentially that it was the marketing campaign, and not some other factor, that was responsible for the high number of sales of the new version of ActiveWeb compared to competing products. One way to support the argument is to rule out one or more other factors that might have been responsible for this phenomenon instead. By implication, choice (E) provides just this sort of evidence. While *favorable* third-party reviews of ActiveWeb would serve to weaken the claim that the marketing campaign was the cause of the sales results, *unfavorable* reviews would accomplish just the opposite.

20. **The correct answer is (E).** One problem with the original sentence is that it makes an illogical comparison, suggesting that a pluralistic democracy is not a system of government, when in fact it is. The solution is to add *other* to the end of the underlined phrase. A second problem with the original sentence is that *in greater degree* is not idiomatic; *to a greater degree* would be the appropriate idiom here. Choice (E) corrects the first error and avoids the second one by replacing *in greater degree* with the concise *more*.

21. **The correct answer is (D).** The words *examination, diagnosing*, and *treatment* are not all grammatically parallel. One solution is to replace *diagnosing* with *diagnosis*. Also, the first clause seems to refer nonsensically to *patients* because of this word's proximity to the clause. The solution is to reconstruct the sentence so that the clause is closer to *physicians* than to *patients*. Choice (D) is the only alternative that corrects both problems without creating any new ones.

22. **The correct answer is (B).** The argument assumes that the proposed course of action—reducing demand for aoli tree bark—is necessary to prevent total depletion of aoli tree bark within fifty years. However, the argument ignores the possibility of increasing supply as an alternative means of achieving this goal. Choice (B) provides this alternative.

23. **The correct answer is (D).** Based on the last sentence of the passage, we can conclude that juvenile criminals associate primarily with other juvenile criminals, and that adult criminals constitute the same group of people who were juvenile criminals. For choice (D) to *not* be readily inferable would require that most adult criminals associate primarily with law-abiding peers as teenagers. But this contradicts what we know about adult criminals, based on the passage information. Thus, choice (D) is strongly inferable.

24. **The correct answer is (B).** In the original version, *both limit of the number* and *limit . . . of the boundaries* improperly use *of*. (In both cases, *limit on* is idiomatic.) Also, the plural *numbers* should be replaced with *number*. Choice (B) corrects both problems.

25. **The correct answer is (A).** The original version is the best one. Choice (B) is wordy and awkward; choice (C) alters the sentence's meaning by suggesting not using waterfront land at all; choice (D) is awkward; and choice (E) contains *utilizations*, which is not a word.

26. **The correct answer is (C).** The passage's author indicates that Elvery was influenced by fifteenth-century Italian art, but the author neither states nor suggests that Elvery was influenced by her French contemporaries. Choice (D) is not explicitly supported in the passage. However, in the third paragraph the author indicates that Keating was a student of Orpen. The fact that Orpen participated in the French avant-garde experiment as a teacher lends strong support to the assertion that Keating was also influenced by the avant-garde movement.

27. **The correct answer is (A).** Although the passage does not indicate the subject matter of the paintings of realists Henry and Keating, the author discusses Lavery and Orpen as depicting in their paintings somewhat romanticized scenes of politically charged subject matter. Yeats'

focus on everyday Irish life is set against, yet complements (i.e., provides a "counterpoint to"), the depictions by Lavery and Orpen.

28. **The correct answer is (E).** The passage's main concern, expressed in the first sentence, is with the transition in Ireland from art that was influenced primarily by Britain's lyrical tradition to art that reflected Ireland's distinct national character. Of the five answer choices, choice (E) is most consistent with this overall concern.

29. **The correct answer is (D).** As a whole, the passage involves the increasing role that Irish tradition and nationalism played in the subject matter of Irish painting, beginning at the turn of the twentieth century. The first sentence strongly suggests that the article would continue in this vein.

30. **The correct answer is (B).** Assuming the number of viable competitors has increased during the last two years, the likely result would be to draw circulation away from already viable newspapers, including the most profitable one. Given that profitability depends primarily on advertising revenues and therefore on circulation, choice (B) actually exacerbates the discrepancy between the two statements.

31. **The correct answer is (A).** The argument is essentially that the proposed law makes no sense because knitting needles are dangerous as well. The argument relies explicitly on an analogy between hypodermic and knitting needles. Thus, the two must be similar in all respects relevant to the argument. Otherwise, the argument is unconvincing. Choice (A) affirms that knitting needles are in fact dangerous, thereby affirming the analogy between the two types of needles.

32. **The correct answer is (B).** The underlined part leaves it unclear whether the Milky Way is the name of our galaxy or the name for the center of our galaxy. Choice (B) reconstructs the underlined part to clear up the ambiguity.

33. **The correct answer is (D).** In the original version, the shift in time frame from past (*were*) to present (*have expected*) is confusing and illogical. Also, the syntax obscures the intended meaning; specifically, one could interpret *neither result of the two experiments* to mean that *each* of the two experiments had two results; but this is clearly not the intended meaning. Finally, the plural verb *were* does not agree in number with its singular subject *neither result*. Choice (D) remedies all of these problems.

34. **The correct answer is (A).** The subjunctive mood is appropriate for this sentence since it ostensibly involves a contrary-to-fact situation. Either of two phrases—*If empty space were* or *Were empty space*—would be perfectly acceptable here. Choice (A) employs the latter phrase. Choices (B) and (C) incorrectly use the present tense *is*, which is inappropriate for expressing the subjunctive mood. Choice (B) is also wordy. Choice (D) is not idiomatic. (*That* should be replaced with *If*.) Choice (E) incorrectly uses the past tense *was*.

35. **The correct answer is (A).** Unless the primary motivation for joining a gym is a concern for health and fitness, the fact that club memberships are in decline is insufficient to show that people are becoming less concerned about their health and fitness. The argument fails to rule out other possibilities as the major reasons people use health clubs—for example, to socialize—as well as other possible reasons people might discontinue using health clubs—for example, because membership fees have become less affordable.

36. **The correct answer is (B).** The high-altitude plateaus are called *puna* or *altiplano*. The passage states explicitly that the soil fertility of the northern altiplano is generally good.

37. **The correct answer is (E).** The passage provides explicitly that, unlike the Northern Andes, the eastern slopes of the Central Andes have a dry season.

38. **The correct answer is (D).** This question focuses on the information in the second paragraph. The author first notes that vegetation patterns correspond generally with climate (as determined primarily by latitude and altitude). Accordingly, altitude and latitude affect vegetation patterns throughout the region. Then, in the final sentence the author points out that, in spite of the general correspondence between climate and vegetation, local patterns may not correspond so precisely with climate, due to a number of local factors. Choice (D) accurately reflects the information in the second paragraph.

39. **The correct answer is (E).** The only evidence the spokesperson has provided that the coasters still in operation are safe is that no fatalities occurred last year involving any one of these coasters. To better assess their safety, it would be helpful to determine the incidence of not just fatal accidents but also non-fatal accidents involving these coasters. Although the investigations described in choices (B), (C), and (D) might shed some additional light on the safety of these coasters, the investigation described in choice (E) relates most directly to the specific coasters that the spokesperson claims to be safe.

40. **The correct answer is (D).** The original version misplaces the modifying phrase *when its people obey and revere the law*. As it stands, the pronoun *its* appears to refer to *Lincoln*; but the intended reference is to *democracy*. Choice (D) clarifies the pronoun reference by positioning *its* after its antecedent *democracy*.

41. **The correct answer is (D).** SubStop complied with the state's cost-of-living raise requirements. (The question stem stipulates that all information in the passage is true.) Therefore, the only explanation for giving either type of raise (discretionary or cost-of-living) to 2 employees last year is that they had worked for SubStop continuously for six months.

ANSWER SHEET PRACTICE TEST 6

ANALYTICAL WRITING ASSESSMENT

_____
_____
_____
_____
_____
_____
_____
_____
_____
_____
_____
_____
_____
_____
_____
_____
_____
_____
_____
_____
_____
_____
_____
_____
_____
_____
_____
_____

answer sheet

answer sheet

INTEGRATED REASONING

1.1 Ⓐ Ⓑ Ⓒ Ⓓ Ⓔ Ⓕ   4.1 Ⓐ Ⓑ Ⓒ Ⓓ Ⓔ Ⓕ   7.1 Ⓐ Ⓑ   10.1 Ⓐ Ⓑ Ⓒ Ⓓ
1.2 Ⓐ Ⓑ Ⓒ Ⓓ Ⓔ Ⓕ   4.2 Ⓐ Ⓑ Ⓒ Ⓓ Ⓔ Ⓕ   7.2 Ⓐ Ⓑ   10.2 Ⓐ Ⓑ Ⓒ
2.1 Ⓐ Ⓑ   5.1 Ⓐ Ⓑ Ⓒ Ⓓ Ⓔ   7.3 Ⓐ Ⓑ   11.1 Ⓐ Ⓑ Ⓒ
2.2 Ⓐ Ⓑ   5.2 Ⓐ Ⓑ Ⓒ Ⓓ Ⓔ   8. Ⓐ Ⓑ Ⓒ Ⓓ Ⓔ   11.2 Ⓐ Ⓑ Ⓒ
2.3 Ⓐ Ⓑ   6.1 Ⓐ Ⓑ   9. Ⓐ Ⓑ Ⓒ Ⓓ Ⓔ   12.1 Ⓐ Ⓑ Ⓒ
3.1 Ⓐ Ⓑ Ⓒ Ⓓ Ⓔ   6.2 Ⓐ Ⓑ   12.2 Ⓐ Ⓑ Ⓒ Ⓓ
3.2 Ⓐ Ⓑ Ⓒ Ⓓ Ⓔ   6.3 Ⓐ Ⓑ

QUANTITATIVE SECTION

1. Ⓐ Ⓑ Ⓒ Ⓓ Ⓔ   9. Ⓐ Ⓑ Ⓒ Ⓓ Ⓔ   17. Ⓐ Ⓑ Ⓒ Ⓓ Ⓔ   25. Ⓐ Ⓑ Ⓒ Ⓓ Ⓔ   33. Ⓐ Ⓑ Ⓒ Ⓓ Ⓔ
2. Ⓐ Ⓑ Ⓒ Ⓓ Ⓔ   10. Ⓐ Ⓑ Ⓒ Ⓓ Ⓔ   18. Ⓐ Ⓑ Ⓒ Ⓓ Ⓔ   26. Ⓐ Ⓑ Ⓒ Ⓓ Ⓔ   34. Ⓐ Ⓑ Ⓒ Ⓓ Ⓔ
3. Ⓐ Ⓑ Ⓒ Ⓓ Ⓔ   11. Ⓐ Ⓑ Ⓒ Ⓓ Ⓔ   19. Ⓐ Ⓑ Ⓒ Ⓓ Ⓔ   27. Ⓐ Ⓑ Ⓒ Ⓓ Ⓔ   35. Ⓐ Ⓑ Ⓒ Ⓓ Ⓔ
4. Ⓐ Ⓑ Ⓒ Ⓓ Ⓔ   12. Ⓐ Ⓑ Ⓒ Ⓓ Ⓔ   20. Ⓐ Ⓑ Ⓒ Ⓓ Ⓔ   28. Ⓐ Ⓑ Ⓒ Ⓓ Ⓔ   36. Ⓐ Ⓑ Ⓒ Ⓓ Ⓔ
5. Ⓐ Ⓑ Ⓒ Ⓓ Ⓔ   13. Ⓐ Ⓑ Ⓒ Ⓓ Ⓔ   21. Ⓐ Ⓑ Ⓒ Ⓓ Ⓔ   29. Ⓐ Ⓑ Ⓒ Ⓓ Ⓔ   37. Ⓐ Ⓑ Ⓒ Ⓓ Ⓔ
6. Ⓐ Ⓑ Ⓒ Ⓓ Ⓔ   14. Ⓐ Ⓑ Ⓒ Ⓓ Ⓔ   22. Ⓐ Ⓑ Ⓒ Ⓓ Ⓔ   30. Ⓐ Ⓑ Ⓒ Ⓓ Ⓔ
7. Ⓐ Ⓑ Ⓒ Ⓓ Ⓔ   15. Ⓐ Ⓑ Ⓒ Ⓓ Ⓔ   23. Ⓐ Ⓑ Ⓒ Ⓓ Ⓔ   31. Ⓐ Ⓑ Ⓒ Ⓓ Ⓔ
8. Ⓐ Ⓑ Ⓒ Ⓓ Ⓔ   16. Ⓐ Ⓑ Ⓒ Ⓓ Ⓔ   24. Ⓐ Ⓑ Ⓒ Ⓓ Ⓔ   32. Ⓐ Ⓑ Ⓒ Ⓓ Ⓔ

VERBAL SECTION

1. Ⓐ Ⓑ Ⓒ Ⓓ Ⓔ   9. Ⓐ Ⓑ Ⓒ Ⓓ Ⓔ   17. Ⓐ Ⓑ Ⓒ Ⓓ Ⓔ   25. Ⓐ Ⓑ Ⓒ Ⓓ Ⓔ   33. Ⓐ Ⓑ Ⓒ Ⓓ Ⓔ
2. Ⓐ Ⓑ Ⓒ Ⓓ Ⓔ   10. Ⓐ Ⓑ Ⓒ Ⓓ Ⓔ   18. Ⓐ Ⓑ Ⓒ Ⓓ Ⓔ   26. Ⓐ Ⓑ Ⓒ Ⓓ Ⓔ   34. Ⓐ Ⓑ Ⓒ Ⓓ Ⓔ
3. Ⓐ Ⓑ Ⓒ Ⓓ Ⓔ   11. Ⓐ Ⓑ Ⓒ Ⓓ Ⓔ   19. Ⓐ Ⓑ Ⓒ Ⓓ Ⓔ   27. Ⓐ Ⓑ Ⓒ Ⓓ Ⓔ   35. Ⓐ Ⓑ Ⓒ Ⓓ Ⓔ
4. Ⓐ Ⓑ Ⓒ Ⓓ Ⓔ   12. Ⓐ Ⓑ Ⓒ Ⓓ Ⓔ   20. Ⓐ Ⓑ Ⓒ Ⓓ Ⓔ   28. Ⓐ Ⓑ Ⓒ Ⓓ Ⓔ   36. Ⓐ Ⓑ Ⓒ Ⓓ Ⓔ
5. Ⓐ Ⓑ Ⓒ Ⓓ Ⓔ   13. Ⓐ Ⓑ Ⓒ Ⓓ Ⓔ   21. Ⓐ Ⓑ Ⓒ Ⓓ Ⓔ   29. Ⓐ Ⓑ Ⓒ Ⓓ Ⓔ   37. Ⓐ Ⓑ Ⓒ Ⓓ Ⓔ
6. Ⓐ Ⓑ Ⓒ Ⓓ Ⓔ   14. Ⓐ Ⓑ Ⓒ Ⓓ Ⓔ   22. Ⓐ Ⓑ Ⓒ Ⓓ Ⓔ   30. Ⓐ Ⓑ Ⓒ Ⓓ Ⓔ   38. Ⓐ Ⓑ Ⓒ Ⓓ Ⓔ
7. Ⓐ Ⓑ Ⓒ Ⓓ Ⓔ   15. Ⓐ Ⓑ Ⓒ Ⓓ Ⓔ   23. Ⓐ Ⓑ Ⓒ Ⓓ Ⓔ   31. Ⓐ Ⓑ Ⓒ Ⓓ Ⓔ   39. Ⓐ Ⓑ Ⓒ Ⓓ Ⓔ
8. Ⓐ Ⓑ Ⓒ Ⓓ Ⓔ   16. Ⓐ Ⓑ Ⓒ Ⓓ Ⓔ   24. Ⓐ Ⓑ Ⓒ Ⓓ Ⓔ   32. Ⓐ Ⓑ Ⓒ Ⓓ Ⓔ   40. Ⓐ Ⓑ Ⓒ Ⓓ Ⓔ
   41. Ⓐ Ⓑ Ⓒ Ⓓ Ⓔ

answer sheet

Practice Test 6

ANALYTICAL WRITING ASSIGNMENT

Analysis of an Argument

1 Question • 30 Minutes

Directions: Using a word processor, compose an essay for the following argument and directive. Do not use any spell-checking or grammar-checking functions.

The following appeared in a memorandum from the vice president of a music recording company to the company's publicity department:

> "The rock band Excess has not had a hit record in more than a decade and is no longer in demand for concerts at major venues. Excess is planning to spend the next year writing and recording new songs. Instead, however, the band should replace its current manager with Jason Stribling, who manages some of today's most popular touring bands. Once Excess re-establishes its popularity as a live concert band, music fans will begin to rediscover the band, and sales of Excess recordings will increase sharply."

Discuss how well reasoned you find this argument. In your discussion be sure to analyze the line of reasoning and the use of evidence in the argument. For example, you may need to consider what questionable assumptions underlie the thinking and what alternative explanations or counterexamples might weaken the conclusion. You can also discuss what sort of evidence would strengthen or refute the argument, what changes in the argument would make it more logically sound, and what, if anything, would help you better evaluate its conclusion.

INTEGRATED REASONING

12 Questions • 30 Minutes

1. A cube is inscribed in a sphere, whose surface area equals its volume. The surface area of a sphere is given by $S_s = 4\pi r^2$, and the volume of the sphere is given by $V_s = \frac{4}{3}\pi r^3$, where r is the radius of the sphere.

   In the table, select a value for the surface area of the cube and a value for the volume of the cube, so that the two values are consistent with the given information. Make only two selections, one in each column.

	1.1 Surface area	1.2 Volume	
(A)	○	○	24
(B)	○	○	36
(C)	○	○	$24\sqrt{3}$
(D)	○	○	$36\sqrt{3}$
(E)	○	○	72
(F)	○	○	36π

2. The table shows the permits issued by building size and borough in New York City in 2010 and 2011. Each percentage in the table shows the percentage of the corresponding Borough's permits that were issued for that particular building size in each year. The Total Buildings columns show the total number of permits issued for each Borough for each year.

Sort By: [Select ▼]

Year/Borough	1-Family		2-Family		3- or 4-Family		5 or More-Family		Total Buildings	
	2010	2011	2010	2011	2010	2011	2010	2011	2010	2011
Bronx	9.2%	1.5%	38.5%	35.3%	23.1%	19.1%	29.2%	44.1%	65	68
Brooklyn	3.6%	0.0%	31.4%	44.3%	27.9%	30.5%	37.1%	25.3%	140	174
Manhattan	0.0%	3.6%	18.2%	0.0%	9.1%	3.6%	72.7%	92.9%	11	28
Queens	12.4%	21.5%	67.2%	57.0%	11.2%	11.9%	9.2%	9.6%	509	386
Staten Island	71.9%	52.5%	27.2%	47.2%	0.6%	0.0%	0.3%	0.3%	349	341

For each of the following statements, select *Yes* if the statement is true based on the information in the table. Otherwise, select *No*.

	(A) Yes	(B) No	
2.1	○	○	Permits issued for 5 or More-Family buildings in 2011 accounted for 13.8% of all permits issued in 2011.
2.2	○	○	More permits were issued in 2011 for 5 or More-Family buildings in Queens than were issued in 2011 for 2-Family buildings in Brooklyn.
2.3	○	○	The decrease between 2010 and 2011 in the number of permits issued for 2-Family buildings in Queens was greater than the decrease between 2010 and 2011 in number of permits issued for 1-Family buildings on Staten Island.

(On the computer test, this will be the end of the question prompt and statements. For this paper test and your convenience, we are providing the various other ways you may sort the data.)

Sort By: | 1-Family, 2010 ▼ |

Year/Borough	1-Family		2-Family		3- or 4-Family		5 or More-Family		Total Buildings	
	2010	2011	2010	2011	2010	2011	2010	2011	2010	2011
Manhattan	0.0%	3.6%	18.2%	0.0%	9.1%	3.6%	72.7%	92.9%	11	28
Brooklyn	3.6%	0.0%	31.4%	44.3%	27.9%	30.5%	37.1%	25.3%	140	174
Bronx	9.2%	1.5%	38.5%	35.3%	23.1%	19.1%	29.2%	44.1%	65	68
Queens	12.4%	21.5%	67.2%	57.0%	11.2%	11.9%	9.2%	9.6%	509	386
Staten Island	71.9%	52.5%	27.2%	47.2%	0.6%	0.0%	0.3%	0.3%	349	341

Sort By: | 1-Family, 2011 ▼ |

Year/Borough	1-Family		2-Family		3- or 4-Family		5 or More-Family		Total Buildings	
	2010	2011	2010	2011	2010	2011	2010	2011	2010	2011
Brooklyn	3.6%	0.0%	31.4%	44.3%	27.9%	30.5%	37.1%	25.3%	140	174
Bronx	9.2%	1.5%	38.5%	35.3%	23.1%	19.1%	29.2%	44.1%	65	68
Manhattan	0.0%	3.6%	18.2%	0.0%	9.1%	3.6%	72.7%	92.9%	11	28
Queens	12.4%	21.5%	67.2%	57.0%	11.2%	11.9%	9.2%	9.6%	509	386
Staten Island	71.9%	52.5%	27.2%	47.2%	0.6%	0.0%	0.3%	0.3%	349	341

Sort By: | 2-Family, 2010 ▼ |

Year/Borough	1-Family		2-Family		3- or 4-Family		5 or More-Family		Total Buildings	
	2010	2011	2010	2011	2010	2011	2010	2011	2010	2011
Manhattan	0.0%	3.6%	18.2%	0.0%	9.1%	3.6%	72.7%	92.9%	11	28
Staten Island	71.9%	52.5%	27.2%	47.2%	0.6%	0.0%	0.3%	0.3%	349	341
Brooklyn	3.6%	0.0%	31.4%	44.3%	27.9%	30.5%	37.1%	25.3%	140	174
Bronx	9.2%	1.5%	38.5%	35.3%	23.1%	19.1%	29.2%	44.1%	65	68
Queens	12.4%	21.5%	67.2%	57.0%	11.2%	11.9%	9.2%	9.6%	509	386

Sort By: | 2-Family, 2011 ▼ |

Year/Borough	1-Family		2-Family		3- or 4-Family		5 or More-Family		Total Buildings	
	2010	2011	2010	2011	2010	2011	2010	2011	2010	2011
Manhattan	0.0%	3.6%	18.2%	0.0%	9.1%	3.6%	72.7%	92.9%	11	28
Bronx	9.2%	1.5%	38.5%	35.3%	23.1%	19.1%	29.2%	44.1%	65	68
Brooklyn	3.6%	0.0%	31.4%	44.3%	27.9%	30.5%	37.1%	25.3%	140	174
Staten Island	71.9%	52.5%	27.2%	47.2%	0.6%	0.0%	0.3%	0.3%	349	341
Queens	12.4%	21.5%	67.2%	57.0%	11.2%	11.9%	9.2%	9.6%	509	386

Sort By: | 3- or 4-Family, 2010 ▼ |

Year/Borough	1-Family		2-Family		3- or 4-Family		5 or More-Family		Total Buildings	
	2010	2011	2010	2011	2010	2011	2010	2011	2010	2011
Staten Island	71.9%	52.5%	27.2%	47.2%	0.6%	0.0%	0.3%	0.3%	349	341
Manhattan	0.0%	3.6%	18.2%	0.0%	9.1%	3.6%	72.7%	92.9%	11	28
Queens	12.4%	21.5%	67.2%	57.0%	11.2%	11.9%	9.2%	9.6%	509	386
Bronx	9.2%	1.5%	38.5%	35.3%	23.1%	19.1%	29.2%	44.1%	65	68
Brooklyn	3.6%	0.0%	31.4%	44.3%	27.9%	30.5%	37.1%	25.3%	140	174

Sort By: | 3- or 4-Family, 2011 ▼ |

Year/Borough	1-Family		2-Family		3- or 4-Family		5 or More-Family		Total Buildings	
	2010	2011	2010	2011	2010	2011	2010	2011	2010	2011
Staten Island	71.9%	52.5%	27.2%	47.2%	0.6%	0.0%	0.3%	0.3%	349	341
Manhattan	0.0%	3.6%	18.2%	0.0%	9.1%	3.6%	72.7%	92.9%	11	28
Queens	12.4%	21.5%	67.2%	57.0%	11.2%	11.9%	9.2%	9.6%	509	386
Bronx	9.2%	1.5%	38.5%	35.3%	23.1%	19.1%	29.2%	44.1%	65	68
Brooklyn	3.6%	0.0%	31.4%	44.3%	27.9%	30.5%	37.1%	25.3%	140	174

Sort By: | 5 or More-Family, 2010 ▼ |

Year/Borough	1-Family		2-Family		3- or 4-Family		5 or More-Family		Total Buildings	
	2010	2011	2010	2011	2010	2011	2010	2011	2010	2011
Staten Island	71.9%	52.5%	27.2%	47.2%	0.6%	0.0%	0.3%	0.3%	349	341
Queens	12.4%	21.5%	67.2%	57.0%	11.2%	11.9%	9.2%	9.6%	509	386
Bronx	9.2%	1.5%	38.5%	35.3%	23.1%	19.1%	29.2%	44.1%	65	68
Brooklyn	3.6%	0.0%	31.4%	44.3%	27.9%	30.5%	37.1%	25.3%	140	174
Manhattan	0.0%	3.6%	18.2%	0.0%	9.1%	3.6%	72.7%	92.9%	11	28

Sort By: | 5 or More-Family, 2011 ▼ |

Year/Borough	1-Family		2-Family		3- or 4-Family		5 or More-Family		Total Buildings	
	2010	2011	2010	2011	2010	2011	2010	2011	2010	2011
Staten Island	71.9%	52.5%	27.2%	47.2%	0.6%	0.0%	0.3%	0.3%	349	341
Queens	12.4%	21.5%	67.2%	57.0%	11.2%	11.9%	9.2%	9.6%	509	386
Bronx	3.6%	0.0%	31.4%	44.3%	27.9%	30.5%	37.1%	25.3%	140	174
Brooklyn	9.2%	1.5%	38.5%	35.3%	23.1%	19.1%	29.2%	44.1%	65	68
Manhattan	0.0%	3.6%	18.2%	0.0%	9.1%	3.6%	72.7%	92.9%	11	28

Sort By: | Total Buildings, 2010 ▼ |

Year/Borough	1-Family		2-Family		3- or 4-Family		5 or More-Family		Total Buildings	
	2010	2011	2010	2011	2010	2011	2010	2011	2010	2011
Manhattan	0.0%	3.6%	18.2%	0.0%	9.1%	3.6%	72.7%	92.9%	11	28
Bronx	9.2%	1.5%	38.5%	35.3%	23.1%	19.1%	29.2%	44.1%	65	68
Brooklyn	3.6%	0.0%	31.4%	44.3%	27.9%	30.5%	37.1%	25.3%	140	174
Staten Island	71.9%	52.5%	27.2%	47.2%	0.6%	0.0%	0.3%	0.3%	349	341
Queens	12.4%	21.5%	67.2%	57.0%	11.2%	11.9%	9.2%	9.6%	509	386

Sort By: | Total Buildings, 2011 ▼ |

Year/Borough	1-Family		2-Family		3- or 4-Family		5 or More-Family		Total Buildings	
	2010	2011	2010	2011	2010	2011	2010	2011	2010	2011
Manhattan	0.0%	3.6%	18.2%	0.0%	9.1%	3.6%	72.7%	92.9%	11	28
Bronx	9.2%	1.5%	38.5%	35.3%	23.1%	19.1%	29.2%	44.1%	65	68
Brooklyn	3.6%	0.0%	31.4%	44.3%	27.9%	30.5%	37.1%	25.3%	140	174
Staten Island	71.9%	52.5%	27.2%	47.2%	0.6%	0.0%	0.3%	0.3%	349	341
Queens	12.4%	21.5%	67.2%	57.0%	11.2%	11.9%	9.2%	9.6%	509	386

practice test

3. A sporting goods company is considering redesigning the soccer section or the baseball section of its Web site. Internal studies suggest that a redesign of the baseball section will have a bigger positive effect on sales than a redesign of the soccer section. Therefore, in order to achieve the greatest possible increase in its sales as soon as possible, the company has decided to redesign the baseball section this year, rather than the soccer section.

Indicate two different statements as follows: one statement identifies an *assumption required* by the company's decision, and the other identifies a *possible fact* that, if true, would provide significant logical support for the required assumption. Make only two selections, one in each column.

3.1 Assumption	3.2 Fact	
(A)	(A)	The company cannot redesign both sections this year.
(B)	(B)	The soccer world cup is going to take place later this year.
(C)	(C)	Baseball is more popular with the company's customers than is soccer.
(D)	(D)	The soccer section redesign will cost more than the baseball section redesign.
(E)	(E)	The company's Web site development team will need at least ten months in order to complete the redesign of either the baseball or the soccer section.

4. An arithmetic sequence is such that the division of the fifth term by the third term gives a quotient of 1 and leaves a remainder of 10, while the product of the first and third terms equals 24.

In the table, select a value for the first term, a_1 of the sequence, and a value for the difference, d, between successive terms of the sequence, that together are consistent with the given information. Make only one selection in each column.

4.1 a_1	4.2 d	
(A)	(A)	2
(B)	(B)	3
(C)	(C)	5
(D)	(D)	7
(E)	(E)	12
(F)	(F)	22

5. For the past few years, the per store sales of a drugstore chain have been declining steadily. However, after a new management team took over last year, there have been promising signs of a recovery. Among the customers who responded to a survey asking them to rate, on a scale of 1 to 5 (5 being highest), how satisfied they were with their shopping experience, 75% of them rated their experience a 4 or higher. This is in sharp contrast with last year, when only 35% of survey responders rated their satisfaction with their shopping experience a 4 or higher. The company's marketing department is trumpeting this improved customer experience in its advertising campaign. Therefore, the drugstore company is poised to reverse the recent trend and increase its per store sales this year.

In the table, select *Support* for the statement that, if true, would provide the strongest support for the argument, and select *Undermine* for the statement that, if true, would undermine most seriously the argument. Make only two selections, one in each column.

5.1 Support	5.2 Undermine	
(A)	(A)	The old management team was focused on customer satisfaction.
(B)	(B)	Studies show that only a score of 5 in customer satisfaction correlates strongly with increased sales.
(C)	(C)	Not all customers who shopped at the drugstore chain, but only a representative sample of them, responded to the survey.
(D)	(D)	A separate survey among consumers who do not habitually shop at this company's stores shows that most of them have an improved opinion of the company now compared to a year ago.
(E)	(E)	The company is planning to open 57 new stores in the coming year.

6. The table shows the results for the years 2009 and 2011 of a citywide survey of students, parents, and teachers regarding the city's schools. In total, 14,700 teachers, 63,200 students, and 41,600 parents responded in 2009, and 15,300 teachers, 67,600 students, and 40,700 parents responded in 2011. Survey responders graded the city's schools on a scale of 1 to 10 in 4 major categories.

Sort By: | Select ▼ |

Category	Students		Parents		Teachers	
	2009	2011	2009	2011	2009	2011
Academic Expectations	7.2	7.5	8.1	7.8	7.6	8.2
Communication	5.8	6.1	7.6	7.9	6.5	6.4
Engagement	6.4	6.7	7.4	7.8	7.2	7.3
Safety and Respect	7.1	7.2	8.4	8.6	6.8	7.0

For each of the following statements, select *Yes* if the statement is true based on the information in the table. Otherwise, select *No*.

	(A) Yes	(B) No	
6.1	o	o	In 2009, the city's schools received an average rating of 7.0 among all survey responders in the category of Engagement.
6.2	o	o	If in 2011 the schools received a rating below 7.0 in a particular category, there is a 67% probability that this rating was given by students.
6.3	o	o	In 2011, the average rating that the city's schools were given by students and teachers combined for Academic Expectations was greater than the rating the schools were given for Academic Expectations by parents.

(On the computer test, this will be the end of the question prompt and statements. For this paper test and your convenience, we are providing you the various other ways you may sort the data.)

Sort By: | Students, 2009 ▼ |

Category	Students		Parents		Teachers	
	2009	2011	2009	2011	2009	2011
Communication	5.8	6.1	7.6	7.9	6.5	6.4
Engagement	6.4	6.7	7.4	7.8	7.2	7.3
Safety and Respect	7.1	7.2	8.4	8.6	6.8	7.0
Academic Expectations	7.2	7.5	8.1	7.8	7.6	8.2

Sort By: | Students, 2011 ▼ |

Category	Students		Parents		Teachers	
	2009	2011	2009	2011	2009	2011
Communication	5.8	6.1	7.6	7.9	6.5	6.4
Engagement	6.4	6.7	7.4	7.8	7.2	7.3
Safety and Respect	7.1	7.2	8.4	8.6	6.8	7.0
Academic Expectations	7.2	7.5	8.1	7.8	7.6	8.2

Sort By: | Parents, 2009 ▼ |

Category	Students		Parents		Teachers	
	2009	2011	2009	2011	2009	2011
Engagement	6.4	6.7	7.4	7.8	7.2	7.3
Communication	5.8	6.1	7.6	7.9	6.5	6.4
Academic Expectations	7.2	7.5	8.1	7.8	7.6	8.2
Safety and Respect	7.1	7.2	8.4	8.6	6.8	7.0

Sort By: | Parents, 2011 ▼ |

Category	Students		Parents		Teachers	
	2009	2011	2009	2011	2009	2011
Engagement	6.4	6.7	7.4	7.8	7.2	7.3
Academic Expectations	7.2	7.5	8.1	7.8	7.6	8.2
Communication	5.8	6.1	7.6	7.9	6.5	6.4
Safety and Respect	7.1	7.2	8.4	8.6	6.8	7.0

Sort By: | Teachers, 2009 ▼ |

Category	Students		Parents		Teachers	
	2009	2011	2009	2011	2009	2011
Communication	5.8	6.1	7.6	7.9	6.5	6.4
Safety and Respect	7.1	7.2	8.4	8.6	6.8	7.0
Engagement	6.4	6.7	7.4	7.8	7.2	7.3
Academic Expectations	7.2	7.5	8.1	7.8	7.6	8.2

Sort By: | Teachers, 2011 ▼ |

Category	Students		Parents		Teachers	
	2009	2011	2009	2011	2009	2011
Communication	5.8	6.1	7.6	7.9	6.5	6.4
Safety and Respect	7.1	7.2	8.4	8.6	6.8	7.0
Engagement	6.4	6.7	7.4	7.8	7.2	7.3
Academic Expectations	7.2	7.5	8.1	7.8	7.6	8.2

7.

Restaurant Owner	Wine Expert

E-mail from restaurant owner to wine expert, March 4.

I have inherited a restaurant from my uncle and need some help with the wine list. At the moment, our wine list is extensive and includes wines from California, France, Italy, Spain, and Chile, but I think it would be better to simplify it. I don't think many of our customers can tell a Bordeaux from a Barolo—and I'm not sure I can, either! They tend to buy more Cabernet, Merlot, and Chardonnay, probably because these are names they recognize. Then again, if they ever think to try a French or Italian wine, I think the cost of some of these bottles often deters them.

Our menu is eclectic and features many pasta dishes, as well as chicken, steak, and lamb plates. I know the basic rule of thumb—red wine with red meat, white wine with white meat or fish—but I'd like to understand wine and food pairings better.

Finally, I'd love to know what you suggest regarding wine glasses.

Restaurant Owner	Wine Expert

E-mail from wine expert to restaurant owner, March 5.

Red with red and white with white is a reasonable place to start, though not an absolute rule. Generally, you should match the body and taste of the wine with the body and taste of the food, so it's a good idea to serve lighter wines with lighter dishes, such as white meat or fish, and full-bodied, rich wines with richer, heavier dishes, such as red meat.

I'm including some brief, introductory notes on various types of wine below.

As for glasses, there are several kinds, but the main idea is that bigger, broader glasses are for red, and smaller, thinner ones are for white. If you're going to have several types of glass, at least one of them must be for red wine, which needs the extra space in order to breathe.

Red Wines:

Barbaresco:	Medium- to full-bodied, rich flavor. Can be expensive. Nebbiolo is a cheaper alternative.
Barbera:	Medium-bodied.
Barolo:	Big, full-bodied. Often expensive. Nebbiolo or Barbaresco are cheaper alternatives.
Beaujolais:	Light body, fruity.
Bordeaux:	Medium- or full-bodied, depending on origin. Based on Cabernet or Merlot grapes.
Brunello:	Big, full-bodied. Expensive. Rosso di Montalcino is a cheaper alternative.
Burgundy:	Medium-bodied, balanced.
Cabernet Sauvignon:	Rich, full flavor.
Chianti:	Medium- or full-bodied.
Malbec:	Somewhat lighter red.
Merlot:	Similar to Cabernet Sauvignon, but milder, fruitier.
Nebbiolo:	Medium- to full-bodied, rich flavor. Similar to Barbaresco and Barolo but cheaper.
Pinot Noir: or watery.	Medium-bodied. Cheaper Pinot Noirs can feel thin
Syrah:	Big-bodied, spice-full.
Zinfandel:	Full-flavored, big wine.

White Wines:

Champagne:	Dry or sweet. From Pinot Noir or Chardonnay grapes.
Chardonnay:	Rich, big white wine.
Gewürztraminer:	Full, big white.
Pinot Grigio:	Light, citrusy.
Riesling:	Light- or fuller-bodied, depending on origin.
Sauvignon Blanc:	Lighter than Chardonnay.

For each of the following statements, select *Inferable* if the statement is reasonably inferable from the information provided. Otherwise, select *Not inferable*.

	(A) Inferable	(B) Not inferable	
7.1	○	○	If in a subsequent message the wine expert recommends Barolo as an ideal wine to pair with a particular dish, the restaurant owner may opt for Nebbiolo instead.
7.2	○	○	The restaurant owner would prefer to include in his wine list a Chianti than a Barbera.
7.3	○	○	If the restaurant owner orders only one kind of glass, the wine expert would recommend that it be a bigger, broader type of glass.

8.

Restaurant Owner	Wine Expert

E-mail from restaurant owner to wine expert, March 4.

I have inherited a restaurant from my uncle and need some help with the wine list. At the moment, our wine list is extensive and includes wines from California, France, Italy, Spain, and Chile, but I think it would be better to simplify it. I don't think many of our customers can tell a Bordeaux from a Barolo—and I'm not sure I can, either! They tend to buy more Cabernet, Merlot, and Chardonnay, probably because these are names they recognize. Then again, if they ever think to try a French or Italian wine, I think the cost of some of these bottles often deters them.

Our menu is eclectic and features many pasta dishes, as well as chicken, steak, and lamb plates. I know the basic rule of thumb—red wine with red meat, white wine with white meat or fish—but I'd like to understand wine and food pairings better.

Finally, I'd love to know what you suggest regarding wine glasses.

Restaurant Owner	Wine Expert

E-mail from wine expert to restaurant owner, March 5.

Red with red and white with white is a reasonable place to start, though not an absolute rule. Generally, you should match the body and taste of the wine with the body and taste of the food, so it's a good idea to serve lighter wines with lighter dishes, such as white meat or fish, and full-bodied, rich wines with richer, heavier dishes, such as red meat.

I'm including some brief, introductory notes on various types of wine below.

As for glasses, there are several kinds, but the main idea is that bigger, broader glasses are for red, and smaller, thinner ones are for white. If you're going to have several types of glass, at least one of them must be for red wine, which needs the extra space in order to breathe.

Red Wines:

Barbaresco:	Medium- to full-bodied, rich flavor. Can be expensive. Nebbiolo is a cheaper alternative.
Barbera:	Medium-bodied.
Barolo:	Big, full-bodied. Often expensive. Nebbiolo or Barbaresco are cheaper alternatives.
Beaujolais:	Light body, fruity.
Bordeaux:	Medium- or full-bodied, depending on origin. Based on Cabernet or Merlot grapes.
Brunello:	Big, full-bodied. Expensive. Rosso di Montalcino is a cheaper alternative.
Burgundy:	Medium-bodied, balanced.
Cabernet Sauvignon:	Rich, full flavor.
Chianti:	Medium- or full-bodied.
Malbec:	Somewhat lighter red.
Merlot:	Similar to Cabernet Sauvignon, but milder, fruitier.
Nebbiolo:	Medium- to full-bodied, rich flavor. Similar to Barbaresco and Barolo but cheaper.
Pinot Noir:	Medium-bodied. Cheaper Pinot Noirs can feel thin or watery.
Syrah:	Big-bodied, spice-full.
Zinfandel:	Full-flavored, big wine.

White Wines:

Champagne:	Dry or sweet. From Pinot Noir or Chardonnay grapes.
Chardonnay:	Rich, big white wine.
Gewürztraminer:	Full, big white.
Pinot Grigio:	Light, citrusy.
Riesling:	Light- or fuller-bodied, depending on origin.
Sauvignon Blanc:	Lighter than Chardonnay.

If the restaurant owner decides to keep the Bordeaux wines on the restaurant's wine list, which of the following strategies would be most likely to increase the number of customers who order these wines?

(A) Increasing their prices to make them seem more prestigious

(B) Advertising in the menu the wines' origin in France's most famous wine-producing region

(C) Mentioning prominently on the wine-list that these wines are blends of Cabernet and Merlot grapes

(D) Ensuring the wait staff is well educated regarding what dishes these wines complement best

(E) Placing them higher on the wine list

9.

Restaurant Owner	Wine Expert

E-mail from restaurant owner to wine expert, March 4.

I have inherited a restaurant from my uncle and need some help with the wine list. At the moment, our wine list is extensive and includes wines from California, France, Italy, Spain, and Chile, but I think it would be better to simplify it. I don't think many of our customers can tell a Bordeaux from a Barolo—and I'm not sure I can, either! They tend to buy more Cabernet, Merlot, and Chardonnay, probably because these are names they recognize. Then again, if they ever think to try a French or Italian wine, I think the cost of some of these bottles often deters them.

Our menu is eclectic and features many pasta dishes, as well as chicken, steak, and lamb plates. I know the basic rule of thumb—red wine with red meat, white wine with white meat or fish—but I'd like to understand wine and food pairings better.

Finally, I'd love to know what you suggest regarding wine glasses.

Restaurant Owner	Wine Expert

E-mail from wine expert to restaurant owner, March 5.

Red with red and white with white is a reasonable place to start, though not an absolute rule. Generally, you should match the body and taste of the wine with the body and taste of the food, so it's a good idea to serve lighter wines with lighter dishes, such as white meat or fish, and full-bodied, rich wines with richer, heavier dishes, such as red meat.

I'm including some brief, introductory notes on various types of wine below.

As for glasses, there are several kinds, but the main idea is that bigger, broader glasses are for red, and smaller, thinner ones are for white. If you're going to have several types of glass, at least one of them must be for red wine, which needs the extra space in order to breathe.

Red Wines:

Barbaresco:	Medium- to full-bodied, rich flavor. Can be expensive. Nebbiolo is a cheaper alternative.
Barbera:	Medium-bodied.
Barolo:	Big, full-bodied. Often expensive. Nebbiolo or Barbaresco are cheaper alternatives.
Beaujolais:	Light body, fruity.
Bordeaux:	Medium- or full-bodied, depending on origin. Based on Cabernet or Merlot grapes.
Brunello:	Big, full-bodied. Expensive. Rosso di Montalcino is a cheaper alternative.
Burgundy:	Medium-bodied, balanced.
Cabernet Sauvignon:	Rich, full flavor.
Chianti:	Medium- or full-bodied.
Malbec:	Somewhat lighter red.
Merlot:	Similar to Cabernet Sauvignon, but milder, fruitier.
Nebbiolo:	Medium- to full-bodied, rich flavor. Similar to Barbaresco and Barolo but cheaper.
Pinot Noir: or watery.	Medium-bodied. Cheaper Pinot Noirs can feel thin
Syrah:	Big-bodied, spice-full.
Zinfandel:	Full-flavored, big wine.

White Wines:

Champagne:	Dry or sweet. From Pinot Noir or Chardonnay grapes.
Chardonnay:	Rich, big white wine.
Gewürztraminer:	Full, big white.
Pinot Grigio:	Light, citrusy.
Riesling:	Light- or fuller-bodied, depending on origin.
Sauvignon Blanc:	Lighter than Chardonnay.

If a customer orders fish and wishes to drink a red wine with it, which of the following types of wine would be the best recommendation?

(A) Barolo

(B) Beaujolais

(C) Brunello di Montalcino

(D) Chianti

(E) Nebbiolo

10. The graph shows the unemployment rates for three cities between 2000 and 2011. During this period, the total population of City X grew from 1.3 million to 1.7 million; of City Y grew from 2.1 million to 2.3 million; and of City Z decreased from 1.2 million to 1.1 million.

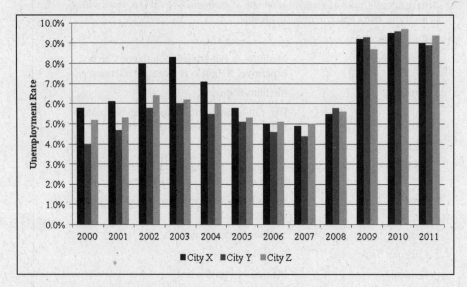

Based on the given information, fill in the blanks in each of the following statements.

10.1. The unemployment rate in City X was _____ times greater than the average of the unemployment rates in Cities Y and Z.

(A) 7

(B) 8

(C) 9

(D) 10

10.2. Among these three cities in the year 2000, _____ had the greatest number of unemployed people.

(A) City X

(B) City Y

(C) City Z

11. The graph shows the per share price of the stock of three companies at the end of each year between 2002 and 2011.

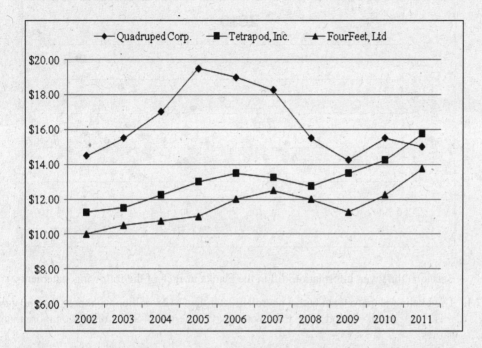

Based on the given information, fill in the blanks in each of the following statements.

11.1. Between the end of 2003 and the end of 2007, the stock of _____ experienced the greatest percent appreciation.

(A) Quadruped Corp.

(B) Tetrapod, Inc.

(C) FourFeet, Ltd.

11.2. At the end of 2005, the per share price of Tetrapod, Inc. was approximately _____ times the sum of the per share prices of Quadruped Corp. and FourFeet, Ltd.

(A) 0.34

(B) 0.43

(C) 0.81

(D) 1.23

12. The graph shows the total payroll and number of regular season wins for the 30 Major League Baseball teams in 2010.

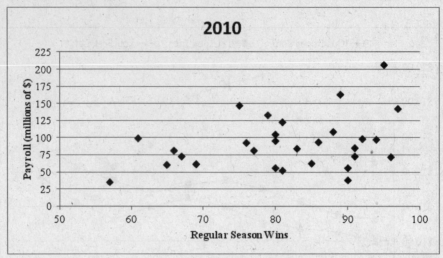

Based on the given information, fill in the blanks in each of the following statements.

12.1. The likelihood that a team with a payroll greater than $125 million won more than 80 games was _____ the likelihood that a team with a payroll less than $75 million won more than 70 games.

(A) greater than

(B) equal to

(C) less than

12.2. The probability that if a team is selected at random, it will be one of the top five teams in terms of both payroll and number of wins is _____.

(A) 2 out of 30

(B) 3 out of 30

(C) 2 out of 5

(D) 3 out of 5

QUANTITATIVE SECTION

37 Questions • 75 Minutes

Directions for Problem Solving Questions: *(These directions will appear on your screen before your first Problem Solving question.)*

Solve this problem and indicate the best of the answer choices given.

<u>Numbers:</u> All numbers used are real numbers.

<u>Figures:</u> A figure accompanying a Problem Solving question is intended to provide information useful in solving the problem. Figures are drawn as accurately as possible EXCEPT when it is stated in a specific problem that its figure is not drawn to scale. Straight lines may sometimes appear jagged. All figures lie on a plane unless otherwise indicated.

To review these directions for subsequent questions of this type, click on HELP.

Directions for Data Sufficiency Questions: *(These directions will appear on your screen before your first Data Sufficiency question.)*

This Data Sufficiency problem consists of a question and two statements, labeled (1) and (2), in which certain data are given. You have to decide whether the data given in the statements are *sufficient* for answering the question. Using the data given in the statements *plus* your knowledge of mathematics and everyday facts (such as the number of days in July or the meaning of *counterclockwise*), you must indicate whether:

(A) Statement (1) ALONE is sufficient, but Statement (2) alone is not sufficient to answer the question asked;

(B) Statement (2) ALONE is sufficient, but Statement (1) alone is not sufficient to answer the question asked;

(C) BOTH Statements (1) and (2) TOGETHER are sufficient to answer the question asked, but NEITHER statement ALONE is sufficient;

(D) EACH statement ALONE is sufficient to answer the question asked;

(E) Statements (1) and (2) TOGETHER are NOT sufficient to answer the question asked, and additional data specific to the problem are needed.

<u>Numbers:</u> All numbers used are real numbers.

<u>Figures:</u> A figure accompanying a Data Sufficiency problem will conform to the information given in the question, but will not necessarily conform to the additional information in Statements (1) and (2).

Lines shown as straight can be assumed to be straight and lines that appear jagged can also be assumed to be straight.

You may assume that positions of points, angles, regions, etc., exist in the order shown and that angle measures are greater than zero.

All figures lie in a plane unless otherwise indicated.

<u>Note:</u> In Data Sufficiency problems that ask you for the value of a quantity, the data given in the statements are sufficient only when it is possible to determine exactly one numerical value for the quantity.

To review these directions for subsequent questions of this type, click on HELP.

1. How long would it take 5 typists to type thirty pages if all 5 typists type at the same speed?

   (1) One typist can type four pages in 30 minutes.

   (2) Three typists can type eight pages in 20 minutes.

2. If $x + y = 8$, if $x + z = 7$, and if $y + z = 6$, then $x =$

   (A) 3.5

   (B) 4

   (C) 4.5

   (D) 5

   (E) 5.5

3. Code letters X, Y, and Z each represent one digit in the three-digit prime number XYZ. If both X and Y are even integers, and if the sum of the three digits is 7, how many different three-digit numbers could XYZ represent?

   (A) one

   (B) two

   (C) three

   (D) four

   (E) five

4. Tom and Jerry were the two owners of a small business, which they sold for $250,000. Tom received 60% of the sale price and Jerry received 40%. The two partners used the proceeds of the sale in the following way: Tom spent $20,000 to buy a car, and placed the rest in a savings account. Jerry spent 10% of his share on a family trip, and placed the rest in a savings account. The total amount that Tom and Jerry placed into savings accounts represents what percent of the total sale price?

   (A) 82%

   (B) 86%

   (C) 88%

   (D) 90%

   (E) 92%

5.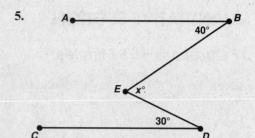

   In the figure, if $\overrightarrow{AB}$ is parallel to $\overline{CD}$, then $x =$

   (A) 60

   (B) 65

   (C) 70

   (D) 75

   (E) 80

6. If $\sqrt{x + 2} = x$, which of the following choices lists all the possible values of x?

   (A) $x = -1$

   (B) $x = 1$

   (C) $x = 2$

   (D) $x = -1$ or $x = 2$

   (E) $x = 1$ or $x = 2$

7. If $x \neq 0$, what is the value of $\left(\dfrac{x^m}{x^n}\right)^p$?

   (1) $p = 1$

   (2) $m = n$

8. A group of students, no two of whom are the same height, are lined up next to one another. What is the probability that they are lined up in order from shortest to tallest, from left to right?

   (1) There are four students in the group.

   (2) Three of the students in the group are females.

9. What is the numerical ratio $P:Q:R$?

   (1) The ratio $P:Q$ is 1:2.

   (2) $R = 5$

10.

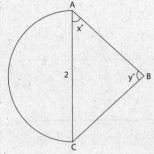

If a semicircle and triangle are pieced together to form the figure shown above, what is the total unit area of the figure?

(1) The length of $\overline{AB}$ is 2 units.

(2) $x = y$

11. What is the arithmetic mean (simple average) of a sequence of consecutive odd integers?

(1) The median of all integers in the sequence is 36.

(2) The sum of the first and last integers in the sequence is 72.

12. If a is divisible by 2, b is divisible by 4, and c is divisible by 6, each of the following must be divisible, with no remainder, by 12 EXCEPT:

(A) $2ab$

(B) $3ab$

(C) $\dfrac{bc}{2}$

(D) $\dfrac{3ab}{2}$

(E) $\dfrac{abc}{4}$

13. Three salespeople—A, B, and C—sold a total of 500 products among them during a particular month. During the month, did A sell more products than B sold as well as more products than C sold?

(1) A sold 166 products during the month.

(2) C sold 249 products during the month.

14. On the xy-plane, if the point $(4,t)$ is equidistant from the points $(1,1)$ and $(5,3)$, then $t =$

(A) $\dfrac{3}{2}$

(B) 1

(C) 0

(D) $-\dfrac{1}{4}$

(E) -4

15.

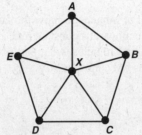

In its initial "trip" starting at point X in the circuit pictured above, a glip jumps to A to B and back to X, then to D and back to X. Each successive trip follows the same pattern of jumps, starting with a jump to the next point clockwise (in this case, B) around the circuit. After jump 472, the glip will be at point

(A) X

(B) A

(C) C

(D) D

(E) E

16. What value of x satisfies the equation $\sqrt{4x - 4} - 4 = 8$?

(A) 26

(B) 37

(C) 42

(D) 47

(E) 51

17. What is the arithmetic mean (simple average) of three numbers?

(1) The absolute value of one number equals the value of one of the other two numbers.

(2) The value of one, and only one, of the three numbers is 0.

18. If x is a non-zero integer, what is the value of x?

    (1) $-4x - 7 > -14$
    (2) $5x + 3 > -2(x + 1)$

19. How many boxes, each of which contains 64 cubic inches, will fit into a larger rectangular box?

    (1) Each of the small boxes is a cube.
    (2) The larger box contains 1440 cubic inches.

20. It takes Paul m minutes to mow the lawn. Assuming he mows at a constant rate, after Paul mows for k minutes, what part of the lawn remains to be mowed?

    (A) $\dfrac{m - k}{m}$

    (B) $\dfrac{m}{k}$

    (C) $k^2 - \dfrac{k}{m}$

    (D) $\dfrac{k - m}{k}$

    (E) $\dfrac{k + 1}{m}$

21. Two pairs of socks are randomly removed from a drawer containing five pairs: two black, two white, and one blue. What is the probability of removing a black pair and a white pair from the drawer?

    (A) $\dfrac{1}{10}$

    (B) $\dfrac{1}{5}$

    (C) $\dfrac{1}{4}$

    (D) $\dfrac{1}{3}$

    (E) $\dfrac{2}{5}$

22. What is the total profit on sales of seven dozen washers?

    (1) Washers are bought at 45 cents per dozen and are sold at four washers for 18 cents.
    (2) Washers are sold for 20% more than their cost, which is $3.75 for 100 washers.

23.

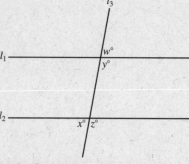

In the figure above, is l_1 parallel to l_2?

    (1) $x + 90 = 280 - y$
    (2) $w + y = x + z$

24. If the letter M represents a digit in the decimal number 0.0M, and if the letter N represents a digit in the decimal number 0.0N, then $0.0M \times 0.0N =$

    (A) $\dfrac{1}{10,000} \times M \times N$

    (B) 0.000MN

    (C) $\dfrac{1}{1000} \times M \times N$

    (D) 0.00MN

    (E) $\dfrac{1}{100} \times M \times N$

25. Critter Kennel currently boards eight fewer cats than dogs. If the ratio of boarded cats to boarded dogs is 5:6, how many cats and dogs altogether are boarded at the kennel?

    (A) 64
    (B) 77
    (C) 84
    (D) 88
    (E) 98

26. On the xy-coordinate plane, points $R\,(7, -3)$ and $S\,(7, 7)$ are the endpoints of the longest possible chord of a certain circle. What is the area of the circle?

    (A) 7π
    (B) 16π
    (C) 20π
    (D) 25π
    (E) 49π

27. In a group of m workers, if b workers earn D dollars per week and the rest earn half that amount each, which of the following represents the total number of dollars paid to the entire group of workers in a week?

(A) $bD + b - m$

(B) $bD + \dfrac{1}{2}mD$

(C) $\dfrac{3}{2}bD + mD$

(D) $\dfrac{3}{2}D(b+m)$

(E) $\dfrac{1}{2}D(b+m)$

28. Distribution D consists of five different numbers. What is the standard deviation of distribution D?

(1) The average of the five numbers in distribution D is 12.

(2) The range of the five numbers in distribution D is 12.

29. The distance from City 1 to City 2 is 825 kilometers. On an accurate map showing both cities, 1 centimeter represents 75 kilometers. On the map, how many millimeters separate City 1 and City 2? [Note: 1 centimeter = 10 millimeters.]

(A) 10

(B) 45

(C) 60

(D) 90

(E) 110

QUESTIONS 30–31 REFER TO THE FOLLOWING CHART.

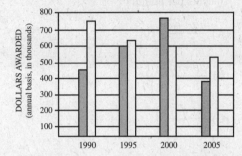

STATE SCHOLARSHIP FUNDS AWARDED (1990-2005)

☐ Non-minority scholarship funds
■ Minority scholarship funds

30. During the greatest ten-year change in non-minority scholarship funds awarded, which of the following most closely approximates the greatest five-year percent change in minority scholarship funds awarded?

(A) 15

(B) 25

(C) 27

(D) 33

(E) 43

31. During the year in which the total amount of non-minority and minority funds awarded was the greatest, the difference between the two amounts was approximately

(A) $130,000

(B) $170,000

(C) $220,000

(D) $270,000

(E) $400,000

32. If integer $x \geq 1$, is x an even number?

(1) $x^3 - x^2 - x$ is an even integer.

(2) $3x + 2x + x$ is an even integer.

33. If $3a = 5b$ and $ab = 135$, then which of the following is the entire solution set for $a + b$?

(A) ± 6

(B) ± 24

(C) 6

(D) 24

(E) All real numbers

34. A merchant mixes a pounds of nuts worth b cents per pound with c pounds of nuts worth d cents per pound. At what price, expressed in cents, should he sell a pound of the mixture if the merchant wishes to make a profit of 10 cents per pound?

(A) $\dfrac{ab+cd}{a+c}+10$

(B) $\dfrac{ab+cd}{a+c}+\dfrac{1}{10}$

(C) $\dfrac{b+d}{a+c}+10$

(D) $\dfrac{b+d}{a+c}+\dfrac{1}{10}$

(E) $\dfrac{b+d+10}{a+c}$

35. If $y=\dfrac{x^5+x^3+x}{3}$, what is $y-x$ when $x=-1$?

(A) -3

(B) $-\dfrac{4}{3}$

(C) -1

(D) $-\dfrac{1}{3}$

(E) 0

36.

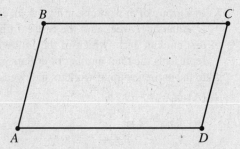

In parallelogram $ABCD$ above, $\angle BAD$ measures $60°$. What is the sum of the measures of $\angle ABC$ and $\angle ADC$?

(A) $60°$

(B) $120°$

(C) $180°$

(D) $240°$

(E) $300°$

37. If $A>B>0$, is $\dfrac{A}{B}$ an integer?

(1) Neither A nor B is an integer.

(2) $A=3B$

VERBAL SECTION

41 Questions • 75 Minutes

1. Could an argument be made that Sagittarius, which has a galactic center, several double and variable stars, and a high proportion of globular <u>clusters, is the most unique of the constellations?</u>

   (A) clusters, is the most unique of the constellations
   (B) clusters, could be the most unique of the constellations
   (C) clusters, are the more unique of the constellations
   (D) clusters, is more unique among the constellations
   (E) clusters, is unique among the constellations

2. Recent biographers of Margaret Fuller <u>have been recently shifting the focus of her accomplishments</u> from contributions to transcendental thinking to contributions to the women's rights movement.

   (A) have been recently shifting the focus of her accomplishments
   (B) have recently shifted the focus of her accomplishments
   (C) were shifting the focus of her accomplishments
   (D) have recently shifted the focus of her accomplishments
   (E) have shifted the focus of her accomplishments

3. Which of the following provides the best completion of the passage below?

   Our nation's public policy dictates that our lands be put to their most economically productive uses. Although farm subsidies help farmers avoid bankruptcy during years in which they lose their crops due to natural disasters, in the long term, subsidies provide a disincentive for farmers to farm productively. Therefore, _____.

(A) the farm subsidy system is ultimately to blame when a farm goes bankrupt.

(B) our nation's public policy should be modified to accommodate farm subsidies.

(C) farmers should strive to make more productive use of their farmland.

(D) in the long term, farmers would operate their farms more profitably without subsidies.

(E) the current farm subsidy system amounts to a violation of our nation's public policy.

4. Many literary critics consider James Joyce's *Ulysses* (1922), <u>a novel once banned as an obscene one,</u> as the greatest novel of the twentieth century due to its remarkable synthesis of mythology, philosophy, and social realism.

(A) a novel once banned as an obscene one, as

(B) which is a novel that was once banned as obscene, as

(C) once banned for its obscenity as a novel, to be

(D) once a banned and obscene novel, to be

(E) a novel once banned as obscene, to be

5. Despite escalating gasoline prices and a slowing economy, Zenith State Park is growing in popularity as a tourist destination. The state authorities who operate the park currently charge a five-dollar entrance fee per vehicle and are concerned that the congestion and noise caused by the steady stream of park visitors, particularly motorists, now detract significantly from the enjoyment of the park, which was once known for its isolation and solitude.

Which of the following courses of actions, if implemented, would most likely address the concerns of the authorities who operate Zenith State Park?

(A) Impose an entrance fee based on the number of occupants per vehicle instead of a per-vehicle fee.

(B) Establish and strictly enforce a limit on the total number of vehicles entering the park each day.

(C) Encourage the public to avoid the park during the peak tourism season and to visit during other times of the year instead.

(D) Require all motorized vehicles to remain outside the entrance gate and allow park entrance only to pedestrians and non-motorized vehicles.

(E) Allow entrance to the park only to visitors who have made reservations in advance.

6. In the sport of maxiball, in which the objective is to score more goals than the opposing team, each team member faces off against one member of the other team. The coach for the Panthers predicts victory over the Cougars in an upcoming match between these two maxiball teams. The chief reason for the coach's prediction is that the Cougars' best defensive player will not be defending against Fonsica, who is the Panthers' highest scoring player.

Which of the following, if true, would cast most doubt on the prediction made by the Panthers' coach?

(A) The Panthers have defeated fewer opponents than the Cougars this year.

(B) Fonsica is the Panther's best defensive player.

(C) The Panthers' best defensive player will not be defending against the Cougars' highest scoring player.

(D) Fonsica is not the Panthers' best defensive player.

(E) The Cougars' highest scoring player will not be defending against Fonsica.

QUESTIONS 7–9 ARE BASED ON THE FOLLOWING PASSAGE.

Line   A decade after its passage, the Sarbanes-Oxley Act of 2002 (SOX) is still maligned. As the RAND Corporation and others noted early on, its effects have taken a quantifiable
(5) and pronounced toll on smaller businesses that have paid a higher cost on a relative basis for the auditing and accounting fees required for compliance with Section 201 and other sections of the act. Furthermore,
(10) the RAND study quantified deregistering in the immediate wake of the act, finding that it occurred more frequently among smaller firms. As the study noted, however, the exit of some small firms from the public
(15) sphere, particularly if they had engaged in financial misstatement, may have also increased investor confidence in the remaining market players.

    In addition to the adverse effect on small
(20) businesses, detractors today cite the effect of SOX on the ability of U.S. firms to compete in the global market, noting the exodus from the NYSE to the less regulated London Stock Exchange, now the true
(25) nexus of international finance. More hyperbolically, they suggest the disruption of the free market.

    Other more recent charges against the act include its having stood in the way of
(30) the creation of new businesses and having cost investors billions of dollars instead of protecting them from losses. Even a 2012 study pointing to the decrease in the number of COOs and the trend toward the
(35) elimination of the COO position from the corporate hierarchy chart, most likely in response to Section 302 requirements, blames Sarbanes-Oxley.

7. It is possible that the author regards all of the following as conceivably legitimate or reasoned complaints against Sarbanes-Oxley EXCEPT:

(A) the pre-eminence of the London Stock Exchange in international finance.

(B) the burden of audit costs borne particularly heavily by smaller companies.

(C) a decrease in the competitiveness of U.S. firms abroad.

(D) the adverse effect on investors of the early deregistration of many smaller businesses.

(E) a general limiting effect on the creation of new businesses.

8. It can be inferred that Section 302 of the Sarbanes-Oxley Act mentioned in line 38

(A) links the COO position to financial misstatements of the past.

(B) does not require COO participation in oversight requirements.

(C) outlines a new corporate hierarchy relative to financial audits.

(D) undermines a reasonable non-intrusive measure to protect investors.

(E) criticizes previous Securities and Exchange Committee filing requirements.

9. Which of the following best expresses the author's attitude toward Sarbanes-Oxley?

(A) It has cost businesses billions of dollars while failing to achieve its oversight purpose.

(B) Its greatest impact has been on smaller businesses, which have suffered disproportionately.

(C) It is a source of continued complaints, some of which are inaccurate or overstated.

(D) The negative criticism it has garnered over the years is, in the main, deserved.

(E) Those calling for the early repeal of the act have been validated over the years.

10. In the late 1940s and early 1950s, when televisions were prohibitively expensive, television viewing often brought two families together in the same living <u>room; in contrast, television viewing today is often a solitary pastime</u> experienced through a personal device.

(A) room; in contrast, television viewing today is often a solitary pastime

(B) room; whereas, in contrast, television viewing today is often a solitary pastime

(C) room, in contrast, television viewing today is often a solitary pastime

(D) room; in contrast, television viewing today, often a solitary pastime,

(E) room, conversely, television viewing today is often a solitary pastime

11. According to Newtonian physics, the greater the distance between two particles, given the so-called gravitational constant, the less will be the gravitational force between them.

(A) the greater the distance between two particles, given the so-called gravitational constant, the less will be the gravitational force between them.

(B) given the so-called gravitational constant, the greater the distance between two particles, the smaller the gravitational force between them.

(C) given the so-called gravitational constant, more distance between two particles will result in a lesser gravitational force between them.

(D) the less of a gravitational force between two objects, the more of a distance between them, given the so-called gravitational constant.

(E) the greater the distance the less the gravitational force between two particles, given the so-called gravitational constant.

12. Now being pulled from the ocean at an unprecedented rate, a relatively recent addition to the ever-growing list of threats to ocean life is the disappearance of forage fish, in part to satisfy the growing market for fish-oil supplements.

(A) rate, a relatively recent addition to the ever-growing list of threats to ocean life is the disappearance of forage fish, in part to satisfy the growing market for fish-oil supplements

(B) rate, in part to satisfy the growing market for fish-oil supplements, a relatively recent addition to the ever-growing list of threats to ocean life is the disappearance of forage fish

(C) rate, in part to satisfy the growing market for fish-oil supplements,

disappearing forage fish are a relatively recent addition to the ever-growing list of threats to ocean life

(D) rate, in part to satisfy the growing market for fish-oil supplements, the disappearance of forage fish are a relatively recent addition to the ever-growing list of threats to ocean life

(E) rate, in part to satisfy the growing market for fish-oil supplements, disappearing forage fish, a relatively recent addition to the ever-growing list of threats to ocean life

13. State X requires employers to pay hourly-wage employees 50 percent more than their regular wage for every work hour in excess of 8, on any workday. State Y requires employers to pay these employees the same overtime rate, but only for work hours in excess of 40 during any given week. Most hourly-wage employees prefer to work in state Y over state X.

Based only on the statements above, which of the following best explains why most hourly-wage employees prefer to work in state Y over state X?

(A) Most hourly-wage employees work at least five days per week.

(B) Most hourly-wage employees prefer to work for employers that do not provide overtime work.

(C) Most hourly-wage employees prefer to work for employers that provide overtime work.

(D) Overtime work hours for most hourly-wage employees exceed regular work hours by at least 50 percent.

(E) Most hourly-wage employees work fewer than 40 hours per week.

14. During the past week, 120 RamTech Corporation employees have reported symptoms of a strain of food poisoning known as disporella, but only 8 of these employees have tested positive for the strain. A Ram-Tech spokesperson claims that the apparent outbreak of disporella can be attributed to contaminated food served two weeks ago at the company's annual employee picnic.

Which of the following, if true, would best support the claim made by the RamTech spokesperson above?

(A) Disporella symptoms generally last only a few days.

(B) RamTech's cafeteria facilities provide lunch to RamTech employees during every workday.

(C) People with disporella do not generally test positive for disporella until at least one week after disporella symptoms begin to occur.

(D) People with disporella often do not exhibit disporella symptoms until more than a week after contracting disporella.

(E) A person can test positive for disporella without exhibiting symptoms of disporella.

QUESTIONS 15–17 ARE BASED ON THE FOLLOWING PASSAGE.

Line   Radiative forcings are changes imposed on the planetary energy balance; radiative feedbacks are changes induced by climate change. Forcings can arise from either
(5)   natural or anthropogenic causes. For example, the concentration of sulfate aerosols in the atmosphere can be altered by volcanic action or by the burning of fossil fuels. The distinction between
(10)   forcings and feedbacks is sometimes arbitrary; however, forcings are quantities normally specified in global climate model simulations, while feedbacks are calculated quantities. Examples of radiative forcings
(15)   are greenhouse gases (such as carbon dioxide and ozone), aerosols in the troposphere, and surface reflectivity. Radiative feedbacks include clouds, water vapor in the troposphere, and sea-ice cover.
(20)   The effects of forcings and feedbacks on climate are complex and uncertain. For example, clouds trap outgoing radiation and thus provide a warming influence. However, they also reflect incoming solar
(25)   radiation and thus provide a cooling influence. Current measurements indicate that the net effect of clouds is to cool the Earth. However, scientists are unsure if the balance will shift in the future as the
(30)   atmosphere and cloud formation are altered by the accumulation of greenhouse gases. Similarly, the vertical distribution of ozone affects both the amount of radiation reaching the Earth's surface and the amount
(35)   of reradiated radiation that is trapped by the greenhouse effect. These two mechanisms affect the Earth's temperature in opposite directions.

15. It can be inferred from the information in the passage that "burning of fossil fuels"

(A) is an anthropogenic cause of radiative forcings.

(B) results in both radiative forcings and radiative feedbacks.

(C) does not affect atmospheric forcings or feedbacks.

(D) is a significant type of radiative forcing.

(E) is an anthropogenic cause of radiative feedbacks.

16. According to the passage, radiative forcings and radiative feedbacks can generally be distinguished in which of the following ways?

(A) Whether the radiative change is global or more localized

(B) The precision with which the amounts of radiative change can be determined

(C) The altitude at which the radiative change occurs

(D) Whether the radiative change is directed toward or away from the Earth

(E) Whether the amount of radiative change is specified or calculated

17. The author discusses the effect of clouds on atmospheric temperature most likely in order to show that

(A) radiative feedbacks can be more difficult to isolate and predict than radiative forcings.

(B) the climatic impact of some radiative feedbacks is uncertain.

(C) some radiative feedbacks cannot be determined solely by global climate model simulations.

(D) the distinction between radiative feedbacks and radiative forcings is somewhat arbitrary.

(E) the effects of radiative forcings on planetary energy balance are both complex and uncertain.

18. As any economist knows, healthy people pose less of an economic burden to society than unhealthy people. Not surprisingly, then, every dollar our state government spends on prenatal care for undocumented immigrants will save taxpayers of this state three dollars.

    Which of the following, if true, would best explain why the statistics cited above are not surprising?

    (A) The state's taxpayers pay for prenatal care of all immigrants.

    (B) Pregnant women who do not receive prenatal care are more likely to experience health problems than other pregnant women.

    (C) State benefits for prenatal care serve to promote undocumented immigration.

    (D) Babies whose mothers did not receive prenatal care are just as healthy as other babies.

    (E) Babies born in this state to undocumented immigrant parents are entitled to infant care benefits from the state.

19. Beautiful beaches attract people, no doubt about it. Just look at this city's beautiful beaches, which are among the most over-crowded beaches in the state.

    Which of the following exhibits a pattern of reasoning most similar to the one exhibited in the argument above?

    (A) Moose and bear usually appear at the same drinking hole at the same time of day. Therefore, moose and bear must grow thirsty at about the same time.

    (B) Children who are scolded severely tend to misbehave more often than other children. Hence, if a child is not scolded severely, that child is less likely to misbehave.

    (C) This software program helps increase the work efficiency of its users. As a result, these users have more free time for other activities.

    (D) During warm weather, my dog suffers from fleas more so than during cooler weather. Therefore, fleas must thrive in a warm environment.

    (E) Pesticides are known to cause anemia in some people. However, most anemic people live in regions where pesticides are not commonly used.

20. With laser technology, vision problems, skin disorders, and even many forms of cancer can now be treated <u>by means of using</u> a quick and painless surgical procedure.

    (A) by means of using

    (B) by means of the use of

    (C) with using

    (D) by means of

    (E) through means of

21. In *The Souls of Black Folk*, <u>the rise of cot-ton mills in the South was chronicled by W. E. B. Du Bois, by observing</u> that "the Cotton Kingdom still lives; the world still bows beneath her scepter."

    (A) the rise of cotton mills in the South was chronicled by W. E. B. Du Bois, by observing

    (B) W. E. B. Du Bois chronicled the rise of cotton mills in the South, by observing

    (C) W. E. B. Du Bois chronicled the rise of cotton mills in the South, observing

    (D) W. E. B. Du Bois chronicled the rise of cotton mills in the South, by means of the observation that

    (E) the rise of cotton mills in the South chronicled by W. E. B. Du Bois, by observing

22. *Justin:* Under current state law, employers must provide worker's compensation insurance, which provides income to employees who cannot work due to injuries sustained at the workplace, to all full-time employees. This form of insurance is vital in protecting workers from financial ruin in the event they are suddenly unable to work.

Bharti: I disagree with your assessment. The high premiums employers are forced to pay for worker's compensation insurance force many of them out of business, thereby serving to increase the state's unemployment rate. Since unemployed people are statistically unlikely to carry health insurance, the state-mandated worker's compensation scheme actually renders workers more vulnerable to financial devastation in the event of bodily injury.

Which of the following, if true, should Justin cite in order to respond most effectively to Bharti's counterargument?

(A) In addition to carrying worker's compensation insurance, most employers in the state also provide health insurance for full-time employees.

(B) Patients without health insurance and who have no money typically receive inferior treatment at hospital emergency rooms.

(C) People are statistically more likely to sustain debilitating injuries at the workplace than elsewhere.

(D) The state agency that compensates injured workers under the current insurance scheme is financially able to pay all foreseeable claims.

(E) Many workers file fraudulent worker's compensation claims, and state regulators often fail to detect such fraud.

23. Casino X advertises that it has the "loosest" one-dollar slot machines in town, which means that the statistical odds of winning money playing a one-dollar slot machine are greater at Casino X than at any other casino. Meanwhile, Casino Y claims to have the loosest five-dollar slot machines in town.

In any event, the statistical odds are always against any slot-machine player. Elaine has five dollars to spend on gambling and has decided to play a five-dollar slot machine at Casino Y.

Assuming Elaine hopes to win money, which of the following, if true, provides the strongest evidence that she made a good decision as to how to gamble her money?

(A) Casino Y's total gambling revenues far exceed those of Casino X.

(B) At Casino Y, more gamblers win money playing slot machines than at any other casino game.

(C) One of the two casinos is providing accurate information about its slot machines, but the other casino is not.

(D) Each of the two casinos has both types of slot machines: one-dollar and five-dollar.

(E) Casino X and Casino Y are the only two casinos in town that claim to have the loosest slot machines of any type.

24. There is the gene that causes hemophilia which, if paired with a healthy gene, the individual will not develop the disease's symptoms.

(A) There is the gene that causes hemophilia which, if paired with a healthy gene, the individual will not develop

(B) The gene that causes hemophilia which, if paired with a healthy gene, then the individual will not develop

(C) There is the gene that causes hemophilia, and if paired with a healthy gene, the individual will not develop

(D) If paired with a healthy gene, the gene that causes hemophilia will not result in the individual's developing

(E) Hemophilia is caused by a gene that, if paired with a healthy gene, will not develop in the individual

25. In the future, any justification for our government's military intervention in the internal political affairs of other nations in the interest of suppressing their civil wars <u>must be weighed against the costs of intervening.</u>

(A) must be weighed against the costs of intervening.

(B) will need to weigh against intervening costs.

(C) are weighed against the costs of intervening.

(D) must also include the costs of such intervention.

(E) must weigh the costs of intervening.

QUESTIONS 26–29 ARE BASED ON THE FOLLOWING PASSAGE.

Line   Matthew Arnold, through his *Culture and Anarchy* (1869), placed the word "culture" at the center of debates about the goals of intellectual life and humanistic
(5) society. Arnold's definition of culture as "the pursuit of perfection by getting to know the best which has been thought and said" helped define the Western world's liberal arts curriculum over the next
(10) century. Although three forms of dissent from his views have had considerable impact of their own, each one misunderstands Arnold.

    The first protested Arnold's designation
(15) of "anarchy" as culture's enemy, viewing this dichotomy simply as a struggle between a privileged power structure and radical challenges to it. Yet, Arnold himself was plagued in his soul by the blind arro-
(20) gance of the world's reactionary powers. Another form of opposition saw Arnold's culture as a perverse perpetuation of literary learning in a world where science had become the new arch from which any
(25) new order of thinking must develop. At the center of the "two cultures" debate were the goals of the formal educational curriculum, the principal vehicle through which Arnoldian culture operates. But
(30) Arnold himself had viewed culture as enacting its life in a much more broadly conceived set of institutions. Today, Arnoldian culture is sustained, if indirectly,

by a third form of dissent, multiculturalism,
(35) which seeks to deflate the imperious authority that "high culture" exercises over curriculum while promoting the idea that we must learn what is representative because we have overemphasized what is
(40) exceptional. Yet, multiculturalism actually affirms Arnold by returning us to a tension inherent in the idea of culture.

    The social critics, defenders of science, and multiculturalists wrongly insist that
(45) Arnold's culture is simply a device for ordering us about. Instead, it is designed to register the gathering of ideological clouds on the horizon. Perfection mattered to Arnold only as the background against
(50) which we could form a just image of our actual circumstances, just as we can conceive finer sunsets and unheard melodies.

26. The author of the passage is primarily concerned with

(A) arguing against those who have opposed Arnold's ideas.

(B) describing Arnold's conception of culture.

(C) explaining why Arnold considered the pursuit of perfection to be the essence of culture.

(D) tracing Arnold's influence on the liberal arts educational curriculum.

(E) examining the different views of culture that have emerged since the mid-eighteenth century.

27. It can be inferred from the passage that the two-cultures debate

(A) emerged as a reaction to the multiculturalist movement.

(B) developed after 1869.

(C) influenced Arnold's thinking about culture.

(D) was carried on by American as well as European scientists.

(E) led to two competing educational systems.

28. In criticizing Arnold's dissenters, the author employs all of the following methods EXCEPT:

   (A) Pointing out the paradoxical nature of an argument against Arnoldian culture

   (B) Presenting evidence that conflicts with a claim made by Arnold's dissenters

   (C) Asserting that a claim made by the dissenters is an oversimplification

   (D) Drawing an analogy between one of the dissenters' claims and another insupportable theory

   (E) Suggesting that the focus of one of the dissenters' arguments is too narrow

29. It can be inferred from the information in the passage that Arnoldian culture is perpetuated today by

   (A) the two-cultures debate.

   (B) postmodernists.

   (C) imperious elitists.

   (D) existentialists.

   (E) social critics.

30. Our school district should not spend its money on a new reading program. After all, our students get all the reading practice they need by studying history and science.

   The argument above depends on which of the following assumptions?

   (A) The reading program involves only reading practice.

   (B) Other reading programs are just as effective but less expensive than the new program.

   (C) The new program would not help the students learn history and science.

   (D) Teaching students history and science is more important than teaching them reading skills.

   (E) The students can already read well enough to study history and science.

31. *City Official:* I cannot deny that sodium monofluoride, which is used in all major brands of toothpaste to help prevent tooth decay, has been shown to be more toxic than lead. Those who oppose our plan to treat the public water supply with sodium monofluoride cite warnings on the back of toothpaste tubes advising the user to contact a poison control center if the user swallows more toothpaste than needed for brushing. But these same opponents ignore the fact that even though nobody reads these warnings, virtually no cases of toothpaste poisoning have ever been reported.

   The passage is structured to lead to which of the following conclusions?

   (A) Sodium monofluoride warnings on toothpaste tubes should be more conspicuous to toothpaste users.

   (B) Fluoride in toothpaste is not so toxic as warnings on toothpaste tubes would lead users to believe.

   (C) Neither fluoridated water nor fluoridated toothpaste contains lead.

   (D) Suppliers of public water treated with sodium monofluoride should not be required to warn their customers about its toxicity.

   (E) Fluoridated water is not so toxic as those who oppose treating water with sodium monofluoride might claim.

32. Contrary to popular myth promulgated partly by Greek classics and partly by the Hollywood movie industry, war heroes rarely earn their status by acting as if they themselves are invincible.

   (A) if they themselves are invincible.

   (B) though they are invincible.

   (C) being invincible.

   (D) if they themself are invincible.

   (E) if they were invincible.

33. Upon appearing first as a tiny speck in the night sky, some comets eventually grow quite large in appearance, although their total mass is miniscule in comparison to the celestial objects we see every night.

   (A) Upon appearing first

   (B) Appearing initially

(C) Their initial appearance

(D) When first appearing

(E) At first, comets appear

34. Improved sonar technology, together with less stringent quotas, <u>account for the recent increase in the amount of</u> fish caught by commercial vessels.

  (A) account for the recent increase in the amount of

  (B) would account for a recent increase in

  (C) accounts for the recent increase in the number of

  (D) is accounted for by the recent increase in

  (E) account for recent increases in amounts of

35. Some of our federal legislators are opposed to government endowments or other financial support for photography as an art form on the basis that much of modern photography portrays nudity and is thus obscene. These legislators are mistaken, however, since even they would agree that Michelangelo's works of art, most of which depict nudity, are not obscene.

Which of the following statements, if true, would most seriously weaken the argument above?

  (A) Due to their relatively high artistic value, the works of Michelangelo that portray nudity are not considered obscene.

  (B) Many modern photographic works of art have been displayed in museums alongside Michelangelo's works.

  (C) The majority of Michelangelo's work was not funded or otherwise supported by the government.

  (D) What these legislators consider to be obscene does not coincide with what the general citizenry views as obscene.

  (E) The artistic level of the works of the vast majority of modern photographers does not approach that of Michelangelo's works.

QUESTIONS 36–38 ARE BASED ON THE FOLLOWING PASSAGE.

Line   In nearly all human populations, a majority of individuals can taste the artificially synthesized chemical phenylthiocarbonide (PTC). However, the percentage
(5) varies dramatically—from as low as 60 percent in India to as high as 95 percent in Africa. That this polymorphism is observed in nonhuman primates as well indicates a long evolutionary history which, although
(10) obviously not acting on PTC, might reflect evolutionary selection for taste discrimination of other, more significant, bitter substances, such as certain toxic plants.

   A somewhat more puzzling human
(15) polymorphism is the genetic variability in earwax, or *cerumen*, which is observed in two varieties. Among European populations, 90 percent of individuals have a sticky yellow variety rather than a dry, gray one,
(20) whereas in northern China these numbers are approximately the reverse. Perhaps like PTC variability, cerumen variability is an incidental expression of something more adaptively significant. Indeed, the observed
(25) relationship between cerumen and odorous bodily secretions, to which nonhuman primates—and to a lesser extent humans—pay attention suggests that during the course of human evolution genes affecting body
(30) secretions, including cerumen, came under selective influence.

36. It can be inferred from the passage that human populations vary considerably in their

  (A) sensitivity to certain bodily odors.

  (B) capacity for hearing.

  (C) ability to assimilate artificial chemicals.

  (D) vulnerability to certain toxins found in plants.

  (E) ability to discern bitterness in taste.

37. Which of the following provides the most reasonable explanation for the assertion in the first paragraph that evolutionary history "obviously" did not act on PTC?

  (A) PTC is not a naturally occurring chemical but rather has been produced only recently by scientists.

(B) Most humans lack sufficient taste sensitivity to discriminate between PTC and bitter chemicals occurring naturally.

(C) Variability among humans respecting PTC discrimination, like variability respecting earwax, cannot be explained in terms of evolutionary adaptivity.

(D) The sense of taste in humans is not as discriminating as that in nonhuman primates.

(E) Unlike nonhuman primates, humans can discriminate intellectually between toxic and nontoxic bitter substances.

38. Which of the following best expresses the main idea of the passage?

(A) Artificially synthesized chemicals might eventually serve to alter the course of evolution by desensitizing humans to certain tastes and odors.

(B) Some human polymorphisms might be explained as vestigial evidence of evolutionary adaptations that still serve vital purposes in other primates.

(C) Sensitivity to taste and to odors have been subject to far greater natural selectivity during the evolution of primates than previously thought.

(D) Polymorphism among human populations varies considerably from region to region throughout the world.

(E) The human senses of taste and smell have evolved considerably over the course of evolutionary history.

39. The city of Exitur recently began providing recycling bins to every household in the city, along with a brochure explaining what types of trash residents should put in the bins for pickup by city workers. Previously, the city's residents had no means of recycling any of their trash. Exitur's residents, who generate a significant amount of recyclables, have all cooperated conscientiously with the new program. Nevertheless, the total amount of trash they have been putting in their garbage cans for disposal—and not for recycling— remains about the same as before.

If the information provided is true, which of the following must on the basis of it also be true about Exitur since the program's implementation?

(A) The city's trash collection workers are not performing their jobs properly.

(B) The average number of trash cans used by each household has increased.

(C) The amount of trash generated by the city's residents has increased.

(D) Some items put in recycling bins are being disposed of rather than recycled.

(E) The city's residents have not been generating any trash that can be recycled.

40. With crude-oil production peaking, the corporate suppliers of energy are aggressively pursuing other energy sources; nevertheless, <u>because oil prices are currently in decline, demand for alternative energy products is lessening.</u>

(A) because oil prices are currently in decline, demand for alternative energy products is lessening.

(B) because of currently declining oil prices, alternative energy products are lower in demand.

(C) in view of the current decline of oil prices, demand for alternative energy products is also declining.

(D) being that oil prices are currently lessening in amount, so too is the demand for alternative energy products.

(E) considering the fact that current oil prices are declining, demand for alternative energy products is lessening.

41. In 2008, more citizens from the country of Monrovia migrated from Monrovia to neighboring Abstania than during any prior year. In 2008, the number of reported violent crimes in Abstania increased dramatically over 2007. The unavoidable conclusion is that Monrovians who migrated from Monrovia to Abstania were responsible for this increase.

Which of the following statements, if true, would most seriously weaken the claim that Monrovians were responsible for the increase in violent crime in Abstania during 2008?

(A) Each year more violent criminals are apprehended in Abstania than in Monrovia.

(B) During 2008, more violent crimes were reported in Abstania than in Monrovia.

(C) In 2008, no Monrovians migrated from either Monrovia or Abstania to any country other than Monrovia or Abstania.

(D) In 2008, the number of unreported violent crimes in Abstania increased as well.

(E) In 2008, fewer Monrovians migrated from Monrovia to Abstania than from Abstania to Monrovia.

ANSWER KEY AND EXPLANATIONS

See Appendix B for score conversion tables to determine your score. Be sure to keep a tally of correct and incorrect answers for each test section.

Analysis of an Argument—Evaluation and Scoring

Evaluate your Argument-Analysis essay on a scale of 1 to 6 (6 being the highest score) according to the following five criteria:

① Does your essay identify the key features of the argument and analyze each one in a thoughtful manner?

② Does your essay support each point of its critique with insightful reasons and examples?

③ Does your essay develop its ideas in a clear, organized manner, with appropriate transitions to help connect ideas?

④ Does your essay demonstrate proficiency, fluency, and maturity in its use of sentence structure, vocabulary, and idiom?

⑤ Does your essay demonstrate command of the elements of Standard Written English, including grammar, word usage, spelling, and punctuation?

The following series of questions, which serve to identify the Argument's five distinct problems, will help you evaluate your essay in terms of criteria 1 and 2. To earn a score of 4 or higher, your essay should identify at least three of these problems and, for each one, provide at least one example or counterexample that supports your critique. (Your examples need not be the same as the ones below.) Identifying and discussing at least four of the problems would help earn you an even higher score.

① Does the argument confuse cause-and-effect with mere correlation between Stribling and the success of the bands he manages? (Perhaps the actual reason for the success of these bands has nothing to do with Stribling, and Excess's current manager is just as effective as Stribling would be.)

② Is it fair to assume that hiring Stribling would be sufficient for the band to regain its popularity? (Perhaps Stribling's specialty is managing hip-hop groups, and he would be far less effective in promoting a rock band like Excess. Also, the band's style of music might be outdated, making it too late for a comeback, regardless of Stribling's talent or efforts.)

③ Would increasing popularity as a touring band be sufficient to increase sales of the band's CDs? (Instead of buying new CDs, the band's old fans might just replay old Excess albums, while new, younger fans might borrow those albums or find another way to listen to the band's songs for free.)

④ Does the argument unfairly limit the band to an either/or choice between two courses of action that are not necessarily mutually exclusive? (Why not hire Stribling and record new songs? If Stribling is successful, the band could promote their new songs at more concerts, sparking more CD sales.)

⑤ Are either of the two plans necessary to achieve sales goals for the band's CDs? (The argument ignores other possible strategies—for example, publicity stunts, image makeovers, or increased television exposure—that might be equally or more effective in boosting CD sales.)

INEGRATIVE REASONING

1.1 E	4.1 A	7.1 A	11.1 A
1.2 C	4.2 C	7.2 B	11.2 B
2.1. A	5.1 D	7.3 A	12.1 C
2.2 B	5.2 B	8. C	12.2 A
2.3 A	6.1 B	9. B	
3.1 A	6.2 A	10.1 C	
3.2 E	6.3 B	10.2 B	

1.1. **The correct answer is (E).** Start by calculating the sphere's radius. Since the sphere's surface area and volumes are equal, then:

$$4\pi r^2 = \frac{4}{3}\pi r^3$$

$$r^2 = \frac{1}{3}r^3$$

$$r = 3$$

Next, the fact that the cube is inscribed in the sphere means that the cube's vertices touch the surface of the sphere. Therefore, the cube's main diagonal, D (that is, the diagonal that goes through the center of the cube), equals the diameter of the sphere. Thus, $D = 2r$. So, the length of the cube's main diagonal is 6.

The main diagonal of the cube is also the hypotenuse of a right triangle whose two legs are (a) an edge of the cube and (b) the diagonal of a face of the cube. Let e be the length of the edge of the cube and d be the diagonal of the cube's face. Then, by the Pythagorean theorem, you have $D^2 = e^2 + d^2$.

You can take this one step further by realizing that the diagonal of a face of the cube is the hypotenuse of a right triangle whose two legs are two of the four edges of the face. Thus, again by the Pythagorean Theorem, $d^2 = 2e^2$.

Combine these two expressions in order to find the length of the edge of the cube:

$$D^2 = e^2 + d^2$$

$$6^2 = e^2 + 2e^2$$

$$36 = 3e^2$$

$$e^2 = 12$$

$$e = 2\sqrt{3}$$

Now that you know what the edge of the cube is, you can find both its surface area and its volume. The surface area equals six times the area of a face:

$$S_c = 6e^2$$

$$S_c = 6\left(2\sqrt{3}\right)^2$$

$$S_c = 72$$

1.2. The correct answer is (C). The volume of the cube equals the third power of the edge of the cube:

$$V_c = e^3$$
$$V_c = \left(2\sqrt{3}\right)^3$$
$$V_c = 24\sqrt{3}$$

2.1. The correct answer is (A). This statement is true. To find the total number of permits in 2011, add the numbers in the "Total Buildings, 2011" column. That total is:

$$68 + 174 + 28 + 386 + 341 = 997$$

To find the number of permits issued for 5 or More-Family buildings in 2011, you must find the number of such permits issued in each Borough. In the Bronx, 44.1% of 68 permits in 2011 were for 5 or More-Family buildings. That means that the number of such permits in the Bronx was 29.988. (It's pretty clear that the actual number was 30, but don't round until the end.)

For Brooklyn, that number was:	$25.3\%(174) = 44.022$
For Manhattan:	$92.9\%(28) = 26.012$
For Queens:	$9.6\%(386) = 37.056$
For Staten Island:	$0.3\%(341) = 1.023$

Thus, the total number of permits for 5 or More-Family buildings in 2011 was the sum of these five numbers:

$$29.988 + 44.022 + 26.012 + 37.054 + 1.023 \approx 138$$

Finally, you can find the percentage of all permits issued in 2011 that were for 5 or More-Family buildings. If 138 is x percent of 997, then:

$$138 = x\%(997)$$
$$x \approx 13.8$$

2.2. The correct answer is (B). This will not require so many calculations. In 2011, 9.6% of 386 permits in Queens were for 5 or More-Family buildings. This number is 37. In Brooklyn, 44.3% of 174 permits were for 2-Family buildings. That number is 77. Thus, fewer permits were issued in 2011 for 5 or More-Family buildings in Queens than were issued in 2011 for 2-Family buildings in Brooklyn.

2.3. The correct answer is (A). The decrease between 2010 and 2011 in number of permits issued for 2-Family buildings in Queens is:

$$67.2\%(509) - 57\%(386) = 342 - 220 = 122$$

The decrease between 2010 and 2011 in number of permits issued for 1-Family buildings in Staten Island on:

$$71.9\%(349) - 52.5\%(341) = 251 - 179 = 72$$

Thus, the statement is true.

3.1. **The correct answer is (A).** The company has chosen to proceed with the baseball redesign only, in order to maximize its sales as soon as possible. An underlying assumption is that doing both redesigns would not have a better result, or that it would not be possible. The latter part of the assumption is articulated in choice (A). Choice (B), if anything, would undermine the company's decision. Choice (C) merely reinforces the validity of the "internal studies" mentioned in the prompt, but it is not a necessary assumption: Baseball need not be more popular than soccer in order to affect sales more positively. (For instance, it could be that baseball equipment sells for more than soccer equipment.) This statement is also not a fact supporting the necessary assumption. As for choice (D), it talks about costs, but the company's decision is geared towards sales—so cost does not come into play.

3.2. **The correct answer is (E).** The possible fact that supports the assumption stated in choice (A) is provided by choice (E). If either of the two redesigns will take the development team at least ten months to complete, then the company cannot undertake both of them in the same year.

4.1. **The correct answer is (A).** If the division of the fifth term by the third term gives a quotient of 1 and leaves a remainder of 10, then $a_5 = 1 \times a_3 + 10$. Since this is an arithmetic sequence, you also know that $a_5 = a_1 + 4d$, and $a_3 = a_1 + 2d$. Therefore:

$$a_5 = 1 \times a_3 + 10$$
$$a_1 + 4d = a_1 + 2d + 10$$
$$2d = 10$$
$$d = 5$$

The product of the first and third terms equals 24, so you have:

$$a_1 \times a_3 = 24$$
$$a_1(a_1 + 2d) = 24$$
$$a_1(a_1 + 10) = 24$$
$$a_1^2 + 10a_1 - 24 = 0$$
$$a_1^2 + 12a_1 - 2a_1 - 24 = 0$$
$$a_1(a_1 + 12) - 2(a_1 + 12) = 0$$
$$(a_1 + 12)(a_1 - 2) = 0$$
$$a_1 = -12$$
$$\text{OR}$$
$$a_1 = 2$$

The second of these answers is listed among the answer choices, so the correct answer for the first term of the sequence is 2.

4.2. **The correct answer is (C).** See the answer explanation for 4.1.

5.1. **The correct answer is (D).** The satisfaction of customers who shop at the company's stores has improved, and the company is advertising this fact. Choice (D) provides evidence that these moves are having a positive effect, and suggests that they may result in higher sales: If people who do not shop at this company's stores think better of the company now than they used to, then there is a possibility that they will be converted to customers of the company. There is no guarantee of this, of course, but there is no other statement that provides stronger support for the argument, so choice (D) is the correct answer in the first column.

Choice (A) seems as though it might weaken the argument, but in fact it does not provide new meaningful information one way or the other: whether or not the previous management team was focused on customer satisfaction, the results are what matters. Choice (C) basically says that the survey results are statistically valid, but it does not give any further evidence that these results will or will not lead to the conclusion presented in the argument. (If, instead, the statement had said that the survey results are not statistically valid, then it would have been a good candidate for the statement that undermines the conclusion.) Choice (E) seems tempting, but is ultimately irrelevant: The conclusion says that the company will increase its per store sales, not its overall sales. You have no information on which to judge how the new stores will affect the company's per store sales. Finally, choice (B) is the one that undermines the argument.

5.2. **The correct answer is (B).** The conclusion that the company's per store sales will increase rests partly on the improved customer satisfaction results. Choice (B) says that only a score of 5 in customer satisfaction correlates strongly with increased sales. Therefore, if most of the 75% of respondents who rated their satisfaction a 4 or a 5 in fact rated it a 4, then the force or the survey results, in terms of predicting increased sales, becomes much weaker. [While choice (B) does not tell you what the breakdown of 4s and 5s is, it does give reason to doubt the significance of that 75% figure.]

6.1. **The correct answer is (B).** Seven is the straight average between the three average scores (6.4, 7.4, and 7.2) given by students, parents, and teachers, respectively. However, a different number of students, parents, and teachers responded, so a weighted average should be considered instead. Without performing the exact calculations, you can tell that, for instance, the 63,200 students weigh more heavily on the average than the 14,700 teachers do, so they will pull the average down compared to the straight average. (The actual average turns out to be 6.8.)

6.2. **The correct answer is (A).** In 2011, the city's schools received three ratings below 7.0: by students in the category of Communication and the category of Engagement, and by teachers in the category of Communication. Thus, among these three ratings, the probability that one of them was by students is 67% (two out of three).

6.3. **The correct answer is (B).** The same principle applies here as in the first question. The straight average of 7.5 (the students' grade) and 8.2 (the teachers' grade) is 7.85. However, the weighted average is 7.61, which is lower than the parents' grade of 7.8.

7.1. **The correct answer is (A).** Nebbiolo and Barolo are similar wines, according to the brief wine descriptions. However, Nebbiolo tends to be cheaper than Barolo. Because the restaurant owner has expressed doubts that his customers will readily buy more expensive bottles, it is reasonable to infer that he would choose Nebbiolo over Barolo.

7.2. **The correct answer is (B).** You cannot infer this. Neither of these is among the easily recognizable wines the restaurant owner mentions, and there's no further information about price or any other consideration that might help you decide whether one is preferable to the restaurant owner over the other.

7.3. **The correct answer is (A).** The wine expert recommends that "if you're going to have several types of glass, at least one of them must be for red wine." With this statement he implies that having the proper glasses for red wine is more important than having the proper glasses for white wine. So, if the restaurant were to carry only one kind of glass, the wine expert would recommend that it be a red wine glass—that is, a glass of the bigger, broader kind.

8. **The correct answer is (C).** The restaurant owner believes that his customers order Cabernet and Merlot more than other kinds of red wine because they recognize those names. He also doesn't believe that they know much about Bordeaux. It is reasonable to infer, therefore, that a way to get around that would be to relate Bordeaux to the more familiar Cabernet and Merlot. Choice (C) describes such a strategy. Choice (A) would be counter-productive, given the cost-conscious nature of the customers, according to the restaurant owner. Next, you have no evidence that prestige is something the customers care about, so choice (B) does not appear to be an attractive option. Choice (D) seems as though it would help, but the restaurant owner does not believe food pairings play so much a role in his customers' wine choices as does price and familiarity. Finally, wine list placement does not come up at all in the e-mail exchange, so eliminate choice (E).

9. **The correct answer is (B).** The wine expert says it's advisable to "serve lighter wines with lighter dishes, such as white meat or fish." If a customer wants red wine with her fish, then the lighter the red the better. All the wines listed in the answer choices, except for Beaujolais, are full- or medium-bodied. Beaujolais is the only one that is specifically described as light. Thus, it would be the best recommendation among the choices provided.

10.1. **The correct answer is (C).** Don't waste time trying to calculate exact averages. Rather, think about the different cases in which City X's unemployment rate would have been greater than the average unemployment rate of the other two cities. One such case is when City X's rate is greater than either of the other two rates. This happened every year from 2000 to 2005. Next, City X's unemployment rate will be greater than the average unemployment rate of the other two cities when City X's rate is between the two other rates, but closer to the larger one of the two. This happened in 2006, 2007, and 2009. In 2011, City X's rate was between the other two but closer to the lower of the two, while in 2008 and 2010 City X's rate was the lowest of the three. Thus, in all but these three years (that is, in a total of 9 years), City X's rate was greater than the average of the other two rates.

10.2. **The correct answer is (B).** In 2000, City X had the highest unemployment rate, but City Y was significantly more populous. The 4% of City Y's 2.1 million residents who were unemployed are more than the 5.8% of City X's 1.3 million residents or the 5.2% of City Z's 1.2 million residents. Thus, the correct answer is choice (B).

11.1. **The correct answer is (A).** Between the end of 2003 and the end of 2007 the stock of Quadruped appreciated from $15.50 to $18.25. This is a 17.74% increase. The stock of Tetrapod went from $11.50 to $13.25, for a 15.22% increase. Finally, the stock of FourFeet went from $10.75 to$12.50, for a $10.75 to $12.50 increase. Thus, the correct answer is choice (A).

11.2. **The correct answer is (B).** At the end of 2005, the per share price of Tetrapod was $13.00, while the per share prices of Quadruped and FourFeet were $19.50 and $11, respectively, summing up to $30.50. If $13 is x times $30.50, then:

$$13 = x(30.50)$$
$$x = \frac{13}{(30.50)}$$
$$x = 0.43$$

12.1. **The correct answer is (C).** There were five teams that had payrolls greater than $125 million. Of those, three won more than 80 games. Thus, the likelihood that a team with a payroll greater than $125 million won more than 80 games was 0.6. Then there were 11 teams with a payroll less than $75 million, and of those, 7 won more than 70 games. Thus, the likelihood that a team with a payroll less than $75 million won more than 70 games was 0.64 (7 out of 11), which is greater than the likelihood that a team with a payroll greater than $125 million won more than 80 games.

12.2. **The correct answer is (A).** Only two of the 30 teams were in the top five in terms of both payroll and number of wins: the one represented by the top-most diamond, and the one represented by the diamond farthest to the right. Thus, the probability that, if a team is selected at random, it will be one of the top five teams in terms of both payroll and number of wins is 2 out of 30.

QUANTITATIVE SECTION

1. D	9. E	17. E	25. D	33. B
2. C	10. C	18. C	26. D	34. A
3. D	11. D	19. E	27. E	35. E
4. C	12. A	20. A	28. E	36. D
5. C	13. A	21. E	29. E	37. B
6. C	14. C	22. D	30. D	
7. B	15. B	23. A	31. B	
8. A	16. B	24. A	32. A	

1. **The correct answer is (D).** The two statements provide essentially the same information: the rate at which a typist types. Since this rate would be sufficient information to answer the question, the correct answer must be choice (D). If you don't recognize this shortcut, you can determine the speed (or rate) at which a typist types, in terms of pages per unit of time, by setting up a general equation to express the time required by a typist to type one page:

$$\frac{(\text{no. of typists})(\text{time})}{\text{no. of pages}} = \text{time per page}$$

Based on the values provided in either Statement (1) or (2), the typing rate of a single typist is $7\frac{1}{2}$ minutes per page:

$$\frac{(1 \text{ typist})(30 \text{ minutes})}{4 \text{ pages}} = 7\frac{1}{2}$$

Once you know the typing rate, you can apply that rate to the numbers given in the question; so the correct answer is choice (D). You don't need to actually answer the question. Just for the record, however, 5 typists could type thirty pages in 45 minutes.

2. **The correct answer is (C).** This problem involves a system of three equations with three variables. One way to solve it is with both the substitution and addition-subtraction methods. Express x in terms of y: $x = 8 - y$. Substitute this expression for x in the second equation: $(8 - y) + z = 7$ or $-y + z = -1$. Add this equation to the third equation in the system.

$$\begin{aligned} -y + z &= -1 \\ \underline{y + z} &= \underline{6} \\ 2z &= 5 \\ z &= 2.5 \end{aligned}$$

To find the value of x, substitute z's value for z in the second equation:

$$x + 2.5 = 7; x = 4.5$$

3. **The correct answer is (D).** Any multiple-digit prime number must end in an odd digit other than 5 (1, 3, 7, or 9). Since the sum of the three digits is 7, Z must be either 1 or 3, and four possibilities emerge: 601, 421, 241, and 223.

4. **The correct answer is (C).** The 40% of the sale price that Jerry received equals $\frac{2}{5}$ of the $250,000, which is $100,000. On his family trip he spent 10% of that amount, or $10,000. Thus, together Tom and Jerry spent $30,000 of the proceeds and placed the remaining $220,000 in savings accounts. Set up and solve a proportion in order to find what percent of the $250,000 they placed in savings accounts:

$$\frac{220,000}{250,000} = \frac{x}{100}$$

$$\frac{22}{25} = \frac{x}{100}$$

$$\frac{22}{1} = \frac{x}{4}$$

$$x = 88$$

5. **The correct answer is (C).** Extend $\overline{BE}$ to F (as shown in the diagram below). m$\angle EFD$ = m$\angle ABE$ = 40°. m$\angle FED$ must equal 110° because the three interior angles of $\triangle DEF$ must total 180° in measure. Since $\angle BED$ and $\angle FED$ are supplementary (the sum of their measures is 180°), m$\angle BED$ = 70° (x = 70).

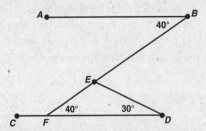

6. **The correct answer is (C).** Begin by squaring both sides of the equation in order to eliminate the radical sign:

$$\sqrt{x+2} = x$$

$$\left(\sqrt{x+2}\right)^2 = x^2$$

$$x + 2 = x^2$$

$$x^2 - x - 2 = 0$$

$$x^2 + (-2x + x) - 2 = 0$$

$$\left(x^2 - 2x\right) + (x - 2) = 0$$

$$x(x - 2) + (x - 2) = 0$$

$$(x - 2)(x + 1) = 0$$

$$x = 2 \quad \text{OR} \quad x = -1$$

It seems there may be two solutions here. However, be careful: squaring the two sides may have introduced an invalid solution. Normally you would plug the two resulting values of x into the original equation to see whether they are both valid. In this case, you can discard the solution $x = -1$ without any further calculations because the original equation tells you that x equals a square root, and square roots are always nonnegative. Next, just to be sure, you can check the other solution. If $x = 2$ then:

$$\sqrt{x+2} = x$$
$$\sqrt{2+2} = 2$$
$$\sqrt{4} = 2$$
$$2 = 2$$

This is a valid result, so $x = 2$ is a valid solution.

7. **The correct answer is (B).** Statement (1) tells you that you can disregard the exponent p; all you need to determine is the value of the fraction given. But since m and n could each be any number at all, so could the value of the fraction. Statement (2) establishes that the numerator and the denominator of the fraction are equal in value, and therefore that the fraction's value is 1. Since 1 raised to any power is still 1, Statement (2) is sufficient to establish that the expression equals 1.

8. **The correct answer is (A).** Statement (1) tells you that there are 4 distinguishable people to be arranged. That's all you need to know to determine the number of possible sequences or permutations. From that number, you'd determine the probability that the 4 students are lined up in any one specific order simply by dividing 1 by the number of possibilities. Statement (1) alone suffices to answer the question. (For the record, to find the number of permutations, you can either list them systematically or apply the factorial $4! = 4 \times 3 \times 2 \times 1 = 24$. Of 24 possibilities, in only one would the 4 students line up in the order given in the question, and the answer to the question is $\frac{1}{24}$.) Statement (2) alone provides no useful information—except that there are at least 3 students in the group.

9. **The correct answer is (E).** Statement (1) alone provides no information about R. Statement (2) provides a value for R, but provides no information about either P or Q. Together, the two statements are still insufficient to answer the question. The values of P and Q relative to R are still unknown.

10. **The correct answer is (C).** You can determine the area of the semicircle in any event—without either Statement (1) or (2). So you need more information only to determine the triangle's area. Given Statement (1) alone, the triangle could be any shape, so its area could vary. Given Statement (2) alone, $\overline{AB}$ and $\overline{BC}$ each could be any length, and so the area of the triangle could vary. Thus, neither statement alone suffices to answer the question. Given both statements together, the triangle must be equilateral, and you can determine its area. (Although you don't need to do the math, the semicircle's area is $\frac{\pi}{2}$, the triangle's area is $\sqrt{3}$, and so the total area is $\frac{\pi}{2} + \sqrt{3}$.)

11. **The correct answer is (D).** The question describes an arithmetic sequence—an evenly spaced, finite sequence of numbers. In any arithmetic sequence, the average of all terms is the same as the median. The average is also equal to half the sum of the first and last number in the sequence. Thus, either Statement (1) or (2) alone suffices to answer the question. For example, the sequence might include four integers {33, 35, 37, 39} or it might include 6 integers {31, 33, 35, 37, 39, 41}. As you can see, regardless of the number of terms, the average and median are each the same as half the sum of the least and greatest terms.

12. **The correct answer is (A).** You don't know whether a, b, and c have any factors other than the ones mentioned, but you don't need to know. You're merely looking for a number that does not HAVE to be divisible by 12 based on the information you have. You need go no further than choice (A). For a number to be divisible by 12, it must have at least one factor of 3, but you don't know of any such factor in 2ab: the only factors you know of are one 2 in a, two 2s in b, and the additional 2. Therefore, 2ab is not necessarily divisible by 12.

13. **The correct answer is (A).** Given that a total of 500 products were sold, Statement (1) alone is sufficient to answer the question. If A sold 166 products, A sold just less than $\frac{1}{3}$ of the total number. Either B or C must sell more than $\frac{1}{3}$, and the answer to the question is *no*. Statement (2) alone is insufficient to answer the question. If C sold 249 products, A could have sold anywhere from 0 to 251 products; if A sold either 250 or 251 products, A would have sold more products than either B or C. However, if A sold 0–249 products, A would not have sold more products than C.

14. **The correct answer is (C).** Since the distance from the two given points to $(4,t)$ is the same, apply the distance formula twice, then equate the results and solve for t:

$$\sqrt{(4-1)^2 + (t-1)^2} = \sqrt{(5-4)^2 + (3-t)^2}$$
$$\sqrt{9 + (t^2 - 2t + 1)} = \sqrt{1 + (9 - 6t + t^2)}$$
$$\sqrt{10 + t^2 - 2t} = \sqrt{10 - 6t + t^2}$$
$$10 + t^2 - 2t = 10 - 6t + t^2$$
$$-2t = -6t$$
$$4t = 0$$
$$t = 0$$

15. **The correct answer is (B).** Each trip consists of 5 jumps, after which the glip starts over at point X. In jumps 1–5, the first jump is to A, as the question stem tells us. In jumps 6–10, the first jump is to B, and so on clockwise around the circuit. After 25 jumps (5 trips of 5 jumps each), the glip begins exactly the same sequence of 25 jumps again:

Jumps 1–5: X to A to B to X to D to X

Jumps 6–10: X to B to C to X to E to X

Jumps 11–15: X to C to D to X to A to X

Jumps 16–20: X to D to E to X to B to X

Jumps 21–25: X to E to A to X to C to X

Since the pattern indicated above begins again after each multiple of 25 jumps, jump 472 is the same as jump 22: from E to A.

16. **The correct answer is (B).** Although trying each answer choice in turn is one way to solve this problem, doing the math, especially calculating and then working with the square root of a large number, might be more trouble than it's worth. A better idea is to solve for x algebraically:

$$\sqrt{4x - 4} = 8 + 4$$
$$\sqrt{4(x-1)} = 12$$
$$2\sqrt{x-1} = 12$$
$$\sqrt{x-1} = 6$$
$$\left(\sqrt{x-1}\right)^2 = 6^2$$
$$x - 1 = 36$$
$$x = 37$$

17. **The correct answer is (E).** Statement (1) alone provides no number values and therefore is obviously insufficient to answer the question. Statement (2) alone provides the value of one number, but the value of all three numbers is needed to compute their average. Considered together, Statements (1) and (2) still allow for many possibilities. Statement (2) tells us that one (and only one) of the three numbers equals 0. Combining this fact with Statement (1), the other two numbers might either have the same positive value or they might be additive reciprocals. If the three numbers are 0, 2, and 2, for example, then the average of the three numbers $= (0 + 2 + 2) \div 3 = \dfrac{4}{3}$. However, if the three numbers are 0, –2, and 2, then the average of the three numbers $= (0 + 2 - 2) \div 3 = 0$. Since both statements considered together allow for more than one answer to the question, the correct answer is choice (E).

18. **The correct answer is (C).** You can solve for x in Statement (1):

$$-4x - 7 > -14$$
$$-4x > -7$$
$$-x > -\frac{7}{4}$$
$$x < \frac{7}{4}$$

You can solve for x in Statement (2):

$$5x + 3 > -2(x + 1)$$
$$5x + 3 > -2x - 2$$
$$7x > -5$$
$$x > -\frac{5}{7}$$

Neither Statement (1) nor (2) alone suffices to determine the value of x. However, considering both statements together, $-\dfrac{5}{7} < x < \dfrac{7}{4}$. Only two integral x-values—0 and 1—fall within this range. Given that x is a non-zero integer, $x = 1$. Both Statements (1) and (2) together suffice to determine the value of x, which is 1.

19. **The correct answer is (E).** Neither statement provides any information about the dimensions of the larger box. (It might be a cube, or it might be only one inch in height, or it might have any other shape.) Without this information, it's impossible to answer the question.

20. **The correct answer is (A).** You can easily answer this question by plugging in simple values for m and k. Assume that it takes Paul 10 minutes to mow the lawn ($m = 10$) and that you want to know what portion of the job remains after 5 minutes ($k = 5$).

Obviously, exactly half $\left(\dfrac{1}{2}\right)$ the job remains after 5 minutes. Now, in each answer choice, substitute 10 and 5 for m and k, respectively, to see which one gives you a value of $\dfrac{1}{2}$. You don't need to go any farther than choice (A):

$$\frac{m - k}{m} = \frac{10 - 5}{10} = \frac{5}{10}, \text{ or } \frac{1}{2}$$

You can also solve this problem abstractly. Here's how. The longer Paul mows, the more lawn is mowed, so the variation is direct. Let x equal the portion of the lawn Paul has mowed after k minutes, set up the proportion, and solve for x:

$$\frac{m}{1} = \frac{k}{x}$$
$$mx = k$$
$$x = \frac{k}{m}$$

Paul has mowed $\frac{k}{m}$ of the lawn in k minutes. Still not mowed, then, is $1 - \frac{k}{m}$, or $\frac{m-k}{m}$.

21. **The correct answer is (E).** When removing the first pair, the probability the pair removed will be black is $\frac{2}{5}$. Four pairs remain, two of which are white. The probability of removing a white pair from among those four is $\frac{2}{4}$. Combine the two probabilities by multiplying: $\frac{2}{5} \times \frac{2}{4} = \frac{4}{20}$, or $\frac{1}{5}$. This is the probability of choosing a black pair and then a white pair. So, the probability of choosing a white pair and then a black pair is also $\frac{1}{5}$. The probability, then, that the two pairs of socks are white and black is $\frac{1}{5} + \frac{1}{5} = \frac{2}{5}$.

22. **The correct answer is (D).** From Statement (1) alone, you know that washers are bought at 45 cents per dozen and sold at 54 (3×18) cents per dozen. Calculating the profit on seven dozen washers is simply a matter of multiplying the difference (9 cents) by 7. Hence, Statement (1) alone suffices to answer the question. (The answer is 63 cents.) From Statement (2) alone, you know that a single washer costs $0.0375 ($3.75 ÷ 100); therefore, a dozen washers cost 0.0375 × 12 = 45 cents, and seven dozen washers cost 45 × 7 cents. The profit would simply be 20% of this total cost. As you can see, you can answer the question based on Statement (2) alone. (Again, the answer is 63 cents.)

23. **The correct answer is (A).** You can express the equation in Statement (1) as $x + y = 190$; thus, x and y are not supplementary angles. (Their measures don't add up to 180°.) This information suffices to establish that the angles created by the intersection of l1 and l3 are different from those created by the intersection of l_2 and l_3. Accordingly, l_1 cannot be parallel to l_2, and statement (1) alone suffices to answer the question. Statement (2) adds nothing to the question. It merely reiterates what is already assumed in any GMAT figure: that all lines are straight.

24. **The correct answer is (A).** Suppose digits M and N are both 1. To find the product of 0.01 and 0.01, you multiply 1 by 1 (M × N), then add together the decimal places in the two numbers. There are four places altogether, so the product would be 0.0001, which is equivalent to $\frac{1}{10,000}$. Thus, whatever the values of M and N, $0.0M \times 0.0N = \frac{1}{10,000} \times (M \times N)$.

25. **The correct answer is (D).** You can solve this problem by setting up and solving a system of two equations in two variables (let c and d equal the number of cats and dogs, respectively):

$$\frac{c}{d} = \frac{5}{6}$$
$$d = c + 8$$

Substitute $c + 8$ for d in the first equation, then solve for c:

$$\frac{c}{c+8} = \frac{5}{6}$$
$$6c = 5c + 40$$
$$c = 40$$

Hence, $d = 48$, and the total number of boarded cats and dogs is 88.

26. **The correct answer is (D).** By definition, the longest possible chord of a circle is equal in length to the circle's diameter. Since the x-coordinates of the two endpoints of chord $\overline{RS}$ are the same (7), the chord is vertical. Accordingly, the length of $\overline{RS}$ is simply the vertical distance from –3 to 7, which is 10. The circle's diameter is 10, and thus its radius is 5. The circle's area is $\pi(5)^2 = 25\pi$.

27. **The correct answer is (E).** The money earned by b workers at D dollars per week is bD dollars. The number of workers remaining is $(m - b)$, and because they earn $\frac{1}{2}D$ dollars per week, the money they earn is:

$$\frac{1}{2}D(m-b) = \frac{1}{2}mD - \frac{1}{2}bD$$

Thus, the total amount earned is:

$$bD + \frac{1}{2}mD - \frac{1}{2}bD = \frac{1}{2}bD + \frac{1}{2}mD = \frac{1}{2}D(b+m)$$

28. **The correct answer is (E).** To determine standard deviation, you need to know the value of each number, not just their average and range. For example, considering Statements (1) and (2) together, here are just two of many possible distributions: {6, 9, 12, 15, 18} and {6, 11, 12, 13, 18}. Notice that the second and fourth terms in the second set are closer to the mean than the corresponding terms in the first set. Accordingly, the standard deviation of the second distribution is less than that of the first set.

29. **The correct answer is (E).** On the map, the number of centimeters from City 1 to City 2 = 825 ÷ 75 = 11. To convert this number to millimeters, multiply by 10: 11 × 10 = 110.

30. **The correct answer is (D).** The greatest ten-year change in non-minority scholarship funds awarded occurred from 1990 to 2000: $750,000 to $600,000 (approximately). During this period, the greatest *percent* change in funds awarded occurred from 1990 to 1995—an increase of approximately 33%—from about $450,000 to $600,000. (The increase from 1995 to 2000 is about the same in dollar amount but less in percent.)

31. **The correct answer is (B).** A quick visual inspection reveals that the aggregate amount awarded in 2000 exceeded that of any of the other three years shown. During that year, minority awards totaled approximately $770,000 and non-minority awards totaled approximately $600,000. The difference between the two amounts is $170,000.

32. **The correct answer is (A).** Statement (1) alone suffices to answer the question. If x is an even integer, all three terms are even, and combining them by subtracting always yields an even integer. If x is an odd integer, x^3, x^2, and x are each odd, and combining them by subtraction always yields an odd integer. Based on Statement (1) alone, the answer to the question must be yes. On the other hand, Statement (2) alone does not suffice to answer the question. $3x + 2x + x = 6x$, which is an even integer regardless of whether x is even or odd.

33. **The correct answer is (B).** First, solve for a in terms of b (or vice versa). Solving for a:

$$3a = 5b$$

$$a = \frac{5b}{3}$$

Substitute this value for a in the equation $ab = 135$:

$$\left(\frac{5b}{3}\right)(b) = 135$$

$$5b^2 = (135)(3)$$

$$b^2 = \frac{(135)(3)}{5}$$

$$b^2 = 81$$

$$b = \pm 9$$

If $b = 9$, $a = 15$. If $b = -9$, $a = -15$. Thus, there are two possible values for $a + b$: -24 and 24.

34. **The correct answer is (A).** The value of a pounds of nuts is ab cents. The value of c pounds of nuts is cd cents. The value of the mixture is $ab + cd$ cents. Since there are $a + c$ pounds, each pound is worth $\frac{ab + cd}{a + c}$ cents. Since the merchant wants to add 10 cents to each pound for profit, and the value of each pound is in cents, add 10 to the value of each pound.

35. **The correct answer is (E).** Substitute $x = -1$ in the expression of y and evaluate $y - x$:

$$y - x = \frac{x^5 + x^3 + x}{3} - x$$

$$= \frac{(-1)^5 + (-1)^3 + (-1)}{3} - (-1)$$

$$= \frac{-3}{3} + 1$$

$$= 0$$

36. **The correct answer is (D).** Given $m\angle BAD - 60°$, $m\angle ABC = 120°$ because the two angles are supplementary. (Their measures total $180°$.) $m\angle ABC = m\angle ADC$. Thus, their sum is $240°$.

37. **The correct answer is (B).** Statement (1) alone does not suffice to answer the question. For example, assume that $B = 1.1$. If $A = 2.2$, then $\frac{A}{B} = 2$ (an integer), but if $A = 2.3$, then $\frac{A}{B}$ is a non-integer. Statement (2) alone establishes that $\frac{A}{B} = 3$ (an integer) and therefore suffices alone to answer the question.

VERBAL SECTION

1. E	10. A	19. D	28. D	37. A
2. E	11. B	20. D	29. C	38. B
3. E	12. E	21. C	30. A	39. C
4. E	13. A	22. C	31. E	40. A
5. D	14. D	23. B	32. E	41. E
6. C	15. A	24. D	33. B	
7. D	16. E	25. A	34. C	
8. B	17. B	26. A	35. A	
9. C	18. B	27. B	36. E	

1. **The correct answer is (E).** The original answer is flawed in only one way: it uses "most unique," a redundant phrase. Choice (E) eliminates the redundancy and also substitutes conventional usage for the words that follow *unique*.

2. **The correct answer is (E).** The original answer is faulty in two ways: it repeats forms of the word *recent*, and it uses the wrong verb tense. Choice (E) remedies both problems by eliminating the word *recently* and replacing the incorrect use of the present perfect continuous (have been shifting) with the present perfect, which is the correct choice for an action completed at an unspecified time in the past, and for an action whose exact moment of·completion is not of particular interest.

3. **The correct answer is (E).** Although the passage's second premise (that farm subsidies discourage farm productivity) doesn't suffice to prove that they will in fact result in lower farm productivity, it does suggest that this result is probable to some degree. Given that a decrease in productivity would run contrary to public policy, it is reasonable to infer that farm subsidies are, or will be, responsible for a public policy violation. Choice (E) expresses this conclusion.

4. **The correct answer is (E).** In the original version, the phrase *an obscene one* is wordy. Also, the correct idiom is either *consider . . . to be* or simply *consider*, not *consider . . . as*. Although choices (C), (D), and (E) each corrects both of these problems, choices (C) and (D) are awkward and confusing. Of the three, choice (E) provides the clearest and most graceful sentence.

5. **The correct answer is (D).** The passage strongly suggests that motor vehicle traffic is the primary cause of the congestion and noise that detract from enjoyment of the park, which is what the park authorities are concerned with. Hence, prohibiting motorized vehicles would clearly be the most effective way to abate the problem. Although the courses of action that choices (B) and (E) propose would each be likely to reduce noise and congestion caused by motorists, especially during peak tourism season, neither would be so effective as an outright ban on motor vehicle traffic.

6. **The correct answer is (C).** If choice (C) is true, then the Cougars are likely to score more goals than if choice (C) is not true. The more goals the Cougars score, the less likely the coach's prediction will come true.

7. **The correct answer is (D).** Choice (D) is the correct answer because the author notes in the first paragraph that the exit from the public sphere of some smaller firms may have actually increased investor confidence. Therefore, the adverse effect on investors of that initial deregistration is not a reasoned or legitimate complaint against the act. Choice (A) must be ruled out because the author mentions this with reasonable objectivity, going so far as to note his or her agreement with the centrality of London in international finance. Choice (B) must be ruled out because the author does suggest that this complaint has been quantitatively legitimized by the RAND study. Choice (C) is incorrect because the author does not comment positively or negatively on the complaint that the act has limited the ability of U.S. firms to compete in the global market. Choice (E) should be eliminated because the author makes no comment, positive or negative, on the act's effect on the creation of new businesses; he or she only mentions this complaint among others.

8. **The correct answer is (B).** Choice (B) is the correct answer because the answer must point logically to both the inferred or known purview of the act as well as to passage facts. The reader must infer that the Sarbanes-Oxley Act is about oversight; furthermore, the reader must infer within that frame of reference that the COO position has been rendered unnecessary. This makes choice (B) the most logical choice, as the discussion of other distractors also shows. Choice (A) must be ruled out because nothing in the passage suggests this; nor is it logical to infer that the act would single out COOs as the sole originators of financial misstatements. Choice (C) must be ruled out based not only on an absence of clues in the passage pointing to this response, but on logic related to the fact that the government would not specify corporate hierarchy. Choice (D) is incorrect because it makes no sense; the intended effect of SOX is just the opposite. Choice (E) should be eliminated because nothing in the passage states or implies this possibility; furthermore, even if the Section were to do this, there is no logical relationship to the COO position.

9. **The correct answer is (C).** Sentence 1 suggests this focus; the remainder of the passage details ways in which the act is maligned or blamed. Throughout, the author shows it as a source of complaints, taking care to note some that are overstated (or "hyperbolic") and those that may be inaccurate, such as the claim about the negative effects of deregistering. Choice (A) is an accusation leveled against SOX, but there is no information given in the passage to indicate the author's agreement with this charge. Choice (B) is tempting because the author clearly makes this point. Nevertheless, this is just one point among many in the passage, and it is only through the accumulation of those points and the author's attitude toward them that the author's attitude as a whole can be accurately inferred. Choice (D) is incorrect because the author states neither agreement nor disagreement with most charges against SOX, though the author does call at least one of them hyperbolic. Choice (E) should be eliminated because the author states neither agreement nor disagreement with most charges against SOX, though the author does call at least one of them hyperbolic.

10. **The correct answer is (A).** The original sentence correctly connects two independent clauses using a semicolon, a conjunctive adverb, and a comma.

11. **The correct answer is (B).** The original version creates confusion by separating the two parallel clauses *the greater* . . . and *the less* . . . . Also, *will be* is unnecessary and undermines the parallel structure of the two clauses. Choice (B) remedies both problems. (The words *smaller* and *lesser* may be used interchangeably here, because both refer to amount rather than quantity.)

12. **The correct answer is (C).** The original sentence contains a misplaced modifier: what is being pulled from the ocean is forage fish, not a relatively recent addition to a list. Choice (C) corrects the problem by causing the introductory phrase to modify "disappearing forage fish."

13. **The correct answer is (A).** If an hourly-wage employee works fewer than five days per week, the employee would need to work more than 8 hours per day *on average* to qualify for overtime pay in state Y. On the other hand, the same employee would need to work more than 8 hours per

day *only on one day* to qualify for overtime pay in state X. Thus, employees working fewer than five days per week would prefer to work in state X. Given that most employees prefer to work in state Y, it is reasonable to conclude that most employees work at least five days per week.

14. **The correct answer is (D).** The argument relies on the unstated assumption that no other event since the picnic could have caused the outbreak. Choice (D) provides some evidence that the employees who have reported disporella symptoms in fact contracted disporella at least one week ago. Accordingly, choice (D) helps support the claim that it was the food served at the picnic two weeks ago that caused the outbreak. Admittedly, choice (D) would provide even stronger support if it indicated that symptoms never appear until one week after contamination. Nevertheless, choice (D) is the best of the five answers.

15. **The correct answer is (A).** The author states in the first paragraph that "[f]orcings can arise from either natural or anthropogenic causes." In the following sentence, the author describes two specific causes of forcings, presumably to illustrate the point of the previous sentence. It can be reasonably inferred by considering both sentences together that the first example (volcanic activity) is a natural cause, while the second (the burning of fossil fuels) is an anthropogenic cause.

16. **The correct answer is (E).** According to the passage, radiative "forcings are quantities normally specified in global climate model simulations, while feedbacks are calculated quantities".

17. **The correct answer is (B).** This choice restates the author's point in the first sentence of the second paragraph. Immediately thereafter, the author discusses clouds as an example of this point: it is difficult to predict the impact of greenhouse gases on clouds and thus on temperature.

18. **The correct answer is (B).** The argument relies on the unstated assumption that prenatal care results in better health and therefore less cost to society. Choice (B) helps affirm this assumption. Choice (E) describes benefits that might decrease the overall tax burden, but only if the prenatal care program serves to reduce the amount of infant-care benefits paid. The argument does not inform us whether this is the case. Thus it is impossible to assess the extent to which choice (E) would explain how the prenatal care would save the taxpayers money.

19. **The correct answer is (D).** The original argument bases a conclusion that one phenomenon causes another on an observed correlation between the two phenomena. The argument boils down to the following:

Premise: X (beautiful beach) is correlated with Y (crowd of people).

Conclusion: X (beautiful beach) causes Y (crowd of people).

Answer choice (D) demonstrates the same pattern of reasoning:

Premise: X (warm weather) is correlated with Y (fleas).

Conclusion: X (warm weather) causes Y (fleas).

20. **The correct answer is (D).** The original version is redundant. Either *by means of* or *using* would be acceptable here, but not both. Choice (D) corrects the redundancy by omitting *using*.

21. **The correct answer is (C).** The original sentence contains two problems: the inappropriate use of the passive voice and the awkward use of "by observing that." Choice (C) corrects these problems by shifting to the active voice and streamlining the sentence through elimination of the unnecessary preposition *by*.

22. **The correct answer is (C).** The less likely it is that a person will sustain an injury somewhere other than the workplace, the lower the person's risk of incurring medical expenses for such injuries. Thus, choice (C), if true, helps to refute Bharti's argument that the worker's compensation scheme actually puts workers at greater risk of financial hardship.

23. **The correct answer is (B).** Choice (B) provides at least some evidence that the slot machines at Casino Y are "loose" and, accordingly, that Elaine's chances of winning at one of those machines is relatively good.

24. **The correct answer is (D).** In the original version, the superfluous *there is* sets up an awkward construction. The sentence should be reconstructed, omitting *there is*. Among the other four versions, choice (D) provides the best solution.

25. **The correct answer is (A).** The original version is the best one. The use of the passive voice by way of the phrase *be weighed against* is idiomatic, and the sentence contains no grammatical errors. Choices (B) and (E) are incorrect because their grammatical construction suggests illogically that weighing is to be done by a *justification* rather than by government. Choice (C) illogically shifts the sentence's tense from the future to the present. Choice (D) ineffectively expresses the sentence's intended meaning; choice (A) is much clearer.

26. **The correct answer is (A).** The author's threshold purpose, articulated in the final sentence of the first paragraph, is to identify the significant forms of dissent to Arnoldian culture. But the author proceeds to do more than merely identify and describe these forms of dissent; the author is also critical of the dissenters because they have misunderstood Arnold. Choice (A) embraces both the author's threshold and ultimate concerns.

27. **The correct answer is (B).** Arnold's *Culture and Anarchy* was published in 1869. The three forms of opposition to Arnold's ideas as presented in this work, therefore, must have emerged later than 1869.

28. **The correct answer is (D).** The only analogy in the passage is found in the final sentence, in which the author compares striving for perfection (i.e., culture) to conceiving "finer sunsets and unheard melodies." Although the author uses this analogy to help the reader understand the author's final argument against Arnold's dissenters, this analogy is not in the nature of "an insupportable theory," which the author compares to a claim made by Arnold's dissenters, as choice (D) suggests.

29. **The correct answer is (C).** In the first paragraph, the author states that Arnold helped to define the purposes of the liberal arts curriculum in the century following the publication of his *Culture and Anarchy*. In the second paragraph, the author claims that today's multiculturalist movement, which opposes Arnoldian culture, is interested in deflating the "imperious authority that 'high culture' exercises over curriculum". It is reasonably inferable, then, that these imperious elitists are modern-day allies of Arnold who have perpetuated his ideas about culture through their authority over today's educational curriculum.

30. **The correct answer is (A).** The argument boils down to the following, including the unstated assumption provided by choice (A):

    Premise: Students get enough reading practice already.

    Unstated assumption (choice A): The program provides only reading practice.

    Conclusion: The program is unnecessary.

    None of the other four choices provides the necessary assumption.

31. **The correct answer is (E).** The argument as a whole can be characterized as an attempt to refute an argument against treating water with sodium monofluoride. To refute that argument, the city official provides evidence tending to show that sodium monofluoride is not as harmful as some might believe. Thus, choice (E) expresses the point that the city official is leading to in the passage.

32. **The correct answer is (E).** The original version intends to express a contrary-to-fact situation, so the subjunctive *were* (instead of *are*) is appropriate here. Also, the reflexive pronoun *themselves* is improper here. (Compare the phrase *consider themselves invincible*, which uses the reflexive form properly.) Choice (E) corrects both problems.

33. **The correct answer is (B).** In the original version, the word *Upon* confuses the meaning of the sentence by suggesting nonsensically that comets grow large in appearance immediately—as soon as they appear as a tiny speck. Choice (B) is concise and clears up the confusion by omitting the word.

34. **The correct answer is (C).** In the original sentence, the plural verb *account* does not agree in number with its singular subject *technology*. The intervening clause (set off by commas) should not affect the verb's case, which should be singular (*accounts*). Also, the word *amount* is improperly used here and should be replaced with either *quantity* or *number*. Choice (C) corrects both problems. Although choice (B) also fixes the problems, using the subjunctive verb form *would account* alters the meaning of the original sentence, transforming it into a hypothetical statement.

35. **The correct answer is (A).** The argument relies on the assumption that Michelangelo's portrayals of nudity are similar to modern photographic portrayals of nudity in all respects relevant to the argument. Choice (A) directly refutes this assumption by stating explicitly that Michelangelo's works are considered *not* obscene for the reason that they have relatively high artistic value.

36. **The correct answer is (E).** In the passage's first paragraph, the author points out that the ability to taste PTC varies among human populations. Then, in the final sentence of that paragraph, the author refers to "other, more significant, bitter substances . . . ." It can reasonably be inferred from these two statements, considered together, that PTC is a bitter substance.

37. **The correct answer is (A).** In the first sentence, the author points out that PTC is an artificially synthesized chemical; thus, PTC has clearly not existed long enough to play any part whatsoever in the evolution of taste discrimination among primates.

38. **The correct answer is (B).** In the first paragraph, the author's main concern is to point out that the variability among human populations regarding sensitivity to PTC might be a trace of the evolutionary process of natural selectivity. In the second paragraph, the author offers a similar suggestion about variability in earwax type. To support these assertions, the author implies that both characteristics still serve useful purposes among nonprimates—from whom humans presumably evolved. This inference is especially clear with respect to identifying bitter substances that might be toxic. Choice (B) accurately reflects the author's main assertion and supporting evidence.

39. **The correct answer is (C).** Based on the facts, it is clear that a large portion of the kinds of trash residents used to throw into their garbage cans for disposal is now being recycled. Thus, the only explanation for the steady (not decreasing) amount of nonrecyclable trash is that Exitur's residents are generating more of it.

40. **The correct answer is (A).** The original version is the best one. Choice (B) is nonsensical; *lower* appears to refer to energy products rather than to demand. In choice (C), the phrase *in view of* distorts the sentence's meaning. Also, the idiom *decline in* is preferred over *decline of*. Choice (D) contains the awkward phrase *being that*. Also, prices are not said to lessen in amount, but rather *decline* or *decrease*. In choice (E), *considering the fact that* is wordy, and it distorts the meaning of the original sentence, unfairly suggesting that the lessening demand for alternative energy products is surprising.

41. **The correct answer is (E).** The argument relies on the unstated assumption that Abstania's Monrovian population either remained stable or increased during 2008. However, choice (E) provides that this population actually declined in 2008, despite the influx of Monrovians. Given that the number of Monrovians residing in Abstania decreased while the crime rate increased, choice (E) reduces the likelihood that it was Monrovians who were responsible for the increase in violent crime in 2008. Choice (A) would appear to weaken the argument by providing ostensible evidence that Abstanians are more likely than Monrovians to commit violent crimes. However, choice (A) does not account for the possibility that in Monrovia far fewer violent criminals are apprehended than in Abstania. In fact, the argument's explicit reference to "reported" violent crimes underscores this possibility, which prohibits us from drawing any firm conclusion as to which group is more likely to be responsible for violent crimes.

APPENDIXES

Resources for GMAT Preparation

How much should you invest in GMAT preparation, in terms of time and money? The conventional wisdom is that since the GMAT is one of the most important tests you'll ever take, you should invest as much time and money as possible. However, the law of diminishing returns applies to GMAT preparation. This book, along with a few other thoughtfully selected resources, can provide virtually all of the potential benefits of a full-blown GMAT prep course.

GMAT BOOKS

The number of GMAT preparation books is overwhelming. Here are some suggestions to help you sort through them:

- Peruse a book carefully before committing to it. Yes, this means visiting your local brick-and-mortar bookstore rather than reviewing a book online.

- Look for a book that emphasizes skill development, not just practice questions.

- Rule out any book that emphasizes so-called secrets and shortcuts or that makes the test seem easier than it appears. Do you really think the Graduate Management Admission Council (GMAC) would devise a test that can be "cracked" like a cheap safe? If you do, think again.

- Limit the number of comprehensive GMAT books you use to two or three at most. Any more and you'll find yourself reading the same strategies and test-taking tips over and over.

- Identify your weakest skill area and supplement this book with a workbook that targets that area.

If you must shop for GMAT books at an online bookstore, don't put too much stock in customer comments and ratings, especially if they are few in number. Laudatory comments can be submitted anonymously by publishers themselves, and derogatory comments tend to be factually inaccurate, unfair, or inflammatory.

ONLINE GMAT RESOURCES

The Web is now littered with GMAT advice and practice questions, all freely available for public consumption. To separate the wheat from the chaff, limit your GMAT Web surfing to the official GMAC site (www.mba.com) and the sites of test-prep publishers who have time-tested reputations for producing high-quality content, such as Peterson's at www.petersons.com/graduate-schools.aspx.

appendix a

GMAT PREP COURSES

Would it be worthwhile to enroll in a live GMAT prep course? Here are some advantages, with counterarguments included:

1. The dynamics of a live classroom setting can help you learn difficult concepts by providing different perspectives. However, you could also start your own study group. You're just as likely to gain useful insights from your peers as from a GMAT instructor.

2. Having made a substantial financial investment, you'll probably be motivated to get your money's worth out of that investment. Some people view this as an expensive head game, however. And if you can't afford the course, it doesn't matter anyway.

3. You're less likely to procrastinate with a set class schedule. On the other hand, if you're disciplined enough, this is no advantage.

4. All the materials are provided, so you don't need to decide which books and/or software to buy. But is this a significant benefit?

5. You can commiserate and compare notes with your classmates. In fact, GMAT prep classes typically become de facto pre-MBA support groups. But again, why not start your own GMAT study/support group?

Here are some drawbacks and caveats to keep in mind if you're thinking about taking a GMAT prep course:

1. They're expensive; you can easily spend $1000 on such courses. If you're near a university, you might find a course sponsored by the university, perhaps through its extension program, for a fraction of the cost of a private course.

2. Despite their claims, private test-prep companies pass along no secrets. In fact, you can find all of the information yourself in good test-prep books.

3. The popular test-prep services require each of their GMAT instructors to have taken the real GMAT and attained a high score (typically above the 90th percentile). But this hardly ensures that your instructor will be an effective teacher.

4. During peak times of the year, you might have difficulty scheduling out-of-class time in the computer lab, at least during reasonable hours.

5. If you don't live in a major urban area or near a large college or university, the class location might be too remote for you.

If you decide to enroll in a GMAT prep course, keep in mind the following points of advice:

1. Ask about the policy for repeating the course. Insist on having the option to repeat the course at least once without charge at any time (not just within the following year).

2. Ask about merit-based or need-based scholarships (fee reductions).

3. If you repeat the course, be sure to arrange for a different instructor; just as with GMAT books, each GMAT instructor has his or her own teaching style, and you may derive greater benefit from a different type.

4. The most significant benefit of a GMAT course is the live classroom, so be sure to attend as many classes as you can.

5. Take full advantage of opportunities to meet other students and set up out-of-class study sessions. As we've already noted, you can learn just as much from your peers as from an instructor.

GMAT AVAILABILITY AND REGISTRATION

The computer-based GMAT is administered year-round at more than 500 locations, most of which are in North America. Testing centers are located at Prometric Testing Centers, Sylvan Learning Centers, certain colleges and universities, and Pearson VUE locations. The official *GMAT Bulletin* contains a complete list of GMAT computer-based test centers; an updated list is available at the GMAC Web site (www.mba.com).

Registering for the GMAT

To take the computer-based GMAT, you must schedule an appointment by using any of the following four methods:

1. Make an appointment online via the GMAC Web site (www.mba.com). Click on "The GMAT®" at the top of the page.

2. Call the test center of your choice directly. A current test center list is available at the GMAC Web site (www.mba.com/mba/thegmat).

3. Call the central registration number: 800-717-GMAT (800-717-4628).

4. Register by mail or fax. To do so, you must first complete the GMAT Appointment Scheduling Form, available at www.mba.com. To complete the form, you'll need the Test Center List for Site ID numbers and the Country Code List, also available at this Web site. To fax your form from North America, dial 952-681-3681; go to www.mba.com for fax numbers for other countries and regions.

If you're registering by mail, send your completed form to:

Pearson VUE
Attention: GMAT® Program
P.O. Box 581907
Minneapolis, MN 55458-1907
USA

Please keep in mind that it may take up to eight weeks for letters to reach the United States from some countries.

You might be able to sit for the GMAT within a few days after scheduling an appointment. However, remember that popular test centers may experience a backlog of up to several weeks. Also, you might find it more difficult to schedule a weekend test date than a weekday test date. So be sure to plan ahead and schedule your GMAT early enough to meet your business school application deadlines.

Mobile Testing Center

GMAC, in collaboration with Pearson VUE, is now offering a limited mobile testing option, available to applicants on military bases, historically black colleges and universities, and schools that are very remote from a testing center. The Mobile Testing Center is a bus that travels throughout the United States for seven months, stopping at select locations so that students may board the bus to take the GMAT. The Mobile Testing Center launched its sixth GMAT North American bus tour (GMAT Bus) in October 2010 and was scheduled to visit approximately thirty campuses across the United States, administering hundreds of tests. To view the GMAT Mobile Calendar, go to www.gmac.com.

The Mobile Testing Center can accommodate 6 test-takers at one time and is wheelchair accessible. Its interior is consistent with that of a Pearson Professional Center (PPC) or Pearson-owned testing center. The testing environment is as secure as that of other GMAT test centers. For more information on registering to take the GMAT at the Mobile Testing Center, go to www.gmac.com or e-mail GMAC at gmatprogram@gmac.com.

Obtaining Up-to-Date GMAT Information

For detailed information about GMAT registration procedures, consult the official GMAC Web sites (www.mba.com or www.gmac.com) or refer to the printed *GMAT Information Bulletin*, published annually by the GMAC. This free bulletin is available directly from GMAC and through career-planning offices at most four-year colleges and universities. You can also download the *Bulletin* from the GMAC Web site. The official GMAC Web site and *Bulletin* both provide detailed and current information about:

- Test center locations, phone numbers, and hours of operation
- Registration procedures
- Accommodations for disabled test-takers
- Requirements for admission to the GMAT
- Registration and reporting fees and refund policies
- Repeating the test
- The paper-based GMAT (availability, registration procedures, etc.)
- Official scoring criteria for the AWA essays
- How GMAT scores should be used by the institutions

The *GMAT Bulletin* is published only once a year, so for the most up-to-date official information, be sure to check the GMAC Web site.

CONTACTING THE TESTING SERVICE

To obtain the *Bulletin* or for other information about the GMAT, you can contact GMAC using any of the following methods:

Phone (in the Americas):
    800-717-4628 (toll-free within the U.S. and Canada only),
    7:00 a.m. to 7:00 p.m. Central Time
    Phone: 952-681-3680,
    7:00 a.m. to 7:00 p.m. Central Time
    Fax: 952-681-3681

E-mail:
    GMATCandidateServicesAmericas@pearson.com

Web sites:
    www.mba.com
    www.gmac.com

Mail:

Pearson VUE
Attention: GMAT® Program
P.O. Box 581907
Minneapolis, MN 55458-1907
USA

Determining Your Score

CAN YOU PREDICT YOUR GMAT SCORE?

The short answer is "no." Because the GMAT is a computer-adaptive test, it's not possible to accurately predict your actual GMAT score based on how you perform on the practice tests in this book. However, you can use the scoring table below to get a *general* idea of how you performed on the practice tests and how they might reflect your GMAT score were you taking the actual computerized test.

To calculate your score on the practice tests, first count the number of correct answers you have in each section. Then find that number in the left column (labeled "C") on the table. Directly across from that number, in the corresponding column labeled "S," you'll see an approximation of your GMAT score.

Quantitative Subscore (C = Correct Answers; S = Score)

C → S	C → S	C → S	C → S	C → S
37 → 60	29 → 46	21 → 30	13 → 14	5 → 0
36 → 60	28 → 44	20 → 28	12 → 12	4 → 0
35 → 58	27 → 42	19 → 26	11 → 10	3 → 0
34 → 56	26 → 40	18 → 24	10 → 8	2 → 0
33 → 54	25 → 38	17 → 22	9 → 6	1 → 0
32 → 52	24 → 36	16 → 20	8 → 4	0 → 0
31 → 50	23 → 34	15 → 18	7 → 2	
30 → 48	22 → 32	14 → 16	6 → 0	

Verbal Subscore (C = Correct Answers; S = Score)

C → S	C → S	C → S	C → S	C → S	C → S
41 → 60	34 → 48	27 → 34	20 → 20	13 → 6	6 → 0
40 → 60	33 → 46	26 → 32	19 → 18	12 → 4	5 → 0
39 → 58	32 → 44	25 → 30	18 → 16	11 → 2	4 → 0
38 → 56	31 → 42	24 → 28	17 → 14	10 → 0	3 → 0
37 → 54	30 → 40	23 → 26	16 → 12	9 → 0	2 → 0
36 → 52	29 → 38	22 → 24	15 → 10	8 → 0	1 → 0
35 → 50	28 → 36	21 → 22	14 → 8	7 → 0	0 → 0

GMAT Score (C = Correct Answers; S = Score)

C → S	C → S	C → S	C → S	C → S
78 → 800	62 → 660	46 → 500	30 → 340	14 → 200
77 → 800	61 → 650	45 → 490	29 → 330	13 → 200
76 → 800	60 → 640	44 → 480	28 → 320	12 → 200
75 → 790	59 → 630	43 → 470	27 → 310	11 → 200
74 → 780	58 → 620	42 → 460	26 → 300	10 → 200
73 → 770	57 → 610	41 → 450	25 → 290	9 → 200
72 → 760	56 → 600	40 → 440	24 → 280	8 → 200
71 → 750	55 → 590	39 → 430	23 → 270	7 → 200
70 → 740	54 → 580	38 → 420	22 → 260	6 → 200
69 → 730	53 → 570	37 → 410	21 → 250	5 → 200
68 → 720	52 → 560	36 → 400	20 → 240	4 → 200
67 → 710	51 → 550	35 → 390	19 → 230	3 → 200
66 → 700	50 → 540	34 → 380	18 → 220	2 → 200
65 → 690	49 → 530	33 → 370	17 → 200	1 → 200
64 → 680	48 → 520	32 → 360	16 → 200	0 → 200
63 → 670	47 → 510	31 → 350	15 → 200	

Why a Graduate-Level Business Degree?

John C. Hallenborg
Business Consultant

WHAT'S HOT IN THE OFFICE IS HOT IN THE CLASSROOM . . . AND VICE VERSA

Ambitious graduate-level business candidates, looking forward to their careers or perhaps to the exciting prospect of entrepreneurship, cannot afford to presume that every graduate-level business program will meet the educational requirements specific to an industry or profession. In today's job market, the advanced business graduate is expected to deliver both technical and nontechnical skills in every business and industrial sector. As in other areas of graduate study and related employment, the focus is on specialized expertise in business management. For businesses, opportunities exist to work with universities to create new graduate-level business programs that prepare candidates to fulfill an array of specialized leadership roles. For schools, this phenomenon continues to spur on the revamping of curricula almost annually to keep pace with the real-world demands that are placed upon future advanced business graduates.

Master's degree holders of all types are on the rise, allowing employers to be quite discriminating in hiring. Of course, the weight assigned to the graduate-level business degree by prospective employers varies considerably, depending on the industry, company, and job assignment. For a programmer at a software development company, the firm's in-house technical training would provide more valuable background than a graduate-level business degree. Conversely, someone applying for a middle-management job in the finance department at a mid-sized company may find a graduate-level business degree indispensable. The point is the two jobs might be represented on the same salary tier, so it is still a maxim in the transitional process from M.B.A. school to the workplace that the degree's importance is job-specific.

If you're holding down a job, it is always prudent to map out your time wisely. The working M.B.A. candidate may, for example, distribute a course load to accommodate a work schedule. An M.B.A. candidate will also need to consider employer assistance whereby the candidate's choice of school or program might be determined solely by which programs are endorsed and subsidized by the candidate's employer.

Holders of a newly minted graduate-level business degree bring new ways of thinking and innovative approaches to problem solving, leadership skills and experience, and the confidence that they can change things and make a difference. For many graduates, acquiring an advanced business degree may signal the difference between a lackluster occupation and a robust, life-affirming career full of welcome challenges and even more welcome rewards.

TWO-YEAR VERSUS ONE-YEAR

Is it safe to presume that the recruitment managers at most major companies are aware of the changing makeup of the leading business school programs? The answer is most definitely yes, and it is apparent in the variety of degree options, concentrations, and alternative courses of study available to today's M.B.A. student. Certainly for the past thirty years or so, benchmark companies and top graduate schools have worked intensively to match academic programs to corporate needs. By all accounts, the composition of the graduate-level business degree and how it is acquired will continue to evolve in the coming years. The trend in graduate-level business programs is toward increased fragmentation and segmentation designed around students' specific needs.

How the degree can be obtained today also closely mirrors current business trends—the expectation of an early return on investment, preferably within one to two years. Future graduate-level business programs will likely continue to reflect the choices seen today: the one-year degree, which often dispenses with core programs in favor of specialized courses tailored to specific career paths, and the more traditional two-year and extended graduate-level business programs, which have been the basis of graduate business degrees for decades.

The upsurge in one-year degrees has been driven, for the most part, by corporate demand. Although two-year programs are still the norm in most business schools, accelerated and specialized one-year degree programs are seeing increases in enrollment.

The primary difference between one-year and traditional two-year programs is that with the shorter version, there is little, if any, overlap with undergraduate business curricula. Thus, it is highly recommended that students who decide on a one-year program enroll soon after receiving their undergraduate degrees and are able to satisfy all core business course requirements. However, some one-year programs require anywhere from two to five years' work experience in lieu of the traditional first-year M.B.A. core study courses. Many one-year programs are dedicated to serving experienced professionals and recent undergraduates with some work experience. One-year elective courses are all but tailored to the applicant's career, so that the graduate can reenter the workforce as quickly as possible. Classic two-year programs most often focus on elective and specialized course work in the second year after completion of core requirements in the first year.

A number of emerging realities highlight the one-year M.B.A. degree: technology-based information media replaces class time in many cases, fewer faculty members may be required as schools combine resources to teach fewer classes to more students, and distance learning replaces some on-campus classes. For most schools and students of the future, technology will certainly dictate the learning medium.

Business schools that have been adversely affected by the trend toward one-year programs are offering degree options that combine an undergraduate business degree with an M.B.A. in a five-year program. The proliferation of all these programs makes the choices more complex for the person considering an advanced business degree.

Corporations have generally been neutral about recruiting one-year program versus two-year program graduates. Part of the consideration comes down to a job applicant's reasons for pursuing a one-year versus a two-year program. Is it someone with plenty of work experience who is looking to advance her skills? Or is the graduate someone who is pursuing an advanced business degree because he is switching careers? Subjectivity on the question of whether an employer has a bias concerning graduates of two-year or one-year graduate-level business programs can come down to the hiring manager.

Albert W. Niemi Jr., dean of Southern Methodist University's Edwin L. Cox School of Business, explains: "I don't see, in the data that we have collected—in terms of starting salaries—that there is any difference in the way one-year people are treated by industry. One-year grads do as well as two-year grads in terms of earning power in the marketplace." Despite Niemi's findings, the proportion of one-year programs is still relatively small compared to the total number of graduate-level business programs offered nationwide.

CHANGES IN THE FINANCIAL SECTOR

There has been a considerable shakeout in the better sectors of the financial job market, and many large financial organizations are as vigilant in maintaining a positive public image as they are about profit levels. Any M.B.A. candidate seeking a spot at one of the top investment banks, for example, will have to be aware of issues of public relations in addition to more predictable questions about money markets. Expect this sensitivity to public opinion to remain high for many years. In fact, a reputation for aboveboard dealings is nearly as important as bottom-line performance in today's financial sphere.

How does this job market realignment affect the M.B.A. holder's chances for a lucrative career in finance? For one thing, M.B.A. graduates may find more opportunities in non-investment banking finance positions. Many small- and mid-sized companies that are doing quite well have neither the staff nor the inclination to recruit on campuses. They prefer to engage executive search firms to ferret out good candidates. It's up to applicants to make themselves known to these employers and their headhunters. Once M.B.A. graduates have their foot in the door, they should heed the message of employers: Bring us good grades from a good school but also bring along maturity and a problem-solving attitude. Despite the fact that compensation at the higher levels in banking is very bonus-oriented, the fresh M.B.A. graduate should avoid being a self-serving maverick. The advanced business-degree holder of tomorrow, more than ever before, will have to display strengths in leadership, teamwork, problem solving, and communication. Upper management will be looking for well-rounded individuals who offer a balanced perspective and are ready and able to apply their education in a real-life setting.

BIG POSSIBILITIES AT SMALLER COMPANIES

The ideal of a "secure job forever" has been replaced by the reality that most Americans will have two or three careers in their lifetimes and may even change jobs every five years or so. Small and middle-market corporations continue to be fertile ground for M.B.A. recruitment.

Preparation for a specific industry niche or, better yet, a specific company or companies, is key to landing those choice spots that feature a daunting 50:1 or 500:1 applicant:position ratio. Most competing M.B.A.'s are aware that the key to landing the desired job is to positively differentiate oneself from other equally qualified candidates. Some graduate-level business students have gone so far as to research potential employers at the beginning of their course work, studying the details of annual reports, product brochures, etc., for the duration of the typical two-year M.B.A. program.

Skills learned in M.B.A. core and specialized courses can be especially valuable in helping to transform technical ideas and concepts into tangible, marketable products. In both large and small businesses in the future, managers will certainly be expected to bring not only technical expertise to the table but also the ability to translate new ideas into profit-sustaining products and services. The small- and mid-sized firm is often the perfect venue for such creative expression coupled with pragmatic implementation.

TOMORROW'S ENTREPRENEUR

There will always be a place for the ambitious M.B.A. holder who cannot wait for others to bring his or her ideas to the marketplace. For many fearless graduates, starting or buying a business may be a quicker and more lucrative route to success. Those with the best chance of making it this way will most likely combine prior experience raising money for and operating a start-up with the marketing and financial knowledge acquired with a graduate-level business degree. Graduate-level business programs are designing support systems for graduates who face the critical test of success within three to five years of launching their companies. This is when most businesses fail. Schools are involving alumni in the education process, developing communities among them to provide ongoing support, as well as bringing them back to teach and mentor current students.

Still, the appeal of running a small business does not get as much media coverage as it should, if a review of Harvard Business School alumni is any indication. M.B.A. graduates have founded such diverse and successful businesses as Intuit; United Bank of Africa; Donaldson, Lufkin & Jenrette; Bloomberg; Software Arts; Staples; and the Weather Channel.

OPPORTUNITIES IN THE TWENTY-FIRST CENTURY

Because management and finance are functions common to every conceivable type of business or industry, it is difficult to make predictions about job growth for M.B.A.s in particular markets. However, Gary Lindblad, assistant dean and director of The Paul Merage School of Business at the University of California, Irvine, mentions that their school's redesigned curriculum emphasizes the three critical drivers of the innovation economy: strategic innovation, information technology, and analytical decision making. For advanced business students who intend to further their careers in the technology sector, M.B.A. programs with a technology focus may be the answer. These programs combine finance, operations, and marketing courses with a solid technical background. Candidates to these programs often have engineering and computer sciences backgrounds. Schools that rank high among recruiters include Northeastern University in Boston, University of Texas at Austin, University of Maryland at College Park, University of Alabama at Tuscaloosa, and University of California at Irvine.

A significant amount of future growth may come from overseas operations of domestic corporations. With the continued advance of telecommunications as the primary medium for data transfer, banks and corporations have permanently erased many commercial barriers between nations. This borderless, global market is an exciting prospect for the ambitious M.B.A. The Internet in particular has created opportunities for companies to outsource a broad array of operations to other countries with lower cost structures. Once content to move manufacturing to other countries, U.S. companies are now looking abroad to skilled, low-wage workforces to carry out certain operations, such as software development and bill processing. Graduate-level business students who graduate with an understanding of how to manage operations that are carried out in countries in different time zones with diverse cultures will find themselves in demand. Clearly, the cosmopolitan M.B.A. will be the first to reap the rewards from emerging international markets in the twenty-first century.

POSTGRADUATE TIPS

With the hiring of M.B.A. graduates trending away from investment banking and consulting, schools have been significantly re-engineering their career services. Many institutions that were once content to stage recruitment fairs must now work closely with candidates to design a career journey strategy. Counselors are advising prospective graduates to approach alumni, involve themselves in student network groups, and undertake very heavy networking among any contacts they may have in the business community. Zero-in on three to five companies that are very attractive, firms wherein you could happily spend the next three to ten years working hard to establish yourself in the business community. If you are a strong writer, parlay your skill by writing a detailed letter expressing your knowledge of the industry and the company and why you would be an asset to that company.

In the case of public companies, get their latest annual report, analyze it, and have your own views on the company's future ready to share with your interviewer. Do not make the mistake of blindly agreeing with everything the interviewer offers about the firm. If you disagree on a point, assert yourself with an explanation of your perspective on the issue. Never shy away from creating polarized discussion during an interview if you truly believe your position to be correct. Hopefully, your interviewer will recognize your willingness to defend your viewpoint as a trait of a successful executive.

Choosing the Right Program for Your Career Needs

Dr. Richard L. White
Director of Career Services
Rutgers University

appendix d

In recent senior surveys, approximately 80 percent of Rutgers University students have indicated that they intend to pursue graduate study at some point in the future. Many are thinking about a graduate-level business degree. The intentions of Rutgers students reflect a national trend: More and more students want additional education, and, in fact, many feel they will need it to achieve their fullest career potential.

From your first thoughts about graduate school to your actual admission and decision to attend a school, you are engaged in an extensive, complex, competitive process. The emphasis of the program you select will greatly influence the direction of your career. In selecting a graduate-level business degree program, it is critical to match your strengths, interests, and goals with the specific offerings of the school and program.

To organize and manage the process, develop a strategy for evaluating your choices and creating a detailed action plan. At the heart of your action plan are four basic questions that are simple to ask but require self-exploration and research to answer.

1. WHY PURSUE AN ADVANCED BUSINESS DEGREE?

You are probably thinking about pursuing an advanced business degree for these basic reasons:

- Your chosen profession demands further skills.
- You want to enhance your marketability and salary.
- You want to change careers.
- You are committed to further study in your current discipline or a new discipline.

Most applicants fit one of these profiles:

- You're currently working with an employer that you would like to stay with for the long term. You've talked to your boss and colleagues, and they believe that your getting an M.B.A. will improve your business and technical knowledge and thus increase your performance and promotional opportunities with the employer. You understand that there probably won't be a big jump in salary when you complete your degree, but in the long term it will pay off. In addition, your employer will pick up the tab through its tuition reimbursement program.

- You're currently working with an employer who doesn't fit into your long-term plans. You're planning to leave in the near future. You see your M.B.A. as the key to opening new opportunities in the same field or a new field and to increasing your salary prospects. You realize that you're on your own financially (no employer assistance), but you see the short-term investment paying off in the long run.

- You're a senior in college. You've surveyed the job market, but you're really leaning toward an advanced business-degree program. You're very interested in pursuing your business education, especially because your bachelor's degree is not in business. You understand that the best business schools accept only a small percentage of applicants directly from undergraduate programs, but you have a strong academic record and some good internship and part-time work experience.

Whatever your profile may be, make sure you can articulate your reasons for pursuing an M.B.A. clearly, succinctly, and persuasively both orally and in writing. Review the evolution of your thinking from first thoughts about an M.B.A. to major influences such as people, courses, positions, and research.

To understand your motivation for pursuing an M.B.A., follow these five action steps:

1. Take notes on yourself.
2. Write or revise your resume.
3. Develop a generic personal statement (two or three typed pages), indicating what makes you special and why you want an advanced business degree. This will serve as the basis of the personal statement that will accompany your applications.
4. Request a sampling of M.B.A. applications and begin crafting sample answers to the questions, using parts of your generic personal statement.
5. Determine job prospects for graduate-level business students in your intended field—both short-term and long-term. The best resources for short-term job prospects are individual placement reports from business schools, which are available online or through the admissions offices. For long-term prospects, talk to relatives, family friends, or professors. Another great source is alumni, if your school has an alumni career network.

2. WHEN AND HOW DO YOU WANT TO PURSUE YOUR ADVANCED BUSINESS DEGREE?

There are four fairly clear-cut options about when and how to pursue your advanced business degree:

1. *Full-time beginning in the fall after your graduation from college.* Keep in mind that graduate-level business programs typically look for candidates with at least one to two years of full-time work experience. If you are a student early in your undergraduate career, one option to explore is a five-year dual-degree (B.S./M.B.A.) program.
2. *Full-time beginning after a year or more of work.* Graduate-level business programs value the diversity and quality of candidates' work experiences, which bring "real-world" perspectives and new ideas into the classroom. Moreover, many graduate-level business students indicate that their course work has even more significance after they continue their professional and career development.
3. *Part-time while working.* In most cases, you will take evening classes. As part of your preliminary research, find out if your employer provides full or partial tuition remission. Also explore whether or not your employer values an advanced business degree and whether it

will really contribute to your long-term promotability. Finally, try to determine how flexible your employer may be if, for example, you need to take a 4:30 class or need one or two days off to complete a school project.

4 *Part-time while not working.* If you're not working, you can take either day or evening classes. But if you're looking for a daytime job, bear in mind that you might want to remain flexible during the day and therefore take your classes at night. The reverse is true if you have a part-time evening job.

To sort out the different possibilities, take these three action steps:

1 Research the schools of your choice. Compare these five key elements: percentage of full-time versus part-time enrollees; percentage of incoming M.B.A.s who came directly from undergraduate programs; average age; average work experience; and costs.

2 Research the profession and prospective employers, utilizing corporate recruiters, friends in the corporate world, career services and admissions professionals, professional associations, alumni networks, professors, and publications. Consider these elements: availability of tuition remission programs; value of the advanced business degree within the profession or company; and balance between a company's B.A./B.S. hiring and M.B.A. hiring.

3 Balance all of the above elements with your personal lifestyle and the lifestyle of the people closest to you.

3. WHERE DO YOU WANT TO PURSUE YOUR ADVANCED BUSINESS DEGREE?

This is the most complex step in the process, because there are many variables. However, by taking these five action steps, you can gain firm control of the process and manage it to your advantage.

Note that these steps are in no specific order. It would be helpful to put them in rank order in terms of importance for you—or at least group them by "very important," "important," and "less important."

1 Determine the availability of degree programs in your specific field.

2 Determine the quality and reputation of the programs of your choice. This is a crucial element. Employers often base their recruiting decisions on quality and reputation, and you will be associated with the name of your M.B.A. school for the remainder of your career. Three key factors in assessing quality and reputation are faculty, facilities, and student body. Talk to professors and professionals and "read between the lines" of the admissions literature and placement reports. Feel free to consult various national rankings, but don't take them too seriously. These are often based on journalistic endeavors rather than hard research and often overlook the special offerings of individual programs.

3 Determine the costs of graduate programs—the simple part—and your ability to pay through loans, income, savings, financial aid, and parental support—the not-so-simple part. Pursue those programs that are affordable.

4 Determine the locations of your preferred graduate programs. Do you prefer urban, suburban, or rural locations? Do you have any personal geographical restrictions or preferences? Think about the time and cost of commuting and travel.

⑤ Determine the size of the programs and the institutions. Most graduate-level business programs are relatively small but the size of institutions varies considerably. Many institutions enhance the breadth of their programs by partnering with other U.S. and international institutions offering programs. Size is critical to the overall environment, character, academic resources, and student–faculty ratios and relationships.

4. WHAT SCHOOLS AND PROGRAMS ARE RIGHT FOR YOU?

Now, put it all together and generate a list of five to ten schools where you intend to apply. Typically, you will want one or two "stretch" schools, a handful of "good bets," and one or two "safety" schools. Rank your preferences at the outset of the admissions process, but remain flexible. As you receive admissions decisions, your preferences will probably change and need to change.

Once your acceptances are in hand, how do you make the final important decision? Consider the following steps.

Rank the five most important features of the graduate-level business experience for you. You might also want a second-tier group of five additional features. Focus on these ten features (feel free to add others to the list):

① Career and placement services (placement report, number of employers recruiting on campus, overall quality of operation)

② Class offerings (day, evening, summer, weekend)

③ Cost (tuition, room, board, travel, living expenses)

④ Curricular focus (ethics, diversity, international)

⑤ Facilities (dorms, classrooms, libraries)

⑥ Faculty (general quality, individual faculty members)

⑦ Location (geographic, urban, rural)

⑧ Personal considerations (spouse, family, friends)

⑨ Quality and reputation (general comments)

⑩ Teaching methodology (lectures, case studies, team projects)

Systematically compare each school and each feature. Rank schools within each feature, assigning a score if you wish.

Once you have completed your analysis, make sure your heart agrees with your head. If it's a toss-up, go with your instincts. They're probably right.

Word List

A

abbreviate (verb) To make briefer, to shorten. *Because time was running out, the speaker was forced to abbreviate his remarks.* abbreviation (noun).

aberration (noun) A deviation from what is normal or natural, an abnormality. *Jack's extravagant lunch at Lutece was an aberration from his usual meal, a peanut butter sandwich and a diet soda.* aberrant (adjective).

abeyance (noun) A temporary lapse in activity; suspension. *In the aftermath of the bombing, all normal activities were held in abeyance.*

abjure (verb) To renounce or reject; to officially disclaim. *While being tried by the inquisition in 1633, Galileo abjured all his writings holding that the Earth and other planets revolved around the Sun.*

abrade (verb) To irritate by rubbing; to wear down in spirit. *Olga's "conditioning facial" abraded Sabrina's skin so severely that she vowed never to let anyone's hands touch her face again.* abrasion (noun)

abridge (verb) To shorten, to reduce. *The Bill of Rights is designed to prevent Congress from abridging the rights of Americans.* abridgment (noun).

abrogate (verb) To nullify, to abolish. *During World War II, the United States abrogated the rights of Japanese Americans by detaining them in internment camps.* abrogation (noun).

abscond (verb) To make a secret departure, to elope. *Theresa will never forgive her daughter, Elena, for absconding to Miami with Philip when they were only 17.*

accretion (noun) A gradual build-up or enlargement. *My mother's house is a mess due to her steady accretion of bric-a-brac and her inability to throw anything away.*

activism (noun) A belief or practice based on direct action. *The young man's interest in activism led him to participate in numerous protest marches against the war.*

adjunct (noun) Something added to another thing, but not a part of it; an associate or assistant. *While Felix and Fritz were adjuncts to Professor Himmelman during his experiments in electrodynamics, they did not receive credit when the results were published.*

adulterate (verb) To corrupt, to make impure. *Unlike the chickens from the large poultry companies, Murray's free-roaming chickens have not been adulterated with hormones and other additives.*

adversary (noun) An enemy or opponent. *The senator became the front runner when most of his adversaries dropped out of the race.* adverse (adjective).

advocate (noun) One who pleads on another's behalf. *The woman's attorney served as an excellent advocate during her trial.*

affability (noun) The quality of being easy to talk to and gracious. *Affability is a much-desired trait in any profession that involves dealing with many people on a daily basis.* affable (adjective).

affected (adjective) False, artificial. *At one time, Japanese women were taught to speak in an affected high-pitched voice, which was thought girlishly attractive.* affect (verb), affectation (noun).

affiliation (noun) Connection, association. *The close affiliation among the members of the team enabled them to outplay all their opponents.*

affinity (noun) A feeling of shared attraction, kinship; a similarity. *When they first fell in love, Andrew and Tanya marveled over their affinity for bluegrass music, obscure French poetry, and beer taken with a squirt of lemon juice.*

aggrandize (verb) To make bigger or greater; to inflate. *When he was mayor of New York City, Ed Koch was renowned for aggrandizing his accomplishments and strolling through city events shouting, "How'm I doing?"* aggrandizement (noun).

aggression (noun) Forceful action or procedure. *Mohandas K. Ghandi argued that aggression on the part of one's oppressors was best met with passive resistance.* aggressive (adjective).

agitation (noun) A disturbance; a disturbing feeling of upheaval and excitement. *After the CEO announced the coming layoffs, the employees' agitation was evident as they remained in the auditorium talking excitedly among themselves.* agitated (adjective), agitate (verb).

alignment (noun) The proper positioning of parts in relation to each other. *If the wheels of an automobile are not in alignment, the car will not function properly.* align (verb).

allocate (verb) To apportion for a specific purpose; to distribute. *The president talked about the importance of education and health care in his State of the Union address, but, in the end, the administration did not allocate enough resources for these pressing concerns.* allocation (noun).

alluded (verb) Made indirect reference to. *Without actually threatening to fire his employee, the manager alluded to the possibility of his being terminated.*

amalgamate (verb) To blend thoroughly. *The tendency of grains to sort when they should mix makes it difficult for manufacturers to create powders that are amalgamated.* amalgamation (noun).

ameliorate (verb) To make something better or more tolerable. *The living conditions of the tenants were certainly ameliorated when the landlord finally installed washing machines and dryers in the basement.* amelioration (noun).

amortize (verb) To pay off or reduce a debt gradually through periodic payments. *If you don't need to take a lump-sum tax deduction, it's best to amortize large business expenditures by spreading the cost out over several years.*

amplify (verb) To enlarge, expand, or increase. *Uncertain as to whether they understood, the students asked the teacher to amplify his explanation.* amplification (noun).

anachronistic (adjective) Out of the proper time. *The reference in Shakespeare's* Julius Caesar *to "the clock striking twelve" is anachronistic, since there were no striking timepieces in ancient Rome.* anachronism (noun).

analogous (adjective) Having a likeness or similarity. *The student pilot quickly learned that flying a plane was only slightly analogous to driving an automobile.* analogue (noun).

analytical (adjective) Separating something into its component parts. *The mathematician's analytical ability enabled him to determine the correct answer to the problem.* analyze (verb).

anarchy (noun) Absence of law or order. *For several months after the Nazi government was destroyed, there was no effective government in parts of Germany, and anarchy ruled.* anarchic (adjective).

animosity (noun) Hostility, resentment. *During the last debate, the candidates could no longer disguise their animosity and began to trade accusations and insults.*

anomaly (noun) Something different or irregular. *Tiny Pluto, orbiting next to the giants Jupiter, Saturn, and Neptune, has long appeared to be an anomaly.* anomalous (adjective).

antagonism (noun) Hostility, conflict, opposition. *As more and more reporters investigated the Watergate scandal, antagonism between the Nixon administration and the press increased.* antagonistic (adjective), antagonize (verb).

antipathy (noun) A long-held feeling of dislike or aversion. *When asked why he didn't call for help immediately after his wife fell into a coma, the defendant emphasized his wife's utter antipathy to doctors.*

apprehension (noun) A feeling of fear or foreboding; an arrest. *The peculiar feeling of apprehension that Harold Pinter creates in his plays derives as much from the long silences between speeches as from the speeches themselves. The policeofficer's dramatic apprehension of the gunman took place in full view of the midtown lunch crowd.* apprehend (verb).

appropriate (verb) Take possession of. *The little boy appropriated his sister's new doll.*

arbitrary (adjective) Based on random or merely personal preference. *Both computers cost the same and had the same features, so I made an arbitrary decision about which one to buy.*

archaic (adjective) Old fashioned, obsolete. *Those who believe in "open marriage" often declare that they will not be bound by archaic laws and religious rituals.* archaism (noun).

argumentation (noun) Forming reasons, drawing conclusions, and applying them to a discussion. *A discussion of the merits and demerits of grass and artificial turf in ballparks provides an excellent opportunity for argumentation.* argumentative (adjective).

arid (adjective) Very dry; boring and meaningless. *The arid climate of Arizona makes farming difficult. Some find the law a fascinating topic, but for me it is an arid discipline.* aridity (noun).

articulate (adjective) To express oneself clearly and effectively. *Compared to George W. Bush, with his stammering and his frequently incomplete sentences, Barack Obama is considered a highly articulate president.*

asperity (noun) Harshness, severity. *Total silence at the dinner table, baths in icy water, prayers five times a day—these practices all contributed to the asperity of life in the monastery.*

assail (verb) To attack with blows or words. *When the president's cabinet members rose to justify the case for military intervention in Iraq, they were assailed by many audience members who were critical of U.S. policy.* assailant (noun).

assay (verb) To analyze for particular components; to determine weight, quality, etc. *The jeweler assayed the stone pendant Gwyneth inherited from her mother and found it to contain a topaz of high quality.*

assertion (noun) A positive statement or declaration. *If he had not sincerely believed that he was the best person for the job, he would not have made that assertion.* assert (verb).

assessment (noun) An appraisal. *The woman's assessment of the situation led her to believe that it was an appropriate time to take some action.* assess (verb).

assimilate (verb) To absorb into a system or culture. *New York City has assimilated one group of immigrants after another, from the Jewish, German, and Irish immigrants who arrived at the turn of the last century to the waves of Mexican and Latin American immigrants who arrived in the 1980s.* assimilated (adjective).

assuage (verb) To ease, to pacify. *Knowing that the pilot's record was perfect did little to assuage Linnet's fear of flying in the two-seater airplane.*

attainment (noun) The act of achieving a goal, or the goal itself. *Had the company's vice president not already reached a certain level of attainment, she would never have been considered for the presidency.*

audacious (adjective) Bold, daring, adventurous. *Her plan to cross the Atlantic in a twelve-foot sailboat was audacious.* audacity (noun).

authoritarian (adjective) Favoring or demanding blind obedience to leaders. *Despite most Americans' strong belief in democracy, the American government has sometimes supported authoritarian regimes in other countries.* authoritarianism (noun).

authoritative (adjective) Official, conclusive. *For over five decades, American parents regarded Doctor Benjamin Spock as the most authoritative voice on baby and child care.* authority (noun), authorize (verb).

autonomy (noun) The quality of being self-governing. *Only in the most progressive companies are managers given the autonomy they really need to effectively do their jobs.*

aver (verb) To claim to be true; to avouch. *The fact that the key witness averred the defendant's innocence was what ultimately swayed the jury to deliver a "not guilty" verdict.*

avow (verb) To declare boldly. *Immediately after Cyrus avowed his atheism at our church fund-raiser, there was a long, uncomfortable silence.* avowal (noun), avowed (adjective).

B

belligerent (adjective) Quarrelsome, combative. *Mrs. Juniper was so belligerent toward the clerks at the local stores that they cringed when they saw her coming.* belligerent (noun) An opposing army, a party waging war. *The Union and Confederate forces were the belligerents in the American Civil War.*

benevolent (adjective) Wishing or doing good. *In old age, Carnegie used his wealth for benevolent purposes, donating large sums to found libraries and schools around the country.* benevolence (noun).

bogus (adjective) Phony, a sham. *Senior citizens are often the target of telemarketing scams pushing bogus investment opportunities.*

bombastic (adjective) Inflated or pompous in style. *Old-fashioned bombastic political speeches don't work on television, which demands a more intimate, personal style of communication.* bombast (noun).

brazenly (adverb) Acting with disrespectful boldness. *Some say that the former White House intern brazenly threw herself at the president, but the American public will probably never know the full truth.* brazen (adjective).

broach (verb) To bring up an issue for discussion; to propose. *Knowing my father's strictness about adhering to a budget, I just can't seem to broach the subject of my massive credit-card debt.*

burgeon (verb) To bloom, literally or figuratively. *The story of two prison inmates in Manuel Puig's play* The Kiss of The Spiderwoman *is testimony that tenderness can burgeon in the most unlikely places.*

burnish (verb) To shine by polishing, literally or figuratively. *After stripping seven layers of old paint off the antique door, the carpenter stained the wood and burnished it to a rich hue. When Bill Gates, one of the wealthiest men in the country, decided to endorse the Big Bertha line of Golf Clubs, many suggested that he was trying to burnish his image as a "regular guy."*

buttress (noun) Something that supports or strengthens. *The endorsement of the American Medical Association is a powerful buttress for the claims made on behalf of this new medicine.* buttress (verb).

C

cacophony (noun) Discordant sounds; dissonance. *In the minutes before classes start, the high school's halls are filled with a cacophony of shrieks, shouts, banging locker doors, and pounding feet.* cacophonous (adjective)

calibrate (verb) To determine or mark graduations (of a measuring instrument); to adjust or finely tune. *We tried to calibrate the heating to Rufus's liking, but he still ended up shivering in our living room.* calibration (noun).

caste (noun) A division of society based on differences of wealth, rank, or occupation. *While the inhabitants of India, for example, are divided into castes, in theory no such division exists in the United States.*

castigate (verb) To chastise; to punish severely. *The editor castigated Bob for repeatedly failing to meet his deadlines.* castigation (noun).

catalytic (adjective) Bringing about, causing, or producing some result. *The conditions for revolution existed in America by 1765; the disputes about taxation that arose during the following decade were the catalytic events that sparked the rebellion.* catalyze (verb).

causal (adjective) Indicating a reason for an action or condition. *The continuing threat of rain was a causal factor in the canceling of the annual school picnic.*

caustic (adjective) Burning, corrosive. *No pretensions were safe when the famous satirist H. L. Mencken unleashed his caustic wit.*

cessation (noun) A temporary or final stopping. *Due to the cessation of the major project he was working on, the architect found himself with a considerable amount of time on his hands.* cease (verb).

chaos (noun) Disorder, confusion, chance. *The first few moments after the explosion were pure chaos: no one was sure what had happened, and the area was filled with people running and yelling.* chaotic (adjective).

chary (adjective) Slow to accept, cautious. *Yuan was chary about going out with Xinhua, since she had been badly hurt in her previous relationship.*

chronology (noun) An arrangement of events by order of occurrence, a list of dates; the science of time. *If you ask Susan about her two-year-old son, she will give you a chronology of his accomplishments and childhood illnesses, from the day he was born to the present. The village of Copan was where Mayan astronomical learning, as applied to chronology, achieved its most accurate expression in the famous Mayan calendar.* chronological (adjective).

circumspect (adjective) Prudent, cautious. *After he had been acquitted of the sexual harassment charge, the sergeant realized he would have to be more circumspect in his dealings with the female cadets.* circumspection (noun).

cleave (verb) A tricky verb that can mean either to stick closely together or to split apart. (Pay attention to context.) *The more abusive his father became, the more Timothy cleaved to his mother and refused to let her out of his sight. Sometimes a few words carelessly spoken are enough to cleave a married couple and leave the relationship in shambles.* cleavage (noun).

coagulant (noun) Any material that causes another to thicken or clot. *Hemophilia is characterized by excessive bleeding from even the slightest cut and is caused by a lack of one of the necessary coagulants.* coagulate (verb).

coalesce (verb) To fuse, to unite. *The music we know as jazz coalesced from diverse elements from many musical cultures, including those of West Africa, America, and Europe.* coalescence (noun).

coerce (verb) To force someone either to do something or to refrain from doing something. *The Miranda ruling prevents police from coercing a confession by forcing them to read criminals their rights.* coercion (noun).

cogent (adjective) Forceful and convincing. *The committee members were won over to the project by the cogent arguments of the chairman.* cogency (noun).

commensurate (adjective) Aligned with, proportional. *Many Ph.D.s in the humanities do not feel their paltry salaries are commensurate with their abilities, their experience, or the heavy workload they are asked to bear.*

commingle (verb) To blend, to mix. *Just as when he was only 5 years old, Elmer did not allow any of the foods on his plate to commingle: the beans must not merge with the rice nor the chicken rub shoulders with the broccoli!*

companionate (adjective) Suitably or harmoniously accompanying. *Even though the two women had never traveled together before, they found each other to be extremely companionate.*

compensate (verb) To counterbalance or make appropriate payment to. *Although the man received a considerable salary for all his hard work and long hours, he did not feel it was enough to compensate him for the time taken away from his family.* compensation (noun).

complaisant (adjective) Tending to bow to others' wishes; amiable. *Of the two Dashwood sisters, Elinor was the more complaisant, often putting the strictures of society and family above her own desires.* complaisance (noun).

complement (noun) Something that completes, fills up, or makes perfect. *Red wine serves as an excellent complement to a steak dinner.* complementary (adjective).

compound (verb) To intensify, to exacerbate. *When you make a faux pas, my father advised me, don't compound the problem by apologizing profusely; just say you're sorry and get on with life!*

compulsory (adjective) Mandatory, required. *Prior to the establishment of a volunteer army, military service was compulsory for young men in the United States.*

conceivable (adjective) Possible, imaginable. *It's possible to find people with every conceivable interest by surfing the Web—from fans of minor film stars to those who study the mating habits of crustaceans.* conception (noun).

conclusive (adjective) Putting an end to debate, question, or uncertainty. *The district attorney was able to provide conclusive proof of the defendant's guilt.* conclude (verb).

concur (verb) To agree, to approve. *We concur that a toddler functions best on a fairly reliable schedule.* concurrence (noun).

condensation (noun) A reduction to a denser form (from steam to water); an abridgment of a literary work. *The condensation of humidity on the car's windshield made it difficult for me to see the road. It seems as though every beach house I've ever rented features a shelf full of Reader's Digest condensations of B-grade novels.* condense (verb).

condescending (adjective) Having an attitude of superiority toward another; patronizing. *"What a cute little car!" she remarked in a condescending fashion. "I suppose it's the nicest one someone like you could afford!"* condescension (noun).

condone (verb) To overlook, to permit to happen. *Schools with zero tolerance policies do not condone alcohol, drugs, vandalism, or violence on school grounds.*

conglomerate (verb) To form into a mass or coherent whole. *When one company buys another, the two conglomerate into a single larger entity.*

congruent (adjective) Coinciding, harmonious. *Fortunately, the two employees who had been asked to organize the department had congruent views on the budget.* congruence (noun).

conjunction (noun) The occurrence of two or more events together in time or space; in astronomy, the point at which two celestial bodies have the least separation. *Low inflation, occurring in conjunction with low unemployment and relatively low interest rates, has enabled the United States to enjoy a long period of sustained economic growth. The moon is in conjunction with the sun when it is new; if the conjunction is perfect, an eclipse of the sun will occur.* conjoin (verb).

consolation (noun) Relief or comfort in sorrow or suffering. *Although we miss our dog very much, it is a consolation to know that she died quickly, without much suffering.* console (verb).

consternation (noun) Shock, amazement, dismay. *When a voice in the back of the church shouted out, "I know why they should not be married!" the entire gathering was thrown into consternation.*

contention (noun) A point made in an argument or debate. *Despite evidence to the contrary, it had always been the president's contention that he was not guilty of any crimes or misdemeanors.* contentious (adjective).

contingency (noun) An event that is possible. *When making plans for the future, it is always wise to prepare for any contingency that may occur.* contingent (adjective).

convergence (noun) The act of coming together in unity or similarity. *A remarkable example of evolutionary convergence can be seen in the shark and the dolphin, two sea creatures that developed from different origins to become very similar in form and appearance.* converge (verb).

conviviality (noun) Fond of good company and eating and drinking. *The conviviality of my fellow employees seemed to turn every staff meeting into a party, complete with snacks, drinks, and lots of hearty laughter.* convivial (adjective).

convoluted (adjective) Twisting, complicated, intricate. *Income tax law has become so convoluted that it's easy for people to violate it completely by accident.* convolute (verb), convolution (noun).

corrective (noun) Something that removes errors or mistakes. *A safe driving course can serve as a corrective for dangerous driving habits.* correctively (adverb).

correlation (noun) A correspondence between two comparable entities. *Whether or not there should be, there is not necessarily a correlation between the amount of work people do and the compensation they receive for it.* correlate (verb).

corroborating (adjective) Supporting with evidence; confirming. *A passerby who had witnessed the crime gave corroborating testimony about the presence of the accused person.* corroborate (verb), corroboration (noun).

corrosive (adjective) Eating away, gnawing, or destroying. *Years of poverty and hard work had a corrosive effect on her strength and beauty.* corrode (verb), corrosion (noun).

cosmopolitanism (noun) International sophistication; worldliness. *Budapest is known for its cosmopolitanism, perhaps because it was the first Eastern European city to be more open to capitalism and influences from the West.* cosmopolitan (adjective).

counterargument (noun) A point made in a discussion contrary to an already stated point. *The lack of proof that the death penalty has historically served as a deterrent to potential murderers is a good counterargument to those who contend that it will do so in the future.*

countering (verb) Offering something opposite or contrary. *Because they were so close to agreeing on a price, the seller believed that countering the buyer's offer would result in their reaching an agreement.* counter (noun).

covert (adjective) Secret, clandestine. *The CIA has often been criticized for its covert operations in the domestic policies of foreign countries, such as the failed Bay of Pigs operation in Cuba.*

covetous (adjective) Envious, particularly of another's possessions. *Benita would never admit to being covetous of my new sable jacket, but I found it odd that she couldn't refrain from trying it on each time we met.* covet (verb).

craven (adjective) Cowardly. *Local gay and lesbian activists were outraged by the craven behavior of a policeman who refused to come to the aid of an HIV-positive accident victim.*

credulous (adjective) Ready to believe; gullible. *Elaine was not very credulous of the explanation Serge gave for his acquisition of the Matisse lithograph.* credulity (noun).

cryptic (adjective) Puzzling, ambiguous. *I was puzzled by the cryptic message left on my answering machine about "a shipment of pomegranates from an anonymous donor."*

culmination (noun) The climax. *The Los Angeles riots, in the aftermath of the Rodney King verdict, were the culmination of long-standing racial tensions between the residents of South Central L.A. and the police.* culminate (verb).

culpable (adjective) Deserving blame, guilty. *Although he committed the crime, because he was mentally ill he should not be considered culpable for his actions.* culpability (noun).

cursory (adjective) Hasty and superficial. *Detective Martinez was rebuked by his superior officer for drawing conclusions about the murder after only a cursory examination of the crime scene.*

cyclic (adjective) Relating to a regularly repeated event or sequence of events. *Since autumn follows summer each year, and is in turn always followed by winter and spring, the year is said to be cyclic.* cyclically (adverb).

D

debilitating (adjective) Weakening; sapping the strength of. *One can't help but marvel at the courage Stephen Hawking displays in the face of such a debilitating disease as ALS.* debilitate (verb).

decelerate (verb) To slow down. *Randall didn't decelerate enough on the winding roads, and he ended up smashing his new sport utility vehicle into a guard rail.* deceleration (noun).

decimation (noun) Almost complete destruction. *Michael Moore's documentary, "Roger and Me," chronicles the decimation of the economy of Flint, Michigan, after the closing of a General Motors factory.* decimate (verb).

decry (verb) To criticize or condemn. *Cigarette ads aimed at youngsters have led many to decry the unfair marketing tactics of the tobacco industry.*

defamation (noun) Act of harming someone by libel or slander. *When the article in the* National Enquirer *implied that she was somehow responsible for her husband's untimely death, Renata instructed her lawyer to sue the paper for defamation of character.* defame (verb).

defer (verb) To graciously submit to another's will; to delegate. *In all matters relating to the children's religious education, Joy deferred to her husband, since he clearly cared more about giving them a solid grounding in Judaism.* deference (noun).

deliberate (verb) To think about an issue before reaching a decision. *The legal pundits covering the O.J. Simpson trial were shocked by the short time the jury took to deliberate after a trial that lasted months.* deliberation (noun).

demagogue (noun) A leader who plays dishonestly on the prejudices and emotions of his followers. *Senator Joseph McCarthy was a demagogue who used the paranoia and biases of the anti-communist 1950s as a way of seizing fame and considerable power in Washington.* demagoguery (noun).

demographic (adjective) Relating to the statistical study of population. *Three demographic groups have been the intense focus of marketing strategy: baby boomers, born between 1946 and 1964; baby busters, or Generation X, born between 1965 and 1976; and a group referred to as Generation Y, those born between 1976 and 2000.* demography (noun), demographics (noun).

deprecate (verb) To express disapproval of. *Even if you disagree with an individual on a given subject, it is not necessary—nor even advisable—to personally deprecate him or her.*

derisive (adjective) Expressing ridicule or scorn. *Many women's groups were derisive of Avon's choice of a male CEO in 1998, since the company derived its $5.1 billion in sales from an army of female salespeople.* derision (noun).

derivative (adjective) Imitating or borrowed from a particular source. *When a person first writes poetry, her poems are apt to be derivative of whatever poetry she most enjoys reading.* derivation (noun), derive (verb).

desiccate (verb) To dry out, to wither; to drain of vitality. *The long drought thoroughly desiccated our garden; what was once a glorious Eden was now a scorched and hellish wasteland. A recent spate of books has debunked the myth that menopause desiccates women and affirmed, instead, that women often reach heights of creativity in their later years.* desiccant (noun), desiccation (noun).

despotic (adjective) Oppressive and tyrannical. *During the despotic reign of Idi Amin in the 1970s, an estimated 200,000 Ugandans were killed.* despot (noun).

desultory (adjective) Disconnected, aimless. *Tina's few desultory stabs at conversation fell flat as Guy just sat there, stone-faced; it was a disastrous first date.*

deteriorated (verb) Made inferior in character, quality, or value. *As a result of having been driven more than 150,000 miles, the salesman's car had deteriorated to the point that it had to be replaced.* deterioration (noun).

determinant (noun) An element that identifies the nature of something or fixes an outcome. *Location is a determinant—one of many—in making a decision about buying a home.* determinantal (adjective).

deviate (verb) To depart from a standard or norm. *Having agreed upon a spending budget for the company, we mustn't deviate from it; if we do, we may run out of money before the year ends.* deviation (noun).

diatribe (noun) Abusive or bitter speech or writing. *While angry conservatives dismissed Susan Faludi's* Backlash *as a feminist diatribe, it is actually a meticulously researched book.*

differentiate (verb) To show the difference in or between. *When considering two offers, a job applicant must clearly differentiate between them to determine which is the better.*

diffident (adjective) Hesitant, reserved, shy. *Someone with a diffident personality is most likely to succeed in a career that involves little public contact.* diffidence (noun).

digress (verb) To wander from the main path or the main topic. *My high school biology teacher loved to digress from science into personal anecdotes about his college adventures.* digression (noun), digressive (adjective).

disabuse (verb) To correct a fallacy; to clarify. *I hated to disabuse Filbert, who is a passionate collector of musical trivia, but I had to tell him that The Monkees had hardly sung a note and had lip-synched their way through almost all of their albums.*

disburse (verb) To pay out or distribute (funds or property). *Jaime was flabbergasted when his father's will disbursed all of the old man's financial assets to Raymundo and left him with only a few sticks of furniture.* disbursement (noun).

discern (verb) To detect, notice, or observe. *With difficulty, I could discern the shape of a whale off the starboard bow, but it was too far away to determine its size or species.* discernment (noun).

discordant (adjective) Characterized by conflict. *Stories and films about discordant relationships that resolve themselves happily are always more interesting than stories about content couples who simply stay content.* discordance (noun).

discourse (noun) Formal and orderly exchange of ideas, a discussion. *In the late twentieth century, cloning and other feats of genetic engineering became popular topics of public discourse.* discursive (adjective).

discredit (verb) To cause disbelief in the accuracy of some statement or the reliability of a person. *Although many people still believe in UFOs, among scientists the reports of "alien encounters" have been thoroughly discredited.*

discreet (adjective) Showing good judgment in speech and behavior. *Be discreet when discussing confidential business matters—don't talk among strangers on the elevator, for example.* discretion (noun).

discrete (adjective) Separate, unconnected. *Canadians get peeved when people can't seem to distinguish between Canada and the United States, forgetting that Canada has its own discrete heritage and culture.*

disparity (noun) Difference in quality or kind. *There is often a disparity between the kind of serious, high-quality television people say they want and the low-brow programs they actually watch.* disparate (adjective).

dissemble (verb) To pretend, to simulate. *When the police asked whether Nancy knew anything about the crime, she dissembled innocence.*

dissemination (noun) Spreading abroad or dispersing. *The dissemination of information is the most important aspect of a public relations person's job.*

dissipate (verb) To spread out or scatter. *The windows and doors were opened, allowing the smoke that had filled the room to dissipate.* dissipation (noun).

dissonance (noun) Lack of music harmony; lack of agreement between ideas. *Most modern music is characterized by dissonance, which many listeners find hard to enjoy. There is a noticeable dissonance between two common beliefs of most conservatives: their faith in unfettered free markets and their preference for traditional social values.* dissonant (adjective).

distillation (noun) Something distilled, an essence or extract; in chemistry, a process that drives gas or vapor from liquids or solids. *Sharon Olds's poems are powerful distillations of motherhood and other primal experiences. In Mrs. Hornmeister's chemistry class, our first experiment was to create a distillation of carbon gas from wood.* distill (verb).

diverge (verb) To move in different directions. *Frost's poem "The Road Less Traveled," tells of the choice he made when "Two roads diverged in a yellow wood."* divergence (noun), divergent (adjective).

diversify (verb) To balance by adding variety. *Any financial manager will recommend that you diversify your stock portfolio by holding some less-volatile blue-chip stocks along with more growth-oriented technology issues.* diversification (noun), diversified (adjective).

divest (verb) To rid (oneself) or be freed of property, authority, or title. *In order to turn around its ailing company and concentrate on imaging, Eastman Kodak divested itself of peripheral businesses in the areas of household products, clinical diagnostics, and pharmaceuticals.* divestiture (noun).

divulge (verb) To reveal. *The people who count the votes for the Oscar awards are under strict orders not to divulge the names of the winners.*

dogmatic (adjective)   Holding firmly to a particular set of beliefs with little or no basis. *Believers in Marxist doctrine tend to be dogmatic, ignoring evidence that contradicts their beliefs.* dogma (noun), dogmatism (noun).

dormant (adjective) Temporarily inactive, as if asleep. *An eruption of Mt. Rainier, a dormant volcano in Washington State, would cause massive, life-threatening mud slides in the surrounding area.* dormancy (noun).

dross (noun) Something that is trivial or inferior; an impurity. *As a reader for the* Paris Review, *Julia spent most of her time sifting through piles of manuscripts to separate the extraordinary poems from the dross.*

dubious (adjective) Doubtful, uncertain. *Despite the chairman's attempts to convince the committee members that his plan would succeed, most of them remained dubious.* dubiety (noun).

dupe (noun) Someone who is easily cheated. *My cousin Ravi is such a dupe; he actually gets excited when he receives those envelopes saying "Ravi Murtugudde, you may have won a million dollars."*

E

eccentricity (noun) Odd or whimsical behavior. *Rock stars may be better known for their offstage eccentricities than for their on-stage performances.* eccentric (adjective).

edifying (adjective) Instructive, enlightening. *Ariel would never admit it to her high-brow friends, but she found the latest self-help bestseller edifying and actually helpful.* edification (noun), edify (verb).

efficacy (noun) The power to produce the desired effect. *While teams have been enormously popular in the workplace, there are some who now question their efficacy and say that "one head is better than ten."* efficacious (noun).

effrontery (noun) Shameless boldness. *The sports world was shocked when a pro basketball player had the effrontery to choke the head coach of his team during a practice session.*

elaborate (verb) To expand upon something; develop. *One characteristic of the best essayists is their ability to elaborate ideas through examples, lists, similes, small variations, and even exaggerations.* elaborate (adjective), elaboration (noun).

emanating (verb) Coming from a source. *The less than pleasant odor emanating from the frightened skunk was enough to send the campers in search of another campsite.* emanation (noun).

embellish (verb) To enhance or exaggerate; to decorate. *The long-married couple told their stories in tandem, with the husband outlining the plot and the wife embellishing it with colorful details.* embellished (adjective).

embezzle (verb) To steal money that has been entrusted to your care. *The church treasurer was found to have embezzled thousands of dollars by writing phony checks on the church bank account.* embezzlement (noun).

emollient (noun) Something that softens or soothes. *She used a hand cream as an emollient on her dry, work-roughened hands.* emollient (adjective).

empirical (adjective) Based on experience or personal observation. *Although many people believe in ESP, scientists have found no empirical evidence of its existence.* empiricism (noun).

emulate (verb) To imitate or copy. *Cover bands are quite open about their desire to emulate their idols.* emulation (noun).

enervate (verb) To reduce the energy or strength of someone or something. *The stress of the operation left her feeling enervated for about two weeks.* enervation (noun).

engender (verb) To produce, to cause. *Countless disagreements over the proper use of national forests and parklands have engendered feelings of hostility between ranchers and environmentalists.*

enhance (verb) To improve in value or quality. *New kitchen appliances will enhance your house and increase the amount of money you'll make when you sell it.* enhancement (noun).

enigmatic (adjective) Puzzling, mysterious. *Alain Resnais' enigmatic film* Last Year at Marienbad *sets up a puzzle that is never resolved: a man meets a woman at a hotel and believes he once had an affair with her—or did he?* enigma (noun).

enmity (noun) Hatred, hostility, ill will. *Long-standing enmity, like that between the Protestants and Catholics in Northern Ireland, is difficult to overcome.*

ensure (verb) To make certain; to guarantee. *In order to ensure a sufficient crop of programmers and engineers for the future, the United States needs to raise the quality of its math and science schooling.*

enumerate (verb) To count off or name one by one. *In order to convince his parents that he was choosing the right college, the high school senior felt it would be advisable to enumerate all the reasons for his decision.* enumeration (noun).

epithet (noun) Term or words used to characterize a person or thing, often in a disparaging way. *The police chief reminded the new recruits that there is no place for racial epithets in their vocabulary.* epithetical (adjective).

equable (adjective) Steady, uniform. *While many people can't see how Helena could possibly be attracted to "Boring Bruno," his equable nature is the perfect complement to her volatile personality.*

equity (noun) The state of being impartial and fair. *Although our legal system is designed to provide equity, it does not always provide justice.*

equivocate (verb) To use misleading or intentionally confusing language. *When Pedro pressed Renee for an answer to his marriage proposal, she equivocated by saying, "I've just got to know when your Mercedes will be out of the shop!"* equivocal (adjective), equivocation (noun).

eradicate (verb) To destroy completely. *American society has failed to eradicate racism, although some of its worst effects have been reduced.* eradication (noun).

erosion (noun) The process of being worn away by degrees. *The process by which the elements reduce mountains to hills over time is an excellent example of erosion.* erode (verb).

erudition (noun) Extensive knowledge, usually acquired from books. *When Dorothea first saw Mr. Casaubon's voluminous library she was awed, but after their marriage she quickly realized that erudition is no substitute for originality.* erudite (adjective).

esoterica (noun) Items of interest to a select group. *The fish symposium at St. Antony's College in Oxford explored all manner of esoterica relating to fish, as is evidenced in presentations such as "The Buoyant Slippery Lipids of the Escolar and Orange Roughy" and "Food on Board Whale Ships—from the Inedible to the Incredible."* esoteric (adjective).

espouse (verb) To take up as a cause; to adopt. *No politician in America today will openly espouse racism, although some behave and speak in racially prejudiced ways.*

estimable (adjective) Worthy of esteem and admiration. *After a tragic fire raged through Malden Mills, the estimable mill owner, Aaron Feuerstein, restarted operations and rebuilt the company within just one month.* esteem (noun).

ethnology (noun) A science dealing with the division of mankind into races and their origins. *The anthropologist Margaret Mead is best known for her study of the ethnology of the natives of New Guinea.* ethnologic (adjective).

euphemism (noun) An agreeable expression that is substituted for an offensive one. *Some of the more creative euphemisms for "layoffs" in current use are "release of resources," "involuntary severance," "strengthening global effectiveness," and "career transition program."* euphemistic (adjective).

exacerbate (verb) To make worse or more severe. *The roads in our town already have too much traffic; building a new shopping mall will exacerbate the problem.*

excoriation (noun) The act of condemning someone with harsh words. *In the small office we shared, it was painful to hear my boss's constant excoriation of his assistant for the smallest faults—a misdirected letter, an unclear phone message, or even a tepid cup of coffee.* excoriate (verb).

exculpate (verb) To free from blame or guilt. *When someone else confessed to the crime, the previous suspect was exculpated.* exculpation (noun), exculpatory (adjective).

executor (noun) The person appointed to execute someone's will. *As the executor of his Aunt Ida's will, Phil must deal with squabbling relatives, conniving lawyers, and the ruinous state of Ida's house.*

exigent (adjective) Urgent, requiring immediate attention. *A two-year-old is likely to behave as if her every demand is exigent, even if it involves simply retrieving a beloved stuffed hedgehog from under the couch.* exigency (noun).

expedient (adjective) Providing an immediate advantage or serving one's immediate self-interest. *When the passenger next to her was strafed by a bullet, Sharon chose the most expedient means to stop the bleeding; she whipped off her pantyhose and made an impromptu, but effective, tourniquet.* expediency (noun).

explicitly (adverb) Clearly, unambiguously. *Using a profit and loss statement, the company's accountant explicitly explained the company's dire financial situation.* explicit (adjective).

extant (adjective) Currently in existence. *Of the seven ancient "Wonders of the World," only the pyramids of Egypt are still extant.*

extenuate (verb) To make less serious. *Karen's guilt is extenuated by the fact that she was only 12 when she committed the theft.* extenuating (adjective), extenuation (noun).

extol (verb) To greatly praise. *At the party convention, one speaker after another took to the podium to extol the virtues of their candidate for the presidency.*

extraneous (adjective) Irrelevant, nonessential. *One review of the new Chekhov biography said the author had bogged down the book with far too many extraneous details, such as the dates of Chekhov's bouts of diarrhea.*

extrapolate (verb) To deduce from something known; to infer. *Meteorologists were able to use old weather records to extrapolate backward and compile lists of El Nino years and their effects over the last century.* extrapolation (noun).

extricate (verb) To free from a difficult or complicated situation. *Much of the humor in the TV show "I Love Lucy" comes in watching Lucy try to extricate herself from the problems she creates by fibbing or trickery.* extricable (adjective).

F

facetious (adjective) Humorous in a mocking way; not serious. *French composer Erik Satie often concealed his serious artistic intent by giving his works facetious titles such as "Three Pieces in the Shape of a Pear."*

facilitate (verb) To make easier or to moderate. *When the issue of racism reared its ugly head, the company brought in a consultant to facilitate a discussion of diversity in the workplace.* facile (adjective), facility (noun).

fallacy (noun) An error in fact or logic. *It's a fallacy to think that "natural" means "healthful"; after all, the deadly poison arsenic is completely natural.* fallacious (adjective).

fatuous (adjective) Inanely foolish, silly. *Once backstage, Elizabeth showered the opera singer with fatuous praise and embarrassing confessions, which he clearly had no interest in hearing.*

feint (noun) A bluff; a mock blow. *It didn't take us long to realize that Gaby's tears and stomach-aches were all a feint, since they appeared so regularly at her bedtime.*

ferret (verb) To bring to light by an extensive search. *With his repeated probing and questions, Fritz was able to ferret out the location of Myrna's safe deposit box.*

finesse (noun) Skillful maneuvering; delicate workmanship. *With her usual finesse, Charmaine gently persuaded the Duncans not to install a motorized Santa and sleigh on their front lawn.*

florid (adjective) Flowery, fancy; reddish. *The grand ballroom was decorated in a florid style. Years of heavy drinking had given him a florid complexion.*

flourish (noun) An extraneous embellishment; a dramatic gesture. *The napkin rings made out of intertwined ferns and flowers were just the kind of flourish one would expect from Carol, a slavish follower of Martha Stewart.*

fluctuation (noun) A shifting back and forth. *Investment analysts predict fluctuations in the Dow Jones Industrial Average due to the instability of the value of the dollar.* fluctuate (verb).

foil (verb) To thwart or frustrate. *I was certain that Jerry's tendency to insert himself into everyone's conversations would foil my chances to have a private word with Helen.*

foment (verb) To rouse or incite. *The petty tyrannies and indignities inflicted on the workers by upper management helped foment the walkout at the meat-processing plant.*

forestall (verb) To hinder or prevent by taking action in advance. *The pilot's calm, levelheaded demeanor during the attempted highjacking forestalled any hysteria among the passengers of Flight 268.*

fortuitous (adjective) Lucky, fortunate. *Although the mayor claimed credit for the falling crime rate, it was really caused by a series of fortuitous accidents.*

foster (verb) To nurture or encourage. *The whitewater rafting trip was supposed to foster creative problem solving and teamwork between the account executives and the creative staff at Apex Advertising Agency.*

functionary (noun) Someone holding office in a political party or government. *The man shaking hands with the governor was a low-ranking Democratic Party functionary who had worked to garner the Hispanic vote.*

G

gainsay (verb) To contradict or oppose; deny, dispute. *Dot would gainsay her married sister's efforts to introduce her to eligible men by refusing to either leave her ailing canary or give up her thrice-weekly bingo nights.*

garrulous (adjective) Annoyingly talkative. *Claude pretended to be asleep so he could avoid his garrulous seatmate, a self-proclaimed expert on bonsai cultivation.*

generic (adjective) General; having no brand name. *Connie tried to reduce her grocery bills by religiously clipping coupons and buying generic brands of most products.*

gist (noun) The main point, the essence. *Although they felt sympathy for the victim's family, the jurors were won over by the gist of the defense's argument; there was insufficient evidence to convict.*

guile (noun) Deceit, duplicity. *In Margaret Mitchell's* Gone with the Wind, *Scarlett O'Hara uses her guile to manipulate two men and then is matched for wits by a third: Rhett Butler.* guileful (adjective).

gullible (adjective) Easily fooled. *Terry was so gullible she actually believed Robert's stories of his connections to the Czar and Czarina.* gullibility (noun).

H

habitat (noun) The place where a plant or animal normally lives and grows. *Even though frogs do occasionally come up onto land, their natural habitat is water.*

hackneyed (adjective) Without originality, trite. *When someone invented the phrase, "No pain, no gain," it was clever and witty, but now it is so commonly heard that it seems hackneyed.*

haughty (adjective) Overly proud. *The fashion model strode down the runway, her hips thrust forward and a haughty expression, something like a sneer, on her face.* haughtiness (noun).

hesitance (noun) Holding back in doubt or indecision. *The young woman was thrilled that her boyfriend had proposed to her but had some hesitance about marrying him because of his dysfunctional family.* hesitantly (adverb).

hierarchy (noun) A ranking of people, things, or ideas from highest to lowest. *A cabinet secretary ranks just below the president and vice president in the hierarchy of the government's executive branch.* hierarchical (adjective).

homogeneous (adjective) Uniform; made entirely of one thing. *It's hard to think of a more homogenous group than those eerie children in "Village of the Damned," who all had perfect features, white-blond hair, and silver, penetrating eyes.*

hone (verb) To improve and make more acute or effective. *While she was a receptionist, Norma honed her skills as a stand-up comic by trying out jokes on the tense crowd in the waiting room.*

humanitarian (noun) One who promotes human welfare and social reform. *In providing millions of dollars to build libraries around the country, Andrew Carnegie showed himself to be a true humanitarian.*

hypothesized (verb) Theorized. *As part of his famous Theory of Relativity, Albert Einstein hypothesized that time travel was a real possibility.* hypothesis (noun).

I

iconoclast (noun) Someone who attacks traditional beliefs or institutions. *Comedian Bill Maher relishes his reputation as an iconoclast, though people in power often resent his satirical jabs.* iconoclasm (noun), iconoclastic (adjective).

idealization (noun) Bringing something to perfection. *Marrying Prince Charming was the idealization of Cinderella's dreams.* idealize (verb).

ideology (noun) A body of ideas or beliefs. *Thomas Jefferson's ideology was based on the assumption, as he put it, that "all men are created equal."* ideological (adjective).

idolatry (noun) The worship of a person, thing, or institution as a god. *In communist China, admiration for Mao resembled idolatry; his picture was displayed everywhere, and millions of Chinese memorized his sayings and repeated them endlessly.* idolatrous (adjective).

idyll (noun) A rustic, romantic interlude; poetry or prose that celebrates simple pastoral life. *Her picnic with Max at Fahnstock Lake was not the serene idyll she had envisioned; instead, they were surrounded by hundreds of other picnickers blaring music and cracking open soda cans.* idyllic (adjective).

illicit (adjective) Illegal, wrongful. *When Janet caught her thirteen-year-old son and his friend downloading illicit pornographic photos from the Web, she promptly pulled the plug on his computer.*

illuminate (verb) To brighten with light; to enlighten or elucidate; to decorate (a manuscript). *The frosted-glass sconces in the dressing rooms at Le Cirque not only illuminate the rooms but make everyone look like a movie star. Alice Munro is a writer who can illuminate an entire character with a few deft sentences.*

immaculate (adjective) Totally unblemished, spotlessly clean. *The cream-colored upholstery in my new Porsche was immaculate—that is, until a raccoon came in through the window and tracked mud across the seats.*

immaterial (adjective) Of no consequence, unimportant. *"The fact that your travel agent is your best friend's son should be immaterial," I told Rosa. "If he keeps putting you on hold and acting nasty, just take your business elsewhere."*

immunity (noun) Being free of or exempt from something. *Polio vaccinations provide children with immunity to the polio virus and thus keep them from contracting the disease.*

immutable (adjective) Incapable of change. *Does there ever come an age when we realize that our parents' personalities are immutable, when we can relax and stop trying to make them change?*

impartial (adjective) Fair, equal, unbiased. *If a judge is not impartial, then all of her rulings are questionable.* impartiality (noun).

impassivity (noun) Apathy, unresponsiveness. *Dot truly thinks that Mr. Right will magically show up on her doorstep, and her utter impassivity regarding her social life makes me want to shake her!* impassive (adjective).

imperceptible (adjective) Impossible to perceive, inaudible or incomprehensible. *The sound of footsteps was almost imperceptible, but Donald's paranoia had reached such a pitch that he immediately assumed he was being followed.*

imperturbable (adjective) Cannot be disconcerted, disturbed, or excited. *The proper English butler in Kazuo Ishiguro's novel* Remains of the Day *appears completely imperturbable even when his father dies or when his own heart is breaking.*

impetuous (adjective) Acting hastily or impulsively. *Ben's resignation was an impetuous act; he did it without thinking, and he soon regretted it.* impetuosity (noun).

implacable (adjective) Unbending, resolute. *The state of Israel is implacable in its policy of never negotiating with terrorists.*

implement (verb) To carry out. *The entrepreneur had to have all his financing in place before he could implement his plans for expanding the company.* implementation (noun).

implosion (noun) To collapse inward from outside pressure. *While it is difficult to know what is going on in North Korea, no one can rule out a violent implosion of the North Korean regime and a subsequent flood of refugees across its borders.* implode (verb).

incessant (adjective) Unceasing. *The incessant blaring of the neighbor's car alarm made it impossible for me to concentrate on my upcoming Bar exam.*

inchoate (adjective) Only partly formed or formulated. *At editorial meetings, Nancy had a habit of presenting her inchoate book ideas before she had a chance to fully determine their feasibility.*

incise (verb) To carve into, to engrave. *My wife felt nostalgic about the old elm tree since we had incised our initials in it when we were both in high school.* incisive (adjective) Admirably direct and decisive. *Ted Koppel's incisive questions have made many politicians squirm and stammer.*

incongruous (adjective) Unlikely. *Art makes incongruous alliances, as when punk-rockers, Tibetan folk musicians, gospel singers, and beat poets shared the stage at the Tibet House benefit concert.* incongruity (noun).

incorrigible (adjective) Impossible to manage or reform. *Lou is an incorrigible trickster, constantly playing practical jokes no matter how much his friends complain.*

incur (verb) To become liable or subject to. *When you have a difficult boss, it's wise to avoid anything that might incur his or her wrath.*

incursion (noun) A hostile entrance into a territory; a foray into an activity or venture. *It is a little-known fact that the Central Intelligence Agency organized military incursions into China during the 1950s. The ComicCon was Barbara's first incursion into the world of comic strip artists.*

indefatigable (adjective) Tireless. *Eleanor Roosevelt's indefatigable dedication to the cause of human welfare won her affection and honor throughout the world.* indefatigability (noun).

indigenous (adjective) Native. *It's much easier for a gardener to cultivate indigenous plants than those that are native to other climates.* indigenously (adverb).

individualistic (adjective) Asserting independence of thought and action. *The woman's insistence on going against the tide of popular opinion was only one aspect of her individualistic nature.* individualist (noun).

inducement (noun) A consideration leading one to action. *In order to compete effectively, some automobile companies offer inducements to potential customers, such as special features at no additional cost.* induce (verb).

inequities (noun) Injustice, unfairness. *Sometimes it takes a person many years to accept the fact that life is full of inequities, and some people simply refuse ever to recognize the basic unfairness of life.*

inevitable (adjective) Unable to be avoided. *Once the Japanese attacked Pearl Harbor, United States involvement in World War II was inevitable.* inevitability (noun).

inextricably (adverb) Incapable of being disentangled. *When a man and woman have lived together for many years, particularly if they've raised children together, their lives become inextricably intertwined.* inextricable (adjective).

infer (verb) To conclude, to deduce. *Can I infer from your hostile tone of voice that you are still angry about yesterday's incident?* inference (noun).

influx (noun) Flowing in. *The influx of immigrants from the former Soviet Union was so great that it overwhelmed the immigration authorities.*

informant (noun) One who apprises, acquaints, or notifies. *In order for police officers to maintain an awareness of the criminal world, it's often necessary for them to have relationships with an informant or two.*

inhibiting (verb) Restraining, holding back. *The boxer's fear of doing serious damage was an inhibiting factor in his attack on his opponent.* inhibition (noun), inhibitory (adjective).

inimical (adjective) Unfriendly, hostile; adverse or difficult. *Relations between Greece and Turkey have been inimical for centuries.*

inimitable (adjective) Incapable of being imitated, matchless. *John F. Kennedy's administration dazzled the public, partly because of the inimitable style and elegance of his wife, Jacqueline.*

inopportune (adjective) Awkward, untimely. *When Gus heard raised voices and the crash of breaking china behind the kitchen door, he realized that he'd picked an inopportune moment to visit the Fairlights.*

inscrutability (noun) Quality of being extremely difficult to interpret or understand, mysteriousness. *I am still puzzling over the inscrutability of the package I received yesterday, which contained twenty pomegranates and a note that said simply, "Yours."* inscrutable (adjective).

insensible (adjective) Unaware, incognizant; unconscious, out cold. *It's a good thing that Marty was insensible to the titters and laughter that greeted his arrival in the ballroom. In the latest episode of police brutality, an innocent young man was beaten insensible after two cops stormed his apartment.*

insinuate (verb) Hint or intimate; to creep in. *During an extremely unusual broadcast, the anchorman insinuated that the Washington bureau chief was having a nervous breakdown. Marla managed to insinuate herself into the Duchess of York's conversation during the Weight Watchers promotion event.* insinuation (noun).

insipid (adjective) Flavorless, uninteresting. *Most TV shows are so insipid that you can watch them while reading or chatting without missing a thing.* insipidity (noun).

insolence (noun) An attitude or behavior that is bold and disrespectful. *Some feel that news reporters who shout accusatory questions at the president are behaving with insolence toward his high office.* insolent (adjective).

insoluble (adjective) Unable to be solved, irresolvable; indissoluble. *Fermat's last theorem remained insoluble for more than 300 years until a young mathematician from Princeton solved it in 1995. If you are a gum chewer, you probably wouldn't like to know that insoluble plastics are a common ingredient of most popular gums.*

instigate (verb) To goad or urge on. *It's never a good idea to instigate a fight between other people, because you might get caught in the middle of it.* instigation (noun).

insular (adjective) Narrow or isolated in attitude or viewpoint. *New Yorkers are famous for their insular attitudes; they seem to think that nothing important has ever happened outside of their city.* insularity (noun).

intangible (adjective) Incapable of being perceived by the senses. *Having a child's love is one of the intangible benefits of being a parent.*

intercede (verb) To step in, to moderate; to mediate or negotiate on behalf of someone else. *After their rejection by the co-op board, Kevin and Sol asked Rachel, another tenant, to intercede for them at the next board meeting.* intercession (noun).

interception (noun) The act of stopping or interrupting an intended course. *Interception of drugs coming over the border is one of the means federal authorities use in their efforts to combat the drug trade.* intercept (verb).

intermediary (noun) One who acts as an agent between persons or things. *When the policemen's union has to discuss a new contract with the city, they often find it necessary to use an intermediary during the negotiations.*

interpolate (verb) To interject. *The director's decision to interpolate topical political jokes into his production of Shakespeare's* Twelfth Night *was not viewed kindly by the critics.* interpolation (noun).

interrelated (verb) Mutually connected or associated. *If all the parts of an automobile engine were not interrelated, the engine would not function properly.* interrelation (noun).

interspersed (verb) Distributed among other things at intervals. *In the library, all the historical biographies were interspersed among the general history books.*

interval (noun) A period of time between events. *Because they wanted to be married quickly, the interval between the couple's engagement and their wedding was an extremely busy one.*

intransigent (adjective) Unwilling to compromise. *Despite the mediator's attempts to suggest a fair solution to the disagreement, the two parties were intransigent, forcing a showdown.* intransigence (noun).

intricate (adjective) Complicated. *Because of the many elements to be included in the company's logo, creating the design was an intricate process.* intricately (adverb).

intrinsically (adverb) Essentially, inherently. *There is nothing intrinsically difficult about upgrading a computer's microprocessor, yet Al was afraid to even open up the hard drive.* intrinsic (adjective).

inundate (verb) To overwhelm; to flood. *The company was inundated with new customers, and thus began the annoying delays in service.* inundation (noun).

invective (noun) Insulting, abusive language. *I remained unscathed by his blistering invective, because in my heart I knew I had done the right thing.*

invigorate (verb) To give energy to, to stimulate. *As her car climbed the mountain road, Lucinda felt herself invigorated by the clear air and the cool breezes.* invigoration (noun).

irascible (adjective) Easily provoked into anger, hot-headed. *Soup chef Al Yeganah, the model for Seinfeld's "Soup Nazi," is an irascible man who flies into a temper if his customers don't follow his rigid procedure for purchasing soup.* irascibility (noun).

irreconcilable (adjective) Impossible to settle or resolve. *The two sides were so far apart in the negotiations that they had to admit their differences were irreconcilable.*

irreversibly (adverb) Incapable of being turned backward. *The car was moving at such a fast rate when the collision took place that it was irreversibly damaged.* irreversible (adjective).

J

jeopardize (verb) To put in danger. *Terrorist attacks on civilians jeopardize the peace talks.* jeopardy (noun).

L

labyrinthine (adjective) Extremely intricate or involved; circuitous. *Was I the only one who couldn't follow the labyrinthine plot of that new mystery thriller? I was so confused I had to watch it twice to see "who did it."*

laconic (adjective) Concise to the point of terseness; taciturn. *Tall, handsome, and laconic, the actor Gary Cooper came to personify the strong, silent American, a man of action and few words.*

laudable (adjective) Commendable, praiseworthy. *The Hunt's Point nonprofit organization has embarked on a series of laudable ventures pairing businesses and disadvantaged youth.*

leery (adverb) Distrustful or suspicious. *Whether deserved or not, car salesmen have a reputation for being dishonest, so many people are leery of whatever they say.*

legitimizing (verb) Making lawful or conforming to accepted rules. *Establishing the man's familial relationship to the deceased was an essential aspect of legitimizing his claim to the woman's substantial estate.* legitimate (adjective).

lethargic (adjective) Lacking energy; sluggish. *Visitors to the zoo are surprised that the lions appear so lethargic, but, in the wild, lions sleep up to 18 hours a day.* lethargy (noun).

levy (verb) To demand payment or collection of a tax or fee. *The environmental activists pushed Congress to levy higher taxes on gasoline, but the automakers' lobbyists quashed their plans.*

lien (noun) A claim against a property for the satisfaction of a debt. *Nat was in such financial straits when he died that his Fishkill property had several liens against it, and all of his furniture was being repossessed.*

loquacity (noun) Talkativeness, wordiness. *While some people deride his loquacity and his tendency to use outrageous rhymes, no one can doubt that Jesse Jackson is a powerful orator.* loquacious (adjective).

lucid (adjective) Clear and understandable. *Hawking's* A Brief History of the Universe *is a lucid explanation of a difficult topic: modern scientific theories of the origin of the universe.* lucidity (noun).

M

magnanimous (adjective) Noble, generous. *When media titan Ted Turner pledged a gift of $1 billion to the United Nations, he challenged other wealthy people to be equally magnanimous.* magnanimity (noun).

maladroit (adjective) Inept, awkward. *It was painful to watch the young congressman's maladroit delivery of the nominating speech.*

malinger (verb) To pretend illness to avoid work. *During the labor dispute, hundreds of employees malingered, forcing the company to slow production and costing it millions in profits.*

malleable (adjective) Able to be changed, shaped, or formed by outside pressures. *Gold is a very useful metal because it is so malleable. A child's personality is malleable and is often deeply influenced by things her parents say and do.* malleability (noun).

mandate (noun) Order, command. *The new policy on gays in the military went into effect as soon as the president issued his mandate about it.* mandate (verb), mandatory (adjective).

marginal (adjective) At the outer edge or fringe; of minimal quality or acceptability. *In spite of the trend toward greater paternal involvement in child rearing, most fathers still have a marginal role in their children's lives. Jerry's test scores were so marginal that he didn't get accepted into the graduate schools of his choice.*

marginalize (verb) To push toward the fringes; to make less consequential. *Hannah argued that the designation of a certain month as "Black History Month" or "Gay and Lesbian Book Month" actually does a disservice to minorities by marginalizing them.*

martial (adjective) Of, relating to, or suited to military life. *My old teacher, Miss Woody, had such a martial demeanor that you'd think she was running a boot camp instead of teaching fifth grade. The military seized control of Burma in 1988, and this embattled country has been ruled by martial law since then.*

mediate (verb) To reconcile differences between two parties. *During the baseball strike, both the players and the club owners expressed willingness to have the president mediate the dispute.* mediation (noun).

mercenary (adjective) Doing something only for pay or for personal advantage. *People have criticized the Bush administration's motives in the Iraq War as mercenary, pointing out that the United States would not have invaded Iraq if that country did not produce oil.* mercenary (noun).

mercurial (adjective) Changing quickly and unpredictably. *The mercurial personality of Robin Williams, with his many voices and styles, has made him one of the most talented comedians of the past three decades.*

metamorphose (verb) To undergo a striking transformation. *In just a century, book publishers have metamorphosed from independent, exclusively literary businesses to minor divisions in multimedia entertainment conglomerates.* metamorphosis (noun).

methodology (noun) A procedure or set of procedures. *Because the methodology the scientist employed was unconventional, the results of his study were questioned by others in the field.* methodical (adjective).

meticulous (adjective) Very careful with details. *Watch repair calls for a craftsperson who is patient and meticulous.*

mimicry (noun) Imitation, aping. *The continued popularity of Elvis Presley has given rise to a class of entertainers who make a living through mimicry of "The King."* mimic (noun and verb).

misanthrope (noun) Someone who hates or distrusts all people. *In the beloved Christmas classic,* It's a Wonderful Life, *Lionel Barrymore plays Potter, the wealthy misanthrope who is determined to make life miserable for everyone, and particularly for the young, idealistic George Bailey.* misanthropic (adjective), misanthropy (noun).

miscreant (adjective) Unbelieving, heretical; evil, villainous. *After a one-year run playing Iago in* Othello, *and then two years playing Bill Sikes in* Oliver, *Sean was tired of being typecast in miscreant roles.* miscreant (noun).

mitigate (verb) To make less severe; to relieve. *There's no doubt that Wallace committed the assault, but the verbal abuse Wallace had received helps to explain his behavior and somewhat mitigates his guilt.* mitigation (noun).

moderated (verb) Arbitrated, mediated. *The professor moderated the debate between the advocates of open enrollment and those who opposed it.* moderator (noun).

monitoring (verb) Watching or observing for a purpose. *Court-appointed parole officers are responsible for monitoring the behavior of criminals who have been released from prison.*

monopoly (noun) A condition in which there is only one seller of a certain commodity. *Wary of Microsoft's seeming monopoly of the computer operating-system business, rivals asked for government intervention.* monopolistic (adjective). *Renowned consumer advocate Ralph Nader once quipped, "The only difference between John D. Rockefeller and Bill Gates is that Gates recognizes no boundaries to his monopolistic drive."*

monotonous (adjective) Tediously uniform, unchanging. *Ambient music is characterized by minimal melodies, subtle textures, and variable repetition, which I find rather bland and monotonous.* monotony (noun).

moorings (noun) Elements providing security or stability. *When her best friend moved to another city, the young woman felt that to a great extent she had lost her moorings.*

morose (adjective) Gloomy, sullen. *After Chuck's girlfriend dumped him, he lay around the house for a couple of days, refusing to come to the phone and feeling morose.*

mutation (noun) A significant change; in biology, a permanent change in hereditary material. *Most genetic mutations are not beneficial, since any change in the delicate balance of an organism tends to be disruptive.* mutate (verb).

N

nadir (noun) Lowest point. *Pedro and Renee's marriage reached a new nadir last Christmas Eve when Pedro locked Renee out of the house upon her return from the supposed "business trip."*

nascent (adjective) Newly born; just beginning. *While her artistry was still nascent, it was 15-year-old Tara Lipinski's technical wizardry that enabled her to win a gold medal in the 1998 Winter Olympics.* nascence (noun).

necessitated (verb) Required. *The college senior's desire to attend graduate school necessitated his taking the Graduate Management Admission Test.* necessity (noun).

negligence (noun) The state of being careless or casual. *The author's negligence in checking his spelling resulted in his editor's having to do more work than she had anticipated.* negligent (adjective).

neutrality (noun) The state of being unallied with either side in a disagreement. *Switzerland's neutrality during World War II was the reason it was not attacked by either the Axis or the Allied powers.* neutral (adjective).

noisome (adjective) Putrid, fetid, noxious. *We were convinced that the noisome odor infiltrating every corner of our building was evidence of a moldering corpse.*

notorious (adjective) Famous, especially for evil actions or qualities. *Warner Brothers produced a series of movies about notorious gangsters such as John Dillinger and Al Capone.* notoriety (noun).

O

obdurate (adjective) Unwilling to change; stubborn, inflexible. *Despite the many pleas he received, the governor was obdurate in his refusal to grant clemency to the convicted murderer.*

oblivious (adjective) Unaware, unconscious. *Karen practiced her oboe solo with complete concentration, oblivious to the noise and activity around her.* oblivion (noun), obliviousness (noun).

obscure (adjective) Little known; hard to understand. *Mendel was an obscure monk until decades after his death, when his scientific work was finally discovered. Most people find the writings of James Joyce obscure; hence the popularity of books that explain the many odd references and tricks of language in his work.* obscure (verb), obscurity (noun).

obsolete (adjective) No longer current; old-fashioned. *W. H. Auden said that his ideal landscape would contain water wheels, grain mills, and other forms of obsolete machinery.* obsolescence (noun).

obstinate (adjective) Stubborn, unyielding. *Despite years of government effort, the problem of drug abuse remains obstinate.* obstinacy (noun).

obtuse (adjective) Dull witted, insensitive; incomprehensible, unclear, or imprecise. *Amy was so obtuse she didn't realize that Alexi had proposed marriage to her. French psychoanalyst Jacques Lacan's collection of papers,* Ecrits, *is notoriously obtuse, yet it has still been highly influential in linguistics, film theory, and literary criticism.*

obviate (verb) Preclude, make unnecessary. *Truman Capote's meticulous accuracy and total recall obviated the need for note-taking when he wrote his account of a 1959 murder,* In Cold Blood.

odium (noun) Intense feeling of hatred, abhorrence. *When the neighbors learned that a convicted sex offender was now living in their midst, they could not restrain their odium and began harassing the man whenever he left his house.* odious (adjective).

opprobrium (noun) Dishonor, disapproval. *Switzerland recently came under public opprobrium when it was revealed that Swiss bankers had hoarded the gold the Nazis had confiscated from their victims.* opprobrious (adjective).

orthodox (adjective) In religion, conforming to a certain doctrine; conventional. *George Eliot's relationship with George Lewes, a married journalist, offended the sensibilities of her more orthodox peers.* orthodoxy (noun).

ossified (adjective) In biology, to turn into bone; to become rigidly conventional and opposed to change. *His ossified view of co-education meant that he was now the only teacher who sought to bar girls from the venerable boys' school.* ossification (noun).

ostentatious (adjective) Overly showy, pretentious. *To show off his new wealth, the financier threw an ostentatious party featuring a full orchestra, a famous singer, and tens of thousands of dollars' worth of food.* ostentation (noun).

ostracize (verb) To exclude from a group. *In Biblical times, those who suffered from the disease of leprosy were ostracized.* ostracism (noun).

P

pantheon (noun) A temple dedicated to all gods; a group of persons highly regarded for contributions to a field or endeavor. *Reviewers praised the author for his exceptional ability to cover the pantheon of twentieth-century physics in his new book on the history of physics.*

parse (verb) To break a sentence down into grammatical components; to analyze bit by bit. *In the wake of the sex scandal, journalists parsed every utterance by administration officials regarding the governor's alleged promiscuity.*

partisan (adjective) Reflecting strong allegiance to a particular party or cause. *The vote on the president's budget was strictly partisan: Every member of the president's party voted yes, and all others voted no.* partisan (noun).

patriarchal (adjective) Relating to a man who is a father or founder. *When children take over businesses from their fathers, they often find it difficult to meet patriarchal expectations.*

peccadillo (noun) A minor offense, a lapse. *What Dr. Sykes saw as a major offense—being addressed as Marge rather than Doctor—Tina saw as a mere peccadillo and one that certainly should not have lost her the job.*

pedantic (adjective) Academic, bookish. *The men Hillary met through personal ads in the* New York Review of Books *were invariably pasty-skinned pedantic types who dropped the names of nineteenth-century writers in every sentence.* pedantry (noun).

pedestrian (adjective) Unimaginative, ordinary. *The new Italian restaurant received a bad review due to its reliance on pedestrian dishes such as pasta with marinara sauce and chicken parmigiana.*

perfidious (adjective) Disloyal, treacherous. *Although he was one of the most talented generals of the American Revolution, Benedict Arnold is remembered today as a perfidious betrayer of the patriot cause.* perfidy (noun).

peripatetic (adjective) Moving or traveling from place to place; always on the go. *In Barbara Wilson's* Trouble in Transylvania, *peripatetic translator Cassandra Reilly is on the road again, this time to China by way of Budapest, where she plans to catch the TransMongolian Express.*

permeate (verb) To spread through or penetrate. *Little by little, the smell of gas from the broken pipe permeated the house.*

personification (noun) The embodiment of a thing or an abstract idea in human form. *Many people view Osama bin Laden as the very personification of evil.* personify (verb).

perturbed (verb) Made uneasy or anxious. *Because she expected her mother to be at home, the woman was extremely perturbed when she called and the phone just rang and rang.* perturbation (noun).

pervasive (adjective) Spreading throughout. *As news of the disaster reached the town, a pervasive sense of gloom could be felt everywhere.* pervade (verb).

phenomenon (noun) An unusual and significant occurrence or person. *Johann Sebastian Bach's extraordinary talent would have made him a phenomenon in his own or any other century.* phenomena (plural).

pith (noun) The core, the essential part; in biology, the central strand of tissue in the stems of most vascular plants. *After spending seventeen years in psychoanalysis, Frieda had finally come face to face with the pith of her deep-seated anxiety.* pithy (adjective).

placate (verb) To soothe or appease. *The waiter tried to placate the angry customer with the offer of a free dessert.* placatory (adjective).

placid (adjective) Unmarked by disturbance; complacent. *Dr. Kahn was convinced that the placid exterior presented by Frieda in her early analysis sessions masked a deeply disturbed psyche.* placidity (noun).

plaintive (adjective) Expressing suffering or melancholy. *In the beloved children's book* The Secret Garden, *Mary is disturbed by plaintive cries echoing in the corridors of gloomy Misselthwaite Manor.*

plastic (adjective) Able to be molded or reshaped. *Because it is highly plastic, clay is an easy material for beginning sculptors to use.* plasticity (noun).

platitude (noun) A trite remark or saying; a cliché. *How typical of June to send a sympathy card filled with mindless platitudes like "One day at a time," rather than calling the grieving widow.* platitudinous (adjective).

plausible (adjective) Apparently believable. *The idea that a widespread conspiracy to kill the president has been kept secret by all the participants for more than thirty years hardly seems plausible.* plausibility (noun).

plummet (verb) To dive or plunge. *On October 27, 1997, the stock market plummeted by 554 points and left us all wondering if the bull market was finally over.*

polarize (adjective) To separate into opposing groups or forces. *For years, the abortion debate has polarized the American people, with many people voicing views at either extreme and few people trying to find a middle ground.* polarization (noun).

ponderous (adjective) Unwieldy and bulky; oppressively dull. *Unfortunately, the film director weighed the movie down with a ponderous voice-over narrated by the protagonist as an old man.*

posit (verb) To put forward as a fact. *It is possible, if ill advised, to posit an argument even if you have little or no evidence to support it.*

positivism (noun) A philosophy that denies speculation and assumes that the only knowledge is scientific knowledge. *David Hume carried his positivism to an extreme when he argued that our expectation that the sun will rise tomorrow has no basis in reason and is purely a matter of belief.* positivistic (adjective).

posterity (noun) Future generations. *Even if a man has no wealth to pass onto his children, he can bequeath his ideals and beliefs to posterity.*

practitioners (noun) Those who engage in a profession or technique. *Those who hold black belts in karate are the most proficient practitioners of the martial arts.*

pragmatism (noun) A belief in approaching problems through practical rather than theoretical means. *Roosevelt's attitude toward the economic troubles of the Depression was based on pragmatism: "Try something," he said. "If it doesn't work, try something else."* pragmatic (adjective).

precedent (noun) An earlier occurrence that serves as an example for a decision. *In a legal system that reveres precedent, even defining the nature of a completely new type of dispute can seem impossible.* precede (verb).

precept (noun) A general principle or law. *One of the central precepts of Tai Chi Ch'uan is the necessity of allowing ki (cosmic energy) to flow through one's body in slow, graceful movements.*

precipitate (verb) To spur or activate. *In the summer of 1997, the selling off of the Thai baht precipitated a currency crisis that spread throughout Asia.*

preclude (verb) To prevent, to hinder. *Unfortunately, Jasmine's appointment at the New Age Expo precluded her attendance at our weekend Workshop for Shamans and Psychics.* preclusive (adjective), preclusion (noun).

precursor (noun) A forerunner, a predecessor. *The Kodak Brownie camera, a small boxy camera made of jute board and wood, was the precursor to the sleek 35mm camera.* precursory (adjective).

prefigured (verb) Showed or suggested by an antecedent form or model. *The stream of consciousness style of James Joyce's* Ulysses *was prefigured to some extent by the nonsense verse of Edward Lear.* prefigurement (noun).

preponderance (noun) A superiority in weight, size, or quantity; a majority. *In Seattle, there is a great preponderance of seasonal affective disorder, or SAD, a malady brought on by light starvation during the dark winter.* preponderate (verb).

presage (verb) To foretell, to anticipate. *According to folklore, a red sky at dawn presages a day of stormy weather.*

prescience (noun) Foreknowledge or foresight. *Even before she saw the characteristic, eerie, yellowish-black light in the sky, Dorothy had the prescience to seek shelter in the storm cellar.* prescient (adjective).

presumptuous (adjective) Going beyond the limits of courtesy or appropriateness. *The senator winced when the presumptuous young staffer addressed him as "Ted."* presume (verb), presumption (noun).

prevaricate (verb) To lie, to equivocate. *When it became clear to the FBI that the mobster had threatened the 12-year-old witness, they could well understand why he had prevaricated during the hearing.*

primacy (noun) State of being the utmost in importance; preeminence. *The anthropologist Ruth Benedict was an inspiration to Margaret Mead for her emphasis on the primacy of culture in the formation of an individual's personality.* primal (adjective).

pristine (adjective) Pure, undefiled. *As climbers who have scaled Mt. Everest can attest, the trails to the summit are hardly in pristine condition and are actually strewn with trash.*

probity (noun) Goodness, integrity. *The vicious editorial attacked the moral probity of the senatorial candidate, saying he had profited handsomely from his pet project, the senior-citizen housing project.*

procreative (adjective) Capable of reproducing. *If a species were for some reason to lose its procreative ability, it would die out with the current generation.* procreation (noun).

procure (verb) To obtain by using particular care and effort. *Through partnerships with a large number of specialty wholesalers, W. W. Grainger is able to procure a startling array of products for its customers, from bear repellent for Alaska pipeline workers to fork-lift trucks and toilet paper.* procurement (noun).

prodigality (noun) The condition of being wastefully extravagant. *Richard was ashamed of the prodigality of his bride's parents when he realized that the cost of the wedding reception alone was more than his father earned in one year.* prodigal (adjective).

proliferate (verb) To increase or multiply. *Over the past fifteen years, high-tech companies have proliferated in northern California, Massachusetts, and other regions.* proliferation (noun).

prolixity (noun) A diffuseness; a rambling and verbose quality. *The prolixity of Sarah's dissertation on Ottoman history defied even her adviser's attempts to read it.* prolix (adjective).

pronounced (adjective) Distinct or strongly marked. *As a result of a leg injury he received during the war, the man walked with a pronounced limp.*

propagandistic (adjective) Relating to the spread of ideas or information designed to help or injure a cause, institution, or individual. *Margaret Sanger's propagandistic efforts to foster the use of birth control were instrumental in making the public aware of its possibilities.* propaganda (noun).

propagate (verb) To cause to grow; to foster. *John Smithson's will left his fortune for the founding of an institution to propagate knowledge, leaving open whether that meant a university, a library, or a museum.* propagation (noun).

prophetic (adjective) Auspicious, predictive of what's to come. *We often look at every event leading up to a new love affair as prophetic—the flat tire that caused us to be late for work, the chance meeting in the elevator, the horoscope that augured "a new beginning."* prophecy (noun), prophesy (verb).

propitiating (adjective) Conciliatory, mollifying, or appeasing. *Management's offer of a 5-percent raise was meant as a propitiating gesture, yet the striking workers were unimpressed.* propitiate (verb).

propitious (adjective) Favorably disposed. *She had learned as a little girl that when her father was in a good mood it was a propitious time to ask for something he might not otherwise have been willing to give her.* propitiously (adverb).

propriety (noun) Appropriateness. *Some people questioned the propriety of wearing flip-flops to a meeting at the White House.*

prospective (adjective) Likely to happen. *The young man's prospective in-laws were more than happy to involve him in planning for the wedding.* prospectively (adverb).

proximity (noun) Closeness, nearness. *Neighborhood residents were angry over the proximity of the proposed sewage plant to the local elementary school.* proximate (adjective).

pundit (noun) Someone who offers opinions in an authoritative style. *The Sunday afternoon talk shows are filled with pundits, each with his or her own theory about the week's political news.*

pungency (noun) Marked by having a sharp, biting quality. *Unfortunately, the pungency of the fresh cilantro overwhelmed the delicate flavor of the poached turbot.* pungent (adjective).

purify (verb) To make pure, clean, or perfect. *The new water-treatment plant is supposed to purify the drinking water provided to everyone in the nearby towns.* purification (noun).

Q

quiescent (adjective) In a state of rest or inactivity; latent. *Polly's ulcer has been quiescent ever since her mother-in-law moved out of the condo, which was well over a year ago.* quiescence (noun).

quixotic (adjective) Foolishly romantic, idealistic to an impractical degree. *In the novel* Shoeless Joe, *Ray Kinsella carries out a quixotic plan to build a baseball field in the hopes that past baseball greats will come to play there.*

quotidian (adjective) Occurring every day; commonplace and ordinary. *Most of the time, we long to escape from quotidian concerns, but in the midst of a crisis we want nothing more than to be plagued by such simple problems as a leaky faucet or a whining child.*

R

rancorous (adjective) Marked by deeply embedded bitterness or animosity. *While Ralph and Kishu have been separated for three years, their relationship is so rancorous that they had to hire a professional mediator just to discuss divorce arrangements.* rancor (noun).

rapacious (adjective) Excessively grasping or greedy. *Some see global currency speculators like George Soros as rapacious parasites who destroy economies and then line their pockets with the profits.* rapacity (noun).

rarefied (adjective) Of interest or relating to a small, refined circle; less dense, thinner. *Those whose names dot the society pages live in a rarefied world where it's entirely normal to dine on caviar for breakfast or order a $2,000 bottle of wine at Le Cirque. When she reached the summit of Mt. McKinley, Deborah could hardly breathe in the rarefied air.*

receptivity (noun) Willingness or ability to take or acquire something. *The student's receptivity to constructive criticism from his teachers helped him improve his grades substantially.* receptive (adverb).

reclusive (adjective) Withdrawn from society. *During the last years of her life, Greta Garbo led a reclusive existence, rarely appearing in public.* recluse (noun).

recompense (noun) Compensation for a service rendered or to pay for damages. *The 5 percent of the estate that Phil received as executor of his Aunt Ida's will is small recompense for the headaches he endured in settling her affairs.* recompense (verb).

reconcile (verb) To make consistent or harmonious. *Roosevelt's greatness as a leader can be seen in his ability to reconcile the differing demands and values of the varied groups that supported him.* reconciliation (noun).

recondite (adjective) Profound, deep, abstruse. *Professor Miyaki's recondite knowledge of seventeenth-century Flemish painters made him a prized—if barely understood—member of the art history department.*

redemptive (adjective) Liberating and reforming. *While she doesn't attend formal church services, Carrie is a firm believer in the redemptive power of prayer.* redeem (verb), redemption (noun).

refractory (adjective) Stubbornly resisting control or authority. *Like a refractory child, Jill stomped out of the car, slammed the door, and said she would walk home, even though her house was 10 miles away.*

regulatory (adjective) Related to controlling or directing according to a rule. *The Federal Communications Commission is the regulatory agency charged with ensuring the broadcast industry's compliance with government rules.* regulate (verb).

reinforced (verb) Strengthened. *His mother's agreement with his father's position reinforced the teenager's belief that, despite what they said, he was making the right decision.* reinforceable (adjective).

relentless (adjective) Unyielding. *After weeks of relentless attacks by the class bully, the boy finally complained to their teacher.* relentlessness (noun).

relevance (noun) Connection to the matter at hand; pertinence. *Testimony in a criminal trial may only be admitted to the extent that it has clear relevance to the question of guilt or innocence.* relevant (adjective).

reparation (noun) The act of making amends; payment of damages by a defeated nation to the victors. *The Treaty of Versailles, signed in 1919, formally asserted Germany's war guilt and ordered it to pay reparations to the allies.*

replicate (verb) Duplicate, copy. *Authors whose first books are very successful often find it difficult to replicate that success with their second efforts.* replication (noun).

reproof (noun) A reprimand, a reproach, or castigation. *Joe thought being grounded for one month was a harsh reproof for coming home late only once.* reprove (verb).

repudiate (verb) To reject, to renounce. *After it became known that Duke had been a leader of the Ku Klux Klan, most Republican leaders repudiated him.* repudiation (noun).

repugnant (adjective) Causing dislike or disgust. *Many people find a lack of honesty repugnant.*

resilient (adjective) Able to recover from difficulty. *A professional athlete must be mentally resilient, able to lose a game one day and come back the next with renewed enthusiasm and confidence.* resilience (noun).

resolution (noun) The act of deciding to do something. *Around New Year's Day, it's not unusual for people hoping to attain some goal to make a resolution or two about the upcoming year.* resolve (verb).

resonant (adjective) Full of special import or meaning. *I found the speaker's words particularly resonant because I, too, had served in Vietnam and felt the same mixture of shame and pride.* resonance (noun).

rumination (noun) The act of engaging in contemplation. *Marcel Proust's semi-autobiographical novel cycle,* Remembrance of Things Past, *is less a narrative than an extended rumination on the nature of memory.* ruminate (verb).

S

salutary (adjective) Restorative, healthful. *I find a short dip in an icy stream to be extremely salutary, although the health benefits of my bracing swims are, as yet, unclear.*

sanction (verb) Support or authorize. *Even after a bomb exploded on the front porch of his home, the Reverend Martin Luther King Jr. refused to sanction any violent response and urged his angry followers to love their enemies.* sanctify (verb), sanction (noun).

satiate (verb) To fulfill to or beyond capacity. *Judging by the current crop of films featuring serial killers, rape, ritual murder, gun-slinging, and plain old-fashioned slugfests, the public appetite for violence has not yet been satiated.* satiation (noun), satiety (noun).

saturate (verb) To drench or suffuse with liquid or anything that permeates or invades. *The hostess' furious dabbing at the tablecloth was in vain, since the spilt wine had already saturated the damask cloth.* saturation (noun), saturated (adjective).

scrutinize (verb) To study closely. *The lawyer scrutinized the contract, searching for any detail that could pose a risk for her client.* scrutiny (noun).

sequential (adjective) Arranged in an order or series. *The courses required for the chemistry major are sequential, since each course builds on the previous one.* sequence (noun).

signatory (noun) Someone who signs an official document or petition along with others. *Alex urged me to join the other signatories and add my name to the petition against toxic sludge in organic foods, but I simply did not care enough about the issue. The signatories of the Declaration of Independence included John Adams, Benjamin Franklin, John Hancock, and Thomas Jefferson.*

sinuous (noun) Winding, circuitous, serpentine. *Frank Gehry's sinuous design for the Guggenheim Museum in Bilbao, Spain, has led people to hail the museum as the first great building of the twenty-first century.* sinuosity (noun).

skepticism (noun) A doubting or questioning attitude. *When someone is making what seem to be grandiose promises, it's always a good idea to maintain a certain level of skepticism.* skeptical (adjective).

specious (adjective) Deceptively plausible or attractive. *The infomercial for Fat-Away offered mainly specious arguments for a product that is, essentially, a heavy-duty girdle.*

spontaneous (adjective) Happening without plan or outside cause. *When the news of Kennedy's assassination hit the airwaves, people everywhere gathered in a spontaneous effort to express their shock and grief.* spontaneity (noun).

sporadically (adverb) Appearing occasionally. *Although the girl's father had left her and her mother years before, he sporadically turned up at the door to ask for money or other favors.* sporadic (adjective).

spurious (adjective) False, fake. *The so-called Piltdown Man, supposed to be the fossil of a primitive human, turned out to be spurious, though who created the hoax is still uncertain.*

squander (verb) To use up carelessly, to waste. *Those who had made donations to the charity were outraged to learn that its director had squandered millions on fancy dinners, first-class travel, and an expensive apartment for entertaining.*

stanch (verb) To stop the flow. *When Edison began to bleed profusely, Dr. Munger stanched the blood flow by applying direct pressure to the wound.*

stint (verb) To limit, to restrain. *The British bed and breakfast certainly did not stint on the breakfast part of the equation; they provided us with fried tomatoes, fried sausages, fried eggs, smoked kippers, fried bread, fried mushrooms, and bowls of a cereal called Wheatabix (which tasted like cardboard).* stinting (adjective).

stipulate (verb) To specify as a condition of an agreement. *When the computer company president sold his operation to another firm, he was required to stipulate that he would not start a competing company for at least five years.* stipulation (noun).

stolid (adjective) Impassive, unemotional. *The popular animated television series* King of the Hill *chronicles the woes of a stolid, conservative Texan confronting changing times.* stolidity (noun).

stringent (adjective) Severe, rigid. *Because their father was stringent about their behavior, the children were always careful to behave well in his presence.* stringency (noun).

subordination (noun) The state of being subservient or treated as less valuable. *Heather left the naval academy because she could no longer stand the subordination of every personal whim or desire to the rigorous demands of military life.* subordinate (verb).

subpoena (noun) An order of a court, legislation, or grand jury that compels a witness to be present at a trial or hearing. *The young man's lawyer asked the judge to subpoena a boa constrictor on the grounds that the police had used the snake as an "instrument of terror" to coerce his confession.*

subside (verb) To settle or die down. *The celebrated lecturer had to wait 10 minutes for the applause to subside before he began his speech.*

subsidization (noun) The state of being financed by a grant from a government or other agency. *Without subsidization, the nation's passenger rail system would probably go bankrupt.* subsidize (verb).

substantiated (adjective) Verified or supported by evidence. *The charge that Nixon had helped to cover up crimes was substantiated by his comments about it on a series of audio tapes.* substantiate (verb), substantiation (noun).

subsume (verb) To encompass or engulf within something larger. *In Alan Dershowitz's* Reversal of Fortune, *he makes it clear that his work as a lawyer subsumes his personal life.*

subterranean (adjective) Under the surface of the earth. *Subterranean testing of nuclear weapons was permitted under the Nuclear Test Ban Treaty of 1963.*

summarily (adverb) Quickly and concisely. *Immediately after I voiced my utter disdain for the new ad campaign, my boss put her hand on my elbow and summarily ushered me out of the conference room.*

superficial (adjective) On the surface only; without depth or substance. *Her wound was only superficial and required no treatment except a light bandage. His superficial attractiveness hides the fact that his personality is lifeless and his mind is dull.* superficiality (noun).

superimpose (verb) To place or lay over or above something. *The artist stirred controversy by superimposing portraits of certain contemporary politicians over images of such reviled historical figures as Hitler and Stalin.*

supersede (verb) To displace, to substitute or supplant. *"I'm sorry," the principal announced, "but today's afternoon classes will be superseded by an assembly on drug and alcohol abuse."*

supposition (noun) Assumption, conjecture. *While most climate researchers believe that increasing levels of greenhouse gases will warm the planet, skeptics claim that this theory is mere supposition.* suppose (verb).

synthesis (noun) The combination of separate elements to form a whole. *Large multinational corporations are frequently the result of the synthesis of several smaller companies from several different countries.* synthesize (verb).

T

tactical (adjective) Regarding a means for achieving an end. *In the early Indian Wars, since the U.S. Cavalry had repeating rifles and the Native Americans had only bows and arrows, the soldiers had a distinct tactical advantage.* tactic (noun).

tangential (adjective) Touching lightly; only slightly connected or related. *Having enrolled in a class on African American history, the students found the teacher's stories about his travels in South America only of tangential interest.* tangent (noun).

tedium (noun) Boredom. *For most people, watching even a 15-minute broadcast of the Earth as seen from space would be an exercise in sheer tedium.* tedious (adjective).

temperance (noun) Moderation or restraint in feelings and behavior. *Most professional athletes practice temperance in their personal habits; too much eating or drinking and too many late nights, they know, can harm their performance.*

temperate (adjective) Moderate, calm. *The warm gulf streams are largely responsible for the temperate climate of the British Isles.*

tenuous (adjective) Lacking in substance; weak, flimsy, very thin. *His tenuous grasp of the Spanish language was evident when he addressed Señor Chavez as "Señora."*

terrestrial (adjective) Of the earth. *The movie* Close Encounters of the Third Kind *tells the story of the first contact between beings from outer space and terrestrial creatures.*

tirade (noun) A long, harshly critical speech. *Reformed smokers, like Bruce, are prone to delivering tirades on the evils of smoking.*

torpor (noun) Apathy, sluggishness. *Stranded in an airless hotel room in Madras after a 27-hour train ride, I felt such overwhelming torpor that I doubted I would make it to Bangalore, the next leg of my journey.* torpid (adjective).

tractable (adjective) Obedient, manageable. *When he turned 3 years old, Harrison suddenly became a tractable, well-mannered little boy after being, quite frankly, an unruly little monster!*

tranquility (noun) Freedom from disturbance or turmoil; calm. *She moved from New York City to rural Vermont seeking the tranquility of country life.* tranquil (adjective).

transgress (verb) To go past limits; to violate. *The Secretary of State warned that if Iraq had developed biological weapons, it would have transgressed the UN's rules against manufacturing weapons of mass destruction.* transgression (noun).

transmute (verb) To change in form or substance. *Practitioners of alchemy, a forebear of modern chemistry, tried to discover ways to transmute metals such as iron into gold.* transmutation (noun).

treacherous (adjective) Untrustworthy or disloyal; dangerous or unreliable. *Nazi Germany proved to be a treacherous ally, first signing a peace pact with the Soviet Union, then invading. Be careful crossing the rope bridge; parts of the span are badly frayed and treacherous.* treachery (noun).

tremor (noun) Shaking or trembling. *Brooke felt the first tremors of the 1989 San Francisco earthquake while she was sitting in Candlestick Park watching a Giants baseball game.*

trenchant (adjective) Caustic and incisive. *Essayist H. L. Mencken was known for his trenchant wit and was famed for mercilessly puncturing the American middle class (which he called the "booboisie").*

trepidation (noun) Fear and anxiety. *After the tragedy of United Airlines Flight 93, many previously fearless flyers were filled with trepidation whenever they stepped into an airplane.*

turbulent (adjective) Agitated or disturbed. *The night before the championship match, Martina was unable to sleep, her mind turbulent with fears and hopes.* turbulence (noun).

turpitude (noun) Depravity, wickedness. *Radical feminists who contrast women's essential goodness with men's moral turpitude can be likened to religious fundamentalists who make a clear distinction between the saved and the damned.*

typify (verb) To serve as a representative example. *Due in large part to post-Civil War minstrel shows, the smiling, shuffling, lazy black man came to unjustifiably typify the African American male.*

tyro (noun) Novice, amateur. *For an absolute tyro on the ski slopes, Gina was surprisingly agile at taking the moguls.*

U

ubiquitous (adjective) Being or seeming to be everywhere at one time. *The proliferation of chain-owned bookstores in malls across the country have made them a ubiquitous feature of American retailing.* ubiquitously (adverb).

unalloyed (adjective) Unqualified, pure. *Holding his newborn son for the first time, Malik felt an unalloyed happiness that was unlike anything he had ever experienced in his 45 years.*

unconventional (adjective) Out of the ordinary. *The manager's unconventional methods for inspiring his staff—such as providing additional vacation days for good work—pleased those who worked for him but dismayed his superiors.* unconventionally (adverb).

undermine (verb) To excavate beneath; to subvert, to weaken. *Dot continued to undermine my efforts to find her a date by showing up at our dinner parties in her ratty old sweatsuit.*

unfeigned (adjective) Genuine, sincere. *Lashawn responded with such unfeigned astonishment when we all leapt out of the kitchen that I think she had had no inkling of the surprise party.*

univocal (adjective) With a single voice. *While they came from different backgrounds and classes, the employees were univocal in their demands that the corrupt CEO resign immediately.*

unstinting (adjective) Giving with unrestrained generosity. *Few people will be able to match the unstinting dedication and care that Mother Teresa lavished on the poor people of Calcutta.*

upsurge (noun) A rapid or sudden rise. *Since no one could explain why it had occurred, the tremendous upsurge in sales in the shoe department was a source of amazement for everyone.*

urbanity (noun) Sophistication, suaveness, and polish. *Part of the fun in a Cary Grant movie lies in seeing whether the star can be made to lose his urbanity and elegance in the midst of chaotic or kooky situations.* urbane (adjective).

usurious (adjective) Lending money at an unconscionably high interest rate. *Some people feel that Shakespeare's portrayal of the Jew, Shylock, the usurious money lender in* The Merchant of Venice, *has enflamed prejudice against Jews.* usury (adjective).

V

validate (verb) To officially approve or confirm. *The election of the president is formally validated when the members of the Electoral College meet to confirm the verdict of the voters.* valid (adjective), validity (noun).

vapid (adjective) Flat, flavorless. *Whenever I have insomnia, I just tune the clock radio to Lite FM, and soon those vapid songs from the seventies have me floating away to dreamland.* vapidity (noun).

variables (noun) Things that are able or apt to have different attributes or characteristics. *When you are considering the purchase of a car, it's necessary to take all the variables—price, size, reliability, etc.—into account in making your decision.* variably (adverb).

venal (adjective) Corrupt, mercenary. *Sese Seko Mobuto was the venal dictator of Zaire who reportedly diverted millions of dollars in foreign aid to his own personal fortune.* venality (noun).

venerate (verb) To admire or honor. *In North Korea, Kim Jong-il is venerated as an almost god-like figure.* venerable (adjective), veneration (noun).

veracious (adjective) Truthful, earnest. *The child's statement was proven to be veracious.* veracity (noun).

verify (verb) To prove to be true. *The contents of Robert L. Ripley's syndicated "Believe It or Not" cartoons could not be verified, yet the public still thrilled to reports of "the man with two pupils in each eye," "the human unicorn," and other amazing oddities.* verification (noun).

veritable (adjective) Authentic. *A French antiques dealer recently claimed that a fifteenth-century child-sized suit of armor that he purchased in 1994 is the veritable suit of armor worn by heroine Joan of Arc.*

victimizing (verb) Subjecting to swindle or fraud. *On the streets of New York City, as well as on those of other large cities, three-card monte players are extremely adept at victimizing gullible tourists.* victim (noun).

vindictive (adjective) Spiteful. *Paula embarked on a string of petty, vindictive acts against her philandering boyfriend, such as mixing dry cat food with his cereal and snipping the blooms off his prize African violets.*

viscid (adjective) Sticky. *The 3M company's "Post-It," a simple piece of paper with one viscid side, has become as commonplace—and as indispensable—as the paper clip.*

viscous (adjective) Having a gelatinous or gooey quality. *I put too much liquid in the batter, so my Black Forest cake turned out to be a viscous, inedible mass.*

vitiate (verb) To pollute, to impair. *When they voted to ban smoking from all bars in California, the public affirmed their belief that smoking vitiates the health of all people, not just smokers.*

vituperative (adjective) Verbally abusive, insulting. *Elizabeth Taylor should have won an award for her harrowing portrayal of Martha, the bitter, vituperative wife of a college professor in Edward Albee's* Who's Afraid of Virginia Woolf? vituperate (verb).

volatile (adjective) Quickly changing; fleeting, transitory; prone to violence. *Public opinion is notoriously volatile; a politician who is very popular one month may be voted out of office the next.* volatility (noun).

volubility (noun) Quality of being overly talkative; glib. *As Lorraine's anxiety increased, her volubility increased in direct proportion, so during her job interview the poor interviewer couldn't get a word in edgewise.* voluble (adjective).

voracious (adjective) Gluttonous, ravenous. *"Are all your appetites so voracious?" Wesley asked Nina as he watched her finish off seven miniature sandwiches and two lamb kabob skewers in a matter of minutes.* voracity (noun).

W

warrant (noun) Authorization or certification. *The judge provided the police officer with a warrant for the alleged criminal's arrest.* warranted (verb).

X

xenophobia (noun) Fear of foreigners or outsiders. *Slobodan Milosevic's nationalistic talk played on the deep xenophobia of the Serbs, who, after 500 years of brutal Ottoman occupation, had come to distrust all outsiders.*

Z

zenith (noun) Highest point. *Landing on the moon in 1969 was the zenith of Neil Armstrong's career.*

NOTES

NOTES

NOTES

NOTES